The Dryden Press

Publications in History

GENERAL EDITOR
RAY ALLEN BILLINGTON
NORTHWESTERN UNIVERSITY

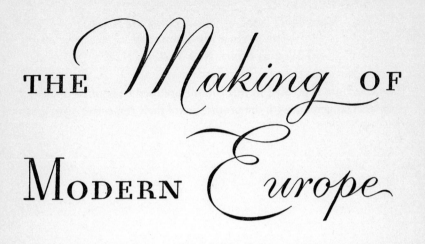

THE *Making* OF
MODERN *Europe*

BOOK TWO:

WATERLOO TO THE ATOMIC AGE

Edited by

HERMAN AUSUBEL
Assistant Professor of History
Columbia University

The Dryden Press · New York

FORMAT

The text has been set in Granjon type, with Nicholas Cochin for the chapter and article titles. The title line on the cover and on the title page is hand lettered. Designed by Stanley Burnshaw and William Bayless, and printed and bound in Scranton, Pennsylvania, by The Haddon Craftsmen.

First Printing, March 1951

Preface

THE PROBLEM of what to do about supplementary readings has disturbed every teacher of European history. He knows that textbooks have become so big and heavy that additional reading assignments would seem to impose too great a burden on students. At the same time, however, he knows that the content of history is so rich and complex that even the most learned textbook writers cannot have a mastery of every topic with which they deal. And he regrets that students should acquire almost all their knowledge of the past from such writers—and not from the experts who have devoted long years of research to the mastery of particular historical subjects.

The result often is that the teacher decides to require several book reviews from his students. Soon, however, he discovers that although reviews are admirable for some purposes, they fail to prepare any large number of students to engage effectively in any large number of class discussions. If he proceeds, therefore, to require scattered weekly readings in specialized secondary works, he soon finds himself in difficulties with the administration. For these days American college libraries are hard pressed. They suffer not only from a lack of money but from a lack of space. As Carl Becker expressed it, "If, some bright afternoon, all the students in philosophy, literature, and the social sciences should take it into their heads to invade the library in order to do what they are conventionally expected to do, there would scarcely be standing room for them, to say nothing about tables to work at. . . ." In short, the teacher continues to be disturbed by the problem of what to do about collateral readings.

The present volume aims to help solve that problem. Designed to accompany any of the standard textbooks in modern European history, it consists mainly of articles that appeared originally in American and British scholarly journals. Written by some of the most gifted of recent specialists in European political, economic, religious, and intellectual history, these articles deserve to be more readily available. First, they are generally interpretative in character; frequently, in fact, they embody relatively new approaches to their subjects. Secondly, they lend themselves readily to classroom discussion; often, indeed, they are provocative enough to give rise to the hope that many a student will descend willingly on the library—despite all the difficulties involved—in order to find out more about particular topics.

For the convenience and guidance of the reader, each article has an introduction and, in almost all cases, a glossary. The introduction is designed to place the selection in its setting and to indicate why the student has been invited to read it. The glossary identifies those names and defines those terms which seem to deserve or require special definition or identification. Except in a few instances—and these are clearly indicated—the articles have been reproduced in their entirety. In order to save space, however, the footnotes which originally appeared with many of the articles have often been omitted. Such omissions have again been clearly indicated.

In conclusion, I should like to express the hope that the reader will find this sampling of the literature of modern European history as stimulating to read as it was to prepare.

H. A.

Columbia University
October 1950

A Note on Sources

The articles in *The Making of Modern Europe* have been selected from both books and periodicals. The periodicals are listed below.

Agricultural History

American Academy of Political and Social Science: Annals

American Economic Review

American Friends of Lafayette: Publications

American Historical Review

American Philosophical Society: Proceedings

American Political Science Review

American Scholar

Association of History Teachers of the Middle States and Maryland: Proceedings

Cambridge Journal

Canadian Historical Review

Catholic Historical Review

Church History

Church Quarterly Review

Columbia University Quarterly

Commentary

Contemporary Review

Current History

Economic History Review

Foreign Affairs

German Life and Letters

Hibbert Journal

History

Huntington Library Quarterly

Isis

Journal of Central European Affairs

Journal of Economic History

Journal of Modern History

Journal of Political Economy

Journal of the History of Ideas

Listener

Lutheran Church Quarterly

Political Science Quarterly

Psychological Review

Public Opinion Quarterly

Queen's Quarterly

Review of Politics

Royal Historical Society: Transactions

Russian Review

Scientific Monthly

Slavonic Review

Social Education

South Atlantic Quarterly

Speculum

Studies

Virginia Quarterly Review

Yale Review

Contents

≫≫≫≫≫≫≫≫≫≫≫≫ BOOK TWO ≪≪≪≪≪≪≪≪≪≪≪≪

XIV · Conservatism vs. Liberalism in Post-Napoleonic Europe

R. W. SETON-WATSON
Metternich and Internal Austrian Policy   578

D. S. MIRSKY
The Decembrists   596

G. M. TREVELYAN
The Great Days of Reform   603

XV · Economic Change in Post-Napoleonic Europe

HERBERT HEATON
"The Industrial Revolution"   616

KENT ROBERTS GREENFIELD
Economic Ideas and Facts in the Early Period of the Risorgimento (1815-1848)   628

ARTHUR L. DUNHAM
Unrest in France in 1848   642

XVI · 1848

OTAKAR ODLOŽILÍK
Storm over the Danube   656

FRIEDRICH MEINECKE
The Year 1848 in German History: Reflections
  on a Centenary   668

XVII · Another Napoleonic Era

ALBERT GUÉRARD
Saint-Simon on Horseback: The Economic and
  Social Policy of Napoleon III   688

LAZAR VOLIN
The Russian Peasant and Serfdom   709

ERICH EYCK
Bismarck and the War of 1870   732

XVIII · Shapers of Nineteenth-Century Thought

KARL PEARSON
Charles Darwin, 1809-1882   742

SOLOMON F. BLOOM
Man of His Century: A Reconsideration of the
  Historical Significance of Karl Marx   765

XIX · Currents in German and Italian History, 1870-1914

SIDNEY B. FAY
Bismarck's Welfare State 784

RAYMOND J. SONTAG
The Germany of Treitschke 796

KENT ROBERTS GREENFIELD
The New Italy Coming of Age: 1870-1915 810

XX · Currents in British and French History, 1870-1914

MICHAEL TIERNEY
Gladstone and Ireland 822

EDWARD P. CHEYNEY
Constructive Reforms [in Britain], 1860-1914 833

J. V. DUCATTILLON
The Church in the Third Republic 855

XXI · Currents in Austro-Hungarian and Russian History, 1870-1914

L. B. NAMIER
The Political Structure of Austria-Hungary Before the War 868

V. MAKLAKOV
The Agrarian Problem in Russia Before the Revolution 881

XXII · Imperialism

ROBERT LIVINGSTON SCHUYLER

The Climax of Anti-Imperialism in England   898

WILLIAM L. LANGER

A Critique of Imperialism   918

KENNETH SCOTT LATOURETTE

The Christian Missionary Movement of the
Nineteenth and Twentieth Centuries   933

XXIII · War and Peace

BERNADOTTE E. SCHMITT

July 1914: Thirty Years After   942

CHARLES SEYMOUR

Versailles in Perspective   992

XXIV · The Soviet Dictatorship

N. S. TIMASHEFF

The Russian Revolution: Twenty-Five Years After   1008

PAUL OLBERG

The Teaching of History under Stalin   1032

XXV · The Fascist Dictatorships

GAETANO SALVEMINI
The March on Rome: Revised Version 1040

FRANCIS O. WILCOX
The Use of Atrocity Stories in [the Ethiopian] War 1050

W. O. HENDERSON
Some Economic Aspects of National Socialism in Germany 1063

R. JOHN RATH
History and Citizenship Training in
    National Socialist Germany 1076

XXVI · World War II and Its Aftermath

L. B. NAMIER
The Russo-German Treaty of 1939 1090

DAVID THOMSON
Third Republic *versus* Third Reich 1097

HANSON W. BALDWIN
The Missing Pages of World War II 1106

SAMUEL J. HURWITZ
Diagnosing the German Malady:
    The Events That Led Up to the Crime 1114

PHILIP E. MOSELY
Soviet-American Relations Since the War 1131

XXVII · Science and Religion in the Twentieth Century

EDNA HEIDBREDER

Freud and Psychology   1148

HENRY D. SMYTH

Fifty Years of Atomic Physics   1158

KENNETH SCOTT LATOURETTE

A Historian Looks Ahead;
    The Future of Christianity in the Light of Its Past   1170

XIV

Conservatism vs. Liberalism in Post-Napoleonic Europe

Metternich and Internal Austrian Policy

R. W. SETON-WATSON

The Decembrists

D. S. MIRSKY

The Great Days of Reform

G. M. TREVELYAN

Metternich and Internal Austrian Policy

R. W. SETON-WATSON

Published in 1939

Few periods in European history have been so dominated by fear as the years following the collapse of the Napoleonic Empire. Memories of the Great French Revolution and of the Revolutionary and Napoleonic Wars were fresh, and fears of a further outbreak of revolution and war were rife. Even Metternich, the leading upholder of the so-called Conservative System, was convinced that revolution and war were inevitable, and that nothing man could do would avert the disasters of the future. Nevertheless, Metternich worked on the assumption that the pursuit of certain policies would, in the short run, promote stability and peace and postpone the coming of revolution and war. He believed that the extensive use of repression, for example, would be most helpful, for, if freedom of speech, press, and assembly were carefully restricted, those who were dissatisfied with existing conditions would be unable to infect others with their dissatisfaction. Furthermore, if the major powers cooperated and supported armed intervention in the affairs of any state that was threatened by revolution, the rest of Europe would remain safe from contagion. But it was not only the techniques of repression and armed intervention which Metternich upheld. He was a firm believer, also, in the need for reform from above, as R. W. Seton-Watson, the dean of British authorities on Habsburg history, points out in the present selection. Indeed, the great tragedy of Metternich's career was that he was unable to convince Emperor Francis of this need.

> "J'ai gouverné l'Europe quelque fois, l'Autriche—jamais"
> ["At times I ruled Europe—but never Austria"]
> —METTERNICH

Metternich. By Heinrich von Srbik. 2 vols. 1925.
Der Zerfall Œsterreichs. By Viktor Bibl. 2 vols. 1922.
Metternich's Nachgelassene Papiere. 8 vols. 1880-4.
Tagebücher des Freiherrn von Kübeck. 1909.
Metternich und Kübeck: ein Briefwechsel. 1910.
Metternich. By Algernon Cecil. 1933.

Metternich after his fall denied the existence of a "Metternich System": but his contemporaries and posterity agree in assigning to him the foremost rôle as defender of the existing order in Europe in the thirty years that followed Waterloo. "Depuis longtemps," he said in 1824, "l'Europe a pris pour moi la valeur d'une patrie" ["For some time Europe has had for me the character of my own country"].

While, however, Metternich's foreign policy has received full attention from historians (though there is still much documentary evidence withheld from us), the part which he played in the government of Austria during his thirty-nine years of office has been unduly neglected. Yet it was upon the methods of government employed at home that the continuity of his foreign policy rested, and the two complemented each other to quite an unusual degree. Abroad the doctrine of Stability allied itself with Balance and Legitimacy against the corroding forces of constitutionalism and nationalism: at home, Stability became absolute rigidity, and the frontiers were in an intellectual sense a Chinese wall designed to keep out all new ideas so far as possible.

If foreign policy revolved round the person of Metternich, home policy was wholly dependent upon Francis himself, who with all his faults was really all-powerful, at any rate in the negative sense that little or nothing could happen without him or against his wishes. With his character and political outlook in the first seventeen years of his reign (1792-1809) we are not concerned here: but it is to be noted that after 1809, the year of Austria's worst disasters—or, it is sometimes argued, after 1807, when he lost his rather frivolous and pleasure-loving second wife—Francis threw off a certain laziness and triviality and not merely became still more autocratic, but devoted a much closer attention to public affairs. In the words of Anton Springer—the Liberal Austrian historian, whose book, though possessing a very definite bias, will always remain a classic for the period before 1848—the Government of Austria first assumed in 1809 "a firm shape and an enduring steadfastness in which the nature of its ruler was sharply and clearly reflected."

Francis was a man of simple tastes who disliked splendour and was devoted to routine. Lacking self-confidence and culture, he was pro-

Reprinted by special permission from *The Slavonic Review*, XVII (1939), 539-555.

foundly suspicious and a born pedant. Thus he developed into the typical bureaucrat in a State where the bureaucracy had already become the cement which held everything together. He became increasingly the slave of protocols and "Akte" ["acts"] and formulæ, with a passion for red tape, officework and audiences in which he listened sympathetically but generally came to no decision. His determination to examine all the details for himself led to a congestion and stagnation of business which grew steadily worse till there were literally thousands of applications awaiting his decision or signature. It was an extreme misfortune that he was not merely surrounded by such men as his adjutant Baron Kutschera, who was both incompetent and of bad morals, but could join the Emperor in his musical quartets, or Baron Stifft, his private physician, or Father Frint, his confessor, men of the narrowest and most pedantic outlook, who really played the rôle associated with witch doctors at a primitive Zulu court—not merely this, but he was extremely jealous of his three able brothers, Charles, John and Joseph; kept the first out of all political life, and, though leaving the latter in Hungary as Palatine, hampered him at every turn. It was only the most shallow and insignificant of them all, Ludwig, with whom he was ever on close terms, and to whom, most unhappily for Austria, he left the political directive at his own death. In the same way he kept able generals like Schwarzenberg and Radetzky at arm's length, following the principle inculcated upon him in his youth by the veteran Lascy: "A general of whom good use is to be made in the field must never be given influence in peace." This method he applied all along the line; as Springer puts it—"To no service the full reward, to no force the entire power, to no man the right part." Metter-

---

FRIEDRICH VON GENTZ: Talented German political writer and statesman. A defender of the conservative position, he translated Burke's *Reflections on the French Revolution* into German. In the Napoleonic period he figured prominently in the struggle against French domination. After Waterloo, he cooperated with Metternich in the attempt to prevent the outbreak of revolution and war.

ADAM MÜLLER: German romantic writer and philosopher of conservatism who served as an official of the Austrian government and as a political observer for Metternich. Critical of the rationalism of the eighteenth century, he defended authority and tradition.

nich was the one memorable exception, and even he was not omnipotent and had surprisingly little say in internal affairs.

There are few more remarkable political partnerships in history and few based on so striking a contrast between the two men—the simple, suspicious, unintellectual, hidebound and straitlaced master, and the elegant, gay dilettante, full of charm and varied interests, dabbling in many subjects, and, though capable of much serious work, always ready to leave drudgery to his subordinates. There was, however, a strong link in their common hatred of the Revolution and in their conviction, amounting almost to an obsession, that it must be challenged at every point, that there can be no concession to it, and that, as Metternich said to Széchenyi in 1825, "if you take one stone out of the arch, the whole thing crashes round it."[1] But there was the further factor of personal affection, which made Metternich turn to Francis for advice about his marriage and Francis draw up his will in terms of special cordiality towards his Minister. "Heaven," wrote Metternich in 1820, "has placed me beside a man who is, as it were, made for me. The Emperor Francis wastes no words, he knows what he wants, and his will is always what it is my duty to wish. Leaving aside secondary considerations, he always goes straight towards this goal. He never throws down the glove, but picks it up if it is thrown to him."[2] This rings true, and Metternich was for good and for ill throughout life "der treue Diener seines Herren" ["the true servant of his monarch"].

He was himself under no illusions on this point, and in 1829 he

[1] Srbik, i, p. 51.
[2] *Nachgelassene Papiere*, iii, p. 341.

ROBOT: Labor service obligation which peasants in the Austrian Empire owed to their lords. Abolished in 1789 by Joseph II, it was restored by his successor. It was abolished again in the period of the Revolution of 1848 but with the provision that compensation was to be paid to the lords.

FRIEDRICH VON SCHLEGEL: A major literary figure in the German romantic movement. In his youth he defended French Revolutionary ideas. Soon, however, he emerged as a spokesman for the philosophy of conservatism. He was employed by the Austrian government and served as an agent of Metternich.

said to the Russian General Krasinsky: "I know the Emperor Nicholas has the idea that I lead at my pleasure the master whom I serve. But this is to misjudge the Emperor of Austria, for his will is firm and no one can bring him to do what he does not want. If he heaps favours on me and trusts me, it is because I go the way which he prescribes to me: and had I the misfortune to stray from it, Prince Metternich would not remain twenty-four hours Foreign Minister."[3] As will appear later, Metternich was by no means lacking in ideas as to the internal government of the State, though he never really knew *Austria* so well as either Germany or Italy, in spite of all his years at the Ballplatz. But he was not able to carry out his views, and after pressing them up to a certain point found it wiser not to press them further.

The real power, then, under the Emperor himself, was always the Ministry of Police, and from 1817 onwards the all-important man was its chief, Count Sedlnitzky, who already found an elaborate system in existence, but made it more all-pervading and irresistible than ever. Though in private life the mildest of men, he was a past-master in the arts of espionage, censorship, denunciation and the intercepting and extracting of letters. He was supreme in his own sphere, and it is utterly incorrect to describe him, as Hormayr did in 1848, as "Metternich's ape" or "police lackey,"[4] or as "the dust on the Prince's soles," to use the phrase of the great Orientalist Hammer-Purgstall.[5] On the contrary, even Metternich was powerless, and in defiance of his orders the police opened letters which Gentz was in the habit of sending to the Hospodar of Wallachia, and which are now a valuable source of our knowledge of what Metternich and Gentz *wished* to be thought of their policy. While Metternich was absent from Vienna, the police even forced Gentz to submit his letters to them.

Next to his system of spies, in which he boasted to have outdone Napoleon's famous Police Minister Fouché, Sedlnitzky's most valuable weapon was the censorship, which on the one hand kept out the foreign Press and the products of foreign literature—and not least of all, of German literature (for instance, Schiller's plays were either prohibited altogether or such obnoxious characters as Vater Moor in *The Robbers* or the Capuchin in *Wallenstein's Camp* were drastically cut)—and

[3] Srbik, i, p. 454.
[4] *Kaiser Franz und Metternich*, p.t.
[5] *Briefe an Menzel*, p. 103, cit. Srbik, i, p. 494.

on the other hand strictly controlled such writers as Austrian soil produced in spite of all official discouragement. The treatment of Grillparzer, the greatest of Austrian dramatists, whose whole outlook and development were warped and stifled by the control and disapproval to which he was subjected, is typical of the reign of Francis, who was not merely indifferent but directly hostile to all real culture, with the one exception of music. Grillparzer received a severe reprimand and threat of dismissal from the Hofkammer because of a poem on "the decay of ancient Rome," and we have it in his own words: "In the Austria of those days there was no place for a poet." "The invisible chains clank on hand and foot." "Depotism has destroyed my literary life." This means very much, coming as it does from an ultra-Conservative, the author of the famous poem to Radetzky and of more than one historical eulogy of the Habsburgs.

Similar restraints checked the careers of Lenau, the famous German-Hungarian poet, of Bauernfeld, even of Prince Auersperg, better known as Anastasius Grün, who, when the authorship of *Viennese Walks* was brought home to him after seven years of denial, had to promise silence in order to avoid banishment. And all this at the very height of German romanticism, when south Germany in particular was full of poets and writers.

It is well worth stopping for a moment to consider the mentality of the Austrian censor. The following passages are extracted from the report of Hagelin, the first official censor, in 1795. "That the death of Cæsar, the Roman Brutus, the expulsion of King Tarquin and such subjects are not allowable, goes without saying. Nor can any events from the history of the Arch-House be acted, such as might be to the discredit of these rulers. For instance, the revolt of the Swiss Confederacy from the Austrian sceptre, item the Swiss hero William Tell, the rebellion of the United Netherlands."

"The clerical Estate must not be brought on to the stage at all, even if represented as virtuous. . . . The military is also to be spared, so that no dishonouring action or criticism be thrown upon this reputable class, whose most delicate side is the *point d'honneur. . . . Dr. Faust* of Weidmann is objectionable, because the Angel in it shows far less sense in his speeches against the tempter, than Mephisto, who shows far more wit in his counter-arguments in favour of crime. . . . The oaths Mordio, Sackerment, etc., are not to be tolerated . . . also such exclamations as Jesus Maria, Holy Saints, etc. . . . The expressions

Tyranny, Despotism, oppression, are to be used as little as possible. . . . Of the word Enlightenment there is to be as little use in the theatre, as of 'freedom' and 'equality.' "[6]

Needless to say, it was equally impossible for a school of historians to flourish. While many of the greatest German historians were in full activity, Austria could boast of nothing but a few harmless collectors of documents such as Chmel and Kurz. The only two who enjoyed a name in their day—Hormayr and Schneller—were of no real consequence whatever, and even they found it necessary to leave the country—the one because he was mixed up in Archduke John's harebrained scheme of a rising, the other because he could not get the censor to permit the publication of his Austrian history, even though it was intended as an eulogy of the House of Habsburg.

The attitude of Sedlnitzky and of Francis towards education generally is altogether of a piece with this. While it was made very difficult for students from the Habsburg Monarchy to go to Germany, those who came from there were closely watched, and at each university special directors of studies were appointed to strengthen the control. This control was applied with even greater severity to the professors, and more than one was deprived on account of his dangerous doctrines.

Specially instructive is the case of Bolzano, who was professor of religious philosophy at Prague, and was denounced for his attempt to provide his students with a rational basis for Christianity. The Maltese Order, whose headquarters were in Prague, and Father Frint, the Emperor's confessor, conducted a kind of heresy-hunt against Bolzano as a disciple of Kant, and against another professor, Fesl, who had endorsed Kant's views on universal peace and had dared to found a Christian Union (Christenbund) at Leitmeritz in Bohemia. His private diaries were seized and minutely inspected by Frint, with the result that Fesl was deprived and interned for four years at the Servite monastery.

During Bolzano's examination Count Saurau, who was then at the head of the Hofkanzlei, laid down the following doctrine, which clearly reflects the mind of Francis himself.[7] "The State," he says, "pays public teachers in order that they may teach those principles which are

---

[6] Grillparzer, *Sämmtliche Werke*, ed. Neckar, i, pref., pp. xv-xvii.

[7] Extract from a Vortrag of Saurau, of 24 Sept., 1819, quoted by Bibl, *Der Zerfall Œsterreichs,* i, p. 264. On Bolzano, see an interesting passage in Ernest Denis, *La Bohême depuis la Montagne Blanche*, ii, pp. 124-8.

approved by the Church and by the State administration, and it is a dangerous error if a professor believes that he may teach the youth entrusted to him according to the tendency of his individual conviction or according to his peculiar views." Francis himself gave public expression to this point of view in 1821, when he addressed the professors of Laibach gymnasium in the following terms:—"Hold to the old, for it is good, and our ancestors found it to be good, so why should not we? There are now new ideas going about, which I never can nor will approve. Avoid these and keep to what is positive. For I need no savants, but worthy citizens. To form the youth into such citizens is your task. He who serves me must teach what I order. He who cannot do so, or who comes with new ideas, can go, or I shall remove him."[8] On 30 March, 1820, he had given orders for the strict observation of all professors and teachers at schools and universities, and an immediate report in the case of anything which might be regarded as "ordnungswidrig" (an infringement of order). So faithfully were his instructions observed that all librarians had to draw up and submit special lists of all books taken out by individual professors in the course of the year!

As the tide of liberalism grew, Sedlnitzky issued after the July Revolution a prohibition upon students visiting foreign universities, and he justified this to Metternich by his desire to prevent them from falling into (here is the police-pedant's list *in ipsissimis verbis*) "philosophical materialism, religious rationalism or mysticism, so called liberalism, the revolutionary principle and the corporative spirit." It was in connection with this veto that a Protestant faculty of theology was founded at Vienna, so that Protestants could for the first time study for the ministry in Austria without going abroad.

As regards the Press, there was nothing whatever except the official organs of the authorities: and this side of things was very closely supervised by Metternich himself, who already as Minister in Berlin in 1805 had been instrumental in the foundation of a journal called "Vaterländische Blätter," which for all its official flavour was the first modern newspaper in Austria, and was edited by such brilliant men as Friedrich von Schlegel, Pilat and Adam Müller, often printed articles drafted by Metternich himself, and aimed at interpreting Austria to foreign opinion, and by its well-informed reports upon east European problems hoped to attract readers in the west of Europe. As Srbik gravely points out, Metternich's whole system rested on "the principle that

[8] *Allgem. Zeitung*, 1821, p. 12, cit. Springer, i, p. 119, and Bibl, i, p. 284.

Press freedom leads to the destruction of the foundations of the State and of society"—a principle which the Austrian historian, writing in 1925, describes as "an sich richtig" ["correct in itself"].

While this police system spread its feelers in every direction, silencing criticism, checking enterprise and encouraging the capital in its habits of superficial pleasure, Francis was confronted with the burning problems of financial and administrative reform. As regards the former, he was really sensitive, and though here, too, he hesitated and often waited too long, he did at last attempt to grapple with a situation which was becoming increasingly grave. The Finanzpatent promulgated by Count Wallis in 1812 had practically amounted to State bankruptcy. Yet the return of peace found Austrian finances in a desperate state—a large State debt with high rate of interest, masses of paper money, low credit, a deficit, and chaos in taxation. In 1814 the place of Wallis was taken by Count Philip Stadion, the former Finance Minister, who made a really valiant attempt to remedy matters. A series of new Finance Patents (1 June and 29 October, 1816, and 21 March, 1818) established a National Bank for the gradual restriction of paper money, and a sinking fund for the reduction of debt, and gave a solemn pledge never to issue any new paper at a compulsory rate, as had been done in 1812. In spite of many difficulties—not the least being the extreme suspicion of the public—he succeeded by 1818 in wiping out debt to the amount of 126,000,000 gulden and calling in 131,000,000 gulden in notes: and loans were concluded with big banking houses in the west. But Stadion stood in permanent conflict with all the great spending departments of State, and though at his death in 1824 there was a noticeable improvement, the annual deficit had not yet been overcome. Meanwhile methods of taxation were gradually brought up to date and the monopolies rendered more profitable to the State, though, for instance, the special Tobacco Office was not erected till 1834. But endless restrictions on trade remained, beginning with the customs frontier between Austria and Hungary, noble privileges and "Robot" and other peasant forced labour, and again special tolls and dues and octroi rights in the towns: and in all these directions there was no real change till the revolution of 1848.

By 1829 the financial situation was again steadily deteriorating, and Count Kolowrat wrote a special memoir for Francis on its dangers.[9] He pointed out that while other Powers had improved their finances

[9] Srbik, i, p. 541, based on the original documents in the Staatsarchiv.

during the long peace, Austria had increased her debt by 180,000,000 gulden. The causes which he assigned for this were (1) the excessive interest paid on the Austrian debt, (2) the undue readiness to repay foreign subsidies (in this respect Great Britain was, of course, the chief creditor), (3) the fact that Hungary contributed far too little to the general expenses of the Monarchy, and (4) above all, that far too much was spent on the Army and on Foreign Affairs.

Francis appointed a commisison of enquiry, but nothing happened, and in January, 1830, Kolowrat asked to be relieved of his post, as his suggestions of economy had not been carried out, and as the problem seemed insoluble under the existing conditions. But though Francis persuaded him to withdraw his resignation, and though he had under him several officials of the highest quality, notably Baron Kübeck,[10] none the less little or nothing was done, and the question of financial reform again vegetated.

Thanks to the energy of Radetzky, the state of the Army was greatly improved after 1832, but in every other respect there was steady decay. One reason why nothing was done is to be found in the rivalry of two men, each of whom Francis had come to regard as indispensable, and whom it often suited his suspicious mind, with its dislike for decisions, to play off against each other. These were, of course Metternich and Kolowrat.

Count Kolowrat, a wealthy Bohemian noble, who had till then held the office of "Oberstburggraf" in Prague, became a Minister in 1826 on the death of Count Zichy, and was not long in acquiring a powerful influence over Francis. He was a man of real ability and knowledge, but vain, ambitious and jealous of all others. He wanted to monopolise the Emperor and enjoy the sole credit for everything.[11] His peculiar character was summed up by Kübeck, who was intimately associated with him, in these words (1832)—"Kolowrat is a man of talent and understanding, but his character is a strange mixture of thirst for action and weak love of quiet."[12] On one occasion Kolowrat burst out to Kübeck: "Believe me, he who has to serve for any length of time in the immediate entourage of the Emperor must be either a philosopher or an intriguer or a mere animal (*ein Vieh*), in order to stick it out

[10] His diaries and correspondence, published in 1908 by his son, throw a flood of light on the inside workings of the old régime.

[11] *Ibid.,* I, p. 293.

[12] *Tagebücher,* I, (ii), p. 623.

(*es auszuhalten*)." To which Kübeck sarcastically rejoined: "Of these three, most people hold to the *juste milieu*, namely, intrigue."[13] In the words of Count Clam-Martinitz, the Archduke Charles's successor as commander-in-chief, "Kolowrat is a child who plays alternately with different dolls, now with the ideal of the all-powerful Minister, and now with that of the independent country magnate." He never lost the outlook of his own class, the feudal aristocracy of Bohemia, and was not without a certain interest for Czech nationality, though he can hardly be said to have advanced its cause in any way.

Kolowrat set himself to undermine Metternich's influence, and so far as domestic affairs were concerned, he succeeded. From Kolowrat's advent to power, Metternich may be said to have hardly counted at home. On the other hand Francis was too intelligent to prefer Kolowrat to Metternich in foreign affairs and here Metternich held his own, though his jealous colleague often hinted that what really mattered was financial reform, and that "Europe might go hang."[14] Kolowrat seems to have taken the opposite view from Metternich almost on principle: for instance, he favoured a reduction of the army, as a sequel to a modest foreign policy, and he was hostile to the Hungarian Constitution, to which Metternich had a strong leaning, especially after his third marriage, with Countess Melanie Zichy.

Kolowrat, it is only fair to add, had many ideas for the improvement of the administration, and for reforms which he regarded as necessary, but he lacked the steadfastness to force them through against the deadweight of Metternich's negative policy and Francis's hatred of all change. He warned the Emperor that what he called "a wood of bayonets" would lead sooner or later to the very Revolution which he wished to avoid, and that social reforms were vitally needed. But though he periodically offered his resignation because he could not carry his point, and retired for a certain time to his Bohemian estates, he was always persuaded to change his mind and give up the big principle for the sake of some petty concessions. He thus created among the general public the impression that he was of more liberal tendencies than any of his colleagues, but in effect he wavered between the rival views and effected nothing.

What made the situation so serious was that Francis came to

[13] *Ibid.*, p. 533.
[14] cf. Srbik, *op. cit.*, p. 541.

depend more and more upon Kolowrat, who occupied in fact, though not in name, the position of a Prime Minister, and that while it suited Francis very well to have two rival Ministers, the result was that, internally at least, most of their energies were spent in counteracting each other, and so nothing got done. This was even more serious than it would otherwise have been because the heir to the throne, Ferdinand, was little better than feeble-minded, suffered from rickets and epilepsy,[15] and had had a very faulty education. He was quite unfit to govern, and it was not at all clear what would happen if he succeeded to the throne. Already under Francis it was possible to say that Austria was administered, but not governed, and this was to become truer as time passed.

At this period the complicated machinery of State may be summed up under seven main heads: (1) the Combined Aulic Chancellory, consisting of one Hofkanzler for home affairs in Austria and Bohemia, and two others for Hungary and Transylvania; (2) the Hofkammer or Aulic Chamber for financial and commercial affairs; (3) the Oberste Justizstelle or Supreme Judiciary, from which Hungary and Transylvania, having their own supreme courts and judicial system, were excluded; (4) the Hofkriegsrat, or Aulic War Council; (5) the Generalrechnungsdirektorium or Accountant's Office; (6) the Polizei-und-Censurhofstelle (police and censorship); and (7) the Haus- Hof-und-Staatskanzlei for foreign affairs and the Imperial Household. At the instance of Kaunitz, Maria Theresa had created the Staatsrat, or Council of State; but the departments of War, Finance and Foreign Affairs were excluded from its sphere, and formed so many watertight compartments, which had no link save written communications. In 1802 Francis, urged on by his brother Charles—who took a very alarmist view of the future unless serious reforms were put in hand— created the so-called "Staats- und Konferenzministerium," consisting of only six members, including the Emperor himself. The object of this was to co-ordinate affairs and to win a general survey. But owing to Francis's peculiar mentality, this proved impracticable. He could not shake himself free from details, and matters were continually referred to the new body with which it ought never to have been troubled. Lack of system or co-ordination remained as great as ever.

[15] The confidential report on Ferdinand's health sent by Dr. Staudenheim to Metternich on Francis's instructions (30 April, 1829) is preserved in the Metternich archives at Plass, and is quoted by Srbik, I. p. 546.

It is highly interesting to note Metternich's attitude to the question of reform. For he combines in a very curious manner the fear of change, the rigid insistence upon order and authority, the detestation of popular sovereignty or democratic institutions, which dominated Francis, with a recognition that it is impossible to govern indefinitely with bayonets, that the monarchical principle is more a matter of convenience and continuity than an eternal, immutable dogma, and that such constitutional machinery as exists must be respected and may even be extended with advantage, so long as the Sovereign is recognised as the source of authority and power. The Hungarian constitution, in particular, was to him a valuable conservative institution, and even the Estates of the various Austrian provinces deserved to be encouraged so long as they did not claim to rest upon popular sovereignty, but merely to represent vested interests and corporations.[16] Above all, Metternich was far too intelligent not to realise the dangers due to red tape, pedantry, slow movement and watertight compartments. One of the first things he did on becoming Foreign Minister was to advocate a reorganisation of the Staatskanzlei archives on modern lines, and this was accepted.[17]

In 1811, however, he made a much more ambitious proposal to the Emperor, which if carried into effect would have revived the old 18th century Staatsrat of Prince Kaunitz, though remodelling it on lines copied from Napoleon's Legislative Council and the Imperial Council of Russia. The root idea—the details of a stillborn scheme need not concern us here—was to have a Reichsrat or Imperial Council for the whole Monarchy, presided over by the Sovereign and consisting of the heads of all the great departments of State—without executive power, but with a mandate to discuss and advise upon such matters of policy as the Sovereign laid before it—and thus to relieve the pressure upon the "Conference of Ministers," which would retain its existing executive powers and would consist more of technical experts, thereby gaining immensely in efficiency.[18] Nothing came of this plan, and the Staatsrat and Conference of Ministers con-

---

[16] The distinction between Parliament and Estates or *Stände*, between parliamentary and *Ständisch* Government, must be recognized as fundamental, if we are to understand the constitutional development of Austria and Hungary, and indeed of Germany, during the 19th century.

[17] *Nachgelassene Papiere*, ii, p. 315.

[18] *Ibid.*, II, pp. 444-53.

tinued on the old lines, working more and more against each other and so paralysing each other's efforts. This became so self-evident that in August, 1814, Metternich, in a series of memoranda, insisted on the need for drawing a clear distinction between the legislative, executive and judicial functions, and argued that it was the lack of this distinction in autocratic States which tended to produce paralysis.[19]

Francis accepted Metternich's ideas, and reorganised the Staatsrat as a purely consultative body, formed of the Ministers on the one hand and specially appointed Councillors (*Staatsräte*) on the other, and divided into four sections, legislative, administrative, financial and military. Foreign Affairs were specially excluded, but a link was provided in the fact that the Staatskanzler was also a Staatsminister, and thus a permanent and, of course, very influential member. But the old system, or rather lack of system, soon drifted back owing to the Emperor's inveterate habits of interference with every detail, and his inability to distinguish between the functions of the various bodies. He never learned the difference between administration and government.

To meet one of Metternich's main criticisms, Francis consented in 1816 to the creation of a real Ministry of Finance, on modern lines, instead of the old department. But it was thoroughly character-istic of his methods that the Hofkammer, of which the department of finance had formed a part, continued to survive side by side with the new Ministry, like the Hofkriegsrat beside the Ministry of War. Metternich's proposal for a new Ministry of Justice was disregarded.

In 1817 Metternich went a step farther and submitted proposals for a reorganisation of the central authority, on lines which Professor Srbik describes as federalist rather than centralist. Knowing his master, he was careful to begin by insisting that his plan "contains nothing harsh (*nichts grelles*), nothing subversive, no single daring principle." It was, however, essential "that already under your eyes and your beneficent (*segnend*) hand the supreme authority should be organised in such a way as will form the best defence against by-paths (*Abwege*) or will at least not render them easy." This was a delicate way of hinting that the heir to the throne was quite unequal to any test that required initiative or reflection. "The machine of State works," Metternich reminded Francis, "because its lower

[19] Srbik, I, p. 459—based on the original archives of the Staatsrat itself, and not hitherto utilised.

mechanism is well constructed and because it has as its head a monarch who is capable of governing." The art of suggestion by implication could hardly go farther.[20] Metternich went on to argue that there are only two alternatives—"complete fusion," which means unrestricted centralisation and is only attainable through revolution, or on the other hand a strong central government, tempered by due consideration for local institutions (*Sonderstellungen*). He therefore suggests the creation of a Supreme Chancellor (*Oberster Kanzler*) who will at the same time be Minister of the Interior and head of the whole administration, and four subordinate Chancellors under him: (1) for Bohemia, Moravia and Galicia, (2) for Austria, (3) for Illyria (including Dalmatia), and (4) for Italy. The Hungarian and Transylvanian Chancellories would in some respects be curtailed, but would remain outside the scheme, more or less on existing lines.

It is important to note in all this that Metternich, who already in 1811 and 1813 opposed the idea of overthrowing the Hungarian Constitution, is still as reluctant as ever to see its infringement. The explanation of this lies in a direction already briefly indicated. Metternich always drew a very strong distinction between the principle of popular representation, deriving from the doctrine of popular sovereignty, and therefore in his opinion inevitably leading to communism, the destruction of property and the propertied classes, and on the other hand the principle of the Estates or *Stände*, which represent classes and vested interests rather than individuals and are the chief bulwark of the aristocratic principle. We therefore find him helping Tirol to recover its old constitution in 1816, and Galicia in the same way in 1817: and again he promotes the creation of Diets in Carniola (1818) and Salzburg (1826). He did not, however, regard these bodies as sovereign, or even as representing the province, but only the Estates. They had no legislative or financial powers, and thus no real initiative, though they could tighten the purse strings and exercise a certain amount of control. In 1819 we find him explaining at Teplitz to Frederick William III this fundamental distinction between "*landständische Verfassungen*" and "*ein sogenanntes Repräsentativsystem*."[21] The former he argues, could safely be granted by Prussia, whereas to introduce a democratic constitution would complete the process of revolution.

[20] *Nachgelassene Papiere*, III, pp. 62-75.
[21] *Ibid.*, III, p. 269.

Even more instructive are Francis's comments on Metternich's meeting with the King of Prussia. Francis thinks it better to leave the idea of "Estates representation" alone, because public opinion is hardly likely to rest satisfied with that. The idea that the Estates might share in legislation he dismisses as "risky" (*bedenklich*), and as for a Commission of Enquiry into "my Universities," he will never allow such a thing, for that would be the surest way of "bringing them into unrest and confusion." Once again then, nothing was done, and so far as Prussia was concerned, Frederick William III never redeemed the constitutional pledge which he had given in the great days of victory: while in Austria what Metternich's son Richard has called Francis's "belief in the intangibility of written law, carried to the point of timidity (Angstlichkeit)," led him now, as ever, to play for time.[22]

Metternich's proposals were laid in a drawer of the Emperor's desk, but in 1826 Francis had a very serious illness which left him an old man; and on his recovery he sent one day for Metternich and said very frankly that he wished to free his mind of a sin which, when he seemed unlikely to recover, weighed more heavily upon him than the illness itself. "I have still not followed out your proposal. I shall make good the omission and have enquiry made without loss of time." Metternich took advantage of this occasion to argue that "it is not enough, as affairs stand today, for Your Majesty to govern. You must assure to your successor the instruments of government."[23] None the less nothing came of these good resolutions, and after the July Revolution the very idea of reform was odious to him. In June, 1831, he said to Pillersdorff—"I won't have any innovations. Let the laws be justly applied: our laws are good and adequate. This is no time for reforms. The peoples are, as it were, badly wounded. One must avoid irritating these wounds by touching them."[24] The last stage is on the last day of the year 1834, when the Chancellor came to pay his New Year respects, and Francis said to him: "I stand once more like a penitent sinner before you: but the year 1835 shall not pass without my debt being paid."[25] Two months later the Emperor died, and the

[22] *Nachgelassene Papiere*, III, p. 8.

[23] Schlitter, *Aus Œsterreichs Vormärz*, IV, p. 40. Bibl, *Zerfall Œsterreichs*, I, p. 318; Srbik, I, p. 465.

[24] Kübeck, *Tagebücher*, I, p. 438.

[25] Srbik I, p. 472, based on letter of Metternich to Hartig, 29 January 1850 (*Plass Archives*).

strange and abnormal situation which arose under his successor put an end to all hope of reform.

This survey shows quite clearly that the chief blame for the stagnation and rigidity of the Austrian system lay not so much with Metternich, after whom popular tradition has named it, as with Francis, who neutralised his Minister's repeated attempts to repair the outworn machine of State. In the later years of his official life Metternich was always repeating the phrase that the first duty of the Crown was to govern, not to administer, and he must have been conscious that that was exactly the opposite of what his master was actually doing. In an autobiographical fragment written after his fall he commits himself to the view that revolutions "only ripen into action through the fault of the supreme authority, whether this consists of misuse or of non-use of its power."[26] He lacked the energy to resign rather than see what he regarded as vitally necessary simply shelved. But no one can fairly accuse him of not diagnosing the trouble, and in economic matters he was even more far-sighted, as is exemplified by his attitude to the whole question of a Zollverein [Customs Union].

It was not without ground that the disappearance of Francis from the scene in 1835 coincided with a widespread outbreak of acute pessimism. Perhaps it would even be more accurate to say that pessimism inside Austria had been steadily gaining ground for a number of years. Gentz in his latter years became highly critical of the system of which he had so long been a mainstay, and quarrelled with Metternich over it. He saw the future, to quote his own words, "about as black as the grave." Then again, Grillparzer, arch-Conservative though he was, wrote in 1830: "The whole world will be strengthened by the new upheaval" (the July Revolution), "only Austria will fall in pieces as a result": and in 1834 no less a man than Kübeck, one of the ablest and most influential officials in the whole Austrian service, records his view that "Anarchy is at the gates."

Stability remained to the last the note of Francis's Government, and stability was proclaimed as that on which his successor was to rest. A Viennese wag circulated the story that some good patriots wept at the loss of Francis and received the official assurance, "Don't cry, children, everything is to stay exactly as it was." Their reply was, "That's just why we're crying." As we saw, his New Year promise to

[26] *Nachgelassene Papiere*, VIII, p. 621.

Metternich remained unredeemed, but on his deathbed he put his signature to two documents containing his political testament and addressed to his son Ferdinand. When Anton Springer wrote his "History of Austria" in the 'sixties they had already been heard of, but on the whole he rejected them as spurious. Since the War, however, Dr. Bibl has had the originals in his hands in the Vienna Archives, and was able to establish their absolutely genuine character. The essence of their doctrine is this: "Don't move in any way the foundation of the State edifice." "Govern and change nothing." (*Regiere und verändere nichts*). In domestic affairs the new Emperor is advised to consult his uncle Archduke Ludwig, while in foreign affairs he is told to give his confidence to Metternich, "my most loyal servant and friend," and to take no decisions without consulting him. No mention whatever is made of Kolowrat. He is also advised to continue his father's unfinished work of modifying the relations between Church and State, in a sense approved by the Pope and in conformity with the decisions of the Council of Trent; and in this he is again to rely upon the advice of Metternich, and also of Bishop Wagner, the Court chaplain.

There is no doubt that there was a deliberate attempt to eliminate Kolowrat altogether, although it did not prove successful. But perhaps the most striking feature was that of all the Emperor's brothers, it should have been Ludwig whom he selected—the one who had the fewest ideas and least to recommend him. Charles, John and Joseph—all three men of brilliance and enlightenment—were strictly eliminated from any deciding influence, though the latter was allowed to remain Palatine of Hungary. Ludwig was the wittiest of the family, in a genial, superficial, Viennese way, but he had no talents or governing capacity. The result of the will was that the real power fell from the hands of the dead Emperor into that of a triumvirate, in which neither of the two subordinates, Metternich and Kolowrat, was strong enough to eliminate the other, while the Archduke adopted his brother's traditional policy of playing them off against each other, in the hope that the balance would rest in his own hands.

The Decembrists

D. S. MIRSKY

⇛⇛⇛⇛⇛⇛⇛⇛ *Published in 1925* ⇚⇚⇚⇚⇚⇚⇚⇚⇚

Despite all the fear of revolution, none took place in any of the major European countries in the first decade after Waterloo. It was only in the minor countries of Europe—in Spain, the Kingdom of the Two Sicilies, Piedmont, and the Ottoman Empire—that revolutions broke out. And when a major country was at last faced with the long-expected revolutionary outbreak, that country proved to be not England or France but Russia. There, in December 1825, the uprising of the Decembrists took place. Poorly organized, it quickly turned out to be a fiasco; and it would probably have been quickly forgotten if not for the manner in which Nicholas I (1825-1855) chose to deal with those who were involved. Seizing upon the uprising in order to give warning to any other Russians who might be tempted to upset the established order, Nicholas made it seem to be far more important than it really was. In short, he played a decisive part in fostering the legend of a Russian revolutionary tradition—a legend that was to inspire successive generations of Russian reformers of all sorts. It is with the significance of this legend, among other things, that Prince D. S. Mirsky, the renowned historian of Russian literature and author of the penetrating *Russia, A Social History,* concerns himself in the present article. The article itself was written at the time of the centennial celebration of the Decembrist uprising.

I t is easy to predict the sort of thing every particular Russian paper will say on the occasion of the Centenary of the Decembrists. The official publicists of the Communist Party, while giving them qualified praise for being the first to rise against Autocracy, will remind the proletarian reader that these rebels were squires and nobles; that the only thing they cared for were the class interests of the middle gentry, and

Reprinted by special permission from *The Slavonic Review,* IV (1925), 400-404.

that their revolutionary importance is not by any means comparable to Razin's and Pugachev's. The *émigré* Socialists and Republicans will be unreservedly enthusiastic in their praise of the Decembrists, and will lament the cruel irony of fate that has crowned the effort started by them with the tyranny of the Communists. The ex-Liberals of the following of Peter Struve will try to ignore the political aspects of the question, but will dwell at length on the religious feeling, the patriotism, and the gentility of the mutineers of December—so unlike the disreputable revolutionaries of later and recent times. The reactionaries' comment will be the bluntest and simplest of all; they will extol Nicholas I. for the unsentimental way in which he dealt with Ryleyev and Pestel, and respectfully regret that his great-grandson was not as drastic with Milyukov and Kerensky.

What would the Decembrists themselves have said if they had been in a position to comment on the Russia of to-day? One can be sure of one thing: they would have shown no unity. All parties would have found partisans among them. I have no doubt that some of them would even be joining with the thick-skulled Bisons of the extreme Right in their panegyrics of Nicholas I. These, however, would be but few; the majority would probably be with the ex-Liberals, deeply disgusted by the turn which the Revolution took. A considerable minority, including, I am sure, the best—Ryleyev, Yakushkin, Batenkov—would rally to the Republicans, disgusted also with the present rulers of Russia, but not stooping to regret the past. At least one or two (and one of them Pestel) would be heart and hand with Lenin and Trotsky. Nor would anyone of them, in all this range of voices, be an apostate from his hundred-year-old youth. The fact is that the Decembrists were not a party, or a sect; they were a generation. They were, in every sense of the word, the *pick* of the generation that came of age during and after the Napoleonic Wars: all those in it who heard the call of civic honour and of patriotic duty; all those who obeyed the dictates of a generous heart; all those who, in the words of Ryleyev's *Citizen* (written in December, 1825, a few days before the Rebellion), were "incapable of dragging on their youthful years in shameful indolence, in the embrace of lust, and of letting their passionate soul waste away under the heavy yoke of tyranny." Eighteen or fifteen years earlier, none of them would have dreamt of rising in arms against the Monarchy; they would have found food for their love of honour and for their activity on the fields of Eylau and Borodino. Many of them had fought there, and were still drunk with the glory of the Napoleonic Wars. They had returned from captured Paris, after restoring freedom to the nations of the West—and found at home a coalition of brutal bullies, hysterical hypocrites, and honest but obsolete dotards, forcing their inglorious rule on a nation and on an army that had been victorious all over Western Europe, and that were still rich in young men, ambitious, capable, avidly progressive. The same conditions prevailed at that time in other countries besides Russia. The last ten years of Alexander I.'s reign were precisely the moment when Russia, in the advanced *élite* of her upper classes, was most thoroughly Europeanised and European. And the Decembrists must not be isolated from their contemporaries in the West. The Revolutions of Spain and Naples, the "Tugendbund" in Germany, the anti-Bourbon conspiracies in Restoration France—were all connected with the armies and with the educated youth of the upper classes. The very organisation of the Russian Secret Societies was modelled on those of Germany and Italy, and the spirit animating them was the same. All that was at all active and alive in the younger generation gravitated round the Secret Societies. It was impossible to have a sense of honour and not to join, or try to join, them. "Honour," in the poetic language of the time, is invariably used in the sense of revolutionary duty. The spirit of the Secret Societies animated the Poets of the time. Of the greater literary men of the day, only quite unpolitical men, like the patriarchal and placid Aksakov and the metaphysical Baratynsky, kept aloof from them. The greatest minds of the generation—Chaadayev, Pushkin and Griboyedov—were of them and with them. If they were not on the Senate Square on St. Philemon's Day, it was in each case by the merest chance.

The Decembrists were a company of young men. And young men

ARAKCHEYEV: Russian general of the early nineteenth century. Hated for his brutal treatment of soldiers, he came to serve, in the eyes of reformers, as a symbol of reaction and of man's inhumanity to man.

BELINSKY: Russian literary critic (d. 1848) who exerted considerable influence upon Russian intellectuals in the nineteenth century. At first an advocate of literature for its own sake, he came increasingly to insist on the principle of social significance, declaring that it was the function of the writer to deal with the problems of his age and to further social progress.

NARODNIKS: Populists. Members of a revolutionary society formed in 1870. The society broke up into several lesser groups, one of which sought to

are not, as a rule, of much use in politics when they are acting at their own risk. Young men are a valuable asset in revolutionary work, but only when they are guided by the old and experienced. The Decembrists had no one to guide them. The story of the conspiracy and of the revolt of the Fourteenth is pathetic, so extraordinary was the muddle-headedness and inefficiency of the conspirators and rebels. Still more pathetically helpless was the revolt of the Chernigov Regiment in the South, its march on Kiev, and its destruction by the government forces. It was not only the youth of the revolutionaries that ruined them; it was also their lack of cohesion. They did not know what they wanted. They were united by a negation, by a moral impulse, by a strong but vague sense of duty—the duty of overthrowing the despotism of the Arakcheyevs—but by no programme, no positive ideal. The only one of them who had a definite idea of what he wanted was Pestel—but Pestel was far too radical for the great majority; they feared his ideas and mistrusted him as a man.

Was a victory of the Decembrists under any circumstances possible? Most certainly. With greater cohesion, it would have been easy for them to win the day of the Fourteenth. The Romanov family was small enough to be easily destroyed; its destruction would have disorganised the Government, and thrown confusion into the army; the middle and lower classes in the towns were distinctly sympathetic; the peasants were indifferent. But a victory of the rebels would also most certainly have led before long to chaos and anarchy; and unless, by some miracle, Ermolov or some other man had proved himself what is called "a Napoleon," the Revolution would have culminated in a general *jacquerie* and in the rapid overthrow of the whole social order—a Pugachev rising on a tenfold magnified scale—or a Bolshevik revolution without Marxists to direct it.

---

provoke a peasant revolution and another of which sought to assassinate the emperor.

PESTEL: Leader of the radical wing of the Decembrists. Politically, he supported the formation of a highly centralized republic. Economically, he advocated a fundamental redistribution of landed holdings in Russia. In an immediate sense he favored the establishment of a military dictatorship.

STENKA RAZIN and PUGACHEV: Cossacks who led the most powerful and fear-inspiring peasant revolts in seventeenth- and eighteenth-century Russia, respectively.

But all this might have happened only if the rebels had been very different from what they were. As they actually were, defeat was the only thing possible.

Nicholas I., in dealing with the Decembrists, showed an astounding lack of sense of realities; in other words, of the sense of humour.[1] He exaggerated the actual and undervalued the latent importance of the revolt and of the rebels. All their behaviour had been a pathetic contradiction between their generous and morally great underlying impulse, and their practical and political inadequacy. There were in the revolt all the elements of comedy. If Nicholas had noticed this, he would have scored a political victory that might have made Russian history very different; he would have proved himself a politician of genius—which he, fortunately or unfortunately (fortunately, I think), was not. Nicholas's conduct was not so much a failure of the politician, as a failure of the man. On 14 December he had seen Fear. All his dealings with the vanquished rebels were dictated by his resentment against those who had made him a coward. In the trial of the Decembrists, he acted, with truly Shakespearean grasp, the part of the victorious coward. The main facts of the trial are too well known to be recalled. They are the darkest and *meanest* blot on the memory of the Russian Monarchy. They are the most permanent influence working against the good name of the dynasty.

Nicholas was given the opportunity of turning the affair into a comedy; he preferred to make it a tragedy. After all, it was only that the fitness of things was emphasised. A humorous, that is to say, a statesmanlike, treatment of the affair would have more cruelly belittled the rebels than the horrors of the trial. Their martyrdom brought out the essential fact of the whole business—the intrinsic moral superiority of the vanquished, impolitic, inefficient Decembrists over the confident victors; their superiority, in the light of the essential and lasting values, to those who were not with them.[2]

[1] A sense of humour, says W. P. Ker, consists in being able to think of more than one thing at a time.

[2] The conduct of some (not all) of the Decembrists during the trial, their recantations and their revelations, does not reflect on their moral worth any more than Galileo's retraction at his trial. The conditions of the trial were in both cases the same, if the instruments of justice were slightly different. Anyhow, the *subsequent* behaviour of the sentenced Decembrists was a splendid *eppur si muove* [act of defiance].

The trial was the first act of a reign whose meanness and moral smallness is unparalleled in history, a reign that made inevitable and irremediable the cleavage between the monarchy and the best part of the nation, and sealed the tragic fate of the Romanovs.

The trial and what followed created the Legend of the Decembrists which, in Russia, was more effective than anything in raising the moral and poetic prestige of the revolutionary movement, and in giving it an almost religious sanction.[3] The principal thing about it was the *unanimity* of public feeling about the Decembrists; irrespective of political bias, all were fascinated by the martyrs' halo round the heads of the first Revolutionaries, and no one refused to respect their moral superiority. This was only inevitable poetic justice.

Apart from the Legend, the Decembrists had little influence on the subsequent development of the Russian revolutionary movement. The first half of the reign of Nicholas I. was one of the crucial periods of Russian history, when old traditions were dropped and new traditions established. Like Pushkin, the Decembrists belonged to the old "pre-Belinsky" formation of Russian society, and like Pushkin they survived into the new age only in the form of a myth. The myth was heavy with significance, but the historical facts that underlay it and the ideas that inspired the facts were lost touch with. The new revolutionary tradition grew out of movements of the 'thirties and 'forties that had no link with the Decembrists. Socialism was the soul of the new movement, and it came to life without any real influence of the December Revolt. Only the generous spirit that impelled the Decembrists was not dead, and the same spirit lived again in the Narodniks of the 'seventies. It is this spirit that is permanently valuable, as the soul of the Decembrist movement: that *multa pars* of them that evades death and becomes the most cherished inheritance of the nation.

The modern world has only one religion—the worship of success. But there are higher values than success; and the universal and supernational significance of the Russian revolutionary movement is that it has emphasised these values, and enhanced them in the eyes of a

---

[3] The heroic conduct of the wives of the Decembrists contributed, of course, very powerfully to enhance the prestige of the exiles. But it would have been insufficient to create it alone; the equal heroism of Princess Nathalie Dolgoruky in the reign of Anne has made her, too, one of the noblest figures of Russian history, but did not succeed in making of the Dolgorukys more than an object of tragic compassion.

world idolatrous of success. The political failure of the Decembrists is patent. Not only did they not command; they did not even deserve success. Their victory would have been for them the worst of defeats. And still we cannot revoke the unanimous verdict of posterity that gives them one of the highest places in the national esteem. What we admire in them is the quality of the impulse that moved them. They remain, and will remain, hallowed in our memory, because in their life and in their death they were the champions of the eternal truth of the chainless spirit against the vegetable powers of sloth and selfishness, which are the soul of social conservatism.

The Great Days of Reform

G. M. TREVELYAN

➤➤➤➤➤➤➤➤➤➤ *Published in 1932* ◀◀◀◀◀◀◀◀◀◀

Restoration France—the France of Louis XVIII (1814-1824) and of Charles X (1824-1830)—saw one long struggle between ultraroyalists and liberals—a struggle which by 1830 ended in the revolution that Metternich had long feared. Hardly had Charles been driven from the throne and Louis Philippe made King of the French than the repercussions of this July Revolution were felt in many parts of Europe. In England, for example, it aroused considerable excitement. The *Edinburgh Review* went so far as to state that "the battle of English liberty has really been fought and won at Paris"; and young John Stuart Mill rejoiced that the Revolution had given him "a new existence." Archconservative Lord Eldon, on the other hand, feared that "to a certain extent it will do work here"; and he was disheartened that there was no Pitt the Younger in power "to allay what is brewing, a storm for changes here, especially for Reform in Parliament." Lord Eldon proved to be entirely right. The July Revolution did "do work" in England: it played an important part in making possible the enactment of the Reform Bill of 1832. It seems hardly necessary to point out that the Bill itself represented a tremendous victory for the Whigs. It is especially appropriate, then, to read an evaluation of its significance by George Macaulay Trevelyan, descendant of the great Macaulay and the outstanding Whig historian of the twentieth century.

I. *Whigs and Tories*

One hundred years ago the great Reform Bill was passed, after 15 months of fierce convulsion in the body politic that made almost as great an impression on contemporaries as the Bill itself. Of the protagonists in that struggle *The Times* newspaper alone survives to-day, triumphing over chance and time.

Reprinted by special permission from the London *Times*, June 7 and 8, 1932.

By the consent alike of friends and foes, the Reform Bill began a new era in the political life of Britain. In our domestic history 1832 is the next great landmark after 1688. But, whereas the institutions in Church and State known as the Revolution Settlement lasted unchanged for nearly a century and a half, the Reform Bill ushered in an era of ceaseless change. We have long ago overthrown the nicely adjusted balance of forces set up by the actual terms of the Bill—a balance between the landlord class and the bourgeoisie, between privilege and modern enterprise. Since then country life has been offered up a sacrifice to the city populations; the squires have gone down before the town middle class; but the victors have to-day the less joy of their victory, because they in their turn are hard pressed upon by classes that were not enfranchised by the Bill of 1832. Contrary to the prophecies of extreme Tories and Radicals at the moment when the Bill became law, Crown, Established Church, and House of Lords still exist, but the last two have been deprived of many privileges that were then considered essential. The Crown, indeed, has greater security and prestige than it had when worn by the sons of George III. But it has less political power than in 1831, when Grey admitted that, if King William had not signified his approval, he could not, under the existing custom of the Constitution, have introduced the Reform Bill into Parliament at all, any more than Pitt could introduce Catholic emancipation without the Royal consent.

Strictly interpreted, the new constitutional era begun in 1832 lasted only till the second Reform Bill of 1867. But in another sense it is still the era in which we live. For the epoch of political change dating from the first Reform Bill has never yet stopped; nor will it ever stop, so long as scientific invention, the blind titan that makes and

WILLIAM COBBETT: Editor of the *Political Register* and the most talented and influential journalist in the England of the early nineteenth century. A leader in the movement for parliamentary reform, he agitated for the introduction of universal manhood suffrage, which he viewed as the starting point for a series of social and economic reforms in the interests of the English lower classes.

LUDDITES: Desperate English workingmen who found it hard to earn a living in the last stages of the Napoleonic Wars because of the loss of markets on the continent. Accordingly, they went about destroying the machinery which they considered to be the cause of their misfortunes. The

moves the world, continues to recast the economic and social structure of the country as fast every decade as it used to change every century. It was to meet the pressure of new social conditions that the political floodgates were opened in 1832, and the water has never ceased to pour through them. If they had not been opened purposely and wisely by skilled and careful hands, the pent waters would soon have burst the barriers, carrying destruction far and wide. That the Reform Bill saved the land from revolution and civil strife, and made possible the quiet progress of the Victorian era, is its great claim to the gratitude of posterity.

Lord Grey's Meaning

When Lord Grey said that in passing the Bill he intended to "stand by his order"—meaning the nobility and the landlord class—the Tory Peers laughed bitterly at such a paradox. But he meant what he said; and in fact the Bill did save "his order" for at least as long as anything could have saved it, and it saved a great many other things besides. Owing to the passage of the Bill, the cultivated upper class was not driven out of politics by a violent revolution, as in America, France, and elsewhere. Like the Revolution of 1688, the Reform Bill was a great Conservative as well as a great Liberal measure.

The opponents of the Bill—Eldon, Wetherell, Walter Scott, and the Duke of Wellington—in their honest attachment to the country's noble past and not ignoble present, refused to consider the possibilities of the future and to take counsel how the best of the past could be preserved for service in a new age. Their mistake did not consist in preferring rural to city life, or aristocracy to bourgeoisie—matters of taste wherein many will agree with them to-day and most of the Whig leaders

name itself is derived from Ned Ludd, a mythical person who was said to have directed the movement from his "office" in Sherwood Forest.

Peterloo Massacre: Massacre in 1819 of some Manchester reformers who had met in St. Peter's Fields in order to listen to a speech by the radical "Orator" Hunt and to draw up petitions in support of parliamentary reform.

Six Acts: Repressive measures of 1819 designed to prevent a revolutionary outbreak in Britain. Enacted shortly after the Peterloo Massacre, they severely restricted the holding of public meetings, limited the freedom of the press, and extended the heavy tax on newspapers to periodical publications in general.

agreed with them then. Nor did their mistake lie in their prophecy that larger changes would follow in the wake of the Reform Bill if once it were passed. The Tory mistake consisted in thinking that no changes would follow if it were thrown out. On the contrary such changes would then have followed as have been seen in less happy lands. Westminster would have been as the Tuileries, and the struggle of churches and classes in the nineteenth century would have been fought out by other weapons than the vote.

The fundamental mistake of the Tories lay in supposing that a world which the Industrial Revolution had already reconstructed socially could for ever retain the same political structure as in the days of Queen Anne. If the Tories wished to preserve the rotten boroughs and the aristocratic constitution in perpetuity, they should have stopped the Industrial Revolution; they should have passed Luddite laws to prohibit the new machines. To prosecute Tom Paine was a mere measure of delay, since they neglected the more important work of hanging James Watt and locking up George Stephenson. When once they had allowed the cotton mills of Lancashire to arise, Peterloo and the Six Acts were mere measures of postponement—strong sweeps of Mrs. Partington's broom against the incoming Atlantic, effective for a season but ultimately of no avail. For, when once the cotton lords had made their fortunes, when once the operatives had come together in great new communities around the factory doors, the old order of society was doomed. Thenceforth the problem of statesmen could only be the orderly and gradual conduct of the process of political change, to answer to social facts already accomplished.

THE WHIG CABINET

It is the merit of the Whigs of 1830-32 that they saw this better than the able men who had been governing England for the previous 50 years. The rising generation of Whig opposition leaders in the twenties—Russell, Durham, Brougham, and Althorp—realized the need of the nation as regards Reform of Parliament better than the Tory Governmentalists, partly because the Whigs, being always in opposition, had been at more leisure to observe and were less bound to vested interests; partly because Charles Fox had a generation before inscribed Parliamentary Reform on the Whig banner in the days when "it was safer to be a felon than a Reformer," and Grey and Holland had preserved that tradition of the elders.

To the older and younger Whigs, who had all been brought up in at least a theoretic attachment to Reform of Parliament, were added in the winter of 1830 a powerful group of reforming Tories, some of them the followers of Canning and Huskisson, lately dead. These recruits of Reform—Melbourne, Palmerston, Graham, and Stanley, "the Rupert of debate"—were welded with the Whigs into the Cabinet that Grey so skilfully formed after the fall of the Duke of Wellington. It was more than a new Cabinet, it was a new party, a party of Whigs and former Tories brought together to reform Parliament. It was an aristocratic Cabinet, and the element of family alliance was strong in it. It was none the worse for that, for the Whig aristocrats, Durham, Russell, Althorp, and Grey himself, were not only able men but advanced reformers— more advanced, oddly enough, than the democratic leader Brougham, who boggled at the total abolition of the rotten boroughs. It was a Cabinet formed to pass a Reform Bill, and it accomplished its task. It is much to be doubted whether in that moment of time any other set of men could have cajoled and forced King, Lords, and Commons into doing what the nation so imperatively demanded. If the aristoc-racy was to be persuaded to abdicate a portion of its powers, the unwelcome medicine had best be prepared and presented to it by aristocrats.

With the *ex post facto* criticisms of later Radicals that the Bill did not go far enough the historian need scarcely concern himself, for he knows that nothing more radical could have been passed by, or even introduced into, the then House of Commons. To contemporaries the only question was why the Bill went so far as it did. That was the surprise which rallied the nation and even the Radicals of the day to support the Whigs, whom otherwise they distrusted and disliked. There lay the wisdom of Lord Grey and the "Committee of Four" whom he appointed to draw up the Bill—Russell, Durham, Graham, and Duncannon. The Bill went far enough to arouse the enthusiasm of the nation because it was more than "bit-by-bit Reform"; it did not go so far as "Radical Reform," for if it had been Radical it would have alienated those forces in Court and Parliament without whose initial aid it could not be passed. It was a bull's eye of legislative marksman-ship, when an inch more to right or left would have been fatal.

AFTER WATERLOO

The reason why the country needed and demanded a measure so extensive, and why nothing short of the total abolition of the rotten boroughs would have united opinion behind the Bill, was that Reform had been so long postponed. Fifty years before milder measures would have sufficed. Between the American and the French Revolutions proposals to abolish some, but not all, the rotten boroughs had been urged by Pitt, Fox, and the Yorkshire Reformers. "Bit-by-bit Reform" would probably have been England's path of progress in the later years of George III., had it not been for the French Revolution and the long Napoleonic Wars. The anti-Jacobin reaction in England, an inevitable result of those foreign events, by stopping change, made rapid change necessary in 1830 if revolution was to be avoided.

The Reform movement, when it revived after Waterloo, revived first as a workingclass movement only. In the years 1817-19 the Radical agitation for the abolition of the rotten boroughs and for universal suffrage, led by Cobbett and Hunt, had been a movement of the suffering working class. In their acute economic distress during the bad times after the war they took up Parliamentary Reform as a means of compelling politicians to pay attention to their miserable state. The Radical and social character of the movement prevented both the Whig Opposition and the middle-class manufacturers from joining at that time in the cry for Reform, although Lord Grey still declared that if ever the nation took up the question of Reform "seriously and affectionately" he would place himself at the head of the movement.

Since for the present both Whigs and middle classes held aloof, it was easy for the Tory Government in 1819 to suppress the working-class movement by Peterloo and the Six Acts. After that the Tories carried on for another dozen years with renewed vitality under Peel and Canning, undergoing a change in a Liberal direction in every subject of home and foreign policy, except only on Parliamentary Reform and the allied question of Municipal Reform. On that the Tory Government, even at its most liberal moment, was adamant. That was the Ark of the Covenant. All else could be touched—Catholics, Test Act, trade union laws, police, foreign policy, tariff policy—but the rotten boroughs, Parliamentary and municipal, were to be sacred.

THE SPIRIT OF THE AGE

For this reason, owing to the Tory refusal to touch Parliamentary Reform, so unwisely emphasized by Wellington in the autumn of 1830, when he declared the British Constitution to be incapable of improvement, the liberal "spirit of the age" had to turn elsewhere and seek some other embodiment than the Liberal Toryism that had dominated the twenties. "The spirit of the age" breathed into the nostrils of the long-moribund Whig party and revived it for another great period of national leadership and government.

For in 1830, under the exasperating stimuli of bad times and of Wellington's Prime Ministership, and in the excitement caused by an orderly bourgeois revolution in France, the middle classes of England suddenly began to agitate "seriously and affectionately" for the destruction of the rotten boroughs—but not for universal suffrage. They cried out for Parliamentary Reform on different lines and in a different spirit from the Radical agitation of the Peterloo period. There was, however, one thing in common between working-class and middle-class Reformers—intense hatred of the rotten boroughs. "Down with the borough-mongers" was the cry in every street. On that platform, and on that alone, the much divided nation might yet be united by a bold and skilful appeal.

Lord Grey and his Whig colleagues put themselves at the head of this new agitation in the winter of 1830, and satisfied it by the Reform Bill of 1831-32. That Bill was a treaty of alliance between the Whig aristocrats and the middle classes, particularly the new middle classes created by the industrial revolution. Many bourgeois families passed over from neutrality or Toryism to Whig allegiance on this issue. They had supported the Tory Government against the Jacobins, against Napoleon, and more recently against the Radical Reformers, though with divided sympathies over the Peterloo massacre. Owing to the Reform Bill the Tories lost them again for a generation.

II. *England's Way*

What, then, were the terms of the alliance struck between the middle classes and the Whig aristocracy? What, in other words, were the essential provisions of the great Reform Bill? First and foremost, the rotten boroughs were all abolished. The principle of appointment of members of Parliament by individual patrons disappeared from the practice of the Constitution. This was effected in two ways. In the first place 150 seats were abolished by the famous Schedules A and B of the Bill; towns or hamlets in Schedule A lost both their members, those in Schedule B lost one. Secondly, some rotten boroughs kept their representation, but ceased to be "rotten" because their franchise was extended, so that they ceased to be in the gift of patrons. This occurred automatically, because a uniform franchise of all householders paying

£10 a year rent was established for all Parliamentary boroughs, whether they were old or newly created by the Bill. The redistribution of seats to make good the gaps left by Schedules A and B went partly to increase the county representation, and partly to enfranchise certain great centres of population, including Manchester, Birmingham, Rochdale, and other towns of the North and Midlands which had been raised to importance by the Industrial Revolution. In the counties, where ever since the fifteenth century the franchise had been confined to freeholders of forty shillings and upwards, the larger tenant farmers were also enfranchised by the Reform Bill.

Such were the main outlines of the Bill in the form in which it became law on June 7, 1832. The chief criticism that is sometimes directed against it to-day is the principle of uniformity. It is argued that Brougham was right when he wanted some of the rotten boroughs to be spared, as indispensable for party managers and Ministers to put in able young men and other persons useful to Government or to Opposition. It is also argued that if, instead of the uniform £10 franchise, the franchise had varied in the different boroughs, a considerable portion of the working class could at once have been admitted to the franchise in some places, while in others something nearer to the old patronage boroughs could have been continued with advantage.

Nothing but the Bill

These criticisms, though by no means devoid of weight, overlook the actual difficulty of making arbitrary discriminations, which would most certainly have been fiercely attacked by an envenomed Opposition, and would moreover have cooled the support of the Bill in the country. Ministers would have been accused, with truth, of "cooking" the new constituencies. Even as it was that charge was made, and was rebutted only because a principle of statistical uniformity had been adopted. Ministers would have had no right to abolish a number of vested interests in certain boroughs of immemorial antiquity if they had preserved others equally abusive and had created a number of new irregularities in the franchise. Such a system might have been ideally better, but it would not have appeared just to plain people, and it could never have been passed through Parliament.

For these reasons the principle of uniformity, which had existed in the country franchise ever since the Act of 1430, was now applied to boroughs also. It had the result of excluding the whole working class for the time being. On the other hand, it made it inevitable that when in the course of time the franchise was further extended, the whole working class would ultimately be enfranchised. The Radicals, Francis Place and Cobbett, foresaw this, and supported the Bill in the interest of their clients. They joined in the cry for "The Bill, the whole Bill, and nothing but the Bill," because the Bill would break down the immemorial barriers of antiquity—the first line of defence which was by far the most formidable; and also because the principle of uniformity, though now working in the interest of the bourgeoisie by the £10 franchise, must in the end work in the interest of the masses at present unenfranchised. Others among the working-class leaders, like Hunt, denounced the Bill because of the restricted franchise. But, though working-class opinion may be said to have been to that extent divided, it was solid against the rotten boroughs, and solid for a fight with the Lords when the Lords threw out the Bill.

The most vigorous and active support of the Bill—particularly in the Political Unions organized by Attwood—came from the middle classes. The term "middle class" was then a less vague description than it is to-day. It meant all who did not belong to the "gentlemen" of the landowning class and of the liberal professions on the one hand, and who were not, on the other hand, weekly wage-earners. The middle class, whom the Whig publicists idealized as "the solid part of the nation" and "the wealth and intelligence of the nation," included every one from the humblest clerk or village shopkeeper up to the wealthiest moneyed magnate. In 1832 the master manufacturers were seldom allied by matrimonial, social, or political ties with the aristocracy or landed interest. Many of them were Dissenters. The law did not allow them to shoot game, even if they hired a shooting; they were not invited to the country houses; and very few of their class could obtain seats in Parliament, or had anything to do with the choice of members for the rotten boroughs. They regarded the "landed interest" with a modified English version of the jealousy that the French capitalists in 1789 felt for the privileged *noblesse*: and the distaste was mutual. These social divisions largely disappeared in the following generation, but they counted in 1832, and put a great mass of wealth and power behind "the Bill."

THE WORLD OF DICKENS

But, most of all, the multitudinous lower middle class, the world of Cruikshank and of Dickens, was stirred by the Bill like the ocean by the attraction of the moon. The £10 franchise seemed to offer them political power and therewith a cure for all their troubles. Yet in fact the £10 franchise did not include all the lower middle class. It left very many of them still unenfranchised; this was perhaps a fortunate circumstance, because the demand for a further extension of the franchise became in later years common ground, under Bright's leadership, between the excluded half of the middle class and the whole working class. That was one reason why Victorian England was not torn by a class conflict of the working class against the rest of society.

In those days politics turned almost as much on religious and denominational jealousies as on social and economic issues. The Dissenters were for the Bill, seeing in it the necessary prelude to the redressing of their grievances such as Church rates and University tests. And this time they had unwonted allies in all the roughs in the country. The mob outrages, which a generation before had been directed against Dissenters and Reformers, were now directed against Bishops and Tories.

The clergy of the Establishment, with a few exceptions like the Rev. Sydney Smith, were more solidly against the Bill than any other class of the community. But the influence of the Church was then at its lowest point and did not carry the congregations. The clergy thought that the Bill would lead to disestablishment and disendowment. Yet in fact the Church retained not only its endowments but even the much-challenged compulsory Church rates and the monopoly at Oxford and Cambridge till after the passing of the second Reform Bill. That is one of many proofs that the immediate change made by the first Reform Bill was less than many people expected it to be.

It is not, indeed, true that the middle classes attained in 1832 to full control of the State. Their power was increased, but so also was the power of the squirearchy proper as against the small oligarchy who until 1832 had owned the borough representation.

THE LANDED INTEREST

If opinion in the towns was united in favour of the Bill, the countryside was divided. Probably half the squires supported it. They feared revolution if it were lost. For that reason many of the propertied classes were "Bill men" in the sombre winter of 1831-32—the winter of the rejection of the Bill by the Lords, the Bristol riots, cholera, and hard times. Many squires, whether Whig or Tory, were pleased by the increase which the Bill made in the county representation at the expense of the rotten boroughs, in which 99 squires out of 100 had no personal interest. The "borough-mongers," 150 individuals all told, must not be confused with the landed class as a whole. Moreover, the squires were delighted at the "Chandos Clause" added in Committee, which enfranchised their large tenant farmers. Under the Bill thus amended the squires obtained even more control over the county representation than before; and at the same time the county representation, previously limited to 82 English seats, was increased to 139.

Yet, actually and relatively, the power of the landed interest was diminished by the Bill. For it would now have to meet, on the floor of the House, no longer the mere nominees of borough owners who were landlords themselves, but the representatives of the triumphant middle class, the members of the newly enfranchised or newly reformed boroughs, elected by £10 householders. The issue between the gentry and the middle class, between the landed interest and the commercial and industrial world, came to a head over the Corn Laws a dozen years after the passage of the Reform Bill. Only then was the full extent of the change apparent. And by then intermarriage and social intercourse were beginning to blur the line previously so visible between the two divisions of the owners of wealth.

PUBLIC OPINION

The total abolition of the rotten boroughs won for the Bill and its authors the fierce support of the great bulk of the nation, irrespective of class and party. Once the Whig Ministers had, in March, 1831, made public their quite unexpected resolve to abolish all patronage boroughs it was necessary to go on and give effect to the policy, or, in the then state of public opinion, chaos would come again. Some of the Ministers and their supporters, like Palmerston, Lansdowne, and Campbell, were frightened by the sweeping character of the Bill. But to retire in face of the popular storm they had aroused in their support would be far more dangerous to the State than to let themselves be driven forward. The dynamics of the situation were not overstated in the emphatic orations with which young Tom Macaulay sprang to House of Commons fame. From first to last public opinion was the decisive element in the situation, and that is a main reason why the first Reform Bill was so important a step in the passage from aristocratic to democratic government. It was not only the actual provisions of the measure and the change it made in representation, but the means by which it was carried in face of the Peers' opposition, which made the first Reform Bill a turning point in political development.

The resistance of the House of Lords to the Reform Bill called forth a tremendous display of popular feeling and determination—orderly and organized, with a few exceptions like the disgraceful Bristol riots. Had it not been for the display of organized popular determination which held the Ministers and the House of Commons to their task, the Lords could have maintained their right of veto and compelled a compromise. For the only constitutional way to overcome their veto was the threat of a wholesale creation of Peers by the King. And William IV., though favourable to the Bill in its early days, was turning hostile to it in the winter of 1831-32, and would never have consented to make the famous threat of Peer making if it had been possible for him to carry on the Government peaceably in any other manner.

DAYS OF MAY

The last stage was the famous crisis in "the days of May," 1832. The Duke of Wellington, ever loyal to his Sovereign, attempted to form a Ministry in order to save the King's face and pass something like the Reform Bill without the appearance of Royal coercion applied to the House of Lords. The country thought that the Duke intended to scrap the Bill, and under that impression, probably a mistaken one, prepared for civil resistance. Such resistance must have been formidable, since the Army was hardly large enough to hold down London, let alone the other cities of England. Fortunately the matter was not put to the test, for Peel and the Conservative minority in the House of Commons declined to face an impossible situation merely in order to save the face of King and Peers, since by that time it was clear that the Bill must in any case be passed.

During this crisis in May the Whig Ministers had never actually vacated their offices. So when the King gave the effective guarantee that he would make Peers if necessary, the machinery of State rolled smoothly forward again, and on June 7, 1832, the Reform Bill became law. A change that in other lands or in an earlier England would have caused bloodshed and the breaking up of laws had been carried like any other Act of Parliament, as the prelude to the great era of peaceful progress that we now know as the Victorian Age. As we look back on it after a hundred years, "all passion spent," it was an affair of which Englishmen of all classes and parties may be proud, and it was a characteristically English business from beginning to end.

XV

Economic Change in Post-Napoleonic Europe

≫≫≫≫≫≫≫≫≫≫≪≪≪≪≪≪≪≪≪≪≪

"The Industrial Revolution"

HERBERT HEATON

Economic Ideas and Facts in the Early Period
of the Risorgimento (1815-1848)

KENT ROBERTS GREENFIELD

Unrest in France in 1848

ARTHUR L. DUNHAM

≫≫≫≫≫≫≫≫≫≫≪≪≪≪≪≪≪≪≪≪≪

"The Industrial Revolution"

HERBERT HEATON

⋙⋙⋙⋙⋙⋙⋙⋙⋙ *Published in 1938* ⋘⋘⋘⋘⋘⋘⋘⋘⋘

Few subjects are more solidly embedded in American textbooks of modern European history than the English Industrial Revolution. Yet the approach to the subject that continues to dominate many of these textbooks has been under fire for several decades. The more specialists in economic history have dug into the sources, the more suspicious have they become of the dramatic and sensational features of the traditional approach to the Industrial Revolution. They insist that this approach is based on a fundamental misunderstanding of the industrial evolution of late medieval and early modern times. No less important, they maintain that it is based on an exaggeration of the rate of industrial change in the late eighteenth and early nineteenth centuries. In recent years, these specialists have written much to dispel some of the misconceptions that have surrounded the history of English industrial development. It would be difficult, however, to find a statement of the newer approach to the growth of English industry that can rival the present essay by Herbert Heaton, of the University of Minnesota. Indeed, readers would not complain so often about the dullness of much of the secondary literature on economic history if more economic historians had Heaton's insight, critical power, sense of humor, and style.

The Editor's letter asked for an article on the industrial revolution, "with the view to bringing teachers up to date on newer scholarship and interpretations." So I spent the morning of Thanksgiving Day examining several recent high school or university history or social science texts to see how they handled economic developments. I soon found I had a new reason for being thankful. One *History of Europe* gives 102 pages out of 845 to economic conditions and trends, and another gives 136 pages out of 1024. This is a mighty advance since the

Reprinted by special permission from *Social Education,* II (1938), 159-165.

'eighties, when Fyffe wrote over a thousand pages and never mentioned a machine or a railroad. It is even better than conditions were thirty years ago, when the *Cambridge Modern History* included only three economic chapters in its fourteen volumes. The "Manor," the "Commercial Revolution," "Mercantilism," and the "Industrial Revolution" have definitely been admitted to the texts. My daughter tells me she has heard the manor described in five different lecture courses, and I notice that in her prescribed books the famous plan of a "typical manor" has been improved: a stork stands forlornly in the swamp, and the landlord is hunting a deer and a boar—simultaneously—in the Woodland.

This flush of gratitude for the many crumbs that are now falling from the general historian's table is, however, tempered a little by the staleness of some of the crumbs. Even the best of the university texts have provoked me to make several query marks in the margin; and some of the high school books ought to have whole paragraphs or even pages torn out. A teacher who said that the Roman Empire fell in 476, that the renaissance began when a Greek scholar migrated from Constantinople to Florence in 1397, that the American Constitution was a popular document, or that Germany was solely responsible for the World War would be accused of being old fashioned. Yet that is what often happens when general surveyors or writers of historical introductions to social science deal with economic history. This is inevitable, for the subject is being overhauled by higher criticism of the contents and the ideas of the founding fathers. Those men began their serious study only about sixty years ago and did a grand job with the limited data at their disposal. The second generation, working with a vastly enlarged mass of material, has revised or scrapped some of the pioneers' conclusions, and the third generation is now knocking at the door, or rather knocking some doors down. Almost every issue of the special periodicals forces us to change an opinion or an emphasis; the subject is as living, as exciting, as contemporary physics. But the task of keeping up with the bright young people on the research front line is hard on the heart and lungs of those of us who are over forty. It is even more strenuous for those who wish to be well informed academic general practitioners.

Such higher criticism has been devastating in two fields well known to history teachers. These are the "Manor" and the "Industrial Revolution." Of the "Manor" there is room here only to say that anyone who thinks he has done justice to the medieval countryside when he has described the manorial system is almost as wrong as he would be if he passed off a picture of a slave plantation as an adequate account of the American countryside. Of the "Industrial Revolution," the sharp lines and strong colors—chiefly rose and black—of the old picture have become so blurred that some of us now put the title in quotation marks or avoid using it.

That old picture, painted about 1880 by Arnold Toynbee, is a triptych, or a melodrama in three acts. First there is "The Eve," still, placid, quiet, at the end of a long day that reaches back to the Normans, Nero, or even Noah. The methods of agriculture, industry, and transportation have changed little in a thousand years. Production is carried on by small manufacturers or farmers. The former, like the latter, live in the country, combine industry and agriculture, and supplement the family labor supply by training an apprentice and perhaps employing a journeyman or two. The wage earner usually works, aided by his family, in his own home on materials put out to him by his employer; but he may work under his master's roof. Between master and man is a "warm attachment"; they call each other by their Christian nicknames. The class of capitalist employers is still "in its infancy"; some merchant-employers put out material to be processed in the homes of their employees or of small masters, and a few factories or central workshops exist. But in general the family firm and the family farm prevail. Division of class and of labor is slight. The worker can express his personality in his work, though what happens if it is crooked is not clear. Production is for local markets or for the producer's larder and wardrobe, since defective means of transportation and mercantilistic policies shut off distant consumers. No one

JOHN U. NEF: Professor of economic history at the University of Chicago, he is the author of numerous articles and books dealing with the economic development of early modern Europe. His two-volume study of *The Rise of the British Coal Industry* (1932) and his *Industry and Government in France and England, 1540-1640* (1940) are basic works for anyone interested in economic history.

DAVID RICARDO: English economist of the early nineteenth century who built on Adam Smith's *Wealth of Nations* and on Thomas Robert Malthus' *Essay on Population*. One of the chief formulators of "classical economics," he was frequently misinterpreted by his contemporaries and his followers,

earns great rewards, but the domestic system insures on the whole a sound and healthy life under conditions favorable to the development of mind, body, and personal dignity. Contentment spins at the cottage door; there is plenty of honeysuckle, ivy, and good ale in this "quiet world" of "scarcely perceptible movement." A comprehensive code of state regulation of production and trade combines with technical inertia to prevent anything from changing.

Then, with a rapidity known in the tropics, "The Night" falls, a night full of noise and action. Seven men—four Lancashire men (Kay, Hargreaves, Arkwright, and Crompton), two Scots (Adam Smith and James Watt), and one Episcopalian parson (Cartwright)—invent some textile machines, improve the steam engine, or write *The Wealth of Nations*. Meanwhile other men revolutionize agriculture and redraw the village map, while others improve roads and rivers or cut canals. But it is the seven men who get their names on the record, for their actions or thoughts "destroyed the old world and built a new one." And what they did was crowded into a brief night that lasted from about 1760 to 1780.

Act Three is "The Murky Dawn," in which the effects become visible. It is a period of "economic revolution and anarchy," as machinery and steam overrun industry, and Smith's plea for laissez faire sweeps the statute book clear of the mercantilistic devil. Population is "torn up by the roots" and dragged "from cottages in distant valleys into factories and cities"; independent farmers, expelled from their lands and impoverished by the extension of sheep raising and the inclosure movement, join the small manufacturing master or journeymen in this rural exodus. In the towns a landless propertyless proletariat is the victim of the seven deadly sins of unrestrained inhuman

---

and his ideas came often to be used as weapons in the struggle against government intervention in economic life. Although in general he defended *laissez faire*, he himself favored government intervention in instance after instance.

Arnold Toynbee: English historian and social reformer after whom the social settlement house Toynbee Hall, located in the East End of London, is named. His posthumously published *Lectures on the Industrial Revolution of the Eighteenth Century in England* (1884) did much to popularize one of the most famous labels in historical literature. He was the uncle of the present Arnold Toynbee, of *A Study of History* fame.

industrial capitalists. The sins are the factory system, long hours, child labor, the exploitation of women, low wages, periodical or chronic unemployment, and slums. If the victims dislike the contrast between their deplorable lot and the fortunes made by fat factory owners; if they object, riot, join labor unions, or become chartists or socialists, they are shot down, put in jail, or sent to Botany Bay. Their economic masters become their political lords by displacing the landowners in the seats of government, and then legislate—or refuse to do so—with one eye on the cashbox and the other on some page of Smith, Ricardo, or Malthus. A dreary, tragic, selfish, sort of dawn! But by lunch time the weather is improving. The exploited grow class-conscious and organized, some employers grow softhearted, laws are passed to permit unions, to regulate child labor, or to provide a better water supply. Mass production makes goods cheaper, the corn laws are repealed, Victoria becomes queen, Albert the Good builds the Crystal Palace, and by the time it is opened in 1851 the grim tragedy is promising to turn into whatever the urban counterpart of a pastoral should be called.

This story has got into the general books, and the title for it has become so widely accepted that some wit has said all college courses now begin with the amoeba, Aristotle, or the industrial revolution. That is—all courses except those given by the economic historian, for he is getting more and more suspicious of the name and of the crisp dramatic conception. In the great university schools of economic history, Manchester admits that the name was useful when first adopted but thinks it has now served its turn and can scarcely be applied aptly to a movement which was in preparation for two centuries and then occupied at least one more. Oxford finds there is "no hiatus in economic development, but always a constant tide of progress and change, in which the old is blended almost imperceptibly with the new." Edinburgh chimes in with the remark that "sudden catastrophic change is inconsistent with the slow gradual process of human evolution." Harvard insists that the technological changes of the eighteenth century were "only the completion of tendencies which had been significantly evident since Leonardo da Vinci." Birmingham reinforces this by asserting that the developments between 1760 and 1830 "did but carry further, though on a far greater scale and with far greater rapidity, changes which had been proceeding long before." Cambridge finds the period presents a study in slow motion, and in London they tell the pass students there was an industrial revolution, but tell the honors students there never was any such thing.

These quotations give a composite picture of the revised view of the industrial revolution. Let me put it in three generalizations. (1) Steam and the textile machines did not break in on an almost unchanging world of smallscale slightly capitalistic enterprise. (2) The rate of technical change was *lento* rather than *allegro* for a long time; it took decades or even generations to transform old industries and build up new ones. (3) The social and economic "evils" were not new; they were not as black or as widespread as is usually asserted; their causes were often due to special or non-economic factors; and they were in no small measure offset by a substantial improvement in the real wages and living standards of a large part of the wage-earning population. Sentimental unhistorical hysteria is not a good approach to a problem, whether present or past, but it dominated much of the discussion a hundred years ago and the description of a hundred years ago.

Let me elaborate these three contentions. In Toynbee's day little was known of sixteenth-century economic life, and little of any eighteenth-century industry except textiles. Now we know that during this period there were important changes in methods of production, and a quickening spirit of scientific inquiry and of inventive curiosity. New methods of extracting and refining metals were discovered; the preparation of silk yarn, the knitting of hose, the weaving of ribbons, the making of clocks, the finishing of cloth, all obtained new or improved equipment, as did shipbuilding, brewing, mining, sugar refining, and the manufacture of chemicals. The harnessing of wind, water, and animal power was made more efficient, and coal was used in increasing quantities by industries which needed heat. Professor Nef has shown that England had an industrial revolution between 1540 and 1640, and that the rate of technical change was possibly as striking during the age of Shakespeare as during that of Wordsworth or Byron. Holland, Sweden, France, and England alike contributed to technical progress, and by 1700 scientists, especially physicists, had learned enough to be able to answer some questions asked by industrialists. True, some industries or processes stood still, and spinning and weaving did not change much; but many were on the march.

At the same time the organization of production was changing.

Small craftsmen did not have the capital necessary for some of the new equipment, or for bridging the long gap between buying raw material and getting paid for the finished article by a dilatory or distant customer. Hence where materials were costly or came from afar, where equipment was expensive, where the market was large or distant, the initiative had to be taken by merchants or large producers. Some of them bought the raw materials and put them out to be processed by small masters or by wage earners. Sometimes they supplied the equipment as well and paid the master only for his labor, just as he in turn might pay wages to his journeymen. Some of them gathered workers in, because the material could not be put out. You could not put out coal mining, smelting, sugar refining, building, cloth finishing, shipbuilding, calico printing, or the making of glass, bricks, paper, leather, or gunpowder. As these industries grew, so did the number of persons working for wages in their employer's plant; and the combined expansion of putting out and gathering in had created a large propertyless proletariat long before 1760. It may be true that in 1640 the great majority of industrial workers "laboured in their homes, in town cellars or garrets, or in village cottages. But that majority was by no means so overwhelming as has been supposed" (Nef) and was declining rapidly before a flying shuttle flew or a spinning jenny was devised, even in Lancashire cotton production. Wherever men worked, many of them were wage earners.

If they were, their wages tended to be low; but so were all returns in an age of low productivity. Their hours were long—twelve or more a day—but so were those of their employers and of independent workers, since the rate of production was so slow. Their children and their wives had to work, for every scrap of labor was needed; but so did all children and wives, except those of the rich. Unemployment was frequent and severe, industrial diseases and accidents were common, living and working conditions were often dank, unhealthy, and malodorous, whether in town or village. Labor unions were formed, class conflicts occurred, and the state usually took the employers' side.

This sketch of the period before 1760 takes much of the melodrama out of the next seventy years. Some of the remainder disappears, when we examine the pace at which the textile machines and the improved steam engines were adopted. The cotton industry, which was the scene of the famous inventions, has been used as a sample case. But it was not typical; various factors, such as the newness of the industry, the suitability of the cotton fiber for mechanical treatment, and the great market existing for cheap cotton cloth, prevent the story of cotton from being typical of the changes in industry at large. The transfer from domestic hand spinning of cotton to factory machine spinning was rapid—a matter of about twenty years. By 1815 "the power loom was entering into effective rivalry with the hand loom in the cotton industry, though another generation was to elapse before the battle was finally decided." But cotton was a lonely hare in an industrial world of tortoises. It loomed far less large in that world than it has done in the textbooks, for even in the 1830's the number of its employees was only two-thirds that of the number of female domestic servants.

When we get our eyes off this exception, we find the pace of change in the rest of industry much more sedate. Wool spinning, on hand jennies instead of on wheels, was still being done in Yorkshire homes in 1850. Power looms had not seriously threatened the woolen hand weaver at that date; the transfer from hand to power weaving came quietly during the next twenty-five years, but even in 1877 I find one manufacturer contending that the old method was as cheap as the new. As for steam power, Watt had only 320 of his engines at work in England in 1800, and in 1830 a quarter of the power used by cotton mills was still drawn from waterwheels. Mining had no great technical change, but a series of little ones. Building remained a manual industry until the concrete mixer came. The pottery industry relied less on machinery than on other factors. Clothes making, glass blowing, and printing were late in getting mechanical equipment, while mechanical engineering only slowly developed the tools it needed for shaping metal parts cheaply and accurately. In 1850 everything was not over except the shouting. Cheap steel, cheap lubricants, industrial chemistry, and cheap electricity were still to come. The railroad had won its battle, but the steamship was still fighting its sailing rival, even on the North Atlantic. Away from Lancashire and the railroad tracks, technical change between 1760 and 1850 had been gradual, slow, and unspectacular.

What then of the social and economic consequences and of the seven deadly sins? In the first place, if we leave out one or two exceptional industries or areas, people were not torn loose from a rural life of pleasant and virtually independent enterprise and plunged almost overnight into the horrible existence of an urban factory slum-dwelling proletariat. Many of them were already proletarian; many of them already lived in industrial towns which now grew large or in villages which grew into towns; and some of them already worked under the employer's roof. For them there was not much shift of habitat or of economic class. There was little mass migration, and little long distance movement, except by the Irish, who swarmed into England before they swarmed into North America, and who made many labor and urban problems much more acute than they would otherwise have been.

In the second place, before we beat our anger to white heat in describing the slums, the foul streets, the smoke-laden atmosphere, the lack of water or sanitation, the ravages of disease, etc., let us remember three controlling considerations. (a) Technical. Cheap bricks, cheap sewer or water pipes, and cheap house fixtures were not available till at least 1840, and knowledge concerning public health was still scanty. Compare conditions in the industrial towns with those of non-industrial communities or with rural housing facilities; then it is evident that the housing and sanitary shortcomings of the manufacturing districts were not wholly due to the new machinery and the factory system. (b) Constitutional. Until 1835 no town government had adequate powers to cope with the new urban problems. (c) Economic. The provision of houses was never, until recent years, regarded as a public duty. It was left to private enterprise and the stimulus of investment or speculation. The potential builder considered whether his capital would yield a better return in houses than in the many other fields that were thirsty for capital; and the amount he put into a dwelling was limited by what the tenant could afford to pay. In one English town 76 per cent of the houses were rented at a dollar a week or less in 1839; the total capital outlay for one house could not be more than six hundred dollars. In view of the western world's housing impasse since 1914, we must speak more kindly of the builder who a century ago put a roof over the head of the poor, without the aid of mass-produced materials, machinery, or government subsidies.

In the third place, few of the factory working conditions were new. Not even the discipline of fixed hours of work was new to industries which had been conducted in central workshops. Night work may have been new, but long and late hours were not. The cruel treatment of some children by foremen was a personal matter; parents had not been free from it in the domestic workshop, and it was part of that streak of cruelty common in prisons, the army and navy, schools, and homes. The thing that was new and revolutionary was not the "evils," but the discovery that they were evils. For that we have to thank those employers who were heartless. We have to thank the factory for making noticeable in the mass what had been ignored in scattered small instances. We can thank onlookers, whether lay or ecclesiastic, and even Tory politicians who saw in factory conditions a new whip with which to flog their Whig industrial opponents. Finally, much credit must go to those employers—and they were many—who treated their workers decently. These men belonged to that growing army of humanitarians who cleaned up slavery, made the penal code less fierce, welcomed the attack on excessive drinking, pushed the cause of education, built hospitals, dispensaries, and charitable institutions, organized the relief of the unemployed in depressed days, established good working conditions, and fought for better factory laws and better town government.

One final comment may help us to understand better the years between 1760 and 1830. Twenty-six of those years (1789-1815) were dominated by the emotions and strain of the French Revolution and the Napoleonic war, and sixteen of them (1815-1830) were filled with the task of readjustment after a generation of war. The first period was torn by the fear of Jacobinism and the stress of war and famine. There could be little tolerance of mutterings of social discontent or of organized protest during those years; and there was little time to think of domestic problems. The second period we understand better because we have lived through a similar one. The legacies of war were high prices which collapsed, high interest rates and taxes which did not, a scarcity of houses, wide agrarian distress, a disarranged currency, a chaotic credit system, economic nationalism, choked trade channels, prohibitive tariffs, demobilized soldiers without jobs, and so forth. Much that has been blamed on the economic transition was not new, and much of the rest has to be put on the shoulders of the war. The remarkable thing is that by 1830 British opinion had got rid of most of its war phobias and was tackling its problems realistically and constructively by a combination of voluntary organization and state action. If anything was rapid and revolutionary in this whole period it was

the change in outlook that between 1824 and 1835 removed the ban
on labor organization, passed an effective factory act, reformed the
poor law, lowered the tariff wall, made a hole in the navigation laws,
remodelled urban government, reformed the House of Commons,
liberated the slaves, emancipated Roman Catholics, fashioned a good
banking system, and sowed the seeds of national education, trade
unionism, and the cooperative movement.

Behind all this was the intense energy of manufacturers and merchants who, either with old equipment or new, enterprised and ad-
ventured. This energy is denounced by some as "an orgy of soulless
cupidity," and praised by others as "a triumph of the spirit of enterprise." In general it was a bit of both. Cupidity, yes, as in all ages
and occupations. Enterprise, yes, but not always triumphant, for the
field was strewn with the wreckage of men who failed. When the
classical economists said profit was the reward of risk and interest the
reward of abstinence, they meant it. Not the abstinence that today
would lead a man to pick a Buick for his twelfth car instead of a
Rolls Royce, but one which meant meager living and the ploughing
back of every spare penny into the business. As for risk, some day
somebody will study the industrial revolution through the bankruptcy
records; but we know enough to realize on what a treacherous sea the
entrepreneur launched his tiny bark.

How does all this affect the teacher's presentation of economic aspects
of modern Europe? It takes out some of the heroics—and the villainics,
if I can coin a word—it cuts down the pace, and leaves the tale that
of a trend rather than of a tumult. But there is enough left, and space
has been made available for more that is of first class importance.
Any survey of the making of modern Europe should have something
to say about the gradual industrialization of parts of the continent,
including the effect of hydro-electricity, industrial chemistry, and
post-Bessemer metallurgical developments; the emergence of intensive
agriculture; the effect of good roads, canals, railroads, steamships,
and refrigeration; the end of serfdom in other countries than Russia
and the evolution of an efficient peasant proprietor economy; the
growing need for more capital and better banking; the unprecedented
growth of population and the mass migration of 50,000,000 Europeans
to other continents in a century; the steady advance of voluntary
association and the influence of the social conscience in producing the

social service state; the instability of a complex capitalistic system in a world economy; the twentyfold increase in the value of world trade; the impact of the new world on the old; and the ability of Europe to raise greatly the standard of living of an expanding population, thanks to better technique, better organization, and freedom for a hundred years from Armageddon. And if textbooks must have illustrations, I would dispense with pictures of the spinning jenny, Louis Blanc, and even Karl Marx, if thereby I had room for two graphs, one of the movement of general prices and one of the business cycle. These two would explain a lot of social, political, and even diplomatic history.

Economic Ideas and Facts in the Early Period of the Risorgimento (1815-1848)

KENT ROBERTS GREENFIELD

➤➤➤-➤➤➤-➤➤➤-➤➤➤-➤➤➤-➤➤➤-➤➤➤-➤➤➤-➤➤➤ *Published in 1930* ◄◄◄-◄◄◄-◄◄◄-◄◄◄-◄◄◄-◄◄◄-◄◄◄-◄◄◄-◄◄◄

It is easy enough to understand why most accounts of nineteenth-century Italian history are overwhelmingly political in their emphasis: the outstanding event in nineteenth-century Italian history was, after all, the establishment of the Kingdom in 1861; no other event could possibly surpass it in importance. Nevertheless, it is unfortunate that the stress on political evolution has resulted in a neglect of Italian economic history. And this is all the more unfortunate in view of the fact that the study of Italian economic development in the nineteenth century throws much light on Italian political development. The American scholar who has done most to remedy this basic deficiency in the literature of nineteenth-century Italian history is Kent Roberts Greenfield, formerly of the Johns Hopkins University and author of the important study *Economics and Liberalism in the Risorgimento* (1934). In the present article, which appeared several years before the publication of his pioneering monograph, Greenfield called attention to the significance of economic life and thought in early-nineteenth-century Italian history.

T he modern student who devotes himself to an attentive study of the standard histories of the unification of Italy soon feels the need of a less strictly political description of the Risorgimento than that which they offer him. The purely political history of the Risorgimento has a discouragingly episodical character, at least until Cavour comes on the scene. The outbreaks of 1820, 1848 and 1859-1860 reveal an un-

Reprinted by special permission from *The American Historical Review*, XXXVI (1930), 31-43. The documentation which originally appeared with this essay has been omitted.

mistakable crescendo in the force of the national movement. But a satisfactory account of the development of that movement in the long intervals between crises is lacking. In the attempt to provide one, the best of the historians, from Tivaroni to Rosi, flounder amid episodes, and end with giving excessive emphasis to isolated acts of patriotic heroism which are far more impressive in retrospect than they could possibly have been in their immediate practical effect. One feels that the main stream must have been taking another course. This feeling is deepened when one contemplates the strength and consistency of the party that rallied to Cavour and the National Society in the period between 1852 and 1859. Such a party could not have been created in a day or even by such a magician as Cavour. To find the main stream, to understand the strength of this party, it is necessary to go back to the period when Cavour and his generation were coming of age, the period between 1815 and 1848; and one realizes at once that their education could not have been political, but was the product of forces primarily economic and social. They were excluded from the political scene, the young men of that generation; or they rushed into it only to make martyrs of themselves. Economic and social questions they were free to discuss openly. They did so with competence and a fine ardor and with a remarkable consistency of direction; and through their discussion they developed a compact and intelligent body of public opinion on which the success of Cavour's masterly project was based.

If one studies this period of preparation, previous to 1848, leaving on one side the revolutionary propaganda of Mazzini and the semi-religious propaganda of Gioberti, one finds that two powerful currents entered into the education of the new generation. One was a current of thought, the other a current of fact, of circumstance. Let us take them in order.

One of the striking phenomena of Italian life in the period 1815-1848 was an earnest discussion of the economic and social interests of the several states of Italy, and of the nation as a whole. This discussion was accompanied by the evolution of a group of publicists. They were recruited from the aristocracy and the middle class. Though originally separated by the barriers that divided their nation into eight thought-proof compartments, they started from a common point of view, a common philosophic preconception. This was economic liberalism. They attached themselves to the school that had been founded by Adam Smith, and that was being carried on by Ricardo, McCulloch, and Mill in England, and by Jean Baptiste Say and Sismondi in France. In their own tradition its doctrines had been brillantly represented by such writers as Genovesi, Beccaria, Carli, and Verri in the eighteenth century, and were receiving fresh elaboration and criticism at the hands of Melchiorre Gioja and Gian Domenico Romagnosi when they themselves came on the stage. They were free traders, and believed in the doctrine and all of its corollaries with a semi-religious faith; they were humanitarians; and finally, they belonged to the "cult of progress" and were animated by the conviction that the nineteenth was the greatest of centuries, destined to witness an unexampled advance in what they enthusiastically called "civilization."

The master-mind of this movement of thought in Italy was Gian Domenico Romagnosi (1761-1835). It was he who gave it the peculiar turn that it took in Italy. The secret of his powerful influence is not to be found in his cumbrous and difficult writings, but in his magnetism as a teacher. He was the Socrates of a group of young scholars, aristocrats, and *borghesi*, which centered at Milan and included Confalonieri, Luigi Azimonti (the Milanese sugar magnate), and such brilliant young thinkers as Carlo Cattaneo, Cesare Correnti, Carlo Tenca, Giuseppe Ferrari, and Cesare Cantù. Romagnosi indoctrinated them with an idea upon which they eagerly seized as the foundation of a patriotic program, namely: that of the inseparability of economic, social, and political processes. An anti-Utopist, Romagnosi insisted that any political order is a function of existing economic and social conditions. He believed furthermore that free institutions, and the unified nation, were the necessary expression of nineteenth century civilization in Europe. Once the condition of society was ripe, and the necessity

CESARE BALBO: Leader in the Italian national movement. His *Hopes of Italy* (1844) proposed the formation of a confederation of Italian princes under the leadership of Piedmont. But Balbo was interested not only in liberating the Italies from Austrian rule; he was also a strong advocate of railroad building and he agitated for the establishment of a customs union among the Italian principalities.

MASSIMO D'AZEGLIO: Political writer who insisted that the national movement would not succeed under either papal or republican auspices. Prime minister of Piedmont from 1849 to 1852, and an advocate of Piedmontese

for a government in harmony with it was generally felt, a political revolution would be inevitable; and unless it came thus naturally, it would fail to produce enduring results. The task for the present, then, was progress in "civilization" and a general discussion of it. Given these, freedon and nationality would follow as day follows night.

Seeking an outlet for this gospel the group of young men to which I have referred acquired organs of expression in a type of journalism which had first appeared in Italy under the French and which they now revived. It was a combination of the journal of literature and of "useful knowledge." The series may be said to have begun with the ill-fated *Conciliatore*, edited by Silvio Pellico, and snuffed out by the Austrian government in 1819. But it assumed a fuller development in such periodicals as *L'Antologia,* published by Vieusseux at Florence between 1821 and 1832, and the *Annali Universali di Statistica,* of Milan, which was founded in 1824 and continued to flourish throughout the period. This journalism reached its maturest expression in the well-known *Politecnico,* founded by Cattaneo in 1839, and the *Rivista Europea* (1838 ff.), edited by Carlo Tenca, which absorbed the *Politecnico* in 1845.

These journals ambitiously aimed to launch their readers into the full current not only of Italian but of European life. They soon brought about an exchange of views and information. This in turn operated to confer a more than local reputation on certain figures who distinguished themselves as leaders in liberal thought, or in public action that was in harmony with it. This included, with the Lombard group whom I have mentioned, such men as Raffaele Lambruschini, Ricasoli and Ridolfi at Florence; the Balbos, Prospero and Cesare, Giovanetti, and

---

leadership in the struggle to attain a united Italy, he did much to prepare the way for Cavour.

GIOBERTI: Italian priest who emerged in the 1840's as the leader of the neo-Guelph group, which looked to the papacy for leadership in the movement to establish a united Italy. Disillusioned by the results of the Revolution of 1848, he lost all hope for his original scheme.

SILVIO PELLICO: Italian patriot of the early nineteenth century who was for many years imprisoned by the Austrians. His personal sacrifices for the idea of a liberated Italy helped to "turn the cult of Italian nationality into a holy cause."

eventually Camillo Cavour, in Piedmont. Finally, the discussion led to the definition of objectives, which, at first vaguely patriotic, eventually took the form of a definite and well-recognized program of national action.

Such, in general terms, was the journalistic phase of that action which D'Azeglio so admirably defined as a "conspiracy in the open sun."

The spirit in which patriotic young Italians dedicated themselves to these journals may best be represented by the following passage from a letter of Cesare Correnti to a friend in 1876:

> Forty years ago . . . our venerable master, G. D. Romagnosi, had begun to see how the science of statistics might be a weapon less worn and blunted than historical lamentations and poetical anathemas manipulated by so many—so well and so uselessly. For this reason I resigned myself, an impatient conscript, to the discussion of averages, tables and numbers, which gave us a chance to talk in jargon and in a cipher, and to withdraw ourselves from the mutilation of the censorship, accustomed as it was from long usage to sniff only at phrases and epithets. The thing was done. Numbers spoke their language only to those who knew how to read their hidden meanings: true language of mutes! Sometimes these guesses piqued the curiosity; sometimes one felt in them a reflection of poetry, a correspondence of sound to sense more intimate and more intellectual than the casual chiming of rhymes.

By 1847 this intellectual group had not only become self-conscious and well organized, but had come to be united by a program. The foundations of this program were certain convictions about the nature of social progress. The corner stone was free trade, in all its implications—among which was a firm belief in commerce as a good in itself, as the great vivifying element in civilization. The liberal publicists sought therefore to stimulate commerce in Italy—by good roads, canals, free ports, steam navigation; by joint stock corporations, insurance companies, and modern banks; by the removal of tariffs and the introduction of uniform weights, measures, and coinage—by every possible means, until the circulation of goods and ideas would acquire a force that would sweep away all barriers of ignorance and municipalism. They desired to promote industrialism by the dissemination of technical science and new inventions; but, horrified by the social misery that had attended the sudden revolution in England and France, they were not ready to go fast in that direction; and some wished to exclude the new industrialism altogether. They were one in recognizing agriculture as the great industry of Italy; and in this field their aim was to substitute the new science for its blind empiricism, and to inject into its sluggish practices the stimulant of the new chemistry, physics, and zoölogy, elaborating for this purpose the precepts of a popular technology, and a program of agricultural societies, model farms, and rural education. They showed the deepest interest in all humanitarian enterprises designed to promote the thrift and enlightenment of the poor and give them a social stake in the coming prosperity: such institutions as savings banks, free public schools, Sunday and holiday schools and kindergartens of the type founded by Owen in England for the children of laborers. In all these enterprises they saw means of promoting that blessed "spirit of association" which they felt to be so lacking in their nation, and which they believed to be the key to all the good things of modern life. In short, sanely recognizing the fact that Italian life must grow in its own way, they aimed to liberate it, and seriously and competently set themselves to the task of exposing it to all the fertilizing influences of modern civilization.

Such a program embodied in fact a consummate strategy. Many, in fact most, of its specific desiderata could be granted by the governments of Italy without a radical departure from their conservative and anti-national policy. Such for instance were free schools, good roads, local railways, the encouragement of agriculture and industry. But it will be seen at once that taken as a whole the program could not be realized without a reconstitution of the political order. If the princes of Italy pledged themselves to it, they would be admitting a camel into their tent. The first step to free trade was a pan-Italian customs union; the indispensable condition of a flourishing commerce was a truly national railway net; the only régime under which a free circulation of technical knowledge and a development of the precious spirit of association was imaginable was one from which the devils of censorship, police suspicions, and bureaucrats had been cast out. A strong group of the propagandists of the journals realized this with an increasing confidence in the strength of their cause. Shunning violence on principle, placing a noble confidence in the force of ideas, and in the irresistible power of economic and social necessities, once thoroughly felt, to break through all barriers, they worked their way forward within the irritating bounds imposed by the law. But there is no doubt of their intimate purpose, which was to create a new Italy. Cesare

Correnti, publishing in the *Annali,* from 1840 onwards, articles passed
by the Austrian censor, could in 1847 launch anonymously, from the
same editorial desk, his terrific indictment *L'Austria e La Lombardia,*
proclaiming his deliberate conviction that the Austrian government "in
every circumstance is our enemy by nature, by choice and by necessity."

It is evident that in this journalistic propaganda, from its inception,
were implicit the spirit and ideas of the well-known program of the
moderate party as formulated by Balbo and D'Azeglio and its other
representatives from 1844 to 1848. One finds in it the same sane oppor-
tunism, the same idealization of "legality," the same "active resignation," based on the conviction that sound and durable progress was
possible only in so far as it was supported by a widespread sense of common interest and necessity, intelligently recognized by the public and
therefore by the princes themselves, if they would face the facts, as a
proper object of policy. One also finds, gradually developing, the specific items of a political program as answering to these necessities. These
were brought together and formulated clearly by Cesare Balbo in his
Speranze d'Italia (1844), and summed up by Massimo d'Azeglio in his
Proposta di un Programma per l'Opinione Nazionale (1847). In these
great "Primary Works of the Risorgimento" anyone who has paged
such a journal as the *Annali* from 1824 onwards finds nothing new
except the political emphasis. The reforms that had been discussed for
twenty years were merely invested with a frankly political character
by Balbo, Durando, D'Azeglio, Cavour, and by the course of events
after 1840 which pointed to an impending opportunity for action.

It was not only by a gathering stream of propaganda that the minds
of Cavour's future associates in the task of reconstituting Italy were
formed. Behind that propaganda was a pressure—the pressure of a
changing environment, of the forces of a revolution in the economic
and social order, which experience as well as books and journals
brought home "to their business and their bosoms." Journals like the
Annali aimed to provide their readers with a mirror of this new and
changing world, or more precisely, a burning glass which would concentrate its rays upon the public consciousness which they were striving to foment in Italy. What were the facts that loomed up before them
as the most imposing and influential?

The foremost was the advent of industrialism, mechanical and
capitalistic. This meant England, Belgium, France, and the United
States. England was a theme on which the writers of the *Annali* never

tired of descanting—England "so industrious, commercially so active, so enterprising, so powerful, in a word the mistress of the earth." Where else prevailed that "union of knowledge, of interests, of power of all sorts that are to be found at London, at Manchester, at Liverpool? No pains were spared to bring home to the reader the tremendous phenomenon. He received a full and competent delineation of England's factories, her trade, banks, finances, poor laws, schools, prisons, cities, political institutions, her possessions overseas. He was familiarized with the idea that the new industrialism was a revolutionary force, that it required a root-and-branch reconstruction of society; and furthermore, that having started in one country it was bound to spread throughout Europe.

If industrialism was impressive, not less so was its inevitable concomitant, the railroad. At first the Italian writers assumed the attitude of curious spectators. But their conversion was rapid. By 1830 they were eagerly reporting every step in the progress of the invention abroad. After 1835, when Austria began to build railways, the discussion became urgent and practical; and it entered the phase of full commitment with Cattaneo's famous article, published in the *Annali* in 1836: "Researches on the Project of a Railroad from Milan to Venice," a project authorized in February, 1837.

The discussion was the more fervid as the writers soon realized that the railroad was the most powerful instrument yet found to advance all of their ulterior purposes both economic and political. They saw in it the triumphant vindication of their philosophy that progress is not a dream, but a fact imposed "by the science of interests." The locomotive would make free trade, at least within the Italian peninsula, a necessity. And after 1840 it began clearly to be seen that the locomotive, if properly directed, was the greatest of national revolutionists, and might be made to "stitch the boot." This is the idea that dominates the discussion of railroads in Balbo's *Delle Speranze d'Italia* (1844), in Petitti's *Delle Strade Ferrate Italiane e del miglior Ordinamento di esse* (1845), and in the famous review of Petitti's work by Cavour in *La Revue Nouvelle* (May, 1846).

While the liberals were discussing the railroad, the steamship began to trail its smoke across the Mediterranean. Steam navigation brought in its train a consequence that was quickly apprehended as having a tremendous importance for Italy. For it was seen to be drawing the line of communication between England and the East back from the

Atlantic and the Cape of Good Hope, to which this had shifted in the Renaissance, leaving Italy to languish, and to be restoring it to the Mediterranean, to the very gates of the Italian cities. The British government became deeply interested in finding a way through the Levant, by Egypt or by the Euphrates. In 1835 the *Annali* announced that in March the British had established a monthly service of steamships from London to Alexandria, connecting with the East India Company's steam packets from Suez to Bombay. By 1835 the traffic of dispatches and passengers from the whole Continent, including England, to the East was passing through France to Marseilles, thence by French packet boats to Alexandria. Austria bid for a share of this traffic at Trieste, and that port grew by leaps and bounds on its trade with the Levant.

The Italian writers watched all these changes with an increasingly anxious sense of the need for prompt and radical action to give Italy its proper place in relation to them. An Italy without partitions must be thrown open to the transit trade between East and West. A railroad line must be built from the Rhine to Genoa to enable that port to compete with Marseilles and Trieste, or better still, a peninsular line from the Alps to Brindisi, which would make Italy once more the thoroughfare between Europe and the East. The effect of this great shift in the trade routes to the Orient upon the national consciousness of the Italian publicists can hardly be overemphasized. It placed Italy, with its antiquated institutions, squarely in the midst of "the new European system." The realization of this reacted on the discussion of railroads, making a truly national network seem imperative; and contributed powerfully to a sense of the urgent necessity of modernizing both the economic and the political equipment of the nation.

Another fact made a profound impression on the Italian journalists as they looked out upon the new Europe, and that was the German Zollverein. The *Annali* hailed the news of the meeting at Berlin in September, 1833, which insured its completion with the exclamation: "Heaven grant that like combinations may be proposed and adopted for the states of Italy!" The event gave a tremendous impulse to the discussion of an Italian customs league. The Zollverein supplied the propagandists of liberalism with an invaluable weapon, for it was a fact that could be discussed openly; it was a working model of what they wanted; it was furthermore a measure at once indispensable to the success of the railways that were being built, and inseparable from the idea of a national network and the dream of making this a link in the transit to the East; finally, the Zollverein indicated a step, counselled by obvious practical interests, which must inevitably be accompanied by an act of political association, and which would, they believed, throw open the doors to Liberty and Union.

The European scene was changing, and we have abundant evidence that in Italy a powerful intellectual minority were eagerly and hopefully studying this revolution; but also in Italy itself the economic and social order was undergoing changes in the critical period between 1815 and 1848. This is not the place for a description of them, and the materials for an adequate description are still painfully scanty. With the scarcity of good studies, and in a few words, one can only offer some cautious generalizations.

In the first place, it is sufficiently clear that when the Italian states were swept by the first war of independence, in 1848, their industries had only begun to feel the effect of the economic revolution that was transforming those of Northern Europe. Agriculture retained an immense preponderance. Nevertheless there was an industrial movement. The factory, though still comparatively rare, had entered the scene; and modern machinery was being introduced and multiplied. The force of this statement is not seriously weakened when one adds that it is applicable only to Lombardy, Tuscany, and Piedmont, and with much less emphasis to the Kingdom of the Two Sicilies.

Also commerce was increasing. It is true that internal circulation of any scope was almost paralyzed by the customs barriers and bad roads, and that commercial speculation was characterized by extreme caution, even in Lombardy where capital was the most abundant. Nevertheless there was movement. In Lombardy-Venetia and Piedmont great transalpine highways were opened, and in Tuscany and Naples, as well as in these states, the period saw a new skeleton system of main roads constructed, and in Lombardy an admirable network connecting these with the rural communes. A steadily increasing mass of goods was cleared at the ancient fairs of Brescia, Bergamo, and Sinigaglia; and the shipments of silk to Switzerland, England, France, Germany, and Russia assumed very considerable proportions. The statistics of the seaports tell the same story of expansion. Insurance companies were established; joint-stock corporations, savings banks, and banks of discount were introduced; and these institutions gave a facility to the mobilization of capital which Italy had not known since the Renaissance. In commerce as in industry it was a period of beginnings, but there was movement.

Finally, in all of the states of Italy agriculture was showing signs of progress—a progress that was a phase in a profound revolution. This had begun in the eighteenth century as a result of the steady pressure of population on the means of subsistence and the general rise in the price of foodstuffs. It received a great impulse under the French régime with the abolition of feudalism, the sale of church lands, and the application of a code of law that exalted the rights of the small proprietor. It is important to note that in this field the Restoration did not seriously disturb the Napoleonic system, at least in the important states of Italy, and the remnants of the old order went on disappearing. Land had become negotiable, and the class of small proprietors multiplied. The result, on the economic side, was the application of individual initiative to the problems of agricultural production. The effect on the social order was to promote an interpenetration of the old nobility with a new proprietary bourgeoisie, which made itself felt as those who had acquired capital in trade or by their labor bought up the land or rented it for speculative purposes. This fact must be kept constantly in mind for it is the key to the social complexion of Italy in the states that were the true centers of the Risorgimento. The proprietors resided, not on the soil, but in the towns and cities, and therefore formed a bourgeoisie, which was conservative, but which was profoundly attached by its interests to the principle of private property and free contract. It was therefore readily penetrated by the economic liberalism which dominated the thought of the intellectuals, and which was founded on the principle of personal responsibility and individual rights. With this gradual social transformation came the introduction of the new scientific technique, eagerly adopted and disseminated by the great liberal proprietors like Porro, Confalonieri, Ridolfi and Ricasoli, Cavour and Balbo, and vigorously propagated by the new journalism and by the agricultural societies, such as the Georgofili of Tuscany, and the Associazione Agraria of Piedmont.

It is not as yet possible, as I have already remarked, to ascertain precisely the extent of the economic changes that occurred in Italy during the Risorgimento. But far more important than a description of those changes are the beliefs about them that were commonly entertained, for it was the picture of them in the mind of the contemporary observer, and not the picture that we can piece together only with difficulty after a century, that determined action. Regarding this our evidence is full and positive. However slight the measurable progress of Italian industry, commerce, and agriculture, the young liberals of Cavour's generation, seeing it as a part of the great revolution that was transforming Europe, attached a tremendous significance to it. Most of them, with their fine dream of human perfectibility, hailed it with joy and eager impatience. But the important fact is that, whether optimistic or not, the liberals were united in representing it to themselves and to their readers as an inexorable destiny. Cattaneo, flaying the opponents of the Milan-Venice railway in 1836, writes: "If they do not want to build it now, they will have to build it later. . . . Willing or unwilling they will have to obey the force of the times which stands over us inexorable." Another writes: "This utility . . . by the law of levels . . . assumes inevitably the character of a necessity." And nothing is more important, in this contemporary discussion, than the rapidly increasing insistence of the note of urgency. The Italians must align themselves with the general movement or be ruined. "In the present state of Europe the *status quo* is the ruin of a nation." "Those who do not progress with the times will by the times be overtaken, overthrown and punished." This insistence upon the need of immediate action reaches its climax in Balbo's *Speranze*: "In these years about the middle of the nineteenth century, perhaps in the few that remain of its fifth decade, our future, commercial, industrial and agricultural, will be decided for centuries and centuries. These are the climacteric years of the public economy of all the nations of Europe, but more than all for that of Italy." For Italy it is a race, a question of "seizing the single advantage that remains to us," the providential advantage of a position on the "reopened thoroughfare to the Orient."

Finally, to understand the relatively rapid penetration and triumph of the propaganda that I have been describing, one must take into account not only the changes in the fabric of Italian society, and the change in Italy's position with reference to the rest of Europe, but also the attitude of the aristocracy of the Italian states, and later, the action of the princes. The Italian communities remaining predominantly agricultural were profoundly conservative. They would not have responded to the leadership of a parvenue bourgeoisie, and it is therefore a fact of capital importance that from 1815 onwards a group of young nobles devoted themselves to the propagation of "improvements" and of the order of ideas associated with them. They traveled in

England and France; they gave of their wealth to introduce the new technique, to found schools and savings banks, to finance new enterprises, to form charitable associations that would bring into coöperation men of all classes and awaken a civic spirit. When, in the 'forties, the princes, the natural leaders of the aristocracy, began to move; when, above all, Charles Albert, King of Sardinia, adopted new civil and commercial codes, reduced the Piedmontese customs duties, projected a railroad, and founded a bank of discount, such steps were immediately interpreted in terms of the whole program of action which had been elaborated and discussed for twenty years and which was inseparably connected with the thought of political liberalism; and the princes almost immediately found themselves caught in an avalanche which swept them towards constitutionalism and union. And in the accompanying outburst of national feeling, the intellectual leadership passed as by right into the hands of those who seemed to be triumphantly vindicated in their affirmation that "independence is not a cry of revolution but a principle of political economy." The hour of the Moderates had arrived.

With the yielding of the princes, the "Moderates"—for by that name was called the party that had rallied to the ideas that I have been discussing—were suddenly swept into the field of political action. Here their lack of experience and of a previous opportunity for free discussion told heavily against them. These shortcomings combined with municipal and sectional jealousies, and with the apathy and clericalism of the masses, to produce the dissensions, the disorientation, and the swift and tragic failures of 1848-1849. But the long campaign of free discussion in the economic field had done its good work. It had cleared the air, and produced a unanimity of sentiment regarding the fundamental principles of economic and social reforms. Between 1852 and 1859 Cavour could carry out a program of such reforms on which substantial agreement had already been reached. For him remained only the task—and a Herculean one it was!—of finding the political and diplomatic combinations that the necessities of the new situation required. It was a factor of the greatest importance in his success that for eighteen years before his political début, as a commercial farmer, tramping the fields at Leri in his "enormous straw hat," he had felt in all of its practical urgency the need of a reconstruction; and as a liberal "of the first hour," active journalist from 1843, editor of the *Risorgimento* in 1847, and therefore a brother craftsman in the group of liberal propagandists, he fully shared their vision, and was recognized by them as one of themselves.

The current of thought which I have sought to define, as distinct from those dominated by the nationalistic idealism of Mazzini, and the Neo-Guelf idealism of Gioberti, together with the gradual changes in the Italian economic and social order on which the hopes of this movement were founded, presents a field of research that has remained unexploited and that is far from being the dusty scrapheap of statistics which it might seem at first. It involves the study of a philosophy and of social and political action in the broadest sense; and it brings into view a most interesting and instructive variant of the liberal democratic movement of the century. Although the theme has been curiously underemphasized by the Italian historians, a foundation has been laid by the precious studies of Ciasca, Prato, Pugliese, Rota, and Tarlé. What is now most needed is a series of monographic studies which will reveal, state by state, the nature and extent of the social and economic changes that took place in the critical period between 1815 and 1848, and will relate these to the thought of the liberal group whose writings determined the impression that they made. The material is abundant in Italy, and is sufficient for a good beginning in such substantial Risorgimento collections as those at Harvard and Yale. The student who approaches it with a sufficiently broad "discourse of reason" could make a most useful and interesting contribution to the history of nineteenth century Europe.

Unrest in France in 1848

ARTHUR L. DUNHAM

➢➢➢-➢➢➢-➢➢➢-➢➢➢-➢➢➢-➢➢➢-➢➢➢ *Published in 1948* ⧏⧏⧏-⧏⧏⧏-⧏⧏⧏-⧏⧏⧏-⧏⧏⧏-⧏⧏⧏-⧏⧏⧏

The France of Louis XVIII (1814-1824), Charles X (1824-1830), and Louis Philippe (1830-1848) remained overwhelmingly rural; but French industrial capitalism continued to grow in relative importance during the course of their reigns. If the factory system with its mass production did not develop more rapidly than it did, the explanation was partly to be found in the strength of the French luxury-goods industries. Even so, mass production was adopted increasingly; and closely connected with this industrial growth were several major economic crises. The severest of these began in the fall of 1846 and gave rise to a serious unemployment problem in the larger French towns. The failure on the part of the government of Louis Philippe to intervene actively in behalf of the unemployed served to increase their dissatisfaction with his regime and to stimulate their demand for change. By February 1848, France had another revolution, and Louis Philippe went the way of Charles X. King by grace of the barricades, he lost his crown by grace of the barricades. In the present paper, Arthur L. Dunham, of the University of Michigan, examines some of the main currents in French economic history in the decades before 1848 and suggests their bearing on the unrest that made possible the Revolution of that year. One of the most learned students of nineteenth-century French economic history, Dunham has done much to clarify the growth of French industrial capitalism.

I

On December 11, 1847, the *Journal des chemins de fer*, founded and edited in Paris since 1842 by an Englishman, declared that the French *rentes* had fallen as much as if the government was about to be overthrown. The King, who was ill in body at the time, yet per-

Reprinted by special permission from *The Journal of Economic History, Supplement*, VIII (1948), 74-84.

fectly comfortable in mind, recovered, but on February 24, 1848, he and his government fell in a revolution that was as sudden and dramatic as it was triumphant. Among its leaders were Socialists, like Louis Blanc, who controlled a considerable body of workingmen, some of whom belonged to the building trades and the domestic industries of the capital, while others had been brought to Paris some years before to work on the fortifications. They were moved first to the barricades; then, after being victorious there, to the national workshops organized by Louis Blanc, now a member of the provisional government, who had proclaimed on behalf of the workingmen the "right to work," as the most important organ of the workingmen, *L'Atelier,* had proclaimed the limitation of hours, the right to organize, and a minimum wage. These demands seem reasonable to us now, but they were thought dangerous then, not only by a majority of the provisional government, but also by the majority of the new legislature and of the French people.

The failure of the Socialists was due to their small numbers in the face of a superiority of peasants and *bourgeoisie,* and to the lack of unity in their views once the government of Louis Philippe had been overthrown. Another cause of failure was the fact that few of the workingmen understood the socialist doctrines. They knew only that the Orleanist government had been that of their bourgeois employers. Their wages had been low and become lower still when business became bad, and their hours of work seem to us to have been incredibly long when the eight-hour day is common except for scholars. The right to work seemed to them natural and just; but, while Paris did for a few weeks have its national workshops, in general it remained true that, although the right to work was admitted, there was no work. In June 1848 the workers of Paris returned to the barricades where they were defeated and where many died for a cause that neither their government nor their fellow citizens supported.

That a serious economic crisis affected the whole of France in the spring of 1848 is clear from contemporary accounts, such as that of Jérôme Blanqui, the economist and the bourgeois brother of one of the most extreme radicals. In Paris on the outbreak of the Revolution the five new banks founded in the 1830's by Jacques Laffitte and others to promote the development of industry promptly failed. In Mulhouse, the industrial capital of Alsace, forty-two mills closed and some never reopened. In Lille and nearby towns, such as Roubaix and Tourcoing, more than half the mills were closed and the others were open only part of the time. In Rouen there was at least as much distress. The paralysis of industry and trade was widespread. But just as the Revolution of 1848 was only partly the result of a revolt of the workers under Socialist leaders, so the economic crisis was only partly the result of the new political situation. The Revolution had not caused the crisis. It had merely intensified a crisis that already existed.

Among the socialistic thinkers of France we should give great prominence to Sismondi who was neither a distinguished theorist nor a democrat, but who saw clearly from afar, at a time when the effects of the industrial revolution in France were first becoming visible, how they affected the workers. The remedies he proposed were futile, but he was a good observer, as was his pupil Eugène Buret. These men had little in common with Utopian landowners and administrators like Gérando, Morogues, and De Villeneuve-Bargemont, who were well described by Vidal in 1846 when he said: "The Pauperists and Philanthropists have analyzed carefully and described minutely the effects of misery; then they have advised the rich to be charitable and the poor to be patient, resigned, thrifty, and chaste." Sismondi, on the other hand, in his book of 1827 asked for the workers the right to combine, wished the state to prohibit the work of children, limit the hours of work of adults, and oblige the employer to care for the worker during illness, old age, and unemployment. With the important exception of the work of children, his ideas resemble closely the wishes of the workers as expressed in *L'Atelier* shortly before the Revolution of 1848.

Two other men carried on the work of Sismondi: Dr. Louis René Villermé, the Parisian, and member of the Academy of Moral and Political Sciences who was commissioned by that body to undertake his well-known travels through France at the suggestion of the Société Industrielle de Mulhouse; and Dr. Thouvenin, a factory inspector at Lille, whose report in 1846 attracted little attention, but was remarkable

---

L'Atelier: A French newspaper which was edited by workers and is therefore a basic source for any study of the ideas and demands of French working-class elements in the period of the Revolution of 1848.

Le Chapelier Law: Measure passed by the National Constituent Assembly in 1791. It forbade the formation of either workers' or employers' associations, outlawed strikes and picketing, and prohibited public meetings of workers.

for its intimate personal knowledge of the poor. Villermé had great influence on his contemporaries in calling attention to the excessive employment of children and the long hours of labor exacted from adult workers in industry, and he had much to do with starting the movement of reform in both cases which was thus well under way before the Revolution of 1848. Dr. Thouvenin, whose voice unfortunately was not heard, realized the same evils quite as clearly, but showed also that much of the suffering of the workers was due to the unwholesome homes in which they were satisfied to live, and to their complete lack of interest in any form of sanitation. He also reinforced the observations of Villermé on the sufferings of workers in domestic industries that were being destroyed by the progress of the industrial revolution.

It is important to realize that just as a part only of the industrial paralysis from which the restless workers of France suffered in 1848 was due to the Revolution, so not all the rest was due to the industrial crisis that began slowly in 1846 and grew worse during the year that followed. An important part of the restlessness was due to technological progress. The power loom was important in the cotton industry before 1848, but very far indeed from universal, only cotton spinning being thoroughly mechanized. The spinning and combing of wool were still domestic in great part and performed under unhealthy conditions because dampness and lack of ventilation were considered essential. The mechanical spinning of flax, scarcely practiced in France or Belgium before 1837, made rapid progress after 1842 and caused intense suffering to unemployed hand spinners. Dr. Thouvenin pointed out that most of the patients in the hospitals of Lille, Mulhouse, Rouen, Amiens, and Ste. Marie aux Mines were hand weavers or combers. For their sufferings the industrial crisis can be blamed only in so far as it hastened technological change. This we know it did in the spinning

---

SISMONDI: Swiss author of the early nineteenth century. Highly regarded in his own time for his writings on Italian history and on the literature of southern Europe, he is now remembered mainly as an economist. At first he believed in Adam Smith's economic liberalism, but he came to be obsessed with the problem of underconsumption and economic crisis, and he moved more and more away from the optimism of Smith. His influence on the growth of socialist thought proved to be considerable.

of flax and in the development of the self-acting spinning machine in the cotton industry of Alsace and of the power loom for cotton in all the important manufacturing districts of France.

While the government of Louis Philippe cannot be held responsible for the hardships endured by the workers during the crisis that began in 1846, it was indifferent to any sufferings not likely to provoke riots and it was believed by many workers to be definitely hostile to them and their interests. This was certainly a factor in the unrest of 1848 and there were reasons for it other than the ignorance of most of the working classes and their excitability, which we sometimes forget is characteristic of all classes of the French people. The most important check on working-class organizations was the prevalence of the domestic system under which most workers toiled in their homes or in small workshops. This was closely connected with the fact, which also has been mentioned, that great numbers of workmen, even when in factories, retained a direct connection with the land. But we could hardly expect the workers to reason on such lines in 1848. To them the government of Louis Philippe was the one that enforced the Code Napoléon which forbade associations of more than twenty persons by incorporating the law of Le Chapelier of 1791; which regularly prosecuted working-class organizations, and which treated strikers as rebels as the law directed. In 1834, after the great strike of the silk workers of Lyons in 1831, and the more recent attempt to assassinate the King, the law was strengthened to forbid any association of less than twenty persons which was part of a larger organization. The government then had sufficient legal authority to prevent all workers' organizations. Through the police and the army it could, and frequently did, break strikes. According to our present knowledge the workers won only two of the recorded strikes of importance: that against the powerful coal-mining company of Anzin in 1833 and that of the carpenters of Paris in 1845. In all the others the workers failed; and in those at Lyons in 1831 and 1834 and in that of the coal miners of Rive de Gier in 1844 the police and army were used, although at Rive de Gier at least, we know that the local authorities and local public opinion favored the strikers.

Since the workers had no effective representation in municipal governments, or even in courts dealing with their immediate interests, such as the *conseils des prud'hommes*, they could do nothing but strike when there seemed a faint chance of success or when conditions were too trying to be borne. That resentment among the workers against the July Monarchy in its last years was widespread I believe to be true, but there is no reason to believe that it was organized, or could have been, in any effective way. The government could have defended itself on the ground that it was not responsible for the hardships suffered by the workers, and did make it clear that it felt it had no right to intervene in disputes between them and their employers as long as the laws were obeyed. If conditions did not suit them they need not work in factories or workshops. If they were threatened with starvation during periods of sickness or unemployment, why did they not save when employment was good?

II

Before considering the crisis that began in 1846 as the most important single factor producing widespread unrest in France in 1848, we must consider three factors which influenced the situation, although they have seldom been mentioned in connection with economic crises in France and almost never in studying the welfare of the French working classes. Most production in France was on a small scale and for local or provincial markets that were often separated from each other and from Paris either by inadequate means of transportation or by provincial differences. These small manufacturers were reluctant to co-operate with each other or with merchants who might have helped them to solve their problems of marketing. Competition within the country was thus restricted, while competition from abroad was reduced excessively by the high tariff of France. In consequence, overproduction at home was frequent, while sales of French goods abroad were both irregular and difficult. It is remarkable that Roubaix accomplished so much when we remember that most of its firms were small and competing fiercely. The same could be said of the manufacturers of silks at Lyons and St. Etienne, who were so numerous and competed so vigorously that they could not deal constructively with the labor problem and shifted the cost of technological change onto their workers. Lyons did have able merchants who handled their foreign trade well, as did Paris, Sedan, Roubaix, Reims, and probably Elbeuf; but St. Etienne, the chief center in France for the manufacture of silk ribbons, did not have such merchants. In general, also, merchants could not get manufacturers to produce regularly for foreign markets, so that, in the majority of cases, foreign sales were large only when domestic markets proved inadequate; that is, in times of overproduction there was dumping rather than a regular foreign trade. There is little evidence of decisive improvement in any of these factors before 1848, although transportation did improve greatly, the number of mills and large firms increased, as did exports, while provincialism diminished. The existence of these factors meant that French industry and trade were not fitted to deal with a great crisis, yet they were at the mercy of both foreign and domestic influences tending to cause overproduction because of the inadequacy of their markets.

The French were so thrifty and the industrial revolution in their country made such slow progress that we should not expect to find any serious amount of speculation. Yet it did occur and on a scale sufficient to cause trouble before each of the depressions that came in 1827-1832, 1837-1842, and 1846-1851. In 1825 we find it in the cotton, woolen, and silk industries; there were rising prices at least in the iron industry, and a building boom in Paris and probably in some other French cities. In 1836 there was speculation in canal shares, in the textile industries, in coal mines, and in asphalt. In 1846, which was a boom year until the autumn, there was speculation on a large scale in railroad shares, especially in promissory ones, and serious overproduction with rapidly rising prices in all the textile industries, while in the iron industry the demand, especially for rails, was so great that there could be no overproduction, but there was a notable increase in prices. There is enough evidence now available to prove the prevalent tendency in several industries in each of the years named, and usually in more than one part of France. It is unfortunate that in France official statistics up to 1850 are notoriously unreliable, while statistics from other sources are few, and those from sources that are trustworthy are rare. The situation in Alsace, in nearly all cases, is the clearest, thanks to the valuable *Bulletin* of the Société Industrielle of Mulhouse which has appeared regularly since 1826.

Foreign influences were, of course, important in bringing on all these depressions. Thus, in 1825-1826 there was a crisis in England due partly to bad investments in the United States and Latin America, and partly to overexpansion of British industry at home. France had, even then, important financial and commercial relations with Great Britain, while she had some direct contacts with the United States also, although not enough to cause her to feel keenly a purely American crisis. In 1837 the crisis very clearly began in America with some causative factors going back at least to 1835. By that time French contacts with the United States were more important, and the French silk industry reacted to the American market as early as 1836; but the main foreign influence on France was from England. It is impossible here to trace these crises in detail in the French economy. If I were to try you would become as restless as the French workers in 1848. It is important chiefly to remind ourselves that they occurred, and that in the midst of the depression that began in 1827 there came the Revolution of July 1830. It is clear that the depression was severe in France in 1827 and 1828, that in the latter year and in 1829 the wheat crop was bad, and that early in 1830 recovery seemed definitely to have begun. I believe it will be possible in time to prove that there was a causative connection between this depression and the July Revolution. It should be kept in mind now as a precedent for the events that occurred in France nearly twenty years later. The earlier revolution was far less formidable than the later one, but so was the crisis that preceded it and that partly caused it.

The coming of the crisis that was so important a cause of the Revolution of 1848 and of unrest among the working classes of France can be seen in 1845, although no one thought of a crisis then because prices were still rising, speculation was common, and it seemed as if the industrial boom would continue indefinitely. Trouble began because the wheat crop that year was bad, and disease cut down seriously the production of potatoes, which was the chief food of swine in France. The same crop failures occurred in the rest of western Europe, including Belgium and Great Britain, and it is well known that the potato disease in Ireland was a disaster of the first magnitude. In 1846 the wheat crop in France failed almost completely from drought, while in the autumn, floods in the basins of the Loire and the Rhone and a cloudburst in that of the Allier interfered seriously with the distribution of imported grain. The most important source of imports, in view of the crop failures throughout western Europe, was Russia whose wheat was imported chiefly through Marseilles and Arles. The railroads were of little use in this emergency because the vital line from Paris to Lyons and the Mediterranean had scarcely been begun.

The government did not act quickly, except to silence alarmists. It admitted grain free of duty and suspended the octroi on grain and flour only toward the end of the year 1846 when official reports showed the situation to be critical. France had to import grain worth 125,000,000 francs in 1846 and 231,000,000 francs in 1847. By January 1847 the price of a hectoliter of wheat had risen from the normal figure of 18-23 francs to 37 francs, and by April 1847 to 42 francs. There were complaints that wheat was being stored in warehouses by the rich, for which there may have been some foundation, for a century later we are only too familiar with what we now call the black market. But it should be remembered that England was importing from four to five times as much grain as usual, and chiefly from Russia, while the rest of western Europe was forced to do the same. It has also been stated that the complete failure of the French wheat crop of 1846 was not realized until the harvest had been completed, that is, presumably, not until September. Even so, the government could and should have admitted grain free and suspended the octroi before the end of November. The inevitable result of these catastrophes, whose effects could only have been mitigated, however, was widespread food riots in the early months of 1847 in northern and central France. The wheat crop of 1847 was good and thereafter there were fine harvests for several years, but the prices were so low by 1850 that, as C. E. Labrousse says, there had been nothing like them since 1787. In short, crop failures were succeeded by overproduction, so that the peasant simply exchanged hunger for financial loss. We must remember that in 1848 approximately three quarters of the French people were engaged in agriculture and that this included many industrial workers in the summer and on week ends.

Next to crop failures one of the great factors in producing the crisis of 1846-1851 was the railroad. The law of 1842 providing a general network for France marked the beginning of a wave of enthusiasm for railroad construction that lasted well into 1847. The immediate success of the railroads from Paris to Rouen and Orleans in 1843 convinced people that all railroads would be highly profitable. This aroused an eagerness to invest in railroad shares that reminds us of the spirit that caused the railroad mania in England, although there could be no mania in France because the network had been planned carefully by the government and no new line could be built without further legislation involving endless public discussion. The railroads contributed to unrest in France in several ways, however, for they absorbed large sums of capital which thus could not be used to buy grain or finance industry, and they caused heavy financial losses in 1847 by their bankruptcies, which threw thousands of laborers out of work. The large sums of capital temporarily frozen in them could yield no profits, and, in most cases, no income as long as the railroads in which they had been sunk had not been completed, and few had been finished in 1847. While much capital was contributed from England, the withdrawal of this began with the first crash of railroad securities in England in November 1845, followed by general panics there in the summers of 1846 and 1847. Most of the withdrawals, however, came after the outbreak of the Revolution of 1848. Such English withdrawals as there were before 1848 were evidently made good by French investors, as they appear to have been on a much larger scale after 1848, but this increased the volume of French capital invested in railroads when it was needed elsewhere.

While the French were making what seemed to them enormous investments in railroads, for they had had little experience with undertakings requiring large capital investment, they were also investing considerable sums in improving their highways, completing their network of waterways, and fortifying Paris. Quentin-Bauchart says that in 1846-1847 the French spent 419,000,000 francs on railroads and committed themselves to spend 900,000,000 francs more, 210,000,000 francs on local roads, and 400,000,000 francs on the fortifications of Paris. He does not mention either main roads or waterways. In all, he says, 1,789,000,000 francs were pledged to these public works, of which 600,000,000 francs were taken from the national savings of those two years. The French market had thus lost most of its elasticity when famine and industrial depression came, while England, the usual source of financial help in time of need, could do little because she herself was faced with even greater financial difficulties. The distress of the French over their heavy investment in railroads was increased by the panic which hit their shares on the Bourse on September 26, 1846, and lasted a week, while their values continued to fall until the end of November. In 1847 the construction of new lines and of old ones not completed had to be stopped, several railroad companies went bankrupt, and thousands of navvies found themselves unemployed at just the time when a large part of the industrial workers also were idle and nearly all the poor were hungry.

Labrousse tells us that the agricultural crisis gave birth to the crisis in the textile industries, and I can confirm the conflict in them all, although there is no reliable and detailed account as a whole. Economic historians must accumulate far more French evidence before we can give an adequate account. Labrousse says rightly that the crisis beginning in the autumn of 1846 was more widespread and more acute than any other under the July Monarchy, by which he really means more acute than the crisis that had begun in 1837, because that was the only general crisis under the July Monarchy, except the one that began in 1827 before the July Revolution and continued as a depression until 1832. From the textiles the crisis in 1847 spread to industry and commerce in general, and in all was severe beyond any known precedent. Wages did not fall as much as in the textile industries, but unemployment spread just as widely.

Financial strain had been felt at the end of 1846, and during the whole of 1847 the Bank of France held its discount rate at 5 per cent, which was quite unusual. Then, late in December, it was lowered to the customary 4 per cent and the financial crisis was thought to be over. But within two months the Revolution broke out and Labrousse describes the effect as like a tornado in the Bourse and the Bank of France. An acute financial crisis existed through March and, although it then grew milder, conditions were not normal until 1851. The crisis in the textile industries was acute until the summer of 1848, then there was prosperity in 1849, followed by two years of uneasiness. Business in general remained poor, and while the working classes gained from the great decrease in the cost of living, they lost from continued unemployment and lower wages.

III

The existence of widespread unrest in France in 1848 is well known and needs no further demonstration. I have tried in this paper to explain what I believe were the principal causes of that unrest. The most important, in my opinion, was the crisis that began in the autumn of 1846 and grew steadily worse. Associated with it in the popular mind was the suffering in dying domestic industries such as hand-weaving and spinning, for which the industrial revolution was more responsible than this crisis. Resentment against the indifference of the July Monarchy to the sufferings or wrongs of the working classes and its undeviating support of their employers was another cause of unrest. Yet it is difficult to say what other government would or could have done better in the existing state of public opinion and knowledge. I believe that the government of Louis Philippe was callous and stupid, but it has been blamed for nearly everything by writers under succeeding governments, even for its heavy expenditures for public works. Recently it has been vindicated on this last ground by the late Marcel Marion, and I cordially endorse that vindication, for most of the public works were roads, waterways, or railroads, and France needed desperately a good system of transportation at any cost.

I have chosen not to dwell upon the influence of Socialists like Louis Blanc and the more original thinkers who inspired them like Proudhon, Fourier, Cabet, or Babeuf; or even Saint-Simon and Rousseau. I do not believe that the labor movement in France was strong enough or sufficiently organized to have been a major cause of the unrest in 1848. It was obviously more important as a cause of the outbreak of the Revolution, as was the political opposition to Louis Philippe and Guizot, which cannot be discussed here. But the Revolution is not the same as the unrest so prevalent in 1848, which, I believe, would have existed even if no revolution had occurred. It is easy, of course, to focus our attention upon the Revolution because it was sudden and dramatic, just as it is easier to study the labor movement in France than the progress of the industrial revolution. In taking this point of view I believe that I am following the late Henri Sée and agreeing with C. E. Labrousse who both see the most important cause of the unrest in France in 1848 in the crisis that began in the autumn of 1846. The outline of that crisis given in this paper is sketchy, for the reliable evidence is scanty. Much work remains to be done on this subject. When it has been done we can fuse economic with social and political causes into a true and sound interpretation of the Revolution of 1848 in France.

XVI

1848

Storm over the Danube

OTAKAR ODLOŽILÍK

The Year 1848 in German History: Reflections
on a Centenary

FRIEDRICH MEINECKE

Storm over the Danube

OTAKAR ODLOŽILÍK

➤➤➤➤➤➤➤➤➤➤➤➤ *Published in 1948* ◀◀◀◀◀◀◀◀◀◀◀◀

Western European and American historians have rarely been able to deal adequately with the complicated revolutions that took place in 1848 in the territories of the Habsburgs. One reason for this is that the study of Habsburg history requires a knowledge of foreign languages that few Western European and American historians have been willing to master. It is not enough to be able to understand German; the scholar who wishes to do justice to the peoples ruled by the Habsburgs must be familiar with the languages those peoples spoke. It is fortunate, therefore, that in connection with the recent celebrations of the centenary of 1848 a great deal was published in English by Central European scholars who have the linguistic equipment that American, British, and French historians almost always lack. One such scholar is Otakar Odložilík, now of Columbia University. An outstanding authority on the history of the Czechs and the Poles, Odložilík is admirably qualified to deal with the revolutions that were such a milestone in the emergence of the Western Slavs in modern times.

Time rolled up the curtain upon a changed world—thus opens the romance concerning the revolutionary year of 1848 written by a Czech poet, Jan Neruda.

The fall of the absolutist régime and the advent of the constitutional era in the Habsburg domains indeed bore the semblance of a sudden change of rôles in a play. After a series of monotonous scenes which even the rivalry of the two principal partners, Prince Metternich and Count Kolowrat, failed to enliven, the curtain fell suddenly and was

Reprinted by special permission from *Journal of Central European Affairs*, VIII (1948), 129-138. The footnotes which originally appeared with this essay have been omitted.

rolled up by an invisible hand upon a new act. Groups of anonymous
players, for whom the producer had reserved modest functions in the
backstage, rushed to the footlights and instantly were joined by the
crowd entering from behind the coulisses. The play changed quickly
from an uninspiring dialogue to lively action, to the applause and
evident satisfaction of the audience. An outburst of indignation among
the crowd prompted Prince Metternich to leave the scene immediately.
His shrewder partner, Count Kolowrat, vanished from the stage
shortly afterwards, almost unnoticed.

The belated collapse of the absolutist régime was the main source
of the difficulties with which the architects of the new order were confronted. To the present generation, which on several occasions witnessed the blunders and miscarried efforts of dictatorial régimes of
different colors and shades, it is not necessary to present in detail
the inadequate training of men upon whom, after the fall of the
autocracy, fell the responsibility for a speedy reconstruction and
reorientation of public life. In no part of the Habsburg monarchy
had there existed, prior to March, 1848, a training ground for self-
government or a free platform for political discussions. It is true that
political problems had been ventilated in the Hungarian diet and that
occasionally the Bohemian or Austrian diets had passed from routine
transactions to discussions of current affairs. These diets, based as they
were on feudal privileges and survivals from the middle ages, were,
however, not truly representative of the population.

The pressure of the omnipresent police was not evenly distributed
among all groups of inhabitants. Its firm hold upon the middle class
contrasted with the comparative leniency of the court in dealing with
the landed aristocracy. The watchful eye of the censor supervised the
literary output of Bohemia more closely than that of Hungary. The
roads leading from abroad to the imperial residence in Vienna were
less effectively guarded than any links which may have been established
between the intellectual centers of non-Germanic peoples and the
outposts of learning beyond the frontiers of the monarchy. With the
passing of time symptoms of an approaching end multiplied and
betrayed the growing uneasiness and weakness of the ruling class.
When the storm swept from Paris over Southern Germany and reached
the Habsburg residence, it carried away the undesirable elements but
failed to supply in sufficient quantity the seeds of progress or to
engender new life in the middle and lower Danube regions.

Historians of political thought when dealing with the early modern era only occasionally refer to the contributions from the lands over which the House of Habsburg had extended its power. The victories which the Habsburgs had won during the seventeenth and early eighteenth centuries over the Estates in various parts of Central Europe gave them virtually unlimited control of religious life, of education, and of literary activities in general. An interval of comparative freedom of thought and of religious toleration came to an end soon after the death of Joseph II in 1790. The specter of revolution which appeared on the horizon in 1789 fomented fear and suspicion. The timid souls of Francis II and his advisers yielded to the loud demands for the reversal of the government's policy made by the assemblies of the nobility since Joseph's death. It was Emperor Francis who directed the course of public life into the stagnant waters of traditional concepts and of deceptive stability.

During the religious and constitutional struggles which the Habsburgs had waged with vehemence and persistence, the landed aristocracy was their principal opponent. Not the extermination of the nobility but its subordination to the almighty ruler was the ultimate goal of Habsburg policy. When it appeared that this aim had been reached, peace on the domestic front was restored by compromise, and the spheres of influence between the court and the aristocracy were carefully delimited so as to prevent further clashes. On more than one occasion the descendants of the rebel families were won over for service either at the court or in the army.

On the other hand, dislike of the burgher class was deeply rooted in the family tradition of the Habsburgs. Its manifestations during the

---

ALEXANDER BACH: Austrian lawyer and political leader. After the failure of the Revolutions of 1848, he emerged as a prominent figure in conservative circles. His "system" involved a policy of Germanizing the whole Empire, strengthening the police and spy forces, and increasing the power of the Roman Catholic Church. His system broke down with the defeat of Austria in the Austro-Sardinian War of 1859.

LAMENNAIS: Radical French clergyman and social philosopher. Having become convinced that the church could be free only in a free society, he upheld the ideas of disestablishment and freedom of conscience. Condemned by the papacy, he refused to recant and was excommunicated in 1834. His

sixteenth century both in the Low Countries and in Bohemia were just as spontaneous as the mistrust of the middle classes displayed by Austrian emperors during more recent periods of history. The fear that the towns might become hotbeds of revolutionary spirit motivated to a large extent the restrictions which were imposed upon public life in the Habsburg empire during the Napoleonic era and the period between 1815 and 1848. The surveillance of education, the control of books and periodicals coming from abroad, the censorship of domestic publications, and similar protective measures were handed over to civil servants recruited mostly from the ranks of the lower nobility and characterized by stubbornness, a lack of imagination, and an instinctive aversion to any novelty or change. The advance of the middle class to the same position in political, economic, and social life as it had in Western Europe was hampered both by the slow progress of economic revival in the Danubian area and by an unremitting pressure from above.

As soon as the mighty storm of the spring of 1848 subsided and calmer days set in, the constructive elements of the population, now freed from their former fetters, set to work to effectuate a smooth transition from absolutist rule to parliamentary government. As to what parts of the population may be included among the constructive elements, both contemporaries and students of the revolutionary period have differed on details. With the exception of Karl Marx, in his *Revolution and Counter-Revolution*, they have, however, been in complete agreement in regard to the active part which the middle class played both in the revolution and in the consolidation of its gains. It was otherwise with the privileged classes. Whenever the high nobility

---

writings were widely read and discussed by liberal Roman Catholics all over the world.

FRANCIS PALACKÝ: Czech historian and patriot. Author of the monumental *History of Bohemia*, he played a major part in arousing nationalist sentiment among Czech intellectuals. Active in the Revolutions of 1848, he believed in preserving the Bohemian link with the Habsburgs but at the same time he insisted on the need for Czech autonomy. In his later years he lost faith in the "Austrian idea."

VORMÄRZ: The period before the outbreak of the March Revolutions of 1848.

appeared in public as a compact body, it endeavored to stem the tide and to save traditional concepts and institutions from total destruction. The entry of the working class upon the stage was signalized during the 1840's by demonstrations against low wages and widespread unemployment. A new source of dissatisfaction arose during the winter of 1847-48 after the poor harvest of 1847 had resulted in shortages in many commodities and in actual famine conditions. Voices of protest and reiterated demands for an improvement in the living conditions of the industrial workers can be found in such documents and manifestoes as the petition to the imperial court adopted by the people's assembly in the Wenceslas Baths at Prague on March 11, 1848. Demands for social changes were made not only by proletarian leaders but by progressive groups of university students both in Vienna and in Prague and defended by journalists of a radical orientation. But the authors of political programs, as they emerged from discussions in small circles or from public meetings, came mostly from the middle class, which saw in the collapse of the absolutist régime the long-denied opportunity for its own advancement and to procure a proportional share in the conduct of public affairs.

Compared with the masses of peasants and manual workers, the middle class in the cities and towns formed only a thin layer of population, especially in those parts of the monarchy where agriculture predominated. With the exception of Vienna and some provincial capitals, the towns in the Danubian area had not awakened from their lethargy before March, 1848. A narrow horizon, mediocrity, and a subconscious fear of the return of the "Jacobins" characterized the mentality of the average citizen of the empire during the *Vormärz* period. Everywhere the comforts of the home were highly appreciated, for apart from one's own living quarters there were only a few places where a citizen could breathe freely and speak his mind. Organizations or societies which might have invigorated political or cultural life were stifled or in constant danger of being dissolved by the government. A *Bürgerressource,* founded with the consent of the police as a social center for the wealthy class, was the Central European counterpart of English clubs. An annual ball topped the program of its activities.

Only a fraction of the middle class freed itself from intellectual bondage and led a more eventful life in dark corners of the stage. Groups of intellectuals who aspired to play an active part in public affairs endeavored to get some training and experience. They maintained contacts with the outside world at a high cost. If they succeeded in importing newspapers, pamphlets, or books from abroad in spite of the vigilant police, they compared conditions in the monarchy with the progress made in other countries and lamented the great lag in Austria.

With the growing inefficiency of the bureaucratic machinery, some organizations which had been authorized by the police broadened their program, and, under the cover of professional interests or of purely literary activities, they encroached upon the strictly guarded field of politics. The *Juridisch-politischer Leseverein* in Vienna, which in the *Vormärz* period counted among its members Dr. Alexander Bach and other men interested in political and constitutional problems, underwent such a transformation. It was under the aegis of the Union for Advancement of Industry in Bohemia, founded in Prague in 1833 and sponsored by Count Karl Chotek as well as by other Bohemian aristocrats, that František Ladislav Rieger and some of his contemporaries who, after the March revolution, formulated the first Czech political program, first studied contemporary problems. The *Gewerbeverein,* founded a little later in Vienna, vied with the Union both in the search for new industrial methods and in its efforts to exert influence upon current affairs.

The police system was not as competent as its originators and tools thought it was. It had gaps and flaws which were not difficult to discover. Obscure cafés or small restaurants were often patronized by opponents of the régime, whom only experienced agents of the police could recognize among the regular clientele. Such was a group of young Czech intellectuals with radical leanings meeting frequently at "The Golden Scale." In the memoirs of some of the members this group is frequently referred to as "Repeal." The term was introduced into Bohemia by a talented journalist, Karel Havlíček, who in a series of articles discussed conditions in Ireland so vividly that nothing was required for the readers but to substitute Bohemia for the name of the distant country in order to realize what evils he was exposing.

Few generations were confronted with such a complex of problems and duties as the comparatively small portion of the population of the Austrian empire which was catapulted into political prominence in March, 1848. The middle class, the students, and the industrial workers greeted the fall of the obsolete régime and the promise of the constitution as their own victory. The overthrow of Metternich filled them with such joy that they paid little attention to the fate of other supporters of the old régime. Statesmen or high civil servants, however, proved, on the whole, to be less dangerous than the imperial generals whose position nobody dared to attack. The dislike of the generals for the revolution and their decision to muster their forces and to reappear on the stage at an opportune moment proved to be the most fatal of all the anti-revolutionary forces in the summer and fall of 1848. To the strong will of the commanders of military garrisons and to their determination to serve the dynasty, the revolutionary elements opposed a fervent desire for far-going political and social changes and a courage and an enthusiasm which the invigorating air of the March days kept at a boiling point. If in the initial period the army was considered a mere instrument of the government that happened to be in control, the course of the struggles in Italy revealed its power and its relative independence from the ministry. At a comparatively late stage the political leaders finally discovered their mistake in allowing the army to play such an independent rôle and sought in vain for means to compel such military figures as Prince Alfred Windischgrätz to be under the orders of the ministry rather than under the influence of the imperial court.

During the spring months of 1848 the progressive forces gained the upper hand in various parts of the Danubian area, and then set to work to lay the foundations for a constitutional system. Until early June the court vacillated and showed a willingness to retreat before the revolutionists rather than precipitate bloody conflicts anywhere. In order not to reveal their real desires prematurely at that time, the commanders of the armed forces marked time.

If, then, we look for causes for the slow progress of the work of reconstruction we must turn our eyes in other directions. Two obstacles stood in the way and marred the work of the architects of the new order. In their attempts to overcome the unfavorable circumstances, time and energy were wasted which might otherwise have been turned to the fulfillment of revolutionary programs and projects.

Through no fault of their own the members of the revolutionary committees possessed little knowledge of the state machinery and its functioning. In pre-March days the ranks of the bureaucracy were closed to keen minds and enterprising spirits. The high percentage of lawyers among the leading figures of the revolution is not surprising, since it was that profession alone which provided both training in legal practices and contacts with reality. Furthermore, the knowledge the revolutionists had about constitutional problems was highly unsatisfactory, since it was chiefly theoretical and, with few exceptions, most fragmentary and scanty.

As long as absolutism ruled triumphant, loud and many were the criticisms made by the liberals. The number of articles, pamphlets, and books attacking Metternich and his collaborators ran into dozens. They were mostly published in Germany, but hardly any of them failed to be widely circulated among liberal circles in Austria. Their authors scrutinized the system of government and all its flaws. Few aspects of public life escaped their seaching eye. One of the best-known of the anti-Habsburg publications of the time appeared anonymously in 1842 under the title *Österreich und dessen Zukunft*. Its author, Baron Andrian von Werburg, struck a better balance between pure criticism and planning for the future than did most of his contemporaries, but even his book was more specific in making charges against the régime than in formulating a program for recovery. Only a few leading principles had passed through the discussion stage to concrete and applicable forms before the March revolutions tore down the ramshackle edifice against which so many arrows had been directed.

Pamphlets and invectives undoubtedly reached a wider circle than did the books on political theory or on government composed by writers in the Western countries. The latter works were not available on the book market, and only a limited number of them found their way to private libraries. The Austrian régime put restrictions upon travel and study abroad, as the Chief of Police, Count Sedlnitzky, explained, in order to protect the young generation from "philosophical materialism, religious rationalism or mysticism, so-called liberalism, the revolutionary principle and the corporative spirit." Few enthusiasts were as successful as Alexander Bölöni Farkas, who, in 1831, travelled from Hungary to the United States, "a happy fatherland where everyone is equally born into freedom and independence." For the majority of the Austrian liberals who wished to see beyond the Chinese wall, such newspapers as the *Augsburger Allgemeine Zeitung* and the *Grenzboten,* which was published in Leipzig, were the easiest media.

The picture of conditions in West European countries and in the United States, as obtained from the press reports and from periodicals or books, was inevitably dim and incomplete. But what Farkas learned during his travels, František Palacký derived from his reading as early as 1820: the hope that the temporary eclipse of liberty in Europe will pass into a new dawn of freedom ushered in from the New World.

These lofty visions, inspiring as they may have been, were of little practical help, if not supplemented by the study of parliamentary government, preferably on the spot. The opportunities for such a study were a trifle greater during the years immediately preceding the revolution than they had been before. The rigid police and censorship system was everywhere breaking down, and as a consequence the writings of Thiers, Victor Hugo, and Lamennais were circulated among both the Magyars and the Poles. The classic work on the American democracy by Alexis de Tocqueville was studied both by Magyar progressives and by František Rieger in Bohemia. Some members of the *Leseverein* made the study of political and social changes in Great Britain their main field. But it would be misleading to assume that these exceptional cases were the general rule or to infer that a knowledge of the workings of constitutional government was widespread within the Habsburg empire.

The inadequate knowledge of the principles of democracy and the lack of training in local government were coupled with another stumbling block: the lack of knowledge of each other's aspirations and aims which the leaders of the various nationality groups within the empire had. This drawback was pointed out by such an eminent authority on Danubian problems as Oscar Jászi when he wrote: "With the exception of some clear-sighted spirits general public opinion did not realize that the Monarchy was based on the co-operation of ten nations and many smaller nationalities but each nation was busy only with its own existence and problems."

The blame for this rested to a great extent upon the absolutist régime. It tolerated, or even promoted, close relationships between aristocratic families in the hope of welding such groups as the Polish, Bohemian, Austrian, and Hungarian nobility into a compact body to serve as the principal support of the throne. But barriers existed between various provinces, and the intellectuals especially found it difficult to cross them. Of all large centers of population Vienna was the most attractive and the easiest to reach. Not only the German-speaking Austrians but also the educated Slavs from both the North and the South often migrated to Vienna in the hope of finding congenial spirits there. Even these contacts were, however, rare and occasional. In the Constituent Assembly which convened in Vienna late in July, 1848, and which after November, 1848, held its sessions in the summer residence of the Archbishop of Moravia at Kroměříž (Kremsier), national units did not dissolve themselves in order to make possible a more organic grouping along political lines.

Ignorance bred suspicion. Traditional prejudices proved to be stronger than the evident need of subordinating local jealousies to common interests. The revolutions in the Danubian basin had been kindled by sparks which had been blown thither from Paris. They had been motivated by the dissatisfaction with the obsolete Habsburg régime which was common to the inhabitants of Vienna, Pest and Prague, Cracow and Zagreb. The barricades, however, never joined one another to form a single contiguous line. Everywhere in the empire the local revolutionary movements remained separated from each other by geographical lines and traditional antipathies. A Czech liberal felt little inclination to place the future of his people in the hands of a German patriot, liberal though he might be in his political outlook. František Palacký, in his letter to the Frankfort liberals on April 11, 1848, resolutely declined the invitation to sit side by side with German deputies to work with them for the unification of Germany. Palacký's aide, the journalist Karel Havlíček, rapped the Viennese publicist Franz Schuselka so successfully in a ditty that his light verses proved a more effective weapon in the struggle between the two nationalities than the dignified message of Palacký. That the deliberations in the Polish-Ruthenian section of the Slavonic Congress in Prague would result in probable failure was foreshadowed by the determination of the Ruthenian delegates to say "no" anytime "aye" would be heard from the Polish benches.

All in all, a spirit of progress had not permeated the population of the Danubian area with the force necessary to surmount all linguistic barriers, dispel fear, and make evident the imperative need of cooperation both during the initial period of the struggle against a common enemy and in the calmer atmosphere of the national Constituent Assembly. Had the Constituent Assembly, in its session of September

7, 1848, not enacted the law freeing the peasants from their personal bondage to the nobility, as recommended by Dr. F. A. Brauner and Hans Kudlich, it would be difficult to point out even a single permanent gain of the revolution.

It would be a hard task to narrate the story of the revolutionary movements in the Danubian basin in a single, comprehensive work. Along the Danube the tide of revolution divided itself into many currents and countercurrents immediately after Metternich's overthrow. Gradually during the winter of 1848-49 the revolutionary movement again united around the single goal of formulating a constitution for the Habsburg monarchy. Discussions went on at Kroměříž both in the constitutional committee and in plenary sessions. Out of these conversations there emerged early in March, 1849, a draft of the long-desired constitution, which, in the words of Oscar Jászi, "was the first consequent and logically consistent attempt to rebuild a large Empire on the basis of supranational unity and to codify the great principle of national equality in all the walks of public life."

At the same time that the liberals were drafting a constitution, the reactionary forces, encouraged by the earlier victories of Prince Alfred Windischgrätz in Prague and Vienna, as well as by the advance of the imperial regiments in Lombardy and Venetia, rallied round the Court, then at Olomouc (Olmütz), a mere thirty miles from Kroměříž. The accession of Francis Joseph to the imperial throne vacated by the resignation of his uncle Ferdinand on December 2, 1848, marked a sudden turn to reaction. In the early days of March, 1849, the consolidated ranks of the guardians of the old order overpowered the progressive forces. On March 7, 1849, the members of the Constituent Assembly found the archepiscopal palace surrounded by armed forces sent there to prevent the taking of a final vote on the constitution in which, after a fiery defense by Rieger, the people and not the monarch were proclaimed the source of all power and sovereignty. Not Prince Metternich, but Prince Felix Schwarzenberg, the brother-in law of Prince Alfred Windischgrätz, appeared in the limelight when on March 7, 1849, the curtain fell over the revolutionary period and rose again with the elected representatives hastily retreating behind the coulisses and bureaucrats and officers taking their places.

For the January 2, 1849, issue of his *Národní Noviny*, Karel Havlíček wrote an editorial, "On the Threshold of a New Year." He summarized the swift course of events since March, 1848, as follows: "One of the most remarkable and greatest years just lapsed into the past and has left a remarkable trace in the memory of all peoples of Europe. Liberty had knocked with a mighty hand at the palaces of the kings and the gates opened. More especially the Slavic peoples celebrated in the past year their resurrection, their revival."

Without changing in any way Havlíček's verdict we may justly extend his evaluation of the events of 1848 to all peoples in the Danubian area. The storm which swept over the mountains and plains was overpowered by contrary currents of air when the storm divided itself and spent its initial speed and vigor. The division of the revolutionists enabled the reactionaries to return to power in 1849. The system of absolutism which they re-established, however, rested on feet of clay. It throve in the atmosphere of depression prevailing on the European continent in the early 1850's but collapsed when the defeat of the Habsburg army in Lombardy in 1859 mercilessly revealed its weakness.

The Year 1848 in German History

REFLECTIONS ON A CENTENARY

FRIEDRICH MEINECKE

>>>->>>->>>->>>->>>->>>->>>->>>->>> *Published in 1948* <<<-<<<-<<<-<<<-<<<-<<<-<<<-<<<-<<<

If German historians held an election to choose their most distinguished twentieth-century representative, there is no doubt that the honor would be accorded to Friedrich Meinecke. A historian's historian in much the same sense that Keats is a poet's poet, Meinecke has exercised considerable influence on some of the best products of twentieth-century German historical scholarship. Even when he was removed by the Nazis from his post as editor of the most important German historical journal, the *Historische Zeitschrift*, he had the consolation that many of his leading disciples were carrying on in exile the tradition of scientific history that he upheld. Meinecke is a difficult writer, whose works require great concentration and thought. This, indeed, is one of the reasons why his works, important though they are, have not been translated into English. One notable exception is his analysis *The German Catastrophe,* which appeared in translation in 1950. Another notable exception is the thoughtful essay that follows, on the significance of the German Revolutions of 1848. Written in connection with the recent centennial celebrations, it deserves the careful attention of anyone interested in the historical background of the German problem.

The popular uprising of the March days of 1848 in Berlin, super-ficially viewed, remained an episode, and the men who were fighting for progress along various lines failed, and were bound to fail, in their aims. The German revolution, said Friedrich Engels in his instructive articles of 1851-52 (which he published in America above the signature of Karl Marx), was a necessity, but its temporary suppression

Reprinted by special permission from *The Review of Politics,* X (1948), 475-492.

was similarly unavoidable. We shall still have to substantiate this, but must turn our gaze first upon the Berlin revolution, and upon the positive comment which it may offer for our contemporary historical situation. Yet for this too it is necessary to search somewhat deeper.

We must set before ourselves today more sharply than before, the problem of critical alternatives in the history of Germany, in order to gain a deeper insight into the infinitely complex web of her dark destiny. The natural task of Germany in the nineteenth century was not only to achieve unification, but also to transmute the existing authoritarian state (*Obrigkeitsstaat*) into commonwealth (*Gemeinschafts-staat*). To that end, the monarchial-authoritarian structure had to be made elastic—if possible, through peaceful reform—so that the result would be an active and effective participation of all strata of society in the life of the state. This was imperatively demanded by the new configuration which was in process within the German society, and which was undermining the former aristocratic foundations of the authoritarian monarchy. An upper middle class arose, the lower middle class increased in large strides, and the beginnings of the industrial proletariat in the middle of the century gave notice of its mighty growth to come. Now, the task of reorganizing and harmonizing within a new commonwealth a people in social transition, bursting with vitality, remained largely unfulfilled, although many liberal and democratic concessions were granted by the old authorities. Which then were the decisive points in this development? When were possibilities first seen, attempts made or frustrated, which could have brought Germany forward upon the path to the commonwealth?

I see, above all, three such moments. The first occurs toward the end of the Prussian era of reform, in the year 1819—the year of the Carlsbad Decrees—when with the dismissal of Wihelm von Humboldt and Boyen, their most fruitful constitutional projects were also buried, and the authoritarian and militaristic principle triumphed in Prussia. The second crisis, when this principle once more won out in the end, was the year 1848. And the third point of decision was the Prussian era of conflict and the year 1866, which, while seeing some progress made toward satisfying the desire for national unity and strength, allowed the liberal and democratic ideas only a partial or apparent success. For it separated the way of the upsurging popular movements from the authoritarian-militaristic citadel of the entire national life.

Of these three fundamental decisions of the nineteenth century, the first was fought out in the more restricted circle of the ruling class it-self, between high-minded and farsighted statesmen on the one hand and a monarch of limited understanding on the other. The third crisis developed as a duel between the liberal upper middle class and Bis-marck, in which that tremendously skilful campaigner understood how to win over at last a large part of the opposition. At no time in the years before 1866, was the weapon of a revolution seriously con-sidered by Bismarck's progressive antagonists; they were fearful of it, in accordance with the instincts of an upper bourgeoisie. The second crisis—that of 1848—offers therefore a unique, and for us today, a moving spectacle: here the whole people, not Prussians alone, but Ger-mans of every class, stepped into the arena, and an actual revolution came about.

Revolutions, fearful as the invasion of irrational forces may be, or turn out to be, have in certain cases their deep historical justification. Such was the case in Germany, and especially in Prussia, in the year 1848. Admittedly the old order, now attacked by the revolution, was not in all aspects characterized by decay or ossification. The *Bieder-meierzeit* with its lovely spiritual flowering had gone before. The Zoll-verein, since 1833 a work of the Prussian bureaucracy, had made secure the indispensable preconditions for the rise of modern economic forces, and thereby also for the social transformation from which the revolu-tion itself had sprung. The psychopathic romanticist who now sat on the throne of the Hohenzollerns was himself inspired with a deep love for German civilization (*Deutschtum*), and was at some pains to bring about a German unity in its own way. But this way contradicted most sharply the urgent needs of the time. It was upon illusions that he based his attempts to reform the wretched organization of the German Bund and to fulfill the promise of a constitution (made in 1815) by the assembling of the united provincial diets in 1847. For the strongly

---

CARLSBAD DECREES: Repressive measures of 1819 sanctioned by the Diet of the Germanic Confederation. Sponsored by Metternich in order to drama-tize the struggle against potential revolutionaries who were infected with French ideas, the Decrees imposed severe restrictions on freedom of speech, press, and assembly.

DAHLMANN: German historian, political writer, and liberal statesman. A professor at the University of Göttingen, he led the protest movement

aristocratic composition of these provincial estates, and the narrow powers which were all that the king would concede to them, were completely inadequate to satisfy the claims of popular representation which grew out of the process of social change. And in everyday life one felt everywhere the old absolutist-militarist police state, unbroken in spite of the isolated concessions to liberalism which the king, giving with one hand and rescinding with the other, might make. But behind the reaction against his personal and self-contradictory rule, and behind all individual grievances, there stood as a deepest source of discontent the feeling that the Prussian military and Junker state must be reorganized from the ground up—that the old authoritarian state must give way to a new commonwealth.

In fact this emotion, spurring on toward revolution, was not actually evoked but only powerfully stimulated, by the February revolution in France and the scattered revolts that were flaring up throughout Germany and even in Metternich's own Vienna. The remarkable circumstance that everywhere they succeeded at once, without encountering resistance, would demonstrate that the moral position of the rulers themselves was already noticeably shaken, that they no longer possessed an unquestioning and naive faith in the viability of the old order. Such a faith was necessary, if the governments were to use against the revolution the physical instrumentalities of power, still amply available to them. When later they realized that these resources were still at their disposal, the authorities did not hesitate to act accordingly, and to suppress the revolution with reaction. But as things were in March, 1848, they all, as Frederick William IV later expressed it, "lay flat on their bellies."

He, the king himself, most of all. And this in spite of the fact that he had actually launched, on the 18th of March, the physical auxiliaries of his power—his faithful army—successfully against the people's barri-

---

against the King of Hanover, who had violated the Hanoverian constitution. Dismissed from the University, he became a hero to German liberals. In the Frankfurt Assembly he led the center group, which favored the establishment of a constitutional empire headed by Prussia. Though a liberal in his views, he was also a staunch German nationalist.

PAULSKIRCHE: The Church in which the Frankfurt Assembly of 1848-1849 met.

cades in Berlin. Yet on the very next day, he permitted, through his own order, these troops—though undefeated—to abandon the inner city which they had conquered, and thereby exposed the person of the king to the severest of humiliations at the hands of the rebels. Let us leave aside entirely the tangled complexity of these events, which have been investigated time and again, and emphasize only this. So feeble and contradictory a policy could not have been conducted by any prince, who, with a pure and undiminished faith in his old world, was simply defending it against a new. This new world had already to some degree insinuated itself, secretly and unsuspected, into his own thinking, distracting and weakening his power for effective action. Sooner or later the new was bound to win out, in spite of many setbacks to come, and to replace the authoritarian state by some form of democracy.

Such an interpretation may be justified, as we look back over the whole century that separates us from the year 1848, and as we think of the task now before us—the task of casting aside all relics of the authoritarian state (of which the Third Reich was, in fact, but a malignant outgrowth), and building up a sound and vigorous democracy. The easy victory—to be sure, not a military but a political and psychological victory—by which the street-fighting in Berlin prevailed over the old military monarchy, suggested symbolically that the latter's downfall was written in the stars; that one day the sovereignty of the people would become a reality. But, at the same time, it was no more than a symbol. For the new world was as yet quite untested and immature, and the old world still possessed many unexploited resources —even the chance of remaining victorious for some time to come. Bismarck and his work, after all, had sprung from it, at once magnificent and ephemeral. But let us now mark clearly the indications of that immaturity in which the new world of democracy then continued to find itself.

First a glance at Berlin. The men on the barricades of the 18th of March certainly fought bravely and fiercely, more fiercely than the Parisians before them had fought on the 24th of February. Such was the opinion of the Frenchman Circourt, who had come to Berlin as the representative of the new republican government, and had witnessed both engagements. But was it really the whole of the Berlin populace that stood behind the fighting or accompanied it with good wishes? Pastor Bodelschwingh, son of the minister whose task it was to pass on the royal command for retreat on the 19th of March, wrote in 1902:* "We youngsters were running about on the streets that Sunday morning (March 19). With the uprising repelled, there reigned a joyful mood among the greater part of our population; everywhere from the houses the troops were plied with food." Of course, most of the individual bits of evidence which we possess concerning the 18th and 19th of March, are colored to some extent by the sympathies of the witness, and so this testimony of Bodelschwingh should not be taken too literally either. But even less does it deserve to be entirely discarded. And a glance at the general attitude of the German upper middle class in the years 1848-49 reveals all the more clearly that large sections of this class were still greatly desirous of tranquillity, and continued to be loyal to the old authorities.

It is necessary to go more deeply into these questions, in order to explain the paradoxical fact that the German revolution of 1848 could everywhere succeed so easily at first, and then in the sequence of events be overthrown with comparatively little effort. To understand this, the character, attitudes, and moral habits of the German people as it was at that time, and those of the various social strata within it, must be taken into consideration. And our contemporary need to attain to an inner relationship with this first attempt at German democracy gives this problem all the more importance.

The German people had only just emerged from the years of thinking, writing, and striving. But the thinking and dreaming continued likewise within the framework of new achievements and new desires. This ideological groundswell is common to all parties and classes within the German people, from Frederick William IV and his devout Christian-German friends—the extremists of reaction—all the way to the extremists of revolution: the men whose forceful minds conceived the Communist Manifesto of 1848, Karl Marx and Engels. For did not Hegel live on with them—a Hegel in reverse and yet preserved (*aufgehoben*)? Was it not true of both these thinkers, who claimed to regard all ideologies as merely secondary efforts of fundamental economic forces, that in them there came to life something distinctly ideological—an unqualified belief in the determining power of the laws of development—set up at a time when they themselves found

---

* Pastor Bodelschwingh is known as the founder of Bethel. The author wrote to him in 1902, requesting information about the revolution of 1848; the above quotation is from his reply.

only a tiny handful of followers? In any case, we ought no more gain-say the strong impulse of idealism which worked in these men, than that operating in Dahlmann and Gagern—the champions of the liberal nation-state—or in the brothers Gerlach, defenders of a divinely or-dained corporative state. The German revolution of 1848, admittedly, shows not only an all-pervading spirit of idealism, which often out-stripped reality and became ideological. It also brought to bear what in actual effect was more powerful—the reality itself, the massive and elemental interests of individuals and social groups. And, because it *was* a revolution, it likewise saw the release of base passions, and out-rages of all kinds, perpetrated by the Right as well as by the Left. But if 1848 is compared with other revolutions—and particularly with the most ignominious of all revolutions, that of 1933—it can be stated that the factor of human depravity played a comparatively insignificant role. This must not be obscured by the fact that the extremist parties took pleasure in accusing one another of disgraceful conduct. Theirs were for the most part "atrocity stories." Neither was there anything which could be termed a "brutalized soldiery," nor were the barricades and the free corps of Hecker and Struve manned by a mere "mob." The German people, considered as a whole, kept in those days to a comparatively high moral level.

It must be admitted that their level of life no longer possessed the spiritual grandeur of the age of Goethe. This decline was unavoidable in any case, since the urgent task of establishing a new political and social way of life compressed men into mass or group patterns, and made it more difficult for the individual to gather within himself the creative force from which proceeds all great culture. But what mattered now was, whether this people would prove to possess the maturity, the strength, the insight and steadfastness, that its new task demanded. Certainly, as we have noted, it was written in the stars that one day the new world would triumph over the old, popular sovereignty over the authoritarian state. But could the victory be achieved at this junc-ture? The fact that the revolution failed does not necessarily prove that the people were not ready; this may have been due to the coincidence of accidental factors. How bitter were the complaints, in the very midst of events, that just such a personality as Frederick William IV should have been for the revolution its "man of destiny"—a man who had actually, out of weakness, bowed before it at the outset, but who had then stubbornly resisted it; and by his refusal of the imperial office on April 3, 1849, had allowed the nation's call for the creation of the liberal nation-state to die away. Certainly another man in his place could have attempted another and possibly more propitious solution of the German problem. Then, however, the success of the attempt would once more have depended, in the last analysis, upon the world situation. This aspect of the problem we shall take up later. Suffice it now to ask again: was the German people really prepared for the task ahead?

Basic attributes and historical experiences, working together, had made the German people parochial, not only outwardly but inwardly as well, to a degree hardly equalled in any other nation of Europe. The princely territorial state, multiplied a hundredfold to the point where it exhibited absurd extremes of dwarfishness, depended everywhere upon a landed gentry which served the state and, in return, held sway over those beneath them. All this had mingled with the German bloodstream and had rendered the German people obedient and lacking in political self-reliance. In this very multiplication of authority, we see the chief means by which the mentality of the authoritarian state penetrated so deeply into the pores of German life.

One need only compare this with the development of England and France, where the royal absolutism—in England short-lived anyhow—had indeed helped to create a unified nation, but had never been able to instil so lasting and thoroughgoing a habit of obedience, as had the multiplicity of small German principalities. How far an original or native trait had helped to bring this about, can only be conjectured. Was it perhaps the spirit of fealty described by Tacitus? But the example of the Germans in Switzerland and their historical development since the Middle Ages indicates that there were other potentialities of a political nature inherent in the German character. Free of princely and therefore of rigid rule, subject only to patrician and—by the same token—more pliable authority, Switzerland was enabled to develop the native democratic tenet of her original cantons into the governing principle of her commonwealth, and thus to build upon historical foundations a modern democracy. No, the German need not submit to any fatalistic dread that because he is a German, he may for ever and ever be condemned to the habits of servility implanted by the authoritarian state. But it takes time, much time, again to tear free of it. Then too, his state has borne the German people, along with evil fruits, many and varied benefits, and thus fashioned much of ethical value that might well be carried over into the new world of the democratic commonwealth.

Good and evil alike, then, grew out of this disposition toward obedience, whose origin may well be placed primarily in the political fragmentation referred to above. Even where a larger political entity was growing up, as in Prussia, the extreme insistence upon this subservient attitude brought out in a manner especially striking the contrast between its good and evil effects. Prussia was, indeed, a state with two souls: the one austere and narrow, withdrawing into itself; the other culturally alive, striving, in Boyen's phrase, toward a threefold alliance of *"Recht, Licht und Schwert"* ["Right, Light and Strength"]. This Prussia, at once forbidding and attractive, now exerted her influence upon the rest of Germany. But how much was this influence again bound to confuse and distract all the aims of revolutionary Germany! The singleness of revolutionary purpose which would have been necessary for a victory over the old order, was thus rendered at the outset far more difficult to achieve. Now the German people, breaking loose from its previous subservience, did indeed reach out tumultuously for unity, power and freedom—only to find itself divided anew when it sought to determine the methods by which these were to be accomplished. How deep was the disintegrating and paralyzing effect of the Austro-German (*grossdeutsche*) problem, which implied what to some seemed an avoidable, to others an inevitable sacrifice of a portion of their fellow-countrymen (*Brudersstamm*), and the break-up of a German national community; how strongly has this problem contributed to the negative result of the revolution! It is hardly necessary, in addition, to recall the particularism of the intermediate German states. In fact, it was not merely the egotistic instincts of the princes, of their court councillors and court provisioners, but particularistic tendencies as well, conscious or unconscious, in the people themselves, which came into conflict with the new yearning for unity.

These were the factors of secular growth, going back as far as the Middle Ages, which weakened and divided in advance any unified revolutionary purpose in the German people. To these, however, were now added problems of the most modern type, arising out of the new configuration of society. It is true that the one part of the people which now broke away from the old attitudes of obedience, and rose up against the authoritarian state and against the splintering apart of the nation, was agreed upon the demand for greater unity, power and freedom; but it fell out once again over the emphasis and interpretation to be placed upon one or another of these three words. For behind the national revolution there was unfolding a social revolution, a class struggle between the old, the newer, and the newest social strata. This fact was recognized most clearly at the time by Marx and Engels, the champions of the newest class—the industrial proletariat—which had only just arisen and was still by no means very numerous. Between this youngest and (as Marx and Engels dogmatically proclaimed) potentially most important class, and that which had ruled so far—the nobility and the higher bureacracy—there lay the two clearly distinct divisions of the bourgeoisie: the upper and lower middle class. The first was of more recent origin; the other dated far back, though it was not nearly as old as the peasantry—who, together with agricultural laborers, still made up by far the preponderant majority of the people as a whole. (The committee on economic affairs of the Frankfurt Parliament estimated that they constituted virtually four-fifths of the total population at that time.) The share of the rural population in the revolution was certainly not unimportant, but created no particularly complicated issue for the fate of the revolution as a whole. Since a general land reform through the dismemberment of the large estates was not yet seriously envisioned, the agrarian problem of 1848 entailed only the casting-off of all remaining feudal encumbrances upon the peasant class and the peasant holdings. That was a comparatively simple task. Even conservative statesmen realized the necessity of solving this question at once, and when the peasants saw that steps in this direction were being taken or being planned, they calmed down again. They still shared sufficiently in the old habits of subservience, in any case. The young Bismarck could well consider using them as tools in the counter-revolution.

Side by side with the working class, the lower middle class provided most of the revolutionary energy. Craftsmen and workers formed the bulk of the fighters on the barricades. Had they not risen up, the revolution could not have achieved dynamic force at all, and all the idealists and theorists of the general movement (reaching into the upper middle class) would have remained officers without an army. There would have been no parliament in the Paulskirche, no draft for a German constitution with an hereditary Prussian emperor at its head. The craftsmen in Germany at that time were badly off. It was related in the Paulskirche that there was one small town with seventy tailors, of whom only seven were able to find employment. Some hardship was caused by guild restrictions which continued here and there. But a genuine guild spirit revived again, as is evidenced in the desperate struggle waged against the new machine by workers who were losing their livelihood, in the excesses committed by the waggoners against the railroads and by the boatsmen against the Rhine river steamers. These were all, in fact, merely symptoms of the basic feature of an age in which the machine, and the modern technology, had revolutionized the entire life of the western peoples, by creating new human masses and new, unsuspected and distressing situations among these masses.

In such a crisis, the old authoritarian state proved unable for a long time to provide effective aid. Its officialdom was vacillating between benevolence and a narrow, pedantic attitude; its police a nuisance; its army—though possessed in the militia (*Landwehr*) of a more popular aspect—aroused bitter opposition by the arrogance and drill-ground manner of the regulars and their officers. Democracy as a cure for all these sufferings was the magic word that echoed through the ranks of the lower bourgeoisie—a class so quietist by nature and so restless now. The working classes took up the same slogan, and added to it their own socialistic demands. The younger generation within the upper middle class in many places espoused the democratic cause with enthusiasm, and imbued it with the impulse of idealism. It was, to be sure, an exceedingly immature and primitive democracy of which these Germans dreamed, more a rejection of the old authoritarian state than a positive affirmation of the people's state resting upon a fully developed common spirit among all classes. The distrust and arrogance with which the various classes regarded one another, once more divided the very groups which had just made common cause against the old authorities. Let us illustrate this and other facts aforementioned, with certain experiences which the young Rudolf Virchow had in the March Days of Berlin.

Eight days before the 18th of March, he had returned from Upper Silesia, where he had been sent as a doctor to study the "hunger-typhus." He was indignant at the inability of the magistrates to take effective measures, and had long been convinced that the absolutist system of government was untenable. He assisted in the building of barricades on the 18th of March, and, armed with a pistol, placed himself at the one which blocked the Friedrichstrasse from the Taubenstrasse. Only six days later, he had to admit in a letter to his father:

"Already there begins a reaction among the citizenry (Bourgeoisie) against the workers (the people). Already they are speaking of a rabble, already plans are being made for withholding equal distribution of political rights among the various groups in the nation." But, he added, the popular party would be alert and powerful, and would see to it "that no bourgeoisie should enjoy the fruits of a battle it had not waged."

One realizes here the closeness of the relationship between events in Berlin and the revolutions of 1830 and 1848 in France. But the problems of the German revolution were nevertheless much more complicated than those of the French uprisings. For the social revolution in Germany and its underlying class struggle was intertwined with the national revolution in a way which finally led to the failure of both. France no longer had need of a national revolution. She had long since achieved her unity, and her centralized power apparatus remained through one regime after another. In Germany both social equality and national consolidation were still to be achieved, with endless pains. And the need of the nation for unity and power was just as elemental and as deeply rooted in history as was the cry for domestic freedom and equality arising from those classes which the authoritarian state had so far kept down. Dahlmann in Frankfurt even voiced the opinion that within the German desire for both power and freedom, the stronger impulse was now directed toward power, which had thus far been denied. The criminal excesses reached in our day by the need for power in Germany should by no means mislead us into condemning the elemental national craving of the men of '48. For theirs was a genuine hunger for something indispensable. Even Goethe had once acknowledged this fact, after the battle of Leipzig. "Art and science," he said to Luden, "are universal, and in view of these the bonds of nationality disappear. But the consolation they afford is but hollow comfort, and cannot replace the proud consciousness of belonging to a great, strong, feared and respected nation." Basically all the cravings of the year 1848 were permeated by kindred feelings and experiences. There was a general desire to leave behind the constricting and now intolerable bonds of the past, as one leaves behind a dark and airless dungeon. Just as the little man felt himself generally neglected and mistreated by the authoritarian state, so did the more cultivated German, who saw himself as a member of a great national community, and yet hemmed in by the irritating boundaries and the often ridiculous parochialism of thirty-eight greater or smaller authoritarian states. And equally neglected and thrust aside did he feel himself and his whole people to be within the entire body of European states.

All three of these desires [the liberal, the national, the European] were now, it was fondly hoped, to find their fulfillment through the Frankfurt National Assembly which, elected by universal and equal suffrage, convened on the 18th of May. Let us consider its social composition; it was noticeably different from what one might have expected as the result of the democratic suffrage imported from France. It contained no workers, only one genuine peasant, few members of the lower middle class, but many lawyers and judges—and, as is well known, many professors; nor were representatives of business and industry lacking. This indicates the still remaining respect of the lower for the upper strata of society, especially for the academically educated and in general for what is termed the upper bourgeoisie. But the same masses who now cast their votes for these people were simultaneously in a state of unruly and turbulent commotion, which must necessarily have boded evil for the upper middle class interests and ideals. One had to rely on such an energetic thrust from below, in order to succeed at all to Frankfurt and the Paulskirche. But now it was a question, indeed, whether one could continue to employ these energies as indispensable weapons against the rulers, and yet keep them within limits, so as to guard against anarchy and the overturn of the social order.

In the last analysis, it was the danger of communism which appeared to threaten the whole bourgeoisie—not only the upper but the lower middle class as well. How real even the latter felt this threat to be, is exemplified by the bloody clash between the civil guard and the workers in Berlin on October 16, 1848. Communistic slogans and demands rang out from the enraged masses. A clearly conceived program, such as that of Marx and Engels, was in truth limited at first to the narrowest circles. But in a broader perspective, it appears that the very existence of a communist movement was perhaps decisive, or at least instrumental, in determining the course of events in 1848— and, in the first instance, the attitude and policy of the Paulskirche. For it was in view of this communist threat that the middle class and its representation in the majority parties of the Paulskirche again and again were forced over toward the Right, toward some kind of compromise with the old authorities and their military resources. The same threat was instrumental in preventing the maintenance of a unified revolutionary purpose within the whole people, to which perhaps the government might at last have been forced to submit. We use the little word "perhaps," because historical questions of this sort cannot be treated like a mere problem in mathematics; because in every case where we have to consider the historical possibility of another kind of development than that which actually took place, an unknown "X" disturbs the calculation.

In any event, the parties of the majority—right and left center—which desired to establish a liberal, constitutional nation-state with an hereditary Prussian emperor as its head, found themselves in an extremely contradictory and precarious position. They needed the resources of a revolution just as much as those of a counter-revolution. But their position did not enable them to make full and unqualified use of either, without endangering the very basis of their undertaking. In their effort, however, to pursue a middle course and to bring both revolutionary and counter-revolutionary resources simultaneously or alternately into play, they incurred the danger, in turn, of becoming powerless themselves, and of seeing their cause wrecked against the forces of the stronger contender of the two—the counter-revolution. This, viewed as a whole, was to be their fate. Let us briefly point out here only the critical stages.

From France the signal had been given in February for the revolution; from France again the signal was given for the counter-revolution in June. In a terrible, three-day street battle, Cavaignac smashed the Paris workers. To be sure, the German middle class heaved a sigh of relief; but for them the ebbing of the revolutionary wave which now followed in Germany as well, was gain and loss alike—while for the reactionary forces of the authoritarian state, this turn constituted a clear gain. With the decline of communist fortunes, those of national liberalism sank as well.

This same dynamic course of events then unfolded during September. When the Prussian government concluded with Denmark the truce of Malmö, which seriously threatened the German claim to Schleswig, the aroused majority in the Paulskirche at first rejected it outright; but shortly thereafter, in view of the impracticable consequences of a refusal, the assembly, once more grown meek, ratified the agreement. And when an uprising from the Left now led to street fighting in Frankfurt itself and endangered the assembly, it was forced to turn for help to Prussian and Austrian troops (from the federal fortress at Mainz), in order to prevent a general landslide to the Left. Once more the fortunes of the authoritarian state rose, once more those of national liberalism sank. And they dropped still lower when the governments of Austria and Prussia, in October and November respectively, put down with their own military forces the rebellious democracy in Vienna and Berlin.

Under such circumstances was born the constitutional project of the Frankfurt National Assembly, culminating in the choice of the King of Prussia as hereditary emperor on March 28, 1849. Doubtless it was a proud achievement of the noblest aspiration toward national unity and freedom. But it lacked the basis of power which would have been necessary to put it through against the particularistic and reactionary forces of the authoritarian state. It was defeated at once when Frederick William IV, on April 3, 1849, refused to accept the new crown offered to him—a crown which in his view could appear only as a product of the revolution, a Danaean gift. And when the genuine revolution now reared its head again, and the disappointment which broad masses of the people experienced over the failure of Frankfurt exploded in the May uprisings in Pfalz and Baden, the equally disillusioned middle class—in order not to be engulfed altogether by revolution and the social upheaval that might follow—was forced once more, as in September, 1848, to lean on the authoritarian state. It had now exhausted its own role as an independent power factor, and had to be satisfied with the scant dole of liberal and national concessions which the insight of those who ruled Prussia might still be willing to grant. The May uprisings, on the other hand, were easily put down by Prussian troops. The fighters of the revolution, be they idealists of the urban educated class, little people of the lower bourgeoisie, or workers, proved completely inadequate to wage a military campaign against the disciplined and dependable fighting force of the authoritarian state.

Upon these rocks was wrecked the German revolution. Only a unified revolutionary purpose, reconciling workers with bourgeoisie and upper with lower middle class, might have been able (as we have noted) to force another result and so to weaken the army's tradition of loyalty as to overthrow the old authorities. But the social transformation of the people, which brought on disruption within the entire middle class, had in fact made impossible from the first the growth of such a spirit of revolutionary unity. Without this social transformation, however—without a rising upper middle class, a lower middle class threatened with disintegration, and an aspiring working class—the revolution itself would have been impossible. Thus strangely and tragically intertwined were the inner necessity of this revolution and its inevitable failure.

We have deliberately emphasized the question whether the year 1848 could already have brought a commonwealth to the German people. For it is this very question which above all burns in our hearts in the dark situation of today. Only as a genuine and healthy commonwealth could Germany win in Europe and in the world a position strong enough to be maintained through all the crises of Europe. The Bismarckian Reich, magnificent as was its undertaking to combine the vital elements, old and new, within state and society, was yet unable to achieve that intense common spirit which is indispensable as an essential bond within the whole, and as the basis of any vigorous democracy.

There has been much talk since Ranke of a primacy of foreign policy, which is supposed to exercise a formative and dominating influence upon domestic affairs. I believe that this doctrine, while containing an indisputable kernel of truth, today requires revision and certain qualifications. The motives as well as the effects of foreign policy—and particularly whether its success is to be lasting or only temporary—depend to a considerable extent upon the inner coherence and sturdiness of the individual state; upon the type and degree of a common spirit which animates it. The Bismarckian Reich, it is true, was built up under a primary impulse of foreign policy—that is, out of the necessity to erect a strong and independent power in the center of Europe. In addition, it certainly lacked no appreciation of the fact that this power must also possess inner coherence, and rest on a sense of national community. But the synthesis which Bismarck attempted to forge between authoritarian state and commonwealth failed the test in the years of decision, when the world wars came. Too much of the authoritarian state remained in Bismarck's work.

But in what way, we must now inquire, is the year 1848 related to the primacy of foreign policy and to the world of European power politics in general? We have already seen that among the aims of the year 1848, there was also present the hope of raising Germany to the status of a great power. And this need was felt not only in the ranks of the middle class—of the party of liberal reform, the advocates of an hereditary imperial crown. More or less consciously, it inflamed also the will of many of those who wished to make of Germany "the republic one and indivisible." The Left too had its power politics—still a totally irresponsible variety—but one already spurred on in no small measure by desires and aspirations, though they were, of course, assumed to advance democracy. Hence war was appraised as an instrument for winning a lasting peace among the democratically united peoples of Europe. This idea of forming an aggressive front is to be encountered often enough—for example, in the proposal of an alliance with democratic France against autocratic Russia. And was it not the Left itself in the Paulskirche—in the September crisis after the truce of Malmö—which demanded the continuation of a national war against Denmark, a war threatening to widen into a European war? It was the opinion of Karl Marx that a world war must assist his cause. Thus democrats were willing enough in such cases—though at first with merely verbal audacity—to take up the sword, the assumption being that in the future it should not be carried by the "brutalized soldiery" of an authoritarian state, but by a people's army. We realize now, that an intensification, a victory of the domestic revolution in Germany, could have led—and perhaps necessarily—into the storm center of a great European war. A realization, once more, that is deep with tragedy.

This danger of a European war, in fact, was like a lowering black storm-cloud overshadowing the whole of the revolution of 1848, and even subsequent events. All the problems of this year which were specifically national, were inflammatory in the highest degree. To gain Schleswig, a war had to be started as early as April, 1848; but it stirred immediate opposition in Russia, England, and Sweden, which eventually did bar the way to this prize. The Polish-German problem of Posen led, even in its first stage, to bloody fighting within the province itself; but it could as easily have eventuated in a Russian intervention. The great Austro-German question, the exclusion of Austria from the federative state envisioned in the Paulskirche, was most clearly burdened with the heavy mortgage of an imminent war against Russia and Austria. And France? There from the outset a common conviction prevailed that a united and powerful Germany could not be tolerated. French "security," they felt, would be endangered by such a development. Thus a new struggle over the Rhine frontier was threatening.

In the French mind, offensive and defensive motives were in this case
—as, perhaps, ever since then!—inextricably intertwined. But were
they not also similarly present in many ways in the German mind?
There was no lack here either of expansionist fantasies, though at first
they were confined to individual imaginations.

Thus did the German revolution of 1848, and especially the work
of the Paulskirche—the imperial constitution of 1849—contain certain
warlike possibilities, which through the succeeding century became
realities, and finally ended in the collapse of Germany. At that time
they remained mere possibilities, because the German revolution (with
the exception of the Danish war) spent itself internally; because internally it could still be held in check through the exercise of the resources of authoritarian power. But by this means were restrained not
only the war-breeding impulses toward unity and power, but also the
urge to freedom of the German people; the insistence upon becoming
a popular, national commonwealth. Once more an inter-relationship
altogether tragic—one whose significance seizes us especially today.

The fact must however be acknowledged that a large part of this fatal interaction lay in the existence of the Prussian military and authoritarian power. Only Prussia—as the party of the hereditary imperial
crown at Frankfurt perceived—was able and destined to fulfill the
hopes of the whole nation for unity and power; but at the cost of the
nation's hope for freedom, if Prussia remained what she was. She
was indeed a state with two souls; yet the Junker-militarist principle
inherited from Frederick William I and Frederick the Great was
stronger in her than the principle of the Prussian reform era, which had
pointed toward the commonwealth. If Prussia should remain what
she was, even within a Germany united under her leadership, then it
was to be feared that the Junker-militarist principle would permeate
the whole, in one way or another. Instead of Prussia merging into
Germany, Germany would merge with Prussia—if not formally, at
least in essence. This danger the sponsors of the hereditary imperial
crown at Frankfurt clearly recognized—as I had occasion to point out
more specifically forty years ago—and therefore they demanded that
Prussia sacrifice her political unity and allow herself to be divided into
provinces directly under the Empire. But this the strong and proud
spirit of the Prussians rejected categorically, and thus the partisans of
the hereditary imperial crown—as they cast their votes for Frederick
William IV—had to comfort themselves with the uncertain hope that

the force of events would some day take effect and integrate Prussia within Germany.

The force of events decided otherwise. The militaristic principle continued to dominate almost the whole of a century, until it over-reached itself in hybrid form; and Prussia was not dissolved from within, but destroyed from without. The tormenting problem today is this: will *Finis Borussiae* also mean *Finis Germaniae*? To desire once more to become a great power in the traditional sense, would be to begin all over again the tragedy of the century gone by. This time let us learn at last from history! In order to avoid new catastrophes —not only for Germany, but for Europe, yes, even for the whole world —new forms of international solidarity must be discovered. And they are in fact already being sought today, with the purpose of safeguard-ing the morally justified and eternally valid need of a nation for strength. Goethe's phrase (from which we quoted) has indeed ex-pressed this demand: to exist as a nation, fully respected by other nations, to whom a like respect is due. The contribution which Ger-mans themselves have to make to the accomplishment of this infinitely difficult task, is at the same time the permanent legacy of the revolution of 1848. The weaknesses resulting from time and destiny, from which this revolution suffered and through which it failed, we have brought honestly into the open. May we succeed, as men who have been tempered by misfortune, in reaching the goal of that pure and noble yearning: national unification within a democratic commonwealth.

XVII

Another Napoleonic Era

⇾⇾⇾⇾⇾⇾⇾⇾⇾⇾⇽⇽⇽⇽⇽⇽⇽⇽⇽⇽⇽

Saint-Simon on Horseback: The Economic and
Social Policy of Napoleon III
ALBERT GUÉRARD

The Russian Peasant and Serfdom
LAZAR VOLIN

Bismarck and the War of 1870
ERICH EYCK

⇾⇾⇾⇾⇾⇾⇾⇾⇾⇾⇽⇽⇽⇽⇽⇽⇽⇽⇽⇽⇽

Saint-Simon on Horseback

The Economic and Social Policy of Napoleon III

ALBERT GUÉRARD

Published in 1943

In the months that followed the February Revolution, the social and economic radicalism of Parisian workers aroused widespread fears among both the peasantry and the middle class, and these fears were intensified by the uprising of some of the Parisian workers in June 1848. The reflections of these fears were, of course, numerous, the most glaring of them being the election, in December, of Prince Louis Napoleon Bonaparte as President of the Second French Republic. Though viewed by many of his supporters as a strong man who would serve as a bulwark against Parisian radicalism, Louis Napoleon was far from conservative in his own social and economic outlook. Years before he was elected to office he had made this clear in a number of pamphlets and tracts; and he continued to make it clear in his years as President Bonaparte (1848-1852) and as Emperor Napoleon III (1852-1870). Insisting constantly that he was the protector of the interests of all Frenchmen, he sought the favor not only of the peasants and the middle class but of the very working-class elements who had inspired the alarm that helped to make possible both his coming to power and his stay in power. In the present selection the venerable Albert Guérard, now retired from Stanford University and author of many volumes on the history of French civilization and culture, presents Napoleon as an economic and social reformer who struggled to improve the lot of the poorer elements in French society. Taken from Guérard's unconventional biography of Napoleon III (1943), this chapter is basic to his stimulating, if not altogether convincing, attempt to rehabilitate "Saint-Simon on Horseback."

The economic and social policies of Napoleon III are no less perplexing than his management of foreign affairs. Here again we find inner conflicts concealed for many years under the veil of apparent success; the reconstruction of the great cities, the display of material progress and almost insolent wealth at the Exposition of 1867 were more than a match for the impressive Congress of Paris in 1856, or for the triumphal return from the Italian campaign. Here again we believe that, deeper than all contradictions, there ran a steady purpose, which belonged to the Emperor alone. And in this case also, the guiding principle is "dark only with excess of light." Louis Napoleon expressed it early, repeatedly, and in plain, unmistakable terms. Dreamers and profiteers, doctrinaires of the Right and doctrinaires of the Left, stubbornly refused to listen; but, after nearly a hundred years, the gentle, persistent voice can still be heard.

Just as the keyword of the First Empire was Glory, that of the Second was Prosperity; for two generations, the "good times" under Napoleon III were remembered. But there are two preliminary problems that demand elucidation. The first is, was that prosperity genuine? The second, if we admit that it was real, to what extent was it due to the regime and to the ruler?

The stock expression comes to our mind again, "the gaudy Empire." It cannot be denied that there was in imperial Paris, particularly during the last few years, a glaring element of parvenu display. The heavy gold service that appeared on the Tuileries table was *ruolz*—not solid, but plated; Charles Garnier's Opera, the architectural masterpiece of the time, was dazzling with gilded bronze and marbles of many colors. It is a truism that we should not be duped by appearances; but we often forget that the caution should work both ways. The drab is not always the good; conspicuous waste may be a sign of genuine wealth; a garish taste is not incompatible with solidity. The barocco churches of Italy and Southern Germany are no less ostentatious than the most questionable buildings of the Second Empire; the Hall of Mirrors at Versailles is as resplendent as the Foyer of the Grand Opera; Bismarck did not lose his narrow vigor of mind and his iron

Reprinted by permission of the publishers from Albert Guérard, *Napoleon III*, Cambridge, Mass.: Harvard University Press, 1943. The footnotes which originally appeared with this chapter have been omitted.

will because he could dress up, magnificently and absurdly, as a white Cuirassier; and if a touch of meretriciousness were sufficient to damn a period, the reign of Queen Victoria would stand condemned with the gorgeous Albert Memorial.

There have been civilizations in which the fabulous luxury of a court stood out brutally against the distress of the masses. This was true of India, of Tsarist Russia, and, not so glaringly, of Mexico under Porfirio Díaz. Such was not the condition of France under the Second Empire. Not only the cosmopolitan adventurers at the Tuileries and in the Faubourg Saint Honoré, but the nobility old and new, Parisian and provincial society, the professions, the staid traditional bourgeoisie, the newer classes of industrialists and business promoters, all were caught in the same whirl. Even the masses had their popular theatres and their cafés. We are quite willing to denounce much of this luxury as vulgar; at any rate, it was very generally spread; and Puritans could accuse the regime of corrupting, but not of impoverishing, the whole nation.

But luxury was only one of the signs of a general activity. If the onyx stairway of La Païva's residence in the Champs-Elysées attained a *succès de scandale*, there was in the same years an enormous amount of slum clearance, and great parks were created for the poor. It is hardly fair to consider an international center of pleasure and display like the Paris Opera as the only valid symbol of the whole period. The Emperor ordered that the reconstruction of the Opera should be kept behind that of the General Hospital, or *Hôtel-Dieu*. In the same captious spirit, critics denounced the concessions at the Exposition of 1867, and overlooked the main exhibits, admirably organized by Le Play. And while Garnier's triumph of the lavish and

---

AUGUSTE COMTE: French social philosopher and founder of positivism (d. 1857). Seeking to reorganize human society, he formulated a religion of humanity designed for the positive, or scientific, era in history. A former secretary to Saint-Simon, he owed many of his ideas to his master. The last years of his life were lived under the Second Empire, and for a time he saw in Napoleon III the man to carry out his ideas.

BARON HAUSSMANN: French bureaucrat who was in large measure responsible for the planning of the public-works program under the Second Empire. The beautification of Paris, in particular, owed much to his efforts.

HECTARE: Roughly two and one-half acres.

ornate has been pastiched all over the world, Baltard's Central Market, *les Halles*, a model of economy and "functionalism," has likewise served as a universal pattern. Everywhere in Paris, in provincial France, in Algeria, the true monuments of the Second Empire are its public works.

There had been in French history moments of artificial stimulation which could give an impression of fevered prosperity: the time of the Mississippi Bubble, a hectic flare under Calonne on the eve of the Revolution, the phosphorescence of the Thermidorian reaction and the early Directoire. They did not go deep, and they did not last long. The Second Empire lasted for eighteen years. Karl Marx said in 1852: "To the four million official paupers, vagabonds and prostitutes that France numbers must be added five million souls that hover over the precipice of life. . . ." If there be any truth in this gloomy picture, it would be the best justification of the Second Empire, for certainly there was no misery on that scale in 1870. Business was grumbling as usual, and the opposition jeered at "the fantastic accounts of Haussmann." But the country was soon to give a striking proof of its substantial wealth. Sedan came, but in the economic field there was no Sedan. The invasion was destructive, as things went in those simpler days; Gambetta's heroic resistance was reckless of cost; the Commune and the repression of the Commune added to the crushing burden; Bismarck exacted five billion francs, assured that France would be bled white for a generation. Within two years, France had liberated herself. The Assembly solemnly praised Thiers for that achievement. Thiers did but organize the modes of payment; the riches which made that miraculous recovery possible had been accumulated under Napo-

---

PROUDHON: French radical reformer (d. 1865) and author of the famous statement that "property is theft." His reform program emphasized such objectives as free credit and equality of exchange without benefit of state intervention. He won some support for his program among the French representatives in the First International, and Marx viewed him, therefore, as a deadly enemy. He was, of course, in constant difficulties with the Napoleonic government.

SEDAN: Battle in the Franco-German War of 1870 and scene of the capitulation of Napoleon III. It brought about the fall of the Second Empire and the establishment of the Third Republic.

leon III; and for nearly a decade, France remained wealthier than her conqueror.

The Second Empire was not favored with miraculous luck. Immediately after the Coup d'Etat, there was a unanimous feeling of confidence and hope; yet the first few years were by no means easy. In addition to the Crimean war, there were disastrous floods, poor crops, a near famine, and an epidemic of cholera; in 1854 and 1855, for the first time in the century, more deaths were registered than births. To the end, the Empire had to contend with economic troubles not of its own making. There was a disease of the silkworms, and at that time France was producing a notable proportion of the silk needed by the weavers of Lyons. The vine, one of the great assets of the country, suffered from two blights—first the oidium, then the phylloxera. The American Civil War disturbed the cotton trade. Mexico engulfed men and goods without return. Yet there were no signs of impoverishment.

But these, although very real, were after all minor difficulties. We have no desire to ignore the dominant fact: the sudden expansion of industry was at that time transforming the face of the world. It happened under Napoleon III; it was not created by Napoleon III; his regime, at its proudest moment, was but a cork bobbing on an irresistible stream.

In this we firmly concur. If history be written on a scale vast enough—and it may be the only scientific manner of writing history—personalities and individual events disappear altogether. Napoleon I has long ceased to be a living influence; he survives only as the hero of a colorful legend. Our successors will be able to describe the evolution of our century without mentioning Lenin or Hitler. What matters is the trend, not the eddy.

But if we are writing on a human scale, in terms of the experience of living men—perhaps in the hope of helping living men in their present perplexities—then individuals and accidents acquire great significance. The "industrial revolution" began before James Watt, and its possibilities are not yet exhausted; within that vast cycle, the foresight, the determination, the blind obstinacy, the frivolous ignorance of actual leaders were of vital importance. We may call the period 1830-1930 the century of the railroads; Thiers, the embodiment of bourgeois common sense, sneered at the new invention; Lamartine had a prophetic vision of its possibilities; it was not a matter of indifference that before 1848 and after 1870 France was ruled by the congeners of Thiers. The stream itself does not care whether you are pulling with it or against it; to you, it means wasted efforts, frustration, defeat, or the full enjoyment of increasing powers. Ultimately, wars do not count; they are but the useless friction caused by resistance to "the wave of the future"; but, in our brief generation, how much blood, sweat, and tears would be spared if we were able to determine the path of the wave!

Now, it is our contention that Napoleon III had, as no French ruler before, that sense of the future; a sense which was not Utopian, not even prophetic, but practical; a sense which impelled him to steer, and not simply to resist or to drift. The transformation of Paris, his personal conception, may serve again as a symbol. In eighteen years, he achieved much more in this field than all the regimes since the downfall of the old monarchy. After 1870, the work was slowed down; by 1940, his original plan had not yet been fully carried out; and we are convinced that, if his spirit had continued to prevail, that plan would not have remained static, but would have been expanded to meet changing conditions. Yet, incomplete and faulty, it was so nobly conceived that, after half a century, it was still adequate. The administrators of Paris today would be well inspired to say, not "Back to Napoleon III!" but "Forward with Napoleon III!" In the same manner, we feel that his whole social plan, like his scheme for the reconstruction of Europe, could still be our starting point. There are manifestoes issued at present, with a bold and confident ring, which to the student of European history evoke the far-off, half-forgotten and derided spirit of 1848; and of that spirit Napoleon III was the servant. To test our own aspirations, it may not be amiss to measure his achievement and probe the causes of his failure.

II

The essential point about Napoleon III is that he was a Socialist. This ought to be a truism: he said so himself; friends and enemies concurred. The English editor of his pamphlet on *The Extinction of Pauperism* remarks: "It will be apparent that this project is only a modification of Socialism or of Communism (we are hardly clear which is which), and as such repugnant to all sound principles of political economy and the dictates of common sense." According to Karl Marx, Guizot, the profound philosopher of history, "characterized the Second of December as the complete and final triumph of Socialism." The reader will remember the dictum ascribed to Napoleon III: "The Empress is a Legitimist; Morny is an Orleanist; my cousin Napoleon is a Republican; *I am a Socialist*; there is but one Bonapartist among us, Persigny, and he is crazy." Discount the definite, epigrammatic form; the substantial truth of the story has never been challenged.

The problem is to agree upon what is meant by Socialism. Was it not Sir William Harcourt, last of the old Whigs, who asserted, "We are all Socialists now"? The socialism of Napoleon III is not hard to define. It was not Utopian, and it was not doctrinaire (or if you prefer, it was not *scientific*). Doctrinaire and Utopian, by the way, are strangely akin. Both imply a radical change in human conditions, due to the discovery of a new principle; the Utopian imagines, the doctrinaire prophesies; each in his fashion is revealing eternal verities. Socialism with him was more than a sentiment, for sentiment revels in its own beauty, or at best gluts itself on charity. It was a *tendency,* that is to say, an incentive to action, and a guide.

There are two kinds of government, the negative and the positive. The first is a police for the protection of vested interests, the second an agent for collective progress. Both the conservatives and the laissez-faire liberals take the negative attitude. The only difference is this: for the conservatives, or pessimists, repression is an essential function; the police performs a sacred duty; according to Joseph de Maistre, society reposes ultimately upon the executioner. For the liberals, or optimists, the police is but a temporary evil. Napoleon III was committed to the positive side, the government as an agent of collective progress. In his mind, the first concern of the State was "to improve the moral and material condition of the most numerous and poorest class."

The second step is even more definite, but much harder to appraise. The good of the community demands confidence, security, *order*. Ay, there's the rub: to many, who deem themselves good citizens, the word *order* has a sinister ring. It evokes at once the shadow of traditional Bonapartism: the rule of a Super-Policeman, with his staff of generals, bishops, and prefects, mounting guard round the money bags. But does the defense of order inevitably mean the protection of privilege? And is stability synonymous with stagnation? The despised Metternich system posed as the champion of order; it was aptly summed up in the phrase "Quiet is the burgher's first duty." This implies a moral and physical passivity, alien to the progressive and somewhat venturesome temper of the Second Empire. What Napoleon III would have said—and did say in almost every one of his addresses —was "The immediate duty of the State is to curb violence." Every government, autocratic or liberal, must be a government, or abdicate; and the function of a government is first of all to enforce the law, that is to say, to put down lawlessness.

The debate between "legitimate resistance to oppression" and "respect for the law" is a very tangled one, and we have no absolute criterion to offer. Every one of us, looking over the record of history, favors in some instances the rebels, in other cases the constituted authorities. There are "great and glorious revolutions" which challenged an "order" identified with injustice. The cost is heavy, but it is injustice that must bear the blame. "The most dangerous enemy of his country," said Louis Napoleon himself, "is the man who makes a revolution necessary." But the purpose of a revolution is not to abolish the concept of law; it is to create, or to restore, a more natural order, a more legitimate law. In the contest between revolt and the forces of an organized government, we cannot assume that insurgency is inevitably the nobler cause; there is no such thing as the divine right of the barricades. If Cavaignac, who was a staunch Republican, shot down the working men of Paris in June 1848, it was not because they were democrats but because they were violently challenging democratic law. In this case, and in the case of the Commune in 1871, there had been criminal clumsiness on the part of the government before the outbreak, and there was criminal ferocity in the repression. Still, although our feelings are divided, we are compelled to recognize that the law had to prevail. The Bolsheviks came into power because the Kerensky government, committed to a suicidal war policy and undermined by White disloyalty, was unable to maintain order. The first step of the Soviets after their hard-won victory was not to proclaim the glorious anarchy of the Golden Age, but to create a discipline compared with which the sternest measures of Napoleon III were idyllic.

We have discussed this point before, and we shall have to dwell upon it again, for it is the very center of his enigmatic career. We are not attempting to disprove the existence of Napoleon III the Policeman; what we are seeking to establish is that Napoleon III the

Policeman was not in contradiction with Napoleon III the Socialist. Socialism is first of all an orderly society, and the first step toward Socialism is the restoration of order. We remember that in London, at the time of the great Chartist demonstration, he offered himself as a special constable, although his sympathies were most probably on the Chartist side. We must add that we are attempting to interpret the sovereign himself, not every one of the five, seven, or eight million voters who chose and endorsed him in 1848, 1851, 1852, and 1870. Among them, it is manifest that many thought of material order more exclusively than he did. There was throughout rural France, after June 1848, a tidal wave of anger against *les partageux*, the "share-the-wealth" people. In the campaign literature that prepared the Coup d'État, a pamphlet, "The Red Specter," has remained a byword; and in 1870, the solid peasant masses swamped the vote of the cities and supported the Empire because they were afraid of revolution and civil war. No doubt Napoleon III had the backing of reactionary elements. But we contend that this fails to tell the more important part of the story. We must repeat that if France had voted in an agony of resentment and fear, it is Cavaignac, the Butcher of June, the ruthless Savior of Society, who should have been elected in December 1848. In the complex triumph of Louis Napoleon, it is hard to analyze the share of the imperial heir, the policeman, the promoter of prosperity, the social reformer.

At any rate, it was upon the constructive aspect of his program that Louis Napoleon constantly insisted, not upon the restrictive. We have seen that for a whole year before the Coup d'État, he engaged in an open duel with the Legislative Assembly and carried the debate before the people. He thus separated himself from "the Party of Order" in the narrower sense. He complained that, supported by the deputies whenever he had to take repressive action, he was thwarted every time he attempted to do anything for the welfare of the masses. The line was clearly drawn. We believe that his paper *Le Dix Décembre* (June 5, 1849) gave a true interpretation of his election when it declared: "In raising him to the highest position, France said: 'I want order . . . but I want that all those who suffer may have reason to hope.' "

We have been attempting to show that a leader could be at the same time a champion of order and a socialist. We are now venturing a bolder paradox: namely, that a true socialist may also seek to foster prosperity. Any regime that deliberately attempts to increase wealth is open to the charge of materialism, and is apt to be called, as the Second Empire was, a Paradise for Profiteers. A monastic, Spartan, Rousseauistic, or Tolstoyan ideal of simplicity is undoubtedly attractive, especially to those who admire it from afar; still, we wonder whether any modern government has avowed virtuous impoverishment as its goal. If "Share the wealth" be the essence of socialism, surely *creating* wealth is at least as important as dividing it.

The Second Empire took pride in the expansion of riches. Its reports on national progress had almost the same lyric note as the great ode by Alfred, Lord Tennyson: "Fifty years of ever-expanding commerce!" With this tone we are familiar enough: it is that of our Chambers of Commerce. But the optimism of our Boosters' Clubs sounds dull and lifeless compared with the lyric clangor of Soviet statistics. The USSR glories in the fact that it is creating wealth at an unprecedented rate; but for the war, the gigantic increase in production facilities would have been turned into consumers' goods, that is to say into comfort and even luxury. Prosperity is not invariably the enemy of the people.

There is a difference. The Soviets, assuming control of an utterly ruined community, had to start from the bottom and attend to the most elementary, the most pressing needs of the masses; as in a besieged city, conspicuous waste became a crime. Napoleon III, taking hold of a country which was bewildered, dispirited, sluggish, but unravaged, healthy, and at peace, did not have to use such drastic methods. His socialism could be progressive, not apocalyptic. But it was genuine socialism, that is to say, genuine concern with the welfare of the most numerous and poorest class; and his policy, social in its intent, was also social in its methods.

For although he was ready to leave the freest field to individual initiative, he was resolutely opposed to *laissez faire*. Government, according to him, was not an "ulcer," but an instrument for the common good. He believed in organization and planning. This conviction he had expressed in his pamphlet, *On the Extinction of Pauperism* (1844). This little work, much briefer than its political counterpart, *On Napoleonic Ideas*, is also, in our opinion, far less able. Still, it presents, sketchily yet definitely enough, two pregnant ideas, land utilization and the organization of labor.

Briefly, his plan was to take over six out of the nine million hectares of uncultivated land, and settle on them colonies of the unemployed, financed by a loan of three hundred million francs from the State. The colonists would be supervised by foremen or *prud'-hommes* elected by themselves, one for every ten; these would be the non-commissioned officers of the labor army. For an army it would be, living on the rough, cheap, and healthy level of army life. Above the *prud'hommes,* there would be technical directors and a governor. Every year, the governors would meet in Paris, to prepare their plans with the Minister of the Interior.

These settlements would not be purely agricultural. They would produce manufactured goods for their own consumption. It was not expected that the colonists would remain permanently in the "collectives." Normally, they would be reabsorbed by free industry. They would form a reserve army of labor, living under decent conditions, doing fairly useful and therefore self-respecting work, establishing a minimum standard below which private enterprise could not fall. This crude scheme of a hundred years ago reminds us of many contemporary proposals and organizations, the CCC, the PWA, and most of all perhaps Upton Sinclair's EPIC plan.

In spite of elaborate and impressive figures, it is difficult to believe that in an old country like France the State could take the worst land, turn it over to the worst workmen (at best not trained agriculturists), and expect to make the scheme self-supporting and even profitable. Louis Napoleon relied on the economy of semi-military life, and the greater efficiency of large-scale production. In this his colonies resembled the Sovkhozes and Kolkhozes of present-day Russia.

Had Louis Napoleon been a mere publicist, this slim pamphlet would have attracted scant notice; in the same line of thought, Louis Blanc, for one, had done far more serious work. But the author happened to be a Pretender; the little book stamped him as a socialist. As soon as he had a free rein, in 1852, he started a program of activities quite in the spirit of his proposals of eight years before. Like Mussolini, he drained marshes, in Sologne for instance; in the Landes, the eighteenth-century plans of Chambrelent and Brémontier, long neglected, were carried out with energy, and the shifting sand dunes were planted with pines. The work was seldom spectacular; but in every rural district some progress was accomplished. Between the Second Empire and the July Monarchy or the Third Republic there was a decided difference in tension; from the "dreamer" at the Tuileries there seemed to radiate a constant flow of energy.

III

Napoleon III was the elect of the small farmers, and he did his best for them. England, through Free Trade, deliberately sacrificed agriculture to manufacturing and commerce; the Emperor of the French did nothing so radical. He was attempting to keep a balance between the different elements of national prosperity; he refused to commit himself to a purely agrarian policy. He understood that the modern world was to be essentially industrial. In the course of many centuries, the best land had been tilled by the hard-working peasants of France; in that domain, there was no room for sudden expansion. The methods of cultivation could certainly be improved, but in many cases, technical progress would reduce the need for human labor. Already, under the Empire, in many country districts the population was decreasing, and the eternal cry of the conservatives "Back to the land!" was futile. Not for three or four decades would the urban population actually overtake the rural; but the trend was manifest, and the thought of Napoleon III dwelt in the twentieth century. In 1852, he read the future of France more clearly than Premier Méline in 1896, or Marshal Pétain in 1940: if France remained attached to an economy of peasant proprietors, her destiny would be irremediable decadence. His chief interest was industry.

That interest was not purely intellectual, it was intimate. Napoleon III felt that, as a Bonaparte, he ought to be a soldier; but he never was fully convincing as a military man. His patronage of the arts was perfunctory, and less disastrous because of that very indifference than the aggressive Philistinism of Louis Philippe. In modern England, even radical leaders fancy themselves as country squires, and Mr. Lloyd George, like a character in P. G. Wodehouse, is proud of his prize-winning pigs. Napoleon III never played that bucolic role. His heart was not in any of these; it was in industry. His very hobbies were mechanical. F. A. Simpson, a sincere admirer, but a don of the old school, makes gentle fun of him as the White Knight of Lewis Carroll, surrounded with gadgets, all of his own invention. When he died, he was working on an economical stove for the poor. Jules Verne, who anticipated so much of our modern world, found his path and wrote his best books under the Second Empire; there was a

Jules Verne, or, if you prefer, an H. G. Wells in Napoleon III—a romanticist whose dreams were of the future, not of the past, and translated themselves into terms of engineering.

France had long achieved fame in the arts and crafts; at no time more brilliantly than in the exquisite eighteenth century. Industry, on the contrary, was comparatively new; and although not alien, it seemed uncongenial. The days of the good artisan, who loved his trade and his tools, who created an individual piece of work for an individual and appreciative purchaser, have not vanished altogether. But the bulk of our goods will have to be machine-made, and the machine demands different methods and a different ideology. This is not yet fully realized even by responsible leaders. The cultural lag is a universal phenomenon: in England, business men are proud to assume feudal titles, and industrialists pose as gentlemen farmers; in America, great engineers cling to the economy of *The Village Blacksmith*; they belong to the eighteenth century, and in some cases to the fifteenth. Napoleon III realized quite simply that, by its very nature, modern industry is *collectivistic*. It implies the necessary coöperation of the many to serve the needs of the many. It is perfectly possible to conceive of socialism, and especially of communism, without machine production: primitive tribes, and the Christians of the apostolic age, are examples in point. But it is impossible to conceive of an industrial age founded on sheer individualism.

In the early nineteenth century, Parisians had water brought up to their lodgings at a few cents a pail by independent carriers, usually robust Auvergnats; in the latter half of the same age, water was piped to each apartment, and the rugged individualist who trudged up four flights of stairs with his few gallons was doomed to disappear. This revolution in technique was collectivistic. It mattered comparatively little whether the management of the waterworks was entrusted to a purely "capitalistic" company, to a company closely associated with the city, or directly to the city itself. Only doctrinaires will maintain that a single abstract principle must prevail, either rigid coördination, which is totalitarianism, or absolutely free competition, which is anarchy. But, in the necessary adjustment between the two, the machine caused a definite shift; in the economic field, collectivism became the norm.

Napoleon III, who had a steady purpose but no hard and fast doctrine, did not much care which form this indispensable collectivism would assume. He encouraged and subsidized the coöperative system; but he knew that it could not be imposed upon consumers or producers, and the French, on the whole, failed to respond. He was not afraid of State Capitalism, or direct operation by the government: if officials could conduct such vital and intricate "big businesses" as the army, the navy, education, the postal service or public works, was it absurd that they should be able to run a mine or a railroad? But he accepted also as a genuine form of collectivism the corporation, created under the State, supervised by the State in the interest of the community. It represented a definite step away from strictly private property, *jus utendi et abutendi*, "I can do what I please with my own."

Of this pragmatic attitude, his railroad policy was a clear example. It was nonsense to consider railroads as purely personal concerns; individuals could not build them and operate them with the same sturdy independence as Auvergnats carried their water buckets. The fiction that railroads should be left entirely to private initiative and unlimited competition simply led to an orgy of speculation, for any one could start a railroad—on paper. Napoleon III consolidated the innumerable lines into six regional systems, with a ninety-nine-year franchise, a minimum dividend guaranteed by the State, and definite responsibilities to the State. It was easy to pass from these six semi-public corporations to a single "National Company," still capitalistic in form; and from that to direct operation by government officials. The collectivistic revolution came with the railroads themselves, not with the change in their administrative set-up.

P. J. Proudhon called this policy "a new feudalism"; he was not wrong. But we must consider that feudalism *in theory* was superior to the eighteenth-century notion of absolute individual ownership. In good feudal doctrine, no one possessed anything outright: authority, which was not clearly distinguished from property, was simply delegated; it conferred privileges, but it entailed obligations. The system—if it ever was a system at all—had become fossilized long before the end of the ancient regime, and deserved to be swept away; but its long-forgotten principle, encrusted with absurdities and abuses, could be revived and prove fruitful under modern circumstances. In that sense, every *concessionnaire* is indeed a vassal, and he may have vassals in his turn, sub-concessionnaires and contractors. The *kolkhoz* [collective farm] also is akin to a fief. The profit motive is not denied, but it is held in definite subordination to the common good. Of this general interest, the sovereign, whatever his title may be, remains the supreme guardian.

In such a spirit, and with such a method, industrial enterprise proceeded with an enthusiasm which was clearly lacking under Louis Philippe, and which waned under the Third Republic. The loss of momentum after Sedan is undeniable. Just as, in many parts of France, we come across churches which were left uncompleted because the medieval dream had faded, so we find many great projects which remained mere indications because the Empire fell. The engineer who created the modern sewers and water supply of the capital, Belgrand, had a very practical plan for making Paris a seaport. In 1940, after seventy years of *petit bourgeois* rule, the scheme was still held in check by a coalition of private interests. In a boundless and untamed land such as America was in the nineteenth century, individualism could mean pioneering and be a creative force; in an old and small country like France, individualism shrank to anxious self-protection— "Let every one stay at home and mind his own business"—a perfect recipe for stagnation. The collective sense, the *social* sense, required an organ. The imperial power was not the ideal solution; but it was a workable solution, and the need was undeniable.

Planning on a large scale and at long range required a revolution in finance, nothing less than the substitution of *credit* for *thrift* as the most efficient method of meeting the cost of a new enterprise. This is so familiar to us now that we hardly realize what a radical change it involved in the thought and habits of the French people. The peasant and petit bourgeois ideal had been: spend a little less than you earn; with the hoarded pennies, buy another field, another house, another government bond; the key to wealth is abstemiousness. As a result, investors were struck with congenital and hardened timidity. The constant trickle of small savings was absorbed by small enterprises; and these had to be safe beyond the least doubt, for it would be criminal to endanger the fruit of so much toil and such long privations. John Law, early in the eighteenth century, had revealed the magic of credit; but he was only a 'prentice wizard, soon drowned by the flood of paper riches he had evoked and could not control. A hundred and fifty years afterwards the safe and sane were still shaking their heads in reproof. For bourgeois and peasant alike, credit meant gambling, and gambling was mortal sin.

Now Napoleon III was not, in this respect, the average French citizen. He was something of a gambler, for the highest stakes; he had ventured and lost three fortunes on his road to power. But he was not a mere gambler, and his reign was not a fabulous Monte Carlo. He was at heart an industrialist, not a financier. He knew that wealth can be created only by intelligent labor; but he knew also that, in an expanding world, it is not absurd to capitalize on intelligence, and to expect from the harvest more than you have actually sown. The origin of wealth is creation rather than abstention. His economy was dynamic.

The term implies danger as well as progress; of the many gambles in which the Second Empire indulged, a few ended in bankruptcy. But these were minor engagements in a great campaign which, on the whole, was a triumph, and seems to us, many decades later, not to have been unduly bold. In the diplomatic, the military, the political field, the Empire closed in a catastrophe—perhaps not wholly deserved. In the economic, it was justified of its works: the State itself, the great cities, the banks, the chief individual enterprises, were in a healthy condition.

Credit means speculation, which is linked in our minds with the enrichment of the parasites; and by the side of Napoleon III we descry, almost a double, the figure of de Morny, his half-brother, and the most urbane of profiteers. We do not deny de Morny; we deny that the Empire was created for him and for his kind. Once more, by whatever name you call a regime, the fact remains that all planning means risking immediate resources for the prospect of future gain. To build a railroad or a canal may be a reasonably safe bet, but it is a bet; for the French, Suez was a profitable venture, Panama a disaster. In constructing their new world, the Soviets are gambling constantly and heavily. Under Socialism, the whole people is staking its labor for the sake of a richer tomorrow—a common investment for common profit. In *pure* Capitalism—if such could be conceived—only a very few would dare, and fewer still would reap, although the losses would be shared by all. The world of Napoleon III was transitional. He tried to escape from the domination of the half-dozen great bankers, particularly the Rothschilds, who held the whole market in fee. He sought to make credit not oligarchic, but bourgeois and ultimately democratic; in this, he was heading in the direction pointed out by P. J. Proudhon with his "universal and free credit."

One of the methods of this financial democratization was to offer State and municipal loans directly to the masses, and not exclusively through the banks; in this way, there could be a State capitalism on the grandest scale, without a special class of capitalists. Another was the development or creation of credit institutions of a semi-public nature, part of that "economic feudalism" that Proudhon had criticized. Among these were the Bank of France, with renewed privilege, closer coöperation with the State, and branches in every department; the *Crédit Foncier* (1852), a national building loan association, lending on mortgages to departments, cities, and private owners; the *Crédit Mobilier* (1852), which with the Pereire Brothers played an immense part in the economic development of the time, financing railroads, ports, public utilities, navigation companies; the *Crédit Industriel* (1859); the *Crédit Lyonnais* (1863); the *Société Générale pour Favoriser le Développement du Commerce et de l'Industrie en France* (1864): a name which sums up the program of the Empire itself. The *Crédit Mobilier* paid the price of excessive daring. The other financiers, jealous of the Pereires, forced them out, and the institution had to be reorganized in 1867, with heavy losses to the general public. It was a defeat for the spirit of the Second Empire, comparable to the humiliations of Sadowa and Querétaro. But the others remained.

They remained, and formed the financial armature of the Third Republic. But after 1870 they were no longer subordinated to a general purpose. Instead of a government using the capitalists, on the whole for social ends, there was a government which distrusted the capitalists, yet did not dare to challenge them. In feudalism, as soon as the suzerain falters, the vassals pursue selfish ends, and the result is anarchy. So it was with the financial feudalism encouraged by the Empire; when the central authority weakened, finance strove to influence the state. Thus it was that the Republic, far worse than the Empire, was the era of politico-financial scandals.

In his campaign for mass prosperity, Napoleon III used every available means and every available man. De Morny was his right hand in the Coup d'État, and Achille Fould had backed him heavily; both of them were first of all financiers, and they were given high positions. Rothschild was not disturbed; he remained a byword for fabulous wealth. On the other hand, the Emperor borrowed ideas from Louis Blanc, and even from Proudhon, who, for many, was

Terror incarnate. And he also welcomed fellow travelers from the right. Auguste Comte, the Positivist Pope, who had become an extreme conservative, endorsed the Empire. Frédéric Le Play was one of the Emperor's most trusted advisers. Now Le Play's attitude was frankly anti-democratic and anti-Caesarian. He distrusted equally the State and the masses. For him the only possible instrument of social progress was *patronage*, by which he meant the enlightened leadership of the upper classes. He recognized that these classes had become intellectually sluggish and morally corrupt; but, purified through religion, they should again assume command, assuring order, prosperity, and social peace. Napoleon III used to the full the good will, the vast knowledge, and the organizing capacity of Le Play, and rewarded him generously; but he did not commit himself to his ideology.

Quite obviously, Napoleon III was not a Marxian, nor a Fourierist, nor an Owenite; and in spite of his indebtedness to Louis Blanc and P. J. Proudhon, he cannot be called their disciple. His relation with Saint-Simonism offers a more difficult problem. He never was, in any definite sense of the term, a member of the sect. His only direct contact with it would have been through Vieillard, his brother's tutor, for whom he retained affectionate respect and whom he made a Senator. Vieillard was once interested in Saint-Simonism, but the subject does not figure in their correspondence. The Saint-Simonian spirit was something much wider than the Saint-Simonian group.

Napoleon III was called "Saint-Simon on horseback." No picturesque epigram has the value of a scientific formula; but the description is strikingly accurate. In order to realize all its implications, we shall have to turn back a full quarter of a century, to the strange career of Henri, Count de Saint-Simon (1760-1825).

This distant cousin of the great Memorialist and very remote descendant of Charlemagne might be considered as the type of the crackbrained Utopians who flourish in an age of revolution and romanticism; and his school, which turned into a religious sect, amused and scandalized Paris in the early years of the July Monarchy. But Saint-Simon, undisciplined though he was, teemed with ideas which proved more vital than those of the scoffers.

His fundamental principle was the necessity of an organic relation between the various aspects of a culture—religion, science, art, government, economics. But he did not assert, as some Marxians were to do, that the spiritual elements should be subordinated to the material; he claimed they must be harmonized. A world which professes brother-hood on Sunday and ruthless competition on Monday is an absurdity: the principle of brotherhood should pervade the whole social order. This was the essence of his "New Christianity," which might be called Christianity restated and applied. As a corollary, the first duty of the (Neo-Christian) State is to promote the spiritual and material welfare of the most numerous and poorest class; for brothers cannot remain indifferent to the distress of their brothers. So far, this is nothing but the humanitarian democratic feeling of Lamennais, which inspired the whole romantic generation.

But Saint-Simon contributed a very definite element: he was conscious of the industrial revolution fifty years at least before Arnold Toynbee gave it a name. Many socialists had been thinking in terms of more equitable distribution; he believed that industry, with its capacity for producing riches, could be made the best servant of the people as a whole. Industry thus assumed in his eyes a quasi-religious character.

Industrial production on a vast scale demands organization; only an economy of individual craftsmen can be satisfied with *laissez faire*. Organization implies hierarchy. Saint-Simon restored the "orders" of the ancient regime, a *clergy* of artists, scientists, inventors, a *nobility* of engineers, managers, bankers, with a sense of *noblesse oblige*. This nobility is a directing, not a fighting, caste; instead of the knight in armor, we need the captain of industry. To keep pace with the expanding power of production, the industrial society requires the pooling of resources, bold investments as a part of general planning, in other terms a vast expansion of credit.

Neglecting innumerable side issues, this close association between the humanitarian ideal on the one hand, the industrial and financial method on the other, is the key to the thought of Saint-Simon as well as to that of Napoleon III. The Saint-Simonians were slow in recogniz-ing him as one of themselves. Their daily, *Le Crédit* (November 1848-August 1850), opposed him. Gradually, the kinship between the two ideals became apparent. The patriarch of the sect, Father Prosper Enfantin, rallied to the new regime. Guéroult, Lambert, Duveyrier, were in accord with the socialist-industrial sovereign. Michel Chevalier, responsible for the commercial treaty with England in 1860, had been a Saint-Simonian. The Suez Canal, so typical of the Empire in its daring and practicality, had been promoted by Enfantin and his group.

Paulin, Talabot, Enfantin, were among the prominent railroad administrators of the time. Emile and Isaac Pereire had a share in all the great enterprises of the reign. This industrial and financial activity does not mean that the Saint-Simonians had recanted and lost their mystic fervor. To the end, these bankers and great executives published books of truly religious inspiration. Once at the Emperor's table, as one of the guests was deriding the theories of the Saint-Simonians about women, another stood up and said: "I am the son of Lambert, the son of Enfantin, the son of Olinde Rodrigues, the son of Saint-Simon." Among those present, one senator and three cabinet ministers could have made the same claim.

This does not mean that Napoleon III was obediently following the blueprints left by Saint-Simon; it means that Saint-Simon and Napoleon III, independently, came to the same interpretation of the industrial era. And it seems to us that this interpretation, in its broad lines, is more valid today than all the conventional sects, parties, and doctrines. We need a thorough reclassification of ideologies. The Second Empire was certainly more akin to the world of Saint-Simon than to the world of Napoleon I. Twentieth-century America, even before the New Deal, looked as though it had been drafted by Saint-Simon rather than by Adam Smith. Soviet Russia is far closer in spirit to Saint-Simon than to Karl Marx. The Saint-Simonians who were religious enthusiasts in 1830 worked happily in the imperial France of 1860; they would have found themselves even more at home in the United States or the USSR of 1942: the three regimes, so glaringly different on the surface, have deep elements in common. But the Saint-Simonian, or the American captain of industry, or the Russian reveling in five-year plans, would have felt himself cramped and chilled in the *petit bourgeois* republic of Grévy or Poincaré.

NOTE

THE ATTITUDE OF THE WORKING CLASS TOWARD THE EMPIRE

The social legislation of the Second Empire, in the narrower sense of the term, was not negligible. During the first decade, the government relied chiefly on charitable institutions and encouragements to the coöperative movement. A definite social policy began in the early sixties. It was best expressed in the Palais Royal pamphlets, published under the patronage of Prince Napoleon. Significant events in its development include the following:

1862: Working-men delegates were sent by the State to the London Exposition; they were impressed by the working conditions, standard of living, and power of the Unions in England.

1863: *Crédit au Travail*, to finance coöperatives.

1864, May 25: Law on "Coalitions," prepared by Émile Ollivier, removing legal ban on strikes.

1866: The Emperor subscribed 500,000 francs to *Caisse des Associations Coopératives*.

1867: Working-men delegates were sent to the Paris Exposition. The Emperor won a prize for plans of workingmen's houses.

1868, March 31: Trade Unions tolerated.

1868, August 2: Abrogation of Article 1781, according to which the word of an employer was to be accepted by a court against that of an employee—last trace of *legal* class distinction.

But the social policy of Napoleon III was much wider than this legislation would indicate. Yet the working class (industrial) was never won over; for twenty years, France offered the paradox of a leader endorsed by those who understood him least and rejected by those whom he was most anxious to benefit. The cause of this absurdity is that the working population of the great cities thought in political, not in economic, terms. They were democrats rather than socialists, and republicans rather than democrats, for, as we must constantly repeat, they never acknowledged the peasants as their equals. All they chose to remember was that Napoleon had destroyed a parliamentary republic. So, in 1863, Paris gave 400 votes to Labor candidates and 153,000 to the bourgeois opposition, including the Royalist Thiers, hater of "the vile multitude." Paris could neither be bribed nor coerced. This stubborn resistance for the sake of an ideal may not have been wise; at any rate, it cannot be called ignoble.

The Russian Peasant and Serfdom

LAZAR VOLIN

⇒⇒⇒⇒⇒⇒⇒⇒⇒ *Published in 1943* ⇐⇐⇐⇐⇐⇐⇐⇐⇐⇐

The comment is sometimes made that Napoleon III liberated the Russian serfs. For it was the defeat of Russia by France and England in the Crimean War that compelled Alexander II, the new tsar who succeeded to the throne in the midst of the war, to abandon the "Frozen Russia" approach of his predecessor and to turn reformer. Thus the series of military and naval disasters that made up the Crimean War became linked with the event that outstripped in importance all other developments in the history of nineteenth-century Russia: the emancipation of the serfs. It is not enough, however, to emphasize emancipation as such; it is also necessary to understand the conditions from which the serfs were liberated. What, in other words, did serfdom mean to the millions of people—peasants as well as aristocrats—whose lives it shaped during the centuries when it existed and whose outlook it continued to shape after it had been formally abolished? It is this basic question that Lazar Volin, of the United States Department of Agriculture and an expert in the field of Russian agricultural history, seeks to answer in the essay that follows.

Serfdom was formally abolished in Russia on February 19 (March 3), 1861. Until the Revolution of 1917, this memorable episode was regarded, especially by the Russian intelligentsia, as an outstanding landmark in the evolution of modern Russia, and worthy of annual commemoration. Such grandiose events as the Revolution of 1917 and its antithesis, the collectivization of the 1930s, overshadow but still cannot completely eclipse the significance of the peasant emancipation, particularly to the historical-minded student of Russian agricultural problems.

Reprinted by special permission from *Agricultural History*, XVII (1943), 41-61. The footnotes which originally appeared with this essay have been omitted.

The Russian emancipation reform of the 1860s did not succeed in solving the peasant question in the sense in which, for instance, the agrarian reforms ushered in by the French Revolution did in the West. Economic and social vestiges of the Russian servile system lingered on. The peasant problem, therefore, continued to be in Russia what it was in the West between 1500 and 1850—"the great social question of the day." Yet there can be little doubt that an important step forward was taken when Alexander II issued the emancipation proclamation, though its full import can hardly be appreciated without a mental picture of the Russian servile system in operation.

While slavery had existed in Russia since time immemorial, the institution of serfdom appeared relatively late. Its development paralleled an agrarian revolution carried out by the Moscow czars in the fifteenth and sixteenth centuries, whereby both the old feudal aristocracy and the free-peasant smallholders were sacrificed in favor of a new landholding class of Czar's servants, both military and civil, which may be referred to as the gentry. It must be spoken of as the landholding rather than landowning class, for the landlords were not full hereditary owners (in fee simple) of the land but held it on condition that they serve the State. Thus land, which was the only form of wealth that the Muscovite State could dispose of freely, was the remuneration for such services. If the latter were not forthcoming, the holding was to be seized and transferred to a more worthy servant.

Because of its abundance, land in old Russia was worth little without a definite supply of labor to till it, especially since the landlords were busy fighting or otherwise serving the Czar. Consequently the landed gentry tried ceaselessly to solve this problem by binding the peasant tenants to the soil, while, at the same time, becoming absolute owners of their estates. The gentry, which was after all the governing class, succeeded in its objectives in spite of the resistance of peasants, which flared occasionally in violent rebellion. But it was a gradual process that

CHERNYSHEVSKY: Nineteenth-century Russian writer and humanitarian reformer. A leader of the radical intelligentsia, he spent much of his mature life in prison or in exile. His novel *What Is to Be Done?* served as a bible for Russian reformers.

KLIUCHEVSKY: Tsarist historian (d. 1911) whose multi-volume *Course of Russian History* remains the outstanding product of Russian historical writing. Inspired by the emancipation of the serfs, he turned to the study

required several centuries. The tightening noose of indebtedness, custom, and legislation all conspired to transform the mass of the peasantry from freely contracting tenants into serfs by the end of the seventeenth century. The gentry became as absolute in the mastery of its peasants as of its acres. Peter the Great merely gave legal recognition to the existing state of affairs when he abolished conditional land tenure and established full private property of the gentry in their estates and merged slaves with other tillers of this land in one all-embracing type of bondage at the beginning of the eighteenth century.

Thus, all estate tenure as well as possession of peasants became hereditary, but compulsory service to the State on the part of the land-owners was exacted even more strictly by Peter. This, however, became much less true under his weak successors, who usually owed the throne to palace revolutions staged by the guard regiments, composed of the landed gentry. Finally, in 1762, the compulsory service of nobles to the State was entirely abolished, and the old justification of national interest for their ownership of serfs completely disappeared, while the position of the latter deteriorated.

> For until the landlord was considered only a temporary holder of public land, the peasants too were considered akin to government workers who temporarily were obliged to maintain by their labor these servants and defenders of the State. Their work for the landlord was something like a state duty imposed upon them in the interest of defending the State from the enemies. The peasants had to feed the landlord in order that he could defend the State and themselves from external enemies. But when the landlord gradually converted the public land into his private property, then he began to look upon the peasants bound to the estate as a part of his real property . . .

Paralleling the growing ascendancy of the landed gentry as a privileged class in the eighteenth century was the degradation of the peasantry to the status of human chattel.

---

of history, concentrating especially on social and economic development. He was a scholar of profound insight, and even though the English translation of his *Course* leaves much to be desired, it is well worth reading.

MIR: The Russian village community. After the emancipation, its powers were tremendously increased. It held title to the land, it distributed and re-distributed the land among the peasants, and it was responsible for the redemption payments that had to be made to the state treasury.

Although the noble landlords were themselves "slaves" of the Moscow Czars, nevertheless, gradually each landlord became also a Czar of a kind on his estate. While he did not possess the power of death or life over his subjects, it was entirely possible for him to dispose arbitrarily of the labor, property and, to a considerable extent, of the person of his serfs. He could punish them in all sorts of ways: whip, beat, and even exile them to Siberia, draft them into the army or sell them. Though the law provided some restrictions for protection of the peasants from the abuses of the landlords, still these restrictions could have only a very precarious application because the law prohibited the serfs from complaining against their masters.

Moreover, the officials who were responsible for the enforcement of even such modest legal safeguards themselves belonged to the nobility or were dependent upon it for their jobs. Therefore they usually sided with the noble lords. What class-bias, self-interest, or fear of offending the powerful and rich did not accomplish in making enforcement lax, official corruption, which was rampant, completed.

As Kliuchevsky, one of the greatest of Russia's historians, put it:

The Government and the nobility shared among themselves the serf; the Government yielded to the nobles its rights to the person and labor of the serf in exchange for the obligation to pay his poll tax and to guard his farming insofar as it was necessary to maintain the productivity of the soil for fiscal purposes, "so that land should not remain idle" as a decree of 1734 expressed it.

Thus, the Russian peasant was delivered body and soul to the mercies of the master, to serve as the latter's "baptized property," to use Alexander Herzen's caustic epithet. No wonder that Kliuchevsky characterized Russian bondage as "the worst form of serfdom in Europe." Indeed, it is necessary to turn to the slave economies of the Orient or the ante-bellum South for analogies to the Russian servile system.

In the economic and social, as distinguished from the legal, position of the peasant under serfdom, differentiation must be made among (1) serfs discharging their obligation to the masters by paying quitrents, and (2) those tilling the demesne (lord's) lands, or (3) rendering personal service in the manorial household.

Of these three principal types of servitude, the quitrent system was the most favorable from a peasant's standpoint. Although heavy tribute was often exacted, this system entailed less personal contact with the masters and less interference on their part with peasant life and consequently was less subject to abuse than other kinds of serfdom. As a rule, moreover, the peasants held all or most of the land of the estate for their own use. What was often more important, they were free to engage in various trades or seek employment in the cities. As was early noted by observers of Russian economic life, such nonagricultural occupations constituted an important source of quitrents. At the same time the quitrent system, by providing a reservoir of necessary labor and business ability, made possible the development of the famous rural handicraft trades as well as of the factory industry of Russia.

To the landlord the quitrent system was especially advantageous where returns from agriculture were low, as in the less fertile, more northern regions of the country—where a considerable area of the estate land would have been needed to feed the serfs. Here was the *locus classicus* of the quitrent system with the proportion of serfs on this basis increasing, according to best estimates, from over a half during the second half of the eighteenth century to nearly two-thirds in the middle of the nineteenth. In these regions various industries, handicrafts, and manufacturing (especially textiles) sprang up, using the surplus labor of the quitrent peasants.

That the peasants themselves benefited under such arrangements by gaining a certain degree of freedom and economic independence is doubtless true. However, it was a precarious freedom, based not on a change in the legal status but entirely on the convenience and whims of the master, who could always shift the quitrent-paying peasants to a more onerous kind of servitude if he desired. Still, some of the peasants in this category had an opportunity to improve their lot and a few even amassed fortunes with which they were able to purchase their freedom and to establish an industrial dynasty such as, for instance, that of the famous textile magnates—the Morosov family, which incidentally contributed in one of its scions a generous financial backer for the Bolsheviks in their early struggling days.

It was not, therefore, merely a poetic fancy on the part of the great Pushkin, who knew the Russian village well, when he made Eugene Onegin, the hero of his *pièce du siècle,* shift the serfs he inherited from the demesne to the quitrent basis in order to lighten the burden of servitude. As a rule such a shift was as welcome to the peasants as the reverse movement was repugnant, for the demesne serfs were much more rigidly bound to the land than those on the quitrent basis. Under this system peasants usually divided their time between the demesne land and holdings of their own. Forced labor, requiring minute regulation and continuous supervision, naturally involved a great deal of interference on the part of the master with the lives of the demesne peasants. Moreover, it was in the interest of the masters, especially in the fertile black-soil districts, to reduce as far as possible the area of peasant landholdings in order to expand that of the demesne land. The landlords were not slow to act on this incentive.

This tendency to expand the demesne area in the black-soil zone became pronounced after the nobility gained freedom from compulsory state service in the middle of the eighteenth century. The nobles began to settle on their estates, exchanging the role of absentee landlords for that of gentlemen farmers, with a predilection for what the Russian scholars called "entrepreneurship," i.e., commercial farming (production for the market).

While the social and, to some extent, the intellectual life of the provinces gained as a result of the settlement of the nobility on the land, to the peasants it meant a tightening of the servile system. For the technique of genteel entrepreneurship, in spite of much flirtation with the new agronomic science among the more advanced landlords, consisted primarily in exploitation of serf labor, the principal "capital" of the estates, as intensively as possible, since only in this manner, as a rule, could large returns be secured. Much ingenuity, therefore, was exercised by the landlords in devising ways and means of more profitable employment of serf labor. The net result was that the exactions from peasants whether in the form of labor or quitrents had increased in the nineteenth century.

The noble "entrepreneurs" did not confine their quest for profits to agriculture, but often also set up factories on their estates. However bad the lot of farm demesne labor, still more distressing was the position of those peasants who were forced to work in these veritable sweatshops. The peasants, according to one observer, regarded the latter with the same horror as the plague.

The darkest spot in the picture, however, must be reserved for the third large type—the manorial serfs. These were the real pariahs. They were not allotted any land of their own for farming and were housed in the manor, where their whole life was devoted to serving the masters. Hence the manorial serf's entire existence depended completely upon the personality of the master, his character, tastes, and whims. There was obviously ample opportunity for abuse of authority. In fact, from testimony of contemporaries with regard to manor serfs there emerges a picture of slavery in its harshest aspects, symbolized best by the rod, liberally applied to the serfs generally, but from which those attached to the manor suffered most. Although the rod forever remained an emblem of the Russian servile system, it was not the only or the most cruel method of punishment employed. In reviewing the evidence, a distinguished Russian historian asserted: "It is difficult to imagine what tortures some masters were able to invent." If it was true that the worst excesses of this kind were exceptional, it was also doubtless true that many cases of cruelty never became a matter of record.

Grievous as was the fate of the male serf, that of the woman serf in the manor was even worse. Her whole life was regimented in its most intimate details, marriage was hindered, and more often than not she became a prey for the lust of the master. This moral evil is much stressed in the literature on serfdom in Russia. It was not confined to the manorial women, although they were the greatest victims, but affected the peasant women in the village as well. Even the practices of *jus primae noctis* and manorial harems were not unknown.

If the lot of the ordinary serf was difficult enough, it was often nothing short of tragic for the serf intelligentsia—those who, by virtue of either special training as actors, artists, musicians, architects, physicians, etc., or exceptional native ability, succeeded in rising intellectually above the low cultural level of the grey peasant mass and naturally were more sensitive to the prevailing brutality of the régime. The very tendency toward self-sufficiency characteristic of the manorial household, the tendency to produce everything, even culture, with the help of serf labor, described so well in the memoirs of Prince Peter Kropotkin, led to the creation of such a class of educated serfs. Some few among such intellectuals, as for instance, the famous actor, Shchepkin, and the great Ukrainian poet, Shevchenko, succeeded in gaining freedom through manumission, although it was often obtained with the greatest difficulty because of the stubbornness of the masters. However, most of these intellectuals ended their days as they had begun, in bondage, often taking to drink or committing suicide.

Such were the salient features of the Russian servile system in its heyday, as it was spreading to new territory and encompassing additional elements of population. In part, this expansion was due to the colonizing efforts of the landowners themselves in settling their serfs on the new cheaply-acquired lands of the south and southeast, a process reminiscent of the creation of the western cotton belt by the slaveholding planters of the American South. But it was largely the governmental policy that was responsible for the spreading of serfdom. For one reason, the periodic censuses of population introduced by Peter the Great for fiscal purposes were also used to drag arbitrarily into the net of bondage various unattached groups such as illegitimate children, foundlings, vagrants, and so forth.

More important was the extension of the Great Russian form of bondage to large regions such as the Ukraine, where it had not existed formerly. And last but not least was the custom of the eighteenth-century Russian monarchs of rewarding their favorite courtiers and officials with "gifts" of inhabited villages. It was estimated that in the course of the eighteenth century more than two million peasants, with the land they cultivated, were delivered into bondage through such lavish grants, before this practice was abolished at the beginning of the nineteenth century. One of the worst offenders in this respect was that enlightened friend of Voltaire and Diderot and disciple of Montesquieu, Catherine the Great (1762-1796), who in her youth recorded her opposition to serfdom as inconsistent with the principles of Christianity and justice and scorned it in her comedies. This did not prevent her, however, from presenting 800,000 peasants of both sexes as gifts to her favorites. Not without cause did her reign become known as the golden age of the serf-owning nobility, while the noose of serfdom was knotted ever tighter around the peasant neck.

Many large estates, especially in east and south Russia, originated in this period. In spite of subsequent subdivision as a result of inheritance, these *latifundia* still accounted at the time of abolition of serfdom for the lion's share of the nobles' holdings. In 1858—three years before emancipation—it was estimated that four out of five serfs were in estates of not less than 1,000 *desiatines* (2,700 acres). Nearly half of all serfs (47 percent) belonged to nobles who possessed more than 500 male serfs each, 34 percent to those with 100 to 500, and less than 20 percent were owned by nobles with fewer than 100 serfs each.

In spite of all this expansion, serfdom nominally never extended to the whole of Russia's peasant population. Nearly one-third of the latter, according to the census of 1833, consisted of so-called "state" peasants, who were legally free men. But their freedom was a very tenuous affair indeed. It is true that they possessed personal and property rights unknown to the serfs; nevertheless the Government looked upon state peasants as public property to be exploited for fiscal purposes and disposed of as it deemed best. Consequently, this class constituted the reservoir that was drawn upon for the imperial grants of "souls" and "villages," thus easily converting supposedly free state peasants into serfs. Even when that practice was discontinued at the beginning of the nineteenth century, state peasants still were used arbitrarily for pet government projects and experiments, such as the "military settlements" of evil memory in the 1820s, whereby they became part soldiers and part tillers of the soil. Some of them were also shifted into a condition of servitude on the estates of the imperial family. However, even apart from such arbitrary treatment, the state peasants suffered from the squeezing tactics of high-handed and often corrupt officials, who regarded them primarily as a source of revenue to the State or to themselves. When finally the factor of uneven distribution of land is added, it should occasion no surprise that these free peasants often fared worse than the serfs of private masters.

A radical change, however, occurred in the late 1830s, when the state peasants were transferred from the jurisdiction of the Ministry of Finance to the newly organized Ministry of Public Domain entrusted to Count Kiselev, who was perhaps the only aide of Nicholas I sincerely and seriously interested in the improvement of the lot of the peasantry. During the nearly two decades of Kiselev's incumbency, he succeeded in effecting many improvements of an administrative and economic character in the condition of state peasants, who became in principle the wards of the State rather than an object to be mulcted. Although impaired by poor administration and excessive paternalism, and soon eclipsed by the great emancipation reforms of the 1860s, Kiselev's was the first really effective step taken by the Russian Government toward improvement of peasant conditions.

Apart from Kiselev's reforms, the discontinuation of imperial grants of serfs, and a few other feeble mitigating gestures, the first half of the nineteenth century witnessed no essential change in the policy of the Russian State with respect to the servile system as it had crystallized during the preceding century. All the heroism displayed during the struggle against Napoleon brought the Russian peasants only "a single line in Alexander's manifesto of 1814, in which the Tsar 'most graciously' thanked all classes and granted them various privileges. This single line ran: 'The peasants, our loyal people, will be recompensed by God.'"

Not that the Russian rulers failed to realize, at a time when one European country after another was entering on a path of far-reaching agrarian reforms, that in Russia too serfdom must eventually come to an end. Certainly they were aware, as expressed by Count Benkerdorf, the powerful head of the gendarmerie under Nicholas I, that "Serfdom is a powder magazine under the state and the peasantry is an explosive mine." Above all else, however, the Government was afraid to disturb the status quo, and accordingly it was faced with a dilemma, well stated by Nicholas I who said, addressing the Council of State on March 30, 1842: "Doubtless serfdom as it exists at present in our country is an evil that is generally evident; but to tamper with it now would be, of course, an even more disastrous evil." How to deal with this problem was a subject of long and secret deliberations of numerous government committees which were barren of practical results.

Only in the western border provinces was a different course pursued. In the Baltic region, where the landowners were Germans, serfdom was abolished during the second decade of the nineteenth century, but the Latvian and Estonian peasants were left landless. In the western provinces of Russian Ukraine with its Polish landowning class, toward which the Russian Government had no reason to feel kindly after the Polish insurrection of 1831, a more "peasantophile" policy was followed. Serfdom was not abolished, it is true, but the services or dues to be exacted from the peasants were strictly defined and limited in so-called inventories for each estate, thus restricting somewhat the arbitrary powers of the landowners.

In the rest of the country, the servile system continued unabated to the end. But did the Russian peasant meekly acquiesce in his enslavement? The evidence seems to be strongly in the negative. As Ignatovich put it: "Serfdom did not make out of the peasants timid, submissive slaves. In various ways, beginning with individual cases of disobedience and ending with formidable mass movements, putting the Government on its mettle, they [the peasants] protested against serfdom." The peasant mind long continued to cling to the idea that the dependence of peasants was conditioned on service of their masters to the State. It was well formulated at the beginning of the eighteenth century by the publicist, Pososhkov, who wrote that "The landowners are not permanent proprietors of the peasant"; that "they own them temporarily and that their direct owner is the autocrat of all Russia." It is natural, therefore, that the freeing of the nobility from compulsory state service in 1762 should have given rise to strong expectations among the peasantry of their own liberation from bondage. Such a step was, however, far removed from the intentions of the Government.

The failure of these hopes contributed to the serious revolt of 1773, which became known in history as the Pugachev rebellion after the name of its leader. Commencing first as a local mutiny in the Cossack settlements in southern Ural, it spread like wildfire west toward the Volga and beyond, drawing into its vortex the masses of serf peasantry. Numerous jacqueries characterized the uprising, sowing panic among the officials and landowning class, many of whom were killed while their estates were pillaged by rebels. It required a powerful army to quell the rebellion. The nightmare of this "Russian mutiny, terrible and senseless," in the words of Pushkin, long haunted the Russian landowning gentry.

Although the peasants were decisively beaten in this major encounter with the State and the landowning class, their hopes of freedom, though dimmed, could never be extinguished. It is true that no general revolt on the gigantic scale of the Pugachev rebellion occurred again for one hundred and thirty years, but unrest and disturbances there were plentiful. A new accession to the throne or a major war such as that with Napoleon in 1812 or the Crimean War of 1854-55 was the signal for a fresh crop of rumors of impending freedom that often led to scattered but nonetheless serious uprisings. In addition there were, of course, local reasons for disturbances, such as excessive exaction or cruel treatment, non-support of the serfs by the masters during a famine, and so forth. Between 1828 and 1854, according to incomplete data, there were 547 local mutinies, which, significantly enough, increased in frequency and number of participants during the latter part of the period.

A study of the geographical distribution of the peasant mutinies reveals an anomalous fact. Most of them occurred not, as might be expected, in the fertile black-soil zone, where the more oppressive demesne system prevailed, but in the less fertile sections of the country, with their widespread quitrent system and greater development of rural trades. This paradox is attributed by Maslov to the fact that it was not so much the actual degree of oppression that led to protests on the part of the peasant masses as the consciousness of oppression, which was likely to be keener among the relatively freer quitrent peasants (who often moved back and forth between the town and the village) than among their fellow peasants bound to the demesne.

Many of these mutinies were simply strikes or collective "disobedience," as they were called—refusals to work and pay dues and taxes. However, peasant antagonism often took more violent form, with calamitous results to the property and life of the masters and overseers. Arson and murder were common. During the twenty years, 1834-1854, there were 144 cases of murder of landlords and their agents, not counting attempts at assassination. During the nine-year period, 1835-1843, 416 peasants were deported to Siberia for murder of landlords.

A more mild method of avenging sometimes resorted to by the serfs was to subject the master to corporal punishment, so liberally applied to themselves. The number of such cases is probably larger than the few that actually came to light, since it was to the advantage of both sides to keep the matter secret. Needless to say, peasant mutinies were usually severely repressed, often by armed forces and with considerable bloodshed. The official attitude was perhaps best epitomized by an inscription on a common grave of victims of one such "pacification" of a particularly stubborn peasant uprising at the end of the eighteenth century, which read: "Here are lying those who committed crimes against God, the Czar and the landlord, justly punished by fire and sword in accordance with the laws of God and of the Czar."

"Pacification" frequently did not lead to the resumption of the normal state of affairs on the estate. Unrest driven underground often resulted in sabotage or flared up in repeated, sometimes more violent, uprisings. In some cases only a continuous quartering of troops insured "law and order." In any event serious economic loss resulted to the landowners; and their estates, once they acquired the reputation of being "troublesome," greatly depreciated in value. Moreover, such disturbances, isolated and scattered though they were, had also some important psychological and political effects. They held continuously before the eyes of the landowning class and the Government the terrifying specter of another Pugachev rebellion, "reminding like a menacing *memento mori* [reminder of death] of the necessity to end serfdom in the landowners' own interest."

The peasant opposition to serfdom was not confined to individual or collective acts of violence, sabotage, or strikes; flight as a manifestation of such opposition was no less, if not more, important, and the problem long taxed the energies of the Government. There were no abolitionist societies in Russia to organize underground railways to havens of freedom, but the dense forests in the north and northeast, and the vast steppes in the east and southeast, for centuries provided an asylum to those who tried to escape from the oppression of the land-lord, the Government, and the established church. It was in this manner that the peculiar institution of the Cossacks originated, the "most radical type of a community known in Russian national history." Even long after the Cossacks came under the controlling wing of the central government, the territory of these turbulent frontier settlers con-tinued to be a refuge for runaway serfs and a breeding ground of insur-rection. It was among the Cossacks in the Urals, it will be recalled, that the celebrated Pugachev rebellion was kindled.

Not only individuals but whole villages, provoked by some wild rumor, sometimes fled en masse. According to Ignatovich, such escapist tendencies during the second quarter of the nineteenth century con-stituted a greater menace to the servile system than mutinies, which were usually confined to single estates. "Hundreds and thousands of peasants would move in the same direction, influenced by a similar rumor and united by the same purpose." Sometimes only the use of armed force stopped such mass flights.

Of the various episodes of this character, those that occurred dur-ing 1854-1856 made a strong impression on public opinion and the Government, coinciding as they did with the disastrous Crimean War and the beginning of the reign of Alexander II. In 1854 and again in 1855, when the Government issued calls for the militia, a rumor spread that freedom would be granted to those who enlisted, and the serfs rushed in mobs to join, leaving the landlords to their own devices. The movement assumed such huge proportions that the Government had to resort to troops to stop it, and blood was shed. In 1856, after the war ended, a rumor again circulated in the southern provinces that freedom would be granted to serfs migrating to the Crimea. As a result, a mass migration that included whole villages began, and troops again had to be employed to halt it.

These incidents illustrate graphically the deep-seated longing of the peasants for freedom, for which no sacrifice, not even the dangers of the battlefield, were too great. Still, mere freedom without land was not acceptable to the masses of the Russian peasants. Their attitude was epitomized by the reply of the serfs given to the liberal landowner, Yakushkin, who in the early 1820s wanted to liberate them but without land; the peasants did not agree, saying: "Well, sir, let everything remain as it was of old: We are yours, but the land is ours." Here, in essence, is the peasant ideology. In such sayings, the peasants formulated their firm conviction of the indissoluble character of the ties that bound them to the "mother soil"—ties which they would not have torn asunder even in exchange for freedom. Recalling the conditional character of land tenure during the early stages of serfdom, this peasant attitude toward land appears to have a more solid historical justification than the opposing claims of the landlords with their conception of absolute property rights in land.

This deep attachment of the peasants to the land, however, was a formidable obstacle to emancipation. Thus, Prince Vasilchikov, who as President of the Council of Empire was one of the highest functionaries of Nicholas I, wrote in a memorandum to the secret committee set up in 1835 to consider the peasant question, that it was necessary:

> To spread and assert at every convenient opportunity the basic rule that the land is an inseparable and inalienable property of the landlord (the state and private landlord) and that the peasant can use it not otherwise than with the consent of the landlord and in consideration for performance of definite services. The unfortunate idea which exists nearly everywhere among the serfs that *they themselves belong to the master but the land belongs to themselves* [italics added] is one of the principal obstacles to the achievement of the desired aims [relaxation of the servile system]. For the introduction of the intended improvements in the position of the peasants can create unrest and give cause for serious disturbances.

In their striving for freedom and land, however, the peasant masses had a sympathizer in the Russian intelligentsia, which was emerging from swaddling clothes just as serfdom reached its pinnacle. Through the "window into Europe" which Peter the Great opened at the beginning of the eighteenth century there penetrated into Russia not only the externals of European civilization, but slowly, with a considerable lag and for upper-class consumption only, European liberal and humanitarian ideas. The eighteenth-century enlightenment, the French Revolution, the romantic movement with its cult of the people, the early nineteenth-century Utopian socialism, and British utilitarianism—all helped to nurture the growing Russian intelligentsia and to develop a critical attitude toward conditions in their native land.

Brought up on such ideological fare, the Russian intellectual could not fail to recognize the moral evil of serfdom. The teaching of the new political economy pioneered by Adam Smith bolstered the ethical antagonism to serfdom by arguments of the superior efficiency of free as compared with slave labor and by the doctrines of natural liberty and laissez faire.

It was, however, one thing to arouse moral consciousness against the servile system and another to do something about it. Not only was freedom of political expression in the western sense unknown but even the most elementary civil liberties were lacking. The Government was constantly in mortal fear lest any public criticism or attack on serfdom, considered the cornerstone of the whole social fabric, should incite the peasants (though they were predominantly illiterate) or irritate the landlords. Hence the subject was taboo, and even official discussion of it was carried on behind a Chinese wall of secrecy.

The tragic fate of Radishchev, one of the earliest Russian abolitionists and a leading intellectual of his time, was an eloquent warning of what was in store for those who dared to break the taboo. In 1790, he published in his own printing house the celebrated *Journeys from St. Petersburg to Moscow,* in which he strongly denounced the horrors of serfdom. The book, although it was passed by the censor, aroused the ire of Catherine the Great, who had long forgotten the liberal ideas of her youth and whose latter-day reactionary leanings were intensified by the outbreak of the French Revolution. The book was ordered destroyed. Radishchev was sentenced to death, but the sentence was commuted to exile to Siberia on recantation of his views.

To enforce the ban against criticism of serfdom was thus the "first commandment" of censorship, behind which lurked prison and Siberia. Its principal canon of operation, according to one authority, was "noli me tangere," meaning "touch me not," or, perhaps better, "do not mention me in public"; and this irrespective of whether a reactionary or a somewhat more liberal spirit prevailed in St. Petersburg. In fact, the political climate, after some relaxation during the early part of the reign of Alexander I, who himself toyed with liberal ideas, became increasingly more reactionary as the years rolled by. The reaction reached its peak during the reign of the "Iron Czar," Nicholas I. The Marquis de Custine did not exaggerate too much when he wrote in his letters on *Russia in 1839* that "In Russia to talk was equivalent to conspiracy, thinking was revolt; also thought is not only a crime, it is a calamity." "The air," recalled a well-known Russian writer, Gleb Uspensky, "was full of fears; 'you will perish,' shouted heaven and earth, air and water, human beings and animals. And everyone was shrivelling and running away from danger and hiding in the first hole to be found."

Scholarship, like all other forms of intellectual life, experienced the stifling effect of the reactionary political atmosphere. Few scholarly works that dealt critically with serfdom were permitted, and then for the most part in a foreign language. Thus, the academician Storch, who taught political economy to members of the imperial family, was able to publish his treatise on the subject, in which he manifested his opposition to serfdom, in a French edition only. Even legally sanctioned publications in a foreign language did not necessarily exempt an author from subsequent persecution, as was exemplified by the sad case of Professor Schad, who, on recommendation of Goethe and Schiller, was appointed in 1804 to teach philosophy in the newly established University of Kharkov. Because of "dangerous ideas" discovered in his work on institutions of natural law, *Institutiones juris naturae,* published in 1814, he was dismissed from his post and deported in 1816, and all his books were ordered to be destroyed.

Belles-lettres, which in Russia have been tinged to an unusual degree with social significance inasmuch as they early became an avenue of escape for the intelligentsia deprived of other means of political and social self-expression, felt especially the heavy expurgating hand of censorship when it touched so burning a question as serfdom. Hardly an illustrious name in the brilliant literary annals of the first half of the nineteenth century was spared in the process. The spirit animating the censorship may perhaps best be fathomed from the prohibition of a Russian translation of Harriet Beecher Stowe's *Uncle Tom's Cabin.*

Nevertheless, the designs of censorship were at least partly foiled. In the first place, the forbidden works were circulated over the length and breadth of the country in many thousands of handwritten copies. Thus, the second part of Pushkin's celebrated poem *In the Village,* written in 1818 and strongly condemning serfdom, was well known among the educated classes in spite of the fact that its publication was not permitted until half a century later. The same was true of the great comedy of Griboedov, "The Mischief of Being Clever," which was completed in 1824 but was kept off the stage until 1834, and many other forbidden literary works. In the second place, it was on occasion possible to elude the censor with novels, such as those of Grigorovich, obliquely attacking the evils of serfdom. Even Turgenev's celebrated *Stories of a Huntsman*, which provided so moving an indictment of the servile system that they were said to have greatly influenced Alexander II in favor of emancipation, were permitted by the censor.

If legal abolitionism was ruled out under Russian conditions, what about illegal underground activity? Such a movement actually developed in the early twenties with the formation of secret political societies of young intellectual nobles, largely officers of the imperial guard and patterned on similar organizations which sprang up at the time in many countries of western Europe. The liberal aspirations of the Decembrists, as participants in this movement became known in history, were thwarted by Alexander I, who had kindled liberal ideas at the outset of his regime. The Napoleonic Wars had brought this aristocratic youth, through service in the Russian army abroad, into closer contact with the west, and thus had thrown into sharp relief the contrast between European civilization and the semi-Asiatic backwardness of Russia. The new consciousness of national pride that the successful struggle with Bonaparte evoked whetted the appetite for reforms that would bring the internal progress of Russia more in line with its lofty international position. Heading the list of such reforms were political freedom and abolition of serfdom. These were, in fact, the cardinal twin tenets of the Decembrist faith.

Since the Decembrist opposition met only a blind and sterile reaction on the part of the Government, it resorted to conspiracy aiming at a constitutional regime via a palace revolution, for which Russian history supplied so many precedents. The death of Alexander I forced the conspirators to act, and they took advantage of the confusion created by the problem of succession to the throne and staged a revolt among the guard regiments in St. Petersburg, on December 14, 1825, from which this movement derived its name. This revolt, as well as a mutiny in one of the regiments quartered in the Ukraine, was rapidly suppressed. Five of the leaders were executed, including Colonel Pestel, author of an interesting political tract entitled *Russkaia Pravda* (Russian Truth) and one of the most remarkable political personalities of his time, and the poet Ryleev, an official of the famous Russian-American Company which controlled Alaska, then still a part of the Russian Empire; the rest of the Decembrists were deported to Siberia.

This abortive revolution, in which the flower of Russian intelligentsia perished, was staged by the intellectuals in "splendid isolation," without contact with or support from the masses, from whom it was separated by a high social barrier which it did little to lower. In fact, there is evidence that the objectives of the Decembrists were frequently misinterpreted by the dark peasant mind as those of resistance by the gentlefolk to the intention of the new Czar to grant freedom to the serfs. Hence the news of arrests among landowners implicated in the Decembrist plot was often welcomed by the peasants. It was as if the intellectuals and the peasants were simultaneously playing in the same drama but on different stages, largely unknown to each other.

After the suppression of the Decembrists, nearly a quarter of a century passed before a new weapon of attack on the servile system was fashioned, consisting of the immigrant literature published abroad and smuggled into Russia. In the year 1847 there appeared in Paris a three-volume work entitled *La Russie et les Russes,* by N. I. Turgenev (not to be confused with the great novelist), who as a political refugee in France was settling old scores with the archenemy of serfdom. More important was the fact that in the same year a young nobleman, Alexander Herzen, who had already made a mark in the intellectual circles of Moscow, left his native land in order better to carry on his vendetta against serfdom and political despotism from a new vantage point. He was the best representative of that type of "penitent nobleman," made familiar by the novels of his friend Turgenev, who was driven by remorse over the "sins" against the people into the revolutionary camp and exile. Herzen combined a passionate devotion to freedom and justice with a clear, skeptical mind, a fighting temperament, an encyclopedic erudition, and a remarkable literary talent for debunking. He was, therefore, well equipped for intellectual leadership in a campaign against the servile system. In this task he was assisted by his friend, the poet Ogarev, who joined him in self-exile to form a politico-literary partnership reminiscent of the famous partnership of Karl Marx and Friedrich Engels.

In 1853, Herzen published a pamphlet entitled *Baptized Property,* which was probably the deadliest sortie against serfdom since the days of Radishchev. However, the most effective new weapon proved to be the Russian periodicals which he founded in London. In 1856, he began the publication of magazines called *Polar Star* and *Voices from Russia,* in which considerable attention was paid to the peasant question, and many articles and memoranda were printed that could not pass censorship in Russia. On July 1, 1857, the first number of Herzen's famous magazine, the *Bell,* left the printing press, and, in the words of a distinguished Russian scholar, "The most powerful and rapidly shooting gun was set off."

The appearance of the *Bell* marked the beginning of a period in which, following the defeat suffered by Russia in the Crimean War and the death of Nicholas I, the question of ending serfdom ceased to be academic and became one of practical politics. The subject was eagerly discussed by the educated public. The Government itself greatly profited from such discussion during the preparation of the new legislation. However, it was slow in relaxing censorship, which was never completely abandoned. The untrammeled *Bell,* therefore, had a vital function to perform in guiding progressive Russian public opinion. The best evidence of and tribute to its influence was the fact that, although theoretically illegal, the *Bell* was freely circulating in Russia and was widely read not only by the intelligentsia but also in official circles, including, it was rumored, the Emperor Alexander II himself.

Ideological cleavages among Russian intelligentsia, which began to appear in the 1840s, did not affect in the least its opposition to serfdom. The conservative Slavophiles with their romantic hankering after the old Moscovite Russia and idealization of the peasant *mir* were engaged in hot debates with the liberal and individualistic westerners. A little later in the 1850s, young Russian radicalism, with an agrarian socialist philosophy, made its debut on the intellectual scene under the leadership of Herzen and Chernyshevsky. The celebrated controversy over the Russian *mir,* which continued for three-quarters of a century, until the Bolshevik revolution, began in this period. Despite all the ideological divisions and disputes, there was, as Chernyshevsky pointed out at the time, complete unanimity on the central issue of the imperative necessity of peasant emancipation.

The intellectual opposition to serfdom was not in vain. In spite of all handicaps, it succeeded by the middle of the nineteenth century in morally discrediting the servile system among the educated class by focusing public attention on its hideousness, its cruel abuses, and its general injustice and inhumanity, brutalizing and demoralizing the slave and the slaveowner alike. Only a decade or two earlier, literary apologetics of serfdom were not uncommon. The leitmotiv was the more favorable status of the Russian moujik as compared with that of the peasant in Western Europe or the factory worker in England. Serious technical magazines were devoted, it will be recalled, to the discussion of the best method of utilizing serf labor, arguing the pros and cons of the quitrent and demesne systems. In the late fifties the only magazine which spoke for the serf-owning class vigorously denied the charge of defending serfdom and resorted to various euphemisms to mask its retrograde policies. When the proponents of serfdom decided to establish another magazine of a similar kind, they had no difficulty in raising the necessary capital but were not able to find an editor, and the project therefore lapsed.

The abolitionist intellectuals, however, did not confine themselves merely to the task of waking up the sleeping social consciousness of the ruling classes, to whom alone they could appeal. From Radishchev to Herzen, abolitionists also conducted a sort of "war of nerves" by playing upon the constant fear on the part of the governing class of a peasant insurrection on a grand scale, kindled by memories of the Pugachev revolt. The strength of those fears was attested by the secrecy with which it was felt necessary to shroud all official deliberations of the peasant question. Herzen, writing from London in 1853, was quite outspoken when calling on the nobility to take a speedy initiative toward emancipation, he threatened: "A Pugachev revolt is terrible, but we shall say frankly that if the liberation of peasants cannot be bought otherwise, even then it is not bought too dearly." Thus the writings of intellectuals tended to bring the danger of peasant unrest, though not without some exaggeration, into the spotlight of public attention.

The terrible jacqueries in 1846 in the neighboring Galicia (then under Austrian control) did not help to assuage the fears of the Russian Government and landlords, and the serious peasant disturbances during the disastrous Crimean War of 1854-55 only tended to confirm the gloomiest forebodings of the ruling classes. It began to be increasingly felt, at least among the more enlightened of the gentry, that "to own serfs became dangerous," and that the landowners were approaching the thin edge of peasant revolt. Alexander II epitomized this feeling in 1856 in his famous dictum that it was better to grant liberty to the serfs from above than to have it seized from below. Count Rostovtsev, who first headed the commission that drafted the emancipation legislation (and one of the few members of Alexander II's entourage who became a convinced abolitionist), often held up before his colleagues the specter of a Pugachev revolt and warned them during the discussion of the land question that, if voluntary concessions were not granted, the peasants would obtain them by using their sledge hammers. Nor was this merely a tactical move on Rostovtsev's part. These warnings were based on a constant stream of information with regard to the threatening attitude of the peasantry, which reached Rostovtsev from the landowning class itself.

Nevertheless the great majority of the landowning class remained implacably hostile to abolition almost to the last. This fact should provide a convincing refutation of the theory that serfdom was becoming unprofitable to the masters and consequently ready for discarding. It is not difficult to understand why such a theory gained considerable acceptance in Russian historical literature, for it fits neatly into the materialistic interpretation of history, which attributes major historical changes primarily to the operation of economic causes. In Russia, the materialistic interpretation in association with the Marxist doctrine of the class struggle had become intellectually fashionable long before it gained the monopolistic exclusiveness of a political orthodoxy after the Revolution. What could be more tempting, therefore, than to explain the downfall of serfdom by the prompting of alleged economic self-interest of the master class, especially when this appears to coincide with the general trend toward economic progress?

As supporting evidence of the unprofitability of the servile system, there was frequently cited chronic overproduction of Russian estate agriculture, the growing burden of indebtedness on the landlords, the decline of the number of serfs as shown by the last census before the emancipation, and other internal strains in the structure of servile economy. The test, however, is simple. If the servile system really had been disadvantageous to the landlords, it would have been more profitable to operate with free than serf labor. If employment of free labor had been more profitable, as Struve argued in a brilliant critique of this thesis, the landowners would have tried to get rid of the serfs. Far from doing this, however, the overwhelming majority of the landowning class not only vehemently resisted any attempt of the Government to mitigate the servile system but made every effort to extend it by settling serfs on new land and expanding the demesne system in fertile regions in spite of the critical attitude manifested by many landlords toward it. The quitrent system in the north, too, constituted, in Struve's words, a "pleasant privilege" for the landlords, with which they were loath to part. Even the thesis of Tugan Baranovsky and other Russian scholars that serf labor was rapidly disappearing in manufacturing industry is shown by more recent historical research to require serious qualification.

At any rate, recourse to free labor was attempted only as a last resort in districts where the supply of serfs was limited, although much was made of such exceptional cases by students of the problem in subsequent years. To say that landlords were precluded from making a shift from servile to free labor because of a shortage of capital only tends to confirm the desire to retain the servile system. There is certainly no reason to believe that landlords were poor judges of their immediate economic interests. On the contrary, much evidence had been adduced by Struve, Liashchenko, and others, indicating that under the servile system the landlords were very well versed in the practical intricacies of the economics of their estates. That is why—and not simply because of inertia and conservatism, although these too played a part—a great majority of the landowning class opposed the abandonment of serfdom. They were certainly not deterred by the fact that the largely self-sufficient and technically backward servile economy was an obstacle to the economic progress of Russia. On the contrary, it was a source of pride to the master that the manor should produce everything from pastry to fine arts as was vividly told by Prince Kropotkin in his reminiscences of the period.

Confronted with this powerful class opposition to emancipation, only something like a catastrophe could jolt the Government into action. Such, for the regime of Alexander II, was the disastrous Crimean War of 1854-55. This fiasco, which showed that the Russian colossus had feet of clay, transcended an ordinary military defeat. It involved a complete loss of face on the part of an autocratic, reactionary, militaristic regime that had a reputation of invincibility; it demonstrated conclusively the bankruptcy of the whole system of statecraft pivoted on serfdom. It gave substance to the indictments of the intelligentsia that were becoming increasingly bolder with the change in the political climate that followed the Crimean War. Blind reaction would no longer do; far-reaching reforms of the state mechanism were inevitable if Russia were to bring its disorganized finances to order, recover its military strength, and survive as a major European power.

Naturally, the starting point for any serious reform was abolition of serfdom—the keystone of the old system. When it is also recalled that the ground swell of peasant unrest gathered force as the Russian armies floundered in Crimea, it becomes clear why considerations of external as well as internal safety of the State dictated the end of the servile system that morally was becoming more and more discredited because of the attacks of the intelligentsia.

However, once it became clear that the Government was firmly decided on emancipation for reasons of state, the landowning class bent every effort to make the reform as painless or even profitable to itself as possible. In this the landlords succeeded only too well; so well in fact that in their success was planted the seed of their future destruction. But that is another story.

‑››‑››‑››‑››‑››‑››‑››‑››‑››‑››‑›‑‑‑‑‹‹‑‹‹‑‹‹‑‹‹‑‹‹‑‹‹‑‹‹‑‹‹‑‹‹‑‹‹‑‹‹‑‹‹‑

Bismarck and the War of 1870

ERICH EYCK

››‑››‑››‑››‑››‑››‑››‑››‑›› *Published in 1940* ‹‹‑‹‹‑‹‹‑‹‹‑‹‹‑‹‹‑‹‹‑‹‹‑‹‹

For almost forty years after Waterloo the major European powers lived
in peace. Then came a series of conflicts. The first was the Crimean War,
a struggle that grew out of French and British concern over Russian
expansionism and out of Napoleon's search for glory. That it proved to be
one of the most poorly conducted wars in all of European history was
partly the result of the long period of peace to which the leading European
powers had become accustomed. The Crimean War was followed by the
Austro-Sardinian War of 1859, which, because of French participation on
the side of the House of Savoy, turned out to be the decisive event in the
establishment by 1861 of the Kingdom of Italy. Next came the Seven
Weeks' War, or Austro-Prussian War, of 1866, which, because of French
neutrality, made possible the Prussian defeat of Austria, the expulsion of
Austria from the Germanies, the Prussian conquest of a considerable portion of the Germanies, and the transformation of the Austrian Empire into
the Dual, or Austro-Hungarian, Monarchy. Four years after the German
Civil War came the Franco-German War, which brought to France the
Third Republic, to Germany the Empire, and to Italy possession of the city
of Rome. Of all the wars of the third quarter of the nineteenth century
it is the Franco-German War which has occasioned the most heated controversies among historians. French scholars, of course, have tended to
attribute the major responsibility for the outbreak of the war to Bismarck;
German historians have been inclined to concentrate on Napoleon and his
court party as the fomentors of the conflict. In the present essay Erich Eyck
examines the famous diplomatic episode—one of the most sensational in
European history—that ushered in the war. A German of liberal convictions, Eyck is the author of a recently published three-volume biography of
Bismarck (1941-1944) that has superseded all previous accounts of the
Iron Chancellor.

How wars arise our generation has twice experienced with a shudder, but the responsibility is not always so manifest as in 1939. When the war of 1870 which determined the fate of Europe for at least two generations broke out, its causes were shrouded in darkness, and only in our days has research succeeded in clearing them up. To-day an almost unbroken series of records has been published. The great French collection, "*Origines Diplomatiques de la Guerre de 1870-1871*," has been published in twenty-nine carefully and impartially edited volumes. The German records of the critical July days, above all Bismarck's telegrams, were made known by the American historian, Professor R. H. Lord, who interpreted and assessed them in an exemplary manner in a book which was almost a scientific sensation. From the Austrian and South German archives the German historian, Professor Hermann Oncken, has edited a collection of three volumes of records, the value of which must be recognised although his commentary may be considered somewhat biased. This article merely investigates the question: why did this particular affair, Prince Leopold of Hohenzollern's candidature for the Spanish throne, at this particular moment, the summer of 1870, lead to war? It does not deal with the question whether the political situation after the Prussian victory at Sadowa, the shifting of the balance of power in Europe, the changed grouping of the states were the causes of the war between France and Prussia. Nobody was more convinced of Sadowa having been a French defeat than Thiers, who opposed the declaration of war on July 15th with admirable courage.

In the masterly twenty-second chapter of his apologia Bismarck represented the candidature as a family matter of the House of Hohenzollern with which Prussian politics and he himself in his quality as Chancellor of the Norddeutscher Bund had had nothing to do. This version had already been refuted when he dictated it to his faithful Bucher, and nobody knew that better than Bucher himself. To-day we know that it is incorrect in all essential points.

General Prim, the Prime Minister and strong man in Spain after the expulsion of Queen Isabella in 1868, looked for a European prince

Reprinted by special permission from *The Contemporary Review*, CLVIII (1940), 196-202. Several paragraphs from this article have been reprinted in Eyck, *Bismarck and the War of 1870*, and these paragraphs are here used with the permission of The Macmillan Company.

whom he could put on the throne. The name of Prince Leopold of Hohenzollern was mentioned for the first time by a Prussian diplomat at a dinner given by Mrs. O'Shea, who as Parnell's mistress was to play such a disastrous part in Anglo-Irish history. Prince Leopold was the son of Prince Anton of Hohenzollern who in 1849 had ceded his little country to Prussia, had become a Prussian prince, was a general in the Prussian army and, from 1859 till 1862, had been the Prime Minister of the then Prussian King William I whose personal friend he was. Leopold's brother Karl had in 1866 in a somewhat curious manner acceded to the Rumanian throne. These Hohenzollerns were, contrary to the Protestant royal family, Catholics. They regarded themselves—and made no secret of it—as Germans, nay as Prussians, though they were connected with many foreign princely houses.

The first efforts to win the Hohenzollerns for the Spanish candidature failed. But already in May 1869 Bismarck sent Theodor von Bernhardi, whom he and Moltke had long been employing for confidential tasks, to Spain. In Bernhardi's diaries there is no mention of this task, and his notes are still unpublished. But no less a person than Lord Acton contended in 1899 that Bernhardi had been granted by Bismarck £50,000 out of the secret Guelph Fund with which to win followers in Spain. That this statement is supported by incontestable evidence Professor Harold Temperley ascertained from Acton's papers; Acton quoted for this fact among others Droysen, the most Prussian of all Prussian historians. Whom Bernhardi bribed will, of course, always be a secret. The fact is that a Spanish politician, Salazar, called on the Hohenzollerns in Germany in September 1869 and offered Leopold the Spanish crown. Leopold refused with the full

LOTHAR BUCHER: Bismarck's secret agent and collaborator in the German Foreign Office. When Bismarck found himself unemployed in 1890, he accepted an offer to publish his memoirs, and it was Bucher who served as his assistant in preparing a work that is notorious for its falsification of Bismarck's career.

CORPS LEGISLATIF: The Legislative Assembly under the Second Empire. Authorized by the Imperial Constitution of 1852, it lacked the right to introduce or to alter legislation. Its powers were increased with the transformation of the authoritarian empire into a more liberal empire in the years after 1860.

approval of his father. Salazar repeated his efforts in February 1870, this time provided with letters of Prim to the prince, the King of Prussia and Bismarck. Prince Anton also wrote to Bismarck. Bismarck received Salazar on February 26th and next day made to the King, who was absolutely against the candidature, a personal report which was energetically in its favour. He explained that in case of a war against France a Spanish Government sympathetic towards Germany would be worth two army corps, and stressed the increase of the Monarchy's prestige in Prussia if the dynasty should be in a European position which "has only an analogy in the old Habsburg model." The same thought was expressed by Prince Anton in his letter to Bismarck: "History has not seen such a dynasty since Charles V." Did not the French Foreign Secretary Gramont say exactly the same thing in his fatal declaration of July 6th before the Corps Législatif, when he protested against "a foreign power intending to set one of their princes on the throne of Charles V"?

On March 15th the conference—afterwards disavowed by Bismarck under various pretexts—on the Spanish question took place under the presidency of the King in the Royal Palace in Berlin. Formally it was not a Council of Ministers—so far Bismarck was right. But that it had been a political council of the first importance is evident even from the list of those present: besides the Crown Prince, the Hohen-zollerns and the Minister Schleinitz there were Bismarck, the President of the Federal Chancellery Delbrück, the Under-Secretary of the Foreign Office Thile, the War Minister General Roon, and the Chief of the General Staff Moltke. Under Bismarck's firm leadership all ministers and generals advocated the candidature; but the King and Crown Prince were against it and Leopold refused again. Bismarck

---

OLLIVIER: Leader of the liberal opposition in the France of Napoleon III. Permitted in 1869 to form a cabinet that represented the majority member-ship of the Legislative Assembly, he was responsible for the introduction of a number of basic constitutional reforms in the months that preceded the collapse of the Napoleonic Empire.

SADOWA: Decisive engagement in the Seven Weeks' War of 1866. The rapid Prussian victory over Austria had not been anticipated by the French gov-ernment, but that victory meant that Napoleon now had as a neighbor the powerful Prussian-dominated North German Confederation.

continued his work. At the end of March he sent his most intimate collaborator, Lothar Bucher, an official of the Foreign Office, to Spain; but the King thought his report in May too *"couleur de rose"* ["rosy"]. Bismarck now pressed Prince Anton to influence Leopold to accept the candidature. As Leopold was still unwilling, Bismarck sent Bucher to Madrid again, this time with a letter to Prim. To the King, who resented Bismarck's negotiating with Prim behind his back, he tried to explain that it was only an act of politeness. In fact he did, through Bucher, agree with Prim about the tactics, the first principle of which was to make believe that Bismarck and the Prussian Foreign Office had nothing to do with the affair. Bucher returned secretly to Germany with Salazar. Now at last Leopold accepted and on June 21st King William, "with a heavy, very heavy heart," gave his consent which, according to the dynastic law, was indispensable.

So far everything had been kept secret. The plan was to make the Cortes, who had to elect the King, suddenly acquainted with the candidate and to have the election carried out so quickly that Europe should learn only the accomplished fact. It failed owing to misunderstandings. When Salazar arrived at Madrid with the acceptance, the Cortes had been postponed, the secret became known, and Prim was compelled on July 3rd to disclose the Hohenzollern candidature to the French Ambassador. Paris was at once immensely excited and Gramont ordered the Chargé d'affaires in Berlin, Le Sourd, to inquire at the Foreign Office if the Berlin Cabinet had anything to do with this "intrigue." For at this highly critical moment all the important persons were absent from Berlin. The King was taking the cure at Ems, Benedetti, the French Ambassador, was doing the same in Wildbad, and Bismarck had withdrawn into "the Pommeranian forests," to his estate Varzin. Le Sourd had to put up with Under-Secretary Thile, who gave him the answer: he knew nothing of the whole affair which did not exist for him, that is for the Foreign Office. This answer naturally made a very bad impression on Gramont, all the more so as he had been informed from Madrid that Bismarck had corresponded with Prim directly. Thereupon he made the politically unwise declaration in the Corps Législatif which suddenly showed Europe that a war was imminent.

There is as little doubt that up to this moment Bismarck had been the driving force behind the candidature, as that his assertion that it had nothing to do with Prussian politics was only a screen bound to be blown down by the strong gale of facts. There is only doubt as to whether he had carried on the affair intending it to lead to war. It would be a reflection on Bismarck's foresight, which surpassed by far that of all contemporary statesmen, to assume that he did not know (1) that the French would regard the candidature all the more as a provocation since they suffered from the continuous diplomatic defeats which he had inflicted on them since Sadowa; (2) that Napoleon would be anxious for the fate of his dynasty if he put up with this provocation; (3) that the candidature of a prince belonging to a ruling dynasty was in opposition to a principle of international practice which had clearly evolved in the nineteenth century. Moreover Napoleon had informed him in 1869 that he would not suffer a Hohenzollern on the Spanish throne. So Bismarck at least knew that he was bringing war within sight. But those who at that time had seen him at close quarters went farther and pretended that he had wanted the war. Bucher, who knew more than anybody else, has called the Hohenzollern candidature a "trap" which Bismarck had put up for Napoleon; and Prince Anton of Hohenzollern said on July 3rd, 1871, to Radowitz, the future Ambassador, that Bismarck had only raised the affair with the intention and expectation of it leading to war.

Much as Bismarck took pains to leave this in obscurity he joyfully confessed to having, after Gramont's speech, been resolved on the war and having pushed it on. Therefore he fought to the utmost against any weakening, unlike his King, who wanted to avoid a war on this issue and was working for the withdrawal of the candidature. That Benedetti called on the King and negotiated personally with him—a thing to which he was entitled according to international law—was the consequence of the negative attitude the German Foreign Office had adopted. But this caused Bismarck anxiety lest the King should substitute his own policy. The contrast is clearly shown in the telegrams exchanged between Ems and Varzin, as much by what they say as by what they do not. For the King avoids informing his Chancellor of all he is doing for the maintenance of peace. He does not tell him that he is sending a letter and messengers to Prince Hohenzollern to urge the resignation on him, nor that he asks Benedetti to stay at Ems till the expected news from the Hohenzollerns shall arrive. One can understand the King's anxiety, if one reads the excited remarks with which Bismarck comments on the telegrams from Ems. A telegram of July 11th contains an utterance of the King: "to Madrid the Prince must express himself directly." To which Bismarck adds: "Express? Why? About what? And what?" The telegram goes on: "Benedetti said he took it upon himself to stay twenty-four hours longer." Bismarck comments: "Very kind!" Telegram: "H.M. has written to Prince Hohenzollern: attitude as before, the prince will decide, he will consent." The last word is underlined by Bismarck who comments: "To what?" When—to crown all—he gets a telegram from Ems on July 12th saying Hohenzollern had telegraphed to the King: "Erbprinz resigns voluntarily," Bismarck vents his anger in a double underlining of the word "voluntarily" and a large mark of exclamation.

When Bismarck saw from Varzin that despite all his telegrams an amicable arrangement was on its way in Ems, he resolved to go there. But when he arrived in Berlin on July 12th and learned that Leopold had resigned, he interrupted his journey. What his motives were we may conclude from his words a week later to the French Chargé d'affaires who presented him with the declaration of war. After having complained about the pressure to which Benedetti had put the "poor sick King," he added: "Do you think I should not, if officially interrogated, have hurried here from the 'depth of the Pommeranian forests'? . . . I agree that if I had gone to Ems I could perhaps have prevented the war. . . ."

The withdrawal of the candidature was a great diplomatic success for France and therefore a great diplomatic defeat for Bismarck. He was resolved not to accept it and, for his part, planned energetic steps to take the offensive which was bound to end in war if France did not give in. He was saved this trouble by Napoleon and Gramont who—contrary to all political reason—were not satisfied with their success. Everybody knows the fatal order they gave Benedetti and the conversation on the promenade at Ems which ended with the rejection of the new demands by the King. Everybody also knows the story of the wording of the Ems telegram which Bismarck wrote with his mature faculty of description. If this wording has been called a falsification, the way Bismarck speaks of it is also to blame for it. Doubtless by his wording he gave the telegram a new meaning which was completely against the King's wishes. Firstly he connected two sentences which in the original had been separated by an important statement and secondly he did not mention that the King had informed the Ambassador of his having received the confirmation of the resignation from Prince Anton. Thus he gave the words of the Ems text, that "the King had told the French Ambassador through his A.D.C. that he had nothing further to tell him," the meaning of a grave and intentional snub which was as contradictory to the facts as to the opinion of the King which Bismarck knew very well. Bismarck had the telegram published in that offending version the same evening by the special editions of the papers which whipped up the people to patriotic excitement. Besides he had—though he denied it in his official declaration on July 18th—all the German and foreign courts officially informed of it. In Munich, London and St. Petersburg he even aggravated this information by the incorrect statement that "Benedetti had provocatively addressed the King against his will on the promenade." In reality the King had addressed Benedetti.

This communication had exactly the effect expected and intended by Bismarck. When King William had read the paper, he exclaimed in alarm: "That means war!" He recognised that the right of declaring war guaranteed to him by the constitution had been usurped by his Chancellor: what remained to do for him was a mere formality. The effect of Bismarck's wording becomes apparent also in Ollivier's speech before the Corps Législatif on the decisive July 15th: *"Il peut arriver qu'un Roi refuse de recevoir un ambassadeur; ce qui est blessant, c'est le refus intentionnel, divulgué dans des suppléments de journaux, dans les télégrammes adressés à toutes les cours de l'Europe"* ["It may happen that a King refuses to receive an ambassador; what is humiliating is the intentional refusal, revealed in newspaper supplements and in telegrams addressed to all the courts of Europe"]. Actually all forms of politeness had been observed towards Benedetti. *"L'offense résulte d'une publication intentionnelle"* ["The affront results from intentional publication"].

Bismarck always prided himself on having had this "intention." Those who were opposed to it he reproached with not having wanted the result of the war, the unification of Germany. To-day we know that the war between Germany and France had also quite different and much more far-reaching political and cultural consequences. Can we therefore speak of Bismarck's "guilt"? That depends on our individual point of view and our opinion on the political situation in Europe in the summer of 1870. We are justified however in speaking of Bismarck's "responsibility." He shares it with others, especially with those who on the French side were not satisfied with the success achieved, Napoleon, the Empress Eugénie, Gramont, and also Ollivier, who despite his better insight did not stop them, and the French journalists who by their unscrupulous incitement had made all reasonable deliberation impossible. But they were all rather pushed than pushing. The only superman who made tools of them all, friends or enemies, because he looked through them and knew in advance how they would react to his moves, was Bismarck.

XVIII

Shapers of Nineteenth-Century Thought

❯❯❯❯❯❯❯❯❯❯❯❯❯❯❯❯❯❯❮❮❮❮❮❮❮❮❮❮❮❮❮❮❮❮❮❮❮

Charles Darwin, 1809-1882

KARL PEARSON

Man of His Century: A Reconsideration of the Historical Significance of Karl Marx

SOLOMON F. BLOOM

❯❯❯❯❯❯❯❯❯❯❯❯❯❯❯❯❯❮❮❮❮❮❮❮❮❮❮❮❮❮❮❮❮❮❮

Charles Darwin, 1809-1882

KARL PEARSON

⇒⇒⇒⇒⇒⇒⇒⇒⇒⇒ *Published in 1923* ⇐⇐⇐⇐⇐⇐⇐⇐⇐⇐

The history of science in the nineteenth century is studded with the names of great men: Lyell, whose *Principles of Geology* (1830-1833) has been fundamental to the development of modern geology; Faraday, whose *Experimental Researches in Electricity* (1839-1855) has been basic to the growth of modern electrical science; Helmholtz, of conservation-of-energy fame; Mendel, the towering figure in the study of the mechanics of heredity; Lister, the vigorous advocate of antiseptic surgery; Wilhelm Wundt, the pioneer in the development of physiological psychology; Pasteur; and Koch, the discoverer of the germs of tuberculosis and of cholera. But of all the distinguished men of science of the nineteenth century, none captured the imagination of his contemporaries to the extent that Charles Robert Darwin did. His *Origin of Species* (1859) proved to be by far the most influential scientific work of the century; and although it injected new life into the study of biology, its influence was not confined to the realm of science. On the contrary, its repercussions were felt in innumerable spheres—in religion, social thought, psychology, anthropology, and historical writing, to mention only a few. Darwin's impact on the thought of his time was so profound that it almost defies analysis. It is fortunate, therefore, that so eminent a scientist as the late Karl Pearson ventured to undertake an appreciation of Darwin's contributions in a remarkable lecture delivered in 1923. An enthusiastic defender of the Darwinian theory of evolution by natural selection, Pearson himself made important attempts to verify statistically the Darwinian hypothesis.

When I accepted an invitation through Sir Robert Blair to lecture to you on one of the "Master Minds of Science" fully six months ago, I did not clearly realise how difficult my task was likely to be. He had asked me to give my discourse on Galileo Galilei, and there indeed was a "master mind" as I understand one. I would define a "master mind" as one who produces a revolution in current thought,—not only in scientific thought, but in the repercussion of science on human thought generally. Galilei was certainly such a master mind; and those of us who were born in mid-Victorian days have seen at least two others in the flesh, Charles Darwin and Einstein. It may seem strange at first that a mathematician should ask to take Charles Darwin, rather than Galilei, for his discourse, but Darwin has lived close enough to us to measure faithfully his personality. Yet he is far enough from us for us to judge fairly the magnitude of his work, and your present lecturer is old enough to tell you at least something of the freedom of thought which Darwin won for the men of his own generation. The fact that I am not a professed biologist might reduce the value of any judgment I might give you of what Darwin achieved in the narrower fields of specialised investigation. But to enter into those matters would require not one lecture but a course, and not one lecturer, but half-a-dozen specialists.

What was the great reversal of thought which Darwin wrought? What great truth did he bring home to you and to me—to the men in the street as apart from a relatively small group of specialised scientists? That limited aspect of Darwin's work must be my chief theme in the brief time at my disposal tonight. Try and grasp what a reversal of thought means to mankind at large. Intelligent man does not merely live and strive to extract pleasure from the universe around him. He searches for some account of that universe and his own existence in it. All living forms have developed for good or evil *curiosity*, and man among his curious next of kin, the apes, is, perhaps, the most inquisitive primate. His success has largely depended on his curiosity. If he can satisfy his curiosity by knowledge, well and good; but if he cannot, he will not consent to await experiment and observation; he fills up the aching void of his ignorance by hypothesis, by

Reprinted by permission of the Cambridge University Press. This lecture was originally published as No. XII of *Questions of the Day and of the Fray*. The footnotes which originally appeared with this essay have been omitted.

imagination based upon general impressions or limited experience often of a very slender character. Ever since so-called civilisation started, men of every race and of every country have built up cosmogonies to explain how the universe came about and how man came to be part of it. The Eskimo, the Zulu, the Hindoo, the Red Indian, the Egyptian and the Jew have each had their own separate cosmogonies, and these beliefs have played no little part in the development of those races. A false cosmogony may aid a race in a deadly struggle, or by want of elasticity may strangle it. Even today every nation has its tribal god.

Now general impressions, or conclusions not based on trained observation and experience, are never to be trusted. Unfortunately man is still close to his childhood, and thus his curiosity, if great, is yet easily satisfied like that of a child. Man's temptation is to think of a thing once, and then to accept the explanation given to him by authority. That explanation becomes a basis for his conduct in life, and he looks with distaste if not with hatred on any one who submits his philosophy of life to questioning. It involves a readjustment of his thought and very likely a readjustment of his rules of conduct, and to think all these things out afresh requires a strong intellectual effort, and even some of the best of us will shirk that. The "reversal of thought" is too severe a task for us; if old and wise, we are prepared to admit the new truth even if we cannot understand it; if old and foolish we express horror and hatred for it, because we will not admit that our mind has grown too rusty to reverse its thought. Here comes in the glory of the young, their impressions are not prescriptive truths; their minds are not too rusty to reverse their thought. Some of you may well realise the tremendous task which is falling to your lot in revising your views on

THOMAS HENRY HUXLEY: English biologist, literary artist, and controversialist. Author of a multitude of monographs on scientific subjects, he had stylistic gifts that enabled him to become a highly effective popularizer of scientific knowledge. An enthusiastic exponent of the Darwinian theory of evolution, he served, in his own words, as Darwin's "bull-dog," for his master was unaggressive and not constituted temperamentally for controversy.

SAMUEL WILBERFORCE: Bishop of Oxford who was a major force in the attack on the *Origin of Species*. At the Oxford meeting of the British Association for the Advancement of Science in 1860, he asked whether Huxley

the universe so that they may accord with the doctrine of relativity. Those who have attempted it know that it means not only a reconstruction of their ideas of the physical universe, but even of their philosophy of life, and possibly of their religious views. Well, what your generation may feel with regard to Einstein, the mid-Victorians felt with regard to Darwin, and at a much earlier date men from one end of Europe to the other felt, when Copernicus and Galilei destroyed the geocentric legend of the Universe. The Church thundered; men imagined their whole creed of life tottering, the sacred impressions of Heaven, Earth and Hell as they had held them from childhood, as Dante and Milton had pictured them were assailed; the old could not reverse their thought; the young *did*, and within half-a-century the earth was accepted as an insignificant planet of a by no means important star.

It was a similar shattering blow which Darwin struck in 1859 at the anthropocentric conception of life. The old felt their intellectual universe totter, and their anger rose against the man who would force them to a reconstruction of their ideas, to a reversal of their thought. And yet as Huxley has put it: "Darwin delivered a thought-reversing doctrine to mankind, with as little disturbance as possible of the deeply-rooted sentiments of the age."

What made Huxley express himself thus? George Fox produced a reversal of thought in thousands and Martin Luther in hundreds of thousands, and yet Huxley's lines would not apply to them. They were desperately earnest men as Darwin was earnest, but they were fanatical in that they struck to wound. Darwin never struck to wound. He was absolutely free of all personal bitterness. Those who knew him intimately all speak alike of the extraordinary charm of his character.

Listen again to what Huxley wrote of him:

"was related by his grandfather's or grandmother's side to an ape." The exact wording of Huxley's rejoinder was not recorded. But he is quoted as having answered that a man had no reason to feel ashamed that he had an ape for a grandfather, but "if there were an ancestor whom I should feel shame in recalling, it would be a *man*, a man of restless and versatile intellect, who, not content with success in his own sphere of activity, plunges into scientific questions with which he has no real acquaintance, only to obscure them by an aimless rhetoric, and distract the attention of his hearers from the real point at issue by eloquent digressions and skilled appeals to religious prejudice."

There are many to whom Mr. Darwin's death is a wholly irreparable loss. And this not merely because of his wonderfully genial, simple and generous nature, his cheerful and animated conversation, and the infinite variety and accuracy of his information; but because the more one knew of him, the more he seemed the incorporated ideal of a man of science. Acute as were his reasoning powers, vast as was his knowledge, marvellous as was his tenacious industry, under physical difficulties which would have converted nine men out of ten into aimless invalids: it was not these qualities, great as they were, which impressed those who were admitted to his intimacy with involuntary veneration, but a certain intense and almost passionate honesty, by which all his thoughts and actions were irradiated, as by a central fire. It was this rarest and greatest of endowments which kept his vivid imagination and great speculative powers within due bounds; which compelled him to undertake the prodigious labours of original investigation and of reading, upon which his published works are based; which made him accept criticisms and suggestions from anybody and everybody, not only without impatience, but with expressions of gratitude sometimes almost comically in excess of their value; which led him to allow neither himself or others to be deceived by phrases, and to spare neither time nor pains in order to obtain clear and distinct ideas upon every topic with which he occupied himself.

One could not converse with Darwin without being reminded of Socrates. There was the same desire to find some one wiser than himself; the same belief in the sovereignty of reason; the same ready humour; the same sympathetic interest in all the ways and works of men.

And again:

None have fought better, and none have been more fortunate than Charles Darwin. He found a great truth, trodden underfoot, reviled by bigots, and ridiculed by all the world; he lived long enough to see it, chiefly by his own efforts, irrefragably established in science, inseparably incorporated with the common thoughts of men, and only hated and feared by those who would revile, but dare not. What shall a man desire more than this?

Or again, read what Francis Galton wrote to his sister two days after Darwin's death:

Dearest Emma, I feel at times quite sickened at the loss of Charles Darwin. I owed more to him than to any man living or dead; and I never entered his presence without feeling as a man in the presence of a beloved sovereign. He was so wholly free of petty faults, so royal minded, so helpful and sympathetic. It is a rare privilege to have known such a man, who stands head and shoulders above his contemporaries in the science of observation. . . . I hope the first wishes of the family may yield and that Charles Darwin may be laid by the side of Newton as the two greatest of Englishmen of science. . . . The world seems so blank to me now that Charles Darwin is gone. I reverenced and loved him thoroughly.

And once more Galton spoke of Darwin at the Royal Society Anniversary Dinner, four years later:

Few can have been more profoundly influenced than I was by his publications. They enlarged the horizon of my ideas. I drew from them the breath of a fuller scientific life, and I owe more of my later scientific impulses to the influences of Charles Darwin than I can easily express. I rarely approached his genial presence without an almost overwhelming sense of devotion and reverence, and I valued his encouragement and approbation more, perhaps, than that of the whole world beside.

Or take this letter of Charles Kingsley to Sir John Lubbock, May 27, 1867:

I was deeply moved at meeting, for the first time, Darwin. I trembled before him like a boy, and longed to tell him all I felt for him, but dare not, lest he should think me a flatterer extravagant. But the modesty and simplicity of his genius were charming. Instead of teaching he only wanted to learn, instead of talking, to listen, till I found him asking me to write papers which he could as yet hardly write himself—ignorant in his general simplicity of my ignorance, and his own wisdom. And yet of that man Owen said to me—"Darwin is just as good a soul as his grandfather and just as great a goose."

Such statements might be largely multiplied, but I will give one more only, that of the celebrated botanist De Candolle, the younger, who visited Darwin eighteen months before his death in the autumn of 1880:

I remarked that Darwin in the seventies was more animated and appeared happier than when I had seen him forty-one years before. His eyes were keen and his expression lively while his photographs shew that his shape of head is rather that of a philosopher of antiquity. His talk, varied, frank and winning, entirely that of the gentleman, reminded me of that of the Oxford and Cambridge scholars. His general tone accorded with that of his writings, and this tone is the stamp of that sincerity which every one recognises as one of the causes of Darwin's success.

To the foreigner De Candolle, to his countryman Huxley and to his cousin Francis Galton, the foremost idea which personal contact with Darwin conveyed was not transcending intellect, but sincerity and simplicity of character. It was this graciousness of character, that even the outside world rapidly came to realise, which was a great factor in the victory which Darwin achieved. It was the chief reason why his thought-reversing doctrines made the minimum of disturbance in the deeply-rooted sentiments of his age. Personal character made the battle infinitely easier than it would have been had Darwin combined the highest powers of mind with truculence and self-assertion. He was so deeply hurt by these characteristics in certain of his opponents, like Wilberforce and Mivart, that he left controversy largely to others, and opposed it only with fuller collections of facts and observations.

Now we have seen that the work of Copernicus and Galilei was the destruction of the geocentric cosmogony. The work of Darwin was the destruction of another neolithic myth, the anthropocentric doctrine of living forms; it was hard to believe that the immeasurable universe had been created for man, when we recognized the insignificance of his earth and his sun. It was still harder to hold that all living forms had been independently created, to be subservient to a special creation, Man, after the work of Charles Darwin. It may be true that Man, physically by his tools, and mentally by his brain development does dominate all other living forms at this epoch. But he would be a rash man who would venture to assert that his ancestry has always done so; and only a still rasher man would venture to predict that anything we should class as man will continue to dominate all life for aeons to come. An intelligent reptile in the age of reptiles might easily have scoffed at the forecast of an inconceivable form of life, a mammal, bruising his head; and can we even assert that among mammals Man is the last word of creative evolution?

Put yourself psychologically in the position of the savages on a Pacific Island. They were men who dominated other forms of life within their ken, and they were surrounded by an impassable element, a void which they might venture on but could not cross. No man was able to grasp what was beyond its bounds. And then came a white being from nowhere, on a moving island, able to destroy the savage from a distance, utterly and wholly dominating him;—utterly and wholly unexpected and beyond his mental forecast. Always remember that there may be forms of life as unintelligible to us, and yet equally able to cross our void. I am not making a forecast, I am merely suggesting that it is not wholly wise to assume that the evolution of life has reached its highest and final form in man on this earth, and that evolution must end with the age of mammals and with man dominating living forms in his small corner of the cosmos.

Well, Darwin broke down this primitive belief that man for all the past had and for all the future would dominate life, the anthropocentric myth. But to understand the relief brought by Darwin to the minds of his generation, we must look into the state of affairs in his time, and see why the season was ripe for the arrival of a Darwin.

I do not know whether you remember what the first words in most English translations of the Bible are or were? They run B.C. 4004. That is the date fixed for the creation of the world by the Church. According to that view the universe and all its types of life were created about 6000 years ago. That is about the time of the 1st Egyptian Dynasty, which marked a fairly developed civilisation, at least two thousand years later than the neolithic woman from Egypt in our Laboratory Museum, perhaps a hundred thousand years later than the first appearance of palaeolithic man. You will say, and rightly say, that nobody now pays any attention to the dates down the margin of the Bible; they are not part of the original scriptures and may be disregarded. Quite so, nobody *now* pays any attention to the church's old dogma that the sun moved round the earth, but they did pay attention to it and had to pay attention to it, until Copernicus and Galilei controverted it. If we have ceased to believe that the world and all its forms of life were created in 4004 B.C. it is because Darwin freed us from that cramping doctrine. I must give you a little historical account of what men believed before Darwin. I can only sketch in broad lines certain features of human belief. I take first John Woodward, born in 1665— died in 1728, the founder of the Woodwardian Professorship and Geological Museum at Cambridge, and a Fellow of the Royal Society. He was one of the early collectors of fossils and he was struck by the great variety of sea shells and other marine products to be found incorporated in the stone of the quarries he visited all over the country.

But for that B.C. 4004 he might have groped his way towards great geological truths; as it was he recollected the history of the flood B.C. 2000, and wrote an "Essay towards a natural history of the Earth and terrestrial bodies, especially minerals. . . . With an account of the universal deluge, and of the effects it had on the earth," 1695. In this essay he asserts that the flood turned all the solid rocks of the earth into mud, and that this mud was gradually redeposited with the débris of the animals drowned in the flood. Dr. Arbuthnot wrote a criticism of this deluge theory; he criticised it not only from the standpoint of the physics of rock and mud, but also from the Biblical story, because if the surface of the earth were covered by mud, and all its strata reduced to a plastic condition, how was it possible that the old rivers should reappear after the deluge? Why as we are told in Genesis, Chapter 11, did the pre-diluvial rivers and pre-diluvial countries re-appear in post-diluvial times? Thus Arbuthnot cited Moses to con-fute Moses. It is needless here to cite various hypotheses to account for the existence of fossils in the lower strata of rock masses. In the 18th century some thought they had been placed there at the creation itself; others believed that the Devil inserted them to tempt man. With a complete history of the world supposed known from its creation in 4004 B.C. no real solution was possible.

Before Darwin there were two great naturalists Linnaeus 1707-1778, and Buffon born in the same year as Linnaeus and dying in 1788, twenty years before the birth of Darwin. Huxley writes of these two that they are the only naturalists comparable with Darwin. Yet Linnaeus directly talks of the separate creation of the various forms of life. In his great work *Systema naturae* he defines man as the ulti-mate purpose of creation. He is cramped as much as Woodward by that B.C. 4004. If we turn to the more free-thinking and more free-acting Buffon do we find that he has thrown off the fetters? No, he is still bound by them. It is perfectly true that Buffon does not accept such explanations as that the fossil shells were dropped by pilgrims or by armies crossing the Alps. He does ask whether the fossil bones of apes were those of apes who carried the shells hundreds of miles inland! The discovery of marine fossils hundreds of miles inland was partially opening men's minds to the immensely long history of the earth. But Buffon had no explanation ready for this enormous variety of life, and his mind like so many of our minds was built in water-tight compart-ments. He recognised that the span of man's life was now and had been in the time of David three-score years and ten. But he felt it essential to reconcile this with the biblical information as to the age of some of the patriarchs. He tells us that the chief source of death in man is the hardening of the tissues, so that they cannot restore themselves. When the world was young gravity had not condensed its materials, everything was more plastic, and all substances were softer. Hence it came about that they did not harden so rapidly. The tissues of Methuselah remained softer longer than those of modern man, and therefore he lived longer! Thus for Buffon the world was young in 3150 B.C. He had not freed himself once and for all from the neolithic myth.

But the mind of man was growing restless in its bondage to this myth. It was not only the mass of fossils in solid rock, which could not be explained by any deluge, but must have taken millions of years to lay down; it was also the study of the classification of living forms which began to make men doubt a single creation of separate species. Erasmus Darwin (1794), Charles' grandfather, was convinced that species vary and that life was deduced from some simple original, but he could not attribute the changes to anything but the inheritance of acquired characters. The individual was continually striving and *willing* to achieve something, attempting to fit itself into an unoccupied corner of nature, and its offspring inherited the modifications the parents had produced in their organs or habits. Lamarck following Erasmus Darwin—probably unconsciously—was a naturalist with a far wider knowledge of living forms, and was able to make out a stronger case for evolution, which he published in the year of Darwin's birth 1809. But his explanation of evolution was as unsatisfactory as Erasmus Darwin's; forms of life *willed* to be other than they were, they then became other and transmitted their modifications to their descendants. The views of Erasmus Darwin and Lamarck have been advocated later by Samuel Butler and Bernard Shaw, but the discussions of these moderns are of little value as they have small if any acquaintance with the immense mass of material which Darwin's theory at once codified. Lamarck and Erasmus Darwin are chiefly of value as indicating how science was struggling before Charles Darwin against the bondage of a special creation.

But that bondage was not broken by the evolutionists before Charles Darwin. Erasmus Darwin was branded as an infidel by more than one writer of his generation. Lamarck died in 1829 a disappointed man, whose views on evolution had been destroyed by Cuvier (1769-1832), who insisted on the permanence of species, and reconciled this with palaeontological evidence by asserting that the earth had been subject to a series of cataclysms which enabled its Creator to produce afresh new series of living forms. Cuvier would save creation by replacing one creation by a number of successive creations. Thus he forged anew the chains which cramped the mind of man.

You may suggest that while science had not solved the problem of evolution, it had at least thrown off the belief in B.C. 4004. I do not think, if you study the writings of men of even great ability between 1850 and 1860 you will press your suggestion. I will take two out of many instances I could cite. Francis Galton had a mind far above the average. In 1854, in addition to many years of academic study, he had travelled widely, and seen men of many races. Well, Galton talks in his *Art of Travel* of the use of fire-sticks, and he says:

> The method of obtaining fire by rubbing sticks together was at one time nearly universal. It seems remarkable that the time of discovery of the art of fire-making is not recorded in the Bible. We may easily imagine that our first parents obtained their fires from natural sources; of which, some parts of the Caucasus at least, abound in examples. But when Cain was sent an outcast, how did *he* obtain fire? It is remarkable that his descendants are precisely those who invented metallurgy, and arts requiring fire. We might almost theorize to the effect that he or they discovered the art of fire-making, and pushed the discovery into its applications.

Do you grasp now what I mean when I speak of that bondage of 4004 B.C.? We are fairly certain now that the art of fire-making was known 40,000 years ago, possibly 100,000. How could man envisage his own history with that dead weight on his mind?

Now take another case, that of Speke the great African traveller writing on Africa in the very early sixties. He writes thus of the Negroes:

> If my account should not harmonise with preconceived notions as to primitive races, I cannot help it. I profess accurately to describe naked Africa—Africa in those places where it has not received the slightest impulse, whether for good or for evil, from European civilisation. If the picture be a dark one, we should, when contemplating these sons of Noah, try and carry our mind back to that time when our poor elder brother Ham was cursed by his father and condemned to be the slave of both Shem and Japheth; for as they were then, so

they appear to be now—a striking existing proof of the Holy Scriptures. But one thing must be remembered; whilst the people of Europe and Asia were blessed by communion with God through the medium of His prophets, and obtained divine laws to regulate their ways and keep them in mind of Him who made them, the Africans were excluded from this dispensation, and consequently have no idea of an overruling Providence or a future state; they therefore trust to luck and to charms, and think only of self-preservation in this world.

We know now that the Negro existed many tens of thousands of years before the date assigned to Ham! How could there be any anthropology, any real study of man's origin and development under such bondage?

I will give you one more illustration of how these Mosaic fetters ate into and cankered the very spirit of scientific investigation. We have seen what difficulties the discovery of fossils caused Woodward and Arbuthnot. An equal difficulty arose when not only fossils were found, but the artefacts, the tools men had made and used tens of thousands of years ago.

As late as 1860 Lartet presented to the French Academy of Sciences a memoir entitled: "On the geological antiquity of the human race in Western Europe"; it was an epoch-making memoir, but *that Academy printed only the title of it*. As Cartailhac notes it was too early to speak such truths to the Academy of Sciences; it did not comprehend that it placed itself on the very outskirts of progress in geology and anthropology by such an action. Three years later the Perpetual Secretary of the Academy, Elie de Beaumont, ventured to say that he did not believe that man had been a contemporary of the mammoth; that the view of Cuvier—i.e. the theory of repeated re-creations after cataclysms—was the product of genius, and it had not been destroyed. He asked if flint tools were not really of Roman origin!

Nay, even ten years later in 1872 the French Academy of Sciences declined to elect Charles Darwin to its zoological section, and an eminent member of the Academy wrote to *Les Mondes*:

> What has closed the doors of the Academy to Mr. Darwin is that the science of those of his books which have made his chief title to fame—the *Origin of Species* and the *Descent of Man*—is not science, but a mass of assertions and absolutely gratuitous hypotheses, often evidently fallacious. This kind of publication and these theories are a bad example, which a body that respects itself cannot encourage.

Darwin was twenty-five years collecting and digesting material for those books; no books written before or since have placed before their readers such a mass of well-correlated facts and observations. Yet both are here dismissed as a mere "mass of assertions and absolutely gratuitous hypotheses" as if they had been the product of a sensation-monger—not an indefatigable worker and cautious thinker like Charles Darwin.

Let us conclude this section of our discourse by citing a few words spoken in Manchester in 1901 by John Morley—now Lord Morley—they show that not only the theologians, not only the high priests of science in France, but the great men of politics failed to understand how Darwin had broken the fetters of men's minds:

> "I remember," Mr. Morley said, "once going with Mr. Gladstone one Sunday afternoon to pay a visit to Mr. Darwin. It was in the seventies. As I came away I felt that no impression had reached him that in that modest, single-minded, low-browed lover of truth, that searcher of the secrets of Nature—that there was no impression in Mr. Gladstone's mind that he had seen one who from his Kentish hill-top was shaking the world."

Such was the shadow that the spirit behind those figures—4004 B.C.—cast across the world of thought!

I am young enough to have escaped the dogmatic teaching which was impressed upon the pre-Darwinian child. But I am not sure it has come to an end even yet. Not so many years ago in a village in Southern Germany the priest with whom I had become intimate in our evening talks in the village inn asked me, if I would like to listen to his lesson in the village school. I readily consented and this is what I heard, starting with his opening words:

> Der Geistliche [Priest]: Wer war der erste Mann? [Who was the first man?]
> Die Kinder [Children] (a hundred and fifty simultaneously): Adam.
> Der Geistliche: Wer war das erste Weib? [Who was the first woman?]
> Die Kinder (a hundred and fifty simultaneously): Eva.
> Der Geistliche: Zu welcher Zeit war die Welt erschaffen? [When was the world created?]
> Die Kinder (a hundred and fifty simultaneously): Viertausend und vier Jahre vor Christi. [4004 B.C.]

Now can you grasp what that means? It means that the astonishing history of life in the world, the glorious story of man's own evolution lasting for far more than 100,000 years has been cut off at its topmost branches. And the result is not only the hopeless fogging of the child's perspective. There is a worse side to it. This legend created, perhaps, 6000 years ago—a mere yesterday in the life of man—has been unfortunately attached to the child's instruction in morals. Thus when he finds later in life that the legend has no relation to our real knowledge of man's past, he is liable not unnaturally, if unreasonably, to discard both.

I have said I am too young,—or perhaps I ought to have said too fortunate in my parentage,—to have been forced under that dogmatic yoke. But let us see what men, who had been, felt about Darwin's teaching.

Let me read to you a letter of Francis Galton to Darwin dated 1869, when Darwin had been reading Galton's *Hereditary Genius*.

Dec. 24, 1869.

My dear Darwin, It would be idle to speak of the delight your letter has given me for there is no one in the world whose approbation in these matters can have the same weight as yours. Neither is there any one whose approbation I prize more highly on purely personal grounds, because I always think of you in the same way as converts from barbarism think of the teacher who first relieved them from the burden of their superstition. I used to be wretched under the weight of the old fashioned 'argument from design' of which I felt though I was unable to prove to myself the worthlessness. Consequently the appearance of your "Origin of Species" formed a real crisis in my life; your book drove away the constraint of my old superstition as if it had been a nightmare and was the first to give me freedom of thought.

And again at the Darwin-Wallace celebration in 1908, Galton turned to the main point on which he felt our generation's gratitude to Darwin should be keenest—the freedom Darwin gave us from dogmatic bondage:

You have listened to-day to many speakers and I have little new to say, little indeed that would not be a repetition, but I may add that this occasion has called forth vividly my recollection of the feelings of gratitude that I had towards the originators of the then new doctrine which burst the enthraldom of the intellect which the advocates of the argument from design had woven round us. It gave a sense of freedom to all the people who were thinking of these matters, and that sense of freedom was very real and very vivid at the time. If a future Auguste Comte arises who makes a calendar in which the days are devoted to the memory of those who have been the beneficent intellects of mankind, I feel sure that this day, the 1st of July, will not be the least brilliant.

I have already indicated that there were keen evolutionists before Darwin but none of them had propounded any reasonable theory of how evolution takes place, still less had they exhibited any correlated system of facts as flowing from their theories. Let us read what Huxley wrote about the matter, for he had felt the pulse of the chief scientists of his generation:

> I imagine that most of those of my contemporaries who thought seriously about the matter, were very much in my own state of mind—inclined to say to both Mosaists and Evolutionists, "a plague on both your houses!" and disposed to turn aside from an interminable and apparently fruitless discussion, to labour in the fertile fields of ascertainable fact. And I may, therefore, further suppose that the publication of the Darwin and Wallace papers in 1858, and still more that of the "Origin" in 1859, had the effect on them of the flash of light, which to a man who has lost himself in a dark night, suddenly reveals a road which, whether it takes him straight home or not, certainly goes his way. That which we were looking for, and could not find, was a hypothesis respecting the origin of known organic forms, which assumed the operation of no causes but such as could be proved to be actually at work. We wanted not to pin our faith to that or any other speculation, but to get hold of clear and definite conceptions which could be brought face to face with facts and have their validity tested. The "Origin" provided us with the working hypothesis we sought. Moreover it did the immense service of freeing us for ever from the dilemma—refuse to accept the creation hypothesis and what have you to propose that can be accepted by any cautious reasoner? In 1857, I had no answer ready, and I do not think any one else had. A year later, we reproached ourselves with dulness for being perplexed by such an inquiry. My reflection, when I first made myself master of the central idea of the "Origin" was, "How extremely stupid not to have thought of that!"

Therein you see the master mind as exhibited by Darwin. He realised that his time was sick of vague hypotheses whether creational or evolutional, and he gave them a theory which at least correlated a multitude of facts,—a theory by the light of which men have found it possible to work fertilely for fifty and more years; a theory which created embryology and anthropology, and which simply caused geology, palaeontology, botany and zoology to be rewritten. Call "natural selection" a working hypothesis, if you please, and you will still find it is the source of all the best work in the science of life for more than half a century. But is not all scientific advance made by the launching by master minds of "working hypotheses"? What else was the law of gravitation as propounded by Newton? He no more explained why things gravitated than Darwin explained why individuals vary. And although the law of gravitation fructified physical science for more than 100 years, we know it is not absolutely the whole truth and now start with a wider "working hypothesis." If we said that of natural selection, we should not in the least detract from the services of Charles Darwin; his would still remain a master mind, worthy to be placed in life as in death alongside Newton's. But if we said that the day of natural selection is passed should we be speaking the truth? We should at least be echoing the cry of some dozens of smaller minds, who declare that natural selection is wanting and give nothing in its place. That is not the line on which the great steps in science have been made. The giant has reached further to the summit, because he stood on the shoulders of the great of the past. Natural selection will cease to be a part of the scientific creed only when a wider working hypothesis is discovered by another master mind, and there is no sign among the biologists of our generation of a greater than Darwin. Their work has been the steady, necessary, if unsensational task of reaping where Darwin sowed, and the harvest is still after 60 years incompletely garnered.

If you read the chapter in Sir Francis Darwin's *Life and Letters of Charles Darwin* which is entitled "Religion," you will understand how carefully Darwin really thought over these matters, although he was reticent with regard to them, and very modest as to the results of his thoughts on religious and moral topics. But he recognised fully that the belief in a creation and flood some few thousand years ago was an intolerable bondage for human thought. He felt also, as Huxley felt and Galton felt, that the argument from design, even if applied to the variations on which evolution was based, was very fallacious.

If some variations seem beautifully adapted to their use, it was impossible to assert this as a general truth. Was it, he asked, direct purpose which caused the frame and mental qualities of a dog to vary so that a breed could be formed of indomitable ferocity, with jaws fitted to pin down the bull for man's brutal sport? He might have cited also the delicate apparatus of the parasite, which enables it to fix itself firmly in the intestines of its host.

Writing his autobiography in 1876 Darwin says:

> Although I did not think much about the existence of a personal God until a considerably later period of my life [later than the 'Beagle' voyage, 1836-39, when he discarded the Old Testament as a revelation] I will give the vague conclusions to which I have been driven. The old argument from design in Nature, as given by Paley, which formerly seemed to me so conclusive, fails, now that the law of natural selection has been discovered. We can no longer argue that, for instance, the beautiful hinge of a bivalve-shell must have been made by an intelligent being, like the hinge of a door by man. There seems to be no more design in the variability of organic beings, and in the action of natural selection, than in the course which the wind blows.

Pain and suffering have been looked upon as instruments designed for man's moral improvement, but other sentient beings suffer without any moral improvement. These things Darwin held were compatible with the view that all organic beings have been developed through variation and natural selection, but not with an anthropocentric universe created for man by an intelligent and just First Cause.

Some of you will remember the wonderful paragraph with which the *Origin of Species* closes. I cannot refrain from citing it again here:

> It is interesting to contemplate a tangled bank, clothed with many plants of many kinds, with birds singing on the bushes, with various insects flitting about, and with worms crawling through the damp earth, and to reflect that these elaborately constructed forms, so different from each other, and dependent upon each other in so complex a manner, have all been produced by laws acting among us. These laws, taken in the largest sense, being Growth with Reproduction; Inheritance which is almost implied by reproduction; Variability from the indirect and direct action of the conditions of life, and from use and disuse; a Ratio of Increase so high as to lead to a Struggle for Life, and as a consequence to Natural Selection, entailing Divergence of Character and the Extinction of less-improved forms. This, from the war of Nature, from famine and death, the most exalted object

which we are capable of conceiving, namely, the production of the higher animals, directly follows. There is grandeur in this view of life, with its several powers, having been originally breathed by a Creator into a few forms or into one; and that, whilst this planet has gone cycling on according to the fixed law of gravity, from so simple a beginning endless forms most beautiful and most wonderful have been, and are being evolved.

This passage is of very great value for (i) it indicates how the commonest objects of our experience—the population of a hedge-row—have since the doctrine of Darwin become replete with the most intensely suggestive problems connected not only with our views of life, but with our religious notions; (ii) the passage is Darwin's own summary of Darwinism, and as Huxley put it in a letter to Galton of 1883, in our possession in this laboratory:

> Which Faith except a man do keep whole and undefiled, without doubt he shall be made a bishop.

(iii) It indicates that in 1859 Darwin still looked to a First Cause having an intelligent mind in some degree analogous to that of man. He says himself:

> This conclusion was strong in my mind about the time, as far as I remember, when I wrote the "Origin of Species," and it is since that time that it has very gradually grown weaker. But then arises the doubt, can the mind of man, which as I fully believe, has been developed from a mind as low as that possessed by the lowest animals, be trusted when it draws such grand conclusions?
>
> I cannot pretend to throw the least light on such abstruse problems. The mystery of the beginning of all things is insoluble by us; and I for one must be content to remain an Agnostic.

Thus modestly, thus temperately, without aggressiveness and only for himself, spoke Charles Darwin nearly half-a-century ago. If there be those today or in the future who feel more certain of their knowledge of the truth, let them give utterance to it, ever remembering that one—a master mind—felt it needful in such matters to avoid all aggressiveness and to apologise for touching a matter so abstruse as probably to exceed the present powers of the human mind.

I have told you that I am young enough to have escaped practically the dogmatic teaching in childhood which placed in bondage the minds of the generations preceding Darwin, and Huxley and Galton.

But I am old enough to remember the battles of the sixties and seventies, and the joy we young men then felt when we saw that wretched date B.C. 4004, replaced by a long vista of millions of years of development. Just as much as the older men we looked upon Charles Darwin as our deliverer, the man who had given a new meaning to our life and to the world we inhabited. And if you will but study him and interpret the universe by his doctrine you will realise that he is still Darwin, the Liberator, for you also. Yet as you study him for his mind, you will discover that he is not only Darwin the Liberator, and Darwin the Naturalist, but beyond the greatness of his intellect, there is a greatness of character, he is Nature's gracious gentleman. Carlyle forgot to include when he wrote his *Hero Worship*, the 'Hero as Gentleman.' We are happy in being able to admire in our Hero of Science alike his intellect and his character.

If we take this Darwinian creed as stated by Darwin on the last page of the *Origin of Species* more than 60 years ago are there points in which we might venture today to modify it? I would speak with all humility when I say that I think there are. Darwin left open possibilities, which I think more recent research would close. He states that variability arises "from the indirect and direct action of the conditions of life and from use and disuse."

Now some variation does and can arise without any variation in the conditions of life. The two dogs I now show you were born in one litter of the same two parents. Their variation from one another can only be due to one source—the germ-plasm in the reproductive cells of their parents was not homogeneous. But if variations so great as these are possible, is it not adequate to suppose the bulk of variation to arise from heterogeneity in the reproductive germs? Darwin thought that environmental conditions would modify an organ and that these modifications could be transmitted to their offspring. I feel sure that no environmental changes could make one of those dogs resemble the other, that heterogeneity of germ-plasm carried by either parent is far more influential in producing variation than any direct or indirect effect of the conditions of life. There would be nothing surprising, however, in two dogs like Chang having offspring like Topsy or two dogs like Topsy having offspring like Chang. For the heterogeneity lies not in their bodily characters, but in their germ cells. The great truths that we have learnt since Darwin's are:

(i) that the chief source of variation lies in the heterogeneity of the germ-plasm of the individual;

(ii) that the bodily characters of an individual are not a complete index to his germ-plasm, but only a general indication of it;

(iii) that an individual is only the bearer of the germ-plasm of his stock or stirp, he does not create it, nor is it substantially modified by his life or environment.

The child is like his parent, not because he is the product of his parent, but because his parent and he, partially, are products of the same germ-plasm, which both his parent and his grandparent have handed on. This continuity of the germ-plasm was first insisted on by Francis Galton, who in 1872 announced for the first time the true relation of parent to child, and gave a very deep extension to the Darwinian doctrine. The continuity of the germ-plasm, the fact that the transient individual is only a conduit pipe—so to speak—for the eternal germ-plasm, the non-perishing source of life, involves the unity of all life. The germ-plasm which finds its place in our reproductive cells has passed through millions of years of selection, indirect selection by the destruction of those bearers of it with unsuitable bodily characters—i.e. the Darwinian natural selection—and direct selection at the reproduction of each new individual—i.e. the Galtonian germinal selection, which produces the phenomena of variation. But the germ-plasma of all living things is and has been through the millions of years of evolution a unity, constantly differentiated in its heterogeneity and as constantly recombined. As one perishable generation hands down its germ-plasm to the next, so each age of living forms has handed on the torch of life to its successor, the age of invertebrates handed its germ-plasm to the age of fishes; the age of fishes to that of amphibia, and the age of amphibia to that of reptiles, and thence it came to the age of mammals. It is a strange but, I think, true conception that while we as individuals perish, we carry with us perpetually multiplying cells which have passed through all the lower forms of life!

A crude analogy might be taken from a tree, representing the germ-plasm as the sap, the branches as genera, the twigs as species and the leaves and flowers as perishing individuals. The leaves and flowers were they capable of sensation might feel themselves the essential units. But they are not, they perish, and the tree as a whole lives on putting forth new branches, new twigs and fresh leaves. It is the real unity, a unity far beyond the comprehension of the individual leaves. So it comes about that the life of the whole organic world, whose purpose we as ephemeral individuals may fail to understand, continues to develop and expand without regard to the fleeting leaves. We are but parts of that larger whole, whose origin and final purpose are beyond the limited scope of human intelligence.

If the geneticists tell you that they have tried in vain to produce new species by germinal selection, there are two valid answers that can be given to them: the first is that it is difficult if not impossible in the laboratory to reproduce those conditions of duration and intensity of physical stress under which it is highly probable that species originated, and the second is: that life is no longer young; our tree is adult, it can no more put forth twigs, much less branches, only individual leaves, and leaves do not produce twigs. In other words the fundamental germ-plasm is now so differentiated, that no further species formation is possible; that was only possible in the heterogeneity of its youth. That the geneticists have not yet produced a new species does not seem to me a valid argument against Darwinism, unless we assume that the production of new species must ever be going on whatever stage the total of living forms has reached. The stages in the life-history of the universal germ-plasm in which differentiation could produce markedly different new forms may be long past. At any rate experiment in this sense should begin with low and little specialised forms— certainly not mammals. It would be absurd to suppose that very specialised man could be obtained from the very specialised apes known to us. But that both might be obtained from a far less specialised primate is not an unreasonable supposition. We are far from having found that ancestral primate as yet, but since Darwin's day our knowledge of the history of man has immensely increased, and we know something of his form and his tools for at least 100,000 years. That knowledge does not run contrary to Darwin's views. We have not yet reached the common link, but what has been found carries us back both in skeleton and form of brain nearer and nearer to a possible common ancestor. The fossil of such a being, which we should fail to classify as either ape or man might be found any day now, and if found would certainly not create the astonishment today that it would have done 50 years ago, because the gap to be filled would be far less. Meanwhile excavators amuse themselves with such modernities as Tutankhamen, when within a relatively few miles of his tomb, at

Fayûm, they might conceivably discover what would be many thousand times of greater scientific importance.

It is time, however, that I concluded this brief survey of what Darwin did for his generation and what he has done for all time. He broke down a barrier and let the waters of scientific inquiry flow out upon as wide and as arid a land as Newton fertilised. To us as everyday men, and not zoologists or botanists or anthropologists by profession, he opened up all the vistas of the ages. We look back through hundreds of thousands of years of growth in living forms, where we were pulled up at a few thousands by a dogmatic beginning of all things. And what have we lost? Not necessarily the idea of an ultimate First Cause, but of a First Cause, which produced in a way unintelligible to us, a multitude of living forms all especially provided with, not only the instinct, but the means of killing each other, a creator who for some inexplicable reason charged the rocks with fossils and produced enormous reptiles in a world just like our own, the climate and conditions of which were totally unsuited to them!

Darwin has expressed definitely his belief that "man in the distant future will be a far more perfect creature than he now is." That belief of Darwin's might almost be spoken of now-a-days as a truth, if we judge from our present knowledge of the history of man for more than 100,000 years, and predict from that experience of the past man's probable future. Evolution has even from the standpoint of anatomist and psychologist worked towards the perfecting of man, as in a certain sense it has worked to the perfecting of most living forms. Evolution is compatible with a First Cause, even with a First Cause which had in view the development of more perfect living forms, if by methods that appear to the reason of man amoral if not immoral. But to all such final problems Darwin would and did reply. They are impossible for me to answer. "The safest conclusion seems to me that the whole subject is beyond the scope of man's intellect, but man can do his duty."

What did Darwin mean by "man doing his duty"? I think we can interpret the phrase by his own doctrine. Man is governed primarily by heredity and by the facts of variation. Nature has driven him harshly forward on the paths towards being a more perfect creature, by the extermination of the physically and mentally less fit. Is it not the duty of man to accelerate Nature's progress? For if there be that First Cause, which gave natural laws to the universe for its development, then these indicate the purpose of its creator, and the interests as well as the duty of man are to hasten the processes of evolution. As Galton, Darwin's cousin said, it is the *religious* duty of man to see that man is better and better born. But that is another story and is an inference, not the moral drawn by Darwin himself from his doctrine. His task lay in breaking our fetters, in producing a revolution in or a reversal of human thought. It is ours to enjoy the immense fields he opened to human inquiry and to study not only the bearing of his teaching on our religious beliefs, but no less its deep significance for our moral judgments. . . .

Man of His Century

A Reconsideration of the Historical Significance of Karl Marx

SOLOMON F. BLOOM

═══════ *Published in 1943* ═══════

Today no scholar would deny that the nineteenth-century book that has proved to be the most influential in world history is Karl Marx's *Das Kapital*. Its first volume appeared in 1867, and the second and third volumes were published posthumously in 1885 and 1894. There are many ironies connected with the influence of this work. Probably the greatest of them is that Marx tended to belittle the importance of ideas in history and concentrated, rather, on the role of impersonal economic forces; but what has happened to his own ideas has belied the insignificance which he generally ascribed to noneconomic forces. The literature on Marx and Marxism is, of course, impressive in a quantitative sense. Qualitatively, however, it is as a rule far from impressive. Most of it is written either by people to whom Marx is God and *Das Kapital* the Bible or by people to whom Marx is the Devil and *Das Kapital* the Devil's book. Because thoughtful and unemotional evaluations of Marx and Marxism are rare, the present essay stands out all the more for its excellence. Written by Solomon F. Bloom, of Brooklyn College, one of the ablest American commentators on Marx, it is notable not only for its content but for its clear and straightforward prose.

I

Some countries may escape the stage of capitalism, and some may perhaps avoid socialism, but none has so far been able to escape a stage of "Marxism." Each great cultural area of the globe seems fated to live through an absorbing and usually bitter controversy over the

Reprinted by special permission from *The Journal of Political Economy*, LI (1943), 494-505. Publisher, the University of Chicago Press. The footnotes which originally appeared with this essay have been omitted.

merits and relevance of the doctrines of Karl Marx. The pattern of this experience has by now become tritely familiar. The controversy is usually preceded by a more or less prolonged period of neglect and indifference. At a moment of social stress the controversialists proceed to divide the nation into opposing camps, taking care to leave no articulate citizen uncommitted. The defenders, setting out from the premise that a literal acceptance of Marx's writings is somehow basic to the Socialist ideal, end up by incapacitating themselves for independent judgment; and the orthodox literature tends to oscillate between the poles of eulogy and apology. The opponents undertake to question the validity of everything he asserted and the decency of everything he desired. This is done so thoroughly that nonbelligerent critics are moved to intervene, as Thorstein Veblen did once, with the suggestion that Marx was "neither ignorant, imbecile, nor disingenuous" and that he ought to be interpreted as though he might make sense. The period of "reconsidering" him anew then begins.

The United States has reproduced this pattern, but naturally in its own way. For a long time Marx was fairly ignored. This was, in fact, the last great country of the West to occupy itself at all seriously with his thought. Before the first World War, only a few academic people, German immigrant circles, certain Europeanized writers, and the small and uninfluential Socialist party troubled themselves about Marxism. If a few were interested, fewer still were won over. Henry Adams thought he should have been a Marxist "by rights, but some narrow trait of the New England nature seemed to blight socialism, and he tried in vain to make himself a convert." In one of his less biting references to Marx, Mr. Justice Holmes wrote to Sir Frederick Pollock: "I have begun Karl Marx's book, but although he strikes me as a great man I can't imagine a combination less to my taste than Hegel

---

CHARTISM: Radical movement in the Britain of the late 1830's and the 1840's. Although the Chartists agreed as to the necessity of political reform in a democratic direction, they disagreed basically about social and economic changes. Some were not interested in nonpolitical reforms; some favored moderate social and economic reforms; and some supported far-reaching social and economic changes. These disagreements within the ranks of Chartism contributed to its decline by the late 1840's.

BENEDETTO CROCE: Twentieth-century Italian philosopher, historian, and

and political economy." This attitude was not unusual in the more enlightened American community.

The first World War forms the cultural watershed in this field,
as in so many others. Specifically, it was the Bolshevik Revolution of
November, 1917, that brought the United States rather suddenly face
to face with Marxism; but it is interesting to reflect, by way of contrast, that if Russia had not become aware of it some two generations
earlier the Revolution could hardly have taken a Marxist form. During
the "normalcy" of the 1920's, however, Marxism still remained an esoteric concern, for all the febrile activity of the Communists. Great men
learn from the experience of others, but great countries apparently can
learn only from their own. And so it was the consequences of the
crash of 1929 and their coincidence with reports of the successful operation of the First Five-Year Plan in the Soviet Union that made Americans more sensitive to the attractions of Marxism, as it also made many
of them responsive to New-Dealism, industrial unionism, and Town-
sendism. The doctrines of Marx were suddenly "taken up" with the
intensity of a fad. Publishers, journalists, teachers, labor leaders, even
clubwomen, discovered an interest in the materialistic interpretation of
history, the theory of the class struggle and the "withering-away" of
the state. "Dialectics" almost became American idiom. But this fashion,
like others, proved fickle; and presently the Russian purges, our own
modest recovery, and especially the Soviet-Nazi pact of 1939 brought
about a considerable revulsion of feeling. From all sides, Marxism was
quite as suddenly questioned, "autopsied," revised. The wheel gradually swung full circle, and American opinion assumed an increasingly
critical, and even hostile, attitude toward Marxism. That was the stage
we had reached when Hitler invaded Russia. Our stake in that campaign and the extent of Russia's resistance softened that attitude but

statesman. A towering figure in twentieth-century intellectual history, he
has been one of the profoundest critics of the materialism of Marx and
Marxism.

LEWIS HENRY MORGAN: American anthropologist whose *Ancient Society*
(1877) is a basic volume in the literature of anthropology. Dealing with
the evolution of culture through successive stages, the work was seized
upon by Marx and Engels to substantiate their materialist conception of
history.

could hardly reverse it. It was too soon, for one thing. There is an unwritten law of fashion that prohibits the early return of a recent favorite.

Now, in a sense, such treatment is high tribute to Marx. For it pits his thought not against that of other men but against history itself. His significance is judged in terms of events rather than of ideas, and interest in his doctrines fluctuates with the fortunes of economic life. At bottom, however, it is the treatment accorded Christianity by King Clovis of the Franks. Pressed in battle, the King promised to be baptised if the Christian God helped him conquer. He conquered —and was converted. But the understanding of Christianity was no more advanced by the action of Clovis than the understanding of Marxism is deepened by following the shuttlecock of domestic and international affairs.

Of course, the history and cultural peculiarity of the reaction of Americans to Marx does not exhaust his relevance to their country. We sense that strongly, and hence the question of his comparative pertinence to his age and our own must remain a concern of American thought for some time to come. Perhaps it is not necessary to review and assay all the wide-ranging work of Marx in order to indicate the implied historical change. It is not proposed here to discuss his theoretical economics or to measure precisely his corrections of Hegelian "dialectics." After all, it was hardly the academic validity of any individual contribution that persuaded the rest of the Western world and eventually also the United States to reckon with him. On the economic side it was rather the occasional striking appositeness of his diagnosis and prognosis of capitalism; on the intellectual and spiritual side it was his broader reflections on the nature of society, culture, and the past and future path of historical development and, especially, the applicability of these reflections to the institutions and movements of his time.

The followers of Marx were not, however, content to look at him in this light. They did not represent his doctrines as a view of the world bearing the earmarks of a great epoch, or Marx as but another theorist and statesman. Instead, they insisted that he had propounded a method of thought so novel and revolutionary and so powerful that we could use it to control in large measure, as well as to explain, the stream of economic and political events. Marx was pictured much in the role of a Vulcan who had forged a key to unlock the social secrets of the past and pry open the door of the future. In short, the world was asked to treat and accept Marxism as an internally consistent, all-inclusive, and fully articulated philosophy of man, society and polity.

It is interesting to re-examine this claim before employing the more customary technique of balancing contribution against limitation and fitting him into the framework of his century. As a crucial test it may be sufficient to consider some of the more important constituents of Marxism regarded as "system." Historical materialism is the speculative premise from which other aspects of the "system" are derivations and conclusions; the Marxist conception of politics represents a most vital application to practical affairs; and the Marxist view of human character must reach close to the core of a system whose chief driving force is an attempt to reorganize society fundamentally and elevate the position of humanity. These three conceptions, then—of materialism, of the state, and of man—are not only intrinsically important; they are representative issues of Marxism.

II

The economic interpretation of history, broadly understood, is, of course, much older than Marxism. From Swift and Mandeville to Turgot and Smith, many leaders of the Enlightenment underlined the economic factor in human affairs. So vigorous, indeed, was this current that the eighteenth century must sometime appear to be more materialistic than the nineteenth. Marx refined that interpretation, however, and—what is more to the point—employed it with great effect. He urged that the character of social and cultural life is shaped by the material forces of production. He drew a distinction between basic forces and "superstructural" ideas or institutions and, by implication, promised to explain their correlation. However, he never elaborated this view adequately, and each aspect of it has been the subject of an indecisive debate.

As closely as one may get to them, the basic forces are a mixture of technological and social factors, which it is difficult to disentangle and isolate. The "economic structure" of society consists of the "sum total" of "the relations of production" that men perforce establish in social work. That is "the real foundation" of the legal and political "superstructure." Yet that "real foundation" itself corresponds to—shall we say, rests upon?—"a definite stage of development of their material powers of production." It now appears that the "powers" of production are causally antecedent to its "relations." In fact, when these "material forces" conflict with "the relations of production," they proceed to overthrow the latter. That is what is meant by social revolution. But whatever its ultimate meaning, whether technological or social or both, "the mode of production conditions the general character of the social, political and intellectual processes of life."

The "general character" turns out to be a crucial phrase, for it is by no means clear that these "processes of life" rest definitely or wholly upon the method of production. One instance will perhaps suffice. In discussing the art of the ancient Greeks, Marx acknowledged that, while there were limiting social conditions for artistic expression (mythological epics, for example, are not usually produced in an age of science), it was impossible to account for the greatness of classical art by reference to the contemporary method of production. His explanation was, indeed, as far as possible from being materialistic: the Greeks belonged to the childhood of the human race; they were normal rather than "ill bred or precocious" children; childhood has an eternal charm; Greek art will therefore always appeal powerfully to men. Under the circumstances it was natural for Marx to make this comment: "It is well known that certain golden ages of art bear no direct relation at all to the general development of society, nor to its material foundation, the skeleton structure of its organization, as it were." There is a similar remark, in the same passage, on the absence of correlation between production and legal relationships. In later years, Friedrich Engels, indeed, admitted in a letter to a friend that he and Marx "are ourselves partly to blame for the fact that our younger disciples at times place more weight on the economic side than is due it. We had to emphasize this central factor because it was denied by our adversaries and there wasn't always time, place and opportunity to do justice to the other factors which participate in the reciprocal interaction." The residue of historical materialism appears to be, strictly speaking, a conviction of the close and frequent interaction of the elements in society and a strong sense of its integral character.

The theory found an immediate application in the division of history into great stages. The inheritance from Hegel at this point takes the form of intellectual entail; Marx takes over from his philosophical predecessor not only the view that each great epoch has a unity which may be reduced to a basic element, whether it be a *Geist* [spirit] or a method of production, but also the actual division and sequence of the stages. This division appears to be the result rather of historical induction than of theoretical deduction: we meet the old familiar ages of the history books. But it is more revealing that Marx does not distinguish them in terms of comparable factors and does not clarify the manner of their change. The Asiatic stage rested on a communal economy but was uniquely characterized by biologic tribal bonds; moreover, it was a stagnant period (here Marx follows Hegel closely) and so belied the "dialectic" of constant social transformation. The "ancient" stage rested on slavery and developed all the requisites of capitalism; it did not reach the phase of industrialism because the industrial arts failed to keep pace with the growth of commerce. There is no explanation of this interesting failure. If we appeal to Marx's general theory, the famous statement in the *Critique of Political Economy* proves hardly helpful; "*No* social order *ever* disappears before *all* the productive forces, for which there is ROOM in it, have been developed; and new higher relations of production *never* appear before the material conditions of their existence have MATURED in the WOMB of the old society [all emphases mine]." The terms I have placed in italics are sharp enough, but the terms I have put in capitals are too indefinite for either proof or disproof. Instead of clarification, we get ever more assumptions; like so many forks in the road, they make us uncertain of our direction.

The next age of windmill, manor, and lord-serf relations supported Marx's purpose a good deal more cogently, especially in the manner of its death. The transition from feudalism to industrial capitalism involved, technologically, the application of new methods of production and, socially, the rise of new classes and new conflicts. Certainly, this view is considerably supported by western European, and notably British, experience. The question, however, is whether the pattern of four or five stages can be accepted as a fair summary of history at large, beyond the West and beyond the last two or three centuries. The answer, it seems to me, must be in the negative. These stages do not appear outside of the West in anything like the prescribed order. Of this fact Marx himself was clearly aware. He expected India to pass from communalism to capitalism, leaving out feudalism and perhaps also another stage, and he considered that Russia had a good "chance" of developing toward socialism without passing through capitalism. We are driven to conclude that Marx regarded his theory of stages merely as a convenient statement of the "normal" sequence of societies in Western areas; certainly, we must regard it in that light.

Was that sequence "natural" and unavoidable even in those areas? This raises the much belabored issue of inevitability. We may sum up the matter briefly by saying that, while the tone and implication of the *Manifesto* and of many of the well-known passages of *Das Kapital* bespeak unqualified inevitability in the process of history and certainly in the collapse of capitalism and the rise of socialism, Marx's analyses, particularly in his political pamphlets, of specific events and movements, past and present, frequently do justice to the importance of ideas, personalities, traditions, chance events—to historical circumstance in general. These factors represent rather generous discounting of a monistic theory. Indeed, Marx in several drafts of a letter, which was never actually sent, to Russian followers, insisted that capitalism had arrived in western Europe not with the necessity of a "law" but catastrophically and drew the correct inference that no rules could be laid down for its arrival (he did not mention its departure) there or anywhere else. In Marx's universe there suddenly appeared a considerable Miltonic realm where

> Chaos Umpire sits

and

> next him high Arbiter
> Chance governs all.

Marx showed, on occasion, that he was aware of the serious implications of these reflections for his doctrines. He once denied quite specifically that he had propounded—or had meant to propound—a set of laws of the process of capitalistic growth and its "negation," laws valid for every society whatever. He would not have his outline of the origin of capitalism in western Europe (in *Das Kapital*) transformed into "an historico-philosophical theory of the general path fatally imposed upon all peoples, whatever their historical circumstances." His generalizations, he went on to insist, constituted no open sesame for unlocking social problems without considering historical differences. It was, however, just such a passport that his followers thought they had inherited. Critics who rated Marx's intelligence more highly and assessed his aims more shrewdly were satisfied that here was no new philosophy, and particularly no systematic philosophy of history. Benedetto Croce was not alone in his conclusion that historical materialism was not a philosophy but a *canon* of history. It was neither "a new *a priori* notion of the philosophy of history, nor a new method of historical thought. . . ." As a canon, and one "most rich in suggestion," it recommended that "attention be directed to the so-called economic basis of society, in order that the forms and mutations may be better understood." Historical materialism was also, as we shall see, a highly theoretical formulation of the "condition-of-Europe question," to paraphrase Thomas Carlyle.

III

If the notion that methods of production shape society is ultimately the most important in Marx's doctrine, the derivative view that it determines political forms and action is of more immediate consequence. For Marx assumed that capitalism and the material requisites of the Socialist order were fairly accomplished facts, at any rate in the countries which largely absorbed his interest. The stress must therefore be placed on the political aspect of the transition to the Socialist society.

As was his wont, he gave theoretical form to this highly practical problem. Thus arose the familiar "theory" of the state. There is a rather sudden remark in the third volume of *Capital* that the "form" in which surplus labor is squeezed from the workers determines "the political form of the relations of sovereignty and dependence, in short, the specific form of the state." Marx was quick to add that "this does not prevent the same economic basis from showing infinite variations and gradations in its [political?] appearance. This is due to innumerable outside circumstance, natural environment, race peculiarities, outside historical influences, and so forth." However this précis may be construed, Marx never implemented it by stating just what forms of the state were associated with what "forms of exploitation." And where does Marx's characteristic remark that Great Britain was the "classic" economic country but France the "classic" political country leave the formal relation between politics and economics? This paradox throws more light on his use of "classic" than it does on political theory. The "classic" was pretty much the normal and understandable, a sort of epistemologic or pedagogic idea: British capitalism had traced a course of progress visible to the naked eye; the evolution of the French state had been drawn, particularly during the Revolution, in sensational strokes that made it eminently comprehensible. However, Marx did not suggest *economic* reasons for the difference. He seems to have thought it unnecessary to do so—a very significant circumstance; but he appears to have underestimated the zeal of his followers in building a full-panoplied philosophy of politics upon his suggestive descriptions of recent events in Western history. But then Marx, as he himself once protested, was not a Marxist.

The theory of class struggle has stood the test of events better. In the leonine rhetoric of the *Manifesto,* "the history of all society has been the history of the struggle of classes." Modern scholarship owes so much to the insight concealed in this doctrine that any brief appraisal must seem inadequate. But, like the effects, the sources of the class-struggle theory are richly varied. "Long before me," Marx acknowledged, "bourgeois historians had described the historical development of this class struggle and bourgeois economists the economic anatomy of the classes [in modern society]." Indeed, the class terms and interpretations were common coinage in the eighteenth century. There was then talk of "factions" which turned out to be something much like classes. Everyone who has looked at *The Federalist* papers will remember James Madison's remarks:

> . . . . the most common and durable source of factions has been the various and unequal distribution of property. Those who hold and those who are without property have ever formed distinct interests in society. Those who are creditors, and those who are debtors, fall under a like discrimination. A landed interest, with many lesser interests, grow up of necessity in civilized nations, and divide them into different classes, actuated by different sentiments and views.

Madison, of course, desired a constitution which would allay the pernicious and socially destructive effects of class struggles—it could not hope to repress the struggles themselves—whereas Marx would have interpreted the constitution as the inevitable expression of "factionalism" or the domination of one of the "factions."

The more technical political conclusions that Marxists have drawn from the prevalence of class conflict have been perhaps as frequently belied by events as they have been confirmed. The deterioration of his doctrine has been pronounced at this point. Proletarian developments in Germany, Great Britain, and the United States have surprised the expectations of the followers of Marx rather unpleasantly, to say the least. Yet what other countries could have provided a better testing ground for his doctrines? If modern production indicated socialism as the optimum type of political organization; if there arises a class whose stake is vitally bound up both with the exploitation of advanced methods and with the establishment of socialism—the proletarians; and if their increasing class consciousness and political drive soon push them into power—the proletarian dictatorship; then these countries should have long ago experienced revolutionary proletarian rule and should now be Socialist societies in which class distinctions have all but disappeared!

IV

Among the more neglected aspects of historical materialism is its implied view of man. It is generally accepted that Marx defended a primarily social interpretation of human character. Yet, hidden in his thought, there are in fact *two* concepts of man, not clearly related to each other or even always distinguished, which he used in a convenient alternation. One was social and relative, the other absolute and—I almost said—divine. "Historical" man was that infinite succession of traits which are created and changed by environmental and social forces. "Generic" man, the more enduring entity, stood for the distinctively human endowments that are striving to be fulfilled: creative imagination, purposeful activity, a drive to combine mental and manual work, and, perhaps derivatively, a tendency to social grouping. Never yet completely realized, these traits are always latent. They inhere in and so define man. "Scientific" socialism has as its transcendent goal their full exploitation and flowering. This concept represented the ultimate criterion of civilization, and the basis for grading societies on the scale of progress. This concept, too, formed the framework of the ethical message of *Das Kapital*. It was the rational justification of the humanitarianism of Karl Marx.

The humanitarian tendency may be allowed to speak for itself. The pertinent question is whether or not the theory of the two human facets contributes substantially toward understanding man, especially in the contemporary circumstances of social collapse, large-scale propaganda, and autocratic movements? The view that a wealth of traits are wholly conditioned by society ("historical" man), while not original with Marx or with any other thinker, has been so influential that we have come to regard it as almost axiomatic; yet so influential that it suggests a converse view that ideas play a considerable role in shaping society!

Quite specifically, however, the "historical" theory would lead us to expect, after a century of continually growing industrialization in several countries, the emergence of the co-operative man. For the machine involves the most extensive scheme of socialist interaction, exchange, and interdependence that men have ever undertaken. Has this expectation been fulfilled? Certainly not conspicuously. The deepening racial hatreds of our day, the embattled and blatant chauvinisms which rend the world, hardly testify to the birth of a new social man. These phenomena seem no less the product of industrialism than the attractive virtues visioned by nineteenth-century optimists. Does it not then come to this, that Marx's view of the feudal, bourgeois, or proletarian man goes further toward explaining the effect of fully formed societies at their point of maturity upon a particular group than the relations between society and man in general? The bourgeois type, for example, sums up the sharply etched tendencies impressed upon the middle class rather than the character of humanity as a whole in the era of the bourgeoisie. This limitation of the idea of "historical" man is especially apparent in a time of transition, when the old society disintegrates and the new is waiting to coagulate. If the new social man is not yet clearly recognizable, the bourgeois of our day barely resembles the liberal, progressive, and sanguine capitalist of the era of Cobden and Bright. Like Gustave Flaubert and, in a different setting much later, Sinclair Lewis, Marx painted the face not of the bourgeois in general but of the bourgeois triumphant. But neither Mme. Bovary, Babbitt, nor the bourgeois of *The Communist Manifesto* can serve adequately as subjects for an "Essay on Man," quite apart from their being somewhat dated.

The "generic" traits form together a better approximation of man as such than do the "historical." The difficulty from the point of view of a strictly materialistic philosophy is rather obvious: Marx's essential man is a *deus ex machina* thrust into the world by a socially unconditioned fiat. The notion that "history is nothing but a continuous transformation of human nature" is invalidated at once by this arbitrary act. The concept itself was bequeathed to Marx by his historical background and his culture; it is a mixed product primarily of the rationalism of the Enlightenment and of the romanticism of the early decades of the nineteenth century. Although the ingredients are varied, the result errs on the side of oversimplicity. Man has latterly come to be regarded as a somewhat more complex and, at some points, even inchoate being. His potentialities seem less pointed toward definite ends; subjective and emotional factors occupy a larger place.

The fact is that the psychological side of the thought of Marx, who in this as in other matters reflected current attitudes, is strikingly weak. I do not have in mind his almost consistent failure to understand and control his closest associates and followers. More important is the fact that humanity is pictured rather stiffly in his works. This does not diminish, of course, their moral or satirical value; quite the contrary. The proletarians of *Das Kapital* are the attractive synthetic types which naturally people all tracts of social protest. Attacks against oppression and exploitation have never been based on a psychological study of the victims. It is proper also, given his aims, that Marx's bourgeois should be caricatures of themselves. *The Eighteenth Brumaire of Louis Bonaparte* and *The Civil War in France* are effective political satires precisely because their victims are executed in black and white. But more colors and shades are needed to depict man—the whole man who is to sustain the weight of a new social order and civilization.

V

A certain disillusionment attends the effort to analyze negatively a great body of thought. When we are done and the object of criticism lies on the floor strewn in a dozen pieces, we may become uneasily aware, as the mystery writers say, of "somebody" in the room. The ghost of the philosophy still hovers about. Surely there is a residual cogency in the intellectual scheme of Marx. His inquiry into the ramifications of the profit motive, his saga of the Faustian drive in capitalism, his conviction that the fate of the modern world will be decided in the West, his account of the recent course of economic progress, his overlooked attachment to the values of Western urban civilization—these and more are positive legacies. Nor can all the objections in the world erase the authentic force of his influence during the past century. A valid interpretation must jibe with that influence, while allowing for the diminishing pertinence of his doctrine, and, as a first rule of criticism, it must permit his thought to appear plausible rather than extravagant, if possible.

We may start with an assumption. Put aside the political striving of Marx; that is now a subject for historical evaluation. Look upon him not as a legislator of human destiny but, in a figurative sense, as a passionate actor and analyst of his time—of the early and middle decades of the nineteenth century. His strong sense of contemporaneity, his all-absorbing concern with a prompt revolution in western Europe, and his most characteristic traits suggest him inevitably as the voice of his immediate world. A good many contradictions, fallacies, and inadequacies which clutter up Marxism *regarded as a system* disappear from Marxism regarded as a description of the problem and promise of modern industrialism and of its historical background. The fact that Marx thought, as he seems to have done, that his views formed a whole of larger, even universal, significance itself reflected the fashion and culture of his day. It was quite natural for him to express himself in philosophical terms, to pass unconsciously from man to Man and from workaday truth to Reality; he was, after all, trained in Germany to become a professor of philosophy, and his master was Hegel. The tendency to generalize characterized many another thinker of the century. Marx's style and habit of mind need not deceive us into wrenching him from the framework of time and place, when, as a matter of fact, they help to define that very framework.

What a man takes for granted may more quickly betray his cultural heritage than what he finds it necessary to demonstrate. To those who would enlarge his economic and political views into a philosophy of society and reality, the fact that he did not concern himself directly with the problem of human nature must surely be disquieting. But others will find it illuminating that Marx expected his readers to accept without question his ambivalent view of man. For them, as for him, that view was a *portemanteau* for many prevailing modes of thought. It reflected the theory of environmental determinism, increasingly influential in that age. Yet it also managed to preserve much of the classical view of man as a simple addition of a few well-defined traits. It made room for the evolutionary idea propounded by Hegel in philosophy and later by Darwin in biology; for the generic traits, while fixed in their essential character, would be exploited more fully as the environment was improved. There is, finally, in the "historical-generic" amalgam a clear strain of romanticism. Marx's man is cast in noble and heroic mold; his capacities are appraised with a sanguine eye; he is the core of the notion of progress. Some of the most influential ideas of the century are present here in solution. Marx's attitude toward human nature shows how avidly he absorbed and assimilated, with greater catholicity than consistency, the tendencies to which he was heir.

Historical materialism belongs in a different category from the concept of human nature. On that subject Marx thought deliberately and with the self-consciousness of the pioneer. We have already suggested some of the weaknesses of his theory. It is remarkable, however, that these weaknesses multiply directly with the geographic distance from western Europe, the socioeconomic distance from capitalism, and the temporal distance from the middle of the last century. This interesting circumstance suggests that it may be advisable to regard the theory, apart from its value as a canon for the study of history, as an account of the rise and flowering of capitalism, couched in the language dear to the heart of the Hegelian. Such an approach may be richly supported. Although Marx stated his view in ambitiously comprehensive terms, he never established the correlation at all times between particular forms of production and noneconomic forces, such as, let us say, the development of science. He hoped, of course, that scientific contributions would confirm his views, but only in the broadest possible sense. For example, he was glad to learn that Morgan had urged that the earliest human societies were communistic, since it stamped communism as not only "natural" but an actual historical fact, in the past at any rate. But such scientific "confirmation" was hardly essential to his principal concern—the overthrow of capitalism. Would Marxists today abandon their socialist program because many modern anthropologists no longer subscribe to Morgan's interpretation of the early societies? The attempt to apply closely the theory of Marx to the field of the physical sciences and to relate closely socioeconomic and scientific developments is one of the most unfortunate aspects of recent Marxist discussions.

But, while the more formal claims of historical materialism cannot be substantiated, its special applicability to—or, perhaps better, its special derivation from—some important aspects of modern European society are visibly apparent. The collapse of feudalism before the attacks of capitalism amply demonstrated the revolutionary role of commerce; the supplanting of individual handicrafts by the division of labor and the machine illustrated the superior viability of the modern productive system; the readjustment of political, ecclesiastical, and social institutions to the needs of capitalism underscored the primacy of the economic revolution in the Western world; the ever spreading wave of political revolutions in state forms, since 1776 and 1789, in the wake of economic advance, persuaded Marx and many other observers of the secondary and derivative character of politics.

His political reflections also gain in substance when placed against the background of western European practice. Whatever may be the fate of his imputed correlation between economics and politics in general, he has undoubtedly presented a convincing class interpretation of the modern history of British parliamentarianism, by pointing to connivance at the inclosure of common fields, the reactionary attitude toward social reform, and the stress on imperialistic expansion. Consider the contemporary realism of the oft quoted statement of the *Manifesto* that "the modern state authority is nothing more than a committee for the administration of the consolidated affairs of the bourgeois class as a whole." As a summary of the modern state from the fifteenth century onward, this sweeping assertion leaves much to be desired. But in 1847, when it was written, it was an apposite summary of British governance: a small propertied electorate ruled through the elective committee of the Commons, although this body shared rule with the aristocratic upper house. Nor was the implied extension of this generalization beyond Great Britain unreasonable, since its liberal, as distinguished from democratic, parliamentary forms were soon copied in many parts of the Continent.

There should be no need to insist that *Das Kapital* is more significant as a critique of modern industrialism, especially in its earlier stages, than as a treatise on the nature of society. The reader will recall Marx's insistence that the various historical "laws" set forth in *Das Kapital* were intended to outline the actual course of capitalist accumulation, expropriation, and development in western Europe, with no necessary "legal" consequences for other areas. The descriptive aspects of the book are, indeed, notable from the account of the working day, division of labor, the introduction of machinery, and the rise of the factory to the illuminating outline, widely accepted nowadays, of the process by which capitalism took hold of the British town and countryside. Indeed, in studying the history of Great Britain in the first half of the nineteenth century, it would not be safe to ignore Marx. The historical aspects of his principal work have largely stood the test of later investigations.

This analysis may be further extended. The Marxian labor theory of value has not won wide recognition in academic circles but has nevertheless played a sizable role in politics. It was an important factor in that confluence of Marxist ideology with proletarian growth that explains, probably better than anything else does, the rise of modern socialism. The significance of *Das Kapital* in general, whatever the final verdict on its scientific value, echoed powerfully, with voices like Shelley's, the cry of the modern proletarian:

> The seed ye sow, another reaps,
> The wealth ye find, another keeps,
> The robes ye weave, another wears,
> The arms ye forge, another bears.

And if, as Lord Halifax once remarked, the best qualification for a prophet is to have a good memory, Marx might feel qualified to foretell the increasing misery of the working class, for he lived in the "hungry forties." His notion that, as that class grows in numbers, its political consciousness and capacity must also grow was forcibly suggested by contemporary movements such as Chartism. It is well to recall that, in the first half of Marx's century, Great Britain possessed not only the most advanced industrial system but the most advanced, articulate proletariat as well. The expectation that the socialist revolution would occur first in the most developed countries was not fantastic in a period when the British workers frequently engaged in directly revolutionary acts.

It was, in fact, a striking pertinence to the contemporary scene that gave Marxism a pervasive and expanding influence. Marx's account of the process of industrialization was so discerning and "abstract" in a realistic sense that it bore pointedly upon the history of any country that might experience it. It is understandable, therefore, that his ideas should have struck deepest root in the areas which reproduce most nearly the conditions of western Europe a century ago and more. Present-day Russia springs to mind at once; but there are other instances as well. Indeed, a comparison with the age on which the work of Marx was a commentary constitutes the starting-point for tracing the varying fortunes of his doctrines in particular countries. Such a comparison would lead us to divide the world into several kinds of regions with distinctive lines of development, distinctive backgrounds, and hence, also, distinctive reactions and immunities to Marxism. The Western, or, perhaps, the North Atlantic, world would have to be treated as a unit. It is at once the home of Marxism and the region which has traveled the greatest distance from the early industrialism which Marx recorded. It is here that Marxism has met the steepest obstacles and has revealed the greatest limitations. The contrasts a century has worked are as striking as the powerful resemblances.

Karl Marx, then, is best understood as a classically rooted western European who functioned in a time when his area was the center of the whole world in a far greater degree than it is now; when Great Britain was the economic and political model she has now long since ceased to be; when France was a reliable catalyst of revolution; and when a predominantly agrarian society was emerging into the phase of early industrialism. His views represent an authentic aspect of the culture of his day; his political program was naturally built around its peculiar conditions. Both his influence and the uneven pattern of his latter-day relevance derive largely from this circumstance. Marx was born eighteen years after his century began, and he died seventeen years before it ended. His life-span fitted into it with a neat symmetry; his work and striving largely summed it up.

XIX

Currents in German and Italian History, 1870-1914

Bismarck's Welfare State
SIDNEY B. FAY

The Germany of Treitschke
RAYMOND J. SONTAG

The New Italy Coming of Age: 1870-1915
KENT ROBERTS GREENFIELD

Bismarck's Welfare State

SIDNEY B. FAY

Published in 1950

In the first two decades of its existence, Bismarck's new Germany came into conflict with several opposition groups on the domestic front: with liberals who wished to transform Imperial Germany into a more progressive state on the English model, a state in which the Reichstag would exercise the authority enjoyed by the House of Commons; with Roman Catholics who saw in the Empire a threat to the liberty and security of their Church; and with socialists, who favored a fundamental alteration of both state and society. It was the struggle with the socialists that loomed especially large in the last decade of Bismarck's period of service as Imperial Chancellor. Nor was this surprising, for the growth of the German socialist movement was intimately connected with the growth of German industrial capitalism; and the decade of the 1880's, momentous in the development of German industry, proved to be no less momentous in the development of the socialist movement. To combat the Social Democrats, Bismarck used several techniques. First, he had recourse to repression. Just as Metternich had his Carlsbad Decrees, so Bismarck had his antisocialist laws. Far more important, however, he organized a system of social insurance that was designed not only to protect workers against sickness, accident, incapacity, and old age, but also to lure them away from the Social Democrats. Although Bismarck's system of social security failed as a weapon in its immediate objective—it did not put an end to the growth of the German Social Democratic Party—it did come to serve as a model for schemes of social reform in many other countries. In the present essay, Sidney B. Fay, professor emeritus of history at Harvard University and one of the chief American authorities on modern German history, analyzes the movement of Bismarckian Germany in the direction of a social-welfare state.

Bismarck's Motives

Many things in connection with Bismarck's social insurance program seem paradoxical or unexpected. Why was it, for instance, that social security originated first in a conservative, strongly monarchical, almost semifeudal state like Germany rather than in a more liberal and more advanced industrial country like Britain? One reason is that Prussia had a strong tradition of paternalistic, monarchical care for the welfare of its population since the days of the Great Elector and Frederick the Great. Furthermore, Bismarck enjoyed sufficient authority in the Prussian-German state to push through social legislation when he finally decided that there was need for it.

This need, Bismarck believed, lay in the early and vigorous growth of a revolutionary, anti-government, political party—the Social Democrats. As early as 1880 he decided that their power and influence must be broken, not merely by negative, repressive measures but also by positive, social welfare legislation which would win their goodwill and support. In Britain, on the other hand, a socialist (or labor) party developed much later and was much weaker than in Germany. It was of little concern to the government until after the turn of the century. In Britain, moreover, the workers' interests were mainly taken care of by the trade-unions which were relatively conservative. But in Germany trade-unions were a relatively late development as compared with Britain and their influence was less. The German worker of Bismarck's day looked for backing and support to the Social Democratic Party instead of to the trade-unions.

It is also curious that the German social insurance laws were proposed and carried through by conservative groups in the face of vociferous opposition by the liberals, progressives, and socialists.

But within a decade after Bismarck's dismissal in 1890 roles were reversed. After 1900 Progressives and Social Democrats usually favored further social security legislation. After World War I they extended "security" measures to a dangerous degree, while the conservatives were helpless to prevent social welfare policies of which they disapproved.

Bismarck's own motives and changes of attitude were no less remarkable. His early social ideas were strongly conservative because

Reprinted by special permission from *Current History*, XVIII (1950), 2-7.

of his religious feelings and his class position in the Prussian landed nobility. Later, in the 1850's he was much impressed by Napoleon III's social policies which were calculated to strengthen the Emperor's power and make the French masses contented: universal suffrage, recognition of workingmen's organizations, public works, rise in wages, housing, state-aided sickness insurance, and savings institutions for small depositors. All these measures did actually seem to strengthen Napoleon's position and gain for him the support of the masses to offset the criticism of the liberal middle and upper classes. Bismarck likewise, after becoming Minister-President in Prussia in 1862, proposed some measures of a similiar kind. But he was not yet strong enough, or perhaps not persistent enough, to get them adopted.

Ferdinand Lassalle's influence on Bismarck at this time was considerable. Bismarck rejected Lassalle's project for state-financed cooperative enterprises, but he did adopt equal, universal, male suffrage, as advocated by Lassalle, as the basis for elections to the German Reichstag. Today we would regard such an extension of the suffrage as a concession to liberalism. But in those days, in Bismarck's mind, as in Napoleon III's, universal suffrage was reckoned as a means for strengthening conservative monarchy by the support of easily led masses against the liberal bourgeoisie. But time often brings remarkable changes of attitude. A quarter of a century later, in 1890, when the German industrial masses, no longer docile, voted for socialist deputies to the Reichstag and attacked Bismarck's policies, Bismarck seriously considered restricting the suffrage—by a coup d'état if necessary.

During the wars of '64, '66, and '70 and the consolidation of the new empire in the following ten years, Bismarck was too busy, as he himself

---

FERDINAND LASSALLE: German labor leader (d. 1864) whose influence was decisive in the organization, in 1863, of the Universal German Workingmen's Association. A state socialist, he stressed the need for universal manhood suffrage, working on the assumption that if the workers had the right to vote they could gain control of the legislature and bring about the enactment of laws that would improve their condition of life. He and Marx were violent enemies, and their hostility to each other's ideas was reflected in the doctrinal controversies of the German Social Democratic Party.

EUGEN RICHTER: German publicist and liberal statesman (d. 1906). Elected to the Reichstag in 1867, he was a frequent critic of Bismarck's economic

said, to give any thought to social legislation. It was not until 1878 that he became seriously concerned over the danger to the state from the socialists. They had steadily increased their popular vote. Their representatives in the Reichstag voted against all his measures for consolidating the new empire. Their speeches and propaganda advocated the Marxian doctrines of social revolution and the overthrow of the capitalist state.

Repression

In 1878 two attempts were made on the life of old Emperor William by two mentally unbalanced young men. They were not indeed members of the Social Democratic Party, but Bismarck used their revolver shots as a justification for introducing a severely repressive bill against the Social Democrats and all subversive agitation. It provided for the suppression of socialist meetings and newspapers and the arrest or expulsion of socialist agitators (with the exception of the socialist Reichstag members who were protected by their parliamentary privilege). Bismarck's first anti-socialist bill was rejected in the Reichstag by an overwhelming majority of 281 to 57, the National Liberals, Catholics, Progressives, and Socialists all voting against it.

Then, after the second attempt on the Emperor, Bismarck at once dissolved the Reichstag, ordered new elections, and called for drastic anti-socialist legislation. This time he was successful. The anti-socialist law passed by a three-to-two majority in October, 1878, for a limited period, was renewed four times until it finally lapsed in 1890 shortly after Bismarck's dismissal. It was rigorously carried out. Socialists later

---

policies. A believer in *laissez faire*, he attacked the state intervention in economic life that Bismarck favored and the projects for economic reform that the Social Democrats advocated.

TARIFF LAW OF 1879: Measure by which Imperial Germany abandoned its relatively free trade policies and moved in the direction of protectionism. A product of the depression that was ushered in by the financial crisis of 1873, it offered protection against foreign competition to German industry as well as agriculture. The measure had the effect of further splitting the German Liberal Party, and it helped to stimulate the growth of economic nationalism in other countries.

reckoned that under it 352 of their associations had been dissolved, 1299 publications suppressed, 893 persons expelled from home, and prison terms imposed amounting to 850 years, 5 months and 14 days.

This anti-socialist measure, however, as usually happens with repressive laws, did not wholly accomplish its purpose. Socialist newspapers and pamphlets printed in Switzerland and England were smuggled into Germany and widely circulated underground. Worse still, under persecution, the Social Democratic Party grew stronger and stronger, increasing its popular vote and its Reichstag members at every successive election.

Bismarck soon recognized that the anti-socialist law was not a wholly satisfactory solution of the socialist menace. The law was merely negative, repressive. Something positive must be done to make the industrial workers better off, and especially to make them feel that the German state was their friend and not their enemy. This was Bismarck's main motive in pushing the social insurance legislation of the early 1880's. This motive is seen in remarks that he let drop and in the provisions that he was very insistent should be included in the insurance laws. He wanted the German state to contribute to the cost of insurance along with employers and employees, so that the worker would feel a sense of gratitude to the state. With less cause for anxiety and with the state as their friend, the workers, Bismarck hoped, would be more contented, and less likely to listen to socialist agitators. In this way, Bismarck hoped, the power of the Social Democratic Party would be undermined. His hope was not realized and after 1890, during his last years, he seems to have felt that, so far as his political motives were concerned, his social insurance laws were a failure and he showed little pride or interest in them. It is significant that in his "Reflections and Reminiscences" he does not discuss them.

An Employer's Liability Act of 1871 was supposed to provide compensation in case a workman was killed or injured by accident. The law, however, was generally recognized to be very inadequate and unsatisfactory. The worker had to prove that the accident was not his own fault, and was consequently often involved in long and costly law suits, and in most cases got no satisfaction at all. During the 1870's Bismarck refused to do anything to improve the law, partly because he was so busy with other matters, partly because he did not want to put upon employers more burdensome cost charges which might weaken their competitive position in foreign markets.

In April, 1880, however, a Rhine-Westphalian mining industrialist, Louis Baare, presented a proposal for insuring workers against accident and injury. It met with Bismarck's approval and marks the beginning of his active interest in social insurance and of his pushing of legislation to secure it. He asked Baare to elaborate his proposal into a draft law. At the same time he instructed Theodor Lohmann, one of his own subordinates in the Ministry of Trade, to study Baare's proposal but also to draw up a government draft law embodying his own views.

Theodor Lohmann, son of a Westphalian Lutheran pastor, was a deeply religious and conservative man of great ability and staunch independence of character. For years he had devoted much theoretical study and practical investigation to the subject of social welfare. His convictions differed considerably from Bismarck's political calculations. He was opposed to having the state make financial contributions toward paying the insurance premiums because charity weakened the worker's sense of responsibility.

More important in his mind was the fact that if employers and employees by themselves contributed the insurance funds and managed them jointly, then labor and capital would build up a common habit of cooperation and mutual understanding, and that was the most important thing of all. But Lohmann had to subordinate his own convictions to Bismarck's wishes, so that the government draft bill as actually worked out represented Bismarck's views rather than Lohmann's. After three years of trying to reconcile his own convictions with Bismarck's orders, Lohmann resigned from the rather unthankful task. It is a tribute to his character and ability that he still retained his official position and also Bismarck's esteem and friendship. He again played an important part in social legislation after Bismarck's fall in 1890.

Bismarck's first accident insurance bill, embodying his own views with suggestions from Baare and Lohmann and drafted by Lohmann, was laid before the Reichstag in April, 1881. Its novel feature was that it imposed statutory compulsion on many classes of workers to be insured against accident. All workers in mining, iron and steel foundries, shipbuilding, and building construction who received less than 2,000 marks a year in wages must be insured. Annual wages of 2,000 marks, i.e., about $500 seem to us today to be painfully small, but it must be remembered that in the 1880's wages and prices everywhere were far lower than they are today. German wages then, as now, were considerably below the American level and somewhat lower than in Britain.

To emphasize Bismarck's idea of the beneficent part played by the government the insurance scheme was to be administered by an Imperial Insurance Bureau which would guarantee the pension and death payments and thus form a paternal bond between the worker and the government. In the case of poorer workers (those earning less than 750 marks a year), the state would also pay one-third of the insurance premiums, the other two-thirds being paid by the employers, and the poorer workers paying nothing. In the case of the better off workers (those receiving between 750 and 2,000 marks annually), the cost of the premiums was divided between the employer and the workers, the state contributing nothing but the cost of administration.

The three main features of the bill on which Bismarck had insisted —compulsion to insure, an Imperial Insurance Bureau, and state contributions—were precisely the points that were most attacked and brought the bill to grief.

The National Liberal Party, which had been Bismarck's main support ever since 1866, had split in 1879 when two-thirds of its really liberal members refused to accept Bismarck's protective tariff law and went over to the opposition. They and the Progressives ably led by Eugen Richter denounced the obligatory clause as contrary to the liberal principles of laissez-faire. They also criticized the state contribution in the case of poorer workers as "class legislation" and feared that the money for the state's contribution would be raised by indirect taxes which bore most heavily on the classes least able to bear them. (Bismarck in fact always strongly favored indirect rather than direct taxes because the indirect taxes were "concealed" and caused less irritation among people who were not so aware of them as in the case of direct taxes.)

The Catholic Center Party, though much divided amongst themselves, were sharply opposed to the Imperial Insurance Bureau as a centralizing encroachment on states' rights. As federalists rather than centralists, and having their main strength in Catholic Bavaria, the Catholic Center members were always fearful of Prussia's dominating power in the Empire. Their fears found an echo in many of the smaller German states who likewise opposed a new central insurance bureau.

The Social Democrats condemned all the insurance provisions of the bill because they were put forward by a government to which they were ideologically opposed, and also because of various specific objections.

The bill was disfigured by so many amendments, including one which placed the whole cost on the employers, that Bismarck withdrew the bill and dissolved the Reichstag. A few days before the new Reichstag elections, he made propaganda for a new revised accident insurance bill by having William I issue an Imperial Message on November 17, 1881. It stated that "the cure of social ills must be sought not exclusively in the repression of Social Democratic excesses, but simultaneously in the positive advancement of the welfare of the working classes." It also promised a threefold program of sickness, accident, and old age insurance.

In spite of the Emperor's message, the opposition parties increased their strength in the Reichstag. The second accident insurance bill drafted by Lohmann and laid before the new Reichstag in May, 1882, fared no better than the first, because Bismarck would not abandon his idea of a centralized, state-aided, bureaucratic institution. After being criticized and amended, it was eventually replaced by a third accident insurance bill which finally passed the Reichstag in 1884.

Meanwhile Bismarck had better success with sickness insurance. A bill to establish this was quickly passed by the Reichstag and became law on June 15, 1883. It made insurance against sickness obligatory for the great majority of wage earners, but not for the professional classes and other white-collar workers. The law wisely made use of many already existing mutual aid societies, friendly associations, guilds, and local sick benefit funds. Where such sickness funds did not exist, they were created by the law and organized by localities. To pacify Catholics and other states' rights critics who dreaded Bismarck's centralizing of state power, the law provided that all the various local sickness funds should be supervised and controlled by the legislatures and insurance bureaus of the different German states instead of being under an Imperial Insurance Bureau.

Contributions were borne jointly, two-thirds by the workers and one-third by the employers as a rule. In return, the insured received many kinds of benefits in case of sickness:

(a) Sickness pay for 13 weeks (increased in 1903 to 26 weeks, and in some cases for a longer period);
(b) Maternity pay for six weeks after childbirth;

(c) Free medical attendance, including free medicines during sickness, and in many cases free maintenance in hospitals, convalescent homes;

(d) Generous funeral allowances in case of death.

Sickness

Each local fund made its own contract with doctors, druggists, and hospitals. Doctors were usually paid either fixed fees for each visit or an over-all lump sum based on the number of the insured. Patients had a free choice of doctors from the panel of practitioners with whom the sickness fund had made contracts.

In 1910 there were over 23,000 statutory sickness funds. Altogether they received 130 million marks from employers and 260 million from workers, and had some small reserves beyond the amounts paid out in sickness benefits. The cost of administration was commendably low— only about five per cent of the contributions received.

Bismarck was more a practical opportunist than a man of theories and principles. Having taken note of criticisms and prejudices which his first two accident insurance bills had encountered, he made many revisions and brought in a third accident insurance bill which was easily adopted by the Reichstag in July, 1884, and came into operation on October 1, 1885. It introduced compulsory accident insurance on all workers receiving less than 3,000 marks a year and engaged in mining, shipbuilding, factories, and building construction (in 1911 the coverage was extended to include workers in these and almost all other undertakings receiving less than 5,000 marks a year).

The whole cost of insurance was placed upon the employers—no contributions by the worker or by the state. For purposes of administration and management, all employers were organized into Mutual Associations according to geographical areas and the nature and accidental risk in different undertakings. In 1911, for instance, there were 66 Mutual Associations of industrial employers, 48 of agricultural employers, and 556 Executive Boards of state, provincial and communal organizations which acted as Mutual Associations in providing accident insurance for their public employees. In 1911 over 28,000,000 workers, male and female, were covered by accident insurance—about 10,000,000 in industry, 17,000,000 in agriculture, and 1,000,000 in government employ.

Each Mutual Association collected from its employer members at the end of the year a sum sufficient to pay all the accident claims incurred during the year. In accordance with Bismarck's wishes, the central German government came into the picture in two ways, more impressive in appearance than in reality. First, the law created an Imperial Insurance Office. It comprised, aside from its regular technical and paid staff, 32 members, 8 elected by the Federal Council (*Bundesrat*) and 12 each by the employers and the insured. But it had little real importance except as the highest authority for awards, decisions, and supervision.

The main supervisory authority and control continued in the hands of the existing local State Insurance Offices. In the second place, the Reich government made the gesture of advancing the money to the Post Office to pay the accident claims as they were awarded during the year. It was then reimbursed at the end of the year by the Employer Mutual Associations which levied the necessary assessments upon themselves.

Compensation for injury by accident usually (in about 96 per cent of the cases) took the form of a pension, rather than the lump-sum payment usually favored by private insurance companies. This was in accordance with the social idea of providing support to the injured during his disability, or in case of death to his dependent survivors. During the first 13 weeks, while the case was being investigated and the amount of the pension determined, the injured person received support at once from his sickness fund which was later reimbursed by the Mutual Association of employers.

The amount of accident pensions for lower income workers was two-thirds of the yearly earnings in case of total disability, and proportionately less for partial disability (e.g., loss of the right hand was generally reckoned as 66 per cent disability, loss of arm or foot as 75 per cent, one eye 50 and both eyes 100 per cent). In the case of higher income workers, where the need was less, the basis of calculation resulted in a pension a little less than two-thirds of the yearly earnings. If accident resulted in death, funeral money equal to about a month's earnings was paid, and a pension of one-fifth the yearly earnings of the deceased was paid to his widow until her death or remarriage.

Additional payments were made for the benefit of his children and grandchildren and parents and grandparents so far as they had been dependent on him. Pensions were always paid through the Post Office, usually in advance monthly.

One of the most important indirect results of the accident insurance law was greater care in the prevention of accidents and a sharp decline in their number. The Mutual Associations were required to issue and enforce regulations for safety and prevention of accidents. These regulations were drawn up after consultation with the workers and then had to be approved by the Imperial Insurance Office. Disregard of them by employer or employees was seriously punished. As an admirable object lesson in accident prevention, there was set up in 1903 in a specially erected building in Charlottenburg, with money granted by the German government, "a permanent exhibition of contrivances for the prevention of accidents." Most of the exhibits were contributed by the various Mutual Associations and had proved of value in practical use. All out-of-date exhibits were promptly discarded in favor of the most modern improvements.

The third great measure of social insurance—provision for disability and old age—passed the Reichstag and became law on June 22, 1889. It was brought about more by the new, young, self-confident Emperor William II than by the old, disappointed, and disillusioned Iron Chancellor. Bismarck had originally planned to push the measure, in accordance with old Emperor William I's propagandist message of 1881, and would have liked to see the Reich government contribute two-thirds of the cost. But he lost interest when the Reichstag made so many criticisms of his accident and sickness proposals and objected so strongly to the idea of large financial contributions by the Reich government. He was also disappointed that his accident and sickness insurance measures seemed to have brought no change of heart on the part of the Social Democrats. They were as hostile and discontented as ever, and their numbers were rapidly mounting at each election. When a great strike of Westphalian coal miners took place in 1888, Bismarck declared that he was ready to use troops to shoot strikers if necessary. William II, on the other hand, did not want to begin his reign with bloodshed. He announced that he would call an international conference to deal with the labor question and ordered that his grandfather's promise of disability and old age insurance should be carried out.

The law of 1889 provided that nearly all wage earners of both sexes over 16 years of age receiving less than 2,000 marks a year must be insured against disability and old age. The cost was borne equally by employers and employees and by a flat contribution from the Imperial Treasury of 50 marks for each person receiving a disability or old age pension. The system was administered by Pension Boards organized by the governments of the various German states. Each Pension Board was made up of elected representatives of employers and employees in equal numbers, presided over by an appointee of the local state government. Disputed matters might be carried to the Imperial Insurance Office created by Bismarck in 1884, but otherwise the principle of states' rights was generally observed.

Disability pensions, so far as not covered by sickness or accident benefits, were paid to insured persons who became disabled and who had paid contributions for at least five years. Old age pensions were paid to insured persons, whether able to work or not, who had paid contributions for 30 years and had reached the age of 70 (which cost far less than old age pensions that begin at age 65 as is generally the case in the United States). All insured persons were grouped into five classes according to wages received. The joint employer and employee contribution was fixed by the Federal Council on an estimated actuarial basis and varied according to class. The disability and old age pensions varied from 110 marks annually in the lowest class to 230 marks in the first class.

By the end of 1910 nearly 2,500,000 pensions had been granted and a million were still in force at that date, about 80 per cent on account of disability and 20 per cent on account of old age.

In 1911 all three kinds of social insurance were somewhat expanded (as so often happens) by including some new groups of persons, raising the wage figure below which insurance became compulsory, and by extending the benefits. But the essential features remained unchanged until after the World War. Such were the beginnings of the insurance aspect of the welfare state in Germany. . . .

The Germany of Treitschke

POLITIK. By Heinrich von Treitschke*

RAYMOND J. SONTAG

Published in 1939

Fear of Imperial Germany was a momentous fact in the history of late-nineteenth- and early-twentieth-century Europe. In part this fear stemmed from economic development—the emergence of Germany as a powerful industrial state and a no less powerful commercial rival. In part the fear grew out of military and naval development—the expansion in the size of the German army and the growing emphasis on building up a German navy second to none. In part the fear came as a response to the writings and speeches of saber-rattling German nationalists, who succeeded in convincing Englishmen, Frenchmen, Russians, and Americans, among others, that Germany was out for conquest. Among the host of German nationalists and publicists who played so important a part in working up anti-German sentiment among non-Germans in the late nineteenth and early twentieth centuries, one of the most influential was Heinrich von Treitschke (1834-1896). Leader of the Prussian school of historians, Treitschke took a strictly utilitarian view of the study of history and of political science, insisting that its function was to make Germans aware of their superiority. The result was that his writings were filled with assertions of a sort that other Europeans would find—to put it mildly—offensive. It is not surprising, therefore, that during World War I his writings were frequently translated and widely circulated by the governments of the Allies in their effort to acquaint their peoples with the nature of their German enemy. Treitschke, as might well have been expected, came once more into his own in the Nazi era; but to view him simply as a forerunner of the Nazis is to misrepresent and to misunderstand both Treitschke and Imperial Germany. It is this point, among others, that Raymond J. Sontag—author of such valuable books as *European Diplomatic History, 1871-1933* and *Germany and England: Background of Conflict, 1848-1894*—makes in the present essay.

* Leipzig: Hirzel, 1897-98, 2 v.

It has been a persistent source of irritation to Englishmen, and on occasion to Americans, that the Germans have almost invariably deserted from the army of liberalism. True, for a brief moment in the middle of the last century—when Metternich was forced to flee for his life and the old absolutism was everywhere under attack—Anglo-Saxons thought that Germany might reform. Then when liberal prospects seemed brightest the German people supinely surrendered their freedom to Bismarck in exchange for the pottage of political unity. In the years that followed, the language used by Englishmen to express their disgust and hatred for Bismarck was even more vivid than that later hurled at Adolf Hitler. Still, they did not entirely give up hope: when Bismarck went, they argued, all would be well. But after Bismarck's dismissal in 1890, British expectations were again dashed: a few years of the erratic rule of William II made men sigh for the Iron Chancellor.

Even these repeated disappointments failed to daunt the more sanguine among British liberals. This charitable attitude is well illustrated by Sir Edward Grey's reaction to Treitschke's books with which he became acquainted only in 1914. Though he found them appalling—"every ideal except that of force is abolished"—and though he was quite willing to believe that Treitschke spoke for the rulers of Germany, Grey refused to believe that the German people as a whole were so bad. "The rest of the Germans are people more akin to ourselves than any other race," he wrote. Three years later, Woodrow Wilson was to draw the same distinction between the evil rulers and the good people of Germany.

During the early postwar years the Anglo-Saxon optimists seemed vindicated. Then came Adolf Hitler, and the old refrain was taken up once more. In December 1938, Neville Chamberlain asserted that his dealings with Nazi Germany showed faith, not in the Nazis, but in history: ". . . the complete subordination of individual independence to something which is called the State but which really only means those who for the time being rule the State, would be insupportable because it runs counter to all our most fundamental conceptions of the framework of human society." He argued, however, that this was no

Reprinted by special permission from *Foreign Affairs*, XVIII (1939), 127-139. With one exception, the footnotes which originally appeared with this essay have been omitted.

reason for refusing to have contact with the authoritarian states. "History teaches us that no form of government ever remains the same."

Optimism is usually an amiable vice, but in politics, as Machiavelli pointed out in an age very like our own, "leave it to time" may be a dangerous maxim, "for time, driving all things before it, may bring with it evil as well as good." And a hundred years, even in the history of nations, is a long time. During the century just past, the "fifty mad professors at Frankfurt" whom Disraeli denounced gave place to "the crazy minister at Berlin," as Palmerston called Bismarck. And Bismarck was followed by William II, who, Lord Salisbury thought, "must be a little off his head." Today we are left to contemplate the future. One war to save democracy led to the substitution of Adolf Hitler for the Kaiser. Would another such war produce—a liberal Germany? If the past has lessons to teach, we shall not be too confident. Perhaps, as the outstanding statesmen and writers of Germany have constantly reiterated during the past century, the German people believe that the liberal creed is not adapted to them. And indeed, is it not possible that they are right? At any rate, we may profitably listen to what they have to say on the matter.

Heinrich von Treitschke, the professor who so terrified Grey and other Anglo-Saxons from 1914 to 1918, is well suited to be our guide. He was the mentor of countless German university students from 1858 to his death in 1896, and throughout most of those years his favorite course of lectures dealt with politics. He had hoped eventually to distill the essence of these lectures into a definitive work on political science. But this hope he never realized. In 1897, however, his lectures were edited from the notes of his students and were published as his "Politik." It was not until the World War that there appeared an English translation—to which Arthur Balfour and A. Lawrence Lowell contributed introductions.[1] President Lowell contented himself

[1] New York: Macmillan, 1916, 2 volumes.

FIFTY MAD PROFESSORS AT FRANKFURT: Refers to the academic and supposedly impractical and visionary group that was so influential at the Frankfurt Assembly of 1848-1849. It should be remembered, however, that there were far more lawyers, magistrates, and higher civil servants present than professors.

WALTER FRANK: German nationalist historian whose function it was during

with some general remarks about Treitschke's "many startling conclusions." Mr. Balfour, like Sir Edward Grey, was shocked by Treitschke's immorality: "His Utopia appears to be a world in which all small States have been destroyed, and in which the large States are all either fighting, or preparing for battle."

Born in 1834, the son of a Saxon general of Czech descent, Treitschke's formative years were spent in the atmosphere of alternating hope and despair which preceded and followed the revolution of 1848. Before the revolution, German nationalists had been liberals in the sense in which Englishmen understood that word, and the Frankfurt Parliament of 1848 had been filled with men who looked to England for guidance and inspiration. By the time Treitschke began the usual tour of universities, the revolution had been crushed, and the liberal nationalists were in exile or living in discouraged silence. The disillusionment of his friends, and his own growing deafness, tempted the young student to seek refuge in the life of a poet. Even his poetry, however, was saturated with political conflict, and he soon took up the teaching of history and politics at Leipzig. These early writings when read today seem confused and contradictory: now he preaches the liberal doctrines of individualism and cosmopolitanism; now he proclaims the necessity for a strong Prussian army to smash the internal and foreign enemies of German nationalism. At the time, these contradictions were an asset because the same confused aspirations were present in the minds of most young German nationalists. His students revered him as a prophet. The Saxon authorities, however, naturally objected to a professor who urged Prussia's conquest of the lesser German states, including Saxony, and in 1863 he was glad to move to Freiburg in more nationalist Baden. Again he won the ardent support of his students. By 1866 his fame was so great that Bismarck sought his services as a scholarly press agent in the impending war with Austria, offering the hope of a professorship at the University of

---

the Hitler era to hasten the Nazification of the teaching and writing of history.

HERDER: Eighteenth-century German advocate of cultural nationalism. No chauvinist, he was very much a product of the age of reason and enlightenment. He sought to revive interest in the German language and in German literature, insisting that every nationality had a contribution to make to the culture of the world.

Berlin as a reward. Treitschke was tempted, and not only because a post at Berlin meant financial security and professional recognition. He was a nationalist, and he felt that Bismarck was setting out to unify Germany in the only possible way—by the Prussian battalions. But Bismarck was ruling Prussia in defiance of the constitution, and a believer in constitutional government like Treitschke could not serve such a master. He therefore refused the offer. When, however, war came and Baden sided with Austria, he resigned his post at Freiburg. The contradictions in his thought had driven him to the sidelines in the great struggle which was to determine the future of Germany.

The success of Prussia in the Seven Weeks' War, and the partial unification of Germany which Bismarck carried through in 1867, ended Treitschke's doubts. In the latter year he returned to Baden as a professor at Heidelberg, and thereafter he was an unquestioning supporter of the Iron Chancellor. In flaming essays he prepared the German people for war with France, steeled their courage during the war when it came, and prepared their minds for the proclamation of the German Empire at Versailles and for the Peace of Frankfurt in 1871.

The completion of political unity was not the end of the story for Treitschke. Germans, he believed, still lacked the spiritual unity, the self-confidence, and the zest for new achievements which characterized the peoples of older states like England. Eagerly, he set out to remedy these defects in the national character. To stimulate pride in the past glories of his country he undertook to write a "History of Germany in the Nineteenth Century" which he had carried to 1848 at the time of his death. In the columns of the *Preussische Jahrbücher* and from his seat in the imperial Reichstag he attacked the enemies of German greatness and exhorted his countrymen to new endeavors. In 1874 he received the coveted call to the University of Berlin. There, as earlier at Leipzig, Freiburg and Heidelberg, he drew crowds to his lectures. Old men waited at the door long before the lectures began, in the hope of getting a seat; more hardy souls listened outside to the raucous, half-strangled voice of the deaf speaker; and newspapers faithfully reported his words.

Adulation there was aplenty, but it was not won by the methods of a sycophant, as Arthur Balfour suggested in his introduction to the "Politics." This became evident after Bismarck's fall, when Treitschke heaped scorn on the new advisers of William II. Other enemies he had in great number—Socialists, Jews, social reformers, capitalists—all of whom he attacked in language as memorable as it was virulent. In combat with foes at home he was tireless; yet the foreign jibes at his narrow patriotic tone he shrugged aside: "But even the foreign world will some day have to accustom itself to the sentiments of New Germany." Even in his last years, when his eyes failed him, he continued to cry out of the silent darkness against the slothful opulence which, he felt, was corrupting the heroic simplicity of German life. His last speech, delivered a year before his death in 1896, was such a castigation of national weaknesses that Germany's enemies were glad to quote it against her in 1914.

Treitschke intended that his "Politics," like all his teaching and writing, should intensify the—to him—insufficient national pride of his countrymen. One evidence of national weakness was the vogue of western, and particularly British, political thought in Germany. Dazzled by the prestige of political economists like Adam Smith and political philosophers like Jeremy Bentham, Germans talked about natural law, the contractual basis of sovereignty, the self-evident natural rights of the individual citizen and the brotherhood of man. The British, Treitschke warned his hearers, had not taken these ideas too seriously themselves. "England, in her rôle of advocate for Liberalism, set all Europe by the ears, and under cover of the latent discontents which she herself had fostered, she conquered half the world." But in the process England herself absorbed some of the poisonous doctrines she was disseminating; as a result, the Merry England of earlier centuries had been converted into a drab and decadent land where only a tradesman could be happy. Treitschke warned that if the Germans were to escape a similar fate, they must forsake fallacious alien teachings. The foundations of a true art of politics, he declared, had been laid in eighteenth-century Germany by such teachers as Herder. On these foundations he would build.

Politics, Treitschke argued, must always remain an art. This did not mean, however, that experience should be disregarded. On the contrary, the weakness of British thought arose precisely from its reliance on abstract theory, while the strength of German thought was its refusal to consider anything which was not supported by the lessons of history. Politics was really applied history. But no two historical situations were alike, and therefore the political scientist could never hope to prophesy with the same accuracy with which the natural scientist could foretell the results of an experiment. History could warn against actions which had invariably proved disastrous. History could provide working principles of action: the statesman must study the trends of history if he was to hope for success. But the margin of error would always be great. ". . . for the real point is to understand how the Divine plan has unfolded itself little by little in all the variety of actual existence."

Using all history as his laboratory, Treitschke set out to discover the nature of the state. Was the state born, and did it live, in accordance with "the laws of nature and nature's God?" Experience, he contended, provided no evidence to support the doctrine of natural law. Of the innumerable states known to history, no two had been alike; each possessed an individual character, determined in every case by time, place and environmental circumstance. Were governments instituted among men to secure the inalienable rights of their citizens, and were they subject to revolution if these rights were not secured? Again, Treitschke argued, history knew nothing of such rights or of such governments. With unimportant exceptions—which, examined closely, proved not to be exceptions—states had grown up as the expression, the essential outward form, of a national society. To Treitschke, the conclusion was obvious. Far from being a mechanism to be set up, altered or dismantled at will, the state was a living personality, "the most supremely real person, in the literal sense of the word, that exists." History was the biography of states, the story of the strength and weakness, the virtues and sins, the achievements and tragedies of collective personalities.

A reader trained in Anglo-Saxon traditions of statecraft, and therefore contemptuous of philosophical abstractions, will naturally be most skeptical as to the validity of Treitschke's reasoning. Nevertheless, think of them what we will, the consequences of his conclusions are, in practice, far-reaching. If it be granted that states are, as he maintained, "thoroughly capable of bearing responsibility and blame," the statesman is no longer bound by the code of private morality; his actions become good or bad as they advance or injure the interests of the state. "The statesman has no right to warm his hands with smug self-laudation at the smoking ruins of his fatherland, and comfort himself by saying 'I have never lied'; this is the monkish type of virtue."

There are further consequences. For the individual, the law of self-preservation has numerous exceptions: life may be sacrificed for family, for country, for God. Above the state, however, is God alone. For Treitschke, history is "the objectively revealed Will of God, as unfolded in the life of the State." If the state is not merely a person, but a God-directed person, then for it there is no exception to the law of self-preservation. And to live means to be strong. With wearisome emphasis, Treitschke insisted that power was the first need and the distinguishing characteristic of the state. He believed that all the resources of the state—physical, intellectual and moral—contributed to the reservoir of national power. But the reservoir itself was the army. As the expression of national power, the army must be truly national, recruited by compulsory universal service. A professional army, no matter how highly trained, would not suffice; such an army did not gather up and intensify the strength of the state. The lack of universal service in England, in his opinion, explained "the want of chivalry in the English character, which strikes the simple fidelity of the German nature so forcibly." A national army is a civilizing instrument in time of peace; in war it is essential, because in modern war all the resources of the state must be thrown into action. The sublimity of war follows from the fact that the battlefield is the ultimate test of national character. "Brave peoples alone have an existence, an evolution or a future; the weak and cowardly perish, and perish justly. The grandeur of history lies in the perpetual conflict of nations, and it is simply foolish to desire the suppression of their rivalry." Since the great national personalities can suffer no compelling power superior to themselves, and since history will always be in constant flux, some nations declining, some growing in power, war must be accepted as part of the divinely appointed order. And as a corollary, it must be obvious that "the large state is the nobler type," while absence of power "accounts for the undeniably ridiculous element which we discern in the existence of a small State."

Such were the practical consequences of the belief that the state is "the most supremely real person, in the literal sense of the word, that exists." What lessons did these truths, founded on historical experience, hold for Germany?

Before the nineteenth century, Treitschke maintained, the teeming resources of Germany had been wasted by statesmen who refused to recognize that the state was a living personality. With mingled anger and pathos he traced the errors of the mediaeval emperors and the Hapsburgs. As early as the seventeenth century, he believed, it was obvious that Prussia alone was true to the Germanic genius; in the march of subsequent events "we see the secret forces of Nature themselves at work, for Prussia's Crown was not always a willing agent." At last men appeared who could read the message of history—William I, Bismarck and Roon. They imposed the Prussian, the truly German, stamp on the other German states; they created a state capable of guiding, controlling, encouraging the tumultuous strength of German society which had hitherto been dissipated.

Treitschke saw nevertheless that there was still much to be done before the national character of Germany would be fully developed. Remnants of provincialism persisted. Worse, the old cosmopolitanism was still strong: Catholics still gave political as well as religious loyalty to Rome, while workmen were seduced by international Jewish Socialism. The Jew found even more dangerous opportunities in the rise of urban commerce and industry: trade knew no frontier, and since the Jew knew no fatherland, he turned instinctively to trade. Jews had always fostered the disintegration of nations, Treitschke believed. They must not be permitted to undermine the hard-won unity of Germany. If the German Jews could not make up their minds to forget what Treitschke described as their international loyalties, a wave of anti-Semitism was inevitable. Until the Jew had made his decision, the German must be constantly on guard against corruption through the Jewish press or through Jewish artists. "Whenever he finds his life sullied by the filth of Judaism the German must turn from it, and learn to speak boldly about it."

Abroad, too, Treitschke pointed out his country's duties. In this age of great states, Germany must expand if she was not to see the world dominated by "the Russian knout or the English money bags." On the Continent, there remained only one task: to obtain control over the mouths of the German Rhine. Holland need not be annexed —a customs union would suffice. Such a union, by opening the Dutch coast, would enlarge Germany's window to the sea. Sea power was the indispensable prelude to colonial power; it was also a good in itself for the sea helped strengthen national morale. "This Germany of ours was once the greatest of the Sea Powers, and God willing, so she will be again." Holland, he continued, also had a colonial empire, and this, added to the colonies of Germany, would serve as a basis for further expansion. We must "see to it that the outcome of our next successful war must be the acquisition of colonies by any possible means." As things stood, German strength was being drained away, and the strength of rival states increased, by the emigration of millions who could not live in the crowded homeland. This drain must cease. The French had solved the problem by not having children. For Frenchmen, this was a logical answer; they were born calculators "and import the arithmetical spirit even into the kindly relations of married life." Such an escape was impossible for Germans. ". . . we hold that every man should be a man, and place his confidence in God. The German is a hero born, and believes that he can hack and hew his way through life. Reckoning and begrudging are not for him."

Such are the arguments most emphasized in the "Politics." It is easy to see why Allied propagandists translated these volumes. They contained, according to Arthur Balfour, an accurate prophecy of German policy; they foreshadowed all those designs which England was fighting to thwart. "They could not have been written before 1870," said Balfour. "Nothing quite like them will be written after 1917."

When Treitschke was discovered by the British, his writings had long been relegated by Germans to the list of unread classics: he was honored, in Prince Bülow's words, as "the prophet of the national ideal." With the advent of National Socialism his works were resurrected. The Nazis, seeking precursors in German history, canonized Treitschke as a prophet of the Third Reich. His "History of Germany" was put on the list of one hundred most acceptable books compiled for the guidance of National Socialist booksellers. A volume of selections from his works appeared in 1933, with a laudatory introduction by Alfred Rosenberg, the high priest of Nazi doctrine. A year later the National Socialist historian Walter Frank published a pamphlet called "Embattled Scholarship," to which the leader of the youth movement, Baldur von Schirach, contributed an introduction. Ostensibly, Frank's tract was written to commemorate Treitschke's centenary. Actually, it was a virulent attack on German scholarship of the generation before 1933. After Treitschke's death, Frank contended, German historians had retreated to an ivory tower, from which they had looked down with indifferent neutrality on the struggles of the German people. They refused to lead, refused to fight, refused above all to admit that a German must see the past through German eyes, and that German historical writing must serve the national cause. In particular, Frank pilloried Hermann Oncken, a scholar whose writings had won international acclaim. All this was past, Frank rejoiced. Now, with Treitschke as a guide, German scholarship would once more take its place in the battle line, would fight for the German idea.

This challenge was accepted by the dean of German historians, Friedrich Meinecke. Unlike that of Frank, Meinecke's career reached back to Treitschke's day; in fact, it was he who had nominated Treitschke as editor of the most important German historical journal, the *Historische Zeitschrift*. Meinecke himself had succeeded Treitschke as editor in 1893, and in 1934 he still held this position of leadership. This legacy he was unwilling to betray. Therefore, although Frank had carefully directed his attack against less revered scholars, Meinecke unhesitatingly struck back. Frank, he maintained, had falsified both the teachings of Treitschke and the traditions of German scholarship. Treitschke, according to Meinecke, had always been the foe of any ideal which threatened the freedom and the sacredness of the individual, whether the threat came from political authorities of the day or from collectivist philosophies. Treitschke had fought throughout his life for freedom of inquiry, and he had never wavered in his recognition that free inquiry meant the certainty of divergent conclusions. In his insistence on the moral importance of the individual personality, he was a child of German idealism: "In his admiration for Bismarck, he did not forget Goethe." Undoubtedly, Meinecke admitted, the generation just past had produced no one comparable in stature to the giants of whom Treitschke was the last; but German historians had been true to the ideals formulated by their great predecessors. Above all, they had defended the right and the necessity of free inquiry, which was the basis of all historical truth.

The result was a foregone conclusion. In November 1935, Meinecke's name was gone from the cover of the *Historische Zeitschrift*, and the first article was contributed by Walter Frank. Contemptuously Frank described the fate of those scholars who, boasting of their impartiality and objectivity, had thought the National Socialist revolution a temporary evil to be lived through in silence until sanity returned. They had been swept aside. Everyone now understood that there was room in Germany only for those who could say, like Treitschke, "The patriot in me is a thousand times stronger than the professor!" Now German scholarship could be brought back into harmony with national life. "The march of the storm columns and the song of the masses and the solitary struggles of the scholar and the artist, will create tones which will blend together, freely and without compulsion, into one great German symphony." However, Frank hastened to add the warning that refusal to speak or teach in harmony with the ideals of the New Germany would be treated as "a revolt of insolent slaves, who must be beaten down with the whip."

Meinecke's voice can be silenced. But will the voice of Treitschke, speaking from volumes which form part of the National Socialist *Acta Sanctorum*, blend into the one great German symphony? Or will it encourage those who would call a different tune?

Treitschke placed the state, the power of the state, the needs of the state, in the foreground of his "Politics" because he believed that Germans lacked reverence for the state, that they were a cosmopolitan, not a national people. But in the last years of his career this belief was unfounded: he had not perceived the changes which had taken place in German ways of thinking since he first began to preach the blessings of unity in the days when there was no German Empire. By the nineties he was preaching to the converted. The "rough national pride, splendid in its one-sidedness" which he had admired in an Englishman like Canning, had become superabundant in Germany. Undoubtedly the uneasiness of foreigners like Austen Chamberlain, who listened to Treitschke's diatribes and observed the ecstasy of young Germans in the lecture hall, was well-founded. Treitschke must stand as one of those who encouraged the blind, uncontrolled lust for expansion in prewar Germany. The "Politics" is valuable today because from its pages we can learn how much of contemporary Germany is rooted deep in the past and therefore unlikely to be easily uprooted.

The "Politics" is no less valuable as a measure of the gulf separating the Third Reich from nineteenth-century Germany. The distinguishing characteristic of German political life today is that it is totalitarian, that neither the individual in Germany nor the rest of the world outside Germany can appeal to any power higher than the "national will." The question as to what agency enforces that will is irrelevant; it is the claim to exclusive power and right which is significant.

Such a claim was not even thought possible by Treitschke, much less upheld by him. Against the older western European traditions of political thought, which exalted the individual citizen and mankind above the state, he urged the central importance of the state. Yet he accepted limitations on the power of the state as self-evident. He did not stress these limitations precisely because they seemed to him self-evident. He urged his students to study Aristotle because the Greeks revered the state. They did, he added, exaggerate the importance of the state, but modern students were in no danger of falling into this error. "The different circumstances of our lives prevent this, and above all that recognition of our undying personality which Christianity has brought us, through which we realize that man can never be merely a member of the State, when he is free to think as he will of God and the Kingdom of God." Modern Europeans, he declared, realized that the citizen could be a member of several different groups, political and non-political, "without identifying his whole personality with any one of them." The state might try to use its power to impair freedom of conscience, "although it would be madness to attempt it amongst us; it would meet with such resistance that it would have to acknowledge its own impotence." He contended that the growth of strong national states would increase the freedom and independence of the individual. "The State feels that its own strength and glory rests ultimately on the freedom of reasonable, thoughtful men." To him, a national army such as that of Germany presupposed political freedom and general satisfaction with the government; otherwise it would be dangerous to put arms into the hands of the people.

And as the state was strong only if the citizen was free, so the state would realize that there was a real family of nations. "Every State will realize that it is an integral part of the community of other States in which it finds itself placed, and that it must live with them on some kind of terms, bad or good, as the case may be." War was the ultimate arbiter in quarrels between states, and treaties could not endure forever in a dynamic world, but "a state which went upon the principle of despising faith and loyalty would be constantly threatened by enemies." International law had no absolute sanctions behind it, only mutual give-and-take; but even on this basis Treitschke thought it possible to look forward to "a harmonious comity of nations, who, concluding treaties of their own free will, admit restrictions upon their sovereignty without abrogating it."

Cold calculation of national interest would suffice to prevent tyranny at home and anarchy abroad, Treitschke believed. He reminded his hearers, however, that, in the ultimate, all power, including the power of the state, was from God. Treitschke insisted that a political philosophy which was indifferent to the means by which power was won and the ends for which it was used was founded on "deep immorality"; ruin awaited the state which made power an end in itself, rather than a means for service to "the highest moral welfare of the human race."

Treitschke and the Germany of his day had not forgotten Goethe in their admiration for Bismarck. Though that Germany had travelled far from the individualism and cosmopolitanism of Goethe's Weimar, it was still far from the Munich of Adolf Hitler and Paul Goebbels. Goethe, Treitschke, Goebbels—here are fixed points through which the line of German history must be traced. If we have supreme confidence in the teachings of history, we may project the line into the future. But whether we will draw comfort from the vista thus opened to the imagination depends on the degree to which we share the optimism of that long line of Anglo-Saxons which stretches back through Edward Grey and Woodrow Wilson to that forgotten liberal, Sir Mountstuart Elphinstone Grant Duff, who admitted in 1866 that Bismarck's influence had been "simply evil," but who remained serenely confident that the Iron Chancellor would fail because, "when any institutions come directly into contact with the spirit of the time, they may resist for five years, or ten, or twenty, but down they must go in the end."

The New Italy Coming of Age: 1870-1915

KENT ROBERTS GREENFIELD

⇛⇛⇛⇛⇛⇛⇛⇛⇛⇛⇛ *Published in 1931* ⇚⇚⇚⇚⇚⇚⇚⇚⇚⇚⇚

In the years before unification became a reality, Italian patriots had rarely thought of the difficulties that would arise in the post-unity period. Almost always they had considered unity a panacea. Yet when the Kingdom of Italy was proclaimed in 1861, and when Venetia and Rome were acquired in 1866 and 1870, it became clear that Italian history had not come to a close; and it did not take Italian patriots long to disabuse themselves of the notion that the establishment of a United Italy meant the end of the time of troubles. In short, the newly established Italian Kingdom was faced with problems of a sort that would have baffled states much older: the persistence of local particularism; strong sectional animosities; the absence of a tradition of self-government; the hostility of the papacy to the new regime; the woeful lack of the natural resources that were all-important in the world of the late nineteenth century; the limited taxpaying ability of most of the population; the backwardness of the educational system; widespread illiteracy; the humiliating emigration of large numbers of Italians to other countries; and numerous diplomatic rebuffs. Small wonder that the new Kingdom of Italy was filled with disillusioned patriots; unity, it seemed, had created more problems than it had solved. In the present article, Kent Roberts Greenfield, to whose contributions to nineteenth-century Italian history reference has already been made (see page 628), examines some of the main difficulties with which the Kingdom of Italy had to contend in the early decades of its existence; and he emerges with the significant conclusion that, all things considered, Italian achievements in the period were remarkable.

The period of Italian history that lies between 1870 and 1915 has usually been regarded as formless, of minor significance, and lacking in plot. Until recently it was the custom of Italian historians to treat it as an anti-climax. Mazzini, Cavour, Garibaldi, Victor Emanuel II were dead, and no redeemer to succeed them appeared. The nation was plunged from the poetry of the Risorgimento into the prose of national housekeeping, with a large and poor family to look after. Its floundering and discouragement lasted so long that the world at large lost interest and acquired the habit of regarding the Italians as a people of whom not much was to be expected under the conditions of modern life. Foreign observers, and the Italians themselves, were impressed with the contrast between the new Italy, bewildered, poor and struggling, and the new Germany, efficient, rich, confident and dominant. The government embarked on imperialistic adventures in Africa that ended in humiliating disasters; its statesmen followed a foreign policy which inspired Lord Salisbury's stinging description of them as "sturdy beggars." The case for a really impressive Italy looked hopeless indeed in view of its illiteracy, its lack of industrial resources, and the swarming emigration of its proletariat to other countries where their frugal, laborious but illiterate and sometimes disorderly life confirmed the outsider in his supercilious conception of all Italians as "dagos." The well-informed were aware that Italy's new constitution had had only a brief test of opportunity. But in modern life fifty years seems a long time, and when the Italians failed to display any sensational evidences of progress, we set it down to Latin inferiority and ceased to expect much of the new Italy.

But the period has ended in such a spectacular outburst of national energy that it now invites a more careful inspection than we have been disposed to give it. Considered as a postlude to the Risorgimento it was an epoch of disenchantment. Considered as a prelude to the present movement it has been found by Italian historians to have contained a poetry of its own and events and tendencies of unsuspected importance. What I wish to do is to suggest a new perspective with regard to it. This may prove to be incorrect, as any historical picture taken close-up is likely to be. But a new perspective is needed to explain a revival

Reprinted by special permission from *Proceedings of the Association of History Teachers of the Middle States and Maryland*, XXIX (1931), 22-31.

that did not await the Fascist movement, but became evident in the late 'nineties and that manifested its effect in both the intellectual and political life of the nation about the turn of the century—an effect that has been steadily cumulative up to the present moment. My apology for presenting the view that I have in mind is that it is one that has been adopted by the most recent historians of Italy, both by those sympathetic and those unsympathetic with the Fascist regime.

The first correction necessary is to give more weight to the difficulties with which the new state was confronted. If one measures the achievements of the period 1870-1915 against the extraordinary handicaps that the nation had to overcome, one has to acknowledge that it made a fine display of the kind of power that a modern state must have at its command.

At the moment when Italy joined them the other nations of Europe were rushing into the present era of industrial and commercial giantism. Unification had made an Italy that was poor in equipment and sadly deficient in the capital, the natural resources and the technical skill to take a place of importance in this expansion. Unification was necessary, but it was only the first step. It merely cleared away the political barriers that had interfered with the improvement of agriculture and the expansion of manufactures and trade. One remembers the old proverb: "In order to have an omelette you must break your eggs." But breaking the eggs does not produce an omelette. Italy had to have railroads, ships, machinery, capital and training in industrial and financial technique. Lacking materials and money the nation had to go into the foreign market to supply her industries with coal and iron and to

---

ADOWA: Battle of 1896 in which Italian troops were decisively defeated by Ethiopian forces. Faced with one of the most humiliating disasters in the history of European imperialism, the Italian government was forced to recognize the independence of Ethiopia and to abandon temporarily the plan to extend the Italian colonial empire in Africa. Mussolini exploited the memory of Adowa on a large scale, and when the Fascist invasion of Ethiopia began in October 1935, the first objective was Adowa.

CARDUCCI: Italian poet, satirist, and literary historian who served as professor of Italian literature at the University of Bologna for many years (d. 1907). A republican in his youth, he became reconciled to the monarchy because it fostered constitutional government and protected civil liberties, but he deplored the evidences of inefficiency and corruption in the political life of the Kingdom.

provide herself with capital. One productive resource she had in abundance and that was labor. But her labor was unskilled and uneducated.

Furthermore the masses of the new nation had the psychology of an agricultural community. Even the trading class was dominated by it. The most cherished social aspiration of the *borghesia* was to establish themselves in the world by obtaining possession of a piece of land. This widespread ambition made for steadiness, but it also made for conservatism, and retarded the process by which capital could be liberated and mobilized for industrial expansion.

Another handicap was the habit of sectionalism which the Risorgimento had only begun to destroy. That movement, carried through by a small and high-minded minority, had left the masses still Piedmontese, Lombards, Venetians, Tuscans, Romans, Neapolitans, Sicilians—speaking different dialects and further isolated by the absence of common enterprises. Localism of speech and habitudes would yield only when Italy was provided with a single system of education and an organized system of communication, and the new government was too poor to provide the one or the other. The worst problem of sectionalism was the contrast between the North and the South. They were then, as they still are, like two different countries. Naples was "the Ireland of Italy." "To harmonize North and South," said Cavour, "is harder than fighting with Austria or struggling with Rome."

The sectionalism of the South was at first actually increased by the act of unification because it was deepened by its economic consequences. With the union and the disappearance of the internal

STEFANO JACINI: Italian economist and political leader (d. 1891). Serving briefly as one of Cavour's advisers, he was active in advancing new railroad construction and in making the older lines run more efficiently. As a senator in his later years, he furthered the investigation of the conditions of Italian agricultural life with a view to increasing the efficiency of methods of production.

MARINETTI: Twentieth-century Italian writer and iconoclastic literary critic. Spokesman for futurism, he revolted against what he considered to be the tyranny of tradition and considered it his mission to deliver Italy from her past. His worship of violence, danger, and sensationalism fitted in well with the outlook of Fascism.

tariff line, the nascent industry of the South was immediately ruined by the competition of the industries of North Italy whose products invaded its market. And time and policy, the construction of railways, still further opening the Southern market, and the inauguration in 1882 of a policy of national protection for Italian industries only widened the chasm, and deepened the misery of the Southern population, who sought refuge in a vast and tragic emigration to Tunis, South America and the United States.

The Risorgimento had left great numbers of Italians still actually separated from their country. Trieste, Fiume and the Dalmatian cities created the painful problem of irredentism; and due to the circumstances of the inglorious war of 1866, the northern frontier was so drawn as to leave not only these cities but 500,000 Italians (in the Trentino and Upper Adige), together with the Brenner Pass, under the hand of Austria.

The new Italy was further torn by a profound moral schism. The settlement of the Roman question had cast multitudes of patriotic hearts into a torment of divided allegiance, made acute by the Pope's command that the faithful abstain from the polls in national elections. Furthermore, the collapse of the old governments left none of the various regions of Italy prepared for the life of a constitutional state. The Piedmontese were ripest in the art of self-government, and they had had only twelve years of it. In general the masses continued to regard the government as a natural enemy. It was the gravity of all these complexities of division that drew from Massimo d'Azeglio his often-quoted exclamation. "Italy is made; now we must make the Italians."

Measured against such difficulties what the Italians achieved before the War is little short of amazing. The government had at once addressed itself to the fundamental task of creating a national network of roads. Railroads that were prodigies of engineering skill were thrust through the mountainous skeleton of the peninsula to its extremities. The pre-War government of Italy must further be credited with an admirable measure of success in its struggle with two of the most deadly enemies of modern civilization—disease and ignorance. By 1921-23 the death-rate had been brought down to about 17 per thousand, as compared with 12 for England, 14 for Germany, 17.5 for France and 20 for Hungary. The figures that show the reduction of illiteracy are equally impressive. The new state inherited in the South a population that was 90 per cent illiterate. In 1872 the average rate of illiteracy for the whole country was a little under 70 per cent. A vigorous attack on this problem had to await an improvement in the financial situation, though the state had committed itself courageously from the beginning to the principle of free and compulsory education. The financial renaissance came with the turn of the century and after 1900 laws were enacted that put life into the lower schools. The ice-cap of illiteracy began to melt away. In 1909 the percentage of illiterates had fallen to 45. In 1915 it was 37.8. By 1921 it had been reduced by another 10 per cent. In Piedmont it is now only 11—about the percentage that the War tests showed in our own army.

To mend the breach made by the antagonism of the Church and the State both time and wisdom were required, and when the new century arrived, the Pope and the King, though still legally unreconciled, had entered into a kind of working accord, to the relief of the national conscience.

To increase the defective economic power of the nation the government had grappled with the task of nationalizing agricultural production, instituting in 1881-1885 the great *Inchiesta agraria* directed by Stefano Jacini, and created the conditions that eventually led to an agricultural renaissance.

Although agriculture remained the leading form of production, perhaps the most significant sign of the powers of the new Italy was the development of its manufacturing industry. The industrial revolution, retarded by the want of iron and coal, had been pushing its way into the life of Italy with the sluggishness and certainty of a burning lava stream. Signs of marked progress towards industrialization began to show in the early '80's. In that decade the importation of raw and partly-wrought iron and steel and of machine parts rose by leaps and bounds. The amount of wool imported was doubled, that of cotton tripled. The handicaps were immense—in the lack of trained ability, in the superior social attractiveness of the liberal professions for young men of intellect; perhaps most serious, in the chasm between the industrialists and the classes whose savings constituted the sole important social reservoir of capital, and who were habituated to investment in savings banks, whether postal or private, or in the purchase of a bit of land. Industrial development was in part spontaneous, in part due to artificial protection, definitively adopted as the national policy in 1887. Among the comparatively large number of small enterprises that struggled into being under such conditions were a few on a large scale, directed by the forerunners of "the captains of industry." For the most part these creators of wealth belonged to a new generation which had to await the passing of the generation who had conspired and fought. To their support they gathered the technicians and the capital needful first from Belgium and France and later from Switzerland and Germany. By 1905 Milan had passed Lyons as the greatest silk manufacturing city in the world. Italian industries, notably the machine and metal trades and the textile manufactures, gained ground in the home market and were successful in thrusting their way into markets abroad. And Italy began to reduce her huge coal bill to England by converting into electricity the white coal of her mountain streams. With an estimated potentiality of five billion horsepower these gave her the resources to become an industrial nation of the first rank. The effect of the advent of a protected industrialism was to raise the prices of industrial commodities, create a hotbed for socialistic propaganda, and incidentally to aggravate the problem of the South. But while it set up new strains and stresses in Italian life, its effect in the long run was to knit the economic tissues of the nation; and in time it rallied to its support those who saw that Italy's political independence would remain incomplete until her economic independence could be effected and she was armed with a formidable industrial power.

Given the poverty, sectionalism and general backwardness of Italy, it is clear to us now that most of the work that needed to be done could be accomplished only by time, by the growth of the nation, the healing of wounds, the knitting of tissues. Much of the credit is due to the patience of the peasant bearing a staggering burden of taxation, for which he received in return but little of the benefit he had been taught to expect from unity. But in retrospect the work of the government, despite the notorious corruption and the political huckstering that disgraced Italian parliamentary politics from the '70's to the present century, leaves a record far from discreditable. Everything else had to wait upon the prosaic work of balancing the budget and developing resources, under the dead weight imposed by the need of building a new navy and maintaining a system of compulsory military service, superadded to the enormous cost of the reconstruction that I have outlined; and the financial policy of men like Sella, Sonnino and Luzzati must be acknowledged a most substantial success. And in foreign affairs, in spite of reverses, the government had at least kept Italy's head above water as one of the Great Powers.

The darkest hour of the new Italy followed the mortifying defeat which the Abyssinians inflicted on her soldiers at Adowa in 1896. The nation was swept by a surge of demoralization and social unrest that threatened the very existence of the monarchy and culminated when King Humbert was shot down by an anarchist at Monza in 1900. But the real strength that the nation had been gaining was manifested by a remarkable rally in the years that followed. The new ruler, Victor Emanuel III, then in his thirty-first year, represented a generation that had been born with the Kingdom and his accession proved to be a turning point. The King was popular and his ministries attacked the problems of the state at home and abroad with a new vigor and resolution. In short the monarchy, after floundering for a generation in a morass in which the abnormal difficulties of its peculiar situation had been increased by scandalous corruption and rash adventures in imperialism, gave evidence of becoming enlightened and progressive. The new independence, optimism and self-respect, strikingly apparent to all students of Italy after the turn of the century whatever their angle of approach, were not due wholly to the spirit of the government. Both reflected the growing prosperity and power of the nation. Italy had gained a strength more nearly equal to its ambitions.

It is not surprising that the world failed to take a fair measure of the progress that pre-War Italy had made. Not only had it been unspectacular, but it had not been appreciated at its true value by the Italians themselves. The literature of the first generation in the life of the new nation, including its historiography, is colored by a retrospective wistfulness and a contemptuous depreciation of the politics of the new state. One remembers the withering lines of Carducci on the ministers Depretis and Sella in the *Ode barbari*. Dreaming of Rome he cries:

> What is it to me that the bristling spectral vintner of Stradella
> Mingles in Montecitorio Allobrogian jests and wiles?
> Or that the tireless weaver of Biella busies himself
> Within his webs, a spider weaving in vain? . . .

The historians, like Tivaroni in his monumental work on the Risorgimento, represented that movement as a splendid epic that had ended in gloom with the death of its great protagonists, a cascade that had leaped in glory only to be lost in a dismal swamp. In general the young intellectuals turned from their own traditions of culture, and dazzled by the stupendous success of Germany, equipped themselves with the scientific method exalted in the German universities and devoted themselves to a Sisyphean effort to imitate German scholarship in rolling up great accumulations of positive knowledge.

The disenchantment and disorientation that marks the literature and the intellectual activity of the new Italy can only be understood if one bears in mind the peculiarities of the idealism that had been dominant in the preceding period. The Risorgimento had been accomplished by a minority of the nation, a small and ardent minority, who were far ahead of the masses of the people. This minority, this Young Italy, were nurtured on memories of the past greatness of the race, of *Roma immortalis*, the medieval papacy, the communes and the Renaissance. They were fired to heroic sacrifices by leaders like Gioberti and Mazzini, whose being was aglow with a conviction of the greatness of Italy that was fundamentally religious, and by whom they were persuaded that when Italy was free the Italians would regain their lost primacy in the civilization of Europe. This idealism was greeted at once with a cold shower of disappointments. To give Italy a power equal to their hopes it was necessary to settle down to a long, grinding effort of reconstruction, and instead of assuming the moral hegemony of Europe meekly to go to school to other nations in order to equip their backward country with a modern technique.

Their reaction was the sharper because the successes of the Risorgimento had been attended by a marvellous luck. Cavour and Garibaldi had succeeded with a facility that dazzled the world. Both of them still seem magicians. A magnificent demonstration of ardor, the struggle for freedom was not prolonged enough to test the patience of the Italians or to teach them the value of discipline. It was natural that they should expect the impossible of their new government. The effect of having their burning idealism plunged into a cold bath of poverty and disappointment was to produce what can only be characterized as a national inferiority complex.

Always in thinking of Italy since the eighteenth century it is necessary to bear in mind the abyss that has separated a minority of patriotic intellectuals, abreast of modern thought, often enriching it with new conceptions, and the backward masses. For the intellectuals of the period after 1870 it meant a tragic sense of frustration.

There are two phenomena of the period which derive an added significance from the state of mind and the situation I have just described.

One is the imperialistic adventures, the foreign policy, of the new Italy, so disproportionate to its resources. They are less ridiculous if taken to represent in part the need of the disappointed idealism of the Risorgimento for national self-assertion, for some earnest of the splendid destiny for which Young Italy had been willing to face martyrdom in the name of Rome. With nothing but failures and failures to show for its action the Italian government was forced to strike out somewhat recklessly in its foreign policy. By 1911, for an important element of the nation success in some form had become a kind of moral necessity.

Another phenomenon which is closely related to the situation of the idealistic minority is the Socialist movement in Italy. Founded in 1892 the Italian Socialist Party quickly effected a powerful and vigorous organization and secured a monopoly of the rapidly multiplying votes of the workingmen. It owed its peculiar effectiveness to the fact that it attracted the best brains of the younger generation of intellectuals. Sick alike of the nostalgic incantations of the veterans of the Risorgimento and the futilities and corruption of Liberal politics they threw themselves into the cause of social reform. In short the Socialist Party became *par excellence* a party of protest through which the disappointed idealism of Italy could vent its disgust with a staggering and inglorious government and express its *Weltschmerz* [weariness of life].

The fate of the Italian Socialist Party confirms this analysis. Whenever it approached success in its more radical proposals it split into factions, and the moderate wing would rally to the support of the government. In 1911 when the soldiers were about to depart for Tripoli the Socialists undertook to stop the War by means of strikes. The strike movement fizzled out; Turati, the Socialist leader, went over to the government; and the nation saw the troops off for Tripoli with an enthusiasm not witnessed in Italy since the great days of the Risorgimento. The policy of the government was such at last as to give expression to a disillusioned nationalism by which the socialist movement had profited for two decades.

But behind this revival of patriotic feeling was a new development in Italian psychology. It manifested itself shortly after the turn of the century as the nation began to feel its new strength. The youthful intellectuals then coming of age had grown up with the nascent industrial civilization of Italy and were fascinated by its vistas of power. They revolted against the old pessimism. No longer charmed by *Das Kapital* of Karl Marx they recited dramas in d'Annunzio's "imperialistic style," such as his play *La Nave*, produced in 1908, with the ringing lines:

> Arma la prora e salpa verso il mondo
> (Man the prow and sail out into the world)

and his lyrics that hymned the glories of the aeroplane. They were Nietzschean; they believed in force, in *élan vital*, in "the religion of the state," in "the religion of race." They denied that imperialism is a disease or an exaggeration, defining it as "the natural development in the collective mass of the nation of the instinct of power, of the desire of expansion, which animates the individual psychology of each of us." Colonies Italy must have; but they were accessory: they were important as an expression of power. With this movement came Marinetti shouting his Futurism, proposing to send the past to the dustbin, fill up the canals of Venice and create an art and a literature all Italian, brand new. Such was the young and militant group and not a weak-kneed bourgeoisie with whom the Socialists found themselves face to face when they opposed the war with Turkey. Italian nationalist idealism had regained its courage.

I shall not trace the mutations of this new psychology through the period of the Great War or into the present. Suffice it to say here that those whom it inspired flocked from all of the older political groups into a new party, the Nationalist Party, which was founded in a Congress at Florence in 1910 on the eve of the Tripolitan expedition. It was this party, led by Federzoni and Forges-Davanzati, which combined with Benito Mussolini and his followers to effect the Revolution of 1922 and to form the National Fascist Party. . . .

XX

Currents in British and French History, 1870-1914

Gladstone and Ireland

MICHAEL TIERNEY

Constructive Reforms [in Britain], 1860-1914

EDWARD P. CHEYNEY

The Church in the Third Republic

J. V. DUCATTILLON

Gladstone and Ireland

MICHAEL TIERNEY

Published in 1939

William Ewart Gladstone served as prime minister four times: from 1868 to 1874; from 1880 to 1885; in 1886 again; and from 1892 to 1894. And during each of his four ministries the Irish question figured prominently. If at the outset of his first ministry he announced that his mission was to pacify Ireland, the reason was that American Fenians were dramatizing and publicizing Irish grievances and causing considerable embarrassment to the British government. Gladstone's answer to nationalistic Fenianism took the form, first, of an act for the disestablishment and partial disendowment of the Protestant Church of Ireland and, second, of the Land Act of 1870, by the terms of which the position of the Irish tenant was to be improved. Despite these reform measures and in part because of them, the Irish question became more troublesome than ever; and so, during the course of his second ministry, Gladstone pushed for further economic reforms in Ireland. This time the result was the Land Act of 1881, which embodied the principle of the "three F's" (fair rent, fixed tenure, and free sale) and recognized the land rights of tenants as well as landlords. Since economic concessions did not succeed in eliminating the Irish demand for an alteration in the political relations between England and Ireland, Gladstone finally became converted to the cause of home rule; and during the course of his last two ministries he introduced the unsuccessful Home Rule bills of 1886 and 1893. In short, Gladstone wrecked the Liberal Party in his search for an answer to the Irish question. In the review article that follows, Michael Tierney, President of University College, Dublin, re-examines Gladstone's Irish policies and raises a number of thought-provoking "if's" concerning Anglo-Irish relations.

It is possible to view the history of Ireland, during the past century and a half, as the working out in an un-English field of a characteristically English principle. In 1690 John Locke justified the glorious revolution of two years earlier by asserting the right to resistance by direct action against misuse of the powers of government. Whether or not his theory was philosophically sound, it was undoubtedly in harmony with the recent history of England and with the spirit which has inspired British constitutional development from his day till our own. Theorists who seek to set that development upon a basis of strict legality always come sooner or later upon the great fissure which renders legalistic continuity impossible. Resistance may be condemned as illegal, but it is none the less constitutional; it represents in fact the negative core of the whole system, which remains intractable when the positive outer layers are stripped away.

This implicit acknowledgment of the right to revolt has given English institutions their peculiar stability as expressing the political genius of the English people. Like other forms of political ideology, it is, however, of doubtful export value. When applied to countries entirely outside the British Empire, it proved itself, in the hands of English statesmen such as Canning and Palmerston, a terrible solvent of the older European order, founded on the very doctrines torn up in 1688. As it has worked itself out by its own force within the Empire, where English statesmen have naturally rather been its reluctant victims than its agents, it has kept the power and right of the British Parliament to govern non-British peoples subject to perpetual question. Indeed it may yet prove, in the long view, to be as great a solvent of Empire as it has already proved itself to be of the European order. In the eighteenth century its operation lost the British Crown its finest colonies in America. In the late nineteenth and early twentieth it has performed an amputation still more drastic and touching nearer the vital centre: the overthrow of the settlement with Ireland in the shape of the Act of Union recommended in sonorous Virgilian hexameters to the House of Commons by William Pitt in 1800.

In the eyes of future historians the Treaty of London in 1921 may come to loom as large as the Treaty of Versailles in 1783. The earlier event, by acknowledging the independence of the United States,

Reprinted by special permission from *Studies, An Irish Quarterly Review*, XXVIII (1939), 24-34.

marked the end of the First British Empire. The later, less than a century and a quarter after Pitt's peroration, finally demonstrated the incapacity of the British Parliament to govern Ireland and thereby changed what had seemed, during the reigns of four sovereigns, the Second Empire's immutable character. Attempts to justify both the resistance of the American colonies and that of Ireland, by showing that Parliament had violated legality in its treatment of them, have constantly failed[1]—for the very reason that in both cases legality was irrelevant. It was by going outside it that the founders of the United States won their victory, and one of the causes which slowed down the progress of the Irish revolt was notoriously the doctrinaire pacifism of O'Connell. Ireland's grievances were no more of a legal character than those of America, and they were infinitely more pressing; but the difference in the time required for victory is easily explained by the vast difference in situation and resources between the two countries.

The struggle for Irish independence, which began after a short interval of quiescence following on the upheavals of 1798-1803, was undoubtedly inspired by the ideas of a section among the eighteenth century ascendancy, and these ideas were with equal certainty of almost entirely English origin. It is true that they acquired great additional strength from their transplantation to Irish soil, fertilised by memories of an ancient culture and by vaguely-formed impulses to a separate political as well as social system. The defeat of Charles Edward in 1745 was almost a greater blow to Gaelic Ireland than to Gaelic Scotland, and one of its ultimate results was that coalescence between the "old inhabitants of the island" and the dissident Anglo-Irish which

---

[1] See *Parliament and the British Empire*, by Robert L. Schuyler (Columbia University Press, 1929), for a criticism of such attempts from that of Molyneux (*Case of Ireland Stated*) in 1698 to McIlwain's application in 1923 of Molyneux's views to America.

LORD RANDOLPH CHURCHILL: English statesman in the House of Commons in the late nineteenth century, and father of Winston Churchill. Officially a Conservative, he was in frequent difficulties with his party leaders. He championed the cause of Tory democracy, calling attention to the desirability of social reforms. At the same time he was a vigorous defender of the Established Church and a vigorous opponent of Irish Home Rule.

TREATY OF LONDON: Settlement of 1921 by the terms of which the British government granted dominion status to Southern Ireland as the Irish Free

has produced the modern complex English-speaking Irish nation. The Union, designed to safeguard both Imperial interests and the interests of the loyal section among the ascendancy, was a failure almost from the start. Its collapse was delayed by many causes, some purely personal and accidental, but chiefly by an English political tendency which is in a sense the corollary to the constitutional right of rebellion: the tendency to yield only to overwhelming pressure backed by the threat or the actual exercise of force. Catholic Emancipation was granted in response to a half-formulated threat. In order to destroy the Union settlement, the maximum force was naturally required; and owing partly to the innate pacifism of the Irish and partly to a series of strange chances, the pressure had to be raised to its highest intensity not once but many times—and even at the last was only partially effective.

Nevertheless it was obvious to almost any but the blindest partisan that the issue was decided long before the final and most violent phases of the struggle. From 1886 to 1916 Irish nationalism, while deepening its roots and strengthening its fibre by means of Sinn Féin, the Gaelic League, and the Literary Renaissance, was only waiting the hour to make its last push upward to full political stature. The defeat of the two Home Rule Bills of 1886 and 1893, if English statesmen could have only realised it, had merely made inevitable larger and more insistent demands at some future date, and nothing could have been more senseless than the attempt, from 1912 to 1920, to repeat the tactics which a generation earlier had been apparently successful but really disastrous. The failure of the Union, the incompetence of the British Parliament to govern Ireland, was first demonstrated and proclaimed in 1886. Only the most elementary lack of knowledge, vision, or even ordinary prudence, can explain the long-continued English effort to impart a feeble semblance of vitality to a system which the

---

State. Northern Ireland continued under the old relationship with Britain. Although the Treaty was denounced by the "Irreconcilables," led by Eamon de Valera, the Dail Eireann ratified it.

CAPTAIN O'SHEA: A follower of Parnell who in 1890 named his leader as corespondent in a divorce suit. The scandal ruined Parnell, who was renounced by Gladstone and by the majority of his colleagues within the ranks of the Irish Nationalists. It also served to weaken temporarily the Home Rule movement.

whole world knew to be dead. The one statesman of first rank who saw the truth and acted upon it was Gladstone; and the Treaty of 1921 was as much a monument—which would have horrified himself— to his statesmanship as were the abortive Bills by which he had tried so long before to anticipate and prevent what he would surely have lamented as a bitter tragedy.

The simultaneous appearance of Mr. Hammond's impressive study and of Dr. Eyck's objective and very readable biography enables us to enter more fully than has yet been possible into the development of Gladstone's Irish policy and its relation to the complex evolution of his sinuous and many-sided personality. Perhaps the highest compliment that can be paid to Mr. Hammond's work is the statement of one's impression that he shows here the same wide sweep of knowledge and sympathy, the same skill in the marshalling of multitudinous detail, the same sensitive sympathy and the same nobility of style as in his classic studies of English social history. His object is at once to explain the growth of Gladstone's almost religious devotion to Ireland's cause as he understood it, to examine the reasons for his failure, and to elicit Irish sympathy as well as English understanding for a man whose services to both countries were almost equally great, and who might have stood forth as the maker of a new, more real bond between them had not the forces against him been too powerful and his time too short. In this multiple task Mr. Hammond has succeeded to such a point that his work is sure to rank as a classic of historical exposition, not only for English but for Irish students, in spite of the fact that circumstances have so irrevocably nullified Gladstone's policy. Dr. Eyck performs the great service of giving us with cool and skilful brevity and yet with much well-applied variety of illustration, the long perspective of the career which ripened Gladstone, all too late, for his Irish tasks. Here and there his orderly narrative enables us to see some of Mr. Hammond's argument in a usefully different light.

The shorter work in which Captain Harrison expands, with fresh emphasis, part of his earlier authoritative vindication of Parnell serves as a sort of third drama in what, from the Irish point of view, is a tragic trilogy. As usual, the hero is changed, but the theme remains essentially the same, and here there is a sharpening of outline, a deepening of shadow as compared with the other books. Captain Harrison's purpose is to convict Mr. Garvin, Chamberlain's distinguished biographer, of what amounts to decided partiality, and neglect, if not deliberate suppression, of evidence which tells strongly against his hero and in favour of Parnell. Presenting the reader with numerous photographs of essential documents, he establishes a very strong case for his conclusion that Chamberlain was not only behind the famous *Times* attack, by way of the Pigott forgeries, on Parnell, but also the moving agent in O'Shea's decision to apply for a divorce and therefore in Parnell's political ruin. Since the appearance of this book Mr. Garvin has published a reply to its charges in the *Observer*[1] of which he is editor. His reply is, however, more assertive and ex-clamatory than convincing; and although there is more to be said, in explanation rather than in justification, of Chamberlain's actions than Captain Harrison perhaps will allow, it will take much new evidence to clear him of having gone to extreme lengths to satisfy his political rancour. It is to be hoped that the new evidence will take the form of an extensive or indeed a complete publication of Chamberlain's letters and papers. As the case now stands, an ounce of fresh documentation is worth a ton of advocacy; and history surely calls, at this distance of time, for the whole truth, whatever its effect on reputations may ultimately be.

The Irish tragedy was only secondarily Gladstone's, but he had in his own character one at least of the elements to be found in that of a Sophoclean hero. As one reads Mr. Hammond's pages, one cannot help being struck again and again by Gladstone's peculiar isolation of intellect and temperament, to which indeed they explicitly draw one's attention. This quality was most marked in relation to Ireland, where circumstances came to meet it in creating the tragic effect. Like Ajax or Oedipus, he stood apart from his fellows, understood fully by scarcely any of them, battling desperately against a threatening doom which he foresaw and whose causes he understood when they were hidden from almost everyone else. He made his Irish effort with magnificent conviction and with heroic power, but he made it years too late when great obstacles, whose growth he could have done much to prevent, stood in his way. Although he knew far more of Irish history than did Parnell, whose ignorance in that respect appears to have been phenomenal, he visited this country only once, in 1877, and then only stayed for about three weeks. His excursion "did not extend beyond a very English Pale," says Morley, and his hosts were mostly prominent Whigs or officials; yet what he saw "made a deep im-

[1] August 21, 1938.

pression on me," as he told the Dublin Corporation, "and has enabled me the better to understand the intense feeling with which an Irishman loves his country." Mr. Hammond's judgment that if the two men had lived in the early years of the twentieth century, it would have been Gladstone and not Parnell who would have been attracted by the Irish literary renaissance, only makes the slightness of his acquaintance with Irish realities the more regrettable.

Another misfortune which was, if only too natural, equally disastrous, lay in his very peculiar history and its subtle effect on the formation of his mind. It has long been a commonplace that there were "two Mr. Gladstones," and many of his contemporaries found reason to accuse him of being more multifarious than merely dual in number. Mr. Hammond shows us how large a part in his personality was played by his profound sense of European unity. It was this more than anything else that at last drew his attention to Ireland, after he had expended it so vainly on King Bomba's prisons. It was closely allied with his religiosity. He said himself that he owed little to living teachers, but enormously to four dead ones, who are named for us by Morley: Aristotle, Augustine, Dante, Butler. To these four should surely be added Homer. Mr. Hammond is probably the first for many years to have extracted something of value from the three enormous volumes of *Studies on Homer and the Homeric Age* which Gladstone published in 1858, and of which Jowett said that a man who discovered the doctrine of the Trinity in Homer must be crazy. In his youth a high Tory, opponent of the Reform Bill, and strong if rather incomprehensible defender of the Church Establishment, he became in his old age, as the result of a process partly due to events but partly spiritual, the leader and spokesman of Liberalism. It has been acutely said that his intricacy in expounding the stages of this transformation was derived from his early study of Aristotle. But his liberal principles, characteristically enough, were not derived from orthodox sources. He shared de Maistre's opinion "that contempt for Locke is the beginning of knowledge," and Mr. Hammond assures us that he owed little or nothing, consciously at least, to Bentham.

When we read the glowing chapters in which Mr. Hammond describes the European and universal sources and quality of his ideas, we feel that he is entitled to a higher place in the history of thought than any liberal leader except Burke. But he had another and very different side to his character, which Mr. Hammond perhaps passes over too easily, although assigning it great importance in regard to his record on Ireland. The creator, more than any other man, of the modern British Treasury system, he united with all this wide-ranging idealism the archetypal Treasury mind. "A peep into the Treasury was . . . fatal to Gladstone's judgment. . . . All his noble enthusiasms were deflated in a cold, dry, unimaginative atmosphere of severity and public thrift." Behind this kink in his psychology there stretched a long record of thorough financial training, begun on his own estate at Hawarden, continued under Peel, and completed in the Budgets in which he carried into practice the teachings of the Utilitarian school. If he owed little to Bentham, he owed much to Adam Smith, to Bentham's disciple Ricardo, and to their joint disciple Peel, whose Tamworth Reading Room Address in 1841 had called forth Newman's classic attack on Utilitarianism. If Gladstone was a Liberal who had reached his principles by devious paths, he began life as a Tory of a thoroughly unsatisfactory doctrinal type. This strange mixture of incompatible creeds, reflected in his often sophistical arguments, was not without its influence, both material and spiritual, on his approach at the end of his long life to the Irish problem. It seriously distracted his attention, affected the composition and therefore the effectiveness of his cabinets, and quite probably delayed his full apprehension of Ireland's real needs and demands.

What first drew his attention to Ireland was unquestionably the Fenian threat, which happened by a peculiar chance almost to coincide with his first term of office as Prime Minister. In this circumstance we find perhaps the most fatal of all examples of the English tendency only to recognise a grievance when it expresses itself in violence. Long before 1868 Gladstone had a European reputation as a Philhellene and a supporter of Italian unity; but Ireland, so long as it was quiescent, though he was much more responsible for its condition and more powerful in its regard, seems to have made little impression on his mind. It is curious to find that a speech of his on Ireland in 1865 was criticised by the future Lord Salisbury as containing "principles that were too harsh and restrictive." When he did find himself face to face with the Irish problem, he approached it in a manner which goes to show that if he had Ireland in his heart, "he had in his brain" (to quote Mr. Hammond) "a disturbing element of England, and of Treasury England." Like Balfour after him, he convinced himself that the problem was one to be solved by the application of certain remedial measures which, great though they were, did not go near its fundamental causes. Concentrating on Church disestablishment and land reform, he postponed till he was too old the real decision that had sooner or later to be made, and found from his own experience that both concessions and their refusal only led to ever larger demands.

It is strange, too, that even when considering reforms that only touched the fringe of the Irish trouble, he did not extend their scope by paying heed in 1873 to the suggestions of Spencer and Hartington for the improvement of the railway system and the institution of local government. His own plans for a new university and for converting the Viceroyalty into a ceremonial office to be held by the Prince of Wales were only half-heartedly pressed, and his first term as Premier thus ended with comparatively slight positive achievement to its credit as regards Ireland. Nevertheless he had done more than any English minister since Melbourne to put the whole complicated problem in a truer and juster light. At the election of 1874 he even used language which seemed to hint at the possibility of Home Rule and which he had a certain difficulty in explaining to his Whig colleagues. It is clear enough that his mind was more flexible when he was not in office. From 1874 to 1880 he was at first in retirement and afterwards engaged on his Bulgarian crusade. When he resumed power, another complex had arisen in his mind: his mission, as ten years before, was still "to pacify Ireland," but by this time he was conscious of his seventy years, and this consciousness led him to set a limit to his policies. After the passage of the Land Act of 1881—an Act whose sweeping terms he had not in the least contemplated a year earlier—he was inclined to regard further Irish reform as a task for his successors.

This great piece of legislation, described by Mr. Hammond as the most revolutionary measure of the century, was carried in an atmosphere of desperate urgency and, though it contained the germs of the settlement which only came to full fruit in the present generation, was to some extent marred by the tension which produced it. In order to overcome the intransigence of the landlords and their powerful English supporters, Irish pressure had to be applied at its fullest, and the resulting disorder and ill-feeling had many unfortunate effects. It prepared the way for the ultimate disappearance of the landlords and, with them, the old social system in Ireland; it brought into English politics a bitterness which was to poison them for a lifetime; and by arousing Gladstone's suspicion of Parnell's motives it postponed for years the understanding between the two men, which only grew at last in time to be shattered by the divorce case. At the same time the rise of Chamberlain and the first disappointment of his ambitions by an unappreciative Gladstone produced the first signs of the split which was to wreck Home Rule.

Gladstone's treatment of Chamberlain is discussed by Mr. Hammond with the fullness it deserves and in a spirit which keeps a middle course between Mr. Garvin's hero-worship and Captain Harrison's unsparing condemnation of the latter statesman. Chamberlain was a man of powerful character, a great political organizer with his mind always sensitive to the movement of electoral opinion, a ferocious opponent with a remarkable capacity for unrestrained invective. As in Gladstone's own case, his personality broke the bonds of party: he began life as a Radical of republican leanings, uneasy and the source of uneasiness in a Cabinet which contained too many Whigs of the old aristocratic school. What determined his fatal evolution into the Tory Jingo was in part his own domineering individualism, which chafed under the necessity of waiting for his chief's interminably-postponed retirement before he could take over the Liberal leadership, in part his unjustified rancour against Parnell, who seems to have treated him with distrust if not actual disdain; but it was also partly his treatment by Gladstone himself. The latter, always rather the lonely prophet than the tactful party manager, while having a very clear judgment of other men, never knew how to handle them successfully, and his curious angularity in this respect lost him not only Chamberlain but probably Hartington and Bright as well. If he could have led his colleagues, or even chosen them, as dynamically and unerringly as he could marshal public opinion behind almost any cause he favored, he would have carried Home Rule in spite of his advanced age and won his magnificent race with time.

As it was, Chamberlain destroyed the hope of an opportune appeasement, rendered inevitable a still more bitter struggle later on, and by grasping at the irresponsible expedient provided by Lord Randolph Churchill's decision to "play the Orange card" prepared the way for the policy of partition whose full possibilities for trouble between England and Ireland have perhaps not even yet been realized. In face of this multiple achievement and its still living consequences, the credit for which is his beyond yea or nay, his exact part in Parnell's personal tragedy, while by no means a question of no importance, is comparatively a minor one. It is curious that, during his final desperate attempts to maintain his impossible position, Parnell should have concentrated so much of his invective upon the "grand old spider" and said so little about the man who made no secret of his hatred both of Parnell himself and of Ireland.

Gladstone's most obvious vindication is the Home Rule Bill which he carried through the House of Commons in 1893 at the age of eighty-four. There is plenty of room, in such an extraordinary set of circumstances, for speculation about what might have been. Had the Irish Party been more adroitly led immediately after the divorce and before the re-election of Parnell, had Dillon and O'Brien been able to come to England or Ireland, had Gladstone been a younger man, or had Parnell not so tragically succumbed to the hardships of his terrific Irish campaign—the whole story might have ended otherwise than in the partial victory of 1893, which only his age prevented Gladstone from bringing to completion. If Parnell could have been induced to retire temporarily, as he had offered to do with far less cause at the time of the Phoenix Park murders, the Home Rule movement might have suffered a brief set-back but only a brief one. If Parnell had not died when he did, he might well have recovered his ascendancy, but only at the cost of an even more terrible split in Ireland in which nationalism would have had to triumph over the Church, to the great disadvantage of both. If Gladstone had been twenty years younger, he would most certainly have carried Home Rule with all its beneficent consequences to both countries; but it is doubtful if in the eye of history he would have had a juster claim to the gratitude and admiration of Irishmen than his record of devoted effort, statesmanlike vision and triumphant ascendancy over what was best in the British character had already secured for him.

Gladstone and the Irish Nation. By J. L. Hammond. (Longmans. 1938.)
Gladstone. By Erich Eyck. (Allen and Unwin. 1938.)
Parnell, Joseph Chamberlain, and Mr. Garvin. By Henry Harrison. (Robert Hale. 1938.)

Constructive Reforms [in Britain], 1860-1914

EDWARD P. CHEYNEY

Published in *1931*

During the decades of peace that preceded the outbreak of World War I, successive British administrations were concerned not only with the Irish question but also with the role that the state should play in social and economic life. The fact that the suffrage had been extended by new reform measures enacted in 1867 and 1884 meant that Britain had for all practical purposes achieved universal manhood suffrage. And this in turn meant that the new voters soon made their impact felt in the House of Commons. Small wonder, then, that the prewar decades witnessed an unmistakable decline in the laissez-faire conception of the functions of government and a marked growth of state intervention. Like industrial Germany, industrial Britain moved in the direction of a social-welfare state. In Germany it was the growth of the Social Democratic Party that speeded up this movement. In Britain, however, despite Marx's predictions, socialism never gained a significant mass following among the working-class population in the years before 1914. Of the many instances of the development of state intervention at the expense of *laissez faire*, the most notable occurred during the Conservative ministry of Disraeli (1874-1880) and during the Liberal ministries of Sir Henry Campbell-Bannerman and Herbert Asquith that preceded the coming of the war. In the present essay the late Edward P. Cheyney, for many years a professor at the University of Pennsylvania and one of the American pioneers in the study of British social and economic history, analyzes the major reforms that reflected the growth of the social-welfare state in the country that had for a time veered more in the direction of *laissez faire* than any other major European country.

A fair instance of reform legislation resulting from pressure by the organized working classes is to be found in the series of Employers' Liability and Workmen's Compensation acts. One of the characteristics of modern industrial life is the toll of death and accident it demands. Accidents have occurred occasionally, indeed frequently, in the ordinary occupations of life in all times, but with the introduction of mechanical devices and artificial power, and with the increased speed and scale of the processes of industry and transportation, losses by accident have become far more numerous. In a careful study of a long series of accidents occurring in England it was found that 87½ per cent arose solely from modern conditions. In the factories, mines, ironworks, and shipyards; on the docks, on trains, and in the railroad yards; on congested streets, in the construction of buildings, everywhere where men are congregated and the busy work of the world is going on, there are tragic falls, explosions, collisions, entanglement in running machinery, bursting of steam boilers, and, in modern times, electric shock, each of which brings death, loss of limb or eyes, permanent or temporary injury to one or more persons.

It seems that manufacturing, commerce, mining, lumbering, agriculture, life itself cannot be carried on without a constant accompaniment of fatal, serious, or slight mishap. In the especially hazardous trades it is possible to work out an average of accidents that will occur almost as certainly as the tables of mortality used in life insurance. Each crane or derrick will once in so many operations on the average kill

Reprinted by special permission from *Modern English Reform: From Individualism to Socialism*, Philadelphia, University of Pennsylvania Press, 1931, pp. 162-196.

JOSEPH ARCH: Agricultural labor leader who tried to organize the farm hands of Britain. Seeing in trade unionism the key to improved working conditions, he founded the National Agricultural Labourer's Union in the early 1870's. Bitterly opposed by landlords, the Union, despite some early gains, soon declined. In parliament Arch sought to dramatize the need for land-law reform and for state-aided emigration.

THOMAS CLARKSON: A towering figure in the antislavery movement in Britain. An impassioned reformer, he wrote extensively in favor of universal abolition of the slave trade, universal emancipation of slaves, and the economic and cultural development of Africa. His death, in 1846, brought to an end some sixty years of agitation.

or crush a workman; from each iron or steel bridge about so many workmen will fall or be struck and killed or injured. It is sometimes said that the construction of each story of a high building costs the life of a man; in railroad yards there is about an average number of men crushed or injured each month, just as there is an average number of passengers or tons of freight carried.

Nor does it seem possible to eliminate these risks. Men engaged day after day, week after week, and month after month in work involving hazards, inevitably develop a psychology which makes them careless of these hazards. Mechanical devices often contain in themselves imperfections which no care can recognize. The traditions and practice of hurried, competitive modern production are none too careful of the human factor involved. A large concern states that in the year 1900 forty-three per cent of its employees suffered injuries sufficient to keep them away from work longer than the day of the accident, though within the next ten years by strenuous effort this particular firm was able to reduce this figure to less than twenty per cent a year. It is a common statement that half of the accidents that occur are preventable by proper guards for machinery, rails, and other precautionary devices. The daily newspaper gives instances enough of accidents happening in the general course of industrial life, whether preventable or not, and a moment's consideration of the steady flow of these accidents through the whole year is quite sufficient to convince any thoughtful person of the fact, and even to some degree of the number of these victims of warfare in time of peace.

Early statistics are hard to obtain, and unimpressive at best when they are but figures. In the four years between 1872 and 1876 there were

SEVENTH EARL OF SHAFTESBURY: Humanitarian social reformer who believed that it was the responsibility of the upper classes to help to improve the position of the poorer elements in society. Active in exposing the abuses to which lower-class Englishmen were exposed, he played an important part in bringing about the passage of such measures as the Mines Act of 1842 and the Ten Hours Act of 1847.

TRADE UNION CONGRESS: Annual meeting of delegates from British trade unions. Dating effectively from the late 1860's, these meetings have been the occasion for stating the grievances of labor and for suggesting desired reforms.

in England 261 explosions of boilers in factories, causing the death of 308 persons and the injury of 535 more. In 1908 in seven principal industries, there were 3,447 fatalities, 296,338 non-fatal injuries. In 1913 there were 3,748 fatal accidents, 476,920 which were not fatal. Thus for recent times the yearly average is between three and four thousand deaths from industrial accidents, between a quarter and a half million lesser injuries. Each of these accidents involves not only suffering but loss, some loss to the employer whose work and plans are disarranged and whose property may be injured, greater loss to the workman whose earning power is temporarily or permanently destroyed, complete loss to his family in case of death. How shall the loss be met? According to the old common law, if negligence on somebody's part is involved, and in the vast number of cases there is some carelessness somewhere, the sufferer from such negligence has a right to obtain damages from the one responsible. Moreover the employer is answerable for the actions of his employees, since one of the most familiar maxims of the law is that the principal is responsible for the actions of his agent. If therefore a watchman on a railroad makes a mistake in his signals the company must pay damages to passengers who lose their lives or are injured in a resulting accident. If a workman in a quarry uses too large a charge and the explosion injures passers-by, or adjacent houses, the owner of the quarry must pay the damages.

This principle would seem to provide means whereby the money loss to an injured employee or his family in accident cases should be reimbursed by his employer. But the common law had been modified in this respect by a decision of 1837, followed as a precedent in later decisions. This was that when a man accepts work he is supposed to know that it entails danger from the carelessness of his fellow employees and to agree to accept that as one of the conditions of the job; therefore when an accident occurs he must not expect damages. This came to be known as the "fellow servant" or "common employment" rule—that although outsiders may get damages, a workman cannot if his loss arises from the negligence of a fellow workman, as it almost invariably does. If he brings suit in such a case the judge rules that he has no case. Such suits were therefore seldom brought and damages for accidents to workmen were seldom obtained.

This seemed to workmen and to many others unjust, and about 1865 an agitation was begun to have workmen put on the same legal footing as other persons. It was sponsored especially by the Miners

National Union and the Amalgamated Society of Railway Servants, among whose members accidents were especially numerous. They argued that the condition of the common law was absolutely wrong. Employers in carrying on their business subjected their workmen to conditions the latter could not control. It should be incumbent on employers therefore to furnish buildings, machinery, trained fellow-workmen, and other conditions that would reduce accidents to an absolute minimum. If they did not, or if accidents should still occur, they should compensate injured workmen, who were powerless to prevent these. Bills were introduced into Parliament almost yearly by workingmen members after 1872. A parliamentary committee on employer's liability was appointed in 1876, took evidence and made a report, but no further action was taken at the time. The discussions were marked by much bitterness. It was a confused issue; whether the common law should be changed or not, and if so with recognition of various self-help associations and insurance companies, or by merely leaving the disputes to be fought out under fairer conditions. The matter came up yearly in the Trade Union Congress and great pressure was brought by the unions on the government. The first success was obtained in 1880 when under Mr. Gladstone an Employers' Liability act was passed. It removed the defense of common employment in five classes of cases, including practically all those involving accidents on railroads. According to the wording of the law, in all the cases included, the workman is given "the same right of compensation and remedies against the employer as if the workman had not been . . . in the service of the employer."

This seemed a moderate and reasonable change, but it still left actual practice cumbrous and expensive. Each case that came to trial involved court and lawyers' fees and much loss of time and money. Although many cases were settled by compromise, without litigation, for some years between 300 and 400 cases came into court each year. These tended to increase, rising for the period 1898-1906 to 700 a year. The question of contributory negligence on the part of the injured employee was difficult, often impossible to decide, and left the result in many cases unsatisfactory. It was one of the regular functions of the trade unions to help their men in suits for damages. The workmen were still dissatisfied and there was evident room for improvement. It was therefore a natural next step when in 1893 a bill removing the common employment and contributory negligence defenses in almost all occupations and in almost all cases was introduced in the House of Commons and passed without serious opposition. It was defeated at this time by the House of Lords but was carried through both houses in 1897 and became the first Workmen's Compensation act.

An entirely new conception of damages was introduced by this act. No negligence on the part of the employer or another employee had to be alleged. It was enough that an accident had occurred and an injury inflicted. It was obvious that the idea of compensation for industrial accident as such was becoming familiar. This was no doubt largely due to the practice of insurance against industrial accident which had recently been added to life, fire, marine, and other forms of insurance. At first many large firms created insurance funds to which their employees were forced to contribute, at the same time being required to "contract out" of the law, a practice allowed, against trade-union protests, by the courts. The law of 1897 forbade "contracting out" but employers could without serious difficulty themselves pay the insurance, at the same time calculating it as part of the costs of production, in which case it would ultimately fall on the consumer. Under such circumstances why need there be a lawsuit in each case? Therefore in 1906 a new Workmen's Compensation act was passed, under which payments in case of accident on an established scale and under government administration are paid to all employees, with a few exceptions, most of which have still later been included under the system.

None of these laws prohibited injured workmen from suing for damages, just as any other sufferer might, under the common law, but the number of such cases diminished rapidly. In 1908 only 200 were taken into court and more than half of these were compromised at some stage and withdrawn. Only one case was brought in from the mining industry, one from quarrying, and seven in the railroad industry. There is of course much litigation as to amount of claims and other points of difference, but the main principle that all costs of industrial accident are to be considered part of the costs of production and to be paid for in the first instance by the employer and ultimately by the general community is fully accepted. Thus an old workingman's grievance has been removed, and in the course of legislation on the subject a whole system of compensation for accident, extending through much of the community, has been introduced. In its first stages this was a trade-union movement solely, in its later development it became part, as will be seen, of a general system of social reform.

Another instance of such general social reform is to be found in the legislation for the protection of sailors, and incidentally of passengers, from being sent to sea in unsafe and overcrowded vessels. About 1870 Samuel Plimsoll, a London coal merchant, more of the type of reformers of the early than of the later part of the century, began an agitation for the safety of seamen. He had published a pamphlet on the coal trade, internal and foreign, and was thus apparently drawn into an interest in the condition of coaling and other English vessels. He became a member of Parliament in 1868, and in 1870 asked permission to introduce a bill on the subject of government oversight of shipping. Mr. Gladstone's first ministry, then in office and well inclined to reform, introduced a bill looking in the same direction. Both were received with the bitter opposition of shipowners and other business men and neither reached a vote. Plimsoll introduced the matter again the next year with the same result. It has been observed before that a regular step in the agitation for some social reform has been the formation of a society for the purpose, and in fact the National Life-Boat Institution already existed as it still does, published a journal *The Life-Boat*, and was in some degree interested in the same objects. It was not, however, valuable for Plimsoll's agitation. Instead he appealed to the trade unions. Since sailors and engineers were most directly affected, at the Annual Congress they took up his campaign and added to it their protests and urgency. Later Plimsoll became a sort of honorary president of the Sailors' and Firemen's Union.

In the meantime, in 1873, he compiled and issued a book *Our Seamen, an Appeal* in which much along the lines of the illustrations in Clarkson's book on the slave trade and the parliamentary report on children in the coal mines he introduced a "Wreck Chart" of the British Isles for 1871, compiled by the Board of Trade, and showing the location and number of wrecks and other accidents at sea suffered by British vessels during that year. He introduced a mass of statement and testimony, explaining the causes of sea disasters—undermanning, deckloading, want of repair, defective construction, overloading, over-insuring, and other avoidable causes of wreck or accident. Much of his evidence was photographed from original, official documents, and therefore not subject to doubt, other parts were more questionable or at least susceptible to argumentation. The next year he issued a cheap edition of his book which was circulated widely. He showed that for the last ten years there had been on the British coast an average of about 2000 vessels a year totally wrecked or suffering from other disaster. Omitting collisions some 700 vessels a year were sunk, some 700 suffered other casualties.

The number of lives lost in these wrecks had risen in some years to more than a thousand; in 1871 they were 626, the smallest for many years; for the ten years previous to the publication of the book, they averaged more than 800 a year. Apart from these were the large number of vessels that sailed and were lost yearly between Great Britain and India, the colonies, and foreign countries. Half of those lost on the coast were colliers, but the greater losses of life were in the larger vessels engaged in foreign trade and with more numerous crews; for these losses, unfortunately, statistics are not available.

Statistics however were not the most important part of Plimsoll's work. It was his charges of incompetency, inhumanity, and greed on the part of some shipowners, recklessly disregarding the safety of their men. Vessels known to be unseaworthy to the verge of rottenness, "coffin ships," as they were called, were sometimes sent out and never reached their first port. Among the wrecks of the year 1871 thirty-six were of vessels more than sixty years old; three of them more than a hundred. Wrecks had occurred when the wind was scarcely more than a breeze, and in open sea; vessels which if well built and preserved might have held together went quickly to pieces when they went on the rocks even in fair weather, and left the crew to drown.

It was pointed out that the temptation to owners to send out old and unsafe vessels for one more voyage, on the chance that the weather would be unusually favorable, was almost irresistible; that the interest of the underwriters was small because the subdivision of risks under the Lloyd's system reduced loss to insignificance to any one insurer; that sailors were usually ready to take chances, though more than one case was reported where sailors had mutinied before actually leaving the Thames, the Clyde, or Bristol Channel rather than go to what they considered certain death, and were taken off the ship in irons for punishment. Attention was called to the fact that laws had been passed protecting workmen in mines, factories, workshops, on railroads and in construction work. Why should not the protecting arm of government be extended to those who went down to the sea in ships, perhaps the most dependent on outside help of all classes of workmen?

This book caused a great furore; it was discussed, abused, contradicted, and corroborated, as such attacks on an old and extensive system with many variations always is. It served an excellent purpose, creating great public interest and forcing the government to take action. A bill was introduced in 1876 and subjected to long and acrimonious discussion. It touched one of England's oldest, proudest, and most essential industries. It professedly legislated, not for women and children, but for grown men; it extended the oversight of government into an entirely new sphere. It was, nevertheless, passed by both houses, signed and became the Merchant Shipping Act of 1880. Since that year every English vessel carries on its hull the "Plimsoll Mark" defining its load line; before it leaves port it is subjected to strict examination, and its papers indicate the number of passengers and crew it may carry. Some instances there have of course been of inadequate enforcement of these rules, and the winds and waves, rocks and sands, fire, fog, and collision still, of course, bring death and loss, but on the whole the noble structure of the British merchant marine is now founded on the solid foundation of wise regulation and willing acceptance of the protection and restrictions of the law.

Parallel with the two bodies of reform legislation that have just been described there was in progress a series of provisions of the law, some restrictive, some creative, which did much to affect the most fundamental of all relations, that of a people to the soil. The land legislation of the period 1860 to 1892 was not so closely connected with the rise of the working classes as were workmen's compensation and the protection of seamen: it was rather an outcome of that wider conception of reform characteristic of the second half of the century, which considered reform a means of securing some permanent benefit for the whole community or for some very large portion of it. The minds of the men and women of influence, who were still the "governing classes," however much the meaning of that term may have broadened, had now come to consider any legislation fraught with possibilities of general well-being reform legislation.

Under the old aristocratic system, the land was the ark of the covenant; it could not be touched. Such legislation as had been enacted had served either to make its control by individual owners more complete or to facilitate its transfer from one owner to another, not to limit its ownership. A vast number of private-enclosure acts had changed intermingled to separate occupation and divided old common lands among particular owners, and a standing body of enclosure commissioners was occupied in carrying on the same process. By 1860 some 4000 private-enclosure acts and the activities of the commissioners had within the last century changed 7,000,000 acres from more or less communal to strictly private possession. This had been largely at the expense of the small tenants and farm laborers and had increased the hold of private possessors on the land. Mr. Chamberlain, with some truculence, declared that as a result of having no representation in Parliament the agricultural laborers "have been robbed of their rights in the commons. They have been robbed of their open spaces and are still being robbed. There is no protection against the steady absorption that is continually going on of open spaces which belong to the people, but which are gradually being included in the estates of the landowners." Even as moderate a man as John Stuart Mill declares in this connection, "I confess that I cannot speak of the existing practice of dividing the common land among the landlords by any other name than robbery—robbery of the poor. It will, of course, be said that people cannot be robbed of what is not theirs, and that the commons are not the legal property of the poor. But if the commons are not the property of the poor they are just as little the property of those who take them."

It is true the abolition of the corn laws in 1846 was distasteful to the landowning aristocracy, but it was not an invasion of the rights of private property in land; it was simply the withdrawal of certain subsidies that had previously been given them; it still came under the head of the application of the principles of laissez-faire, in this case to the production of grain and the use of the land.

But with the advance of the century new conditions were coming into existence that brought the question of the control of land to a crisis. Wealth was enclosing more land as deer parks, grouse moors and pleasure grounds. It was making constantly new demands upon previously unused and more or less open ground. The suburbs of the towns were stretching far into the country. At the same time the old wild commons, wolds, moors, forests, and downs, the hunting grounds of kings and the playgrounds of the people from time immemorial, were being closed in by fences. England was fortunate in possessing such tracts, large and small, scattered widely through the island, too sterile to cultivate, covered with rough furze, broom, bracken, and heather, or with a poor growth of hawthorn, oak and other scrub, the resort of wild birds, beasts, and men; the delight of gipsies, loiterers, poets, and writers of romance; of questionable ownership and until recent years in use by every one indiscriminately. Even these were being closed in and put to private use. The open spaces of the country were visibly disappearing.

By 1860, however, the population had risen to 20,000,000. Where should they go for recreation? Except for such small or large spots as each might have claim to, roads, public parks, and the rights of way that were still fortunately guaranteed to the people by the common law, were the only places of refuge from increasing congestion of population. Yet there were those who felt, as was said in Parliament, that consideration must be given to "that which the people of this country want almost as much as food—the air which they breathe and the health which they enjoy." Under these circumstances pressure for the preservation of such open spaces as were left began to appear. Its earliest form was a series of suits in chancery by the community or interested parties to prevent enclosure of open commons, the title to which by the encloser was to say the least tenuous. It was somewhat a matter of surprise that the decisions in these cases so generally upheld the contentions of the commoners against lords of manors who were pushing their rights to enclose. In 1865 the inevitable organization of the advocates of reform took place; the Commons Preservation Society, which still exists, was founded.

During the next decade the influence of this society was helpful in the winning of suit after suit to resist, prevent, or even to reverse the process of enclosure. In the same year as the foundation of this society the House of Commons appointed a committee to investigate the title to all open spaces near London, and in 1872, by the Enclosure of Commons act, the enclosure commissioners were ordered to reverse their former practice of encouragement of enclosures and to disapprove all not to the manifest advantage of the public. The commissioners established park regulations for all open spaces within fifteen miles of London and many other open commons and old forests were transferred to the administration of a public board. Thus Hampstead Heath and Epping Forest and Wimbledon Common and Battersea Park and a series of other open spaces were rescued for the public from private invasion. The jagged edges and little islands of private property that border and lie scattered even yet through these commons testify to the relative suddenness with which the process of their enclosure was stopped. To prohibit the action of a few which leads to the disadvantage of the many is one of the bases of modern reform. Legislation and community action came just in time. It can be seen clearly enough now that less than three-quarters of a century ago the open spaces of England were in grave danger of destruction. Their inestimable value as a possession of the whole English people becomes constantly more clear. The hordes who rush to them for release from the great cities on Sundays and holidays, on railroad trains, busses, and tram cars, testify to this valuation.

There was much to bring the whole question of the land into discussion in this second half of the century. In 1870 the Land Tenure Reform Association was founded by John Stuart Mill and others and began its active campaign. From 1872 to 1874 was the great agricultural laborers' lockout and the formation of the National Union of Agriculture Labourers. In 1874 the report of a government survey which had been made during the last two years at the request of Lord Derby showed that only 2250 persons owned more than half the land of England. In 1879 *Progress and Poverty* was published, and from 1880 to 1882 Henry George was in England, lecturing and disseminating the ideas of that work. In 1882 Alfred Russell Wallace published his *Land Nationalization*; in 1884 the Third Reform bill gave the franchise to the agricultural laborer. There was much emigration abroad and immigration to the city from the country. That the young and vigorous should leave the countryside and only the old, the weak, the unenterprising, and those bound by special circumstances should remain gave a deplorable outlook for the future. How could such depopulation of the countryside be prevented and the people be kept on the land? To many the question took the form: how could more land be brought into the possession of the people? Thus a renewed agitation for either ownership or use of the land by the many began. Jesse Collings, Sir Charles Dilke and Joseph Chamberlain, all members of Parliament and the last two members of the ministry, were influential and prominent advocates of land reform, supporting the efforts of Joseph Arch, George Edwards, and other representatives of the laborers or tenants.

As a result of this agitation, in meetings, in magazines, and in Parliament, a series of acts was passed along two parallel lines. One was for the increase of "allotments" to agricultural and other laborers, the other for the increase of small holdings on which a hard-working farmer might make a plain living. Allotments were an old institution. They were pieces of land, usually of less than an acre, carved out of the arable lands of a neighborhood by parish authorities or land-owners, and rented at the usual rate for agricultural land to laborers for gardens in which to work after hours to supplement their wages or to save them from actual pauperism. They had been advocated and created at least from the beginning of the century, had received the distinction of a special essay by Southey, and the steady though languid support of the law as a form of poor relief. Now, however, they were advocated more vigorously, supported by advanced re-formers as a right of the laborers, as partial recompense for the com-mons of which they had been deprived, and in 1882 the Allotments Extension Association was formed. Three other associations were formed for only slightly varying objects, the Free Land League, the Leasehold Enfranchisement Association, and the Land Law Reform Association. In 1882 the first Allotments Extension act was passed, largely by the energy of Jesse Collings. Small results followed from a purely permissive act administered by a reluctant class of land-owners. In 1887 the reform wing in the new Unionist party, consist-ing of the same men as had formerly been the advocates of land reform in the old unbroken Liberal party, were able to carry the Labourers' Allotments bill, which gave to the parish authorities the right of compulsory purchase of land for any allotments up to one acre asked for by workingmen, and to acquire by voluntary purchase land for common pasture. In 1890 the act was amended in the direc-tion of greater extension, and in 1894 its administration was handed over to the new democratic parish councils. The number of allotments is a somewhat changing one depending on the demands of laborers and the interest of the authorities. In 1873 there were in existence about 250,000; by 1890 this had risen to 450,000; and it rose to almost 600,000 by 1895. On the outbreak of the Great War in 1914, dread of a food shortage led to their formation in vast numbers, under the pressure of government and public opinion, until there were a million and a half in existence, and whole tracts of England were cut up into checkerboards. After the war their numbers declined and in 1928 there were only 600,000, though there were, at the time of that report, some 14,000 applicants not yet provided for.

Small holdings involved more serious questions, the relative desirability of large and small farms, of ownership and tenancy, the difficulty of obtaining enough land without compelling landowners to sell, and the reluctance of Parliament to authorize compulsion, and all this in a period of serious agricultural depression. English farm tenants and farm laborers show little of that passion for possession of the soil which animates the peasantry of Ireland, France, Russia, and many other countries. Three centuries of landlordism and two of large farming may have habituated them to tenancy and wage labor, or they may by a process of reasoning have decided that the best thing for them is favorable conditions of renting their land. Whatever the cause, the force exerted in favor of recreating a peasant proprietorship or even an extensive system of small tenant farms has come rather from reformers outside of their class than from small farmers themselves. This force has however been steadily and, so far as law is concerned, effectively exerted. The same influential men, organizations, and political parties that pressed through the legislation for creating allotments did in the main the same for small farms.

In 1883 an act was passed which gave to the tenant some compensation at the expiry of his lease for improvements he had put upon the land; from 1888 to 1890 a royal commission on Small Holdings under the presidency of Joseph Chamberlain sat and took evidence, and published its report in 1890. In accordance with the recommendations of this report a law was passed in 1892, providing complete machinery, short of the right of compulsory purchase, for local authorities to create small farms up to fifty acres in size, encourage and help in their purchase, and in default of purchase to rent out farms of ten acres or less to small farmers. These, like allotments, were placed under the parish councils after 1894, and in 1900 a Small Holdings commission was created under the Board of Agriculture by act of Parliament for the further administration of this system.

The success of the creation of a body of small owners or even tenants of agricultural land has been but moderate. Up to 1914 some 12,584 small holders had been established on the land through the intervention, direct or indirect, of Parliament, involving the transfer of about 200,000 acres of land from its former owners. There has been nothing to correspond to the transformation of Ireland from a country of landlords to a country of peasant owners. When in the year 3000 A. D., according to Mr. Shaw in *Back to Methuselah*, an

Irish peasant is asked what is meant by a "landlord," he says, "There is a tradition in this part of the country of an animal with a name like that. It used to be hunted and shot in the barbarous ages. It is quite extinct now." In England landlords still exist, if they do not flourish. The breaking up of the large estates as a result of the Great War has proceeded rapidly, but what is to succeed them is not even yet clear.

The great land act of 1928 was intended to codify the land law as it exists, not to introduce any change in it. Nevertheless the land system of England has been completely transformed according to the ideas of reformers and by act of Parliament in the second half of the nineteenth century. The trend toward complete private ownership has been stopped and later reversed. Open spaces have been transferred from semi-private to public ownership and use, much land has been set aside by public authority for the use of workmen after hours, and the legal position of tenants has been much improved, and a class formerly practically excluded from tenancy or ownership of land has now by parliamentary action been admitted to it. Having in view the traditional control of the land by the old aristocracy there is probably no part of the whole domain of public interest where the spirit of reform has shown itself more powerful. Each of the three great political parties has its announced program for the improvement of the condition of the rural classes. They differ in details, rather than in essence, and each party when in power has shown itself slow in carrying the plan out. What the future will show is quite obscure, but whatever it may be, legislation will not be prevented by any great respect for the older "rights of property" or any reluctance to utilize the powers of government in obtaining the desired end. That contest has already been fought out.

The movement for the better housing of the working classes in cities and towns passed through much the same course as legislation for better conditions in the rural districts, and in fact has reached much the same *impasse*. The population more than doubled in the first half of the century and a greatly disproportionate part of this increase was in cities and towns. As England became more and more industrial, manufacturing, and commercial, population became more concentrated. Men must live near their work. Moreover, within the towns, there was a constant replacement of dwelling sections by manufacturing buildings and offices, railroad stations and yards, and the cutting through of new streets. It was calculated that between 1860 and 1865, 50,000 people were displaced in this way in London. Workingmen and their families seldom had the means, the time, or the enterprise to go far from their accustomed neighborhood. The result was extreme congestion, ill housing, and poor sanitation. The conditions that have been described at the beginning of the century grew steadily worse. In London and only to a less extent in the other large cities there were vast areas of small houses, much subdivided, in narrow streets and courts, like the parish of St. Giles in which there were seventy courts, small streets, and alleyways running into one another, without access to a single large street. Overcrowding, lack of sunlight, air, and drainage, and high rents forced men down physically, morally, and in economic ability. Even the thrifty and better-paid workmen were often in scarcely better surroundings. The aphorism that "slum people make slums, not slums slum people," if ever true anywhere, was certainly not true in the large English towns of this period. It was rather physical and economic conditions against which the individual was powerless and against which the community had so far taken no action that were responsible.

The laissez-faire attitude, however, gradually passed away. The unsatisfactory living conditions in the towns were manifest to everyone that had eyes to see. It is not a matter of surprise therefore that improved living of the working classes, in the broadened conception of reform, became a familiar object of attention. In fact even before the middle of the century, in 1841, an "Association for Improving the Dwellings of the Industrial Classes" was formed, largely under the kindly influence of Lord Shaftesbury, and it was just after the middle of the century, in 1853, that the first attempt to regulate city building by law was made. This bill, however, was defeated in the House of Lords, and the first serious attempts to meet the difficulty were due to private philanthropy, the Peabody Trust, the Waterlow Company, and the Octavia Hill plan, all of which were inaugurated between 1860 and 1865. Their object was rather the provision of better dwellings for workingmen than a direct attack on congestion. Even the first legislation, the Artisans' and Labourers' Dwellings act, the so-called "Torrens act," of 1868, only empowered city authorities by voluntary agreement with the owner to pull down unfit houses and replace them by new.

It was obvious that these means, however beneficial to those who profited by them, were quite ineffective as a solution of the general problem, for up to 1875 but 30,000 persons had been provided with satisfactory dwellings in London, whereas the increase of population in that city was 40,000 a year, an appreciable proportion of whom were slum dwellers. The pressure for doing something was however very strong, the report of Shuttleworth to the Charity Organization Society in 1873 being particularly outspoken in its demands for government action. In 1875 therefore under Mr. Disraeli's government the Housing of the Artisan and Working Classes act made it incumbent upon city authorities to condemn dwelling sections, where existing conditions were especially unsatisfactory, take them over by compulsory purchase, and erect new houses. Other acts followed upon this, and in 1890 a general codifying act was passed. There has been no lack of attempts at reform in this field; it is a typical instance of acceptance by all of the need and propriety of social reform directed by government. If not much has been accomplished, if the problem has not been yet solved, it is because of its extreme difficulty or because it cannot be solved except after a still fuller acceptance of social control.

The culmination of constructive social reform during this period is to be found in the group of laws placed upon the statute book in the years from 1906 to the outbreak of the Great War by the combination of efforts of the Liberal, Labour, and Irish Nationalist parties. During these eight years a greater body of reform legislation was passed than in any earlier similar stretch of time. Neither the years from 1832 to 1836, the period of the first parliamentary reform bill and its resultant legislation, nor the years from 1868 to 1874, Mr. Gladstone's "great administration," can compare with its achievements in far-reaching reforming legislation. The old familiar power of the House of Lords, used to block advanced social legislation, was taken away from them, and at the same time a notable step toward democracy was taken by the payment of salaries to the members of the House of Commons, who might now more readily be workingmen. New principles of taxation, asserting the right of the state to look into the sources as well as to estimate the amount of the taxpayers' income, and to use taxation as a means of redressing some of the inequalities of the competitive system, were introduced into the annual budget. Trade unions were finally legalized and protected against economic as well as against criminal prosecution, and their powers extended. Workmen's compensation, housing and town planning and development obtained the full acceptance and extension already described. A series of "Children's acts" did much to make the mass of school children veritable wards of the state.

Four great reforms met or attempted to meet, one after another, as many of the fundamental needs of the lower ranges of society, support in old age, relief in sickness, regular occupation, a living wage. For these ends old age pensions were provided, labor exchanges for securing employment were established, trade boards were appointed for setting authoritative rates of wages in poorly paid industries, and national insurance in sickness and time of unemployment was introduced. The objects of these acts are sufficiently clear. The main questions, so far as this work is concerned, are how such far-reaching and fundamental laws came to be adopted, and what light their adoption throws on the general trend of reform. It may be observed that most of these projects had long been ripe for action; the driving force to carry them through alone was lacking. For instance, all parties had accepted the necessity for some support of the aged other than private philanthropy or the poor law afforded. The Old Age Pension act of 1908, only gave special shape to a plan already more than half approved, and the million old men and women who were drawing pensions under it by the year of the outbreak of the war would probably have received them from any party which happened to be in power. When an old woman of sixty-four now remarks, "I'll get my Lloyd George next year," she is paying tribute to the chancellor of the exchequer who but chanced at that time to be the champion of aged indigence.

The inclusion of seamen, domestic servants, and government employees in the system of compulsory compensation for accident and industrial disease in 1906 was an extension of the Workmen's Compensation act of 1898; the passage of such an act had already been attempted by the Conservatives in 1905. The threat to the funds of the trade unions involved in the Taff Vale decision alarmed Conservatives and Liberals, as well as rousing the apprehension of the Labour party. The Conservative party itself introduced, though it was not successful in carrying, a bill to protect trade-union funds from suits. It was an extension of the principle of this bill which was embodied in the Trade Disputes act of 1906 and the Trade Union act of 1913. A long series of parliamentary investigations of wages, from 1892 forward, the activities of the Anti-sweating League and successive bills concerning wages introduced into Parliament from 1895 to 1905 found their completion, not their initiation, in the Trade Boards act of 1909. The early example of

Germany and somewhat later of other continental countries had long suggested the compulsory sickness and unemployment insurance plans introduced by the act of 1911.

The debates were rather on the details than on the principles of these measures. Nevertheless, although the greater part of this reforming legislation of 1906-1914 had been proposed and even prepared for before, it was the peculiar combination of progressive elements in the grouping of parties in that period and their domination by a few bold reforming spirits that brought that body of legislation actually to the birth. A ministry which could count for progressive legislation on 378 Liberals, 83 Irish Nationalists and 53 Labour members, altogether 514 votes, against an opposition of only 156 was all-powerful and needed only leadership to carry reform far forward. If any Parliament ever had a mandate to experiment in social progress and the power to carry it out, it was the Parliament that met in 1906. The principal ministers were deeply pledged to reform. Mr. Asquith, chancellor of the exchequer, declared in Parliament in 1907, "Beyond there lies the whole still unconquered territory of social reform. . . . This is a House of Commons which was elected more clearly and definitely than any other House in our history in the hope and belief on the part of the electors that it would find the road and provide the means for social reform . . . there is nothing that calls so loudly or so imperiously as the possibilities of social reform."

Lloyd George when in a similar position in 1909, introducing his budget demanding large appropriations for old age pensions, insurance, and administrative expenses, in addition to military and naval requirements, declared: "There are hundreds of thousands of men, women and children in this country, now enduring hardships for which the sternest judge would not hold them responsible; hardships entirely due to circumstances over which they have not the slightest control. . . . Is it fair, is it just, is it humane, is it honorable, is it safe to subject such a multitude of our poor fellow-countrymen and countrywomen to continued endurance of these miseries until nations have learned enough wisdom not to squander their resources on these huge machines for the destruction of life? This is a war budget. It is for raising money to wage implacable warfare against poverty or squalidness. I cannot help hoping and believing that before this generation has passed away we shall have advanced a great step towards that good time when poverty and wretchedness and human degradation which always follow in its camp will be as remote to the people of this country as the wolves which once infested its forests." When such views were held by the leading ministers it is no wonder that these measures were pushed at last to completion. If there was any flagging on the part of the Liberals, they were urged to their task by the Labour members, whose support was so important to the ministry, and by the Nationalists who were not only well inclined to reform but were anxious to bring these projects to completion so that attention might be given to their own more special desires. The dark shadow of the war had not yet settled down on the country, England as a whole was rich and prosperous, however dire the need for a better distribution of its prosperity, and men generally believed with Lloyd George that poverty could be exorcised by appropriate reform measures. So as the principal work of the eight years a good baker's dozen of new laws were passed, each carrying some old and hopeful line of reform a long step forward or initiating a new and still more hopeful effort to bring about social welfare. The work was only brought to a close by the catastrophe of war.

The trend of reforming legislation from the beginning of the last century to the Great War is by this time sufficiently clear. Its progress has been from the meager gifts of a kindly if somewhat frigid justice, wrested by upper-class reformers from a stolid Parliament and bestowed upon a few victims of servitude, misfortune, crime, or poverty, to constructive laws given openhandedly by a democratic Parliament to the whole or a great part of the population. Reform has passed from the slight and grudging deviation from the principle of laissez-faire of a hesitant Parliament to the aphorism of a recent prime minister that "political machinery is only valuable and is only worth having as it is adapted to and used for worthy social ends." It has shifted from the few to the many, from negative to positive, from abolition of old abuses to creation of new institutions, from things done by some for others to things done for all by all.

This development has followed, as indicated at the beginning of this book, an inner law of its own. It has been largely independent of political parties. Although Whigs and Liberals have been on the whole rather more willing to pass reform measures than Tories and their successors, Conservatives and Unionists, yet these measures have been pretty equally attributable to both parties. The first law legalizing trade unions, that of 1824-25, was passed by the Conservatives, the law of 1871 by the Liberals, that of 1875 by the Conservatives, that of 1906 again by the Liberals. The Employers' Liability act of 1880 was adopted by a Liberal, the Workmen's Compensation act of 1897 by a Conservative Parliament. The fountainhead of factory legislation is to be found in a strictly Tory Parliament, in 1802, its main principles were accepted under Conservative ministers in the forties and the Factory and Workshop Consolidation act of 1878 was also the work of a Conservative administration. On the other hand later developments in that field have been under Liberal auspices. Land reform has been on the whole the work of Liberal majorities, but some of the most important acts were passed by Unionists and Conservatives between 1880 and 1890.

Some of the reasons for this development irrespective of parties are obvious. Propagandist bodies have been usually non-partisan and their work of conversion has been done in both parties alike. The royal and even the parliamentary commissions of investigation whose reports have been so influential in producing legislation have included men from all parties and men without known party affiliation, and they have often reported, moreover, in the frequent changes of English politics, to a Parliament with a different majority from that under which they were appointed. There have been natural reformers in high position, Peel, Gladstone, Disraeli, Chamberlain, Lloyd George, in all parties. Social legislation has been largely a response to pressure from outside of Parliament and party organizations, and whatever party was in power when this pressure became sufficiently strong has performed the work of placing it upon the statute book. For the ultimate and efficient causes of reform, search must be made much deeper in society than the ups and downs in the strife of political parties.

All of the reforms so far described, both those that came early and those that came late, have been detached reforms, each directed toward the removal of some special abuse, the alleviation of some particular form of suffering, or the establishment of some distinctive beneficial practice. The activity of reformers, so far as we have traced it, has consisted in taking up one object of social reform after another and securing legislation upon it, partially and tentatively or boldly and constructively, yet in neither case with any general plan including all needed or desirable reforms. Running like a slender stream parallel to the main river of reform through the whole century has been a quite different ideal. This has been the advocacy of some fundamental change in social organization that would produce the same results and many more by a single transforming process. Such a change would preclude the necessity for separate reforms by introducing one general all-inclusive reform. Such a proposed deliberate remodelling of society is, of course, socialism, which has been urged in one form or another continuously through the nineteenth century, and has already put a perceptible impress upon legislation. . . .

The Church in the Third Republic

J. V. DUCATTILLON

Published in 1944

The early decades in the history of the Third French Republic were filled with crises. The Republic itself, proclaimed in September 1870, was the product of the Franco-German War. And hardly had France been defeated than it was faced with civil war—the uprising of the Paris Commune. Then came a number of major attempts to overthrow the republic. The 'seventies, for example, saw a series of strong offensives to restore the monarchy— offensives that came close to succeeding. The 'eighties saw the rise in popularity of General Boulanger, "the dictator who failed" but who might not have failed. And the 'nineties saw the beginnings of the Dreyfus affair, which soon developed into a test of strength between republicans and those who sought to get rid of the republic. To understand the power of the antirepublican elements in the France of the late nineteenth century is not difficult. Despite the growth of rationalism and skepticism, France remained a Roman Catholic country, and many devout Roman Catholics associated republicanism with anti-Catholicism, an association that had its roots in the Great French Revolution. The upshot was that devout Roman Catholics filled the ranks of the monarchists, the Boulangists, and the opponents of Dreyfus. It is significant, however, that some leaders of Roman Catholicism saw the danger of linking their Church with opposition to the Republic. Accordingly, they urged their coreligionists to rally to the support of the Republic. In the present selection, J. V. Ducattillon, of the Order of Preachers, discusses this *ralliement* as well as other significant developments in French church and state relationships in the late nineteenth and early twentieth centuries.

The history of the Third French Republic is, in one of its fundamental aspects, that of a great politico-religious crisis. In this
period the political and religious problems were very closely inter-
related. In fact, the religious problem was in large part stated in political
terms as the political problem was stated in religious terms. The
political conflict and the religious conflict coincided rather closely.
André Siegfried, observing this fact in his book, *Tableau des partis en
France*, quotes the humorous explanation of a Leftist candidate who
had been defeated in a department of central France: "The amusing
part of the election was that my disagreement with my fellow citizens
was not about the things of this world, but about those of the next.
Because my opponents repeated it to me so many times, I now believe
they would have willingly trusted me with the things of this world if
we had only been able to agree on those of the next. I was defeated as
politically incompetent for theological reasons."

The amusing side of this story should not deceive us. This close interconnection of politics and religion is certainly one of the principal
characteristics of the history of the Third Republic. It is impossible

Reprinted by special permission from *The Review of Politics*, VI (1944), 74-85.
The footnotes which originally appeared with this essay have been omitted.

LEO XIII: Late-nineteenth-century Pope who formulated the Roman
Catholic approach to modern social and political problems and fostered
the study of the ideas of St. Thomas Aquinas. His *Rerum Novarum* (1891)
proclaimed the need for trade unions and for state intervention to protect
the working classes. Embarrassed by the involvement of Roman Catholics
in the Boulanger fiasco, he emerged as a strong advocate of the *ralliement*.
He believed that French Roman Catholics should rally to the support of
the Republic.

EDGAR QUINET: French publicist and historian (d. 1875). An intense
republican and no less intense an anti-Catholic, he insisted that the great
mistake of the leaders of the French Revolution was their failure to uproot
Roman Catholicism from France. He viewed republicanism and Roman
Catholicism as basically incompatible.

SILLON: An association of young Catholic republicans, organized at the

to understand it if we do not try to grasp this phenomenon. From this interconnection came a heated conflict of fundamental importance which is at the heart of the whole drama of modern France.

Let us note at the beginning that this crisis placed the Republic and Catholicism in conflict with each other. Protestantism and Judaism were not involved.

The reason for such a conflict certainly comes from the fact that in France, a predominantly Catholic country, the Catholic Church played a fundamental role in the historical development of the nation. The bonds between Catholicism and the institutions of the country were so close that any profound transformation of these institutions must also affect religion. One of the fundamental aspects of the problem of the Republic was whether or not and in what way the destiny of the nation would continue to be linked with Catholicism.

We believe, however, that we must go even further and ask whether the problem raised by the conflict we are studying does not result from certain characteristics peculiar to Catholicism.

From our point of view the history of the Third Republic divides into two very distinct periods. The first extends from the beginnings of the regime to the First World War, the second from the First World War to the armistice of June 1940.

---

end of the nineteenth century by Marc Sangnier. They aroused the hostility of conservative Roman Catholics, who viewed them as heretics. Condemned by the papacy, the Sillon was forced to dissolve itself in 1910.

DIANA VAUGHAN: Invention of Léo Taxil, the anticlerical pornographer, who proclaimed his conversion to Roman Catholicism in 1885 and denounced his former associates, the Freemasons, as worshippers of the devil. He attracted considerable attention by his disclosures of the activities of a certain Miss Diana Vaughan, who knew all the secrets of the Luciferians. When he was about to be exposed, he made a public confession in 1897 to the effect that his revelations had been one vast hoax.

LOUIS VEUILLOT: French journalist (d. 1883) and long-time editor of the conservative Roman Catholic newspaper *Univers*. Militantly opposed to liberalism in all its forms, he was constantly engaged in controversies with his liberal coreligionists, who believed that Roman Catholicism and republicanism were not incompatible.

I

From 1870-1914

The first period is on the whole one of mutual hostility between the Catholic world and the world of the Republic. This hostility attained its most acute stage between 1898-1905. From 1905 on signs of a pacification became noticeable.

We must see first the nature of this mutual hostility and how it expressed itself.

Father Lecanuet in his *Histoire de l'Église de France sous la Troisième République* characterizes the general attitude of the clergy at the beginning of the regime: "There were hardly any Republican priests in 1871. For most priests, the Republic meant terror, hatred of the Church and persecution. Although as a group they voted "yes" in the plebiscite of 1870, neither were they attracted by the Empire which had abandoned the Holy Father. Only a very few prelates like Cardinal de Bonnechose remained faithful to Napoleon III. The majority of the clergy, both priests and bishops, inclined rather toward a restoration of the monarchy. It was royalist by temperament, because it saw in such a regime the greatest good for the Church and for France."

At the time the National Assembly had to decide upon a new regime all the Catholic members of the Assembly, and the whole Catholic world of France with them, showed themselves definitely in favor of restoring the monarchy. It is to be noted that this was not only true of the intransigent Catholics led by men like Bishop Pie of Poitiers and Louis Veuillot, editor of the *Univers,* but even of the liberal Catholics like Bishop Dupanloup of Orleans and Archbishop Lavigerie of Algiers.

Bishop Dupanloup, for example, played a very active role in the course of the quarrel between the pretenders to the throne and on the question of the flag. Liberal as he was, he was sincerely royalist. He used all his power and made many attempts to persuade the princes to achieve what at the time was called a "fusion," that is, the union of the royal families around the Count of Chambord. His efforts contributed to the at least apparent success of this fusion. He was less successful with the heir to the throne when he tried to make him accept the tricolor flag. The stubbornness of this prince in holding to the white flag provoked the definitive failure of the monarchists.

The case of Bishop Dupanloup is significant for this prelate represented the advanced wing—we would say the Left—of the Catholic movement.

Here are the reasons which led him to take this definite royalist attitude. He expressed them in a letter of January 23, 1873, to Pope Pius IX in which he tried to obtain the intervention of the Sovereign Pontiff with the Count of Chambord in the hope of softening the Prince's stubbornness on the question of the flag. "Things have reached such a point that crucial events may take place from one day to the next. There may be not only a political crisis but a return of the revolution with a dreadful civil war in which popular passions will be unleashed and go to the worst extremes. And everyone foresees that the Church will necessarily be involved. In such a situation, there is only one hope of salvation: the traditional and hereditary monarchy of the house of France."

Fear of revolution and of religious persecution appears therefore to have been the dominant reason for the total opposition of the Catholics to the Republic.

It is certain that the republicans of the time, as a whole, showed little sympathy for the Church and for Catholics. The Church linked with the monarchy and all it represented, was for them as much the enemy as the monarchy itself.

Edgar Quinet, who played a very important role in the formation of the republican thought, said: "Every Catholic people is a people in eternal tutelage." The Republic which stood for the emancipation of the people could triumph only if it overthrew Catholicism which had to be extirpated.

Without going so far, President Jules Grévy wrote to Pope Leo XIII on May 12, 1883: "Your Holiness rightly complains of antireligious passions. But can one ignore that these passions, of which I disapprove, come principally from the hostile attitude of a part of the clergy toward the Republic?"

Thus we find, on one side, the clergy and the fervent Catholics attached to the monarchy out of fear of revolution and persecution which they identified with the Republic; and on the other hand the republicans, enemies of the monarchy and the Church, which, in their eyes, represented the rampart of the monarchy.

In the first years of the Republic, once it was definitely constituted, a certain number of Catholics, at first only a very small minority, tried to remove this misunderstanding. They were found among those called liberal Catholics in opposition to the traditionalists or authoritarians. They were in the tradition of the movement inaugurated by Lamennais, Lacordaire and Montalembert in the first part of the nineteenth century. They emphasized strongly the fact that the Church by definition and by tradition had not and could not identify itself with any political party or regime. There was therefore no objection in principle to a Catholic being a republican; his Faith authorized him to be one just as it did his being a royalist.

They saw as the principal cause of the hostility of the republicans to the Church the collusion in fact of Catholics with monarchy and their hostility to the Republic. "A sad and fatal conjuncture" wrote Father Didon, "occurred to the great detriment of peace. . . . Almost all of the militant Catholics belonged politically to the defeated parties. . . . We will never realize how deplorable was the confusion engendered by this singular coincidence. . . . Where then has it been proved that Catholicism could not live in a modern society?"

With the same idea in mind Bishop Guilbert of Gap wrote in a pastoral letter of July 1, 1876, entitled "Some Duties of The Priest As Regards Politics and a Catechism Lesson": Does it not both compromise unworthily the Church and the clergy and involve defending a flagrant error to link and identify religion with a system or a given form of government? . . . The clergy should not allow itself to become involved in the political storms and tempests of our time. It should not support any party because it owes itself to all parties, the losing as well as the winning parties, in order to bring them together and to unite them in harmony and in peace. It is only on this condition that it can exercise efficaciously a salutary action and accomplish the divine mission with which it is charged.

"We shall admit frankly," he continued, "that it is not without concern and profound regret that we have seen in recent years certain newspapers, supposedly Catholic above everything else, attach a party flag to Catholicism. No doubt they do not say openly—for they do not dare—that one must accept their opinions absolutely in order to be a good Christian, but that crops out too often in their ardent polemics, and their regular readers must naturally conclude as much.

"The result, which was easy to foresee and predict without being a prophet, has been an anti-religious reaction. It has meant at this moment a fomenting of unjust hatred against the Church, the war against clericalism as they call it, that is, against the whole clergy which they wrongly suppose to share the extremist ideas and exaggerations of these imprudent journalists. For if in a time of divisions and struggles such as ours and in the presence of several regimes of government each of which has its enthusiastic followers, you support one party to the detriment of another, is it not evident that you infallibly arouse against you and, what is even more deplorable, against religion itself the partisans of the others.

"The priest is undoubtedly, like every other citizen, perfectly free to have his own personal political opinions, and nobody has the right to call this a crime. He can believe that one form of government is better than another for his country; he can prefer the Republic to monarchy, or monarchy to the Republic. He is likewise free, but always outside of his pastoral work, to express his personal opinion and to defend it as such with a prudence and moderation becoming his sacerdotal dignity.

"But what we do blame is wishing to link religion and politics —because religion is and ought to remain completely foreign to these systems and to use it to support a party is a sacrilegious abuse which compromises it unworthily."

This attitude which began to manifest itself at the beginning among a certain number of Catholics certainly found a response among those who were called moderate republicans. They too wanted religious peace but felt that it would be possible only if the Church, faithful to her teachings, consented to remain in her own sphere and renounce all political allegiance.

"Yes," exclaimed M. Ribot to the Chamber of Deputies in the session of February 1, 1890, "this increasing hostility to religion is a misfortune for the country. I deplore it as much as anybody in the Chamber. . . . I want religious peace. I want the priest free and respected in his church, but I also want to maintain the rights of the civil power, to follow the tradition of this country, to conform to the profound instinct —to the genius of the French people; I want the priest outside of politics. In the Church, yes; on the public square, on the platform, never."

Mindful of this state of mind, Pope Leo XIII made himself from 1890 on, the protagonist of what was called "the policy of *ralliement*."

It was the Pope who gave the most definite impetus to the movement in favor of a reconciliation of the Catholics of France with the Republic. It is well-known that Leo XIII asked Archbishop Lavigerie of Algiers to express the papal view. On November 12, 1890, the Archbishop at a reception he gave to the officers of the French squadron in the Mediterranean, then at Algiers, and to all the civil and military authorities of Algeria, offered his famous toast in which he asked all Catholics to give their loyal support to the Republic. "When the will of a people has clearly asserted itself," he said, "when the form of government, as Leo XIII has recently declared, has nothing in itself contrary to the principles which alone make Christian and civilized nations live; when, to save one's country from the disasters which threaten, it is necessary to support without reserve this form of government the time has come to declare for the acceptance of this government which has been tried, and in order to put an end to our differences to sacrifice all that our conscience and honor permit and order each of us to sacrifice for the salvation of the country. This is what I teach those about me, and what I hope to see taught in France by all our clergy. In speaking as I do I am sure I will not be disavowed by any recognized authority. Without this resignation, without this patriotic acceptance, nothing can be done to preserve order and peace, to save the world from social peril or to save the very religion of which we are the ministers."

It is enlightening to compare, by way of measuring the progress made, this declaration of Cardinal Lavigerie with that made by Bishop Dupanloup seventeen years earlier. Bishop Dupanloup then expressed the unanimous opinion of the Catholics (and at the time that of Archbishop Lavigerie himself) when he asserted that the salvation of the country, of society, and of religion could be achieved only under a monarchy, that they would be lost under a republic. In 1890 Cardinal Lavigerie, in agreement with the Pope, states that "without this patriotic acceptance [of the Republic] nothing can be done to preserve order and peace, to save the world from social peril or to save the very religion of which we are the ministers."

It has often been said that this policy of *"ralliement"* urged by Leo XIII failed. Certainly it failed by far to gain the unanimous support of the Catholics. The general impression made upon them by the Algiers toast was one of consternation, of defeat if not one of revolt. Only two Bishops dared to approve Cardinal Lavigerie publicly. Most of them kept silent. A few, like Bishop Freppel of Angers, protested vehemently: "No invitation, no matter from whom it comes, will make us change our mind," he declared alluding to the Pope. Certain Catholic papers and a flood of letters, often anonymous, heaped insults upon Cardinal Lavigerie. He was treated as a freemason, a "sans-culotte" and ranked with apostates and the defrocked clergy.

It is also certain that the policy of *"ralliement"* does not seem to have produced, at the very time the Holy See was following it, any pacification of the systematic and persistent hostility of the republican government toward Catholicism. No doubt there was between 1889-1895 a period of quiet during which "the new spirit," as Minister Spuller called it in a famous speech, was manifested. Nevertheless the policy of *"ralliement"* was inaugurated, in 1890. Before this date, obviously unjust decrees and laws had already been promulgated which limited the Church's freedom of action, struck at its most fundamental rights, and stung to the quick the Catholic conscience in its most sacred convictions: dissolution of the Jesuits and decrees against unauthorized congregations in 1880, education laws of 1882, fiscal laws on unalienable property in 1889. It was particularly during the years following 1890 that the most harmful measures were taken. I will not name them here. Let it suffice to point out the two most important ones among many others: the Associations Act passed July 1, 1901, of which certain clauses struck seriously at the existence of all the religious congregations; and the law of 1905 on the separation of Church and State which involved the suppression of the Concordat of 1801. This law left the churches and their property in a juridical situation which Catholics could not accept. Such legislation, however, provoked decisive criticism, particularly from the eminent non-Catholic jurist Leon Guguit, dean of the Law Faculty of Bordeaux, in a famous interview.

Far from favoring the long sought pacification, it seems therefore that the policy of *"ralliement"* sharpened animosities. This policy offered Catholic monarchists the occasion to show their stubbornness. The republicans, on the other hand, saw in this hostility so openly confirmed, the justification of their anti-Catholic feeling and their troublesome acts. As each of the measures unfavorable to the Church increased in its turn the animosity of the recalcitrant Catholics the crisis could not help developing and becoming acute. This is precisely what happened.

Yet, at this same time another profound change was likewise taking place in the Catholic world as a whole. This was a positive work of wisdom and common sense, and one which certainly could not have taken place as it did without the firm and prudent action of Leo XIII. The impassioned violence, often narrow and sometimes clearly unjust, of the intransigent Catholic monarchists likewise contributed to it in good part. Again they did not blunder with impunity in such events as the Dreyfus affair, Boulangism, the farce of Diana Vaughan (inspired by Leo Taxil), etc. It was after all quite a paradoxical attitude taken by those Catholics who pretended only to be against the Republic in order to save religion and the Church but who on this very point found themselves opposing the head of religion and of the Church.

In short, as the years passed the number of Catholics who acquiesced in the Republic kept increasing and we can say that when the first World War broke out in 1914 a very large majority of the Catholics were in this category. In like manner the hostility of the government of the Republic toward the Church quieted down. From 1908 on the effect of this pacification was clearly felt and this was only the beginning. One might well have wondered, however, what was the precise nature of this reconciliation of the Catholics with the Republic.

The term *"ralliés"* used to designate those who obeyed the directions of Leo XIII does not fail to present many problems. Was the support of the Republic by these *"ralliés"* very sincere? Did they not accept the Republic as a makeshift because they couldn't do otherwise, or because the chances of a restoration of monarchy were becoming fewer and fewer? Was not their support of the Republic thus simply one of resignation? "Resignation," the very term used by Cardinal Lavigerie in his famous toast: "Without this resignation, without this patriotic acceptance, nothing can be done." It was this word "resignation" which the Cardinal of Algiers kept repeating to explain his position to all his critics.

The republicans asked themselves, therefore, why the Catholics participated in the Republic. Was it not in order to be better able to down it and strangle it? Or was it not, as Catholics admitted openly, to Christianize the Republic? It is clear, for example, that the Catholics and Leo XIII first of all never failed to make a clear distinction between the republican regime considered in itself as the established power, on the one hand, and the legislation and spirit of the Third Republic on the other. They made perfectly clear that their support of the Republic proceeded from the traditionally professed indifference on principle of the Church to republican or monarchial regimes and from its constant doctrine of recognition of established powers, but that this in no way implied either recognition of the injurious laws against religion or, much less, the spirit and doctrine on which the Third Republic rested in fact. If they accepted the Republic it was in order to modify its legislation and to transform its spirit and doctrine. That spirit and doctrine, derived from the Declaration of the Rights of Man and from the French Revolution of 1789, was the foundation of what is called the modern world. Now it was precisely in the name of this Declaration of the Rights of Man that the French Revolution destroyed the order established by eighteen centuries of Christianity. The Third Republic which found its inspiration in the Declaration and continued the Revolution of 1789, was by that fact anti-Christian. It could only be Christianized by modifying completely this spirit and doctrine. This was how Catholics summed up their reasoning.

But then, the republicans asked, what would remain of their Republic? Did they not have the right to think that there was a radical incompatibility between the Republic and the Church?

We must recognize that the really fundamental problem was as follows, Was the participation of Catholics in the Republic possible without their renouncing the exigencies of their religion, or without mortal danger to the spirit of republican institutions, if not to the very institutions themselves? Was it possible for a Catholic to be truly and sincerely republican? The whole politico-religious drama of the Third Republic centered around this problem.

From the beginning of the nineteenth century a certain number of Catholics had already seen and proclaimed that the ideal of Liberty, Equality and Fraternity of the French Revolution, far from being incompatible with Christianity was, on the contrary, possible only with and by its inspiration. They were those, already mentioned above, who constituted the liberal Catholic school and who opposed during the whole century the traditionalist and intransigent school. We have seen how most of these liberals were nevertheless partisans in 1871 of a restoration of the monarchy.

It is needless to say that it was among these Catholics that the policy of *"ralliement"* of Leo XIII found most of its sincere followers. Under the influence of the encyclicals of this pope they were able to form a more exact conception of the Christian nature of democracy. They did not, however, consider themselves authorized, in so far as they were Christian, to accept all the spirit and doctrine of 1789 and everything that animated the institutions and laws of the Third Republic. They opposed particularly the exaggerated individualism of the French philosophy of the eighteenth century. The socialist movement in the very heart of republican democracy was likewise reacting, often excessively, in what was for Christians the opposite direction.

They also reproved, of course, the religious persecution for which the proclamation of liberty served as a pretext. But they considered as a fatal equivocation and piece of nonsense the identification which tended to become fixed, between democracy and irreligion on the one hand, and Catholicism and reaction on the other. They held that an authentic Christianity far from perverting democracy would rather purify it and provide it with a real equilibrium.

Thus in the period following 1890 Catholics encouraged this democratic movement which, through the "Christian Democracy" of Fathers Lemire, Naudet and Garnier, the Sillon movement of Marc Sangnier and the Catholic Association of French Youth, continued to develop right up to the outbreak of the war in 1914.

We must recognize that this Christian democratic movement did not in every case have all the doctrinal certitude, all the clearsightedness and prudence desirable. Often the generous zeal of these militants led them to excesses which served as pretexts for the attacks and sarcasm of the "right thinking" people against those they called Christian reds and "democratic priests." Some of them did not always avoid being influenced by modernism. Some even thought it necessary to sacrifice a little of the strictness of doctrine in order to assure agreement between the Church and democracy. The Church felt obliged to intervene in certain cases by condemning certain ideas and the Sillon movement. But it took the occasion to repeat and to state more clearly that she was not hostile to democracy, but simply condemning deviation from it and its abuses. She did not wish either to consider it as being in every case the uniquely and exclusively acceptable political and social ideal.

These attacks and condemnations resulted in purifying, in provoking deeper thought about, and in strengthening in people's minds the just conception of, the relations between democracy and Christianity. The Christian democrats profited by them to fortify their two-fold fidelity to the Church and democracy. They were thus in a better position than ever to prove that there was no incompatibility in this two-fold ideal. The authenticity of their democratic position forced itself upon those who considered themselves the most faithful defenders of republican orthodoxy. And the fervor of their religious life expressed itself positively on many occasions.

*   *   *   *   *

XXI

Currents in Austro-Hungarian and Russian History, 1870-1914

The Political Structure of Austria-Hungary
Before the War

L. B. NAMIER

The Agrarian Problem in Russia
Before the Revolution

V. MAKLAKOV

The Political Structure of Austria-Hungary Before the War

L. B. NAMIER

Published in 1921 ≪≪≪≪≪≪≪≪≪≪≪

Within less than a decade the Habsburg Monarchy was twice defeated in war: by France in the Austro-Sardinian War of 1859 and by Prussia in the Seven Weeks' War of 1866. The most striking domestic result of these defeats abroad was the *Ausgleich*, or Compromise, of 1867, by the terms of which the Dual Monarchy of Austria-Hungary was created. This Dual Monarchy lasted for five decades and then, under the strains of World War I, collapsed. During the half century of its existence it was confronted with many basic domestic problems. To a remarkable extent, however, the statesmen of the monarchy sought to avoid these domestic problems by exploiting foreign adventures. Nor are the reasons for the constant attempts to avoid dealing with these problems at home hard to understand. The peasant problem, after all, depended on the willingness of the monarchy to bring about changes in the system of landholding, and changes would have aroused almost universal opposition among members of the landed aristocracy in Austria-Hungary. Likewise, the nationality problem raised many serious difficulties, for, although Germans and Magyars constituted only a minority of the population, they were determined as a rule to preserve their privileged position and no less determined to keep the other nationalities in their place. In the selection that follows, L. B. Namier analyzes the impact of the nationality problem on political life in the Dual Monarchy. One of the finest minds in twentieth-century British historical circles, Namier has written with rare brilliance not only on Austria-Hungary but on eighteenth-century England, the Revolutions of 1848, and the origins of World War II.

1. *The Austrian 'Staatsidee.'* 'The idea of the Austrian State' (*die österreichische Staatsidee*) was in recent years habitually in the mouth of those who defended Austria-Hungary's existence. The concrete meaning of the term was never explained; in fact, it had none which its votaries would have cared to explain, and the Austrian State, to which it primarily referred as being conterminous with the Habsburg dominions, did not exist except in reminiscences of the past and pious wishes for the future. The Habsburg Monarchy consisted of two separate, sovereign States, Austria and Hungary, with Bosnia-Herzegovina held by them in common. Since 1867, Austria was that which remained of the amorphous mass of the Habsburg possessions, the "home-farm" of the dynasty, after national States had arisen in Germany, Italy and, in certain aspects, also in Hungary; for nearly fifty years (until 1916) this residuum, which in proportion to its size displayed more frontier and less coherence than any other State in Europe, went officially by the colourless designation of "the Kingdoms and Provinces represented in the Reichsrat." The name of Austria, currently given to them, was kept in reserve in the hope that some day it might once more cover all the dominions of the Habsburgs, *des Hauses Oesterreich*.[1] The Austria of 1867 was regarded by the Habsburgs as but a phase in the history of their dynastic power, their *Hausmacht*; for them there was nothing final about it, indeed they shunned finality—principles when arranged suggest or imply limitation. Every piece of driftwood carried to their shore was to them a promising sprig which might yet grow into a crown. Their outlying western possessions were gone, their age-long dreams of dominion over Germany and Italy were dead; their face was now to the east. Through Galicia and Dalmatia, Austria's fantastically shaped body, enveloping the massive block of Hungary, stretched out its arms towards Poland, the Ukraine, Rumania, and Serbia, which all found their place in the war-dreams and schemings of the Habsburg dynasty. The Habsburgs were the one dynasty which had never linked up its fate with that of any single nation; they had a capital and a territorial base, but no nationality; they developed schemes territorially coherent, though devoid of all national idea. Their instincts were purely

Reprinted by permission of the Royal Institute of International Affairs and the Oxford University Press from H. W. V. Temperley, *A History of the Peace Conference of Paris* (London, 1921), IV, 58-69.

[1] [Footnote omitted.]

proprietary, the one meaning of an Austrian State to them was that they possessed it; to the outside world, that it existed. For the few, and mostly interested, exponents of an Austrian State, its existence was an aim in itself: and this was the pivot of all that there was in the alleged Austrian *Staatsidee*. But it was by no means this exceedingly frail basis which sustained Austria-Hungary's continued existence.

2. *The Partnership of Magyars on one side and Germans and Poles on the other.* There was more shape and sense in the remaining Habsburg dominions than appeared on the surface and more than the Habsburg Idea recognized or admitted; there was less justice to nationalities than the dynasty could theoretically have put up with. Although inhabited by eight, and, counting sub-divisions, even by eleven peoples, the territory of the Habsburg Monarchy was completely covered by the historic, "imperialist" claims of three nationalities—the claim of the Magyars to the lands of the Crown of St. Stephen, of the Germans to "Western" Austria,[2] and of the Poles to Galicia; each claim was tenaciously asserted, though, unless statistical forgeries were committed and unless the Jews were excluded, none of the three nationalities formed a majority in the territory it claimed. If conceded dominion, the master-nations were ready to defend every inch of the Monarchy against the national claims of its neighbours, the co-racials of the subject nationalities—the Southern Tyrol and Trieste against Italy, the Illyrian provinces against Serbia, East Galicia against Russia,

[2] "Western Austria" is here meant to denote the western hereditary provinces which had been under the Habsburgs since 1526, had been included in the Holy Roman Empire and then in the Germanic Confederation of 1815, and lay within the orbit of German settlement, influence, and ambitions. It excludes the outlying provinces in the east and south-east Galicia, the Bukovina and Dalmatia, acquisitions of the late eighteenth century, unconnected with the original block of the Habsburg possessions in geography and history, in nationality (except for the newly-planted German settlers in the Bukovina) and also in their economic structure.

JULIUS ANDRÁSSY: Hungarian political leader (d. 1890) who figured prominently in the War of Independence of 1848-1849 and who served as president of the parliamentary subcommittee for the development of the *Ausgleich* with Austria. Appointed Minister of Foreign Affairs in 1871, he signed the all-important Austro-German Alliance of 1879.

STEPHEN TISZA: Hungarian political leader (d. 1918) and defender of the

Transylvania against Rumania; whereas the subject nationalities, if conceded national self-government, would naturally have bethought themselves next of national reunion. The Germans and Poles in Austria, and the Magyars in Hungary, in their own interest, not from any attachment to the dynasty, had to become the "State-preserving elements" (*die staatserhaltenden Elemente*).

In turn the Habsburgs, for reasons of internal as well as of international policy, had no choice but to base their rule on the supremacy of the Magyars in Hungary, and of the Germans and Poles in Austria. It had its roots in history and was opposed to the national principle, like the Habsburg Monarchy. It rested on past empire and on consequent social superiority, and was therefore conservative, a feature essential to a Monarchy which lived by survival alone. The upper classes were Magyar throughout Hungary, Polish throughout Galicia; in "Western" Austria even in 1914 they still remained predominantly German. The choice between nationalities implied therefore a choice between classes—a mediaeval, clerical dynasty does not lead social revolutions, nor impose the rule of peasants on their landlords. Lastly, the German-Magyar combination alone could supply the Habsburgs with a suitable foreign alliance to safeguard their possessions against a coalition of the neighbouring States, each of which saw national territory of its own included in their Monarchy. The Germans within Austria were sufficiently strong to permeate the State and thus to accept dominion in lieu of complete national reunion; Germany alone seemed sufficiently powerful to preserve Austria-Hungary's existence and sufficiently concerned in it to attempt doing so; and moreover Germany had no interests conflicting with those of Austria-Hungary in the Adriatic and the Balkans, which now became the main sphere of Habsburg ambitions. Hence the German alliance. The logical result of that alliance upon the internal affairs of the Habsburg Monarchy was once more the predominance of the Magyars in Hungary and of

domination of the Magyar nobility. Determined to preserve the privileges which Hungary enjoyed by the terms of the *Ausgleich*, he opposed any remaking of the Dual Monarchy into a federation of many nationalities. Not surprisingly, he was bitterly hated by the leaders of the subject nationalities in Austria-Hungary.

the Germans (with their indispensable associates, the Poles) in Austria. No one had chosen his partners, no special sympathy bound either the Poles or the Magyars to the Germans—in fact, when necessary, they could show strong dislike of one another—and few statesmen except Bismarck, Julius Andrássy the elder, and, more recently, Stephen Tisza, seem to have understood and accepted all the implications of the system. It had been imposed on the contracting parties by the inherent necessities of their political situation and by the logic of events. Its intricacies were such that no human mind could have thought out, nor any human skill readjusted them. Its inherent force was so great that it survived to the very end, till October 1918.

In 1848, when the national and constitutional movement among the gentry and bourgeoisie found expression in revolt against the non-national, proprietary character of the Monarchy, the dynasty appealed to the subject peasant-races, the Czecho-Slovaks, the Yugo-slavs, Ruthenes,[3] and Rumans, for help against their masters, the Germans, Magyars, and Poles. In 1867 the Habsburgs surrendered their late supporters to their late opponents. Reconciled to the most powerful and most articulate of their subjects, they proposed to resume the struggle against their hereditary enemy, Prussia. A German-Magyar veto prevented them from doing so in 1870. In 1879 the alliance with Prussia-Germany was concluded. The ideas of separation from Germany and of reform within the Habsburg Monarchy, which arose once more in the course of the War and in the hour of defeat, were froth and bubble, and the last desperate attempts of October 1918 bore no more resemblance to action based on a political system than the mad antics of a drowning man do to the movement of swimming. The political developments of Austria-Hungary obeyed the necessities of its internal structure; illusions there were of dynastic power to shape—in reality these developments were pre-determined as the movements of the stars, and subject to iron laws.

It had not been within the power of the Habsburgs and their

[3] The Little Russians in the late Austro-Hungarian territories are usually known by the name of 'Ruthenes,' although in language and race they are absolutely identical with the Little Russians of Southern Russia. A group of Little Russians, which claimed to form a nation distinct from that of the Great Russians and not merely a branch of the Russian nation, to avoid all resemblance, adopted the fanciful name of 'Ukrainians.' Thus they have come to be known by three interchangeable names.

centralist followers to refuse the claims of the Germans, Magyars, and Poles; as far as Austria was concerned, it had been within their power, and to their interest, to prevent the complete establishment of the system. Its full logical development would have left the Habsburgs stripped of all authority, without a "home-farm," with an exceedingly limited base for dynastic schemings, with very little scope for an independent foreign policy, bound hand and foot to the three dominant nationalities. They would have changed into shadowy suzerains of excessively powerful subjects, the real masters of their possessions; in short, the Habsburgs would have been reduced to the position of constitutional monarchs in three "imperialist" States, each based on the artificially secured rule of a dominant minority. It was in opposition to the complete establishment of a system, of which the principle had to be admitted if the Habsburg Monarchy was to be held together, that the interest of the dynasty coincided with that of the submerged nationalities. Cautiously, and as far as Hungary was concerned, in a purely Platonic fashion, the Habsburgs sympathized with the outraged national rights of races whom they themselves, in their own dynastic interest, had surrendered to the master-nations. This was the outstanding peculiarity of the Habsburg system, the only concrete meaning of the so-called Austrian *Staatsidee*.

3. *The Magyar System.* In 1867 Hungary had crystallized once more into the "imperialist" domain of the Magyars and was, in its constitution, completely separated from the remaining Habsburg heritage, the Austrian Hereditary Provinces. The frontier drawn between Austria and Hungary cut across the lands *minorum gentium*, of "the minor nations," the Czecho-Slovaks, the Yugo-slavs, the Ruthenes, and the Rumans, whose national territories were thus partitioned even within the borders of the Habsburg possessions, an obvious fact which, during the War, was only too often overlooked or deliberately left out of count when internal reform and national autonomy within the Habsburg Monarchy were discussed. By forming Croatia into a separate, though absolutely dependent, State, the Magyars had secured for themselves a majority in Hungary proper, and by means of a narrow class franchise in a country where the upper classes were Magyar or Magyarized, they had given an almost exclusively Magyar character to their Parliament. This was an artificially constructed and delicately balanced system which did not admit of any radical changes within Hungary nor of a material extension of its borders; strongly con-

scious of this fact, Stephen Tisza was a bitter opponent of democratic reform at home and of any considerable increase of territory at the expense of Serbia or Rumania. Hungary was not to be used or manipulated in the Habsburg interest; it was neither to be enlarged nor reduced. There were no Magyars outside Hungary's frontiers, and within they were to be dominant. They held the most convenient strategic frontiers, the Carpathian arc and the Transylvania mountain-bastion, and had access to the sea. Hungary was complete.

The Magyars would have gladly seen the Germans and Poles attain the same position in "Western" Austria and in Galicia, respectively, which they themselves held in Hungary. It was not to their interest that in Austria the subject races should remain in immediate touch with the dynasty, and enjoy more favourable treatment than in Hungary, nor that the dynastic power of the Habsburgs should survive anywhere, and threaten with the help of the subject races once more to include or engulf the Magyar domain in the amorphous mass of the Habsburg possessions. In September 1866 Count Julius Andrássy the elder emphatically declared to the Austrian Minister Hübner that the Magyars "could not suffer a federalist system to be established in Austria, a probable centre for future attacks against Hungary." Had full self-government been conceded within Austria such a system would have affected the nationalities oppressed in Hungary; the Magyars would have had to break off all connexion with Austria and the Habsburgs—every extant link and all reminiscences of a common past would then have kept suggesting to the subject races of Hungary that through a reunion in a dynastic Habsburg State lay the road to national self-government. But as changes in the Austrian constitution required a two-thirds majority, and such a majority could not have been obtained in the Reichsrat against the German vote, federalist devolution could have been introduced by means of a dynastic *coup d'état* alone. In the Agreement of 1867 the Magyars therefore explicitly stipulated that the connexion between the two States was to continue only so long as both were governed in a constitutional manner. They thus reserved for themselves the power of vetoing any unconstitutional act even with regard to exclusively Austrian affairs—but they naturally never protested when the Austrian constitution was infringed to the disadvantage of the Slavs.

The Magyars desired Austria to be centralized, and its centralism to bear a distinct German character. But with Galicia as an integral part of Austria, the Austrian State was ill poised. It would therefore have been to the interest of the Austrian Germans, as well as of the Polish and the Magyar oligarchs, had a separate constitutional status been conceded to Galicia. The exclusion of the Galician members from the Austrian Reichsrat would have given a decisive majority to the Germans over the Czechs, Yugo-slavs, and Italians, whilst the Poles would have been left to deal with the Ruthenes in the Galician Diet, where, by means of electoral devices, they had secured for themselves a majority almost as good as that of the Magyars in the Hungarian Parliament. As long as within Austria no single nationality had a decisive, permanent superiority over its opponents, the Habsburgs were able to preserve their dynastic power, without reproducing the strictly "constitutional" Magyar system of government. Although they never seriously questioned the predominance of the Germans and Poles over the subject races, they used the contending nationalities as checks on each other. They could do so the more easily as they invariably had the support of the German clericals and of the Poles. Nationality was not the dominant, or at least not the exclusive, political instinct and interest of the German clericals, whilst the Poles had to think of the wider, international aspects of the Polish question and could not consider a settlement within the narrow frontiers of Galicia, which formed one province only of Poland, as anything but temporary. Neither for the German clericals nor for the Poles was there finality in the frontiers of Austria, as there was for the Magyars in those of Hungary, and neither therefore felt the same overwhelming interest in the complete and definite establishment of the triple Magyar-German-Polish scheme.

4. *Austrian Centralism and German Nationalism.* In the central, purely German districts of Austria national feeling had never completely divested itself of an Austrian imprint; it oscillated between the German national idea on the one hand and a peculiar Austrian sentiment on the other. In the Czech provinces of Bohemia, Moravia, and Silesia, bordering on Saxony and Prussia, the German minority developed an uncompromising nationalism, neither softened nor clouded by religious sentiment; so also, to some extent, in the southern Slovene borderlands. But in the centre, especially in Vienna, the population felt too closely associated with the Habsburgs in their power, and its profits and glory, to adopt the purely German point of view. The phantoms of the mediaeval Roman Empire, of the non-

national world-idea centring in Imperial Vienna, surrounded the throne of the Habsburgs—*ils vivaient de l'ombre d'une ombre* . . . [they lived in the shadow of a shadow . . .] For the devout peasantry of the Alpine provinces and for the Vienna petty middle classes, Roman Catholicism was a further link with the dynasty, and even with the clericals of other nations, Czech, Slovene, or Italian. The *intransigeant* German nationalists turned their backs upon Hungary and Galicia in order to concentrate on the Czech and Slovene provinces, in which they were directly concerned through their German minorities. The "Austrians" could not become indifferent to any part of the Habsburg dominions, their old inheritance, and upheld the conception of the *Gesammtmonarchie* (a State embracing them all) with even more fervour than the dynasty itself. But whilst German nationalism and Austrian "imperialism" were clearly distinct in theory and in the minds of their most extreme exponents, they blended in the middle ranges, and most Austrian Germans were something of the one and something of the other. Austrian imperialism with Vienna for centre was German in its essence, and the Germans were in Austria the most important centripetal force.[4]

The idea of the *Gesammtmonarchie* was a direct negation of the Magyar scheme. "As long as a Magyar is left alive he will not allow his nation to be forced under such a superior State organization," declared Count Tisza on the 1st January 1916. The centralist Austrian "patriotism" was by all means agreeable to the Magyars, but only if enclosed within the frontiers of the western half of the Monarchy, i.e. whilst directed against Czech and Yugo-slav national ambitions. "I consider this feeling equally sacred as our own patriotism," Count Tisza went on to say in his exposition of the Magyar creed. "I sympathize with it and value it, provided it does not turn against the independence of the Hungarian nation. . . . It is in our own interest to strengthen over there the centripetal as against the centrifugal forces . . . . Before now the Magyar nation tried to fulfill its mission, to promote and strengthen the centripetal forces in Austria. . . . And if in the past it has not achieved full success, this was because Austrian patriotism has not been able to divest itself of the old tendencies in favour of a Monarchy including all the Habsburg dominions. . . ." Tisza spoke of an "Austrian patriotism"; he meant it. The Magyars

[4] On this subject cf. L. B. Namier in the *Nineteenth Century and After* of July 1916, "The Old House and the German Future."

wanted Austria, but not too much of it. They wanted it to be German, but not too German. It was to be sufficiently German to prevent the nationalities which were subdued in Hungary from forming national States across Hungary's border, but not so German as to lead to a fusion of Austria with Germany. The weaker Austrian partner would then have been replaced by an overwhelmingly, indeed dangerously superior German neighbour, and the Magyar system in international politics, a marvellous machine which through a multitude of wheels and levers made one of the smallest nations in Europe into a Great Power, would have broken down. "A proper centralization of Austria will secure the State against excessive Germanism (*Deutsch-tümelei*) on the part of the Germans by their being mixed up with the Slavs, whilst the Slavs will be prevented by the Germans from following out a centrifugal policy," explained the elder Andrássy to the Emperor Francis Joseph I in July 1866. The aim of German nationalism was Great Germany—comprising all territories of the former Germanic Confederation—even *Mittel-Europa*; the logical expression of "Austrian" patriotism was Great-Austria—*die Gesammtmonarchie*. The Magyars wanted neither. For them, and them alone, the Dual Monarchy, as they had reconstructed it in 1867, was final.

The Austrian federalist schemes of 1860-73 were based on the historic provinces into which Austria was divided. There were seventeen of these, differing widely in size and population—e.g. Galicia had 22,000 square miles and, in 1910, 8,000,000 inhabitants, Salzburg 2,000 square miles and 200,000 inhabitants. Only some of the small German mountain provinces were nationally homogeneous. All the rest had their national minorities and their national problems. Whereas in the Austrian Reichsrat and government the Germans were practically dominant, there were Slav majorities and German minorities in Bohemia, Moravia, and Carniola; on the Adriatic coast there were practically no Germans. Complete centralization in the Austrian Reichsrat alone could save the Germans in the Slav provinces from becoming minorities subject to non-German rule, and to achieve this was for the German Nationalists the purpose of Austria's existence. But again the particular interests of the German clericals produced divergences within the German camp. To the clericals, who were strongly entrenched in several of the Alpine Diets, provincial autonomy safeguarded certain interests against a possible or actual anticlerical majority in the Vienna Parliament. This was a further obstacle to German centralism in Austria.

5. *The Poles and the Habsburgs.* The Austrian Poles were neither federalists nor centralists, merely Habsburgites. They had been federalists at times, but half-heartedly; they did not really wish for an increase in the power and independence of the pro-Russian Czechs and Yugoslavs. They could not be centralists as long as Galicia remained an Austrian province. For themselves they demanded from Austria national liberty and dominion over the Ruthenes of East Galicia; on every other point they were prepared for compromise. They were willing to co-operate with the dynasty because they counted on Habsburg support in the reconstruction of Poland. Whilst Russia in partitioning Poland had aimed at re-establishing her own national unity (White Russia and the Western Ukraine) and Prussia at consolidating her eastern frontier (West Prussia and Posnania), Austria had merely demanded her pound of flesh as counterpoise to the acquisitions of her neighbours. The same reasons which had moved the other two Powers to partition Poland maintained their opposition to its reconstruction; the Habsburgs were prepared to give up their pound of flesh provided they could get the entire man. Hostility to Prussia and Russia, and the common Roman Catholic religion were bonds between the Poles and the Habsburgs, even before the agreement on the basis of Galician autonomy was reached; that agreement was the logical outcome of a community of interests. The idea of an "Austro-Polish solution" can be traced as early as 1794, 1809, and 1830; after 1848, and still more after 1867, the belief in "Austria's historic mission" with regard to Poland became a fundamental article of the Polish creed in Galicia. Reluctantly the Poles accepted even the German Alliance as necessary for safeguarding Austria and of course also their dominion over the Little Russian territory of East Galicia against Russia. The anti-Russian and generally anti-Slav policy continued to bind them to the Habsburgs and Magyars. It was not an accident that M. de Bilinski, one of the chief leaders of the Galician Poles and Minister for Bosnia-Herzegovina in 1914, was one of the main authors of the Ultimatum to Serbia—which fact did not prevent him in 1919 from attaining Cabinet rank in the reconstituted Poland.

6. *The Yugo-slav Problem.*[5] One stone in the structure of the Habsburg Monarchy was very loose—Bosnia-Herzegovina, acquired

[5] [Footnote omitted.]

in 1878 for dynastic reasons, not coveted then either by the Austrian Germans or the Magyars. Yugo-slav throughout in nationality, though partly Mussulman in religion, and surrounded by Yugo-slav territory— by Croatia, a nominally self-governing kingdom under the Hungarian Crown, by Dalmatia, an Austrian province nowhere bordering on Austria, and by the independent Yugo-slav kingdoms of Serbia and Montenegro—Bosnia-Herzegovina had no political connexion with any of them but remained under the joint Austro-Hungarian government, which itself was not a government but a contractual formation based on the Agreement of 1867. The Austrian Prime Minister, Baron Hussarek, in his speech of the 1st October 1918, described Bosnia-Herzegovina as *ein staatsrechtlich undefinierbares Neutrum*.[6] The dynasty would have willingly accepted a union of all Yugo-slav territory provided it was effected under their sceptre. The Austrian Germans would not allow the Slovene territories, their sea-coast, to be detached from "Western" Austria, but would probably have agreed to a Serbo-Croat State or at least to a Great Croatia—consisting of Croatia, Dalmatia, and Bosnia-Herzegovina. But as such a union of Yugo-slav territories would have changed the balance within Hungary and the Habsburg Monarchy to the disadvantage of the Magyars, these naturally objected, and there was no way of fitting the Yugo-slav stones into the structure of the Habsburg Monarchy. For different reasons the other national problems of the Habsburg Monarchy were internationally more or less dormant during the year preceding the outbreak of the War. The unsolved Yugo-slav question opened up the problem of Austria-Hungary's existence and brought about the War.

The War, in which Russia and Germany opposed each other, unrolled the Polish Question which could not have been reopened in any other way, and the Polish Question raised all the other problems of Austria-Hungary's inner structure. Austria-Hungary, as it existed from 1867 till 1914, the creation of Magyar statesmanship, fully and finally satisfied none but the Magyars; on everybody else, not excluding even the dynasty, the Austrian centralists and the German Nationalists, it imposed sacrifices and renunciations, offering them merely half-solutions and a *modus vivendi*. The War and the possibility, nay the certainty, of change unhinged at one blow the delicate system of compromise and balances, and liberated wildly divergent desires and

[6] "A nondescript creation, which cannot be defined in terms of political science."

forces. "Great" Austria, "Great" Germany, a reunited Poland threatened to destroy the balance and nature of the Dual System, the national ambitions of the subject races threatened to destroy the very existence of the Habsburg Monarchy and the "integrity of Hungary." Whichever side was to prove victorious, the Austria-Hungary of pre-War days was dead, and everything was once more unsettled. Long-forgotten visions stirred up somnolent forces, leading them towards an unknown future.

The Agrarian Problem in Russia
Before the Revolution

V. MAKLAKOV

Published in 1950

The emancipation of the serfs did not end the peasant problem in Tsarist Russia; on the contrary, it aggravated it. For the last decades of the nineteenth century saw the outbreak of numerous peasant uprisings—uprisings which clearly testified to peasant dissatisfaction with the conditions under which emancipation had taken place in 1861. Russian peasants wanted more land to cultivate, and they wanted to be rid of the burdensome redemption payments which they owed to the state in return for the lands that they had received at the time of emancipation. With the Russian defeat in the Russo-Japanese War and with the consequent outbreak of the formidable Revolutions of 1905, the Tsarist government sought to curb the revolutionary spirit that had flared up in one village community after another. Accordingly, it abolished all future redemption payments as well as those redemption payments that were in arrears. Nor was this all. The government also authorized the reform measures known as the Stolypin Laws, which were designed to enable Russian peasants to withdraw their holdings from the jurisdiction of the *mir*, or village community. The intention was to create a class of independent peasant proprietors who would have a stake in Russian society and would therefore serve as a conservative and stabilizing force, a bulwark of the Romanov dynasty. The Stolypin Laws were never really tested, for their operation was seriously affected by the outbreak, first, of World War I and, then, of the March Revolution of 1917. In the present article, V. Maklakov analyzes the peasant problem in pre-Revolutionary Russia and discusses the solutions to the problem that were favored by the more important political groups. A leading spokesman for Russian liberalism, he is the author of volumes on the first and the second Dumas.

Τhe agrarian problem in Russia presented several paradoxes. A country of boundless territorial expanse, with a sparse population, suffered from a *shortage of land*. And the peasant class, elsewhere usually a bulwark of order, in Russia, evidenced in 1917 a revolutionary temper.

These peculiarities are rooted in history. I can deal here only briefly with their historic causes.

By the beginning of the nineteenth century, Russia had evolved a social order based upon serfdom. The landed class owned not only the land upon which the peasants were settled, but the peasants themselves. This crucial fact was reflected in the whole political system. The usual functions of the state—police, jurisdiction, collection of taxes, recruiting of the army—in rural Russia were performed by the landlords through the medium of their serfs, and the landlords were answerable for them to the state.

In 1861, with the emancipation of the serfs, the axis which supported the whole body politic disappeared. Other reforms became unavoidable; and the agrarian, judiciary, military reorganization filled the following years, known in history as the Era of the Great Reforms.

Serfdom became a thing of the past, but in its stead there arose the "peasant problem." Remnants of the old feudal relationships survived into the new era. In 1861, the emancipated peasants had been endowed with land bought for them by the state from their former owners and had to pay off their debt to the state in instalments. In order to protect the peasants against the loss of their land, these "allotted lands," as they were called, were declared by law "inalienable" and made the joint property of the whole village commune composed of former serfs of

Reprinted by special permission from *The Russian Review*, IX (1950), 3-15.

FIRST DUMA (1906): Lower-house legislature created by the tsar as a result of the Revolutions of 1905. It was elected on the basis of universal manhood suffrage, but it was limited in its powers. Since it was boycotted by the more radical groups, the largest party proved to be the liberal Constitutional Democratic Party (Cadets). Even so, it was too radical a body to please the tsar. As a result, it was dissolved after some two months.

RUSSIAN POPULISM: *Narodnichestvo*. Russian intellectual movement which should not be confused with American populism of the General Weaver

the same master. This commune was given the right of periodical re-allotment of the land among the individual homesteads. In this way the threat of "landlessness" was mitigated; but on the other hand, the peasant was made dependent on his commune in a manner unknown to the other social classes and alien to Russian law. It must be admitted that as a transitional phase from "slavery" to "freedom" this was a bold concept. Rural self-government going so far as to include the distribution of common lands, judges and officials elected by the peasants themselves, the application to rural life of "customary law" instead of the general Code—all this represented a democratic solution of the chief problem posed by the historic situation: that of finding a substitute for the authority of the landlords over their serfs.

However, this provisional solution should not have hampered the process of the gradual extension of general civil legislation to the peasantry. After all, the transformation of the serfs into full-fledged citizens had been the chief purpose of the reforms. The reform of the judicial system and that of local self-government (*Zemstvo*) expressly recognized this goal. The same principle of "equalization" should have been applied to the problem of the "allotted lands" and the relationship between the individual peasant and the village commune. Autocracy, which in 1861 had used its absolute power to liberate the slaves and to endow them with land, surely would have been able to complete the process of "equalization." However, all great reforms have a tendency to change their pace—to slow up at times and even to give way to backward movements. "Revolution" and "reaction" are closely interlocked and feed each other. . . . So it happened in Russia in the late sixties. The reforms of Alexander II came to a standstill; and the seventies became a decade of intense revolutionary action directed against the person of the Sovereign. On March 1, 1881,—the very day

---

variety. The name applied to the non-Marxist Russian socialism associated with Herzen, Chernyshevsky, and Lavrov.

ZEMSTVO LAW OF 1864: One of the major reforms that followed emancipation. The law authorized the organization of a system of local self-government. Local boards, consisting of elected representatives of the nobility, the peasantry, and the townsmen, were given limited powers to levy local taxes for schools, hospitals, prisons, and road and bridge construction. It was on these local boards that many a Russian liberal leader received his training.

when Alexander II signed the decree introducing a kind of "popular representation"—which might have developed into a genuine constitutional system—he was killed by a terrorist's bomb. The reign of Alexander III began.

It is understandable that the new Tsar, who succeeded to the throne under such tragic circumstances, felt no inclination to give up absolute power, and declared in his Manifesto of April 29 that he would "preserve autocracy for the good of the people."[1] The great mistake of Alexander III, to which he was driven by his new advisers, was not the preservation of absolute monarchy, which only a short while ago had fully justified itself, but that for its sake he repudiated the great reforms of his father and initiated reactionary legislation in the fields of education (1884), local self-government (1889), and the judiciary. The same thing happened to the peasant problem. A backward movement set in, and the peculiar features which had been considered temporary, now came to be regarded as the groundwork of the state.

It was this attitude that lent its unusual character to the peasant problem in Russia. Everywhere the peasantry forms a social class of small landowners. In Russia it became a kind of *caste*. Since it possessed the exclusive right to the lands allotted in 1861, and these lands had been made "inalienable" and inaccessible to the other classes, few outsiders could enter this "caste."

That was not all. Whenever a peasant was able to make his way up the social ladder, to obtain a university education, to achieve rank and position in government or military service, he was automatically raised into the higher social group of "honorary citizens" and ceased to be a "peasant,"—losing as a result his right to the allotted land. This system inevitably influenced the status of the peasant class. The élite of the peasantry, those who ought to have been the champions of its interests, withdrew from their class, and this kept alive the antiquated tendency to regard the peasants as an inferior social group. The state subjected them to all kinds of special impositions. Before the emancipation, these might have been justified by their status as serfs (so long as the system itself was not questioned). The peasants themselves, their time, and their labor belonged to the landlord. The civic duties actually

---

[1] The revolutionary party made public a letter to Alexander III upon his accession, promising to stop terrorism if autocracy were replaced by a constitution. Nothing could have been more compromising for all advocates of liberal reforms. As to the revolutionary party, it was soon crushed.

performed by the serfs were imposed by the state upon the landlord who was responsible for their execution. The routine of local administration—the repair of roads and bridges, the fight against floods and fires, the maintenance of the lower police—all this was the obligation of the landowners within the boundaries of their estates, and it was carried out by their serfs. After the emancipation, these services became the responsibility of the peasants' elective authorities—who, in addition to looking after the needs of the peasants, were thus compelled to carry out the orders of the general administration. The heavy load of these impositions—which served the interests of the whole population—was borne *exclusively by the peasants*, who provided both the labor and the necessary funds.

This was not only a crying injustice but also a technically inefficient system. The obligation of the peasant class to "run errands" for the general administration was an intolerable burden which distracted them from their real work, the cultivation of the land. The "elections" no longer were a matter of choosing the best men, but became a system of rotation. Some official attempts were made to correct the ensuing chaotic conditions in the villages. In 1889, the institution of "rural superintendents" (*Zemsky nachalnik*) was created—officers appointed by the government from among the local landowners. They not only replaced the former justices of peace elected by the organs of the local self-government (representing all classes), but were put in control of the peasants' elective authorities. Their decisions could be appealed only to their own District Assembly, presided over by the District Marshal of the Nobility. This innovation, which was meant to introduce some order into rural life, strongly reminded the peasants of their recent subjection to the landlords.[2]

Thus originated the "peasant problem" in Russia. Their legal status alone would have explained the peasants' discontent. But to this was added the economic burden. The land allotted to them in 1861 may have been sufficient to support them at that time, but the population increased, and the load of taxes and duties grew from year to year, while the land area at the peasants' disposal remained the same. The system of communal land tenure kept farming on the lowest level. To leave the village in order to seek supplementary work, one

[2] In addressing a delegation of village elders at his coronation, Alexander III said: "Obey the orders of your Marshals of the Nobility!" There could have been no clearer reminder of things that should have been better forgotten.

needed the permission of the commune, which was not given without compensation. The average peasant could obtain additional earnings only through renting some land from a big landowner, or hiring himself out to work on a big estate. The peasants were fully justified in resenting their condition; and it so happened that all the measures of the government directed their discontent against the landowners.

This had important consequences for the land problem proper. The peasants became convinced that they had a rightful claim to the land of their former masters. Under the system of serfdom, the master had the obligation either to provide his serfs with land or else to support them as his house servants. After 1861, if the emancipation had been completed, there would no longer have been any foundation for such a conception. But the government itself had turned the situation into a "class problem," with peasants and landowners in opposite camps. The subjection of the peasants to the landowners and their right to the latter's land were inextricably linked in the peasants' consciousness. The keener the peasant was made to feel his inequality with regard to the landowner, the stronger grew his conviction that he was entitled to the latter's land. (It is significant that the peasants, as was shown in 1917, usually claimed only the land of their own former masters.) The idea that land was God's gift, and as such should not be the object of private ownership, had little to do with the peasants' conviction. That was a fond illusion of many Russian idealists. The Russian peasant, like any other peasant, was a believer in private property. He wanted the gentry's land for his very own.

One of the consequences of the peasants' attitude was the artificial aggravation of the land shortage. Russia had enough land for all who wished to cultivate it; but this presupposed an organized redistribution of the population and the settlement of vacant areas. It was not only the inertia of the government and the selfishness of the landowners— who profited from the availability of cheap labor near their estates— which prevented this redistribution: the peasants themselves resisted it, reluctant to abandon their right to the allotted lands and to give up the hope of coming into possession of the remaining lands of their former masters. In this way an artificial land shortage was created in the vicinity of the big estates.

The men at the helm of the state should have realized the danger that threatened Russia from this source; but under Alexander III they were in the grip of a violent reaction against the Great Reforms and blinded by their successful suppression of all revolutionary attempts. They believed in the necessity of upholding the old order. Their agrarian policy, accordingly, was based upon the preservation of some of the most outdated features of the traditional era: class division, isolation of the peasantry, its subjection to special laws and special authorities; in a word, the perpetuation of its inequality. The statesmen who shaped the agrarian policy of that reign were nurtured on these ideas. Witte alone of all the prominent men of that time understood that absolute monarchy could be saved only through a further development of the great reforms of the sixties. In charge of Russia's financial policy, he was determined to promote the industrialization of the country; and he realized that this presupposed a vast domestic market—a well-to-do farmer class instead of an underprivileged and pauperized peasantry. Witte's ideas were taken up under the successor of Alexander III, when the whole problem was posed in a different way.

It is impossible here to go into details, but it is generally known that under Tsar Nicholas II the question of the fundamental transformation of Russia's political system—of the replacement of autocracy by a constitutional monarchy—definitely came to the fore. The public had reached the conclusion that no real improvement of conditions was possible under absolute monarchy and what was needed was a thorough "Reform" instead of partial "reforms." The movement which called itself "liberating" steadily grew. Its slogan was: "Down with Autocracy!" Any concrete amelioration of conditions was appraised by this movement only as another stepping-stone in the struggle for a new order.

This did not come about all at once. The régime still could have gone back to the Great Reforms—with the full support of public opinion. Witte actually attempted to approach the problem in such a way. In 1897, in his report on the national budget, he stressed for the first time the necessity of *equalizing the status of the peasantry* with that of the other classes. In the eyes of the conservatives this smacked of revolution. Witte sought the support of the wider public. A special conference on agricultural economy was convoked under his personal chairmanship and with the participation of prominent public leaders. This led to a conflict between Witte and the diehards of the old order; the conference was finally dissolved and Witte resigned. Only then did the "liberating movement" gain momentum. Now the illegal "Liberation League" (*Soyuz Osvobozhdeniya*), as well as the revolutionary parties, came to the fore. What solutions did they offer for the agrarian problem?

Let us begin with the Social-Democratic party. A minority of this party, known as "Bolsheviks," has won power in Russia at the price of giving up not only the name but the very ideals of social democracy. The S.-D. party had been an outgrowth of world capitalism, and in the fight against it favored *universal methods*. In Russia, industrial capitalism was still in the embryonic stage; the party, nevertheless, was determined to apply the tactics tested in Western Europe. Here, as elsewhere, it appealed to the factory workers and regarded the capitalists as the chief enemies. The Social-Democrats realized that the class struggle could take a normal course only under a system of "rule by the people"; their program, therefore, called for the establishment of a Republic, with all power residing in a parliament elected by universal suffrage. Even then, however, a minority of the party, the future Bolsheviks, insisted that democracy should be preceded by a *dictatorship* that would achieve the total destruction of the existing order without interference—and thus clear the way for socialism.

The Social-Democrats' treatment of the peasant problem was ambiguous. Owing to the government's mistakes, the peasantry was in a revolutionary mood, and the S.-Ds were willing to take advantage of this. They were aware that the elemental destructive force of the peasantry was far beyond that of the urban working class, but they had little real sympathy with the peasantry, which was, after all, a class enemy of the proletariat. Hence the party's equivocations with regard to the problem.

At first the party was true to its ideology. In 1903, at its second convention, its platform included the abolition of all laws restricting the peasants' right to dispose of their land. As a result of this, the economically weakest members of the peasant class would have lost their plots. The S.-Ds would have welcomed this as a *step forward*— a strengthening of capitalism, but at the same time the growth of the social-democratic army. What the peasants themselves wanted, however, was *more land*; and to gratify them, the party was willing to give them the so-called "segments"—those strips of land indispensable to the peasants, which in 1861 had been left in the hands of the landlords, and had become a source of the peasantry's economic dependence. This was better than nothing, but it was so little that the

S.-Ds themselves felt embarrassed. And so, when the other parties, including the Social-Revolutionaries (S.-R.) and the Constitutional-Democrats ("Cadets") made public their agrarian program, the S.-Ds, at their Stockholm convention in 1906, amended their own program, and began to advocate the confiscation of *all* lands belonging to the landlords. In conformity with their socialist ideology, they recommended that the confiscated lands be made the property not of individual peasants but of their organs of self-government—an idea that had not been advanced by the peasants themselves. History failed to give the S.-Ds a chance to show how they would have actually solved the problem and reconciled the "rule of the people" with the ideology of the "proletariat." Events outran them and left them behind. Only the Bolshevik section of the party has been able to put its ideas into practice. Under its dictatorship, the confiscated estates, instead of being turned over to the peasants, remained in the hands of the state and became the *Sovkhozy*—state farms. As to the "allotted lands," which had belonged to the peasants since 1861, the Communists did everything to crush the individual peasants settled on them and to replace them with compulsory collective farms—the *Kolkhozy*. Collective farming represented a technical advance and might have proved an advantage, but the Soviet government insisted on doing everything with a high hand, using violence and coercion. The peasantry as a social class of small landowners was destroyed. The official slogan was "liquidation of the kulaks" (well-to-do peasants), but every individual owner of a plot was branded a "kulak" and treated accordingly. As a result of the Soviet agrarian reform, all the land came under state control and the peasants were compelled to work for the state—which was in fact a restoration of serfdom, but with a new ruthless master, the all-powerful state. As in 1861, the situation today cries for the emancipation of the peasants. Since technical progress has made the small individual farm unprofitable, it is difficult to foretell the future pattern of agriculture, but first of all, the peasant must be "liberated" once again.

The other socialist party—the Social-Revolutionary—based itself upon the peasantry. The interests of that class were the constant concern of the trend known under the generic name of "populism." It held no menace for the state; the improvement of the peasants' lot was possible within the framework of the then existing political and social system.

Unfortunately, the government followed a different course. And so it came about that in the beginning of the twentieth century, when the "liberating movement" got under way, the peasant class could be readily incited to revolutionary action. The peasants regarded the landowners as their chief enemies. Frictions that grew out of petty local causes could be easily turned by agitators into mass movements directed against the landowners. Such revolts, whenever they happened, would be ruthlessly put down by the government, with the result that the interference of the authorities undermined the people's faith in the Tsar as the protector of the common people against the "masters."

The Social-Revolutionary party was an outgrowth of this frame of mind. Its agrarian program had two sides.

On the one hand, the party demanded the requisition of *all privately owned land*. In this it went farther than the peasants themselves who claimed only the land of their own former masters. The land problem was thus severed from the Russian past and considered on the plane of an *international* ideology.

On the other hand, the S.-Rs as a socialist party were opposed to the principle of private property, and the idea of turning over the confiscated estates to the peasants as their individual property, was repugnant to them. Their program, therefore, called for the transfer of the land to the "democratically organized rural communes for use on an equalitarian basis." The party was convinced that this was in harmony with the peasants' own conception of the land as the property of all. Only he who tills the land should be allowed to use it—but it should not belong to him as his property.

This idea has been often attributed to the Russian peasantry; and indeed, history had not taught the peasants to stand up for their individual rights, nor had it accustomed them to individual ownership of land. They had never enjoyed it, neither under the system of serfdom, or after their emancipation. Nevertheless, to assume that the Russian peasant did not aspire to become the rightful owner of his plot would be a rash conclusion. The opposite is probably true. The peasants submitted to the periodical reallotment of land by the communes as required by the law; but as time went on it became less frequent, the peasants managed to withdraw their homesteads from redistribution, despite all exhortations they failed to adopt "communal farming," and every single agricultural task was divided in such a way that everyone worked *on his plot for himself*. It cannot be determined whether the agrarian program of the S.-Rs was true to the peasants' own ideas or did violence to them. Today the question is academic: the party was not given the opportunity to convert its program into reality, although it won the majority in the elections to the Constituent Assembly. The Assembly was forcibly dispersed by the Communists after its first meeting. Later, the Communists boasted of having put into effect the whole agrarian program of the S.-Rs. The latter would have disclaimed this. What the Communists did was to restore the forced labor of peasants upon land that was not theirs—something very different from the dream of the S.-Rs.

Now let us consider the "liberal parties"—those who wanted to carry out their ideas within the framework of the constitutional system. Their influence varied in the course of time. The era of constitutional monarchy in Russia can be roughly divided into two periods: the first lasting from the introduction of the constitution (February 23, 1906) to the "coup d'état" of June 3, 1907; and the second, from the latter date to the Revolution in February, 1917.

During the first period, the Constitutional-Democratic party ("Cadets") played the dominant part. It originated within the circle of seasoned Zemstvo workers and had participated in the "Liberation League"; it possessed an elaborate legislative program, as well as cadres of faithful supporters, long before the Revolution. It was victorious in the elections to the first Duma and assumed leadership in that assembly. What solution of the peasant problem did it offer at the height of its influence?

This problem had two aspects: the legal status of the peasantry on the one hand; and its provision with land on the other. Progressive public opinion had advocated "equal rights" for peasants for a long time. The Cadet party in the first Duma immediately introduced an "equal rights" bill. A special commission was charged to prepare four groups of laws based upon the principle that "all citizens of both sexes are equal before the law." It was assumed that this would incidentally solve the peasant problem. Such an assumption was obviously superficial. Next to the laws restricting the peasants' civil rights—which could be annulled without difficulty—there existed vast "special" legislation protecting their interests: the laws governing land tenure, the inalienability of the "allotted land," communal property, the right of the village commune to reallot the land among the individual homesteads. The general Code ignored all these relation-ships. It would have been impossible to determine the respective rights of the commune and the individual member on the basis of the "equal rights" bill. The Cadet party gave no clear answer to these concrete questions.

The party's agrarian bill also failed to provide the answers. The party was very proud of it, complacently asserting that its adoption would have prevented the revolution. Its main feature was the "com-pulsory alienation of all private lands with compensation of the owners at a fair rate." "Compulsory alienation" doubtlessly conformed to the wishes of the peasantry. The Cadet party tried hard to lend it an appearance of legality. Confiscation with compensation is admitted by all legislations in *exceptional* cases. The party, admittedly, did not deny the right of ownership to the land; why then did it have to turn the "exception" into a general rule? The gradual transfer of the land-owners' estates to the peasants was already under way; it could have been accelerated by fiscal pressure and other *legal* means. There was no need for such an extraordinary measure. The bill calling for "compulsory alienation" undermined the very foundations of the principle of private property which, after all, at that time was still the basis of the whole social order. Moreover, so long as the technique of peasant farming remained unchanged, it was economically harmful, because it lowered the profitability of the land; in restoring the "class" approach, it ran counter to the principle of "equality"; and it was incompatible with the "protection of individual rights" to which liberalism was pledged. To rob the landlords of their property in order to give it to the peasants was a prefiguration in 1906 of the brutal and violent measures applied in 1928 by the Communist state to the "individual peasants."

Insofar as the demand for "compulsory alienation" was intended to win the support of the peasants, it was successful. But what were the party's plans regarding the tenure of the confiscated lands? It proposed to create a "state fund for allotment of land to the people who cultivate the soil by means of individual labor." The most urgent task—that of bringing order into the conditions of communal tenure and of pro-tecting the rights of the individual member against the encroachments of the community—was ignored by the bill. Rural life was still to be governed by the principle described by the Duma member N. N. Lvov as "a rightless individual against a tyrannical crowd." The Cadet program, moreover, concentrated such an immense land fund in the hands of the state that the dependence of the peasantry upon the state and its organs would have been nothing less than a new slavery. This, too, anticipated on a small scale what was witnessed later, in 1917. Since the Duma insisted on that point, and its discussions kept the public in a state of excitement, the government finally dismissed the Duma (July, 1906) and attempted an agrarian reform itself.

Under Alexander III, the government's agrarian policy had taken a wrong turn. Now, after the dissolution of the Duma, the head of the government, P. A. Stolypin, put forth a "progressive program." Liberal parties still nurse a bitter memory of Stolypin's policies. This is understandable: in his merciless fight against the revolutionary surge he respected neither the constitution, nor the law, nor justice itself. Many were his sins,—and yet in his agrarian policy he was on the right track. It was *his* course, and not the agrarian bill of the Cadets, which might have stopped the revolution.

Without waiting for the second Duma to assemble, Stolypin put into effect two measures under Article 87 of the *Fundamental Laws* which enabled the government to carry out necessary measures in the absence of the two Houses (Duma and State Council), provided a corresponding bill be introduced during the first two months of their next session. A rejection of such a bill would nullify the measures already taken. The attempt to transform the whole system of land tenure under such a proviso was indeed a bold undertaking; but the reforms in question were so important and so long overdue that Stolypin consciously disregarded the formal irregularity of his steps.

Stolypin's first decree (October 5, 1906) abolished the most notorious legal restrictions of the peasant class in the matter of freedom of movement, of education, etc. The necessity of this was so indisputable that the Duma—when the corresponding bill was brought in—didn't even take the trouble to consider it. Only ten years later, in 1916, was it taken up by the Duma then in session; not to reject it, but to broaden its scope. Article 87 in this respect offered certain advantages: the Upper House could not reject the amendments approved by the Duma without abrogating the whole measure. I reported the bill to the Duma, and I remember that after the adoption of various amendments the reporter of the same bill to the State Council conferred with me regarding a possible compromise. The February Revolution put an end to these conciliatory moves.

The second decree under Art. 87 (November 9, 1906) concerned the system of land tenure. It allowed the rural commune to divide the common land among the homesteads for good, to be owned privately; and it enabled those who so desired to withdraw their share from common ownership even without the approval of the commune. Such a delicate matter could not be settled without a special law. Only a law could define the share every homesteader could rightfully claim for his own, and how it should be apportioned. Stolypin's decree settled these questions, although not always fairly. Anyway, it liberated the peasant from the stranglehold of the commune.

The respective bill was introduced in the second Duma. The socialist parties could be hardly expected to support it—for didn't it actually promote bourgeois private property? The Constitutional-Democrats, although not socialists and avowed supporters of law and order, also opposed the bill, on the ground that it failed to mention "compulsory alienation of the land," which the party considered essential. Before any agreement with them could be reached, the Duma was dismissed once again. In violation of the constitution, the electoral law was changed in such a way as to ensure a majority of representatives of the landed class in the next Duma ("coup d'état" of June 3, 1907).

When in November, 1907, the third Duma convened, the "Cadets" had lost their leadership to a party farther to the right—the Octobrists. The passage of Stolypin's bill was now a certainty, since the Octobrists were in full agreement with it. On the other hand, the opposition of the left was joined by the extreme right, which wanted to preserve the special status of the peasants and their dependence on the village commune. For the same reason the passage of the bill was threatened in the State Council, where it was finally adopted in a very close vote.

The opponents of the bill maintained that the peasantry would repudiate it, because private ownership of land was contrary to its sense of equity. Nevertheless, during the seven years that the law remained in force, 27 million *dessiatins*—nearly 80 million acres— were divided up among individual farmers, and 1613 thousand new homesteads were created. This result could not have been achieved through coercion alone: after all, the methods of government were not yet those of the Bolsheviks. The success of the reform was the best proof that the government had taken the right course.

Russia's evolution, however, was arrested first by World War I and then by the Revolution—which now threatens to become universal. What new order will be born out of it, how in the end the agrarian problem will be solved, how the interests of the "toilers" will be reconciled with the industrialization of agriculture and the necessity of large-scale farming—cannot yet be foreseen. This is not only a Russian, but a general problem. But in backward Russia, history has posed the problem under special conditions—as a survival of serfdom and feudal relationships. Within these limits it could have been settled without a revolution. If this was not done, and the social revolution broke out, of all places, in agricultural Russia, the responsibility for it rests on the one hand, upon the government which in its fight to retain power was afraid of reforms: and on the other hand, upon the inexperience of our political parties, who strove to solve world problems for which the time had not yet come in Russia. The history of the agrarian problem in Russia serves to illustrate this.

XXII

Imperialism

The Climax of Anti-Imperialism in England
ROBERT LIVINGSTON SCHUYLER

A Critique of Imperialism
WILLIAM L. LANGER

The Christian Missionary Movement of the Nineteenth and Twentieth Centuries
KENNETH SCOTT LATOURETTE

The Climax of Anti-Imperialism in England

ROBERT LIVINGSTON SCHUYLER

⇒⇒⇒⇒⇒⇒⇒⇒⇒⇒⇒ *Published in 1921* ⇐⇐⇐⇐⇐⇐⇐⇐⇐⇐⇐

It is impossible to understand modern British history except in the context of imperial expansion, but it is often forgotten that the stress on empire building was not equally pronounced in all periods in the history of modern Britain. Indeed, there was a time when a powerful movement to dismember the Empire got under way; and optimistic anti-imperialists predicted that in almost no time at all Britain would be relieved of the burdens of empire. The intellectual father of this movement was Adam Smith, who set forth in his epoch-making *Wealth of Nations* (1776) one vast indictment not only of mercantilism but of the imperialism that had accompanied the historical development of mercantilism. Smith had many influential disciples in nineteenth-century Britain—disciples with whose ideas and interests his position harmonized; and it was they who continued his attack on imperialism. They insisted that colonies did not pay; that they were more of a liability than an asset; that eventually they would demand independence anyhow; and that therefore it was wise to anticipate this demand by liberating them. In the years after the repeal of the Corn Laws in 1846, anti-imperialist sentiment gained additional backing among influential elements in British society. Now that Britain had moved in the direction of freer trade, what was the point in retaining colonies that dated from the mercantilist-minded era? Even Disraeli, who in later years was to emerge as the chief hero of the imperialists, insisted, in 1852, that colonies were nothing more than "a millstone round our necks." In the present essay, Robert Livingston Schuyler, of Columbia University, one of the most gifted of American authorities on modern British history, discusses the powerful anti-imperialism of the 1860's, which textbook writers have so often overlooked.

No nation ever voluntarily gave up the dominion of any province, how troublesome so ever it might be to govern it, and how small soever the revenue which it afforded might be in proportion to the expense which it occasioned. Such sacrifices, though they might frequently be agreeable to the interests, are always mortifying to the pride of every nation; and, what is perhaps of still greater consequence, they are always contrary to the private interest of the governing part of it, who would thereby be deprived of the disposal of many places of trust and profit, of many opportunities of acquiring wealth and distinction, which the possession of the most turbulent, and, to the great body of the people, the most unprofitable province, seldom fails to afford.

Adam Smith could not foresee when he wrote these words that the time would come when, thanks in great part to the general acceptance of his own teaching, many of the leading statesmen of England and the officials most closely concerned with colonial administration would contemplate the break-up of the British Empire with feelings ranging from resignation to pleasure.

The old British colonial system, it is well-known, was essentially commercial; it was part and parcel of the mercantile system. The colonies were valued on account of the advantages supposed to be derived from the monopoly of their commerce. They never yielded the mother country a revenue or military forces for her defense, but on the contrary, they imposed heavy financial burdens upon her. It is not strange, therefore, that when free trade swept away the restrictions on colonial commerce, Englishmen complained of the encumbrances of empire or that some of them advocated openly the independence of the colonies. At a time when it was the habit to regard imperial dominion as a scheme of commercial monopoly it was difficult to justify heavy expenditure on colonies that were free to trade where they pleased, and when these colonies began to impose protective duties on the produce of the mother country the quintessence of anomaly seemed to have been attained.

The same era that witnessed the removal of the old restrictions on colonial trade saw the establishment of responsible government in the

Reprinted by special permission from *Political Science Quarterly*, XXXVI (1921), 537-560. The footnotes which originally appeared with this essay have been omitted.

North American and Australasian colonies, and there were many who regarded this as the prelude to their independence. Lord John Russell declared in 1837 that responsible government in the colonies would be incompatible with the maintenance of imperial authority over them, and though he changed his mind subsequently not all of his country-men kept pace with him. The assumed tendency of colonies to separate from their mother country was often elevated to the dignity of a natural law which could not be controlled by the will of man. Some even of those who were called colonial reformers looked upon reform as preliminary to emancipation.

The decade 1861-70 may fairly be called a critical period in British imperial history, for it was during those years that tendencies in England toward the disruption of the Empire reached their climax. The doctrines of the Manchester School were at the height of their influence. Free trade, having justified itself by its fruits, had been accepted by all parties as the settled policy of the nation, and the Anglo-French Commercial Treaty of 1860 was taken to herald it as the future policy of all nations. Prosperity, peace and progress were about to supplant the unholy trinity of protectionism, militarism and imperialism. So at least it seemed, for untoward events had not yet shown this faith of Manchester to be unwarranted. Were free-trade principles to be followed to the limit of logic; was the Empire to be dissolved? There was much to indicate that the answer to this question would be in the affirmative. This subject has, however, received little or no notice in the standard histories of England or in the biographies of the leading British statesmen of the day. Perhaps this is not to be wondered at, since the insularism of English historians, against which Seeley lodged a memorable protest a generation ago, has been only slightly modified since his day, and the revival of imperialism in England during the last

---

ANGLO-FRENCH COMMERCIAL TREATY OF 1860: Cobden-Chevalier Treaty by the terms of which England and Napoleonic France moved in the direction of freer trade relations with each other. A victory for the antiprotectionist forces in both countries, the treaty was widely criticized by protectionist-minded groups in France; and in Britain it was widely held to be too favorable to France. It seems clear that Napoleon favored the measure because, among other reasons, he wished to win British support for his acquisition of Nice and Savoy from the Kingdom of Sardinia.

fifty years has no doubt predisposed Englishmen, as historians, against dwelling upon what, as citizens, they would prefer to forget. Sometimes when an English historian does vouchsafe to touch upon the anti-imperial sentiment of the mid-Victorian era the reader gets the impression that a regrettable episode is being glossed over.

Probably the foremost advocate of the dismemberment of the Empire was Goldwin Smith. While Regius Professor of Modern History at Oxford, he wrote a series of letters that appeared in *The Daily News* in 1862 and 1863 and were published in the latter year in a volume entitled *The Empire*. He pointed out that conditions were very different from what they had been when the old colonial system was established. "The time was," he said, "when the universal prevalence of commercial monopoly made it well worth our while to hold colonies in dependence for the sake of commanding their trade. But that time has gone. Trade is everywhere free, or becoming free; and this expensive and perilous connection has entirely survived its sole legitimate cause. It is time that we should recognize the change that has come over the world." Every hour that an adult colony was kept in a state of dependence, an injury was done to its political character. If Canada was unable to stand by itself, it must eventually join with the United States. As things were, Great Britain's dominion there kept her constantly on the brink of war with the American Republic. The West Indies had become "a mere burden." The case of India was different; there England had assumed responsibilities which she must discharge if possible, but if she could not transform India from a dependency into a colony by settling there as a governing and civilizing class, the days of her rule were numbered. Even military dependencies like Gibraltar had been rendered to a great extent unnecessary by the triumph of free trade. There was no longer

---

MANCHESTER SCHOOL: Label assigned to the intellectuals, manufacturers, and businessmen who, under the influence of Adam Smith and Ricardo, proclaimed their faith in *laissez faire* and free trade. The most vocal and influential leaders of the School in nineteenth-century Britain were John Bright and Richard Cobden.

SIR JOHN SEELEY: Late-nineteenth-century publicist and historian. A strong believer in the British civilizing mission, he sought to arouse interest in imperial expansion. His *Expansion of England* (1883) was a forceful attempt to justify British imperialism from the historical standpoint.

any need for the British to post themselves all over the globe in order to make way for their commerce; trade had become its own protection. British policy had of late become favorable to colonial self-government, "and, therefore, theoretically favorable to emancipation," but it would be difficult for statesmen to take the decisive step of freeing a colony unless urged on by public opinion. Like other anti-imperialists of the day, Goldwin Smith hoped that the independence of the colonies would be achieved peacefully, without the rancor and animosity that had accompanied the separation of the United States from the Empire and survived to mar Anglo-American relations for a hundred years. He believed that what was best in the colonial relationship—the ties of blood, sympathy and ideas—would not be affected by political separation, and he looked forward to the time when, the colonies having become independent nations, something in the nature of an Anglo-Saxon Federation might develop spontaneously out of "affinity and natural affection."

Goldwin Smith's letters provoked a debate in the press and attracted attention not only in England but throughout the Empire. The London *Times* poured ridicule upon his ideas by comparing them with "projects for general disarmament or for equalizing the political rights of the sexes." Disraeli alluded to him in a contemptuous reference which he made in the House of Commons to "prigs and pedants." He was referred to as the apostle of anti-imperialism, and the dissolution of the Empire came to be spoken of as his "colonial policy." The colonial press in general, and especially that of Australia, was bitterly hostile to his proposals. In his *Reminiscences* published in 1911 Goldwin Smith wrote of his *Daily News* letters: "The whole series was Anti-Imperialist, advocating the concession of independence to adult Colonies so that England might become indeed the mother of free nations." Though his doctrines were submerged in the tide of imperialism that began to flow in the early seventies, he himself seems never to have wavered in his opinions.

In 1865 Henry (afterwards Lord) Thring published a pamphlet entitled *Suggestions for Colonial Reform*, in which he urged that the independence of the colonies ought to be looked forward to and prepared for as the natural termination of a temporary connection. His views are not to be regarded as those of a visionary, remote from the realities of practical politics. He was at the time Home Office Counsel, and as such was called upon to draft all important Government measures; probably no man knew more of the inner history of parliamentary legislation than he. For years he had taken an interest in colonial questions, and in 1850 had prepared a plan of colonial reform for Sir William Molesworth, which the latter introduced into Parliament as a series of amendments to a bill for the government of New South Wales. In the tract of 1865 Thring proposed a comprehensive scheme defining the relations between the mother country and the colonies at every stage of their existence. It included rules regulating the conditions on which adventurers might settle in unoccupied territory, provisions for their temporary subjection to the authority of the Crown and their subsequent organization as a colony with representative institutions, and arrangements by which a colony, having arrived at maturity, might declare its desire for independence. The author was strongly influenced by current events. He believed that the union of the British North American provinces, then pending, would be followed by their independence, and the War of Secession in the United States, then in progress, confirmed him in his belief that the British colonies would eventually secede from the Empire.

As an expert parliamentary draftsman Thring naturally threw his scheme of colonial reform into the form of a parliamentary bill, which was printed in an appendix to his pamphlet. It consists of four parts, of which only the last, entitled "Independence of Colony," concerns us here. This outlined the procedure to be followed by a colony when it desired to withdraw from the Empire. It provided that if a resolution asking for independence should be adopted by the legislature of a colony, by a two-thirds majority of both houses, and confirmed after an interval of not less than three months by a similar resolution passed during the same session by a like majority, the governor should notify the Secretary of State for the Colonies, whereupon it should be lawful for the Queen to grant or withhold her assent to the petition of the colony. If the assent were given, it should be proclaimed in the colony, which should thereupon become independent. A colony, when it had become independent, would be in all respects in the same situation as an independent state, but it should be deemed to have entered into a treaty with the former mother country providing (1) that no law should be passed in the former colony impairing the obligation of any contract made before the date of the colony's independence; (2) that no differential duty should be laid on imports from or exports to any part of the British dominions;

and (3) that no privilege should be conferred on the subjects of any foreign power that was not equally conferred on British subjects.

Shortly after the publication of Thring's pamphlet there appeared a work by Viscount Bury entitled *Exodus of the Western Nations*. Though the book was historical, the author, in a concluding chapter, turned his eyes to the future. He was firmly convinced that the separation of the colonies was a matter of time only, and that it should be prepared for with prudence and foresight so that it might take place peacefully and with mutual goodwill. "The wisest statesman," he said, "is not he who would by any shift postpone the inevitable day, but he who most clearly recognizes signs of maturity and seizes the right moment for separation." He proposed to supplement Thring's bill, of which he approved, by a treaty between Great Britain and a seceding colony. Believing that the British North American colonies, then about to confederate, would be the first to become formally independent, he submitted, as an indication of his views, a draft treaty in the form of "Articles of Separation" between Great Britain and British North America, the latter being referred to as the "New Nation." This provided, among other things, that the Imperial Government might at any time, either with the consent of Parliament or at the request of the colonists of the New Nation, give twelve months' notice of its intention to discontinue the exercise of authority over the New Nation and to recognize its independence; that Great Britain, to the utmost of her power, should protect the New Nation if the latter were attacked by an external enemy; that neither should discriminate against the other's commerce; and that citizens of each should enjoy the rights of citizenship in the other.

The British public at large was uninterested in the colonies and ignorant of colonial conditions. The popular apathy, of which the colonial reformers of the thirties and forties had complained, was still general. Relatively trifling matters of home politics outweighed the gravest problems of colonial policy. Scarcely any of the campaign speeches made during the General Election of 1868 touched upon colonial questions; and even in Parliament they evoked, as a rule, little if any debate. In discussing British anti-imperialism we are concerned, therefore, not with "the man in the street" but with the limited circle of those who had opinions on matters of colonial policy. How general, among such, were the views of Goldwin Smith, Lord Thring and Lord Bury? In his *Reminiscences* Goldwin Smith tells us that his opinions on the colonial question were prevalent in influential circles. "Some of our statesmen avowed them, more were inclined to them." Let us test the truth of this assertion.

In a debate on the army estimates in March, 1865, John Bright thus expressed what may be taken as the view of the Manchester School:

> I suspect, from what has been stated by official Gentlemen in Government and in previous Governments, that there is no objection to the independence of Canada whenever Canada may wish it. I have been glad to hear those statements, because I think they mark an extraordinary progress in sound opinions in this country. . . . I do not object to that separation [of Canada from Great Britain] in the least; I believe it would be better for us and better for her.

Sir George Cornewall Lewis was one of the few English politicians who had given systematic attention to questions of colonial government. His *Essay on the Government of Dependencies*, first published in 1841, was a standard treatise on its subject. In that work he wrote:

> If a dominant country understood the true nature of the advantages arising from the relation of supremacy and dependence to the related communities, it would voluntarily recognize the legal independence of such of its own dependencies as were fit for independence; it would, by its political arrangements, study to prepare for independence those which were still unable to stand alone; and it would seek to promote colonization for the purpose of extending its trade rather than its empire, and without attempting to maintain the dependence of its colonies beyond the time when they need its protection.

In 1862, when Secretary of State for War, he said in the House of Commons: "I, for one, can only say that I look forward without apprehension—and, I may add, without regret—to the time when Canada might become an independent state."

In defending his Government against the charge that it had adopted a new policy of imperial disintegration, Gladstone, in April, 1870, made the following statement:

> If you look back to the history of the colonial connection between European Powers and trans-Atlantic possessions you find that it is the nature of those possessions to grow, and so to grow as to alter essentially, in obedience to laws stronger than the will of man, the conditions of their relation to the countries with which they were

originally connected, until they arrive at that stage of their progress in which separation from the mother country inevitably takes place. It is impossible, however, to look back with satisfaction to the mode in which that separation has occurred. In every instance it has been brought about by war and bloodshed, involving an inheritance of pain, hatred and shame; whereas in reason there ought to be nothing to preclude the hope, when the growth of a colonial possession is such as to make separation from the mother country a natural and beneficial result, that the separation, so far from being effected by violence and bloodshed, might be the result of a peaceful and friendly transaction. Surely it is a great object to place, if possible, our colonial policy on such a footing, not for the purpose of bringing about a separation, but of providing a guarantee that, if separation should occur, it should be in a friendly way. That is the sense, the principle, and the secret of our policy with regard to colonial reform . . .

Earl Granville, who was Colonial Secretary in Gladstone's first Ministry, at a time when imperial relations reached their most critical stage, undoubtedly shared the views of his leader. "Our relations with North America," he wrote in 1870, "are of a very delicate character. The best solution of them would probably be that in the course of time and in the most friendly spirit the Dominion should find itself strong enough to proclaim her [*sic*] independence."

Robert Lowe, afterwards Viscount Sherbrooke, who was Chancellor of the Exchequer in Gladstone's first Ministry, said in the House of Commons in 1865 that Canada ought to be given to understand that she was quite free to establish herself as an independent republic if she desired.

Disraeli, in a famous party pronouncement made in 1872, asserted that the Liberal Party had been striving for forty years, continuously, subtly and energetically, to disrupt the British Empire. Surely his imperialism must have been above reproach. Yet he wrote privately in 1852 to Lord Malmesbury, then Foreign Secretary: "These wretched colonies will all be independent too in a few years and are a millstone round our necks." Nor was this an outburst of mere momentary irritation, as we are assured by Disraeli's biographers. Sir William Gregory, a veteran parliamentarian, who knew Disraeli intimately, tells us that his expressions with regard to the colonies "were always those of contempt and a contented impression that we should sooner or later be rid of them." No doubt real empire, such an *imperium* as Britain wielded over India, appealed powerfully to Disraeli, but the conception of the British Empire as a commonwealth of nations does not seem to have stirred his imagination. In September, 1866, he wrote to his party chief, Lord Derby:

It never can be our pretence or our policy to defend the Canadian frontier against the U. S. . . . Power and influence we should exercise in Asia; consequently in Eastern Europe, consequently also in Western Europe; but what is the use of these colonial dead-weights which *we do not govern?* . . . Leave the Canadians to defend themselves; recall the African Squadron; give up the settlements on the West Coast of Africa; and we shall make a saving which will, at the same time, enable us to build ships and have a good Budget.

While in London in 1866, as one of Canada's delegates to a conference to arrange for the enactment by the Imperial Parliament of the draft constitution for the new Dominion of Canada, framed by the Quebec Conference of 1864, Alexander T. Galt, one of the "fathers" of Confederation, was forcibly impressed by the desire of British statesmen to wash their hands of Canada. In a private letter, dated January 14, 1867, he wrote: "I cannot shut my eyes to the fact that they want to get rid of us . . . I much doubt whether Confederation will save us from Annexation. Even Macdonald is rapidly feeling as I do."

No one who recalls Charles Buller's ironical attack on the Colonial Office is likely to underrate the influence on colonial policy exerted by the permanent officials of the department. Long tenure of office and thorough familiarity with the routine of official business enabled the permanent under-secretary as a rule to guide his official superior, who was selected for party reasons and whose tenure of office was usually brief. Sir James Stephen, called by the colonial reformers in derision "Mr. Mother-Country Stephen" and "Mr. Over-Secretary Stephen," while serving under a succession of secretaries of state, virtually ruled the colonial empire for twenty-five years. In 1848 he was succeeded as permanent under-secretary by Herman Merivale, who, while professor of political economy at Oxford, had delivered a course of lectures on colonies which made a great impression and led to his appointment to the Colonial Office. Merivale believed that the colonies would ultimately become independent, as did his successor,

Sir Frederic Rogers, afterwards Lord Blachford, who held the office of permanent under-secretary from 1860 to 1871, during the entire decade under review. Goldwin Smith's statement that Rogers shared his views on colonial policy is certainly not an exaggeration. In some autobiographical notes which he left, Rogers wrote:

> I had always believed—and the belief has so confirmed and consolidated itself that I can hardly realize the possibility of anyone seriously thinking the contrary—that the destiny of our colonies is independence; and that, in this point of view, the function of the Colonial Office is to secure that our connection, while it lasts, shall be as profitable to both parties, and our separation, when it comes, as amicable as possible. This opinion is founded first on the general principle that a spirited nation (and a colony becomes a nation) will not submit to be governed in its internal affairs by a distant Government, and that nations geographically remote have no such common interests as will bind them permanently together in foreign policy, with all its details and mutations.

So strong were Rogers's convictions that he was not swept into the imperial reaction of the seventies and eighties.

An intimate friend of Rogers's was Sir Henry Taylor, the author and playwright. Taylor served in the Colonial Office in subordinate positions for nearly fifty years, from 1824 to 1872. His anti-imperialism was clear and emphatic. In 1852 he wrote to Earl Grey, then Colonial Secretary, that he regarded the British North American colonies as "a most dangerous possession for this country, whether as likely to breed a war with the United States or to make a war otherwise generated more grievous and disastrous." He added: "I do not suppose the provinces to be useless to us at present, but I regard any present uses not obtainable from them as independent nations to be no more than the dust of the balance as compared with the evil contingencies." Twelve years later, in 1864, he wrote in a letter to the Duke of Newcastle, then Colonial Secretary:

> As to our American possessions, I have long held and often expressed the opinion that they are a sort of *damnosa hæreditas;* and when your Grace and the Prince of Wales were employing yourselves so successfully in conciliating the colonists I thought that you were drawing closer ties which might better be slackened if there were any chance

of their slipping away altogether. I think that a policy which has regard to a not very far off future should prepare facilities and propensities for separation.

Some anti-imperialists feared that an independent Canada would be annexed to the United States, but Taylor saw nothing to be alarmed at even in this eventuality.

The anti-imperial movement reached its climax in the early part of Gladstone's first Ministry, which was formed in December, 1868. Lord Granville, Bright and Lowe, whose anti-imperial utterances have been quoted, were members of the Cabinet, the first-mentioned presiding over the Colonial Office. Certain events soon occurred to create a belief, which became widespread in the colonies and in England, that the Government was contemplating, if it had not positively decided upon, the dissolution of the Empire.

In the first place a crisis was reached in the relations between the Imperial Government and the colony of New Zealand. For some years before the Gladstone Ministry took office, successive Governments had been carrying out a policy of withdrawing imperial military forces from the self-governing colonies. In May, 1868, at a time when hostilities were in progress between the colonists of New Zealand and some of the native tribes, the Duke of Buckingham, then Colonial Secretary, notified the Governor of New Zealand that the last of the British troops would soon be removed; and even after a massacre of some thirty colonists had occurred at Poverty Bay in the North Island, the Colonial Office declined to grant the colony's request that the recall of the troops should be delayed. Lord Granville, upon taking office, announced that he would adhere to his predecessor's policy. Early in February, 1869, a representative of the New Zealand Government asked for an imperial guarantee of a loan to aid the colony in borrowing money to cover contemplated war expenditure, but this request also was peremptorily refused by Lord Granville in a dispatch to the Governor of New Zealand (March 21, 1869), which aroused the deepest indignation throughout the colony and no little hostile criticism in England. A protest signed by Sir George Grey, formerly Governor of New Zealand, and several other persons who had held office in the colony, declared that the policy of the Imperial Government was calculated to drive New Zealand out of the Empire. Lord Granville's dispatch was reprinted in the New Zealand and Australian newspapers, which strongly resented its content, and especially its tone; and part of the New Zealand press went so far as to advocate openly the annexation of New Zealand to the United States. A later dispatch of the Colonial Secretary (October 7, 1869) still further embittered the feeling of the New Zealand colonists. In this, although he had been informed that the New Zealand Parliament had passed an act binding the colony, in the event of the Imperial Government sanctioning the retention of the troops, to pay whatever contribution might be demanded, Lord Granville stated that under no conditions would the recall of the troops be further delayed. The New Zealand ministers officially recorded their conviction that the "tone and purport" of this document would be taken in the colony to indicate a desire on the part of the Imperial Government to sever the colony's connection with the Empire. Writing from New Zealand in January, 1870, the *Times* correspondent said:

> As the immediate consequence of Earl Granville's expressions and his declaration of the Imperial policy towards New Zealand, the expediency of declaring the independence of the colony, of refusing to maintain the Viceregal establishment, and even of annexation with the United States has been freely discussed, and it is only because the case of the colony appears to have attracted considerable attention and called forth the sympathy of a large and influential section of the English people that no decided steps have been taken in one of these directions.

The conduct of the Imperial Government gave rise to a long debate in the New Zealand Parliament, in the course of which bitter resentment was expressed at the tone of Granville's dispatches, and the view was freely voiced that the dissolution of the Empire was at hand.

In England the alarm was sounded in the press by the Liberal *Spectator* and the Roman Catholic organ, *The Tablet*. Both professed to see in the dispatches of the Colonial Secretary and the utterances of supporters of the Ministry evidence that the Government had adopted a policy of dismembering the Empire, and both demanded that the sense of the country should be taken on such a policy. "It is clear," said *Spectator* (July 24, 1869), "that Mr. Goldwin Smith's colonial 'policy' . . . has not only been accepted by the existing Government, but that they are acting on it. It is not only New Zealand which is to be dismissed, but Australia, not only Australia, but the Canadian

Dominion . . ." In the House of Commons attention was called to the New Zealand crisis, and some opposition was expressed to the withdrawal of all imperial protection from the colony; nevertheless the Government's course was light-heartedly defended by the parliamentary under-secretary for the colonies and no member of the Cabinet deemed it necessary to participate in the debate. Official denials by the Government of any intention to bring about the separation of New Zealand from the Empire failed to satisfy the colony or to silence the critics of the Government in England.

The attitude of the Imperial Government in its relations with New Zealand led to a meeting of colonists resident in London at the Palace Hotel, Westminster, on August 4, 1869, at which it was decided by those present to enter into communication with the colonies on the subject of their relations with the mother country. A few days later letters were sent to the governments of the self-governing colonies in which the view was expressed that British policy seemed to point to the disintegration of the Empire, and the proposal was made that a conference of representatives of the self-governing colonies should be held in London early in the following year for the purpose of considering such changes in colonial administration and in imperial relations as might seem desirable. The Colonial Office discountenanced the project, and the responses of the colonial governments were not favorable to it. The conference was never held, though the proposal elicited a good deal of interest and discussion.

It was not the New Zealand crisis alone that lent support to the view that the Imperial Government was aiming at the dissolution of the Empire. There was at this time a considerable sentiment in Canada in favor of independence, and though it was caused principally by the friction between the United States and Great Britain during and after the American Civil War and a belief among Canadians that the British connection subjected them to constant danger from their southern neighbor, it was certainly not diminished by the conviction of many Canadians that Great Britain would welcome the separation of the Dominion from the Empire. The course taken by the Imperial Government, far from allaying the movement for independence in Canada, was calculated to strengthen it.

Early in 1869 Lord Granville, through the Governor of Canada, offered Alexander Galt the Order of St. Michael and St. George.

Feeling that it would be improper to accept the honor without informing the Imperial Government precisely of his political views, Galt wrote in reply: "I regard the Confederation of the British North American Provinces as a measure which must ultimately lead to their separation from Great Britain. . . . I believe the existing relations would be safer if the future state were clearly recognized, and, if possible, a term fixed therefor." In spite of this plain statement of his views, the distinction was conferred upon him; and when in February, 1870, in a debate in the Canadian Parliament his opinions were spoken of as disloyal, he replied that, inasmuch as the honor had been bestowed upon him, he did not consider himself more disloyal than Her Majesty's ministers. It was natural to draw the conclusion that the Imperial Government and Galt were at one in their desire for the political future of Canada, especially as Lord Granville refused to permit the publication of one of the letters which he had written in the course of the correspondence.

The decision of the Government to withdraw almost all of the few British troops still left in Canada seemed to point to the same conclusion. The question was not so much the withdrawal of the troops as the motive for the withdrawal; and many Canadians undoubtedly believed that the motive was to show them that they could stand alone. In the House of Lords the Earl of Carnarvon, who as Colonial Secretary in a preceding Government had himself been instrumental in withdrawing British troops from the colonies, professed to see nothing but disaster to the Empire in the "shabby policy," as he called it, which the Government was pursuing. "I hope," he said, "that Her Majesty's Government are serious in the belief that the course they are now taking will not lead to the dismemberment of the Empire; but I warn them—as everyone who stands calmly and impartially by must warn them—that, whatever may be their meaning, they are doing the very acts, they are taking the very steps, which must accomplish that result." It was important, he added, that the Government should announce its colonial policy. "There are whispers abroad that there is a policy on foot to dismember this Empire. . . . If there is such a policy, in God's name let us know it; if there be not, let it be disavowed." As tending to confirm the rumors, he referred to a public meeting at Halifax in the summer of 1869 at which the Governor-General of Canada threw out what was taken to be an intimation that the time had perhaps come for Canada to consider whether she was not ripe for independence, and to a recent dispatch of Granville's which, he said, might lead to the inference that the Government desired to wash its hands of British Columbia.

Early in General Grant's first term as President it was seriously urged by members of his Administration and especially by Senator Sumner, chairman of the Senate committee on foreign relations, that the claims of the United States against Great Britain for damages sustained during the Civil War should be settled on the basis of the withdrawal of Great Britain from the western hemisphere and the annexation of Canada to the United States. In his illuminating essay on the Treaty of Washington Charles Francis Adams shows that this grandiose project, in view of the anti-imperialist sentiment expressed by the British minister in Washington and by the British press of the day, was not as preposterous as it would otherwise appear to have been. "Mr. Sumner," he says, "certainly had grounds for assuming that a not unwilling hemispheric flag-withdrawal by Great Britain was more than probable in the early future." In December, 1869, and January, 1870, Hamilton Fish, the American Secretary of State, in conversations with the British minister, Sir Edward Thornton, urged the complete withdrawal of Great Britain from Canada. "Oh, you know that we cannot do," Thornton replied. "The Canadians find fault with me for saying so openly as I do that we are ready to let them go whenever they shall wish; but they do not desire it." And later, in 1870, he reiterated that his Government was willing and even anxious to have the colonies become independent.

To the Australian colonies the recall of imperial troops was not so vital a matter as it was to New Zealand, for Australia was not vexed with warlike native tribes. However, Australian public opinion was naturally affected by what was happening in New Zealand, and many Australians believed that independence was the ultimate destiny of their country. There was certainly a widespread impression that such an outcome would be welcomed by the Imperial Government.

At the Cape of Good Hope it was openly stated in the parliament that independence was impending in Canada, Australia and New Zealand. "In North America," said Sir Philip Wodehouse, formerly governor of the colony, "we have unmistakable indications of the rapid establishment of a powerful independent State. In Australia it is probable that its several settlements, with their great wealth and homogeneous population, will see their way to a similar coalition. *In New Zealand the severance is being accomplished under very painful circumstances.*" *Spectator*, in an article on "The New Colonial Policy" (March 26, 1870) remarked that in view of Wodehouse's declarations and Galt's declarations, and the "unparalleled severity" of the Government's dealings with New Zealand, "any politician of ordinary sagacity will draw the inference that a deliberate colonial policy of no insignificant moment has been, at all events, *provisionally* adopted by the present Cabinet, which they are not willing to confide to Parliament and to have discussed in Parliament as yet." It was the duty of the Government, *Spectator* insisted, to take the sense of the nation "on the boldest and most startling innovation in modern statesmanship."

There are evidences that even before the formation of Gladstone's Ministry a revival of imperialism was at hand. In the summer of 1868 a society, later named the Royal Colonial Institute, was organized in London to arouse interest in colonial questions; the advantages of closer union between England and the colonies were beginning to be canvassed; and there are other indications that a change in public opinion was at hand. The imperial reaction was naturally strengthened by the suspicions entertained of the intentions of Gladstone's Government. The earlier public apathy passed away. Relations between the mother country and the colonies became a subject of lively discussion in the press and in public meetings. A series of conferences were held in 1869 at the Cannon Street Hotel in the City of London by persons interested in promoting closer imperial union. Questions of colonial policy were seriously debated in Parliament.

It was very soon apparent that the country would not sanction any policy of cutting the colonies adrift. Nor must it be supposed that the ministers, whatever the individual opinions of some of them may have been, had, collectively, as a Government, adopted such a policy. Had they done so, Mr. W. E. Forster, who openly stated his conviction that public opinion would not permit the dismemberment of the Empire, could not have remained a member of the Ministry. The imperial question must have been discussed at Cabinet meetings, though what was said upon it we do not, of course, know. In view, however, of the anti-imperial sentiments of some of the ministers, and the declarations of Lord Granville and Lord Kimberley, who succeeded him at the Colonial Office in July, 1870, to the effect that the Government was not seeking to dismember the Empire, it seems not unreasonable to surmise that it was left an "open" question, on which members of the Government were not bound to unanimity. In an article entitled "Greater or Lesser Britain," published in *The Nineteenth Century*, in July, 1877, Sir Julius Vogel, who had been a member of the New Zealand Ministry at the time of the crisis in the relations between the colony and the Imperial Government, conjectured that a decision was reached by the British Cabinet to the effect that, whatever might be the opinions of individual ministers, the Government should not commit itself to the dismemberment policy. "But without any policy of the kind," he added, "a strong conviction might have been entertained that the colonies would in course of time be detached from the Empire, and that the sooner that result ensued the better."

In May, 1870, an accommodation was reached in the New Zealand dispute, which was taken to indicate, both in the colonies and by critics of the Government in England, that the Imperial Government had changed its attitude, not only toward New Zealand but on the imperial question in general. The Government of New Zealand sent special commissioners to England to negotiate for the retention of the troops and for assistance to the colony in creating a colonial military force. One great object hoped for from the mission, as stated by the New Zealand premier, was the re-establishment of harmonious relations between the Imperial and the New Zealand Governments. The commissioners were unable to induce the Colonial Office to yield on the question of the withdrawal of the troops, but they offered to accept an Imperial guarantee of a loan of £1,000,000 to cover expenditures incurred in aid of immigration and the construction of public works in the colony "as a measure of conciliation which would be taken throughout New Zealand as proof of the continued goodwill of the Imperial Government, and of its desire that the relations between the Imperial and Colonial Governments should be maintained on the most friendly footing." The knowledge in New Zealand that such an agreement had been reached would, the commissioners informed Lord Granville, "put an end to irritation and discontent."

The Colonial Office, which had previously refused so peremptorily to accede to a like request, now yielded and agreed to introduce the necessary legislation in Parliament. "If we have not been able to induce your lordship to regard in the same light as the Assembly [of New Zealand] did, the question of military assistance," wrote the commissioners in a letter to Granville thanking him for the concession that had been made, "still the chief object of our mission has been gained. It is not a mere matter of money that has been arranged; a lasting tie has been made between the two Governments by their engaging together in objects in which the nation has a common interest with her Dependency. . . ." In a reply, in which graciousness of language took the place of the blunt uncompromising tone of his earlier dispatches, Granville wrote: "I trust that the decision of Her Majesty's Government to waive the objections which attach to the guarantee of Colonial loans will be received by the colonists of New Zealand as a proof of the deep interest which they feel in the welfare and prosperity of this great possession of the Crown." In New Zealand the concession made by the Imperial Government was regarded as a peace offering, and the colonial legislature resolved to let bygones be bygones.

Spectator was jubilant, insisting that nothing less than a revolution in British colonial policy had taken place. "Ministers have changed their policy, have changed it very abruptly, and have changed it for the best of all reasons,—because they had begun to discover that their line was not the line of the people of England, and would, if pushed to its logical results, end in events which would bring down the bitter displeasure of the people of England. . . ." The Liberal press, which was supporting the Government through thick and thin, might try to show that the concession to New Zealand was in harmony with the previous course taken by the Colonial Office, but that, according to *Spectator*, was all nonsense, and it was important for the people of New Zealand to know that it was all nonsense. The difference between military aid and financial aid was merely administrative; there was no difference in policy. Nor was *Spectator* alone in its opinion that a change in colonial policy had occurred. "I am happy to see," said Earl Russell in the House of Lords, "that my noble Friend, the present Secretary of State for the Colonies [Earl Granville] seems in some respects to have changed his opinion; and I always thought that when he had further studied colonial questions and the position of this country, he would be of opinion that it was necessary not only to allow the Colonies to pay their allegiance to this country, but to give them from time to time such encouragement as to make them pay that allegiance happily and contentedly."

From the summer of 1870 onward, anti-imperial sentiment waned rapidly. When in July Lord Granville was transferred to the Foreign Office, all imperialists breathed more easily. His successor, Lord Kimberley, was not suspect as he had been, and official assurances that the Government cherished no anti-imperial designs carried greater conviction. Disraeli skilfully seized upon imperialism as a party issue, and probably no part of his political program appealed more powerfully to the British electorate than his pledge to maintain the integrity of the Empire. The Conservative victory in the general election of 1874 drove Little-Englandism completely from the field of practical politics.

A Critique of Imperialism

IMPERIALISM: A STUDY. By J. A. HOBSON[*]

WILLIAM L. LANGER

➤➤➤➤➤➤➤➤➤➤➤➤ *Published in 1935* ⫷⫷⫷⫷⫷⫷⫷⫷⫷⫷⫷⫷

In the last decades of the nineteenth century there took place virtually everywhere in Europe a revival of interest in imperialism—a revival that has often been accounted for in economic terms. According to the traditional explanation, the European countries needed raw materials for their domestic industries, markets for the sale of their manufactured goods, and outlets for the investment of their surplus capital; hence they undertook to gain control over backward areas which they could exploit in their own interests. The weakness of this standard economic interpretation of imperialism is that it grossly oversimplifies an enormously complicated historical movement. Often, in fact, it is clear that economics was not so much a cause of imperialism as a justification of it employed by politicians who sought foreign victories which they could exploit for political reasons on the domestic front. Disraeli's imperialism, for example, was intimately linked with his attempt to strengthen the Conservative Party and to increase the popularity of the Crown; Jules Ferry's imperialism was intimately linked with his attempt to consolidate the position of the Third French Republic; Bismarck's with the struggle to stop the growth of the Social Democratic Party; and Crispi's with the attempt to enhance the prestige of the Kingdom of Italy. Wishing to convince economy-minded businessmen that costly imperialistic ventures would pay off in the long run, politicians tried to win support for their foreign policies by advancing the stock economic arguments which every high school student now learns by heart. The literature of imperialism is, of course, often highly controversial and emotional; sober-minded treatments of it are hard to find. It is fortunate, therefore, that so dispassionate a historian as William L. Langer, of Harvard University, has devoted a large part of his scholarly life to its study. Author of *European Alliances and Alignments, 1871-1890* (1931)

[*] London, 1902, 400 pp.

and *The Diplomacy of Imperialism, 1890-1902* (1935), Langer is well qualified to deal with a subject, the discussion of which has often generated more heat than light.

It is now roughly fifty years since the beginning of that great outburst of expansive activity on the part of the Great Powers of Europe which we have come to call "imperialism." And it is about a generation since J. A. Hobson published his "Imperialism: a Study," a book which has served as the starting point for most later discussions and which has proved a perennial inspiration for writers of the most diverse schools. A reappraisal of it is therefore decidedly in order. The wonder is that it has not been undertaken sooner.

Since before the outbreak of the World War the theoretical writing on imperialism has been very largely monopolized by the so-called Neo-Marxians, that is, by those who, following in the footsteps of the master, have carried on his historical analysis from the critique of capitalism to the study of this further phase, imperialism, the significance of which Marx himself did not appreciate and the very existence of which he barely adumbrated. The Neo-Marxians, beginning with Rudolf Hilferding and Rosa Luxemburg, have by this time elaborated a complete theory, which has recently been expounded in several ponderous German works. The theory hinges upon the idea of the accumulation of capital, its adherents holding that imperialism is nothing more nor less than the last stage in the development of capitalism—the stage in which the surplus capital resulting from the system of production is obliged by ever diminishing returns at home to seek new fields for investment abroad. When this surplus capital has transformed the whole world and remade even the most backward areas in the image of capitalism, the whole economic-social system will inevitably die of congestion.

That the classical writers of the socialistic school derived this basic idea from Hobson's book there can be no doubt.[1] Lenin himself

Reprinted by special permission from *Foreign Affairs*, XIV (1935), 102-115. With one exception, the footnotes which originally appeared with this essay have been omitted.

[1] I strongly suspect that Hobson, in turn, took over the idea from the very bourgeois American financial expert, Charles A. Conant, whose remarkable article, "The Economic Basis of Imperialism," in the *North American Review*, September 1898, pp. 326-340, is now forgotten, but deserves recognition.

admitted, in his "Imperialism, the Highest Stage of Capitalism," that Hobson gave "a very good and accurate description of the fundamental economic and political traits of imperialism," and that Hobson and Hilferding had said the essentials on the subject. This, then, has been the most fruitful contribution of Hobson's essay. When we examine his ideas on this subject we refer indirectly to the larger part of the writing on imperialism since his day.

As a matter of pure economic theory it is most difficult to break down the logic of the accumulation theory. It is a fact that since the middle of the last century certain countries—first England, then France, Germany and the United States—have exported large amounts of capital, and that the financial returns from these investments in many instances came to overshadow completely the income derived by the lending countries from foreign trade. It is also indisputable that industry embarked upon the road to concentration and monopoly, that increased efficiency in production led to larger profits and to the amassing of ever greater surpluses of capital. We must recognize further that, as a general rule, the return from investments abroad was distinctly above the return on reinvestment in home industry. In other words, the postulates of the socialist theory undoubtedly existed. There is no mentionable reason why the development of the capitalist system should not have had the results attributed to it.

But, as it happens, the actual course of history refutes the thesis. The course of British investment abroad shows that there was a very considerable export of capital before 1875, that is, during the climax of anti-imperialism in England. Between 1875 and 1895, while the tide of imperialism was coming to the full, there was a marked falling off of foreign investment. Capital export was then resumed on a large scale in the years before the war, though England was, in this period, already somewhat disillusioned by the outcome of the South African adventure and rather inclined to be skeptical about im-

---

Rosa Luxemburg: Polish-German Marxist theoretician who denounced those who were attempting to "revise" the teachings of Marx. Author of *The Accumulation of Capital* (1913), she argued that capitalism was incapable of finding an indefinitely expanding market at home and that imperialism was the result. Instrumental in founding the German Communist Party in 1918, she led a workers' uprising in Berlin and was assassinated shortly thereafter.

perialism. Similar observations hold true of the United States. If the promulgation of the Monroe Doctrine was an act of imperialism, where was the export of capital which ought to have been its condition? Let us concede that the war with Spain was an imperialist episode. At that time the United States was still a debtor nation, importing rather than exporting capital. In Russia, too, the heyday of imperialism coincided with a period of heavy borrowing rather than of lending.

There is this further objection to be raised against the view of Hobson and his Neo-Marxian followers, that the export of capital seems to have little direct connection with territorial expansion. France, before the war, had plenty of capital to export, and some of her earliest and most vigorous imperialists, like Jules Ferry, declared that she required colonies in order to have adequate fields for the placement of this capital. But when France had secured colonies, she did not send her capital to them. By far the larger part of her exported funds went to Russia, Rumania, Spain and Portugal, Egypt and the Ottoman Empire. In 1902 only two or two and a half billion francs out of a total foreign investment of some 30 or 35 billion francs was placed in the colonies. In 1913 Britain had more money invested in the United States than in any colony or other foreign country. Less than half of her total export of capital had been to other parts of the Empire. The United States put more capital into the development of Canada than did England; and when, after the war, the United States became a great creditor nation, 43 percent of her investment was in Latin America, 27 percent in Canada and Newfoundland, and 22 percent in European countries. What she sent to her colonies was insignificant. Or let us take Germany, which in 1914 had about 25 billion marks placed abroad. Of this total only three percent was invested in Asia and Africa, and of that three percent only a small part in her colonies. Pre-war Russia was a great

---

LORD NORTHCLIFFE: Journalist and newspaper owner (d. 1922). Appealing to the semiliterate element in British society, he built up a syndicate that numbered some seventy newspapers and magazines. His position of dominance in the newspaper world made it possible for him to bring great pressure to bear on successive British ministries.

imperialist power, but Russia had to borrow from France the money invested in her Far Eastern projects. In our own day two of the most outspokenly imperialist powers, Japan and Italy, are both nations poor in capital. Whatever the urge that drives them to expansion, it cannot be the need for the export of capital.

At the height of the imperialist tide, let us say from 1885 to 1914, there was much less talk among the advocates of expansion about the need for foreign investment fields than about the need for new markets and for the safeguarding of markets from the tariff restrictions of competitors. It is certain that in the opinion of contemporaries that was the mainspring of the whole movement. But this economic explanation, like the other, has not been borne out by the actual developments. Very few colonies have done even half of their trading with the mother country and many have done less. Taken in the large it can be proved statistically that the colonial trade has always played a relatively unimportant part in the total foreign commerce of the great industrial nations. These nations have always been each other's best customers and no amount of rivalry and competition has prevented their trade from following, not the flag, but the price-list. The position of Canada within the British Empire did not prevent her from levying tariffs against British goods, nor from developing exceedingly close economic relations with the United States. In the prewar period German commerce with the British possessions was expanding at a relatively higher rate than was Britain's.

If one must have an economic interpretation of imperialism, one will probably find its historical evolution to have been something like this: In the days of England's industrial preëminence she was, by the very nature of the case, interested in free trade. In the palmiest days of Cobdenism she exported manufactured goods to the four corners of the earth, but she exported also machinery and other producers' goods, thereby preparing the way for the industrialization of the continental nations and latterly of other regions of the world. In order to protect their infant industries from British competition, these new industrial Powers threw over the teachings of the Manchester school and began to set up tariffs. The result was that the national markets were set aside, to a large extent, for home industry. British trade was driven to seek new markets, where the process was repeated. But the introduction of protective tariffs had this further effect, that it made possible the organization of cartels and trusts, that is, the concentration of industry, the increase of production and the lowering of costs. Surplus goods and low prices caused the other industrial Powers likewise to look abroad for additional markets, and, while this development was taking place, technological improvements were making transportation and communication safer and more expeditious. The exploration of Africa at that time was probably a pure coincidence, but it contributed to the movement toward trade and expansion and the growth of a world market. Fear that the newly opened areas of the world might be taken over by others and then enclosed in tariff walls led directly to the scramble for territory in Asia and Africa.

The socialist writers would have us believe that concentration in industry made for monopoly and that the banks, undergoing the same process of evolution, were, through their connection with industry, enabled to take over control of the whole capitalist system. They were the repositories of the surplus capital accumulated by a monopolistic system and they were therefore the prime movers in the drive for imperial expansion, their problem being to find fields for the investment of capital. This is an argument which does violence to the facts as they appear historically. The socialist writers almost to a man argue chiefly from the example of Germany, where cartelization came early and where the concentration of banking and the control of industry by the banks went further than in most countries. But even in Germany the movement towards overseas expansion came before the growth of monopoly and the amalgamation of the banks. In England, the imperialist country *par excellence,* there was no obvious connection between the two phenomena. The trust movement came late and never went as far as in Germany. The same was true of the consolidation of the banking system. One of the perennial complaints in England was the lack of proper coördination between the banks and industry. To a certain extent the English exported capital because the machinery for foreign investment was better than the organization for home investment. In the United States, to be sure, there was already a pronounced concentration of industry when the great outburst of imperialism came in the last years of the past century, but in general the trust movement ran parallel to the movement for territorial expansion. In any event, it would be hard to disprove the contention that the growth of world trade and the world market brought on the tendency toward better organization and concentration in industry, rather than the reverse. It is obvious not only that one large unit can manufacture more cheaply than many small ones, but that it can act more efficiently in competition with others in the world market.

But this much is clear—that territorial control of extra-European territory solved neither the trade problem nor the question of surplus capital. The white colonies, which were the best customers, followed their own economic interests and not even tariff restrictions could prevent them from doing so. In the backward, colored, tropical colonies, which could be more easily controlled and exploited, it proved difficult to develop a market, because of the low purchasing power of the natives. The question of raw materials, of which so much has always been made, also remained open. The great industrial countries got but a fraction of their raw materials from the colonies, and the colonies themselves continued to show a tendency to sell their products in the best market. As for the export of capital, that continued to flow in an ever broader stream, not because the opportunities for investment at home were exhausted, but because the return from foreign investment was apt to be better and because, in many cases, foreign investment was the easier course. Capital flowed from the great industrial countries of Europe, but it did not flow to their colonies. The United States and Canada, Latin America (especially the Argentine) and even old countries like Austria-Hungary and Russia, got the bulk of it. The export of capital necessarily took the form of the extension of credit, which in turn implied the transfer of goods. Not infrequently the granting of loans was made conditional on trade concessions by the borrowing country. So we come back to the question of trade and tariffs. In a sense the export of capital was nothing but a device to stimulate trade and to circumvent tariff barriers, which brings us back to the coincidence of the movement for protection and the movement toward imperialism.

This may seem like an oversimplified explanation and it probably is. Some may argue that imperialism is more than a movement toward territorial expansion and that financial imperialism in particular lays the iron hand of control on many countries supposedly independent. But if you try to divorce imperialism from territorial control you will get nowhere. Practically all writers on the subject have been driven to the conclusion that the problem cannot be handled at all unless you restrict it in this way. When Hobson wrote on imperialism, he had reference to the great spectacle of a few Powers taking over tremendous areas in Africa and Asia. Imperialism is, in a sense, synonymous with the appropriation by the western nations of the largest part of the rest of the world. If you take it to be anything else, you will soon be lost in nebulous concepts and bloodless abstractions. If imperialism is to mean any vague interference of traders and bankers in the affairs of other countries, you may as well extend it to cover any form of influence. You will have to admit cultural imperialism, religious imperialism, and what not. Personally I prefer to stick by a measurable, manageable concept.

But even though Hobson's idea, that imperialism "is the endeavor of the great controllers of industry to broaden the channel for the flow of their surplus wealth by seeking foreign markets and foreign investments to take off the goods and capital they cannot sell or use at home," proved to be the most stimulating and fertile of his arguments, he had the very correct idea that imperialism was also a "medley of aims and feelings." He had many other contributory explanations of the phenomenon. For example, he was keenly aware of the relationship between democracy and imperialism. The enfranchisement of the working classes and the introduction of free education had brought the rank and file of the population into the political arena. One result of this epoch-making change was the rise of the so-called yellow press, which catered to the common man's love of excitement and sensationalism. Northcliffe was one of the first to sense the value of imperialism as a "talking point." Colonial adventure and far-away conflict satisfied the craving for excitement of the industrial and white-collar classes which had to find some outlet for their "spectatorial lust." The upper crust of the working class, as Lenin admitted, was easily converted to the teaching of imperialism and took pride in the extension of empire.

No doubt this aspect of the problem is important. The mechanization of humanity in an industrial society is a phenomenon with which we have become all too familiar, and every thoughtful person now recognizes the tremendous dangers inherent in the powers which the demagogue can exercise through the press, the motion picture and the radio. In Hobson's day propaganda was still carried on primarily through the press, but later developments were already foreshadowed in the activities of a Northcliffe or a Hearst. Hobson himself was able to show how, during the war in South Africa, the English press took its information from the South African press, which had been brought very largely under the control of Rhodes and his associates. Even at that time Hobson and others were pointing out how imperialistic capital was influencing not only the press, but the pulpit and the universities. Indeed, Hobson went so far as to claim that the great inert mass of the population, who saw the tangled maze of world movements through dim and bewildered eyes, were the inevitable dupes of able, organized interests who could lure or scare or drive them into any convenient course.

Recognizing as we do that control of the public mind involves the most urgent political problems of the day, it is nevertheless important to point out that there is nothing inexorable about the connection of propaganda and imperialism. Even if you admit that a generation ago moneyed interests believed that imperialism was to their advantage, that these interests exercised a far-reaching control over public opinion, and that they used this control to dupe the common man into support of imperial ventures, it is obvious that at some other time these same interests might have different ideas with regard to their own welfare, just as it is evident that public opinion may be controlled by some other agency—the modern dictator, for example.

But the same thing is not true of another influence upon which Hobson laid great stress, namely the biological conception of politics and international relations. During the last years of the nineteenth century the ideas of "social Darwinism," as it was called, carried everything before them. Darwin's catchwords—the struggle for existence and the survival of the fittest—which he himself always refused to apply to the social organism, were snapped up by others who were less scrupulous, and soon became an integral part of popular and even official thought on foreign affairs. It not only served to justify the ruthless treatment of the "backward" races and the carving up *in spe* [as they hoped] of the Portuguese, Spanish, Ottoman and Chinese Empires and of other "dying nations," as Lord Salisbury called them, but it put the necessary imprimatur on the ideas of conflict between the great imperialistic Powers themselves, and supplied a divine sanction for expansion. It was currently believed, in the days of exuberant imperialism, that the world would soon be the preserve of the great states—the British, the American and the Russian—and it was deduced from this belief that survival in the struggle for existence was in itself adequate evidence of superiority and supernatural appointment. The British therefore looked upon their empire as a work of the divine will, while the Americans and Russians were filled with the idea of a manifest destiny. It will be at once apparent that glorification of war and joy in the conflict was intimately connected with the evolutionary mentality. Hobson, the most determined of anti-imperialists, was finally driven to define the whole movement as "a depraved choice of national life, imposed by self-seeking interests which appeal to the lusts of quantitative acquisitiveness and of forceful domination surviving in a nation from early centuries of animal struggle for existence."

The last phrases of this quotation will serve to lead us to the consideration of what has proved to be another fruitful thought of Hobson. He speaks, in one place, of imperialism as a sociological atavism, a remnant of the roving instinct, just as hunting and sport are leftovers of the physical struggle for existence. This idea of the roving instinct has made but little appeal to later writers, but the basic interpretation of imperialism as an atavism underlies the ingenious and highly intelligent essay of Joseph Schumpeter, "Zur Soziologie der Imperialismen," the only work from the bourgeois side which has had anything like the influence exerted by the writers of the socialist school. Schumpeter, who is an eminent economist, worked out a most convincing argument to prove that imperialism has nothing to do with capitalism, and that it is certainly not a development of capitalism. Capitalism, he holds, is by nature opposed to expansion, war, armaments and professional militarism, and imperialism is nothing but an atavism, one of those elements of the social structure which cannot be explained from existing conditions, but only from the conditions of the past. It is, in other words, a hang-over from a preceding economic order. Imperialism antedates capitalism, going back at least to the time of the Assyrians and Egyptians. It is, according to Schumpeter, the disposition of a state to forceful expansion without any special object and without a definable limit. Conquests are desired not so much because of their advantages, which are often questionable, but merely for the sake of conquest, success and activity.

Schumpeter's theory is in some ways extravagant, but it has served as the starting point for some very interesting speculation, especially among German scholars of the liberal persuasion. It is now fairly clear, I think, that the Neo-Marxian critics have paid far too little attention to the imponderable, psychological ingredients of imperialism. The movement may, without much exaggeration, be interpreted not only as an atavism, as a remnant of the days of absolute monarchy and mercantilism, when it was to the interest of the prince to increase his territory and the number of his subjects, but also as an aberration, to be classed with the extravagances of nationalism. Just as nationalism can drive individuals to the point of sacrificing their very lives for the purposes of the state, so imperialism has driven them to the utmost exertions and the extreme sacrifice, even though the stake might be only some little known and at bottom valueless part of Africa or Asia. In the days when communication and economic interdependence have made the world one in so many ways, men still interpret international relations in terms of the old cabinet policies, they are still swayed by out-moded, feudalistic ideas of honor and prestige.

In a sense, then, you can say that there is, in every people, a certain indefinable national energy, which may find expression in a variety of ways.

As a general rule great domestic crises and outbursts of expansion follow each other in the history of the world. In many of the continental countries of Europe, and for that matter in our own country, great internal problems were fought out in the period before 1870. The energies which, in Germany and Italy, went into the victory of the national cause, soon began to project themselves beyond the frontiers. While the continental nations were settling great issues between them, England sat "like a bloated Quaker, rubbing his hands at the roaring trade" he was carrying on. In those days the British cared very little for their empire. Many of them would have felt relieved if the colonies had broken away without a fuss. But, says Egerton, the best-known historian of British colonial policy, when the Germans and the French began to show an interest in colonial expansion, then the British began to think that there must be some value as yet undiscovered in the colonies. They not only started a movement to bind the colonies and the mother country more closely together, but they stretched out their hands for more. In the end they, who had the largest empire to begin with, got easily the lion's share of the yet unappropriated parts of the world. Some thought they were engaged in the fulfillment of a divine mission to abolish slavery, to spread the gospel, to clothe and educate the heathen. Others thought they were protecting the new markets from dangerous competitors, securing their supply of raw materials, or finding new fields for investment. But underlying the whole imperial outlook there was certainly more than a little misapprehension of economics, much self-delusion and self-righteousness, much misapplication of evolutionary teaching and above all much of the hoary tradition of honor, prestige, power and even plain combativeness. Imperialism always carries with it the connotation of the *Imperator* and of the tradition of rule. It is bound up with conscious or subconscious ideas of force, of brutality, of ruthlessness. It was these traits and tendencies that were so vividly expressed in the poetry and stories of Kipling, and it was his almost uncanny ability to sense the emotions of his time and people that made him the greatest apostle of imperialism.

We shall not go far wrong, then, if we stress the psychological and political factors in imperialism as well as its economic and intellectual elements. It was, of course, connected closely with the great changes in the social structure of the western world, but it was also a projection of nationalism beyond the boundaries of Europe, a projection on a world scale of the time-honored struggle for power and for a balance of power as it had existed on the Continent for centuries. The most casual perusal of the literature of imperialism will reveal the continued potency of these atavistic motives. In a recent number of this very journal a leading Italian diplomat, explaining the policy of the Duce, recurred again and again to the failure of the other countries to appreciate the fact that Italy is a young and active country "animated by new spiritual values." By the much-decried Corfu episode of 1923, Mussolini, to give a concrete example, "called Europe's attention to the respect due to the new Italy and to the reawakened energies of the Italian people." In the present Ethiopian crisis there is not very much suggestion of economic or civilizing motives on the part of the Italians; rather the Duce holds before his followers the prospect of revenge for the defeat at Adua (reminiscent of Britain's thirst to avenge Gordon) and promises them a glorious future. Not long ago he spoke to a group of veterans among the ruins of ancient Rome and told them that every stone surrounding them should remind them that Rome once dominated the world by the wisdom of her rule and the might of her arms and that "nothing forbids us to believe that what was our destiny yesterday may again become our destiny tomorrow." In much the same spirit an eminent Japanese statesman expressed himself recently in Foreign Affairs: "As soon as the Meiji Restoration lifted the ban on foreign intercourse, the long-pent-up energy of our race was released, and with fresh outlook and enthusiasm the nation has made swift progress. When you know this historical background and understand this overflowing vitality of our race, you will see the impossibility of compelling us to stay still within the confines of our little island home. We are destined to grow and expand overseas." It is the same emphasis given by the Italian diplomat to the need for an outlet for surplus energies.

It is, of course, true that both Italy and Japan have a serious population problem and that Japan, at any rate, has an economic argument to back her imperialistic enterprises in Manchuria and China. But it has been shown long ago that the acquisition of new territory has no direct bearing on the population problem and that emigrants go where their interest calls them, not where their governments would like to have them go. As for Japan's economic needs, it may at least be questioned whether she would not be better off if she avoided political and military commitments in China. Her cheap goods have made very extensive inroads in all the markets of the world, and her eventual conquest of the whole Chinese market is perhaps inevitable. Far from having gained much from her recent policy, she has had to face boycotts and other forms of hostility. In this case, certainly, one might debate whether the game is worth the candle.

Baron Wakatsuki, whose statement is quoted above, was careful to avoid mention of a factor in Japanese imperialism which, as every well-informed person knows, is probably the real explanation of Japanese policy. After the Meiji Restoration it was more the exuberance and bellicosity of the military caste in Japan than the enthusiasm of the country at large which determined the policy of the government. If one reads modern Japanese history aright one will find that from 1870 onward the military classes were constantly pressing upon the government for action in Korea. Only with the greatest difficulty did the civil authorities stave off this pressure. In 1894 the Tokyo government more or less rushed into the war with China in order to avoid a dangerous domestic crisis. In other words, the ideas of honor and patriotism were appealed to in order to divert attention from the parliamentary conflict which was then raging. After the Japanese victory it was the military men who, against the better judgment of men like Count Ito and Baron Mutsu, insisted on the cession of the Liaotung Peninsula, which netted Japan nothing but the intervention of Russia, Germany, and France. We need not pursue this subject in all its minute details. The point I want to make is that in the case of Japan, as in the case of many other countries, it is easier to show that the military and official classes are a driving force behind the movement for expansion than to show that a clique of nefarious bankers or industrialists is the determining factor. Business interests may have an interest in the acquisition of territory, or they may not. But military and official classes almost always have. War is, for the soldiers, a profession, and it is no mere chance that war and imperialism are so commonly lumped together. For officials, expansion means new territories to govern and new jobs to be filled.

Hobson, with his pronouncedly economic approach to the problem, held that "the struggle for markets, the greater eagerness of producers to sell than of consumers to buy, is the crowning proof of a false economy of distribution," of which imperialism is the fruit. The remedy, he thought, lay in "social reform." "There is no necessity to open up new foreign markets," he maintained; "the home markets are capable of indefinite expansion." These contentions sound familiar enough in this day of world depression. Whether the home markets are capable of indefinite expansion is a question on which the economic internationalists and the advocates of autarchy hold different opinions. The interesting thing for us to consider, however, is the fact that movements towards autarchy should have developed at all and that so much stress should now be laid upon the problems of redistribution of wealth, of building up purchasing power, and, in general, of domestic social reform. The current of activity has shifted distinctly from expansion to revolution, peaceful or violent. Perhaps it may be argued from this that the socialist thesis regarding imperialism is now being proved; that capitalism has already transformed the backward areas to such an extent that the markets are ruined, and that the capitalist system is rapidly choking. This view might be acceptable if it were not for the fact that the colonies and backward areas are still very far from developed and if it were not for the further fact that before the depression the colonial trade with the older countries was steadily increasing. In the last five years, to be sure, international commerce has sunk to an unbelievably low point, but the difficulty has been chiefly with the trade between the great industrial Powers themselves. It is quite conceivable that the crisis is primarily due to the special situation arising from the World War and that the root of the trouble lies in the impossibility of fitting tremendous international payments into the existing framework of trade relations. The fantastic tariff barriers which have been set up on all sides have simply aggravated a situation which has been developing since the teachings of Cobdenism first began to fall into disrepute.

But whatever the true explanation of our present difficulties, very few voices are raised in favor of a solution by the methods of imperialism. Indeed, the movement toward autarchy is in a way a negation of imperialism. Economically we have been disillusioned about imperialism. We have learned that colonies do not pay. Britain's expenditure for the defense of the empire alone is enormous, yet she has never yet devised a method by which anything like a commensurate return could be secured. The French military outlay on the colonies in 1913 was more than five hundred million francs, at a time when the entire trade of France with her colonies came to hardly three times that figure. Similar statistics could be quoted for Germany, and it is a well-known fact that the colonies of both Spain and Portugal were much more of a liability than an asset.

In the same way it has turned out that foreign investments of capital are not all that they were expected to be. The higher returns from colonial investments have often been counterbalanced by the greater insecurity that went with them. European countries had more than one opportunity to learn the lesson even before the war. We need only recall the Argentine fiasco of 1890 and the wildcat Kaffir Boom in South African securities in 1895 as classical examples of what might happen. But of course all these instances are completely dwarfed by the experiences of the postwar—or perhaps better, the pre-depression decade. Foreign investments have caused acute international tensions and have resulted in phenomena like American dollar diplomacy in Latin America. The expenditure has been immense and what has been salvaged has been unimpressive enough. The nations of the world are still on the lookout for markets, as they have been for centuries, but the peoples of the world have become more or less convinced that the markets, if they can be got at all, can be got only by the offering of better and cheaper goods and not by occupation, political control or forceful exploitation. As for foreign investments, no one has any stomach for them and most of those fortunate enough to have money to invest would be glad to learn of a safe investment at home. The assurance of needed sources for raw materials is as much if not more of a problem today than it was a generation ago, but there is little sense in taking over the expensive administration of tropical or other territory to guarantee a source of raw materials, because somehow or other it usually turns out that the other fellow has the materials that you want, and it has long since become obvious that the idea of controlling sources of all the materials you may need is a snare and a delusion.

*   *   *   *   *

The Christian Missionary Movement
of the 19th and 20th Centuries

Some Peculiar and General Characteristics

KENNETH SCOTT LATOURETTE

➤➤➤➤➤➤➤➤➤➤ *Published in 1937* ◄◄◄◄◄◄◄◄◄◄

Christian missionaries were among the most effective agents of late-nine-teenth-century imperialism. Remarkably active in many of the "backward" areas of the world, these missionaries sought to spread their particular form of Christianity in the very years when religion was on the defensive in Europe—when it was being assailed by those Europeans who could not reconcile their traditional religious beliefs with Darwinism and with other disclosures of nineteenth-century science. Yet it was not only the Kingdom of God which the missionaries sought to advance; many of them sought also to further the dominion of their national state. Arousing the enthusiasm and the financial support of their countrymen and coreligionists, many of them were doubtless more successful in winning Europeans to im-perialism than in converting heathen peoples to Christianity. Although improved means of transportation and communication seemed to make missionary activity less difficult than it had been in earlier centuries, the fact remained that it was not easy to work for the spread of Christian civilization as long as native peoples found that civilization taking the form of machine guns, gin, and venereal diseases. In the present essay, Kenneth Scott Latourette, of Yale University, the author of a major multi-volume *History of the Expansion of Christianity* and a sympathetic student of Chinese and Japanese history, discusses some of the main currents in the recent development of Christian missions.

Christian missions is one of the subjects most neglected by historians who deal with recent history. Yet here is one of the major movements of the past century and a half. Regardless of what one's religious convictions—or lack of convictions—may be, and whether one believes the missionary movement to be good or bad, because of its extent and its influence it deserves careful study from all historians who wish to understand the age out of which we now seem to be passing. In a paper necessarily as brief and yet as comprehensive as this must attempt to be, all that can be done is to call attention to the extent of the movement and to suggest some of the features which set apart the Christian missions of the past century or century and a half from those of any other period.

First of all, as to the extent of the movement. Never has any religion—or, for that matter, any set of ideas, religious or secular—been propagated over so wide an area by so many professional agents as has Christianity in the twelve decades since the Napoleonic Wars. Christian missionaries have accompanied European peoples in their prodigious *Völkerwanderung* [migration] of the past century and a quarter and have held the immigrants to the Christian faith. In the United States, in Canada, in the Southern republics of Latin America, in Australia, in New Zealand, and in South Africa, the millions of professedly Christian immigrants have been followed to their new homes. For them churches and schools have been built and a native clergy trained. In extent this is one of the major cultural achievements of the modern age. It is, moreover, a religious achievement of unprecedented magnitude. In addition, Christian missionaries have penetrated to the great majority of the tribes and nations which are traditionally denominated non-Christian and there have established themselves. To aid in their labors they have reduced to writing more languages than

Reprinted by special permission from *The Catholic Historical Review*, XXIII (1937), 153-159.

ANIMISM: The belief that all objects have souls.

MANICHAEANS: Followers of the religion developed in the third century by the Persian philosopher Mani. Although denounced as heretical and suppressed by Zoroastrians and Christians, Manichaeism spread both eastward and westward. It embodied an attempt to synthesize elements from

had been given a written form in all the previous history of the race. They have introduced schools and medicine of a Western type and they have gathered groups of converts. Their activities have extended from the frozen North to the steaming heat of the tropics. They have covered the Far East, India, the Near East, parts of Central Asia, the islands of the Pacific, Africa, and many of the Indian and Eskimo tribes of the Americas.

Some of the most obvious features of this missionary movement can quickly be mentioned: (1) It has been almost entirely limited to the Catholic Church and to the various Protestant churches and denominations. Except for some activities of the Russian Orthodox Church before 1914, in it the various Eastern Churches have had almost no share. (2) For the first time in its history Protestantism as a whole has become active in spreading its forms of the Christian faith among non-Christian peoples. Before the nineteenth century some Protestant minorities had been so engaged, but the masses of Protestants had not been interested. (3) Christian missions of the nineteenth and twentieth centuries have been closely associated with the industrial revolution and the expansion of European peoples. With some striking exceptions it is from industrialized countries and sections that missions have had their chief support. Thus it was in industrial Lyons that the Society for the Propagation of the Faith had its inception. It is from lands which have been most active in the expansion of Europe that a large proportion of missionaries has come. For instance, of the Catholic powers in the nineteenth century France both acquired the largest colonial possessions and also led in Catholic missions. Of the Protestant powers, Great Britain led in colonial expansion and long held the leadership in Protestant missions. This generalization must not be pushed too far—for the United States, with very small colonial possessions outside the Americas, now leads in Protestant missions in the Far East and the Near East and provides a large proportion of the Protestant missionaries in India and Africa. So, too, the recent rapid growth

---

various existing religions and was designed for universal adoption. Mani's objective was to provide both the Orient and the Occident with a single faith.

SYNCRETISM: The reconciliation of conflicting religious beliefs.

of Catholic missions from the United States has been directed chiefly to areas in which the United States has no colonial possessions. It is, however, clear that Christian missions, whether Catholic or Protestant, and whatever the nature of their origin, have been intimately associated with the spread of Western culture. They have been the pioneers of some phases of it—notably education, medicine and various humanitarian movements—and have been an almost invariable accompaniment of European expansion.

It is, however, to some of the less frequently noted .features of nineteenth and twentieth century Christian missions that I wish to call attention, and especially to characteristics which are unique in the history not only of the spread of Christianity but also in the expansion of other faiths.

First of all, nineteenth and twentieth century missions, both Catholic and Protestant, have depended for their financial support upon the gifts of millions of donors. The contributions of hundreds of thousands of individuals have made possible the impressive incomes of the Society for the Propagation of the Faith, of the Association of the Holy Infancy, and of the various Protestant missionary societies. A few large gifts have come from wealthy individuals, but they have constituted only a minority of the whole. Endowments have been accumulated but in the case of a number of organizations the return from them is less than a half of the total income. Pre-nineteenth century Catholic missions had been predominantly financed either by governments, by endowments, or by gifts of a few wealthy individuals. This had been less general in pre-nineteenth century Protestant missions, but the latter had not been very extensive and several of such Protestant missions as had existed had derived their financial support from the state. The missions of non-Christian religions, Buddhist, Moslem, or Hindu, have never enjoyed a wide financial support from the masses of their adherents. In other words, more than any other missionary enterprise in history, Christian missions of the nineteenth and twentieth centuries have been a popular movement, made possible by the active support of a large proportion of those who have called themselves Christians.

A second unique feature is the part played by women. The majority of Catholic missionaries—if one may use the latter word in a non-technical sense to embrace all the foreign agents who are professionally engaged in propagating the faith—are women; and, if one includes wives, the large majority of Protestant missionaries are also women. It is no novelty to see women as missionaries. One recalls the large part played by them in the English missions which Boniface directed in eighth century Germany. However, the large proportion of women on the staffs of nineteenth and twentieth century Christian missions is new, in the history of the spread both of Christianity and also of other religions. Why is this so? What effect upon the newly emerging Christian communities has this prominence of the woman missionary had? Into these and other interesting and highly significant questions suggested by this characteristic I must not here take the time to enter.

A third feature is the relatively high standards set up for admission of non-Christians to baptism. This has been true of both Catholics and Protestants. One of the features of pre-nineteenth century missions which most impresses the student is the ease with which admission was gained to the Christian community. In the early Christian centuries, to be sure, pre-baptismal instruction seems usually to have been required. On some occasions it was also demanded in the Middle Ages. In much of the conversion of Western Europe, however, and in the Spanish and Portuguese missions from the fifteenth to the nineteenth century in general, the pre-baptismal preparation was brief and its amount slight. In the relatively few pre-nineteenth century Protestant missions the practice was not uniform. Some had almost no pre-baptismal instruction: others had a long catechumenate with careful preparation. In contrast, in general, the trend of nineteenth and twentieth century Christian missions, whether Catholic or non-Catholic, has been toward a fairly long period of probation and instruction before baptism. Here, as in other centuries, practice has varied. The general direction seems clear. This, too, is unique in the history of the spread of religions. Usually, admission to the general community (not, of course, to the Buddhist monastic groups or the inner circles of the Manichaeans) was easy and involved little or no preliminary instruction in the tenets of the faith.

A fourth characteristic, related to the above but not entirely a result of it, is the relative absence of large group movements into the Church. Entrance into Christianity, as into other religions, has generally been a matter of group decision. Usually a few individuals have led the way, but the majority have come through a popular movement. In a certain sense, the conversion of the Roman Empire was a matter of group choice, especially after Constantine and his successors gave to the Church the support of the state. So, too, was the conversion of the various peoples of the British Isles, of Scandinavia, and of Germany. The Indians of the Americas tended to come into the Church by groups or by tribes. The nineteenth and twentieth centuries have witnessed some group movements—as among the depressed classes and animistic tribes of India, in some of the islands of the Pacific, and in Africa. As a rule, however, conversion has been that of individuals or families or, on occasion, of villages, not of tribes or nations.

This seems to have been, in the main, for three reasons. First, it is because of the high standards set for the baptism of non-Christians. Second, it is because nineteenth and twentieth century Christian missions have dealt so largely with enormous, highly civilized masses of mankind, notably those in the Near East, India, China, and Japan. Here, so far, only a relatively few individuals or smaller groups have come into the Church. In the brief time that nineteenth and twentieth century missions have been operating, the bulk of these populations have not been moved from their traditional religious allegiances. In the third place—and this has to do chiefly with non-Catholic missions— the stress laid by Protestantism upon individual judgment in matters of religion has emphasized bringing individuals one by one into the faith.

A fifth feature of nineteenth and twentieth century missions, closely related to the two last characteristics, has been the relatively small percentages of the population approached who have been won to membership in the Church. In Japan and China it has been less than one per cent of the population, in India less than two per cent, and in the Near East, aside from converts from the Eastern non-Catholic churches, very much less than one per cent. The exceptions to this are significant. In a number of the smaller islands of the Pacific the majority of the native peoples have become Christian. In certain areas of Africa—the Union of South Africa and Uganda, for instance—a fairly large percentage of the population has been baptised. As a rule it has been among formerly animistic folk that the percentage of converts has been highest. The more advanced religions have offered more marked resistance. However, it must be noted that in Japan, China, and India the percentage growth of the Christian groups is more rapid than that of the population as a whole; and this is by conversion as well as by the natural increase through births.

To give a well-rounded and accurate picture, a sixth characteristic must be added. It is true that in general higher standards than heretofore have been maintained for admission of non-Christians to baptism, that mass or group conversions have been less prominent than in other centuries, and that in the major lands of Asia the percentage of professed Christians is small. It is also true that in another sense the latter part of the nineteenth and these opening decades of the twentieth century have witnessed in Asia a remarkable molding by Christianity of enormous congeries of peoples. It has been a kind of mass adoption of certain of the Christian ideals without formal acceptance of the Christian name or without entrance into membership in the visible Church. This is particularly noticeable in India, where nineteenth and twentieth century missions were prominent half a century earlier than in China and Japan. It is seen in the tendency toward the elimination of those features of non-Christian religions which are most repugnant to the Christian ethical sense, in the adoption of some of the methods and the holydays of the Christian Church, in a slight intermixture of Christian beliefs about God, particularly in some syncretistic sects, and in the spread of humanitarian ideals which historically have had their springs largely in Christianity.

This permeation of non-Christian peoples by a certain amount of Christian ideals and practices has not been due entirely and in some instances not primarily to Christian missionaries. For instance, the use of the Christian Sunday as a day of rest in government offices and schools is attributable more to contact with the general practice in the Occident. This, too, is probably the main source of the celebration of the Christmas festival in Japan. Much, however, is from the activities of mission schools, hospitals, orphanages, and other missionary philanthropic institutions. Whether this kind of mass transformation will be followed by formal conversion, the historian must not dare to predict. He must note, however, that it is a relatively new phenomenon. History has seen only one parallel to it on a large scale—the permeation of Chinese life by Buddhism. It is well known that the percentage of simon-pure Buddhists in China has never been very large. Only the monks and nuns and the lay members of some of the strict vegetarian groups can be classed as such. Yet Chinese life as a whole has been widely modified by Buddhist ideology. Today in India, China, Japan, and in the Near East Christianity seems to be having a similar effect.

This paper has not sought to distinguish between Catholic and non-Catholic missions. Their differences are many. To note them would require another essay. However, their similarities are so numerous that in a series of generalizations such as I have attempted they can be treated as two wings of a common movement. Together they constitute one of the most amazing and influential features of the age through which the race has just passed. I must repeat the conviction with which I began. They deserve more of the attention of the dispassionate student of recent history than they have thus far received.

XXIII

War and Peace

July 1914: Thirty Years After
BERNADOTTE E. SCHMITT

Versailles in Perspective
CHARLES SEYMOUR

July 1914: Thirty Years After[1]

BERNADOTTE E. SCHMITT

≫≫-≫≫-≫≫-≫≫-≫≫-≫≫-≫≫-≫≫-≫≫ *Published in 1944* ≪-≪≪-≪≪-≪≪-≪≪-≪≪-≪≪-≪≪-≪≪

Hardly had World War I broken out in the summer of 1914 than the belligerents issued their respective official reports, the purpose of which was to shift onto the enemy the blame for the outbreak of hostilities. From the beginning of the war, in other words, the question of war guilt was an important one; and when the peace treaties which concluded the war were drawn up, the Allied version of war guilt was written into them. By the very nature of things, therefore, the question of the origins of the war could not become academic. Each of the governments involved found itself compelled to justify the position it had taken in the crisis of 1914, the more so because other governments were authorizing the publication of basic documents. In particular it was the states that underwent revolutions in the last stages of the war that took the lead in issuing all kinds of secret sources. The example of these governments proved to be irresistible, and within just a few years of the conclusion of hostilities, historians were deluged with an almost unbelievable quantity of source material relating to the origins of the war. This source material made necessary numerous revisions of wartime views, and many scholars all over the world proceeded to attempt, on the basis of the new materials, to rewrite the story of the coming of the war. Of these scholars one of the outstanding is Bernadotte Schmitt, now professor emeritus of history at the University of Chicago.

[1] Since the author's *The coming of the war 1914* was published in 1930, the Russian and French documents for the period of the crisis have been made available (reviewed at length in *Foreign Affairs*, XIII [1934], 133-53, XV [1937], 516-36), as well as the reports of the Baden, Bavarian, Saxon, and Württemberg ministers and military attachés in Berlin. A few memoirs or biographies of important personages have also been written. These materials do not solve all the problems of the crisis, and nothing decisive has been revealed about the murder at Sarayevo; probably these mysteries will never be cleared up. A revised edition of the book being out of the question at the present time, this article is offered as a summary which takes account of the new material.

A moderate revisionist, Schmitt makes it clear that the Kaiser was not the ogre many people made him out to be, but he believes that the main responsibility for the coming of World War I rests with Germany. For a very different approach the reader should turn to the writings of Harry Elmer Barnes.

O n Sunday, June 28, 1914, the Archduke Francis Ferdinand, nephew of the Emperor Francis Joseph and heir to the throne of Austria-Hungary, and his wife the Duchess of Hohenberg were assassinated at Sarayevo, the capital of Bosnia-Herzegovina. The crime was the culminating incident in the long quarrel between Austria-Hungary and Serbia and provided the occasion for the war of 1914-18.

In July 1914 not much was known about the circumstances of the crime except that the assassin and his accomplices had been armed in Belgrade by minor officials of the Serbian government and smuggled across the frontier. The Austro-Hungarian government laid the responsibility for the murder on a Serbian society called *Narodna Odbrana* ("National Defense"), and it circulated a dossier intended to prove the "culpable tolerance" by the Serbian government of "unwholesome propaganda" organized in Serbia against the Dual Monarchy. Except in Austria-Hungary and Germany, however, the general opinion was that the complicity of the Serbian government was not established and that Austria-Hungary had not proved the necessity of going to war.

Since 1914 considerable new evidence has come to light, such as the minutes of the conspirators' trial, the report of the trial at Salonika in 1917 of Serbian officers alleged, among several charges, to have been involved in the plot, and numerous disclosures by Serbian politicians and officers and by officials of the former Austro-Hungarian government. This evidence is full of contradictions, discrepancies, and anachronisms; and the full story of the murder is not known.

The *Narodna Odbrana* was organized in October 1908, after the annexation of Bosnia-Herzegovina by Austria, in order to "protect and promote [Serbian] interests in the annexed provinces." Its membership embraced prominent members of the Radical party and representatives of the army, including Dragutin Dimitriyevich and Voya Tankosich, who had taken part in the assassination of King Alexander and Queen

Reprinted by special permission from *The Journal of Modern History*, XVI (1944), 169-204. Copyright, University of Chicago Press.

Draga in 1903. For a time the new society carried on a subversive agitation in Bosnia-Herzegovina (not to speak of the stimulation of national enthusiasm in Serbia itself); but it was gradually replaced, so far as propaganda abroad was concerned, by another society, the *Uyedinyenye ili Smrt* ("Union or Death"), or, as it was popularly called, the "Black Hand," which was organized in 1911 by army officers, with Dimitriyevich at the head, to work for the union of all Serbs. This secret society operated through terrorism and succeeded in combining the self-effacing loyalty of the Jesuits, the ruthless spirit of Russian nihilism, and the symbolism of the American Ku Klux Klan. Beginning its work in Macedonia, it extended its activity to Bosnia, especially after the Balkan wars; but it was clever enough (according to a prominent member) to hide behind the *Narodna Odbrana*, so that, although the Austro-Hungarian government knew of the existence of the *Uyedinyenye ili Smrt*, it failed to ferret out the connection between the two societies (a member of the *Uyedinyenye ili Smrt* became secretary of the *Narodna Odbrana*) and in 1914 presented to the world a confused picture of the actual situation.

How close was the connection of the Serbian government with the Black Hand is uncertain. At first the government was willing to use the society in Macedonia; but after the Balkan wars a bitter quarrel ensued between the civil and military authorities, and the Black Hand was generally credited with supporting the army against the Radical party, for Dimitriyevich was the leader of the military party as well as the chief spirit in the secret society. So sharp was this conflict that in June 1914 King Peter retired from the government and Crown Prince Alexander was appointed regent; only the intervention of the Russian minister, Hartvig, enabled the Radical leader, Pashich, to remain as prime minister. In view of this situation, it seems unlikely that the Serbian government would have connived at any activity of the Black

---

SOME LEADING FIGURES IN THE SARAYEVO CRISIS

BERCHTOLD: Austrian foreign minister.
CONRAD: Austrian chief of staff.

BETHMANN HOLLWEG: German imperial chancellor.
FALKENHAYN: German minister of war.
JAGOW: German foreign minister.
LICHNOWSKY: German ambassador to Britain.
MOLTKE: German chief of staff.

Hand in Bosnia; after the Balkan wars Serbia needed peace, and the policy of Pashich was to avoid provocation of Austria-Hungary and even to cultivate tolerable relations with it. On the other hand, it was not easy for the authorities in Belgrade to put a stop to the secret activity of a secret society.

Dimitriyevich—"Apis," as he was often called—was a remarkable man. "Gifted and educated, honorable, a convincing speaker, a sincere patriot, personally brave and full of ambition, energy and capacity for work. . . . he possessed the qualities which fascinate men. . . . he was in every way an excellent organizer. . . . he saw only the goal in front of him and went his own way recklessly and without scruple. . . . others were to obey him and execute his instructions without opposition." One writer represents him as an inveterate conspirator; but the principal charge against him, that he attempted to assassinate Crown Prince Alexander in 1917, may now be considered disproved.[2] In 1923, however, it was alleged that "Apis" had organized the murder at Sarayevo.

The story ran thus: In June 1914 "Apis" was informed by the Russian general staff that at a meeting at Konopischt earlier in the month William II and Francis Ferdinand had planned an attack on Serbia, and from his own agents he had obtained plans for the Austrian maneuvers to be held along the Serbo-Bosnian frontier. To forestall this disaster, Dimitriyevich decided to have the archduke assassinated. While he was in this mood, his confidant Voya Tankosich appeared with two young Bosnians, who declared that they wished to murder Francis Ferdinand, the great enemy of the Yugoslav people. Dimitriyevich thereupon had Tankosich instruct the Bosnians in the use of weapons and smuggle them across the frontier. Dimitriyevich later

[2] The evidence presented by Svetozar Pribichevich in *La dictature du roi Alexandre* (Paris, 1930), pp. 277-319, seems conclusive.

ZIMMERMANN: Undersecretary in the German foreign office.

IZVOLSKY: Russian ambassador to Paris.
SAZONOV: Russian minister of foreign affairs.

POINCARÉ: French president.
VIVIANI: Premier of France.

ASQUITH: British prime minister.
GREY: British foreign secretary.
GOSCHEN: British ambassador to Germany.

informed the executive committee of the *Uyedinyenye ili Smrt* of what he had done; they protested, and yielding to their pressure, Dimitri-yevich sent orders to the young men not to commit murder. But his orders were either disobeyed or not received. There are many diffi-culties about this story, which is now generally regarded with much suspicion. But it led other people to reveal what they claimed to know about the plot, and from this evidence a more plausible explanation can be constructed.

Gavrilo Printsip, the assassin of Francis Ferdinand, and his im-mediate accomplices, Nedelyko Chabrinovich and Trifko Grabezh, were Bosnians, hardly out of their teens, caught up in the revolutionary movement *Mlada Bosna* ("Young Bosnia") in the annexed provinces. Inspired by the ideal of Yugoslav unity and being constantly in trouble with the school authorities, they emigrated to Belgrade and associated with members of the *Narodna Odbrana* and the *Uyedinyenye ili Smrt*, from whom they received financial support and still more revolutionary zeal. The exact relationship is impossible to determine. For example, Chabrinovich was at one time supposed to have been under the protection of the Austrian consul in Belgrade; later it was suggested that his father had been an Austrian secret agent[3] and that the son, out of resentment, had joined the Serbian agitation in Bosnia; a third story had it that he was once presented to Crown Prince Alexander at the state printing office, where he was employed. But such details probably do not matter greatly, for all three men were deep in the revolutionary movement and ready to strike a blow against Habsburg rule.

When it was announced, in March 1914, that Austro-Hungarian maneuvers would be held in Bosnia and that Francis Ferdinand would visit Sarayevo on June 28—a day (St. Vitus' Day [*Vidovdan*]) sacred to Serbian patriots as the anniversary of the battle of Kossovo—Printsip and Chabrinovich decided to assassinate the archduke, and they persuaded Grabezh to join them. Through one Milan Tsigano-vich, a Bosnian employed by the Serbian railways and a member of the Black Hand, they obtained weapons from Tankosich which came from the government arsenal at Krageyuvats and were instructed in their use. Whether Dimitriyevich was informed of this and of the

---

[3] This view is discounted by Rebecca West (*Black lamb and grey falcon* [New York, 1941], pp. 414-29) as the result of an interview with the sister of Chabrinovich in 1937; she suggests that the story was circulated by a rejected suitor of the sister, who sought thereby to discredit the family.

journey of the young men to Sarayevo cannot be asserted positively, although it is probable that he did know; it is also possible that he did not take the young men seriously, thinking them too young and inexperienced, and that he was genuinely alarmed when he learned what had happened. Be that as it may, the conspirators left Belgrade at the end of May, passed across the frontier through a "tunnel," i.e., with the aid of officials, and reached Sarayevo several weeks before the visit of the archduke. They concealed their weapons in the house of Daniel Ilich, a schoolteacher, who was a member of the Black Hand and enlisted three more young men as "reserves."

If Dimitriyevich, who was chief of the intelligence section of the Serbian general staff, knew of the plot, the question arises: Was the Serbian cabinet involved? That it was directly responsible or even aware of the plot was not charged by Austria-Hungary, and the general circumstances of Serbia at that moment made any connivance seem most unlikely. In June 1924, however, Lyuba Yovanovich, minister of education in the Pashich cabinet of 1914, stated that "at the end of May or the beginning of June" 1914 Pashich had informed the cabinet that "there were people who were preparing to go to Sarayevo to kill Francis Ferdinand, who was to go there to be solemnly received on *Vidovdan*." This startling declaration precipitated a lively controversy, first within Serbia (Yugoslavia) and then throughout the world. After a long delay Pashich impugned the veracity of his former colleague, but he did not produce convincing proof that Yovanovich had not told the truth. The latter did not take up charges that he had been guilty of exaggeration in order to magnify his own importance. Both statesmen died before the matter was satisfactorily cleared up; and it is still impossible to say whether the Serbian government knew of the plot, for the revelations made after the first statement of Yovanovich are full of discrepancies. Another version has it that some time before Printsip, Chabrinovich, and Grabezh crossed the frontier, some other agitators were caught by the Serbian police trying to pass into Bosnia, that this incident was reported to the cabinet, and that Lyuba Yovanovich, writing ten years later, had this in mind when he asserted that Pashich had spoken about Printsip's expedition. But whatever the Serbian government may have known, there is no evidence to suggest that it approved of the plot or assisted in its preparation.[4]

[4] The charge has also been brought that Russia was privy to the conspiracy. According to some writers, Hartvig, who was an ardent supporter of Serbian national aspirations, was involved; others suggest that Dimitriyevich was in

If the Serbian government knew anything about the plot and if, especially, as alleged, its efforts to prevent the conspirators from crossing the frontier had failed, it should have warned Vienna of what was brewing. Apparently it did not do so, although both in 1914 and after the war statements were made that it had done so. Here again the evidence is conflicting; but the positive statement of the Serbian minister in Vienna, Yovan Yovanich, has not been disproved. Being aware of the inflamed state of mind of many circles in Bosnia which resented the approaching visit of Francis Ferdinand and fearful of some incident which might disturb the relations of Austria-Hungary and Serbia, he decided to speak to Bilinski, the minister in charge of Bosnian affairs (his own relations with Berchtold, the foreign minister, being somewhat strained). He explained that the army maneuvers would be regarded as a "provocation" and that some Serbian youth might "put a live cartridge in his rifle or revolver instead of a blank one" and shoot at the archduke; "it would therefore be well and wise for the archduke not to go to Sarayevo." Bilinski promised to inform Francis Ferdinand, but apparently did not do so; whether Bilinski spoke to Berchtold is uncertain.

Equally uncertain is it whether warnings, more or less specific, were received from other sources by the Austrian authorities. The evidence does suggest that some kind of warning was received by Francis Ferdinand himself and that he was reluctant to go to Sarayevo, but the stories lack definiteness. Whatever the truth, it is generally recognized that the measures taken in Sarayevo for the protection of the royal visitors were inadequate. For reasons of economy, the local police were not greatly increased; and, because of the jealousy existing between the civil administration and the military authorities, the latter insisted on controlling the arrangements, since the visit of Francis Ferdinand was made in connection with the army maneuvers. When the Emperor Francis Joseph visited Sarayevo in 1910, a double cordon of troops lined the streets; but on June 28, 1914 General Potiorek, the commander of the garrison, failed to take this precaution—although he had been

___

touch with the Russian general staff through Colonel Artamonov, the Russian military attaché. The evidence is not very convincing, and the fact that both Hartvig and Artamonov were absent from Belgrade on June 28 weakens what evidence there is; if they knew that Francis Ferdinand was to be assassinated, they would surely have remained in Belgrade, in order to keep in immediate touch with their Serbian protégés.

constantly complaining of the restlessness of the Bosnian population. He may have felt that this would spoil the good effects which were hoped for from the royal visit, but he must be held accountable for the consequences of his carelessness.

The archduke and his wife arrived at Ilidzhe, a resort near Sarayevo, in time for the maneuvers, which were held on June 26-27; and they were cordially received when they drove through the city on the afternoon of the 26th. On Sunday, the 28th—the anniversary of Kossovo, of the Austro-Serbian treaty of 1881, and of the marriage of the august visitors—they made their official visit. As they were driving to the town hall, Chabrinovich hurled a bomb at the archduke's car; the missile injured, however, not the intended victim but his adjutant, riding in the next car. So, after the ceremonies at the town hall, Francis Ferdinand insisted on visiting his adjutant at the hospital. Although this involved a change of route, the chauffeurs of the motor cars were apparently not told and adhered to the directions originally given them. In consequence, the archduke's car took a wrong turn and was forced to stop and back up—at the very point where Printsip happened to be standing. Printsip seized the moment and shot both Francis Ferdinand and his wife, who died before medical aid could be brought. But for this accident or oversight, it is unlikely that Francis Ferdinand would have met his death on that day, for neither Grabezh nor the local "reserves" whom Ilich had collected took any steps. But for this murder, a general European war would probably not have broken out in the summer of 1914.

In Austria-Hungary the reaction to the crime was instantaneous and significant. Sarayevo was the scene of demonstrations against the Serbs, and in many other places the anti-Serbian feeling so carefully nourished for years manifested itself. The newspapers were at first cautious; but official circles, including church and army, assumed that an hour of reckoning between the Dual Monarchy and Serbia had arrived. General Conrad von Hötzendorf, chief of the general staff, declared that "Austria must draw the sword against Serbia"; and Count Berchtold, the foreign minister, agreed with him. But the emperor and Count Stürgkh, the Austrian premier, wished to postpone a decision until the investigations at Sarayevo, while Count Tisza, the Hungarian premier, was opposed to military action because "we do not have sufficient proof to be able to place the responsibility for the crime on Serbia." Tisza's attitude was partly determined by his belief that on account of William II's supposed prejudice in favor of Serbia, Germany would not support energetic action by Austria-Hungary; so when Tschirschky, the German ambassador, hinted that his government was likely to be in a receptive mood, Berchtold conceived a master-stroke.

Four days before the murder at Sarayevo a memorandum on Austro-Hungarian policy in the Balkans had been completed in the foreign office. Written to be transmitted to Berlin, it declared that the alliance with Romania had become almost a liability and that, in order to bring Romania to reason, Bulgaria should be taken into the Triple Alliance. Germany was to be asked to join with the Monarchy in opposing the "united action of France and Russia" in the Balkans. To this memorandum Berchtold added a few paragraphs, showing that after Sarayevo the proposed action was "more imperative" than ever. Inasmuch as the policy advocated in the memorandum had been originally suggested by Tisza (in March 1914), the document could be safely transmitted to the German government—and by the ordinary diplomatic channels. Berchtold, however, sent the document, along with a letter written by Francis Joseph to William II, by his *chef de cabinet*, Count Hoyos.

Although the imperial letter covered much the same ground as the memorandum, it added that the aim of creating a new Balkan league, with Bulgaria as its center, was possible "only if Serbia, which at present serves as the pivot of Panslav policy, has been *eliminated as a factor of political power in the Balkans*," for "*a reconciliation of the antagonism that now separates us from Serbia is no longer to be thought of*"; Austro-Hungarian policy must, therefore, "in the future be directed toward the isolation and diminution of Serbia." This letter might also have been sent in the diplomatic pouch, for Tisza, although he objected to the words italicized, approved of the "isolation and diminution of Serbia."

But Berchtold had in mind more than a diplomatic campaign against Serbia, and his purpose in sending Hoyos to Berlin was to have him explain to the German authorities his real plans, with the hope that he could use the promise of German support as a lever for overcoming the opposition of Tisza. Incidentally, by leaving the choice between diplomacy (Tisza) and military action (Conrad-Berchtold) to the German emperor, the Austro-Hungarian foreign minister astutely saddled him with the responsibility for the policy to be adopted by the Dual Monarchy.

In Germany the news of Sarayevo was received with a certain bewilderment. The press naturally showed strong sympathy for Austria-Hungary, but it did not demand an aggressive policy on the part of Germany or a free hand for its ally. Zimmermann, the under-secretary in the foreign office, advised Serbia to neglect no step necessary to call to account the persons involved in the plot, and suggested to Austria that "humiliating conditions" should not be proposed to Serbia. William II was so upset that he immediately returned from Kiel to Potsdam. When he learned that his ambassador in Vienna was advising against "too hasty steps," he declared that "the Serbs must be disposed of, and that right soon!" On the other hand, less than two weeks before, both the emperor and the chancellor had been deeply concerned over the mounting armaments of Russia; and the latter had recognized that in the event of a new crisis in the Balkans, Russia would probably take a much stronger stand than it had done in 1912-13. In view of their past record, both William II and Bethmann might have been expected to pursue a cautious course. Military circles, however, were of the opinion that the moment was favorable for war (even though the emperor was personally for peace).

Hoyos arrived in Berlin on Sunday morning, July 5, and, after handing over to the Austro-Hungarian ambassador, Count Szögyény, the memorandum and the imperial letter, proceeded to the Wilhelm-strasse for a discussion with Zimmermann (Jagow, the foreign minister, being away on his honeymoon). He explained that his government would like to undertake "a surprise attack on Serbia without any preliminary preparation"—that is, without a mobilization—and that "a complete partition of Serbia was under consideration." Zimmermann made no objection, and later in the day declared to the German ambassador in London, Prince Lichnowsky, who happened to be in Berlin, that "if war was now after all inevitable for [Germany] in consequence of the unfriendly attitude of Russia, it would perhaps be better to have it now rather than later" (on the next day Bethmann expressed the same opinion to Hoyos).[5]

At Potsdam, Szögyény communicated to William II the memorandum of the Austro-Hungarian government and the letter of

---

[5] So Hoyos declared in a letter written in July 1917, first published by Maurice Muret in the *Journal des Débats* on November 11, 1931 and, later, with other documents, in the original German by Jan Opocenský in the *Journal of modern history*, IV (1932), 426-28.

Francis Joseph. The emperor at first replied that the plans adumbrated in Vienna made him "foresee serious European complications" and that he would have to consult his chancellor. But, after luncheon, William II said that Austria-Hungary might "rely on Germany's full support" and that the action against Serbia "must not be delayed." He sympathized with Francis Joseph's "well-known love of peace"; but, if Vienna "really recognized the necessity of warlike action against Serbia," "he would regret it if [Austria] did not make use of the present moment"; for, while Russia would doubtless be hostile, it "was in no way prepared for war," and, in any case, Germany would stand by Austria-Hungary "with its accustomed loyalty." William further promised to see to it that Romania observed "a correct attitude," and he raised no objection to the inclusion of Bulgaria in the Triple Alliance. The emperor did declare that he must "hear the opinion of the chancellor," but he authorized Szögyény to telegraph to Vienna his personal approval of the Austrian proposals.

Later in the day the emperor received General von Falkenhayn, the Prussian minister of war, who, on hearing that Austria intended to "march into Serbia," urgently begged that "adequate preparations for war be made on the part of Germany." William declined to sanction such preparation, "in order not to disturb the diplomatic situation"; nevertheless, Falkenhayn took it upon himself to write to General von Moltke, the chief of staff, who was on leave at Carlsbad, that "the situation is acute," although he said that he did not expect a decision "in the next few weeks."[6]

After Falkenhayn, came Bethmann and Zimmermann. The emperor, without waiting to hear what the chancellor might say, recited what he had done. There is fair evidence to support the view that the latter was disturbed to find the emperor already committed to a policy which, according to Bethmann's repeatedly expressed opinion, was likely to lead to a general European war and that he tried to oppose it. But, in the end, he was talked around; and on the following day he officially confirmed the emperor's promise.

[6] Falkenhayn wrote to Moltke after a conversation with Bethmann, who, as noted in the next paragraph, had discussed the situation with the emperor. Falkenhayn represents the chancellor as not taking the situation too seriously and as being skeptical as to whether the Austrians were in earnest. Since Bethmann, at bottom, was disturbed by the emperor's policy (which he loyally accepted), he naturally tried to minimize its dangers when talking with the minister of war; the latter, however, was not deceived.

Still later that evening and on the morning of the following day, July 6, William II received representatives of the general staff, the navy department, and the naval staff. To these persons he expressed the opinion that Russia would probably not fight in defense of Serbia; but he clearly recognized that war was a possibility, and he faced the prospect without hesitation, on the assumption that Great Britain would remain neutral. The emperor then departed for Norway, where he remained until July 24.

On July 6 Bethmann and Zimmermann officially received Szögyény and Hoyos and replied to the overtures of the Austro-Hungarian government. Bethmann accepted the proposal to take Bulgaria into the Triple Alliance and promised to bring pressure on Romania to stop the Romanian agitation against the Dual Monarchy. As for Serbia, Germany left it to Vienna to decide what was to be done "to clear up the situation" and would always stand behind its ally. The chancellor also stated that both he and the emperor considered "immediate action" against Serbia as "the best and most radical solution" of the problem and that neither Italy nor Romania should be informed in advance of "an eventual action against Serbia," although, under Article VII of the Triple Alliance, Italy was entitled to notification.

The German and Austro-Hungarian records leave no doubt that the German emperor and the German government understood that Count Berchtold desired to undertake an immediate military action against Serbia, without any diplomatic preparation, and that he contemplated a partition of Serbia; they accepted and approved this policy and urged its immediate execution, even at the risk of war with Russia. The German reasons appear to have been: (1) there was the feeling that the Dual Monarchy must either restore its prestige by a successful war or face disintegration; (2) a good case seemed to exist against Serbia; (3) if this case were properly exploited, other powers would not interfere; (4) if, however, Russia did interfere, it would be better for Germany to fight at that time rather than later, for Great Britain would remain neutral. The German government gambled on the chance that Russia would not intervene, and the circumstance that this gamble proved wrong does not diminish the responsibility of Germany for what happened.

This view is not affected by the fact that no far-reaching preparations were made for war. On the side of the army, nothing was done, so far as has ever come to light, because, as the deputy chief of staff remarked, they were "all prepared" and "ready to jump." What naval preparations were made were ordered by word of mouth and kept strictly secret; but the construction of new ships was speeded up, a battleship was sent through the recently widened Kiel Canal, and the naval flying forces were put in shape. Also, certain ships away from German waters received orders as to what to do in case of war. No financial precautions appear to have been taken; but grain supplies were bought up privately, and the minister of the interior went over "all the measures necessary in case of war."

Immediately after Hoyos's return from Berlin, on July 7, a ministerial council was held in Vienna. Berchtold stated that he had obtained the promise of "the unconditional support of Germany in the event of a warlike complication with Serbia" and advocated a "reckoning" with Serbia, even though "a passage-at-arms with Serbia might lead to a war with Russia." The Austrian premier, the joint ministers of war and finance, and the representatives of the army and navy agreed with this proposal. Only Tisza objected. The Hungarian premier, who had already protested against what Hoyos had said in Berlin about a partition of Serbia, refused to sanction "a surprise attack" and insisted that Serbia must first be given an opportunity for diplomatic submission; hard demands might, indeed, be made, "but not such as cannot be complied with." In face of this attitude, which was made known to Francis Joseph by Tisza himself in writing, Berchtold had to temporize and agree that any military action against Serbia must be preceded by an ultimatum.

The wily foreign minister, however, easily outplayed the Hungarian statesman. He determined to include in the ultimatum demands which would be unacceptable to Serbia (which did not prevent him from giving assurances in the opposite sense to the Russian ambassador!), and he won over the hesitating emperor to this course. He then informed Tisza of a conversation with the German ambassador, who had said that "in Berlin action by the Monarchy against Serbia is fully expected" and that Germany would not understand why the opportunity was neglected. Stung by these reproaches and irritated by the language of the Serbian press, with his protests to Francis Joseph ignored and public opinion in Hungary becoming steadily more chauvinistic, Tisza on July 14 accepted the plan of a short-term ultimatum and "introduced a sharper tone in places."

The final decisions were taken at a ministerial council held on

July 19. An official of the foreign office, Wiesner, who had been sent to Sarayevo to ascertain the results of the investigation carried on there, had indeed reported that there was no proof of the complicity of the Serbian government in the murder and that there were reasons for believing this unlikely. Apparently Berchtold did not inform the ministers of this verdict; but, since Tisza had agreed to his plan, whether the Serbian government was involved or not did not matter. Therefore, the note adopted for presentation to the Serbian government contained an indictment of Serbia's general policy and only incidentally a demand for satisfaction for the murder of the archduke. Berchtold agreed that the Monarchy should not annex any of Serbia, but "by the cession of as much of its territories as possible to Bulgaria, Greece, and Albania, and perhaps also to Romania, should endeavor to reduce its size so that it would no longer be dangerous." Thus the idea of partition was maintained, although Tisza insisted on a resolution being passed stating that the Monarchy "is not conducting a war of conquest and does not plan the annexation of Serbia"; "rectifications of frontier which are strategically necessary" were declared "not excluded" by the resolution.

The German government was kept pretty well informed about the Austro-Hungarian note. Although the text was not received until the evening of July 22, the main points were known and approved; and Zimmermann was of the opinion that "Serbia cannot accept any such demands, which are incompatible with its dignity as a sovereign state" and that "the result would be war." Therefore, on July 21, Jagow renewed the assurances that "Germany would stand by Austria-Hungary with all its strength." He also suggested that the presentation of the note in Belgrade, originally timed for 5:00 P.M. on July 23, should be postponed for an hour, in order to insure that its content would not be known in St. Petersburg until after the president of the French Republic and the French premier, who were on a visit to the tsar, had left the Russian capital. After the war, Jagow asserted that when he received the text of the note, he had thought it "pretty sharp," but that it was too late to make any change. Actually, in July 1914, Jagow declared that he "agreed entirely" with the contents of the note; and since he had twenty-two hours at his disposal before its presentation, there was ample time for objection and change.

On July 20 the text of the note was forwarded to Baron Giesl, the Austro-Hungarian minister in Belgrade, with instructions to present it to the Serbian government on Thursday, July 23. On the next day it was submitted to the emperor for approval; and, before that approval was given, it was communicated to the German ambassador in Vienna, who sent it by mail to Berlin.

The note was framed with the expectation that Serbia would reject its demands and that an excuse for war would thereby be provided. The minutes of the ministerial councils show that the decision for war against Serbia was taken in the full realization that this would in all probability also mean war with Russia: which was precisely why no decision was taken until German assistance was absolutely assured. Apparently, the ministers and advisers of Francis Joseph had persuaded themselves that only by military action against Serbia could they hope to crush the Yugoslav national movement and stay the disintegration of the Monarchy and that, even though this would involve the danger of war with Russia, the military situation was more favorable than it would be later. On the other hand, they could not comprehend that the Yugoslav problem and the other symptoms of internal unrest were the result of the Dual system which they insisted on maintaining or that their policy of war would be opposed by a majority of the peoples of the state. If ever there was a vicious circle, this was one.

Hoping to take Europe by surprise, the Austro-Hungarian statesmen volubly offered assurances of their pacific intentions. In three speeches to the Hungarian parliament Tisza conveyed the impression that serious complications were not probable; the chief of staff and the minister of war went on leave. Berchtold assured Shebeko, the Russian ambassador, that Austria "in no way intended to provoke a conflict" with Serbia, and on July 20 the latter departed for Russia. The French ambassador, Dumaine, was told, on July 22, that the Austrian demands would be "acceptable to the dignity of the Serbs" and that he could count on "a peaceful result."[7]

The German government co-operated in this scheme of reassuring the other powers. When the restless emperor, who was cruising in Norwegian waters, grew nervous as the day of the ultimatum ap-

[7] On July 16 Count Lützow, one-time Austro-Hungarian ambassador in Rome, visited Sir Maurice de Bunsen, the British ambassador in Vienna, and gave him a hint as to the seriousness of the situation. Bunsen told Shebeko (but apparently not his French colleague) and telegraphed to London; but it is not clear that the warning was taken very seriously. A French agent managed to obtain a fairly accurate summary of the impending note, but his information was not received in Paris until July 24, after the ultimatum had been handed in at Belgrade.

proached, particularly about the German fleet, the chancellor telegraphed to him that "any premature recall of our fleet might cause general uneasiness." The press was kept well in hand, and not until July 20 did the *Norddeutsche Allgemeine Zeitung* assert that Austria's relations needed to be clarified and that any dispute should be localized. The foreign office suggested to Albert Ballin, head of the Hamburg-American Line, that he should get in touch with English friends; Ballin came to Berlin and, on learning that Austria would address "a very sharp note" to Serbia, was easily persuaded to go to London to study the situation.

If it is easy to understand why Vienna and Berlin were anxious to keep the Entente Powers ignorant of their plans, the decision not to inform Italy is less comprehensible, for, under the Triple Alliance, Italy was entitled to notice of any projected Austrian action in the Balkans, so that it might demand compensation for its approval. Berchtold professed to fear that Italy would reveal his intentions to Serbia and Russia; he was also greatly annoyed by the attitude of Italy in respect of Albania, where the Prince of Wied was having endless difficulties. But the main reason was, no doubt, that the Austrian plan for the subjection of Serbia was obviously contrary to the interest of Italy, and to keep Italy in the dark seemed the only sensible course to take.

The Italian government suspected that something was brewing and continually urged moderation, pointing out, in passing, that an aggressive policy would defeat its own ends. The German ambassador in Rome, Flotow, warned that without compensation Italy would certainly not march with its allies. Jagow was sufficiently impressed by this argument to urge upon Berchtold the desirability of winning over Italy by promising it the Trentino; but the Austrian statesmen were deaf to argument, declaring that, as Austria intended no territorial aggrandizement for itself, the Italian claims would have no standing; and the German government finally decided to let events take their course.

In the countries of the Triple Entente, the death of the archduke was greeted with expressions of sympathy, but the general feeling was one of relief that a somewhat enigmatic personage had been removed from the scene. In Great Britain, which was facing a crisis over Irish Home Rule, the Balkan situation was not taken seriously. Nevertheless, Sir Edward Grey, the foreign secretary, twice advised Prince Lichnowsky, the German ambassador, that, out of regard for Russia, Austria should keep its action against Serbia "within certain bounds"; these warnings were duly transmitted to Berlin by the anxious ambassador but had no effect. To the Russian government Grey expressed the opinion that "it would be very desirable that Austria and Russia should discuss things together if they become difficult." To Serbia he gave the advice that it should offer "the utmost assurances" of good behavior in the future. To Austria itself Grey offered neither warning nor advice until July 23, when he pointedly referred to "the awful consequences involved in the situation" and remarked that "it required two to keep the peace." Throughout these weeks the British government had to think not only of Europe but also of Persia, where the activities of Russian agents were causing much irritation. The tsar had promised to stop the activities; but, at the same time, Sazonov, his foreign minister, was pressing Grey to accept a triple guarantee of their Asiatic possessions by Russia, Great Britain, and Japan. In the event of a serious European crisis, British policy was bound to be influenced by the fear of repercussions in Asia in the event that Russia should feel that it had not been adequately supported by Great Britain.

In France, also, the early summer of 1914 was marked by political turmoil. The Left bloc in the chamber of deputies desired the repeal of the three years' military service restored in 1913; and only with difficulty had a cabinet been formed under René Viviani, a Republican Socialist, which was willing to maintain the three years' law until an effective substitute could be devised. In July a startling indictment of the deficient organization and equipment of the army was issued by Senator Humbert, so that several newspapers began to play up the excellent condition of the Russian army. The general public, however, was chiefly interested in the trial of Mme. Caillaux, the wife of a prominent politician, for the murder of a newspaper editor during the spring. On the question of Sarayevo, the French press took the side of Serbia; the attitude of the government was, however, correct and reserved, and the Quai d'Orsay was not greatly alarmed by the reports received from Vienna (no news came in from Belgrade after July 14 because the minister was taken ill and his successor did not arrive until July 25). On July 15 President Poincaré and Viviani left for a visit to Russia. Inasmuch as Viviani was inexperienced in diplomacy, the Quai d'Orsay prepared a number of memoranda to guide him in his discussions with Sazonov, the Russian foreign minister; the crime of Sarayevo occupied the fourteenth place in the list of seventeen subjects.

The position of Russia was difficult. The government did not wish to see the Near Eastern question reopened, but Russian opinion took a keen interest in the fate of the Balkan peoples and was exceedingly resentful of the Austrian and German policies as manifested in the Bosnian crisis and the Balkan wars. Early in July, Sazonov issued a friendly warning to Austria not to search for the instigators of the crime on Serbian territory and not to make demands which would threaten "the national independence of Serbia." At the same time he advised Serbia to remain calm and to be prepared to make redress to Austria if the latter could establish grounds for complaint.

On July 20 the two French statesmen arrived for three days of intensive entertaining and discussions. Unfortunately, no records, French or Russian, of the conversations have been preserved; but there is no doubt that the Franco-Russian alliance was reaffirmed and that a decision was taken to try to restrain Austria-Hungary from an intervention in the internal affairs of Serbia and to maintain the balance of power in Europe. Poincaré rejected a British suggestion for direct Austro-Russian conversations as "very dangerous" and reminded the Austrian ambassador, Count Szápáry, that since Serbia had "friends," a Balkan crisis might lead to "regrettable consequences"; Sazonov warned Austria of the "dangerous consequences" which might result from its making demands "incompatible with the dignity of Serbia." The German and Austrian ambassadors, however, were not greatly impressed by the French visit and discounted the manifestations of solidarity, perhaps because serious strikes were taking place at the moment in the Russian capital and the demonstrations in honor of Poincaré were said to have been organized by the police. The French statesmen departed from St. Petersburg late on July 23, without knowing that at 6:00 P.M. an Austro-Hungarian ultimatum had been presented in Belgrade.

When the news of Sarayevo was received in Serbia, public opinion was torn between satisfaction over the disappearance of a hated enemy and fear of what Austria-Hungary might do. Certain newspapers indulged in reckless and vituperative language; and the fact that the official organ of the Serbian government observed all the proprieties failed to undo the damage, for the language of the Serbian press had much to do with the conversion of Tisza to a belligerent program (see above). The government also made a blunder by failing to inaugurate an investigation into the antecedents of the crime and by allowing Tsiganovich to disappear "somewhere out of Belgrade." Its position was indeed difficult, for an election campaign was in progress and any concession to Austria-Hungary would have been denounced by the Black Hand. Pashich did not, therefore, do more than promise the co-operation of his government when the inquiry at Sarayevo had been completed, so far as was "compatible with international usage," and proclaim the desire to "maintain friendly relations with Austria-Hungary."[8]

From Russia no advice was received, except to drop negotiations for a Serbo-Montenegrin union; from Great Britain came only a general admonition to give Austria "the utmost assurances" against any future plots; from France came no word of any kind. But what Serbia did or did not do probably made little difference, for the Dual Monarchy had determined on war.

At 6:00 P.M. on Thursday, July 23, Giesl presented the Austro-Hungarian demands in a note which Grey described as "the most formidable document [he] had ever seen addressed by one state to another that was independent" and required a satisfactory reply within forty-eight hours. Fortunately, the premier, who was off campaigning, was located in southern Serbia and was able to reach Belgrade the next morning.

The note began by quoting the Serbian declaration of March 31, 1909, by which Serbia promised to "live on good neighborly terms" with Austria-Hungary. This promise had not been fulfilled; on the contrary, Serbia had connived at "a subversive movement," which had culminated in the crime of Sarayevo; that crime had been planned in Belgrade; and Serbian officials had helped in its execution. The Serbian government was, therefore, to publish a declaration on July 26, condemning and repudiating all activity directed against Austria-Hungary, and, in addition, to accept ten specific demands:

[8] On July 10 the Russian minister to Serbia, Hartvig, returned to Belgrade from a short vacation and died the same evening, while visiting his Austrian colleague. In spite of fantastic stories about the cause of death, which actually resulted from a heart attack, the funeral was held quietly, and the incident deserves mention only because of Hartvig's immense prestige in Serbia. In Giesl's opinion, Hartvig would have advised the Serbian government to accept the Austrian demands.

1. To suppress any publication directed against Austria-Hungary;

2. To dissolve the *Narodna Odbrana* and to suppress similar societies in the future;

3. To eliminate anti-Austrian propaganda from the public schools;

4. To remove army officers and civil functionaries guilty of propaganda against the Monarchy;

5. To accept the collaboration of Austrian representatives for the suppression of the subversive movement;

6. To take judicial proceedings against accessories to the Sarayevo plot, with Austrian delegates taking part in the investigation;

7. To arrest Tankosich and Tsiganovich;

8. To prevent the illicit traffic in arms and to punish the officials who had helped the conspirators to cross the frontier;

9. To explain hostile utterances of Serbian officials;

10. To notify the Austro-Hungarian government of the execution of these measures.

The note was not a demand, on legal and juridical grounds, for the punishment of criminals but a political *démarche*; and it was regarded as such particularly because Point 5 involved, at least in the opinion of the Entente Powers, interference with the sovereignty of Serbia. For that reason it has been condemned by most neutral, and even some German, historians.

The ultimatum was communicated to the powers for their information on the morning of July 24, together with a statement that a dossier supporting the Austrian demands was available.[9] These demands, it was urged, were "in full accordance with the feelings of all civilized nations," which did not tolerate regicide and were unwilling for "the peace of Europe to be continually disturbed by movements emanating from Belgrade." The German government asserted that the Austrian action was "equitable and moderate" and argued that the matter ought to be "settled exclusively between Austria-Hungary and Serbia" because "every interference of another power would, owing to the different treaty obligations, be followed by incalculable consequences." In other words, war was to be the alternative to accepting the Austro-Hungarian program.

[9] The dossier was not ready until July 25, and then only in German. It was not circulated to the foreign offices until the following week, until after the declaration of war against Serbia; and it had no influence on the decisions of the Entente Powers.

In Rome the reception of the ultimatum was very cold, the foreign minister, the Marchese di San Giuliano, declaring that "Italy could not consider itself under any engagement with reference to the further consequences of this action"; the press was highly critical. In Paris the acting foreign minister, Bienvenu-Martin, hardly knowing what to say in the absence of Poincaré and Viviani, uttered some guarded commonplaces about "the duty of Serbia to proceed energetically against any accomplices of the murders of Sarayevo" and expressed his desire for a peaceful settlement; the language was optimistically interpreted by the German and Austrian ambassadors. The press, however, was critical and was not impressed by the argument for "localization." In London the press, especially the Liberal and Radical papers, was more friendly. Grey, on the other hand, was exceedingly stern. He refused to "discuss the merits of the dispute" and told Count Mensdorff, the Austrian ambassador, that he "felt great apprehension"; to Prince Lichnowsky he spoke about the "danger of a European war." He declined to exert any pressure on Russia in favor of localization and proposed that England, France, Germany, and Italy should undertake to mediate between Russia and Austria.

What really mattered was the impression in St. Petersburg. When Sazonov read the note, he exclaimed, "That means a European war," and summoned a council of ministers for the afternoon. To the Austrian and German ambassadors he insisted that the matter at issue was "a European affair," not a mere Austro-Serbian quarrel—an attitude reaffirmed by a communiqué which stated that Russia "cannot remain indifferent" to the dispute. The press was practically unanimous in condemning the Austrian action.

Sazonov's first move was to address an appeal to Sir George Buchanan, the British ambassador, that "His Majesty's government would proclaim their solidarity with France and Russia," arguing that this would deter Austria and Germany from going to war. As Buchanan could give no such assurances, Sazonov telegraphed to Vienna to ask for an extension of the forty-eight-hour time limit and to Belgrade to advise the Serbs that they "should make no attempt whatever to offer resistance" but should retire and appeal to the powers.[10] But he counted very little on any extension of time, for the

---

[10] Sazonov urged "extreme moderation" on Spalaykovich, the Serbian minister in St. Petersburg, but did not advise the Serbian government how to reply to the Austrian note; and he declined to make any specific promises of help.

council of ministers sanctioned, in principle, the mobilization of the four southern military districts against Austria and the Black Sea fleet, the purchase of military stores, and the withdrawal of funds from Germany and Austria. On the following day (July 25) Sazonov renewed his appeal for British solidarity (this time in the name of the balance of power) and drafted a letter for the Emperor Nicholas to send to King George; he likewise advised Serbia to address a request for mediation to the British government. But, he told Buchanan, "Russia cannot allow Austria to crush Serbia and become the predominant power in the Balkans, and, secure of the support of France, [it] will face all the risks of war."

On the military side, the measures recommended by the ministers were formally sanctioned by the tsar, who authorized the mobilization of the Baltic fleet as well; but the mobilization was not to be ordered "until Austrian troops have crossed the Serbian frontier." At the request of the general staff, troops in summer camps were recalled to barracks, cadets in military schools were promoted to officer rank, martial law was proclaimed in fortresses on the frontier, and, above all, the "period preparatory to war" was proclaimed as of July 26, which permitted the taking of a large number of measures preliminary and necessary to mobilization—measures which would have to be taken along the German, as well as the Austrian, frontier.

From the moment that the Austrian ultimatum was known in St. Petersburg, the highest officials of the Russian government and the leading generals assumed that Austria would make war on Serbia and that Russia must go to the assistance of the little Slav state; the only hope for peace lay in Germany's restraining Austria. But since there was no evidence of Germany's doing this, the Russian government began immediately to prepare for war; at the same time, it decided to await overt action by Austria, and to offer a diplomatic compromise which would allow Austria a large measure of satisfaction. Russia preferred peace; but if Austria insisted on war with Serbia, it must also face war with Russia. Possibly because Poincaré and Viviani were at sea, these military decisions were taken without the French government being consulted; but the decisions were communicated to Paléologue, the French ambassador, who reported them to Paris, and no objections were raised by either the French foreign office or the French general staff. The British government, as a desirable ally, was also informed.

Meanwhile, both Great Britain and France were supporting at Vienna the Russian request for an extension of the time limit of the Austrian note, and were urging Serbia, in general terms, to offer every satisfaction compatible with honor and independence. To St. Petersburg, Grey telegraphed an Austrian statement that a rupture with Serbia would be followed by military "preparations" (rather than actual operations); and to Berlin the forecast of a conciliatory Serbian reply, together with an expression of hope that Germany might induce Austria to "take a favorable view of it." At the same time the Entente Powers endeavored to make clear the probable consequences of Austria's refusal.

The German press almost unanimously approved of the Austrian note; and the German government, on July 24, declared that it was "now unable to advise Vienna to draw back." Jagow, the foreign minister, denied that he had known the Austrian demands until they were communicated on the morning of July 24, and his effrontery knew no bounds: while "passing on" to Vienna Grey's request for an extension of the time limit, he deliberately delayed taking even this step until too late; similarly, he put off receiving the Russian chargé until an hour before the time limit expired. But this was not all. On learning that Austria intended to follow up the diplomatic rupture with Serbia by mobilization rather than by immediate war, the German foreign office protested strongly to Szögyény and urged both an immediate declaration of war and military operations, in order to avoid "the danger of intervention of other powers." Austria, Szögyény was told, "should go ahead at once and present the world with a *fait accompli.*"

If Jagow was dishonest and deceitful, Berchtold exhibited both bravado and ingenuity. He solemnly told Prince Kudachev, the Russian chargé, that "nothing was further from our minds than to humiliate Serbia" and that he had tried "to eliminate from the note everything which might create such an impression"! But since his instinct told him that the Entente representatives would be wishing to see him, he conveniently betook himself to Ischl on Saturday, July 25, in order to be with the Emperor Francis Joseph when the ultimatum should expire. Consequently Kudachev, who had received Sazonov's instructions to ask for an extension of the time limit, was reduced to telegraphing to Berchtold en route and getting a noncommittal reply from the officials of the Ballplatz. Meanwhile, everything was made ready for immediate mobilization if Serbia refused the Austrian demands.

Since the Belgrade archives have not been opened by the Yugoslav government, the course of events in the Serbian capital on July 24-25 is somewhat obscure. Certain of the Austrian demands were unacceptable, especially the dismissal of army officers and the participation of Austrian officials in any investigation, and the cabinet was in continuous session. According to one account, Pashich persuaded the other ministers to reserve final decision until an answer could be received to an appeal for help which the prince regent telegraphed to the tsar on July 24; but, when at noon on July 25 no word had been received from Russia, it was decided to accept the Austrian demands, including "a mixed commission of inquiry, provided that appointment of such commission can be proved to be in accordance with international usage." But in the early afternoon, telegrams were received from Russia urging Serbia to resist and promising help. The reply was thereupon recast and the participation of Austrian officials refused, and mobilization was ordered at 3:00 P.M.

In spite of some circumstantial evidence to support it, this version is of doubtful authenticity. In the collection of Russian documents published by the Soviet government, there are only two telegrams from St. Petersburg to Belgrade—one, on July 24, advising Serbia not to resist an Austrian invasion, and a second, on July 25, urging an appeal to British mediation; it seems inconceivable that the Soviet editors would have omitted telegrams encouraging Serbia to war.[11] This version, in short, rests upon the *ipse dixit* of several journalists. Another story to the effect that the Serbian reply, at least in its main lines, was formulated by an official of the French foreign office, Philippe Berthelot, also lacks documentary foundation. It seems more probable that the Serbs were left very much to their own devices.

The Serbian reply to the Austrian note was handed to Giesl a few minutes before 6:00 P.M. on Saturday, July 25. Since the Serbian note did not accept the Austrian demands *in toto*, Giesl at once broke off diplomatic relations and left Belgrade at 6:30. Arrived at Semlin, across the river, he telephoned to Vienna. The news was promptly relayed to Ischl; and at 9:23 P.M. Francis Joseph ordered the mobilization of eight corps, or half his army, for operations against Serbia, the first day of mobilization to be Tuesday, July 28.

[11] The Serbian minister in St. Petersburg, Spalaykovich, denied sending such telegrams; but until the Serbian documents are published, his statement cannot be verified.

The Serbian reply went much further toward conciliation than had been expected. Although not an integral acceptance of the Austrian demands, for there were numerous reservations, on only one point was there a definite refusal: the participation of Austrian officials in the judicial inquiry (Point 6); but the offer was made to refer the whole dispute to the great powers or to the arbitration of the Hague Tribunal. The Austro-Hungarian government was able to pick out many flaws in detail, some of which were justified; and, undoubtedly, a cursory reading creates an unduly favorable impression. Nevertheless, the verdict of history is likely to be that, not of disappointed Austrian officials who hoped for out-and-out rejection, but of the two highest personages of the German Empire. The chancellor, Bethmann Holl-weg, declared that "the Serbian reply had in fact agreed to the Austrian wishes except on unimportant points." The German emperor was even more explicit: "This is more than one could have expected! . . . With it every reason for war disappears. . . . I am convinced that on the whole the wishes of the Dual Monarchy have been acceded to. The few reservations which Serbia makes in regard to individual points can, in my opinion, be cleared up by negotiation." Unfortunately for all concerned, Austria-Hungary was determined on a military solution.

To achieve this solution as easily as possible, the Central Powers desired to "localize" the dispute; that is, they were anxious to prevent the intervention of Russia. Austria accordingly issued assurances to Russia that "territorially the Monarchy is saturated and does not wish to possess itself of any portion of Serbia"; it further promised to "con-sider the great political interests of Russia" in the Balkans. It declined, however, to assume "any binding engagement."

German policy was more complicated. Very reluctantly Berchtold and Conrad, on July 27, yielding to German pressure, promised to declare war at once, instead of waiting for the completion of Austro-Hungarian mobilization on August 12. Germany had, therefore, to "keep the ring" while its ally acted. So a sharp telegram was sent to St. Petersburg:

> Preparatory military measures on the part of Russia aimed at us in any way would compel us to take military measures for our own pro-tection, which would have to consist in the mobilization of the army. Mobilization, however, would mean war.

And for three days, July 26-28, German diplomacy tried to drive a wedge between Russia and France. Five times the German ambassador in Paris, Baron Schoen, attempted to extract from the officials of the Quai d'Orsay some kind of statement manifesting the "solidarity" of France and Germany and implying, consequently, a reluctance on the part of France to follow Russia. All he got for his pains was reiteration of the French view that France could not restrain Russia unless Germany was prepared to do likewise with Austria—which Schoen recognized was impossible. The Russian ambassador, Izvolsky, was quite pleased with "the correct understanding of the situation manifested" by the French officials. The French press also grew steadily stiffer in tone and began to prepare public opinion for meeting the Austro-German challenge. By July 28 the German maneuvers had produced just the opposite effect of what Berlin desired.

From the practical point of view, what mattered was the evident determination of the military authorities not to be caught napping. They assumed that war was coming and promptly began to take measures, such as the recall of troops to barracks and the suspension of leaves—necessary preliminaries to mobilization. Whether they were only keeping pace with what the Germans were doing, as they claimed, or were going faster than the Germans, as the latter asserted, cannot be determined, and was immaterial if either the French government or the German had decided to fight rather than accept diplomatic defeat at the hands of the other—which was, in fact, the situation. On the evening of July 27 the Russian military attaché, Colonel Ignatyev, asked the French generalissimo, Joffre, whether, if Germany mobilized only part of its forces against Russia, France would feel itself compelled under the Franco-Russian alliance to order mobilization. Joffre's reply that the government would have to decide shows that the French general staff was not pushing for war, but it is worth noting that he did not suggest that Russia should not order mobilization without consulting and without the consent of France.

Although Russian opinion was considerably excited by the Austro-Serbian rupture, Sazonov did not let himself be carried away. He "urgently" begged for German assistance to get the Austrian ultimatum modified in "some of its points" and appealed to Italy as well; just as Germany was trying to separate the western powers from Russia, so the latter endeavored to detach the allies of Austria. Much more to the point was Sazonov's proposal to Vienna, inspired by a suggestion of the German ambassador, Count Pourtalès, for "a private exchange of views" between himself and the Austrian ambassador, Count Szápáry, "in order to redraft certain articles of the Austrian note." The Russian minister recognized that Austria's desire to stop the Serbian agitation was "perfectly legitimate," and he "guaranteed the result" of the proposed conversation. Pourtalès and Szápáry were very pleased, all the more so because the minister of war assured the German military attaché that "nothing but preparatory measures" were being taken. In court circles there was confident hope in the mediation of the German emperor, and Pourtalès reported to Berlin that "there is little enthusiasm for war."

Actually, the Russian attitude was stiffening. On July 27 the tsar telegraphed to the prince regent of Serbia that if the efforts for peace failed, "Russia will in no case disinterest itself in the fate of Serbia"; and Sazonov informed Paris and London that, "if there is a question of exercising moderating influence in St. Petersburg, we reject it in advance, for we have adopted at the outset a point of view which we cannot change." He refused to be impressed by assurances of Austrian territorial disinterestedness. Also, the military authorities went ahead with their measures, reports of which now began to reach Berlin. The period preparatory to war was extended to the Caucasus and Asia; the export of horses was forbidden; and the minister of war asked that the sale of liquor be forbidden in the districts slated for mobilization. Numerous directives were also issued to the naval commanders in the Baltic. There is no evidence that the soldiers were trying to control policy, but they, like their French colleagues, were determined to be ready if war came.

In the Russian view the best chance of preventing war lay in a declaration of British solidarity with France and Russia; and both Sir Arthur Nicolson, the permanent undersecretary of the British foreign office, and Sir Eyre Crowe, the assistant secretary, agreed with Sazonov. But Grey was resolved that he would not have on his head the "blood guilt" of promising British help when it might not be forthcoming, for, whatever his personal feelings might be that the interests of Britain required it to fight by the side of France, he knew it to be "very doubtful whether the cabinet, parliament, and the country would take this view on the outbreak of war." To Sazonov's appeals he therefore replied that he could not do more than point out at Vienna and Berlin that "if the war became general, it would be difficult for England to remain neutral."

Since this was bound not to satisfy Russia, Grey, on July 25, told Lichnowsky that he "counted with certainty on the Austrian mobilization being followed by that of Russia" and that he would not urge Russia not to mobilize; he therefore proposed that the four powers not directly interested should try to "arrange matters" between Austria and Russia. Grey then informed Count Benckendorff, the Russian ambassador, of this proposal; but in order to allay Benckendorff's fears, Grey added that he had made his proposal to Germany "on the assumption that Russia would mobilize" (which Grey thought it would be justified in doing, because of the severity of the Austrian demands). German writers bitterly criticize Grey for what they consider open encouragement to Russia to mobilize.

During the next twenty-four hours the situation grew more and more ominous. Austria had broken with Serbia and ordered partial mobilization. The German fleet had received orders to concentrate off the Norwegian coast. Russia was ready to mobilize 1,100,000 men. The British admiralty, at the instigation of Prince Louis of Battenberg, the first sea lord, therefore decided to hold together the First Fleet, which had been scheduled to disperse on the following day; and this was announced on Monday morning, with the hope of "sobering the Central Powers."

As early as July 24, the French ambassador in London, Paul Cambon, had urged upon Grey the necessity of mediation by the four powers, not between Austria and Russia, but between Austria and Serbia; Grey thought it imperative to discover whether Germany would join in mediation, and his proposal for mediation between Austria and Russia would serve to "smoke out" Berlin. The German government accepted this proposal on July 26; but before the news was received in London, Grey decided to propose a conference of the four powers not directly interested, "in order to endeavour to find an issue to prevent complications," and to request of Vienna, St. Petersburg, and Belgrade that "pending results of the conference all active military operations should be suspended." This proposal was accepted by Italy immediately and by France on the following day; Sazonov declared that he preferred direct negotiations with Vienna but that if these failed, he would accept the British plan, for its purpose was to prevent an Austrian invasion of Serbia, which would almost certainly lead to Russian intervention—and which Germany had been urging upon Austria.

The British proposal was "extremely inopportune" for the German government, because Austria, though reluctantly willing to declare war on Serbia, would not be ready to commence military operations until August 12—so that a conference would have several weeks in which to work out a compromise. In these circumstances the obvious course for Germany was to reject the British proposal. Prince Henry, the emperor's brother, had reported a conversation with King George V in which the latter had said: "England would maintain neutrality in case war should break out between the continental powers."[12] Albert Ballin had returned from England full of hope. The news from Russia was also optimistic, for Pourtalès was misrepresenting the calmness of Sazonov as irresolution and weakness. Accordingly, on July 27, shortly before the return of William II from Norway and without his knowledge, the German government declined the conference on the grounds that "we cannot summon Austria before a European court of justice in its business with Serbia" and that a direct understanding between St. Petersburg and Vienna appeared to be "feasible." In the light of subsequent events, it appears correct to say that the German refusal destroyed the last chance of preventing a European war.

William II reached Potsdam on the afternoon of July 27 and summoned his principal advisers. According to the biographer of Falkenhayn, "it was decided to fight the business through [*die Sache durchzufechten*], cost what it might." The precise meaning of the phrase "fight the business through" may be open to doubt, but the conduct of the German government speaks for itself. The conciliatory Serbian reply had been communicated to Jagow about noon (that is, *before* the conference was rejected); yet it was apparently kept from the emperor, for, when he read it the next morning, he was fairly bowled over. In the next place, when news was received from Rome that "Serbia would be willing to agree to the Austrian demands if they were presented by Europe" (i.e., by the Concert), the suggestion was not sent on to Vienna. Thirdly, Jagow held up for some hours, before transmitting to Vienna, Sazonov's wish for direct conversations with Berchtold, and even then omitted the vital feature of Sazonov's proposal, namely, that Russia would advise Serbia to accept what might

[12] There is every reason to believe that King George made no such statement, but it was eagerly accepted by William II.

be agreed on by Russia and Austria. Jagow also expressed to Szögyény his regret at the postponement of the Austrian military operations. Finally, considerable pressure was put on Berchtold to accept the Italian demand for compensation, in order that the solidarity of the Triple Alliance might be maintained. Clearly, Germany was not prepared to make the slightest concession. No military measures were taken except to recall troops to barracks and to guard the railway lines; but the minister of war ordered grain purchases in the areas of military concentration, and the minister of the interior urged the mayor of Berlin to arrange that "Berlin is sufficiently provisioned for any event."

German policy had been predicated on the assumption that Britain would remain neutral in a general war. But on the evening of July 27 the news came that the British fleet was being kept together: which "changed the situation with a single stroke." It was also learned that the British government regarded the Serbian reply favorably and wished to take it as a "basis for discussion and pause"; Lichnowsky declared flatly that in the event of war "England will place itself unconditionally on the side of France and Russia." Lichnowsky was disliked and distrusted in Berlin; but his opinion was transmitted to Vienna, and Bethmann informed Berchtold that "by refusing every proposal for mediation [Germany] would be held responsible for the conflagration by the whole world and be represented as the veritable instigator of the war." He therefore could not decline to transmit Grey's proposal that the Serbian reply should be taken as the basis of negotiation. But he refrained from advising Berchtold to *accept* either this proposal or that of Sazonov: he was content to ask Berchtold's "opinion." Thus he was able to appear in the role of mediator without doing any mediating. And even this was a shabby trick.

For, earlier this same day, Jagow had told Szögyény that while Germany was transmitting to Vienna British proposals for mediation, it did not identify itself with them and was, in fact, opposed to them. In other words, the *démarche* of the chancellor was for form's sake only, in order that he might be able to say that he had acted as London desired, while his subordinate quietly sabotaged the plan. Grey accepted Bethmann's assurances and suspended his plan for a conference. It is further to be noted that although Berlin learned on the evening of July 27 that Austria would declare war the next day, the German government made no effort to stop this action, as it should have done if it had been in earnest about the British proposal.

Informed by Szögyény of Berlin's real attitude, Berchtold sent a declaration of war to Serbia on the morning of July 28. Tschirschky put off executing his instructions from Bethmann until the afternoon, thus permitting Berchtold to say that the German advice had been received "too late." Berchtold obtained the consent of the emperor only by assuring him that Serbian troops had attacked at Temes-Kubin; but he deleted this charge from the declaration of war because, as he informed Francis Joseph, it "has not been confirmed."

When Sazonov learned of the Austrian declaration of war, "he was carried away by the idea that a general war was inevitable"; and he promptly renewed his appeal to England for a declaration of solidarity. At the same time he notified Berlin that Russia would mobilize the military districts of Odessa, Kiev, Moscow, and Kazan, that is, the troops intended for use against Austria. This step was taken without consultation with France; but no doubt this seemed unnecessary, for the Russian diplomatic and military representatives in Paris were unanimous in affirming the resolution of France to fulfil its obligations. Although Buchanan repeatedly warned against any kind of mobilization, Benckendorff's telegrams from London, while cautiously worded, could be interpreted to mean that Grey sympathized with the Russian attitude and would not object to military action. Since Jagow had said that Germany would mobilize only if Russia mobilized on the German frontier or invaded Austria, partial mobilization seemed not only logical but well calculated to impress Austria without causing Germany to move.

This was, however, opposed by the chief of the general staff, General Yanushkevich, and the chief of the mobilization section, General Dobrorolsky, who had not prepared plans for partial mobilization and represented that a scheme concocted *ad hoc* would endanger general mobilization if that became necessary. Since Sazonov, for diplomatic reasons, opposed a general mobilization, two ukases were prepared, on the evening of July 28—one for partial, the other for general, mobilization; both were to be signed by the tsar, but the decision as to which should be published was left open.

What happened on the following day, July 29, is uncertain. Relying on the recollections of Russian generals and the diary of Baron Schilling, Sazonov's *chef de cabinet,* historians of the crisis have generally agreed that the tsar, albeit reluctantly, signed the ukase for general mobilization sometime during the day and that by evening the ukase had received the countersignatures of the ministers of war, the navy, and the interior, so that all was ready for issuing the order of general mobilization. Yet, in the documents published by the Soviet government, the only mention of mobilization on July 29 refers to *partial* mobilization.[13] Probably, therefore the tsar signed both ukases with the understanding that partial mobilization would be ordered at once and the question of general mobilization deferred (in spite of the insistence of Yanushkevich).

Sazonov was considerably ruffled to learn from Szápáry that Berchtold would not permit conversations about the Austrian demands on Serbia; and while they were still talking about this, Sazonov was informed by telephone that Austrian forces had bombarded Belgrade, which threw him into "a state of great excitement." He had not recovered when Pourtalès appeared to call his "serious attention to the fact that further continuation of Russia's measures of mobilization would force us [Germany] to mobilize and that a European war could then scarcely be prevented"—which meant that Germany had abandoned the attitude that it would not mobilize so long as Russian measures were confined to the Austrian frontier.

While Sazonov was still pondering this communication, the tsar telephoned to say that he had received a telegram from the German emperor urging him not to allow events to develop into a war,[14] which was in contradiction with what Pourtalès had just said. With the tsar's permission Sazonov at once got in touch with the generals; and it was decided that "in view of the small probability of avoiding war with Germany," general mobilization could not be longer delayed. The tsar was informed by telephone and consented. But just at the moment when Dobrorolsky was on the point of telegraphing the order for general mobilization to all points of the Russian Empire, a message arrived from the tsar to stop the mobilization. He had received another and more conciliatory telegram from William II, to whom he had already suggested that the Austro-Serbian problem be referred to the Hague Tribunal; Nicholas II therefore canceled the *general* mobilization; but in face of the objections of the minister of war and

[13] Sazonov told Buchanan that only partial mobilization had been decided on, and this may well have been true at the moment of the conversation.

[14] This telegram crossed with one from Nicholas to William, to much the same effect. The two monarchs appear to have turned to each other spontaneously, as if conscious that events were getting beyond their control.

the chief of the general staff to further delays, he allowed the *partial* mobilization to stand.

Meanwhile Sazonov had informed Paris and London of Pourtalès' *démarche* and declared that he had to assume that "war is inevitable"; he counted on France and once more appealed for British solidarity. He also informed Buchanan and Paléologue that it had been decided "to commence preparations for general mobilization." Buchanan transmitted the news to London. Paléologue drafted a telegram to the same effect; but before it was sent, the general mobilization had been countermanded, and on hearing this the ambassador omitted the relevant sentence from his message; apparently he did not think it necessary to inform his government that the Russian government had actually decided on general mobilization and then had changed its mind.

While the Russian government was thus hesitating between partial and general mobilization, a new diplomatic situation was shaping itself. Grey and his principal advisers were of the opinion that Britain must support France, in the event of war, in order to prevent German domination of Europe; but the cabinet was badly divided and gave Grey no lead. When, therefore, Germany had rejected his proposal for a conference, he fell back on a direct exchange of views between Austria and Russia, which was "the most preferable method of all," and invited Jagow to suggest how mediation of the four powers might best be applied. By way of precaution, the First Fleet put to sea late on July 28 and took up its war station at Scapa Flow.

On the morning of that day the German emperor received the text of the Serbian reply and one of three warning telegrams sent the day before by Lichnowsky. William II thought the reply "a great moral victory for Austria," by which "every reason for war is removed"; and he straightway suggested to Jagow that Austria should occupy Belgrade as a guarantee that the Serbian promises were actually executed. This put the German foreign office "on the spot," for to do as the emperor desired would be tantamount to reversing the policy of July 5. Seemingly nothing was done until the news arrived that Austria had actually declared war on Serbia. Then, some twelve hours after the emperor's suggestion was received, Bethmann communicated it to Vienna; but he spoke of obtaining "the complete fulfilment of the Austrian demands" (rather than of the Serbian promises) and instructed Tschirschky to "very carefully avoid giving the impression that we wish to hold Austria back." The real object of the *démarche* was, as the chancellor naïvely explained, to put Russia in the wrong and once more to give the appearance of mediation without actually mediating. At the same time Bethmann telegraphed to St. Petersburg that "the declaration of war in no way changes the situation"! The only military measure taken on this day was the recall of troops to which "definite special tasks" had been assigned— probably the seizure of Liége by brigades on a peace footing before mobilization. Pressure from Vienna for some kind of declaration in St. Petersburg against Russian mobilization was indeed resisted; but the Austrian chief of staff was getting nervous, for his scheme of mobilization made it imperative for him to know by Saturday, August 1, at the latest, whether he would have to convert the mobilization against Serbia, already under way, into a general mobilization against Russia; and on July 29 Szögyény once more asked Jagow to act in this sense. It was probably because of this *démarche* that shortly after noon Bethmann warned St. Petersburg that "further continuance of Russia's measures of mobilization would force us to mobilize, and that a European war could then scarcely be prevented."[15]

In Berlin, as in St. Petersburg, Wednesday, July 29, was an exciting day. Falkenhayn desired the proclamation of "threatening danger of war" (to meet the measures reported from Russia); but he was opposed, first by Bethmann and later by the emperor, who insisted on awaiting the result of the German *démarche* in Vienna. Even Moltke did not press for military steps. He was convinced that war was coming, and he preferred to fight in 1914 rather than later; but, like Bethmann, he was anxious that Germany should not seem to be precipitating the war, and, since he knew that Germany could wait two or three days with its mobilization, he was determined not to show his hand too soon. Consequently, the only step taken was to order military protection of the railways.

What really worried the German authorities was the situation in the west. Here the plan of campaign called for the seizure of Liége by peacetime units maintained at full war strength and the rapid invasion of Belgium—a *coup de main* the success of which was threatened by the preparations which Belgium was feverishly making. Three days previously Moltke had drafted an ultimatum to be pre-

[15] A warning was also sent to France that, in view of French preparations for war, "Germany would have to take measures of self-protection."

sented to the Belgian government in due course: it alleged that "French forces intend to march on the line of the Meuse by Givet and Namur," and stated that for "self-preservation" Germany must "anticipate such a hostile attack"; if Belgium maintained "a friendly attitude," Germany would make good all the damage done by its troops. On the evening of July 29 the text of this document was dispatched to the German legation in Brussels, to be held ready for presentation later.

Much more significant was the action of the chancellor. During the latter part of the day, consultations had taken place at Potsdam between the emperor, the chancellor, and various military and civil officials; William II seems to have made much of his brother Henry's report that, according to King George, England would remain neutral. At any rate, after his return to Berlin, Bethmann sent for the British ambassador, Sir Edward Goschen, and made "a strong bid" for British neutrality, declaring that "Germany aimed at no territorial acquisitions at the expense of France"; but he declined to give a similar assurance in respect of the French colonies, and he evaded a question from Goschen about the neutrality of Belgium. Bethmann's query is intelligible only if he regarded a European war as practically certain.

Shortly after making his overture, Bethmann received staggering news from London. Grey, considering the situation "extremely serious," had proposed that Austria should occupy Belgrade and then announce its conditions for negotiation. This was very much the scheme hatched by William II and nominally sponsored at Vienna by the German government; but Grey had also given Lichnowsky a "friendly and private" warning that if France were drawn into the war, "the British government would see itself compelled to make decisions promptly." In other words, Great Britain would enter the war. There was also, at the moment, no prospect of an Austro-Italian understanding, owing to the stubbornness and touchiness of Berchtold and San Giuliano; and Romania was also apparently going to remain neutral, instead of lining up with Austria. Worst of all, perhaps, no answer had come from Vienna to the German *démarche* of the night before.

So Bethmann gathered himself together for a last move, which, if it did not prevent war, would at least saddle Russia with the responsibility for it. First of all, he sent a string of telegrams to St. Petersburg asking Russia to hold its hand (the news of the Russian decision for partial mobilization had reached Berlin) while Berlin tried to mediate in Vienna. To Vienna he sent six telegrams, urging Austria to negotiate with Russia—a reversal of the policy which had pushed Austria into war with Serbia and advised it to refuse all mediation! Bethmann urged Berchtold to accept the *Halt in Belgrad* and tried to minimize the importance of the Russian partial mobilization. He explained that if war came because Austria refused all mediation, "England will be against us and Italy and Romania will according to all signs not go with us." If Austria declined to negotiate with Russia, it would be impossible to make Russia responsible for the war. "We are ready to fulfil the obligations of our alliance," Bethmann concluded, "but must refuse to be drawn into a world conflagration by Vienna lightheartedly and without regard for our advice." It is to be noted, however, that he did not ask Austria not to invade Serbia—which was the essence of the Russian demands.

Vienna showed no disposition to follow Berlin's advice. Berchtold on the one hand renewed his request for a German declaration in St. Petersburg against Russian military measures and on the other hand maintained his refusal to allow Szápáry to discuss the note to Serbia with Sazonov, being content to give only vague assurances about the future status of Serbia. When Tschirschky presented Bethmann's demand for acceptance of Grey's proposal of mediation, Berchtold refused to answer until the next day, on the ground that Tisza would have to be consulted, and declined to discuss a limitation of military operations.[16] Late in the day (July 30), a threefold decision was reached: (1) to continue the war against Serbia; (2) to reject the British proposal; and (3) to order general mobilization on August 1. Since Bethmann had said that he did not wish to "hold Austria back," Berchtold took him at his word!

Berlin was not yet informed of these decisions; and Bethmann was getting desperate, for, in view of the Russian partial mobilization, he could not much longer resist the demands of the German military authorities for countermeasures, and, if he yielded to their demands, war and not peace would be the result. By July 30 Moltke and Falkenhayn were pressing for mobilization; but Bethmann held out, continuing to hope for a favorable reply from Vienna about the *Halt in*

---

[16] Technically the *Halt in Belgrad* was objectionable, for there were no troops available, the Austrian plan calling for an invasion of Serbia from the west.

Belgrad. As a result of "endless negotiations," it was finally settled, says Falkenhayn's biographer, that "a decision on the proclamation of 'threatening danger of war' must be made by noon the next day at the latest." While the language is not entirely clear, it seems to mean that Bethmann agreed to the proclamation of "threatening danger of war" not later than noon on July 31; and, since he had stated that "declaration of 'threatening danger of war' meant mobilization, and mobilization meant war," the conclusion may be fairly drawn that the decision for war was made in principle on July 30, on the basis of the Russian *partial* mobilization and at least twelve hours before any news was received of Russian *general* mobilization.[17] This view is supported by an extraordinary incident which was not revealed until after the war. Moltke saw Bethmann about noon; after the conference, he sent for the Austrian military attaché and dictated a message to Conrad, the substance of which was that "he considers the situation critical unless Austria-Hungary mobilizes at once against Russia" and that this would create the *casus foederis* for Germany. Italy should be offered an "adequate compensation," and the British proposal rejected. "A European war offers the last chance of preserving Austria-Hungary. Unconditional support of Germany." Later Moltke personally telegraphed to Conrad in the same sense. It is often asserted that these telegrams were sent behind the back of Bethmann, for they ran counter to the advice which the chancellor had sent the evening before and there is no evidence that he knew of them. But they are not inconsistent with the decision come to by the chancellor that "threatening danger of war" should be proclaimed not later than noon of July 31.

Germany now forced the situation. At the suggestion of Pourtalès, Sazonov had drafted a formula which at least offered the possibility of negotiation:

> If Austria, recognizing that its conflict with Serbia has assumed the character of a question of European interest, declares itself ready to eliminate from its ultimatum those points which infringe on the sovereign rights of Serbia, Russia agrees to stop all military preparations.

[17] Early in the afternoon of July 30 the *Berliner Lokal-Anzeiger* published an extra edition, announcing German mobilization. The edition was at once confiscated by the police, and the news officially denied by the foreign office. The incident has never been satisfactorily explained.

This was rejected by Jagow on the ground that it was "unacceptable" to Austria (although Vienna was not consulted). Several hours earlier Bethmann had sent an "urgent" telegram to Vienna stating that "if Vienna refuses every concession and especially declines the last proposal of Grey, it will hardly be possible any longer to place the blame for the European war on Russia"; and Tschirschky was instructed to speak "at once and most emphatically" to Berchtold in favor of Grey's proposal. Yet, shortly after Sazonov's formula was rejected, the instruction to Tschirschky was canceled, because, according to the general staff, "the military preparations of our neighbors, especially in the east, will force us to a speedy decision unless we wish to expose ourselves to the danger of surprise." What these preparations were was not specified. Conceivably, the Russian general mobilization (ordered late on July 30) was meant; but, since it is reasonable to suppose that if this step were known in Berlin[18] the fact would be mentioned in some document, the presumption must be that the soldiers persuaded the chancellor that his instruction to Tschirschky would have the effect of postponing the Austrian general mobilization —which Moltke was urging on Conrad. A laconic telegram to Paris, "Departure of Germans advisable," certainly supports the view expressed above that, in principle, the die had been cast for war; the next morning both Berchtold and Conrad learned that Germany intended to address an ultimatum to Russia on account of its military preparations. It seems clear that Bethmann yielded to the importunities of the military *before* the Russian general mobilization was known in Berlin. But, in order to place the blame for war on Russia, he relayed to Vienna, early on July 31, a telegram from King George to Prince Henry, received after he had canceled the instructions to Tschirschky, urging German support of the *Halt in Belgrad* plan; thus Bethmann could represent Germany as co-operating with England for the maintenance of peace.

On the morning of July 31 Berchtold, Stürgkh, Tisza, and Conrad met to take their final decisions. When Conrad read out his telegrams from Moltke, Berchtold exclaimed that "the most competent military authority" in Germany had now reassured them that Germany was not weakening; and the general mobilization was ordered immediately (instead of for the next day), before any news had been received of

[18] There is no evidence that the Russian mobilization was known in Berlin until the morning of July 31.

the Russian general mobilization.[19] Francis Joseph telegraphed to William II rejecting German advice to accept Grey's proposal, and this was formally confirmed by a ministerial council; not only that, but it was decided to formulate "new demands on Serbia" and to accept Italy's demands for compensation only if Austria-Hungary acquired territory permanently in the Balkans. At the same time, with the object of confusing them, Great Britain and France were now officially informed that Austria did not intend to make "any territorial acquisitions" in Serbia or to "infringe the sovereignty of the kingdom." Thus to the bitter end Berchtold refused all concessions. But, since he had explained his intentions to the German government and received its approval, he was entitled to go ahead, while the manner in which Germany, quite belatedly, urged concessions in the interest of peace could fairly be interpreted as meaning that this was for diplomatic reasons only and need not be taken seriously.

During these hectic days French diplomacy was passive, largely because the chief of state and the head of the government were absent; but all the precautions necessary for mobilization were taken. The problem facing France was extremely difficult: to avoid war if possible and at the same time to be prepared for it; not to rebuff Russia and thus endanger the alliance, lest France become isolated; and at the same time not be dragged into war by Russia in a cause not of direct concern to France. Upon the return of Poincaré and Viviani at noon on July 29 a cabinet meeting was held which lasted all afternoon; at its conclusion Viviani confirmed to Izvolsky "the firm determination of the French government to act in agreement" with Russia, a decision which, he said, was supported "by all classes of society and by all parties." During the night Izvolsky communicated a telegram from Sazonov reporting the German warning against Russian military measures and stating that "war is probably inevitable." Early on July 30 Viviani therefore telegraphed to St. Petersburg that while France was "resolved to fulfil all the obligations of the alliance," it hoped that "Russia should not immediately take any step which may offer Germany a pretext for a total or partial mobilization of its forces"; in other words, diplomacy should be given a final chance. The telegram

[19] A telegram from Warsaw reporting the Russian mobilization was received in Vienna at 9:00 A.M. on July 31, but the news was apparently not communicated to the council of ministers; at least it is not mentioned in the protocol of the meeting, and it was not put forward as justification for the Austrian mobilization.

was shown to Izvolsky, who was somewhat puzzled by it; the political director of the Quai d'Orsay, Margerie, explained that France did not wish to interfere with Russia's military preparations but wanted them to be "as little public and challenging in character as possible"; this was interpreted for the military attaché, Ignatyev, by the minister of war, Messimy, to mean that Russia should "refrain as far as possible from movements of troops on a large scale." What the minister had in mind was that Russia might order mobilization secretly but should not concentrate troops. At the demand of the commander-in-chief, General Joffre, the covering troops along the Franco-German frontier were ordered into position, but were to keep ten kilometers back from the frontier in order to avoid any incidents and to convince Britain of France's desire for peace.

The French advice was not followed by the Russian government. The general staff claimed, on July 30, to have received alarming news of German military preparations[20] and urged the tsar by telephone to consent once more to the general mobilization which he had rescinded the night before; but he refused. Thereupon Sazonov asked for an audience, which Nicholas II reluctantly granted for the afternoon. Before seeing the tsar, Sazonov received Pourtalès and, at the urgent request of the latter, drew up a formula according to which Russia would stop its military preparations if Austria would eliminate those demands which violated the sovereign rights of Serbia. It was natural, as Sazonov informed Izvolsky, that, "until we receive a thoroughly satisfactory answer from Austria through the German government, we shall continue our military preparations." But, instead of giving time for Berlin to secure such an answer, Sazonov proceeded to Peterhof and, after much argument, wrung consent for general mobilization from Nicholas, who realized that, however justified mobilization might be from the Russian point of view, it would be answered by German mobilization and would lead to war.[21] Sazonov telephoned the decision to the anxious generals at 4:00 P.M. At that time the false news of German mobilization circulated by the *Berliner Lokal-Anzeiger* had not been received in St. Petersburg; nor had a somewhat threatening telegram from William II reached Nicholas.

[20] The Russian documents published by the Soviet government do not contain reports of such preparations.

[21] Since Berlin rejected the formula without consulting Vienna (see above), Sazonov's slipperiness did not affect the march of events.

Thus the Russian government disregarded the French advice not to give Germany "any pretext" for partial or general mobilization. It is true that some effort was made to keep the order secret, in accordance with the French suggestion; but this proved impossible, for in the early morning of July 31 red posters announcing the mobilization were put up in the cities. Sazonov, however, evidently had a guilty conscience, for he only told Paléologue that in consequence of the disquieting news received about German preparations, the Russian government had "decided to proceed secretly to the first measures of general mobilization"; and he failed to notify the ambassador in Paris of the great decision.

Two interpretations of the Russian mobilization may be offered. In the negotiations for the Franco-Russian alliance it was stated that "the mobilization is the declaration of war," and Germany several times warned Russia that "mobilization means war." When, therefore, Russia ordered general mobilization on July 30, she "willed" and was responsible for the European war. So, at any rate, the German government and German writers have argued since 1914.[22] Actually, the matter is not so simple. In the winter of 1912-13 the Russian government adopted the plan of mobilizing and continuing to negotiate at the same time, for the longer the negotiations continued, the stronger the Russian position would be; hostilities were to begin only when ordered by the minister of war. This explains Sazonov's disingenuous conduct in proposing that if Germany could get negotiations started, Russia would stop its preparations, while at the same time he took steps to accelerate the preparations.

Obviously, the question cannot be answered in military terms exclusively. Russia possessed interests in the Balkans which it thought it must defend. Russia offered to negotiate about them, but Austria refused to negotiate. To be sure, Austria proffered assurances that it would not take Serbian territory for itself or infringe the sovereignty of Serbia. But the Russian government suspected that these assurances were not trustworthy, and the German and Austrian documents published in 1919 prove that the Russian suspicions were entirely justified. In face of the Austrian attitude, Russia's only course, if it were to defend its interests, was to exert pressure on Austria by

[22] The Austrian general staff, however, did not contend that "mobilization means war," Conrad being quite ready to negotiate after both Austria and Russia had mobilized.

mobilizing. Partial mobilization was technically impractical and was, moreover, denounced by Germany, who threatened mobilization and war. Russia was, accordingly, driven to general mobilization, although in the full realization that this step would lead to war. This general mobilization could have been postponed another day without danger; but, since Austria refused to make any concession under the pressure of the Russian partial mobilization (because it felt sure of German assistance), the general mobilization was only a question of time.

Russia and Austria-Hungary each ordered general mobilization without being aware of the other's action. The news of the former reached the other capitals on July 31; of the latter, except Berlin, on August 1. So there remained a bare chance for a diplomatic compromise: to which Grey addressed himself. Confronted on the morning of July 30 with the German bid for British neutrality, he rejected it as "a disgrace from which the good name of this country would never recover." But he declared that if peace could be preserved in the present crisis, he would try to promote an "arrangement" between Germany and the Entente Powers which would amount to what would now be called a treaty of mutual guarantee. He declined once more to proclaim the solidarity of England with France and Russia; and, finally, toward the end of the day, he produced a new formula, according to which Russia and other powers were to suspend their military preparations on condition that Austria, having occupied Belgrade, stopped there and consented to negotiate. Grey admitted that this offered only "a slender chance"; but, for the first time since the crisis began, he had asked Russia to stay its hand.

This "slender chance" was destroyed by the impetuous action of the German government. On the previous day Bethmann had promised the soldiers that the question of proclaiming "threatening danger of war" would be settled not later than noon on July 31; this was intended as the prelude to mobilization and war. But the consent of the emperor had apparently not yet been secured. As it happened, at 11:40 A.M. news arrived from St. Petersburg of the Russian general mobilization; and William II promptly agreed to the proclamation of "threatening danger of war," which was made at 1:00 P.M.

From this time on, political considerations yield to the military timetable, so that some exposition of the position of the German government is necessary. Down to 1913 the general staff had two plans of operations—one (the older) for defensive war in the west and an offensive campaign against Russia, the other (the Schlieffen plan) for an attack on France and defensive war in the east. But, on the assumption that both France and Russia would be involved in any European war, the older scheme had been abandoned; and in 1914 only one plan of campaign was available: the invasion of France, preceded by the violation of Belgian neutrality, this latter to be justified by the war with France. But on July 31 Germany had no quarrel with France: so that in order to force the situation as against France, it was necessary to address an ultimatum to Russia, which, if rejected, would justify a declaration of war on Russia; to this France, as the ally of Russia, was expected to reply with a declaration of war. Accordingly, at 3:30 P.M. ultimatums were addressed to both Russia and France. Russia was required to suspend all war measures against both Germany and Austria within twelve hours. France was given eighteen hours in which to state whether it would remain neutral in a Russo-German war; a negative answer was expected, but if an affirmative one was given, then Germany would demand the surrender of Toul and Verdun as a pledge of neutrality. Already Bethmann had informed Vienna that Germany would mobilize within forty-eight hours and expected from Austria "immediate active participation in the war with Russia." The German government was the first among the great powers to declare, in effect, that the issue at stake must be settled by war.

This being so, appeals were dispatched to Rome and Bucharest with the hope of keeping Italy and Romania in line, the latter power being offered Bessarabia as a reward; and a Turkish offer of an alliance was accepted on the Turkish terms. Nor had Bethmann given up hope that England might yet be induced to remain neutral. When informing London of the ultimatums to St. Petersburg and Paris, he declared that the British proposals for mediation, which Germany had strongly recommended, were still being considered at Vienna when the news of the Russian general mobilization arrived; this was not true (and it was not affirmed in the ultimatum to Russia), but Lichnowsky was instructed to make the most of it in the British press.

Throughout the week the British cabinet had been continuing its daily sessions without coming to any decisions; apparently, a small group, headed by Grey, wished to support France, but the majority was against war. Consequently, on July 29, 30, and 31 Grey had to resist the pleas of Cambon and to refuse any kind of pledge. On the afternoon of July 31, however, news was received of the Russian general mobilization and of the German intention to mobilize if Russia did not desist from mobilization. Since this brought war appreciably nearer, Grey was able to inquire whether France and Germany were prepared to respect the neutrality of Belgium so long as no other power violated it and whether Belgium would defend itself. This question would force Germany to show its hand and at the same time compensate the French, to some extent, for the refusal of a positive promise.

Because of the British hesitation, President Poincaré, on July 31, addressed a personal appeal to King George V. Before any answer could be received, the news reached Paris from Berlin that because of the Russian general mobilization (not yet reported from St. Petersburg), Germany had proclaimed "threatening danger of war." Immediately the cabinet allowed Joffre to order the covering troops into position, with instructions, however, not to violate the ten-kilometer line. At 7:00 P.M. Schoen presented the German ultimatum, only to be told that France knew nothing about "an alleged total mobilization of the Russian army and navy"; it was not until 8:30 P.M. that Paléologue's telegram reporting the mobilization reached the Quai d'Orsay. When the cabinet met to discuss the German ultimatum, it knew of Grey's question about the neutrality of Belgium, which was a good omen; and it had received assurances of Italian neutrality. During the session the Austrian ambassador, Count Szécsen, had notified the Quai d'Orsay officially that his government would respect the integrity and sovereignty of Serbia and had let it be known that if Serbia appealed for peace through a third power, Austria would state its terms. But these overtures were not known to the cabinet; and about midnight the Russian representatives in Paris were informed that France was "firmly resolved on war," while the military commanders were warned to prepare for mobilization on the afternoon of August 1. Whether war would come now depended on the Russian answer to the German ultimatum, which was to expire at noon on Saturday, August 1.

Once it had ordered general mobilization, the Russian government could only await developments. On July 31 Sazonov saw Szápáry, who insisted that Berchtold was ready to negotiate with Russia but carefully avoided any discussion of the Austrian ultimatum. Either through a misunderstanding or, more likely, in order to gain time for the mobilization to get under way, Sazonov telegraphed to the other capitals that Austria was "prepared to enter into an exchange of views regarding the contents of the ultimatum" and proposed that the negotiations should be held in London.[23] But the tsar told the German ambassador that "only One [pointing upward] can help us," and Sazonov instructed his minister in Bucharest to find out if Romania would go over "to our side" in return for Transylvania. Pourtalès delivered the German ultimatum at midnight of July 31/August 1. Sazonov made no reply then, or the next day.

Since a reply had not been received in Berlin by noon of August 1, a declaration of war was dispatched to St. Petersburg at 12:52 P.M.;[24] and at 5:00 P.M. William II signed the order for the mobilization of the German army. At 7:00 P.M. Pourtalès presented the declaration of war to Sazonov, being so excited that he handed in two versions; when the minister refused thrice to accept the German demands, the ambassador broke down and wept.[25] Several hours earlier Buchanan had received a long telegram from King George for the tsar expressing the opinion that there must be "some misunderstanding" between Germany and Russia and making a "personal appeal" for the continuance of negotiations. Before the ambassador could be received, the German declaration of war had been presented; in the reply which Nicholas and Buchanan composed, the tsar stated that he had been compelled to order mobilization "in consequence of complete Austrian mobilization," which was not true. No such statement was made in the draft provided by the Russian foreign office; how the charge came to be made remains a mystery.

[23] Berchtold had very cleverly handled Grey's proposal for the *Halt in Belgrad*: he accepted it, but on conditions unacceptable to Russia. Consequently, the notion prevailed for a time that Austria was willing to consider British mediation between itself and Serbia. Sazonov's telegram naturally created the impression that Austria was ready to negotiate with Russia. On August 1, therefore, there seemed, in London, to be some prospect of an accommodation—whereas there was none at all.

[24] Moltke proposed to commence operations in the west without a declaration of war; but Bethmann insisted on a formal declaration, in order thereby, as he hoped, to force France into the war and thus regularize the situation. The chancellor also believed that he would be surer of socialist support, for the Social Democratic party was willing to accept war against tsarist Russia.

[25] Late that evening, some six hours after the declaration of war was supposed to have been presented, William II sent a curious and final telegram to Nicholas II, asking the latter to forbid his troops to cross the frontier.

The Austro-Serbian quarrel developed into a European war because Russia took up the cudgels for Serbia. Yet once a state of war existed between Russia and Germany, Austria and Russia showed great reluctance to go to war with each other, for obvious military reasons. It was not until Germany had used sharp language at Vienna that on August 6 Austria finally declared war on Russia. Even so, this action was hardly in accord with the Austro-German alliance of 1879, which provided for mutual assistance if either were attacked by Russia; and it was Germany which declared war on Russia.

Circumstances led Germany to declare war on France also. At 11:00 A.M. on August 1, when Schoen came for an answer to the German ultimatum, Viviani replied that "France will be guided by its interests," which prevented Schoen from asking for the handing over of Toul and Verdun. The order for French mobilization was issued at 3:55 P.M., or five minutes before that of Germany; as in the case of Austria and Russia, each mobilized without knowledge of the other's action. But, even after news was received of the German declaration of war against Russia, the French government refrained from declaring war on Germany, as required by the alliance with Russia, because it wished to complete mobilization before beginning military operations—and even more because of the relations with England.

On Saturday, August 1, Grey was still unable, because of dissension in the cabinet and the attitude of parliament and the country, to give any assurance to Cambon, who pressed him very hard, that England would enter the war; the most he could do was to say that he had refused to define, to Lichnowsky, the conditions under which England would remain neutral.[26] By the next day, when it was known that Germany had declared war on Russia, the situation changed quickly.

[26] In reply to Grey's query concerning the neutrality of Belgium, Germany had replied that it could not answer without disclosing its plan of campaign: which was interpreted in London to indicate that Germany intended to violate the neutrality of Belgium. On August 1 Lichnowsky asked Grey if England would remain neutral on condition that Germany respected Belgian neutrality, but Grey declined to be pinned down. On this same day, confused negotiations for the neutrality of England went on between London and Berlin; but nothing came of them because Grey's understanding was that Germany might remain neutral in a war between Russia and Austria, whereas Lichnowsky and his superiors in Berlin were thinking of Germany not attacking France, which would induce England to remain neutral.

Many members of the Conservative party had been greatly alarmed by the apparent hesitations of the government. So on the morning of August 2 the leaders met and sent to the prime minister, Asquith, a statement that, in their opinion, "it would be fatal to the honour and security of the United Kingdom to hesitate in supporting France and Russia at the present juncture." With this promise of Conservative support, Grey was able to persuade the cabinet to allow him to promise Cambon that "if the German fleet comes into the Channel or into the North Sea to undertake hostile operations against French coasts or shipping, the British fleet will give all protection in its power." The promise was subject to the approval of parliament and did not carry the assurance that a British army would be sent to the continent; but Cambon, who that morning had failed to move Grey by reports of the German violation of Luxemburg, was satisfied, for "a great country does not really make war by half." The first lord of the admiralty, Churchill, did not wait for parliamentary approval and immediately got in touch with the French navy.

Meanwhile, France and Germany, each having ordered mobilization, sat glowering at each other like *chiens de faïence* [mad dogs]. Each charged the other with violations of frontier; and most of these reports were communicated to London, which in turn passed them on to the other capital. How true these charges and countercharges were, it is impossible to say—and it does not matter. The French government, with an eye to public opinion both at home and abroad, was determined to leave the initiative to Germany. In Germany there were divided counsels. The soldiers, arguing that "the war is already here," were moving their troops into France. But Bethmann and the legal officials of the foreign office insisted on a declaration of war; and since France made no sign of obliging with one, a document was prepared in Berlin and sent to Paris on the afternoon of August 3. It alleged numerous violations of German territory by French troops and airplanes and concluded with the statement that "yesterday French airmen dropped bombs on railways near Karlsruhe and Nuremberg." The telegram was received by the German ambassador in garbled form. Instead of asking to have it repeated, he put together a statement which included the charge that bombs had been dropped at Karlsruhe and Nuremberg and on this basis declared that Germany found itself in a state of war with France. The German charges were formally challenged by Viviani; and they were, in fact, untrue. Thus

France was able to argue that Germany had gone to war on a pretext; this was of incalculable value to France in the maintenance of its own morale and in the war of words which soon began throughout the world. Viviani was able to make a telling case when he addressed the French parliament on the following day.

Although Great Britain had committed itself to France by the declaration of August 2—a declaration given because British interests were thought to require the continued existence of France as a great power—Britain's entrance into the war was determined by the issue of Belgian neutrality. From the very beginning of the crisis the Belgian government was fearful of the course events might take, in spite of the assurances received from both Germany and England that its neutrality would be respected; and on July 31 mobilization was ordered. At 7:00 P.M. on August 2 the German minister in Brussels, Below, presented the ultimatum which had been drafted by Moltke a week previously. It gave Belgium twelve hours in which to agree to the free passage of the German army. The Belgian government sat during the night, under the presidency of King Albert, and decided unanimously on rejection. A manly reply was handed to the German minister at 7:00 A.M. on August 3. Both documents were promptly given to the press. King Albert appealed to King George for the "diplomatic intervention" of Great Britain; but the government refused to seek assistance until its territory was actually invaded, which happened at Gemmerich on the morning of August 4. That afternoon, the German chancellor, speaking in the Reichstag, admitted the "wrong" done but promised to "make it good" after the war; he justified the "breach of international law" on the ground of military "necessity" and did not charge that Belgium had in any way violated its obligations as a neutral.

In a last desperate effort to secure the neutrality of England, the German government on August 3 offered not to attack France by sea or make use of the coast of Belgium and Holland; but Grey declared this "far too narrow an engagement," and, in fact, the cabinet had decided to make the violation of Belgian neutrality a *casus belli*. This was certainly not the fundamental cause of England's going to war, but it was a real factor and the issue best calculated to appeal to parliament and the country. During the afternoon Grey spoke in the house of commons, and his masterly address persuaded a reluctant assembly to sanction his policy. He revealed the notes exchanged

between the French ambassador and himself in 1912; he expressed
the opinion that British honor and British interests required England
to protect France against a German attack; and he read out the
promise given the day before. As regards Belgium, he quoted
Gladstone's views that England was under a definite obligation to
defend the neutrality of Belgium. While he was speaking, the news
arrived that Belgium had rejected the German ultimatum and would
resist aggression. By tumultuous acclamation the government's policy
was approved, but John Burns and Lord Morley resigned from the
cabinet.

For some reason it was not until the morning of August 4 that
the British government formally demanded of Germany that it respect
the neutrality of Belgium. Somewhat later, when the news was
received that German troops had entered Belgium at Gemmerich, an
ultimatum was sent, to expire at midnight. Jagow made a final bid for
British neutrality with an assurance that "Germany will, under no
pretense whatever, annex Belgian territory"—an offer naturally deemed
quite worthless in London. At 7:00 P.M. the German foreign minister
formally rejected the British demand; and a little later the chancellor,
in speaking with the British ambassador, asserted that Britain was
going to war "just for a word 'neutrality,' just for a scrap of paper"—
a winged phrase which he later vainly tried to explain away and
which Germany was never able to live down.

Ever since 1914 the question has been debated whether peace could
have been preserved if Great Britain had indicated at the beginning
of the crisis that it would participate in the war. Since both professional diplomatists and historians disagree, no answer is really
possible. What does seem certain is that, when the crisis broke, British
public opinion did not understand the issue involved and would not
have sanctioned a declaration of solidarity with France and Russia;
for that reason, Grey refused to make such a declaration, and it was
not until the question of Belgian neutrality arose that British opinion
swung around and accepted the necessity of war.

On July 31 Berchtold reluctantly accepted the Italian contention
that Austria should make compensation to its ally, according to
Article VII of the Triple Alliance; but the concession came too late,
for the Italian government proclaimed its neutrality on the ground
that Austria's procedure constituted an "act of aggression." On the
other hand, Germany and Turkey signed a treaty of alliance on

August 2 (this was not revealed until long afterward). The other Balkan states remained neutral, although they were all subsequently to enter the war. On August 12 France and Great Britain declared war on Austria-Hungary; on August 27 Austria-Hungary declared war on Belgium. The Scandinavian countries, Holland, Switzerland, Spain, and Portugal remained neutral. On August 15 the Japanese government sent an ultimatum to Germany "advising" it to withdraw German men-of-war from Chinese and Japanese waters and to surrender to Japan the leased territory of Kiaochow, "with a view to the eventual restoration of the same to China." When no reply had been received by August 23, Japan declared war on Germany. The United States proclaimed its neutrality on August 4.

Although the ten years preceding the murder at Sarayevo witnessed numerous international crises concerning Morocco and the Balkans, they all ended in compromises. In the spring of 1914 the international atmosphere was relatively calm, except for some polemics in the Russian and German press. The crisis of July 1914 was not resolved peacefully because the Austrian demands on Serbia, which were supported by Germany, seemed to Russia, and then to France and Britain, designed to establish Austro-German control of the Balkans and of Europe. Thus the balance of power and the operation of the existing alliances served, not to keep the peace, but to transform a local quarrel into a general war. The Austrian demands were intended to precipitate war between Austria and Serbia; and Austria refused all mediation, even though Serbia in very large measure accepted the demands. Germany not only approved the Austrian policy but urged immediate action against Serbia. While both powers would have liked to restrict the war to Serbia, they faced the prospect of a general conflict with complacency and confidence; they also conducted their diplomacy in a manner which aroused the deepest suspicions, first of Russia and then of France and Britain. They believed that they could easily defeat Russia and France, and Germany made only halfhearted and insincere efforts to change course when the intervention of Britain became probable. On the other hand, the Entente Powers proposed mediation in various forms and offered several compromises, but in vain. Since Austria would not have acted without German approval and support, the primary responsibility of Germany for the fatal ending of the crisis is clear and overwhelming.

Versailles in Perspective

CHARLES SEYMOUR

Published in 1943

Europe has seen many wars and many peace settlements. It is doubtful, however, that it has ever witnessed a settlement that occasioned more violent objections than Versailles did. The individual who emerged as the leader of the attack on the Versailles system was, of course, Hitler. Indeed, Hitler's outlook and approach cannot be understood unless one bears in mind his constant use and abuse of Versailles as a scapegoat. He regarded the peace settlement as intolerable and insisted that "its economic fulfillment necessarily means political slavery and its political fulfillment means economic slavery. The abolition of this treaty, therefore, is a necessity." Nor was it only Hitler and his Nazis who denounced Versailles. All the leading German political parties in the pre-Nazi era also condemned it; these parties conveniently forgot how mild a treaty Versailles was in contrast to the treaty of Brest-Litovsk, which Germany had meted out to Bolshevik Russia in March 1918. Versailles was also attacked by Mussolini's Fascists. And increasingly in the 1930's many a Briton, Frenchman, and American joined the attack. Doubtless some of the criticisms had a sound basis in fact. On the other hand, there is no doubt that Versailles was often blamed for dislocations with which it had little or nothing to do—dislocations that were really the results of the war itself. In the essay that follows, Charles Seymour, now president emeritus of Yale University, re-examines the work of the peace conference of 1919. Himself a member of the American delegation, he recognizes that the men of Versailles made mistakes; but he also makes it clear that to stress only their mistakes is to deal in half-truths.

W e are the executors of Metternich." The phrase ran up and down the corridors of the Quai d'Orsay during the last Peace Conference. It was generally attributed to Balfour and had in it sufficient wit to make such parenthood possible. Moreover, as in the case of all true wit, the phrase expressed a good deal of truth although by no means the whole of it. Whether from necessity or temperamental inclination, the European leaders of the Peace Conference looked to the past rather than to the future; their main interest lay in the reparation of previous mistakes, the restoration of the more benevolent of nineteenth-century conditions purged of the factors that had led to war and revolution.

Such a backward-looking tendency, which to Clemenceau seemed merely a recognition of the importance of historical experience, was natural and perhaps inevitable. A Peace Conference representing a generation that has lived through a long and costly war is in search of something solid upon which to base its hope of security; the past offers known facts as a guide, the future is uncertain. Thus the Congress of Vienna adopted Talleyrand's motto of "Legitimacy" as its basic principle and inaugurated a period of "Restoration." The Tsar Alexander was not very slow to apostatize from his mystic dreams and ended by accepting with a whole heart the reactionary philosophy of Metternich. In the same sense, and in response to the mood of the age, President Harding called for a "return to normalcy." It would appear that in the wake of modern warfare the haze of unrealistic nostalgia distorts in a favorable sense the conditions of the pre-war period, emphasizes the perils of experiment.

The mood results not merely from a longing for something solid; it is also a reaction against the exaggerated dreams of idealism that accompany the moment of victory after a long war, before the hard problems of existing fact are clearly faced. The advent of the Congress of Vienna was heralded with phrases announcing the birth of a new world: "the reconstruction of the moral order"; "the regeneration of the political system of Europe"; "an enduring peace founded upon a just redistribution of political forces." Such idealism was rapidly transformed into Metternich's interpretation of the Holy Alliance. In 1919 hope of establishing a permanent system of international justice and peace, which would discard all the factors of evil that had brought

Reprinted by special permission from *The Virginia Quarterly Review*, XIX (1943), 481-497.

on the holocaust of war, was even more widespread and certainly more sincere. Harold Nicolson has recorded his frame of mind on leaving for the Peace Conference, typical of most of the younger British and Americans: "We were journeying to Paris, not merely to liquidate the war, but to found a new order in Europe. We were preparing not Peace only, but Eternal Peace. There was about us the halo of some divine mission. We must be stern, righteous and ascetic. For we were bent on doing great, permanent and noble things."

I

The prophet of the new order, Woodrow Wilson himself, was emphatic in his determination that the Conference should embark upon a new path and should build for the future. In a small conference on December 10, 1918, he told a group of advisers on the *George Washington* that if the Conference did not succeed in writing the Fourteen Points into the peace, he would be ashamed to go back to Washington, "would look around for an out-of-the-way spot, Guam, perhaps, to retire to." Admitting the difficulties of establishing the new order because of the temperament of Conference leaders, he insisted, "If it won't work, it must be made to work, because the world is faced by a task of terrible proportions and only the adoption of a cleansing process would recreate or regenerate the world."

The history of the Conference belied such hopes and Wilson's fervid determination. The statement does not imply any concession to those critics who have made of the Versailles Treaty the root of all international evil. As we look back at it, with the advantage of twenty-five years' perspective, it is clear that most of the diatribes against the injustice and unwisdom of that treaty and the others which formed the settlement of 1919 have small foundation in fact; on the contrary, the treaties created ample opportunity to accomplish recovery

---

CLASS B MANDATES: One of the three categories into which the former German colonies and Turkish possessions on the Arabian peninsula were divided at the Paris Peace Conference. German East Africa, for example, was made a Class B mandate in keeping with the relative backwardness of its political and economic development. Britain was delegated to serve as it steward until it was prepared for self-rule.

in the economic sense and maintain peace in the political, if only those who followed had been able to capitalize it. But even so, the Versailles Treaty cannot be regarded, as Wilson once insisted, as attaining ninety per cent of his expressed aspirations. The comparison of what was accomplished with what had been hoped brought to many a sense of almost complete failure. Even those who, like Colonel House, saw the situation with clear eyes, appreciating both the need of a fresh approach to international organization and the difficulties of discovering it, confessed their disappointment. On the day after the signing of the Versailles Treaty, House set forth his regrets in his diary:

"There seemed to be no full realization of the conditions which had to be met. An effort was made to enact a peace upon the usual lines. This should never have been attempted. The greater part of civilization had been shattered and history could guide us but little in the making of this peace. How splendid it would have been if we had blazed a new and better trail! However, it is to be doubted whether this could have been done, even if those in authority had so decreed, for the peoples back of them had to be reckoned with . . . We have had to deal with a situation pregnant with difficulties and one which could be met only by an idealistic and unselfish spirit, which was almost wholly absent and which was too much to expect of men come together at such a time and for such a purpose. And yet I wish we had taken the other road, even if it were less smooth, both now and afterward, than the one we took. We would at least have gone in the right direction and if those who follow us had made it impossible to go the full length of the journey planned, the responsibility would have rested with them and not with us."

In his later years Colonel House laid a good deal more emphasis upon the positive accomplishments of the Peace Conference than he did upon its failures, and he stressed the difficulties which attended

---

NEO-MERCANTILISM: The movement in the direction of state intervention in economic life that took such forms as high protective tariffs and subsidies.

HAROLD NICOLSON: Member of the British delegation to the Paris Peace Conference and author of *Peace-making, 1919* (1933), one of the best treatments of the problems and difficulties with which the peacemakers were faced.

the effort to blaze "a new and better trail." Not many weeks before
his death in 1938, when the clouds of another World War were
gathering, he reiterated the eternal truth that treaties do not create
conditions, they reflect them. It could not reasonably be expected that
an "idealistic" peace should emerge from the confusion of passionate
hatred that persisted long after the enemy had laid down arms. In
such a climate and at the very moment of making peace, the seeds
of the next war easily take root. Sir Arthur Salter has quoted, in this
connection, the inversion of the old Latin phrase to read, *si vis bellum
para pacem;* "if you want a war, call a peace conference." He goes on
very justly to point out that there would be less wit but more truth in
the recognition that war by its very nature cannot serve as a healthy
preparation for peace; indeed, it breeds factors violently hostile to
peace which are not eliminated by the signing of a document called a
treaty. These factors can only be conquered over the years by developing more powerful factors that make for conditions of tranquility.

There is another aspect of House's expression of regret at the
course taken by the Peace Conference which deserves emphasis;
namely, his doubt whether its leaders, even had they wished, would
have been able to set out on the "new trail," for the peoples back of
them "had to be reckoned with." It was the paradox of a war waged,
if not to make the world safe for democracy, at least to protect the
democracies from future aggression, that by reason of democratic
control the political leaders were forced to decisions that later stimulated the defeated enemy to renewed aggression. Popular ignorance
and prejudice could not be denied their seats at the peace table.

Wilson went to the Conference as the apostle of the wisdom of
the common man, convinced that the European governments did not
represent their peoples, equally convinced that his own program
voiced a popular feeling which would be irresistible if the people were
not throttled. On the *George Washington* he expressed himself explicitly in this sense:

"We would be the only disinterested people at the Peace Conference and the men with whom we were about to deal did not represent
their own people . . . Unless the Conference was prepared to follow
the opinions of mankind and to express the will of the people rather
than that of their leaders at the Conference, we should soon be
involved in another breakup of the world and when such a breakup
came it would not be a war but a cataclysm."

The self-deception of the President in this regard, despite the enthusiasm of the first greeting given to him by the peoples of Europe, is an unavoidable fact. When, in the controversy over Fiume, Wilson followed the method he had tried on various occasions in his university and political career, that of the direct appeal to popular feeling, he was roughly disabused. The burst of indignation that followed his Fiume manifesto made clear that the Italian people were even more selfishly nationalistic than their leaders. The European governments, had they been free, would have framed wiser provisions than were actually inserted in the treaties. The chief of each of the delegations was invariably hampered in every case by his responsibility to the people at home. Popular opinion forced upon Clemenceau the inclusion of the guilt clause and prevented the writing in of a reasonable sum of reparations. His resistance to the demands of Foch and Poincaré for the dismemberment of Germany cost him his election to the Presidency of France. Whenever Lloyd George suggested more moderate treatment of Germany, the Northcliffe press howled for his head. Orlando's willingness to compromise Adriatic controversies led to his overthrow. The American voters of 1920 repudiated Wilsonism largely because it seemed to them to imply surrender of our national interest for the benefit of foreigners or in behalf of vague international utopias. The power of an ill-educated, democratic nationalism always threatened. We may ask whether at the end of this war our democracies at home and abroad will be better educated or less nationalistic.

The fault was not entirely that of the people, who were never authoritatively informed of the primary aims of the Peace Conference. Mr. Walter Lippmann has commented upon the unfortunate effects of American failure to recognize frankly that we had in reality entered the war to protect our own security threatened by a German victory. It resulted that during the Peace Conference the American public did not know whether Wilson's policy was actually conceived in the interest of the United States or whether we were not indeed yielding that interest to pull the traditional chestnut out of the fire for the British, or serving some distant and evanescent ideal. Such uncertainty interfered with American leadership, since the European chiefs of government were never sure whether Wilson would receive the support of the people back home.

Confusion of purpose was made worse confounded by looseness of phraseology. The Conference was unfortunately dominated by "principles" expressed in very general terms. Perhaps this was a re-action against the attitude of Talleyrand, who is reported to have said: "The best principle is to have none." Phrases such as "justice," "viabil-ity," "self-determination," were freely bandied about without clear definition of their meaning. Inevitably they made for controversy and confusion. They contradicted each other in application and they blurred the real reason for the decision finally taken. Was it "just" to separate East Prussia from Germany by the Polish Corridor, or would it be "just" to exclude Poland from the sea and leave Polish popula-tions under German rule? The principle of viability demanded that Czechoslovakia be allowed to maintain the historic Bohemian frontier; the principle of self-determination demanded with equal force that the frontier be altered so as to throw the anti-Czech, German-speaking Bohemians into the Reich. Abstract principles exercise an emotional attraction, but they provide a wobbly basis for reasoned decisions.

The natural tendency of everyone to rationalize his temperamental proclivities intensified this confusion. Advocates of new methods of international organization appeared at times to rest their case upon the assumption that novelty was in itself desirable or that the methods of the past were inherently vicious. This assumption is implicit in the general criticism of the Peace Conference which alleges that its failure lay in its tendency to look too much to the past. Some of the more emi-nent figures of the Conference were not innocent of this *penchant* for rationalizing evil into traditional procedures. Mr. Wilson's blanket condemnation of the Balance of Power rested upon his assumption that the wars of the past had resulted from the application of this principle and that the peace of the future must be protected from it. He and his adherents made no attempt to analyze the significance of what is, after all, an eternal principle of social organization. We were hypnotized by a phrase. Conversely, those who were temperamentally opposed to change idealized the value of historical experience far above any level that an objective historian could approve. Their recognition of self-in-terest as a predominant factor in social relations was justified; not so their failure to appreciate the extent of the revolution through which the external world was passing and to which man must adjust his conception of self-interest or perish. This emotional conflict between the advocates of the new and the old confused the real issue that arose in the case of each decision,—what is wise in the circumstances, what is unwise?

II

These difficulties which the peacemakers confronted and which impeded the road to wise decisions were to a large extent unavoidable. They were inherent in the conditions bequeathed by war and in the nature of the warring peoples and their representatives. If there is any lesson to be drawn from them to serve future peacemakers, it can hardly extend beyond a warning to be on the lookout for similar difficulties and to prepare to meet them intelligently and vigorously. But there were other factors that controlled the conduct of the Peace Conference and its aftermath which, it may be argued, sprang directly from the mistaken policy of the leaders. It is fruitless to blame those leaders for the course they adopted or to ask of them a wisdom of judgment which the passing of years alone confers upon the historian. But it is important to take careful note of those mistakes, if such they were, to serve as a warning post for the future.

It was a great mistake, it seems to me, for the Peace Conference to attempt to legislate in a single congress a comprehensive world settlement. Success in this attempt would have taxed the capacities of a conference of archangels. We must remember that those who gathered in Paris to draft the treaties found themselves facing a vast variety of immediate problems which had to be met without delay if Europe was not to degenerate into chaos. Social and economic conditions following the fall of the Hapsburgs and the armistice of November 11 were in a state of almost complete disorganization. The return of the demobilized armies further confused the operation of political and industrial agencies. Germany was starving. Bolshevism threatened. The ambitions of the liberated peoples soared into violent competition with each other, so that, as the great war ended, a half-dozen minor wars got under way. Serbs and Italians, Slovenes and German-Austrians, Czechs and Poles, Rumanians and Magyars were less interested in making the peace than in asserting their claims by dint of arms.

The Peace Conference was the only body with authority supported by force sufficient to compose these conflicts, provide for the distribution of food and other supplies, and reorganize industrial activity. During the earlier days of the Conference such administrative functions formed the most important aspect of its work, and long hours were spent by the Supreme Council in the direction of plans for pacification and rehabilitation. Without any formal designation and simply to fill a pressing need, the Council served as an international government for Europe and for many regions outside of Europe. This vital task of supervising and controlling the transition from war back to peace was obviously of surpassing importance. By its nature it was a task demanding qualities different from those essential to laying down the bases of ultimate settlement, and it was carried on under conditions not conducive to wise decisions affecting the peace as a whole. It was asking too much of the peacemakers to serve as an executive committee for the world, at the same time that they deliberated the terms of a comprehensive and permanent peace.

Long previous to the calling of the Peace Conference, when President Wilson and Colonel House first discussed the procedure that ought to be set up following the victory over Germany, the latter suggested that there be two phases in the process of peace-making: the first, in which rapid action must be taken in order to re-establish stable local governments, begin the revival of industrial life in a creative sense, determine frontiers in their main lines; the second, in which there should be leisurely deliberation regarding the larger aspects of international organization both in a political and an economic sense. House advocated calling a peace conference immediately after the armistice, which should conclude its decisions just as soon as disorder had been overcome and conditions no longer demanded international control. The second phase, in House's mind, would be represented by a later conference or conferences, perhaps postponed until belligerent emotions had subsided to some extent, which could embark upon consideration of the larger problems of world organization without being hurried by the need of hasty decisions. When he came to the armistice conferences in the fall of 1918, House still advocated such procedure.

As we look back, the attractiveness of the proposal is obvious. The first conference would have dealt only with problems of immediate necessity. It might have been convened by November 15, for the Supreme War Council already had at its disposal all necessary administrative agencies. It might have been dissolved or adjourned by February 15, with the essential military and territorial decisions made. But Wilson's determination to attend the Peace Conference himself compelled postponement until mid-December; political considerations in Great Britain, France, and Italy led to further postponements. Thus the preliminary Conference did not formally convene until January 18, and it undertook so many functions that it dragged along tardily and was in the end unconsciously merged into the final Conference at a date never determined by historians.

It is not true, as so often stated, that Wilson's insistence upon the League of Nations delayed the signing of the Versailles Treaty. As a matter of fact, the Covenant had been approved before many other provisions of that treaty. But Wilson's determination that the Covenant should be an integral part of any treaty with Germany, preliminary or final, did break down the distinction between the settlement of immediate problems which demanded prompt action, and the larger problems of world organization. Because of this the latter, in so far as they were decided, reached a conclusion in an atmosphere not favorable to ultimate wisdom. It is, of course, arguable that the time to draft comprehensive plans for international peace is while the realization of the horrors of war is vivid. One heard at Paris many times repeated, "If we don't get the League now, we never shall have a league." The answer to this argument, which today is rehearsed in not dissimilar terms, is that no lasting organization can be the product of momentary sentiment; unless it is to be supported by the sober afterthought of those who must make the plans effective, it is futile and dangerous self-deception to launch it upon the froth of emotion.

A second mistake and one that permeated all the discussions of the Conference resulted largely from this attempt to determine large issues in the atmosphere of short-range problems. Economic and social questions of inestimable significance were subordinated to political questions of immediate pertinence. It is true that a great deal of time was given by the Conference to economic and financial issues, engaging some of the best brains in the world. But they became merely the football of politics, as in the case of reparations. To the long-term economic and financial questions involving trade, tariff, shipping, and currency policies from the international point of view, no adequate consideration was given. Nor is it likely that in the time allowed to the peacemakers fruitful conclusions could have been reached.

It is possible that this over-emphasis upon the political aspects of the peace was what Colonel House had in mind in voicing his regret that "an effort was made to enact a peace upon the usual lines." The international problems characteristic of the revolution through which the world was proceeding, but which went largely unheeded, far transcended the political relations of peoples with each other. The fixing of political frontiers was of small importance compared with the determination of their economic significance. President Wilson appreciated the vital nature of this question when he included the "lowering of trade barriers" in his Fourteen Points. But that point was not pursued by the Peace Conference. Thereby, and because of the attitude of the political leaders who followed the Conference, the world lapsed into a neo-mercantilism already under way before the World War, which led to the disasters of the later twenties and thirties.

This apparent faith in political formulae and political controls as the keys to peace was closely related to the third great mistake of the Conference, which I conceive to have been the attempt to give political coercive powers to the League of Nations. It has taken the perspective of twenty-five years to show that this was a mistake. I do not know how anyone could foretell in 1919 that the skeptics were right and that the Powers composing the League would prove unwilling to operate this international institution as they had agreed. Such, however, proved to be the case. The peoples simply did not wish to abide by an international constitution with political and coercive commitments.

Professor Alfred Zimmern, a determined and sagacious protagonist of international co-operation, has pointed out that an institution, if it is to prosper, must be the outward and visible expression of a corporate sentiment. "The ideology of the League of Nations," he wrote in the early thirties, "has been based upon the assumption that there exists today an international community the members of which are linked together by a common consciousness, a corporate tie, comparable to that upon which national institutions depend for their successful working. And this initial confusion of thought, or deliberate make-believe to which statesmen and peoples have found themselves committed, has vitiated first the intellectual and then the moral atmosphere until the hiatus between appearance and reality has become visible to all the world."

The political functions of the League were furthermore directed, at least in the public mind, primarily toward a negative purpose—the prevention of war—rather than toward the positive end of removing the causes of war. The hiatus between appearance and reality was thereby widened, since the mere prevention of war has never been and probably never will be the primary purpose of any national policy. Where the clear interest of the nation demands the use of force, war will continue as an instrument of policy until some preferable substitute for attaining or compromising that interest can be made acceptable.

The development of such a substitute as a means of settling disputes in a world community depends upon a sense of the general corporate interest, which was lacking in 1919 and the years that followed.

III

In certain respects, accordingly, it would appear that the Peace Conference instead of merely looking backwards, attempted too much and in too short a time. In other respects, notably in its over-emphasis upon political factors, it was guilty of a reactionary myopia. Let us note, furthermore, that the positive and valuable achievements of the Conference resulted in part from traditional and in part from progressive tendencies.

The Versailles system, whatever its defects, did respond to the overwhelming demand of the moment: it did provide a security which gave opportunity for recovery and which might have been maintained over a much longer period if it had not been for the moral weakness of the victor nations. This security did not proceed from the League of Nations. It was based upon military control of strategic areas, an old principle, with no relation to "national justice," and by many regarded as vicious. But it offered security against a rearmed and revengeful Germany. So long as the Rhinelands were disarmed and the western flank of Germany lay open to invasion, while at the same time the Czechs occupied the bastion of Bohemia, the general peace of Europe was safe. It was only after 1936 when the French and British permitted the destruction of the Locarno Pacts and the rearmament of the Rhinelands that Hitler was able to concentrate upon Bohemia and establish his control of central Europe. The failure of this system of security, temporary but effective while it was maintained, was the fault not of the Peace Conference but of those who followed.

The League of Nations was helpless, in the circumstances, to prove of any assistance in the maintenance of political security. But it achieved outstanding success in its development of international organization and activity in non-political fields; and therein the criticism of the backward tendencies of the Peace Conference is belied. In a great variety of such fields Geneva was given a creative purpose which it carried forward effectively to serve the interests of individuals and international groups. The League was responsible for setting up and operating through its Secretariat instruments of co-operative research and action to meet problems of finance and trade; of control of drugs; studies in nutrition and public sanitation; through its International Labor Organization it provided a basis for the attempt to elevate labor standards as well as to protect nations with existing high standards from unfair competition. Of great importance, although rarely appreciated, was the success of the League in the administration of Class B Mandates, where the attitude of the Mandatory was affected by economic rather than political factors, and from which valuable lessons may be drawn in future efforts to organize international control of dependent areas.

Thus in contrast to the failure of the League to control political nationalism was its success in sublimating national feeling to a higher internationalism in such non-political activities. Secretary of State Hull has declared that the League "has been responsible for the development of mutual exchange and discussion of ideas and methods to a greater extent and in more fields of humanitarian and scientific endeavor than any other organization in history." Beyond its practical accomplishments it furnished the example of the natural development of an institution when it is truly representative of a corporate spirit. By its actual practice in the workings of internationalism it enriched what President Wriston has called the "subsoil of peace." It is such a subsoil that produces the common consciousness of an international community which, as Zimmern asserts, is a condition precedent to the success of any political league or federation.

IV

The wiser historians are usually cautious in attempting to draw specific lessons from the past; even when they do so, public opinion and its leaders are not apt to pay very strict attention. But it would be foolish of those who guide the policy of the United Nations not to take careful account of the experience of the past Peace Conference. And it would be of tremendous advantage if public opinion could be educated as to what might reasonably be expected of the next Peace Conference.

Clearly, it ought not to expect too much. The difficulties of 1919 which sprang from the disasters of a four years' war and from the spirit of democratic nationalism will be no less at the end of this war. If we promise ourselves any ready-made solutions to the problems that must be confronted, we run the danger of another period of cynical disillusionment.

We shall gain much if the conference which must meet to work some order out of the chaos that will follow the war be convened promptly after the armistice. Such a conference might usefully be set up even before the end of hostilities, ready and accustomed to utilize the international agencies already developed during the war.

It should be sharply differentiated from the organization responsible for laying permanent foundations for the peaceful welfare of the world. The latter organization, indeed, might not take the form of the traditional peace conference. It might rather consist of a number of conferences to consider the larger problems of the peace as the time became more propitious for approaching this or that. Inevitably and properly, these conferences will be primarily concerned with economic and social problems rather than with political. A revived League of Nations at Geneva, deprived of political coercive functions and not directly responsible for the prevention of war would be, in my opinion, of the utmost service.

There must, of course, be a political basis for any system of international organization. But the experience of the past twenty-five years indicates that a political league or federation of nations, created with a formal constitution, and broad commitments depending upon wishfulness rather than existing facts and tendencies, offers the probability of renewed failure. Whatever the nature of any future international organization, its success will depend to a large degree upon its simplicity of mechanism. There is eternal wisdom in a letter of Lord Clancarty to Castlereagh, written in 1818: "The more simple and less multiplied the means by which the great Powers are kept together for mutual defense and the preservation of peace, the less likelihood there will be of interruption to their union."

The aftermath of Versailles reinforces a reasoned conviction of the necessity of developing international institutions; but it also points to the danger of creating them before public opinion is ready to operate them, or beyond the limits set by the true interests of the individual nation. There is no indication that national feeling has lost any of its intensity. It is probably the strongest spiritual force in the world today; any attempt to suppress it would be futile and criminal. It must be channeled into international operation, but these channels can be cut only by the popular will as it becomes educated to their value. Salvador de Madariaga has given wise counsel: "Our eyes must be idealistic and our feet realistic. We must walk in the right direction but we must walk step by step. Our tasks are: to define what is desirable; to define what is possible at any time within the scheme of what is desirable; to carry out what is possible in the spirit of what is desirable."

XXIV

The Soviet Dictatorship

The Russian Revolution: Twenty-Five Years After

N. S. TIMASHEFF

The Teaching of History under Stalin

PAUL OLBERG

The Russian Revolution

Twenty-Five Years After

N. S. TIMASHEFF

⇢⇢⇢⇢⇢⇢⇢⇢⇢⇢⇢⇢⇢⇢⇢⇢⇢⇢ *Published in 1943* ⇠⇠⇠⇠⇠⇠⇠⇠⇠⇠⇠⇠⇠⇠⇠⇠⇠⇠

When the Bolsheviks overthrew the provisional government headed by Kerensky in late 1917, few observers would have predicted that they would remain in power for any length of time. In Russian upper- and middle-class circles the expectation was that the Bolsheviks would quickly discredit themselves. Even Lenin was surprised when the Bolsheviks managed to hold on for more than a few months. Opposition quickly developed to the political, diplomatic, military, economic, and religious policies that the Bolsheviks carried out in the years immediately following their seizure of power; and the fact of this opposition promoted the belief that their collapse was imminent. With the introduction of the so-called New Economic Policy in 1921, the belief was again encouraged that the Bolsheviks had failed and would soon be dislodged. When, by the late 1920's, the era of the Five Year Plans was inaugurated and accounts spread of violent peasant opposition to the collectivization program, the overthrow of the Bolsheviks was again anticipated. So, too, the frequent purges of the 1930's seemed to indicate that the Bolsheviks could not last much longer. And when the Communists and the Nazis fell out with each other in 1941, many an observer expected the Stalin regime to be a war casualty just as the tsarist monarchy had been. Yet despite all the evidences of domestic opposition, the dictatorship of the Communist Party was not overthrown. On the contrary, it seemed to succeed in strengthening its hold on the peoples of the U.S.S.R.—even though the Five Year Plans, which placed small emphasis on the production of consumers' goods, had done little to improve the material conditions of their life. In the present essay, N. S. Timasheff, of Fordham University, evaluates the results of the Russian experiment from the vantage point of the twenty-fifth anniversary of the Bolshevik Revolution. Author of a valuable study of *Religion in Soviet Russia* and of numerous articles in scholarly journals, Timasheff knows how to ask meaningful questions and how to exploit the might-have-been approach to history.

Pre-revolutionary Russia was a rapidly advancing society in which a number of definite trends could be detected. Assuming that this development had not been interrupted by war and revolution, certain conjectures of the effects of these trends might be formulated.

We may assume that without the revolution the political forces of Russia would have achieved the transformation of the "dual" or "constitutional" monarchy, which ruled Russia since 1906, into a parliamentary monarchy in which the Crown would have yielded actual power to representatives of public opinion. The franchise of the Douma would have been gradually democratized. The establishment of *Zemstvos,* that is, provincial and district self-government, which, between 1866 and 1914, had contributed so much to Russia's advance in the fields of public education and public hygiene, would have been extended throughout the Empire, with perhaps the exception of some semi-colonial territories; these agencies would have received a significant re-enforcement through the modernization of obsolete institutions of peasant self-government. The excellent judicial system which Russia had already enjoyed since 1866, curbed during the reactionary period before the Russo-Japanese war, but partly restored under the Douma, would have been expanded and improved.

The agrarian reform inaugurated by Stolypin in 1906, if peacefully continued, would have proved to be one of the greatest agrarian revolutions in history. By 1935, no agrarian communities would have existed, and the Russian country-side would have consisted of 20 million farms run on the basis of civil law of the *code Napoleon* type. Only a few landed estates would have survived: were the pre-revolutionary trend maintained, by 1935 the peasants would have acquired almost all the remnants of the former quasi-feudal estates. The atomization of land ownership would have been balanced by a strong development of rural co-operation which had already attained notable successes in Siberia and in Northern Russia. It is difficult to judge what would have been the impact of these changes on agricultural production. In Russia, the parcelling of landed estates usually decreased the crops, but increased the number of cattle bred in a given area: since, in 1916, only 10% of the arable surface was tilled by the landlords, the impact of parcelling could not have been very important. A moderate, but steady advance of agricultural production could have been expected.

Reprinted by special permission from *The Review of Politics*, V (1943), 415-440. The footnotes which originally appeared with this essay have been omitted.

It would have been accelerated by the spread of general education and of special training in agronomy.

In industry, the rapid advance of the last twenty-five years of Imperial Russia would probably have continued throughout the period actually covered by the Revolution. The natural resources of Russia offered the opportunity, and the expanding population of Russia, in combination with improvements in agriculture, would have created a big internal market. For Western European capital, Russia would have remained a welcome field for investment; American capital, very probably, would have been added.

A quantitative statement on the probable increase in production is possible. During the twenty-five years from 1888 to 1913, Russia's production of coal increased from 5.3 to 29 million tons, or 5½ times, that of pig iron from 0.7 to 4 million tons, also 5½ times, that of oil from 3.2 to 9 million tons, or 2.8 times. Assuming the maintenance of the geometric ratio of expansion, in 1938 Russia could have produced 160 million tons of coal, 22 million tons of pig iron and 25 million tons of oil. The possibility of a slowing down of this expansion in heavy industry cannot be denied, but a tremendous increase of the productive capacity of light industry might have been expected with certainty. Such figures as 5 million tons of sugar, 8 million meters of cotton fabrics, 0.5 million tons of paper in 1938 are rather conservative estimates, since between 1890 and 1912 sugar production had increased four times and cotton and paper consumption three times.

A tremendous expansion of railways was also to be expected. In 1915 a governmental committee drew up a ten years' plan of expansion which would have added 30 thousand miles to the 49 thousand miles which were then in operation. That plan would not have imposed on Russia anything beyond her capacity, because an increase of the railway net by 2,500 miles a year actually took place for many years previous to the decision. Assuming some slowing down after 1925, a network of

---

DALTON PLAN: Educational scheme organized by Helen Parkhurst at Dalton, Mass., and widely imitated all over the world. A revolt against the old-fashioned school with its class work and its uniformly timed assignments, it is a scheme of individual work. Each student receives a month's assignments for each subject he studies; he works in the "laboratory" or study room set aside for each subject; and he can discuss with the teacher in charge of each laboratory any problems that arise. Although the student allots his

100 thousand miles by 1938 could have been achieved without difficulty.

Expanding industry and railways would have produced a rapid numerical increase in the labor classes, and with this quantitative advance, qualitative progress could have been expected: skilled labor was gathering in old industrial centers and tremendous efforts had been made to disseminate technical education in various fields. Russian labor was "class conscious" and, with the liberalization of political institutions, would easily have evolved mighty and well organized labor unions. The social security laws of 1912 were considered by the government, business and labor as just a modest beginning. On the basis of the consciousness of "social service" which prevailed in Russia at that time, a magnificent development along this line could have been foreseen. A significant improvement in wages and labor conditions could be expected in conditions of expanding industry and organized labor, which would continue that of the pre-Revolutionary decades.

Had agriculture and industry expanded rapidly, Russia would have been, even today, far from becoming a "saturated area" in which the increase of population is inhibited. Consequently, the continuation of the population trends of pre-revolutionary years could have been expected and on this basis, an *ex-post-facto* "prediction" of 180 million in 1938 is rather conservative. Gradual urbanization, as a result of industrialization, would probably have resulted in 30% of the population living in urban areas by 1938.

In the field of culture, the main achievement would have been that of overcoming illiteracy. The magnificent efforts of the *Zemstvos* would have been continued and significantly accelerated on the basis of a law passed in 1910 which could be termed a "ten years plan for national education." By 1920, all children in Russia except in semi-colonial areas would have had access to schools; by 1930, this ideal would have been achieved everywhere. Since no special device was foreseen for the older age groups among which illiteracy was high, a

---

time to each subject as he sees fit, he must work during school hours and must complete his assignments at the end of the month.

SOCIAL SECURITY LAWS OF 1912: Measures which introduced health and accident insurance into Russia. Based on the German model, they were in a real sense a working-class equivalent of the Stolypin Laws. They embodied an attempt to give working-class elements a stake in the tsarist regime.

complete elimination of illiteracy could not have been expected before their passing away. Still, by 1938, an index of literacy of 78% could have been foreseen.

By a parallel assumption, a great expansion of high schools, universities and other institutions for higher learning might have been assumed. It is impossible to conjecture the probable achievements in science, literature and art, since in these fields unpredictable "personal coefficients" are decisive. But one thing is certain: in each field, different schools of thought and work would have persisted; criticizing each other, even fighting each other, but enriching themselves and the nation through competition.

In the field of religion, the liberalization of political institutions would probably have resulted in the decline of the privileges of the Established Church. The resulting liberty would have compensated it for the loss of part of her flock to competing denominations and, perhaps, to religious indifferentism. The back-to-Church movement which had started among the Russian intellectuals would have definitely reenforced the position of religion in Russia.

This picture may seem over-optimistic, and perhaps over-emphatic about Russian similarity to this country. But a striking similarity of conditions did actually exist. Like this country, Russia is a continent. Her natural resources are second to none. She is far from the state of demographic saturation. The pioneer spirit has been displayed by the Russians when colonizing the southern steppes (now the larger part of the Ukraine), the trans-Volga region, the Northern Caucasus and Siberia. The democratic spirit was well developed in institutions of peasant self-government, later on in the *Zemstvos*, and in co-operative societies. Among the intellectuals, the spirit of social service was at least as well developed as among the best social workers of this country. Taking into account the similarity of underlying conditions, the similarity in part of our hypothetical picture with the actual state of things in this country is an additional argument in favor of these conjectures. They were established above, through extrapolation of observable trends, in the assumption that the development would not have been disturbed by external and internal causes. But the second part of this assumption is contrary to fact: the geographical location of Russia did not permit her to isolate herself from the rest of the world as this country did during the period of rapid expansion, and in her history many tensions were accumulated which, in combination with the disorganizing effects of war, caused an internal explosion. In these matters conditions were not equal in the two countries and there resulted significant differences in the actual course of events in them.

II

The revolution of March, 1917, overthrew the Imperial government and for eight months introduced into the Russian tragedy a quasi-democratic intermission. Had the order of things then created lasted, many of the trends discussed above would have been given accelerated actualization, but quite a few significant departures would probably have taken place, especially concerning the social order: a drastic agrarian reform would have immediately destroyed the remnants of quasi-feudal landownership and restored the agrarian communities, reversing Stolypin's policy. Very probably, after having secured possession of all arable land, the peasants would have insisted on "full ownership"; thus, after a significant deviation, the goal of 20 million "little masters" in the Russian countryside would have been achieved. It is hard to judge to what an extent socialist ideas would have been carried out in industry, but very definitely, the laboring class would have made an extraordinarily rapid advance, both social and economic.

But the March revolution was only a prelude which was not permitted to develop into a real play. For twenty-five years, Russia's fate was determined by the tremendous shock of the Communist Revolution of November, 1917. This revolution was highly "programmatic"; in other words, its leaders had a complete plan of social reconstruction which, they believed, was the best means to make men happy. In their program, two aspects must be distinguished; the exoteric and the esoteric. The exoteric program was simplicity itself: the four slogans of land, peace, bread and "all power to the Soviets" which meant the abolition of bureaucracy, gave them for a short while the decisive support of the masses. The acquisition of power was the necessary premise for the realization of the esoteric program. What was to happen to Russia, if this realization was permitted to proceed according to plan?

First of all, Russia had to disappear, becoming a part of the International Proletarian Society of Marx's and Lenin's dreams. In this society, no room was preserved for political institutions: the state, a "bourgeois" institution, had to wither away. No bureaucracy was to be maintained, all citizens would direct in turn the corporate activities foreseen by the plan: according to Lenin, every cook was able to govern the state. The standing army was to be abolished and replaced by civil militia. In that society, of which Russia was to be a part, no individual ownership of the means of production would exist any longer; these means of production were to be collectivized, transferred to the society of the future which had to be purely economic, devoid of political functions: state capitalism was considered as bad as private capitalism. In the new economic order, the "capitalist anarchy of production" was to be overcome: no efforts would be wasted and artificial scarcity would be replaced by plenty, permitting, after a short period of transition, the realization of the ideal of remunerating everybody for his work according to his needs; since human needs are essentially equal, this implied social and economic equality. Naturally, this new social and economic order could not be realized within a society holding to the cultural traditions of the bourgeois age. But, since, in the opinion of the leaders, existence determines consciousness and culture is a function of the socio-economic order, after the shift to collective production and exchange, human ideas would change rapidly, old superstitions would die out and new systems of motivation would arise to replace those acquired by men in the bourgeois state of their existence. This natural development could be accelerated by planned actions of the leaders. As a result, religion had to disappear quickly, the stable family of patriarchal Russia was to be replaced by free unions integrated in the proletarian style of life. Living in conditions of plenty, working only so much as would be required by collective needs, liberated from any kind of exploitation and political coercion, free from "religious superstition" and from artificial inhibitions of the sexual instinct, men would be happy for the first time in history.

III

It is beyond the scope of this paper to describe the actions of the new rulers aiming at the realization of their blueprint and the reactions of the population. Only a short survey of the actual state of things, twenty-five years after the outbreak of the revolution, will be given for comparison with both the conjectural state of things described and with the blueprint of Russia's new masters.

In contrast to the Communist plan, but in accordance with the basic expectations of the pre-revolutionary period, Russia did not disappear. In the turmoil of 1917-21, Russia proved to possess much more internal cohesion than was assumed by her foes. She was not merely an agglomeration of provinces ruled by an autocrat, but was the natural organization of a "continent." The centrifugal trends were easily overcome and, by 1922, with the exception of the western borderlands, Russia was again one. In the turmoil of 1939-40, the larger part of the western provinces lost in 1917-21 was regained; the final outcome is not yet certain, but there is much probability that, except for Finland and Poland proper, Russia will have the same frontiers as in 1914 after this war.

But the major fact is that the frontiers are there and quite certainly will be there: Russia has not been dissolved in the International Society which failed to be born. It is true that, for a certain period of time, the name of Russia was carefully avoided, at least as related to the whole of the political entity ruled from Moscow: in 1923, the USSR was created of which the Russian Socialist Republic was but a part. But, approximately ten years later, the leaders started using the term Russia vicariously with that of the USSR. Very soon, the term "patriotism" reappeared designating love of a specified country. In the beginning, the idiom was "Soviet patriotism," but, with every year, the number of cases increased when the idiom "Russian patriotism" was used. In the course of the present war, Russia has definitively prevailed over the USSR in official proclamations, in literary works fostering the war effort, in sermons preached for the same effect, and the like; evidently, the term Russia possesses a much higher emotional appeal and greater motivating strength than the term USSR. Now, people currently speak of the glorious deeds of "the peoples of Russia," of their incomparable artistic production, of their courage, etc. The term "the peoples of Russia" points to a very significant phase in the situation: the new nationalism is not an ethnic or racial nationalism limited to the most numerous of the ethnic groups living within the borders of the Soviet state; it is a kind of corporate nationalism, involving all the groups forming the family of "the peoples of Russia." This neo-nationalism is more akin to the older "imperial" policy which prevailed in Russia up to 1880 than to the narrower "nationalistic" policy of the last few decades before the revolution.

This neo-nationalism seems to be stronger than nationalism ever was before the revolution. The explanation is that the attempts to uproot the national sentiment merely repressed it and, so to say, condensed it; when, anticipating the coming war, the rulers of Russia reversed their policy and began to foster this sentiment, it not only awakened but became overwhelming. Very fortunately, it was not only intensified, but also modified: lacking the narrow shape of racialism, this sentiment remains compatible with the recognition of human values and, therefore, will not necessarily prove to be a new source of disturbance in the post-war world.

The Russian nation, which has become so self-conscious, continues to be politically organized, in other words, to be a state. The withering away of the state, foreseen in the blueprint, did not materialize; bureaucracy, police, courts, jails, a standing army, all these essential attributes of the state are there, and nobody can doubt that the degree of "coercion," that is, of the enforcement of the officially recognized order, has increased as compared with pre-revolutionary times.

That the state would continue to exist, was part of the basic expectation of the pre-revolutionary period. This expectation, and not the opposite expectation of the revolutionists has been fulfilled. But the state was to evolve toward democracy. Has anything of this kind taken place? To this question, the answer cannot be but emphatically negative, and this despite the Stalin Constitution which, taken at face value, grants to the population both freedom and participation in the exercise of power, the essentials of democracy. Only a superficial observer, however, takes a constitution at face value. What actually matters, is constitutional practice and, in contemporary Russia, the practice is as follows: (1) freedom of religion is reduced to the freedom of worship in private homes and church buildings, whereas religious education and propaganda are forbidden; (2) freedom of the press is interpreted as the transfer of all instruments of printing from Capital (to which they are supposed to belong in a "bourgeois" state) to Labor represented by its "vanguard," that is, the Communist Party; (3) similarly, freedom of assembly means the transfer, to the Communist Party, of all facilities relating to human gatherings, so that no assembly may be convoked except under its auspices; (4) the freedom of associations is limited to non-political associations, and the political monopoly of the Communist Party is explicitly recognized; in practice, only such non-political associations are permitted to exist which are entirely controlled by the Party. Under such conditions, the control of government through public opinion is impossible; elections are meaningless since their outcome is known in advance.

On the strength of these facts, it can be said that the Communist Revolution has not only reversed the trend toward democracy, but has disposed of a number of institutions which in pre-revolutionary Russia could be considered as precursors of democracy. In very modest limits indeed, the essential liberties existed in Russia after 1905-6; from 1866, the courts were independent and, in general, good. Today they are neither independent nor good, because their personnel does not master the "stuff of law." After 1866 Russia possessed an excellent system of self-government, but contemporary Soviets are merely agencies of decentralized administration, not of self-government. To find, in Russia's past, a political order similar to that of our day, one must go back to the reign of Nicholas I.

The creation of the dictatorial structure was a natural response of the Communist leaders to the situation which obtained immediately after their ascent to power: since their blueprint was by no means connected with Russia's historical tradition and did not correspond to the trends ingrained in her pre-revolutionary state, the leaders had to abandon either the "withering away of the state" phase or the "collectivization of production" phase of their plan. To socialize production intensified coercion was necessary; on the contrary, were coercion to be permitted to "wither away," Russia would have rapidly evolved towards a nation of farmers owning land, the most important of the means of production in a predominantly agricultural country.

The dictatorial structure was employed to realize the socio-economic phase of the blueprint. In this phase, success, that is the materialization of an order conforming to the plan, has been more complete than in any other one. Except for a small number of "individual," that is, non-collectivized peasants, and of "non-cooperated" artisans, nobody can call his own any means of production; no private trade whatsoever is legally permitted to exist. Arable land, almost in totality, is distributed among 242,000 kolhozes. Trade and industry, as well as transportation, are managed by the state. Still, there is a significant departure from the blueprint resulting from the great deviation in the field of politics: industrial enterprises as well as agencies of distribution are state agencies and not of the stateless productive society of the blueprint. Collective farms seem to fulfill better the expectations of the fathers of Marxism, but this judgment must be reversed if one examines things, not at their face value, but as they actually are: these farms are managed by a special branch of bureaucracy, obeying the orders of the political leaders and paying only slight attention to the desires of the members. Therefore, in the opinion of the majority of the Socialists, not socialism, but state capitalism has emerged in Russia.

Let us not argue about terms. The facts are clear: the means of production and exchange have been taken away from the former owners, according to plan, but placed at the disposal of a mighty bureaucracy, and not of that society of producers which, according to Lenin, could be run by every cook. In this phase of human activity, the development has been in direct opposition both to the pre-revolutionary expectations and to the blueprint of the new rulers.

A new social order has arisen. In the minds of its creators, this was not the ultimate end: the order had to be created to make men happy, primarily by satisfying their material needs. Thus, an extremely difficult question is posed: what has been the impact of the Communist Revolution on the material well-being of the population of Russia? The best way to answer this question is to establish what the new system yields as national dividend. But since the new rulers claim that they had to sacrifice present needs for the preparation of a better future, the question of change in national equipment must also be discussed.

Food supply is the basic function of any national system of economy. The crop of 1913 has yielded 0.52 ton of grain per capita, that of 1938—0.57. The number of cattle, per capita, has evolved as follows:

	Horned Cattle	Sheep	Pigs
1913	0.36	0.59	0.36
1938	0.38	0.61	0.38

These figures show a certain increase, as compared with pre-revolutionary times, which is further significant if one takes into account that the export of food has almost stopped. On the other hand, let us not forget that improvement was to be expected on the basis of pre-revolutionary trends. It is noteworthy that the improvement as appearing from figures for 1938 was, then, quite recent: a few years earlier, the situation was quite definitely worse than that before the revolution.

Light industry has been sacrificed to heavy industry throughout the three five-year plans. Therefore, up to 1934, absolute figures were not higher than in 1928 when the pre-revolutionary level had once more been reached, after the catastrophe of War Communism. Between 1934 and 1938, figures were rapidly increasing; in 1938, 2.42 million tons of sugar, 0.83 million tons of paper and 3.5 billion meters of cotton fabrics were produced; the first and the second of these figures mean a significant improvement as compared with 1913, but the last testifies to a stagnant situation. In regard to sugar the development has lagged behind expectation. It is only in the production of paper work that the advance has been very rapid: a natural feature in a country ruled by the greatest bureaucracy in history.

The industrial equipment of the country has improved tremendously. This improvement can be measured by comparing figures of production for the years 1913, 1938 and 1940, since, in all these years, plants were operated at full capacity.

	1913	1938	1940	1938:1913
	(in millions of tons)			
Coal	28.9	132.9	164.7	4.6:1
Cast iron	4.3	14.5	14.9	3.4:1
Oil	9.4	32.2	34.2	3.6:1

One might be inclined to say that never in history has there been an equally magnificent advance. To refute such a statement, one has only to recall the ratio of advance of industry between 1888 and 1913, given above. Without revolution, the curve would have been different: instead of a slump in 1917-21, followed by a seven years period of recovery and ten or twelve years of feverish activity to make up for the delay caused by the revolutionary events, a relatively smooth advance would probably have taken place. But it is significant indeed that, around 1938, two curves, the hypothetical curve based on pre-revolutionary trends and the curve of actual production, reach approximately the same level and that, after this point had been reached, further advance slowed down. Does it not signify that the almost incredible efforts displayed in 1928-38 were analogous to the display of energy by an organism recovering from a sickness up to the point when the normal state of things had been regained?

Other items of national equipment have evolved according to different patterns. In respect to railways, none of the five-year plans has been even approximately fulfilled, and the present day network is incomparably smaller than that which could have been expected to exist already in 1925, if the ten years plan of the Imperial government had been materialized. As a counterpart, post-revolutionary Russia possesses a large system of airways and produces around 400,000 automobiles a year, whereas pre-revolutionary Russia did not possess any airline and had only 8,000 cars. But airlines belong to post-war achievements throughout the civilized world, as does also, throughout Europe, the diffusion of the "automobile civilization." No definite comparative judgment is possible, but to put the automobile and the airlines on the credit side of the revolution is obviously wrong. The same applies to tractors of which there were nearly one million at the outbreak of the war, compared to a few thousands before the revolution. By the way, the mechanization of agriculture has hardly compensated the country for the loss of half of her horses (31.7 million in 1913, 17.5 million in 1938). In the course of this war, mechanization has proved to be of dubious value, by making agriculture in the richest provinces of Russia dependent on oil supply (so badly needed for the war effort) and on transportation. Had Hitler succeeded at Stalingrad, not to speak of the occupation of Baku, half of Russia's agriculture would have been forced to stop.

An additional item in the national equipment which has fared rather badly is housing. There is unanimity among the recent observers of Russia that the Russian cities are incredibly overcrowded and that the Russian workers often have to live in sub-human conditions. Despite feverish building activity, Russian workers, not to speak of intellectuals, have, per-capita, less living room at their disposal than they had before the revolution. This shortcoming is all the worse since, once more according to unanimous opinion of recent reporters, the new buildings are very poor and display signs of decay a few years after their erection. Therefore, not only must additional buildings be built, but also those of which the five-year planners are so proud, must be replaced in the near future.

To sum up the economic achievements of the Communist Revolution, it may be said that: (1) heavy industry has advanced according to expectations, but with an unequal and unsound distribution in time; (2) the advance in light industry, railways and housing has lagged behind expectations; (3) the food supply is nearly up to expectations; (4) the mechanization of agriculture is a dubious advantage; (5) no paradise on earth, foreseen by the blueprint, has emerged from the Communist revolution.

In addition to this, the "anarchy of capitalist production" has not been overcome, but simply replaced by recurrent blunders of the planners and the executors of the plan. Never have people wasted more energy and raw materials by starting three or more times anew to work on a plan before possessing a final blueprint, or by producing mountains of wrecked commodities, than they did in Russia in the early thirties. Never has there been a less harmonious economic system than that created according to the famous plans. To be convinced of this, one does not have to apply any foreign yardstick to the system in question, but has merely to compare the achievements with the plans, especially the first one: what they expected and recommended was harmonious and rational advance, securing the complete integration of parts into the whole; enormous departures, sometimes meaning acceleration, sometimes retardation, sometimes substitution and modification, made the results bear almost no resemblance to the blueprint. The art of rationalizing the economic machinery has not yet been invented, whereas the existence of such an art was one of the fundamental premises of the whole enterprise.

In this enterprise, the collectivization of the means of production was conceived not only as a means of producing plenty, but also as a means of creating social justice through the abolition of classes and the materialization of socio-economic equality. To what extent did the new rulers succeed in this direction?

According to the census of 1939, only 0.04% of the population continued to belong to the group of "non-toilers" whereas the rest was distributed among the groups of manual workers, intellectual workers and peasants. What was not conceded was the fact that, within the statistical group of intellectual workers, a real group has arisen, comprising the leaders of the bureaucracy, both political and technical, and the upper level of professional men, including authors, actors, and artists. At the outbreak of this war, the differential between their earnings and those of the toilers in the narrow meaning of the word and, consequently, between their standards of living, was at least as great as in capitalist society. The new *élite* is not yet a closed group: membership in it does not depend on birth and may be terminated at any time with the loss of the favor of the Supreme Leader. The trend, however, is towards stabilization. In this regard, the decree of October 2, 1940, is symptomatic, abolishing as it does free education in the two upper grades of high school and in institutions for higher learning; fees are rather high, so that complete education becomes the privilege of children of the members of the new *élite*. Moreover, saving and investment in governmental bonds is not only legal, but highly recommended; naturally the members of the *élite* are in the best position to use this opportunity; since the institution of inheritance exists in the Soviet state, the savings of the fathers enhance the social status of the children. The rise of a new social class, consisting of high ranking Communists and of persons whom Stalin has designated as "non-Party Bolsheviks," is imminent. This signifies the complete disruption of one of the fundamental aspects of the original blueprint and the return of Russia to a situation which would have obtained if no revolution had occurred. As usually happens in revolution, the distribution of individuals among social classes has been strongly affected, but, despite the revolution, social classes have persisted.

In the new class society which is emerging from the revolution, Labor does not occupy the summit: it is placed below the "non-Party Bolsheviks" and is probably not better off than the peasants. Whether real wages have increased is a highly controversial question; but even if they have, let us not forget that, in pre-revolutionary Russia, they were increasing, and without revolution they probably would have continued to increase, as, between the two world wars, they did in industrial societies. But, in any case, Labor has lost the rudiments of organization which it possessed in pre-revolutionary society and lost also the prospect of acquiring the role of one of the main social forces which belongs to it in industrially advanced societies. On the other hand, Labor has gained security; unemployment no longer exists and could hardly return for a long time to come. This is one of the real achievements of the revolution and, very probably, that degree of security would not have been obtained in the background of "capitalist" development. It is noteworthy that only industrial labor, not the peasants transformed into workers in agricultural enterprises of the state, have gained in this regard. Members of collective farms continue to depend on the fluctuations of harvests, and, in case of bad harvests, the Communist government applies no other measures than those which, under similar conditions, were applied in Imperial Russia after the hunger catastrophe of 1891; loans in kind (seed, food and fodder) formed their central part. It is also noteworthy that, under the new social order, two unprecedented demographic catastrophes occurred in Russia, one in 1921-22, another in 1932-33; the cost of each is measured in millions of human lives. The former was a direct effect of the War Communism policy: depriving the peasants of any incentive to produce more than they needed in their homesteads, this policy exposed Russia to a terrible famine. The latter was a direct effect of the policy of the wholesale collectivisation of homesteads, which met desperate resistance on the part of millions of peasants and which, destroying the traditional structure of agriculture, could not immediately replace it by another even moderately adequate organization of food production.

The two catastrophes did not, however, check the general trend in the population movement. After the catastrophes, the increase was resumed and so accelerated that, in 1939, the population reached the figure of 170 million, a little below the figure which would have been reached, if the pre-revolutionary ratio of increase would never have been interrupted. The level of urbanization (33%) has surpassed expectation.

The people of a country is the bearer of culture and also the object of cultural efforts of the *élite*. In backward countries to which Russia quite definitely belonged and continues to belong, the main cultural effort aims at endowing all members of the national community with elementary education. In this regard, the Communist government is very proud of having overcome the secular illiteracy of Russia. The census of 1939 has shown that 81% of persons above the age of 10 could read and write, and that half of the illiterate persons belonged to the older age groups (above 50). This is, however, just one of the phases of socio-cultural life where the imputation of an achievement to the revolution is obviously wrong: without the revolution, in 1939, the index of literacy would have been 78%, a figure only slightly below the actual one; moreover, universal school education would have been reached quite a few years earlier.

As concerns secondary and higher education, comparison is very difficult. It is noteworthy that, after the failure of the pedagogical experiments of 1923-32, the Communists drastically reversed their policy and, in general, restored the school system which had prevailed in the eighties of the 19th century.

Among cultural activities of the higher level, natural and technical sciences have prospered; a large number of important contributions have been made by Russian scholars. Up to the present time, however, scholars who were famous before the revolution or at least graduated from institutions of higher learning before the revolution are still on the top, and it remains to be seen what the contribution of that generation which played the part of *corpus vile* in the pedagogical experiments up to 1932 will be.

On the other hand, the humanities in the broadest meaning of the term have suffered severely by the imposition on them of the official doctrine of Marxism. No great work in philosophy, history, economics, law, or government has appeared in the course of the twenty-five years; how could they, since a great work is necessarily a piece of independent thinking which could not be tolerated in the framework of a totalitarian dictatorship? In some specialized fields, namely in that of law, a very curious phenomenon can be observed. What Soviet lawyers have to say about the law, is now, after 1936, very much like what German Hegelians said 60 or 80 years ago. Thus, for instance, in criminal law punishment is once more conceived as retribution or retaliation for crime, and the sociological approach to crime which dominated in Russia since the early twentieth century up to 1936 is now declared to be one of the contemptible "petty bourgeois deviations" from Marxist orthodoxy.

The cause is clear: the "central theme" of contemporary Soviet culture is Marxist theory created one hundred years ago. Consistent efforts to focus the scientific thought on that theory have naturally resulted in the amazing "reaction" just mentioned. It is hard to say whether this "reaction" corresponds to the Communist blueprint; but one may assert that nothing of that kind would have happened if, in Russia, the humanities would have developed according to the pre-revolutionary trends.

Similar statements must be made concerning art and literature. No great monument, sculpture or picture has embodied the revolution; today, in painting, the style of the 1880's prevails, and in architecture the "Empire" style of the 1820's. In literature, quite a few good works have appeared during the periods of relaxation (1922-27 and after 1936); but, as a whole, literature very obviously suffers from the necessity of being "produced" in an imposed style, today that of a Socialist realism. The great richness of schools and nuances which charactered pre-revolutionary Russia is gone, as the result of Communist interference with culture.

Finally, what has happened to the family and to religion, the two great guardians of culture? After many tribulations, the new rulers were compelled to restore the ideal of the stable family, in direct contrast to their blueprint. After the failure of persistent efforts to uproot religion, the Communists had to look for a compromise with it, on the basis of a partial reformulation of their creed. The revolution has severed the ties between the state and the Established Church which probably would have occurred without revolution, through the gradual liberalization of political institutions. The sufferings inflicted by the revolution have purified the Orthodox Church; this is an advantage, but, very probably, without the revolution, acute atheism or religious indifferentism among the younger generation of our day would not have obtained the "successes" which are undeniable. Where, in regard to the family, the Communist blueprint has proved a complete failure and the historical tradition has prevailed, in regard to religion the blueprint has been materialized, say, by 50%.

IV

On the basis of the preceding survey, the following generalizations are permissible: (1) In regard to many important phases of socio-cultural life, twenty-five years after the Communist revolution Russia was approximately where she would have been, if no revolution would have occurred. Russia continues to exist as a state; the population of this state is almost exactly the same as could have been expected without revolution; this population possesses that industrial equipment which could have been foreseen 25 years ago; the struggle against illiteracy is near termination, but it also accords with pre-revolutionary expectations.

(2) But, as concerns political organization, Russia has been thrown back at least a century; her philosophy is that of the middle of the 19th century; her school system repeats that of "the dark age" of the eighties of the 19th century. Light industry and railways lag behind pre-revolutionary expectation. Her creative capacity in the highest aspects of culture has been very definitely crippled through the imposition of a "managed culture."

(3) Out of the Communist blueprint, the collectivization of production and exchange has been completely realized; religion has been shaken, but not uprooted by far. The country is endowed with heavy industry and has overcome her illiteracy; but in these regards the blueprint did not differ from the historical trends. In other aspects the blueprint has proved a failure. Russia is more nationalistic than ever;

social classes and social inequality continue to exist; an economy of plenty has not been created; no grand art or literature has arisen; the family returns to the stable type; the school is rather "reactionary."

(4) The revolution has produced a new society which is neither that which could have been mentally constructed by projecting into the future the main trends of pre-revolutionary times, nor that which would have corresponded to the plans of the revolutionary leaders. To a certain extent, this new society may be viewed as a blending of the two models, but elements are also present which do not fit into either; these are, first of all, elements of "reaction" and, secondly, elements invented in the course of the revolution, mainly as instrumentalities for the achievement of revolutionary ends.

The cause of the departures is clear. As revolutionary leaders usually are Utopians, they do not recognize the natural limitations of human actions and strive for goals which cannot be attained. They succeed best in those phases where they continue historical trends, which were temporarily inhibited before the outbreak of the revolution. But to achieve these successes, the nation has to pay a heavy price. Everybody knows that revolution means destruction of human lives, of material and spiritual values. It is less well known that revolution, as shown by the Russian example, may mean retrogression. In any case, revolution is the most expensive mode of social change. Very probably, the costs of the Russian revolution have been without precedent.

This cost is to be estimated the higher as the Russian revolution took place in a society fully conscious of its background and displaying sincere efforts to overcome it. Only to a slight extent was the Communist revolution launched to eliminate the partial inhibitions which opposed advance; to a much greater extent it was launched to fulfil a "social plan," to create an entirely new society. To take care of this aspect of the revolution, its balance sheet must include a special account of the original patterns used by the revolutionary leaders and of those which they borrowed from various sources.

The leaders of the Russian revolution were Marxists and, in their opinion, very orthodox Marxists; no wonder that, in their blueprint and activities based on it, Marxist patterns have prevailed. The idea of abolishing private ownership of the means of production and exchange and of founding a classless society is purely Marxist; of purely

Marxist origin also has been the emphasis on internationalism, the implacable fight against religion, the animosity toward the stable, that is "bourgeois," family.

But before the revolution, Marxist thought was known to be highly abstract and to avoid any concrete planning of socialist society. Therefore, when the revolutionary leaders had to materialize their blueprint, it became immediately apparent that the means to the end had to be either borrowed, or invented. Since inventions are not necessarily made any time they are needed, borrowing is often the only possibility. Borrowing was very frequent during the initial phase of the Communist revolution; under War Communism, the general pattern of economic organization was, with deterioration, that of the so-called German War Economies highly appreciated by Lenin. The pattern of "planned economy" which underlies the Five-Year Plans was borrowed by Lenin from two "bourgeois" writers, W. Rathenau and the "white guardist" Grinevetsky whose book, published under the auspices of Denikin's army, Lenin ordered to be reprinted. In art and literature, the problem of new patterns was solved by declaring that Futurism was congenial to Communism, a proposition which very soon was refuted by facts. In regard to the schools, "progressive education," especially the Dalton plan, was hastily borrowed and imposed on the absolutely unprepared Russian system, to start the Communist experiment in that field.

There have also been social inventions. They, more often than not, must be seen in the acts rather than in words, for the Communists never were very proud of their inventions. The most important one has been the One-Party system, in which Lenin embodied the vague ideas of the international revolutionary movement of the early twentieth century. This invention has given rise to a social structure which probably will persist so long as the political system created in November, 1917. And this is an invention which has received widespread appreciation outside of Russia: structurally, the Fascist Party in Italy and the National Socialist Party in Germany are exact counterparts of the Russian Communist Party, as well as the "ruling parties" in minor dictatorships and the Communist and Fascist movements which have struggled for power in democracies.

Another original invention has been that of the Soviet state, developing the rudimentary representation of the Labor class tried out by

Russian revolutionists in the course of the abortive revolution of 1905-6. The Soviet state, based on the ideas of 1) representing the toilers only, 2) organizing elections on the basis of labor units, 3) emphasizing the sovereignty of local bodies, and 4) creating the central political bodies out of representatives of the local ones, was embodied in the Soviet Constitution from 1918 to 1936. In that year, it received a deadly blow from the Stalin Constitution which preserved only the name, but not the principles of the Soviet state.

A third invention can be seen in the "Two Sectors Economy" of the NEP period, leaving the "key positions" in the hands of the rulers and returning the rest of economic activity to "private masters" from whom they had been expropriated under War Communism. In Russia, this structure was destroyed by the shift to the Five Year Plans policy. Outside of Russia, it has very much impressed the Socialists; the de-Man *Plan de travail* is a very strict imitation of the Russia pattern of 1921-8.

Finally, the principle of managed culture is also one of the social inventions of the leaders of Russian Communism, an invention of which the *Gleichschaltung* of the Nazis is merely an expansion. The idea of managed culture is that, in every field of culture activity, the pattern is to be established by official agencies to the official doctrine, so that individual culture agents have only to follow them in their production. This order is obviously very different not only from the liberal one, but also from that of pre-liberal society where trends held subversive were eliminated, but no positive interference with culture was attempted. Just as that of the "One Party," the principle of managed culture has persisted and, obviously, will persist so long as the political regime will; as has already been mentioned, it has found entrance into Fascist and National Socialist Society.

There is no need to evaluate these four inventions. Two of them, the Soviet system and the Two Sectors Economy, have proved to be unworkable and have been abandoned in Russia. Two others, the One Party system and managed culture, have become essential parts of any totalitarian structure. Their location in the value system is thus clearly established.

Such is the meager and rather negative contribution of the Russian revolution to the human treasury of social patterns. This special balance sheet does not, therefore, offer any reason for changing anything in the judgments previously made when comparing the achievements of the Communist revolution with pre-revolutionary expectations.

V

If the achievements and contributions of the Communist revolution in Russia have been so meager, for what do the Russians fight? Why did the Russians display that indomitable will to resist and survive which seems to have been absent in a number of more advanced nations of Europe? Does not the fact of this resistance, of this will to gain victory, invalidate the previous deductions?

These facts do not at all contradict the judgments above, if both the facts and the judgments are correctly interpreted. (1) In the conceptual scheme used in this discussion, the statement that the Russian revolution has been rather poor in valuable accomplishments is not identical with the statement that Russia of 1941-3 has not changed as compared with Russia of 1914. The Russia of our day is much better educated and much better economically equipped than the Russia which fought in World War I; but, in these improvements, Russia's *élan vital* has been manifested; in other words, under the revolution deeds have been accomplished which might have been effected without revolution.

(2) The social environment for the maintenance of which the Russians fight is only partly determined by the Communist plan of social reconstruction. Russia entered this war after at least seven years of retreat from integral Communism, after a far reaching restoration of national tradition had taken place. The Russians of 1941-3, in contrast to the Russians of 1918-1933, are not only permitted, but encouraged to be proud of their culture and history. They fight for their own home, the value of which has been once more officially recognized, and not for an imaginary World Home of the Proletariat which they were, unsuccessfully, invited to love up to 1933. The very character of official propaganda throughout the years of war testifies to this fact: Russia comes first, and the International Communist Revolution is never mentioned; very probably, the dissolution of the Comintern (May 22, 1943) has been hailed in Russia as enthusiastically as among Russia's allies.

The significance of the return to national values as the background of resistance is enhanced by the particular configuration of the conflict in which Russia is involved. Whereas, in previous wars, the point at issue was a claim on some province or sphere of influence, leaving beyond doubt the mutual recognition of the foes as members of the Family of Nations, in this war Russia's foe denies the value of Russian culture and even the right of the Russian people to continue living in areas occupied by them for one thousand years. Acts of the foe, especially the systematic demolition of monuments of Russian culture in the occupied provinces, have proved that he meant business. The great masters of propaganda, which the Communist leaders are, have skillfully used these facts to bring Russian morale to the highest possible level, the same which had been reached, say, in 1812: officially, this war is called "The Second Patriotic War," the term Patriotic War being used by Russian historians to designate Russia's victory over Napoleon.

The Russians fight for their home which is largely the expansion of their old home with slight modifications introduced by Communist architects. It is not quite sure that they would have displayed the same stubbornness and will to victory if the Communist architects had been permitted to reconstruct fully the old building. In 1932, when such a reconstruction threatened, many symptoms of defeatism were observable in Russia. This was probably one of the major reasons of the shift to the "nationalistic policy" of the Communist government inaugurated in 1934.

(3) It must be emphasized finally that people are accustomed to act much more on the basis of short than of long perspectives. In other words, their attitudes are much more determined by the comparison of today with yesterday than with the day before yesterday. In contemporary Russia, people no longer think of pre-revolutionary times and possibilities; but they know very well that, economically and culturally, they are much better off today than they were in 1933. To take an example: the religious situation is still far from religious freedom; but, in 1939, a new religious policy was started which has been substantially accentuated after the outbreak of the war. Religious-minded people cannot fail to be influenced by obvious improvement and are willing to obey the directions of the Church leadership to support the government in the struggle for the preservation of Russia's independence.

Thus it appears that the magnificent war performance of the Russian nation does not contradict our judgments about the Russian revolution. It is very possible that a large number of Russians would like substantial change in many phases of the existing order. But they understand that first things must come first: to secure national independence is the first thing, and getting rid of obsolete survivals of Communism can follow after victory.

In this war, Russia has proved, by deeds, her right to be one of the Big Four among the United Nations. But she had to prove it against the dominant expectation that her strength had been badly undermined through the revolution. Russia's part in the war has shown that, in her history, the Communist Revolution had been a dangerous sickness, but that Russia possessed enough vital energy to overcome it. At the outbreak of this war, she was obviously recovering from it. Whether a new challenge, this time in the form of a titanic war, will accelerate the recovery or be conducive to a relapse, we do not yet know.

The Teaching of History Under Stalin

PAUL OLBERG

➤➤➤➤➤➤➤➤➤➤ *Published in 1939* ᐊᐊᐊᐊᐊᐊᐊᐊᐊᐊ

In Soviet Russia—as in Fascist Italy and Nazi Germany—the study of history took on new significance. Like literature, art, science, and even music, history was regarded as a weapon with which to bolster the new regime. The attempt to find out the truth about the past was in large measure abandoned; the important thing was to present a version of the past that suited present needs. Rarely, if ever, had historical writing been so present-minded. In the 1920's and the early 1930's, Soviet historians stressed class conflicts and economic forces as the keys to an understanding of the past. M. N. Pokrovsky was the most influential historian of the time, and his *History of Russia* was "the pabulum that nourished the rising generation of Russian historians." After Pokrovsky's death in 1932, however, some major shifts took place in the Communist approach to the past. Especially remarkable was the patriotic emphasis that came increasingly to figure in historical writing. Hardly less remarkable were the tendency to glorify Russian military prowess and the attempt to root the Communist regime in the Russian tradition. Lenin and Stalin became the heirs of Ivan the Terrible, who was viewed as the unifier of the Russian state, and of Peter the Great, who was viewed as the first Bolshevik. Of course, this "new" history came as a shock after the sort of approach that Pokrovsky had upheld; but by the late 1930's Communists had had years of experience in learning how to keep up with the frequent changes in the party line. In the present essay Paul Olberg analyzes the conception of the Russian past that dominated the Soviet study and teaching of history on the eve of World War II.

The new Russian School History calls for special attention from European public opinion. It is entitled *School History of the Soviet Union*. It is the work of several authors under the editorship of Professor Schestakoff, and is intended for instruction in the elementary schools. As the Soviet newspaper *Trud* was careful to point out, it "was planned on the initiative, and by the direct advice, of the great leader of the nations, Comrade Stalin." The same paper describes it as "a valuable contribution, not only to the educational literature of our schools, but also to the Marxist Science of History." The *Pravda* recommends it as "a genuine gift from Stalin to our children."

In principle, this book implies a new phase in the Soviet teaching of history and, in fact, in the political education of the rising generation. Hitherto, Russian history and Russian culture were said to begin with the Bolshevist Revolution of 1917. Similarly in pre-Bolshevist ages Russia, like the earth in the legendary account of the Creation, was said to have lain in chaos and darkness. Now, however, we read in the *Pravda*: "This book winds up the dismal period which forced upon Soviet school children the dreary impression that the history of the U.S.S.R. started only in 1917, and that otherwise the past could offer them nothing more interesting or important than the vicissitudes of insignificant social forms." An interpretation of the past in Russia would certainly be very welcome. Looked at in this light, the new method of teaching history would imply a certain degree of progress. Unfortunately, the new School History is far removed from an objective and critical elucidation of former Russian policy: on the contrary it surveys the worst elements in Russia's earlier development, accepts them, and actually does not hesitate to justify them. The tendency is specifically nationalist and full of the spirit of political reaction. The official Soviet historians have rushed from one extreme to the other. The will of the ruler in each successive period of Russian history is glorified as the decisive factor. This will, be it noted, was nearly always clear, wise and strong. Ostensibly, therefore, the rulers could register great success. Earlier school books utterly denied the part played by personality in history: the new book ascribes virtually Divine powers to personality, compared with which all the other factors

Reprinted by special permission from *The Contemporary Review*, CLV (1939), 464-469.

—climatic, geographical, economic and political—of the rise and consolidation of the vast Russian Empire are presented as insignificant. In like manner, the policy of force pursued by Ivan the Terrible and Peter the Great is appraised with kindliness and reverence. For Ivan the Terrible's government the book discovers the following extenuating circumstances: "As a child Ivan grew up under the autocratic Bojars, who wounded his feelings and developed bad qualities in him." With such an argument do the historians believe they can justify his policy. The terrorism of the Opritschina, whose business it was to uphold the Czar's dictatorship "with blood and iron," is characterised as a necessity of State; the Czar himself is extolled as a great statesman, who "strengthened Russian Imperial autocracy," and "founded a mighty State out of many scattered provinces." This picture of power-politics is untrue to life. Even conservative Russian historians, like Kluchewsky, who have given conscientious study to the age of Ivan the Terrible, have condemned the Czar's rule unequivocally.

Why are the rulers of old Russia treated thus benevolently? The answer is found easily between the lines of the *School History*, and runs as follows: Because they must be looked upon as the historical forerunners of "the modern leader of the people, Stalin." Stalin, of course, according to these commentators, must not possess the bad qualities of his predecessors. Unlike Ivan the Terrible, for example, he probably had an excellent education in Georgian Caucasus, obviously based on the humanitarian principles of Komensky, Rousseau, Pestalozzi, Froebel and other world-famous pedagogues. The *School History* contrasts the wise, good Czars with the bad, stupid Bojars, nobles and "rich people" in general. All these "parasites" were only occupied in stirring up rebellions and treason against the ruler, for which they deserved, and received, severe punishment. This picture is also not difficult to explain: the Bojars, minor princes and nobles must be painted as ancestors of the opponents of Stalin, Trotzky, Zinovieff,

---

BOJAR or BOYAR: Landowner.

BUCHARIN: Communist theorist and editor of *Pravda*. Because he favored more concessions to the peasants in keeping with the spirit of the New Economic Policy, he was expelled from the Communist Party in 1929. In 1938 he was labeled a Trotzkyite and executed.

GORKY: Russian short-story writer, novelist, playwright, and autobiographer.

Kameneff, Bucharin and so forth. The teacher must understand how to make clear the danger of opposition throughout the ages.

The nationalist and militarist spirit of the book comes out particularly in the accounts of the waging of wars. As a rule, all Russia's wars have been forced upon her by her enemies; and, equally as a rule, Russia is victorious, for the mighty Soviet Union is invincible. Of course there were exceptions; but these only confirmed the rule. It is not disputed that Russia had to undergo numerous defeats; but it was never the enemy's military, economic or cultural superiority that caused them. Heaven forbid! Russia was always invincible: defeat was the result of "treason" alone. Only a few prominent examples need be quoted: Ivan the Terrible lost the war with Poland, Lithuania and Sweden because the Bojars practised treachery against him. In the Great War Russia was unable to gain victories because "the Russian Ministers and Generals, together with the Empress, betrayed military secrets to the Germans." Thus the same legend of the stab in the back which was launched by the German generals and Nazi demagogues as the cause of the German defeat is similarly made use of in the Russian school book.

It is known from official Soviet documents that the peace negotiations with the Germans at Brest-Litovsk were carried out by Trotzky strictly under Lenin's directions. The *School History* maintains, however, that Russia made a bad bargain because "the traitor Trotzky and his accomplice Bucharin sabotaged the peace negotiations." For this reason Russia is stated to have lost vast tracts of land. It is vain, of course, to search in the book for mention of Trotzky's having organised the Red Army after the signing of peace at Brest and having been Minister of War for some years; nor are the school children allowed to know that for years Bucharin was officially recognised as the leading mind of the Bolshevist party and chief editor of the *Pravda* and *Isvestia*. Concerning the close of the Russo-Polish War

---

His best-known work is his play *The Lower Depths* (1902). Despite his disapproval of Bolshevik methods, he came out in defense of the Soviet dictatorship. Until his death in 1936 he was the leading Russian literary figure.

IVAN PAVLOFF: Russian scientist who, in the early years of the twentieth century, conducted his famous experiments on conditioned reflexes. His success in conditioning the salivary reflex of dogs has been influential in shaping psychological studies of learning and habit formation.

(1920) and the catastrophic defeat of the Red Army near Warsaw, the *School History* states: "The Red Army did not take Warsaw: it was ordered to retire." Everything, clearly, in perfect order. A chauvinist soldier's witticism follows: "The Polish gentlemen were taught such a lesson in the war that they have not forgotten it to this day."

The glaring lies and unscrupulous demagogy of modern Russian history teaching reach unparalleled excesses in its picture of the development of Russia in the last two decades. This section of the book opens with the assurance that "from the first days of the victorious Bolshevist Revolution Lenin and Stalin set about organising the Soviet State." . . . "The Soviet Government gave the Russian people complete liberation—such a liberation as has been conferred on no other nation in the world." To be sure, let there be no premature rejoicings: the constructive work of Lenin and Stalin was disturbed again and again. By whom? By foreign Powers, who cherish bitter hatred against this happy Socialist country. They work hand in hand with the "internal enemies." Who are these "internal enemies"? Hear the answer: the old Bolshevist gang that did not agree with Stalin's policy. Their activities are described as follows: "That contemptible enemy of the people, the Fascist agent Trotzky, and his contemptible friends, Rykoff and Bucharin, organised within the Soviet Union bands of murderers, ruffians and spies. They assassinated the ardent Bolshevist Kirow. They also plotted the murder of other leaders of the proletariat. The Fascist scoundrels who followed Trotzky and Rykoff organised train-wrecking, explosions, fires in coal-mines and factories; ruined machinery, poisoned workmen and did damage wherever they could." All of them, so runs the legend, sought to restore the yoke of Capitalism. "But the bandits were convicted and punished."

The reasons for pouring ignominy on the former Bolshevist leaders, who for years held the highest posts, are as follows: to be able to pass off the failures of the Dictator system as the result of sabotage; to find some justification for the terrorism of late years; and to contrast the "honourable" and "statesmanlike" figure of Stalin with those "despicable internal enemies." There are no limits to the abuse in the legends of "traitors" and "spies." It goes so far that the children are actually asked "to track down carefully all suspicious persons, so that Fascist agents may be trapped." Lenin once coined the saying "A good Communist is a good Tschekist"—i.e. a good agent of the political police.

As befits invincible super-men, Lenin and Stalin have overcome the greatest difficulties caused by the "counter-revolutionists" and the "hostile powers": they have brought the building-up of the Socialist State to a happy conclusion. To our great astonishment we read that "even in 1933 the Soviet Union caught up with, and outstripped, quite a number of European States." The States, however, are left unnamed. The legend is put forward, cloaked by revolutionary and socialistic phraseology, that the Russian State under Bolshevist leadership has become the Chosen Land. It is stressed that only "our fatherland" is "a socialistic country": once the most backward country in the world, it has now become the mightiest and the most progressive. This is the reason why "we love the Soviet Union so much and are so proud of it." The Soviet Constitution is, of course, the best in the world. "Soviet aeroplanes fly higher and traverse longer routes than any others." Where is the finest and best Underground in the whole world? Why, in Moscow, of course. Similarly, art and science flourish better in Soviet Russia than anywhere else. "The musicians and actors of the Soviet Union are known as first-rate artists. Soviet pianists and violinists gain first prizes in international competitions." So it is obvious that all Russian composers, musicians and actors of earlier days, whose fame extended throughout the world, did not exist. The story about Professor Pavloff is particularly pungent—an illustration showing that scientists of the Soviet Union live and work as in Paradise. We read in the *History*: "It was only under the Soviet Government that Pavloff, as member of the Academy of Science, could develop his talents. Cherished by the care of the Russian people, supported by the power of the Soviet, Pavloff made many new discoveries about human life." In reality Professor Pavloff received the Nobel Prize for his achievements in physiology as early as 1904. At that time the Bolshevists did not even picture a Soviet State in their dreams. It is not improbable that he suffered less deprivations under the Soviet than hundreds of other professors. On the other hand, it is equally certain that the conditions under which he worked were tolerable only because, as mentioned above, he was already world-famous: his name could be exploited for purposes of Soviet propaganda.

In painting the work of Stalin himself, the *History* glorifies his personality to such an extent as to remind us of the Caesars. The Soviet Dictator is named only "Leader of the Nations—the great Stalin." In the preface we read that "the oldest State" of the Russian Empire, Georgia, is the home of Stalin. Then everything is praised to high heaven that Stalin has done or even merely wanted to do. We are told, for example, that after the overthrow of the Revolution of 1905, "Lenin abroad and Stalin in Russia carried on, against the law, the great struggle for Socialism; they were ready to sacrifice their last drop of blood for the cause of the workers." In 1917, when Lenin was living, for a time, hidden, under Kerenski, Stalin presided over the Fourth Party Congress. The Report of the Congress proves, how-ever, that his part was quite insignificant. Further: "Stalin was com-missioned to defeat Denikin's army." Stalin "worked out the First Five Years' Plan." Nor is mention forgotten of the great honour done to Gorky by his personal friendship with Stalin. Stalin "gave the people the best Constitution in the world," which is therefore extolled as the "Stalin Constitution." Like Figaro in *The Barber of Seville*, he appears everywhere, marching from one triumph to another. If other people have also played a considerable part in the Soviet State, they are generally described as his colleagues or disciples. Truisms uttered by him are quoted as pearls of political and philosophical wisdom. A picture of a Bolshevist Council of War from the time of the Civil War portrays Stalin in the attitude of a military leader, explaining the war map with a gesture of assurance. Amongst the numerous photographs illustrating the book, only four people are allotted a full page—all the others have to be satisfied with a half or a quarter. The chosen ones are: Marx, Engels, Lenin and "the leader of the nations, the great Stalin."

The reader closes the *History*, in which satire and tragedy meet, with a heavy heart—with pity for the rising generation of Russia to be brought up on a book so far removed from historical truth, and for the fate of Russia, where a ruthless Dictatorship is taught officially, ostensibly in the name of Socialism. The new teaching of history reflects the mentality of the Kremlin of to-day and the mentality of the personal dictatorship of Stalin. From this point of view it is a valuable record of the dramatic phase through which Russia is passing.

XXV

The Fascist Dictatorships

᠁᠁᠁᠁᠁᠁᠁᠁᠁᠁᠁᠁᠁᠁᠁᠁᠁᠁᠁᠁

The March on Rome: Revised Version

GAETANO SALVEMINI

The Use of Atrocity Stories in [the Ethiopian] War

FRANCIS O. WILCOX

Some Economic Aspects of National Socialism in Germany

W. O. HENDERSON

History and Citizenship Training in National Socialist Germany

R. JOHN RATH

᠁᠁᠁᠁᠁᠁᠁᠁᠁᠁᠁᠁᠁᠁᠁᠁᠁᠁᠁᠁

The March on Rome: Revised Version

GAETANO SALVEMINI

Published in 1932

Postwar Italy was rife with discontent. In part, this discontent was the result of the maltreatment which Italians—rightly or wrongly—thought that they had received at the hands of the Allies at the Paris Peace Conference. In part, it was the product of the difficult economic conditions—unemployment and high prices—that accompanied the readjustment from war to peace. The fact that economic discontent was widespread among different elements in the population was clearly reflected in the strength shown in the parliamentary elections of 1919 by the Socialist Party and by the Partito Popolare, the Roman Catholic group that favored a program of fundamental agrarian reform. It is important to note, however, that by late 1921 and early 1922 conditions in Italy were much improved. By then the humiliating experiences associated with Versailles were, if not ancient history, at least remote from the contemporary scene. No less important, economic conditions were definitely on the upgrade. In short, the fact that conditions were improving in Italy throws much light on the decision of the Fascists to act without delay. To delay was to run the risk of a further diminution of discontent and, without discontent to exploit, the Fascists could not exist. So it was that the notorious "march on Rome" of October 1922 was arranged. It is with this much publicized march that Gaetano Salvemini deals in the present essay. One of the foremost historians and journalists in pre-Mussolini Italy, Salvemini quickly emerged as a vigorous opponent of Fascism and its outrages on human dignity. Small wonder that he was compelled to leave Italy. In England and in the United States he continued to denounce the Fascist regime even in the years when it was fashionable in some circles to speak of Mussolini's wonder-working power: that he could make Italian trains run on schedule.

The well-known English writer, Israel Zangwill, was staying in Florence during the last days of October, 1922, at the moment of the political crisis which placed the government of Italy in the hands of Mussolini. In his eyes the events of those days resembled comic opera more than real revolution. Curzio Malaparte, one of the Fascist leaders in Tuscany, describes the episode in his little book *Coup d'Etat: The Technique of Revolution* (New York: E. P. Dutton & Co., 1932). He endeavored to persuade Zangwill that he was witnessing a revolution, and to convince him Malaparte drove Zangwill to the gas works, the telephone exchange, the telegraph office, the bridges and the railway stations. All these "strategical positions" were in the hands of Black Shirts. The result of this demonstration was disastrous for Malaparte's thesis. Zangwill observed that the Fascists had seized all these positions without striking a blow, while the police had taken refuge in the Prefecture behind rows of carabineers, royal guards and armored cars. Not only that, "the troops of the garrison, the infantry and cavalry regiments were under orders to remain in barracks; for the time being the authorities were observing a benevolent neutrality."

Malaparte called Zangwill's attention to the fact that the Prefect of Florence could not communicate with the other authorities because the Fascists held all the telephone and telegraph offices. He neglected to tell him that in Florence the military headquarters are only 200 yards from the Prefecture and that in five minutes the Prefect could have sent orders to the commanding officer to clear out the Fascists from their "strategical positions." Even without knowing this significant detail Zangwill might well have wondered why the Prefect made no use of the police, concentrated in the Prefecture, to expel the Fascists from the telephone and telegraph offices and from the central railway station—all of them within a quarter of a mile of the Prefecture.

The attitude of General Gonzaga, the commanding officer of the garrison of Florence, as described by Malaparte, was, if anything, still more ambiguous than that of the Prefect. After confining all troops to barracks and thus enabling the Fascists to seize the "strategical points" without striking a blow, he learned from the newspapers that the

Reprinted by permission of the New York *Times* from *Current History*, XXXVII (1932), 38-43.

King was negotiating with Mussolini and likely to invite him to become Prime Minister. At the moment the news was fictitious. But General Gonzaga wirelessed to the Ministry of War in Rome for confirmation—apparently the military authorities still had at their disposal the wireless service which the Fascists had forgotten to commandeer. The Ministry of War refused to answer directly, replying that the name of the King must not be brought into party quarrels and that the news was probably premature. The General's next step was to go to the Fascist headquarters in Florence and ask if the news was correct. He was assured that it was. This "good news put an end to his conscientious scruples and lifted a great responsibility from his shoulders"—that of dislodging the Fascists from those "strategical points."

Almost all the Generals commanding military forces in other cities acted more or less as did General Gonzaga at Florence. One needs only to read the accounts in the *Popolo d'Italia* for Oct. 28, 29 and 31, 1922, by the local correspondents in Siena, Piacenza, Cremona, Vicenza, Alessandria, Verona, Mantua and Bologna. Everywhere the Generals confined the troops to barracks and allowed the Fascists to take possession of the railway stations, telegraph and telephone offices, arsenals and newspaper buildings. Wherever the Fascists advanced, the army chiefs tactfully retired. In the rare instances when the military authorities did their duty the Fascists did not move an inch, or if they attempted to seize "strategical points" they were easily dislodged.

A typical case brought to my notice by an eyewitness occurred at Padua. General Boriani, the commander of the garrison of that town, was away on leave, or apparently so, on the night of Oct. 27. General Emo-Capodilista, who was in temporary command and did not belong to the military set who were in collusion with the Fascists, was preparing to take the necessary steps to dislodge the latter when

---

GIOVANNI GIOLITTI: Political leader who dominated the Italian scene in the decade before the outbreak of World War I. Intent on preventing the growth of socialism, he supported government intervention in behalf of the poorer elements of Italian society and did much to promote social-welfare legislation and educational reforms. He was also largely responsible for the achievement of universal manhood suffrage. Insisting that Italy should remain neutral in World War I, he was widely denounced as unpatriotic by those who favored intervention. Although he supported Mussolini in the early

General Boriani hastily ended his leave, took over the command again in the middle of the night and confined the troops to barracks.

As early as Sept. 29, a month before the "march on Rome," the headquarters of the Fascist party had been assured "that the army would remain neutral." This essential fact was divulged by Alessandro Chiavolini, Mussolini's private secretary, in the *Popolo d'Italia* for Oct. 27, 1923. Mussolini himself in a speech on Oct. 30, 1923, declared that he knew that "at the opportune moment the government machine guns would not fire on the revolutionaries." Richard Washburn Child, the American Ambassador in Rome in Oct., 1922, writes in his book, *A Diplomat Looks at Europe*, that he had it on good authority that "the army" secretly favored the movement; but by "army" must, of course, be understood "army chiefs."

A retired General, De Bono, was one of the "quadrumvirate" who on Oct. 27 directed the movement from Perugia. Five other retired Generals, Fara, Maggiotto, Ceccherini, Zamboni and Tiby, commanded the Fascist groups which on the night of Oct. 27 were "marching" on Rome. While these retired Generals were directing the sedition around Rome, other officers, some pensioned, others in service but on official leave, were commanding the Fascist groups which were seizing "strategical points" in the towns.

A Fascist who with his comrades occupied the railway station of Cancello, south of Rome, says in an account of his adventures: "The rumor reached us that the carabineers were proposing to break our lines. We were posted with a one day's ration of bread and corned beef. But it was a false alarm. They never appeared. Instead of that a quartermaster came, singing the praises of Mussolini, and offered us a truckload of all sorts of good things."

Had he known these facts Zangwill would have been still more confirmed in his opinion that he was witnessing a comic opera.

---

years of Fascism, he became the leader of the parliamentary opposition to the Fascists.

Antonio Salandra: Italian nationalist prime minister who pushed actively for Italian intervention on the side of the Allies in World War I. In the postwar atmosphere of disillusionment, he was frequently blamed for the sorry state of Italy. He was willing to cooperate with Mussolini in 1922 to the extent of giving the Fascists several posts in a cabinet that he planned to head.

The King, who had been at his country home of San Rossore, near Pisa, was informed of what was happening and arrived in Rome on the evening of Oct. 27. He was indignant. "Rather than give in," he said in the Piedmontese dialect, "I will go right away with my wife and my boys." That night the Cabinet decided to declare martial law, and while awaiting the King's signature to the proclamation they forced the Prefects of the provinces to hand over their powers to the military authorities.

The Ministers were sure that the King would sign the decree without discussion. In the twenty-two years of his reign he had never refused a signature to a Minister. While neither stupid nor wicked, he is incapable of initiative. His use of the royal prerogative has always been confined to signing the laws and decrees laid before him by his Prime Minister. When a Cabinet resigned, he would call in those who, according to etiquette, were the proper people to be consulted in such circumstances; he would ask each one whom he would suggest as the next Prime Minister, making a note of each recommendation. In the end the man whose name had been put forward by the greatest number would be sent for. Having performed this duty, the King would resume his habit of signing the decrees which the new Prime Minister laid before him.

Feeling certain that the King would sign the proclamation of martial law, the Ministers had the decree publicly posted at 10 A. M. on Oct. 28. As soon as the news was known the Fascists of Rome were seized with panic. They feared that the army chiefs, recalled to their oath of allegiance by a peremptory order from the King, would set the machinery of repression in operation. From 10 A. M. until noon not a Fascist was to be seen on the streets of Rome. One of the Fascist leaders, the present Minister Acerbo, then a member of the Chamber of Deputies, clad in his black shirt, took refuge in the Palazzo Montecitorio, where the Deputies sit, and asked, trembling all over, whether he could be sure of not being arrested if he remained there.

Meanwhile, Luigi Facta, the Prime Minister, took the decree to the King for signature. But he had been forestalled. During the night of Oct. 27 Admiral Thaon de Revel had "advised" the King to yield to the "revolution." On the morning of Oct. 28 General Diaz—one of the army chiefs—arrived at the Palace. He had been in Florence during the previous afternoon when the headquarters of the Fascist party ordered the "mobilization" of the Black Shirts and their "march on

Rome." He received an ovation from the Fascists, gave an interview to *La Nasinie*, a Florence daily, in which he expressed his complete faith in the Fascist movement and rushed off by car to Rome to "inform" the King that the army would not fight against the Fascists. News also reached the King that his cousin, the Duke of Aosta, was at Bevagna, near Perugia, in touch with the "quadrumvirate" which was directing the sedition, ready to have himself proclaimed king as soon as the actual ruler should abdicate or be deposed by the Fascists. It is not for nothing that the Duke of Aosta was the husband of an Orleans Princess.

The King was frightened by all this "advice," "information" and "news." But Premier Facta was still more afraid than the King; moreover, he imagined that he was going to be asked to form a new ministry with the collaboration of the Fascists if he aided in finding a compromise. Therefore he did not advise the King to sign the proclamation. "Sire," he said to the sovereign, "think it over." The King thought it over—and refused to sign; it was easier not to sign. He acted exactly like the Generals commanding provincial garrisons; he left the way open to the Fascists.

Having obtained the revocation of martial law, Thaon de Revel, Diaz and General Cittadini, aide de camp to the King and a supporter of the Fascist movement, suggested that the King send for the man on whom they could depend—Antonio Salandra, who had been informed several days previously of the high destiny which awaited him, and was already in Rome waiting to "sacrifice himself." But the King's advisers soon discovered that they had reckoned without their host.

The revocation of martial law was made known to the press at 12.15 P. M. and the news sent a thrill of triumph through the Fascists all over Italy. Leaving their "strategical points" they poured into all the streets, stormed the trains and thus "marched on Rome." It was impossible to stem the tide. The carabineers themselves left their barracks, fraternized with the Fascists and accompanied them on the "march." By refusing his signature to the decree of martial law, the King not only disarmed the Cabinet but lost his own freedom to choose the new Prime Minister. Until 12.15 P. M. on Oct. 28 Salandra might have negotiated with the Fascists with a view to giving them some subordinate place in the Cabinet. But from that time on Mussolini was master. For twenty-four hours, Salandra tried in vain to assemble a new Cabinet; during the afternoon of Oct. 29 he was obliged to acknowledge his failure. The King had no alternative but to call Mussolini.

The "mass suggestion" of Oct. 28, the failure of Salandra and the putting forward of Mussolini for the Premiership had been foreseen by no one. Mussolini had not been pleased in Naples, on Oct. 26, with the decision of the general staff of his party to order the "mobilization" of the Black Shirts. He distrusted the Nationalists, who were insisting that the order should not be postponed. He knew that the Nationalists wanted a Cabinet with Salandra at its head and with an openly conservative program. He did not like the idea of being dragged along in their wake. While the Nationalists were working for Salandra, Mussolini was negotiating on the one hand with Giolitti and on the other with Nitti, both of them being not only political but also personal enemies of Salandra and the Nationalists. He stipulated for posts in the Cabinet for his friends, and immediate dissolution of parliament and a general election. He was anxious not to compromise the success of his negotiations by violent measures whose outcome could not be foreseen. He brandished the threat of the "march on Rome" to make the politicians bend to his will, but he did not intend that the sword should be drawn from its scabbard.

After the Nationalists had carried their demand for immediate mobilization, Mussolini left Naples, crossed Rome without stopping, and instead of going to the headquarters of the movement at Perugia proceeded to Milan. If he had foreseen the sudden and overwhelming victory of Oct. 28 he would have gone to Perugia, to avoid sharing with others the glory of the "battle" and victory. But having no faith whatever in the adventure he betook himself to within two hours' journey from the Swiss frontier, ready for flight if things should turn out badly. Even the revocation of martial law did not bring a realization of his triumph. On the evening of Oct. 28 he was still negotiating— by telephone—with Salandra about the number of seats in the Cabinet which should be given to his party. It was Finzi, one of his friends with him in the offices of the *Popolo d'Italia*, that cut short negotiations by suddenly taking the receiver from Mussolini's hand and declaring to Salandra that he must make way for Mussolini. The Nationalists in Rome who were backing Salandra were furious at the demands from Milan, but they too were obliged to give way. At the invitation of the King, Mussolini left Milan the next night and "marched on Rome" in a sleeping car.

How many Black Shirts on the morning of Oct. 28, 1922, "marched" on Rome? A Fascist paper, *La Patria*, in a highly colored account of the "epic" days which had just passed, stated on Oct. 31 that "the Fascists encamped at the gates of Rome during the night of Oct. 29 numbered almost 70,000" (quoted by the *Popolo d'Italia*, Nov. 1, 1922). This number was repeated in 1923 by an English journalist, Sir Percival Phillips, in his book *The Red Dragon and the Black Shirt*. In that case the conquest of Rome was the achievement of 117,000 Fascists, of whom 70,000 formed the front line. Again in 1924, in his work *Awakening Italy*, Luigi Villari, the Fascist propaganda agent in Anglo-Saxon countries, gave the figure as 70,000 for the troops in the front line, but put the rear guard at only 20,000. But two years later in the *Manchester Guardian* for March 27, 1926, he raised the total who "marched" on Rome to 200,000. Sir Ernest Benn, an English publisher and student of politics and economics, judged 200,000 not enough and raised the figure to 300,000. None of these gentlemen ever asked himself how many trains and trucks would have been required to transport in one night 70,000 men, much less 200,000 or 300,000. Mussolini's own organ, the *Popolo d'Italia*, on Nov. 3, 1922—a date too early for the Fascist legend to have been invented—stated that between Oct. 30 and Nov. 1 the railways had evacuated from Rome 45,000 Fascists. But in a speech on March 24, 1924, Mussolini said that he had had at his command 52,000 men; by June 17 he had increased the number to 60,000, although in a letter written on Oct. 28, 1924, he reduced it again to 50,000. Probably, then, his "troops" on the fateful Oct. 30 numbered between 50,000 and 60,000.

But the Fascists who entered Rome on Oct. 30 were more numerous than those who on the morning of Oct. 28 might have been called upon to face the regular army. The big rush of Black Shirts to Rome took place only after the revocation of the decree of martial law. During the morning of Oct. 28, according to a staff officer who was in Rome, not more than 8,000 Fascists were in the city. During the afternoon of Oct. 28, all the next day and the following night, thousands of Fascists "marched" on Rome and joined those who had reached the city during the night of Oct. 27 and on the morning of Oct. 28. A few of them, like Mussolini, "marched" in sleeping cars; the majority "marched" in the trains they took by storm, in trucks, on horseback, or even on foot.

Wherever they passed there was a prodigious slaughter of chickens and draining of wine casks. Any peasant indiscreet enough to claim rights of ownership over his poultry or wine ran the risk of being given short shrift as a "Communist" and an enemy of his country. Amid this "marching" anarchy Mussolini made his entry into Rome.

The Black Shirts were divided into four groups. Those who had been transported by the railway which links Rome with Pisa had been prudently halted at Santa Marinella, a seaside village near Civitavecchia, thirty miles west of Rome. Others, coming from Umbria, were at Orte, thirty miles north of Rome. The Fascists from the Abruzzi were halted at Tivoli, fifteen miles east of Rome. The "insurgents" from the south were at Valmontone on the Rome to Naples railway, forty-five miles from the capital. Between these scattered groups there was no direct contact. They had a few machine guns, rifles, revolvers and a small amount of ammunition, bludgeons, table legs and branches of trees. Such is the description of them given in the *Popolo d'Italia* for Nov. 1, 1922—a source not open to suspicion—by the Belgian Member of Parliament M. Pierard, by the American journalist Carleton Beals, and by the Spanish journalist Sanchez Mazas, who were at Rome at the time.

The contingents of the regular army stationed in Rome numbered 12,000 men and could have easily dispersed these badly armed and ill disciplined groups. A pitched battle would have been unnecessary. It would have been enough to have left them without food and water in the desert of the Roman Campagna, cut off from their several bases. After twenty-four hours of this treatment a few judiciously administered kicks would have sufficed to have sent them home in a chastened mood. An old Roman prelate, who had been at the Vatican with Pius IX in 1870 when the Italian forces occupied Rome with a loss of twenty men, commented on the defense of Rome in 1922 with the pithy remark: "We in our day put up a better defense."

Was it a revolution? The "march on Rome" no doubt possesses certain of the elements of a "political revolution," in that a group of men, though armed only with table legs, took advantage of the weakness of the King and the Prime Minister and seized the government. But in a political revolution the army is beaten by the revolutionaries or is unable to resist them, while the army chiefs remain faithful to the regular government. In the case of the "march on Rome" the new men seized the government with the connivance of many military chiefs. Thus the "march on Rome" should rather be classed as a military *coup d'état.*

A military *coup d'état* is made with the help of the army by men who are in the highest posts in the government, as, for instance, the *coup d'état* in France on Dec. 2, 1851, when Louis Napoleon seized control of the Second Republic. In Italy in 1922 the King did not dare to abolish Parliament, nor did any general have the courage to compel the King to abdicate, or by a *coup d'état* to abolish Parliament.

To annul the parliamentary prerogatives the Italian military clique made a "pronunciamento" against the King in order to force him to carry out a *coup d'état* against Parliament. They camouflaged their "pronunciamento" as a popular "revolution." The King found himself caught between a civil government represented by an incompetent Prime Minister and a military uprising masked as a popular insurrection. He was forced to choose between giving in to the "advice"—the masked "pronunciamento" of the military clique—or abdicating in favor of his cousin. He yielded to the pressure and disarmed the civil government by depriving it of its indispensable means of legal repression.

So Israel Zangwill was right in regarding the "march on Rome" as a comic opera when the Fascists wanted him to believe it a genuine revolution. He would have regarded it as a serious matter had he realized that he was witnessing a military "pronunciamento" directed against the civil government. The pretended popular "revolution" was only the civic mask hiding the abolition of parliamentary institutions in Italy.

The Use of Atrocity Stories in [the Ethiopian] War

FRANCIS O. WILCOX

⇢⇢⇢⇢⇢⇢⇢⇢⇢⇢ *Published in 1940* ⇠⇠⇠⇠⇠⇠⇠⇠⇠⇠

The seventeen years that separated the "march on Rome" from the outbreak of World War II saw many changes in political, economic, and cultural life in Italy. Mussolini had insisted that the Italian people needed more action and less talk: "It is not, alas! programs that are wanting in Italy but men to carry them out. All the problems of Italian life—all, I say—have long since been solved on paper; but the will to put these solutions into practice has been lacking. The Government today represents that firm and decisive will." So it was that the Fascists brought to the Italian people a restricted suffrage, a joke of a legislature, a highly centralized bureaucracy; severe limitations on freedom of speech, press, and assembly; the loss of the right to strike, increases in the length of the working day, and a much-touted corporative state; rearmament and naval and air expansion which imposed heavy strains on the limited resources of so poor a country as Italy; and an expensive program of imperialism and war in Ethiopia and active participation in the Spanish Civil War. In the present article, Francis O. Wilcox, formerly of the University of Louisville and now a foreign-relations analyst for the United States Government, approaches the Ethiopian War through a medium that has rarely been employed. He examines the propaganda techniques which the Fascists used in order to justify their aggression in Ethiopia.

Modern warfare is waged on at least four fronts through the coördinated efforts of military, economic, diplomatic, and progaganda weapons. Not the least of these is propaganda. Conscious as never before of the castastrophic effect of war upon humankind, the people of a nation must be convinced, before they can be called upon to make the supreme sacrifice, that they are fighting in the name of Truth and Right. It is desirable, therefore, to portray the enemy as a wicked, murderous aggressor, a fit subject for the collective hatred of the state. Once a people become convinced of the blamelessness of their own government and aroused by a spirit of righteous indignation against the enemy, the problem of motivation becomes much easier.

One of the most time-honored propaganda devices to mobilize public animosity against the enemy and to justify military action is the atrocity story. This technique, says Professor Lasswell, has been used "with unvarying success in every conflict known to man." Certainly from the time of the Irish Rebellion down to the present, the circulation of stories about the atrocious and fiendish acts of the enemy have been utilized to maintain martial morale within the state and to bid for neutral support. During the World War, the tall yarns circulated by the Allied propaganda machine about the wicked Germans who cut off the hands of Belgian children, crucified Canadian soldiers, and operated a corpse factory where they distilled glycerine from the bodies of the dead, increased the blood pressure of honest Americans by leaps and bounds.

Germany's Atrocity Story Campaign. In displaying before the bar of public opinion numerous documents relating to Polish acts of atrocity against the German minority in Poland, the German government in the present war is pursuing a relatively normal course. Given the conditions in western Poland during the first few days of the war, it was only natural that a certain number of outrageous acts should be perpetrated against the Germans residing there. It was only natural, too, that these excesses should be seized upon as an opportunity to justify Hitler's action by trying to convince the German people and

Reprinted by special permission from *The American Political Science Review*, XXXIV (1940), 1167-1178. The footnotes which originally appeared with this essay have been omitted.

the world at large of the fiendish nature of the Polish government, egged on as it was by British imperialists.

The atrocity documents published by the German government in the United States follow the usual pattern. The reader is confronted with an imposing array of official documents, sworn testimony, and expert medical opinion. "Rumor, hearsay, unverified statements are rigidly excluded." Foreign (especially Allied) authorities are cited to assure the world in an impartial way that the Poles are a barbarous people. Numerous pictures are included; "the camera never lies." Then comes a series of depositions, startling examples of the terrible treatment accorded the German minority group. There are ghastly tales of mass murder. There are bloody reports of eyes gouged out, tongues torn out, teeth knocked out, abdomens ripped open, skulls crushed, brains spattered, arms and legs broken, feet, fingers, and legs hacked off, victims emasculated, noses and ears cut off. There are the usual frightful stories of women and girls being violated. The reader is told of pregnant women who were mercilessly bayonetted. Numerous other samples portray the Pole in all his barbarous cruelty; somewhat typical, perhaps, is the account of the Polish laundress who " 'foamed at the mouth' with blood lust."

Evidence is not available to permit a study of the veracity of these depositions, or even to measure their possible effect on world opinion. In 1935-36, however, the Italian government, under much the same circumstances, issued a series of documents calling attention to Abyssinian atrocities. A survey of these documents would seem desirable at this time, since they throw additional light on the atrocity story technique and its effectiveness when utilized by aggressor nations.

Italy's Use of Atrocity Stories in the Abyssinian Campaign. Since one of the chief functions of the League of Nations had been to act as a public forum from which world opinion could be crystallized,

---

HOARE-LAVAL PLAN OF 1935: A scheme designed to settle the Ethiopian situation and to keep Mussolini from joining with Germany. It provided, among other things, that Ethiopia make basic territorial concessions to Italy. The Plan was rejected by both Italy and Ethiopia. Several days before it was formally submitted to the League, its contents leaked out and caused an uproar in both England and France. There was little question that this attempt to appease the Italian aggressor encouraged further attempts at aggression.

it is not strange that Italy took advantage of her position at Geneva to exploit the atrocity story technique in connection with her invasion of Abyssinia. It will be recalled that by September, 1935, all efforts at conciliation or arbitration had failed and the Abyssinian problem child was found once more on the League doorstep. In accordance with League procedure, the two governments were summoned to appear before the Council: Abyssinia obviously the underdog and Italy quite as obviously the guilty party. Then it was that Mussolini played his trump card. Well aware that world opinion was tipping the scales of international justice in favor of Abyssinia, Italy went to Geneva, not as the defendant in the case, but as the plaintiff. Holding high the banner of the white man's burden, the Italian government submitted a flood of documentary evidence denouncing her adversary as a barbarous and uncivilized country unfit for membership in the League—a veritable black sheep in the family of nations.

The first bombshell of the Italian barrage came in the form of a "Memorandum by the Italian Government on the Situation in Ethiopia," under date of September 4, 1935. This heavily documented indictment charged that Abyssinia had consistently violated her treaty engagements with Italy. Her failure to prevent the raids and aggressions of native tribes in outlying territories had constituted an ever-present menace to the security of Italian colonial possessions.

Furthermore, Abyssinia had failed to live up to her obligations under the League Covenant. The slave trade continued, even with the connivance of public officials, who winked at the law and received a handsome bonus for each transaction. Domestic slavery, too, continued an Ethiopian custom, so that there was "not a chief's or notable's house in Abyssinia, from the Imperial Gebbi downwards, which is not at all times supplied with slaves of both sexes."

This possession of human life naturally carried with it all the

KELLOGG-BRIAND PACT (PACT OF PARIS): Antiwar pledge of 1928. By its terms the signatory powers renounced aggressive war as an instrument of national policy and agreed that "the settlement or solution of all disputes or conflicts of whatever nature or of whatever origin they may be, which may arise among them, shall never be sought except by pacific means." The treaty contained no penalties at all for those who violated its provisions.

horrors of domestic slavery. "Children grow up like beasts." Slaves were often under-nourished and many received exceedingly inhuman punishment from their masters—such as being scalded to death, burned with red hot irons, or hanged by the feet, head down, and slowly suffocated by the acrid vapors emitted from burning pepper-corns.

Numerous other atrocious practices were charged in the Italian Memorandum. Emasculation was still practiced by victorious Ethiopian tribes, who used the genital organs of the captured foes as trophies of victory. Tales of trade in eunuchs, cannibalism, bleeding of infants, and extreme torture were advanced to prove the barbarous tendencies of the Ethiopian.

The Memorandum further held up to ridicule the backward state of Ethiopian law, with its atrocious forms of punishment. Cited, for example, was the case of the would-be assassin whose limbs were tightly bound in strips of muslin impregnated with honey-wax and then slowly burned like a living torch. Almost as horrible was the sentence given to a native woman found guilty of murdering her husband. She was "taken to the high road, buried up to her neck, and left there till she died." She survived for three days, "when a large stone was dropped on her head, squashing it as flat as a pancake."

"Such are the barbarous customs and archaic laws in force today in Ethiopia," concludes the report. "By her conduct, Ethiopia has openly placed herself outside the Covenant of the League and has rendered herself unworthy of the trust placed in her when she was admitted to membership. Italy, rising up against such an intolerable situation, is defending her security, her rights, and her dignity. She is also defending the prestige and good name of the League of Nations."

Following the opening of hostilities in October, a steady stream of complaints against Ethiopian atrocities flowed from the Italian Foreign Office to the League, being published in the Official League Documents. The extensive circulation of League documents, it was assumed, would assure world-wide publicity for the Fascist cause. While allegations were made in regard to the use of dum-dum bullets, misuse of the Red Cross emblem, and bombardment of Red Cross hospitals, the most damaging testimonials (and the ones with which this paper is chiefly concerned) related to the treatment of Italian prisoners and workmen by the Ethiopians.

The Convention Concerning the Treatment of Prisoners of War

(1929) provides that such prisoners "shall at all times be humanely treated and protected, particularly against acts of violence, from insults and from public curiosity." According to Italy, therefore, the atrocious practices of Abyssinia in respect to Italian prisoners flagrantly violated the moral code of the civilized world as well as specific rules of international law.

Most common was the allegation that Ethiopian soldiers had emasculated Italian prisoners, decapitated them, slit their throats, and mutilated their bodies with sharp cutting instruments. In a letter to the Secretary-General dated January 16, 1936, the Italian government reported some 36 such cases. At Dekri, on December 3, an Italian soldier had been killed and "subsequently the Abyssinians disemboweled him and split his skull." Following the battle of Abbi Addi (December 18), they had mutilated the body of Lt. Martino "castrating him and cutting off his hands." Likewise of the 44 Italians killed at Makale (December 28), "25 were afterwards found castrated and mutilated by the Abyssinians." Still more serious was the case of pilot Minniti, who was reported horribly tortured, "killed and decapitated and his head . . . carried in triumph to the Abyssinian headquarters." These barbarous acts, argued Italy, "violate every principle of humanity and law and, in particular, the rules established in the Geneva conventions."

Scores of similar incidents were cited by the Italian government, some of the most damaging being sworn to by "impartial" observers. Among other depositions are those of M. Lipmann, a *French* officer on leave, who stated that "*he was told* at Diredawa, in the presence of witnesses," of the Minniti case; Joseph Jonka, an *Austrian* previously an instructor in the Ethiopian army; the secretary of the *Greek* consulate at Diredawa, who certified that Italian prisoners were massacred "in a most barbarous manner"; eight statements made by persons said to be returned members of the *Egyptian* Mission in Abyssinia; Armand Frère, formerly *Belgian* military adviser to Ras Desta; and various others, mainly of lesser importance.

The climax to Italian accusations came with the transmission to the League of certain statements sworn to by members of the Egyptian Medical Mission in Abyssinia. According to these depositions, Italian soldiers who were unfortunate enough to fall into the hands of their savage enemies were maltreated in every conceivable fashion: beaten, chained, bound with iron shackles, their throats cut, and "vilified and insulted in the most atrocious manner." Thus one Labib Hassan Ibrahim reported (this was corroborated by three other members of the mission) that on the morning of December 10, 1935, at Daggah Bur [Dagabur], he saw a parade of 2,000 Ethiopian soldiers with two headless corpses being borne in front of the procession. "At a short distance came other soldiers carrying the heads of the two corpses [Italians captured the previous day] stuck on spears."

But even Ibrahim's statement is somewhat mild when compared to the deposition of one Abdel Mohsen El Wishy, confirmed by two other members of the mission, who—according to the Italian report— *"have heard corroboratory statements from reliable persons in Ethiopia."* Mohsen related that on December 24, 1935, at Bolali, he saw a group of Abyssinian soldiers drag an Italian airman (apparently the case of one Minniti which the Italians had previously denounced by telegram) to a tree, place shackles on his legs, and bind him there. They then proceeded to emasculate him and cut off his fingers. Shortly afterwards the sergeant in charge began to flay the skin from the chest of his unfortunate victim in order to make a cigarette case "which he would use only on great occasions. The horrible operation completed, the body was cut into pieces. The head and feet were stuck on bayonets, while an attempt was made to burn the other wretched remains with petrol taken from a camp of Somali camel-drivers near by."

The Reliability of Such Evidence. While it is not the purpose of this paper to prove or disprove the accuracy of the Italian charges, evidence advanced by the Ethiopian government indicates that certain of the most damaging depositions were of doubtful validity. In her verbal counterattack, Ethiopia charged that the Italian memoranda were a "mass of inaccuracies"; that incompetent and unreliable witnesses had been cited; that photographic evidence had been "manufactured"; that sworn statements were too often of the "hearsay" variety; and that many general and specific accusations could not be proved. A few samples will illustrate the point.

It was amply demonstrated during the World War that modern photography might well "create" good atrocity pictures, one of the most effective types of war propaganda that can be used. In at least one instance, however, in the Italo-Abyssinian controversy, a specific complaint was registered against this technique by one Joseph Van Mollé, a Belgian, who charged that Italy had been "a too zealous collaborator in using a photograph" taken by him in Abyssinia in 1927-28. The photograph in question showed the chaining of a murderer at Gambo just after he had been declared guilty by an Abyssinian tribunal. The interpretation given by the *dossier* of the Italian government represented the scene as follows: "A thief condemned to have his hands cut off is about to suffer the penalty." As the photographer himself said, the interpretation placed on the photograph was "completely inaccurate," for it "does not deal with a thief whose hand is being cut off, but with a murderer who is being put in chains."

Furthermore, the Ethiopian government, in its report of May 2, 1936, presented a veritable flood of depositions (largely from members of the Egyptian Medical Mission) which cast considerable doubt upon the veracity of the statements of the Egyptian Medical Mission members referred to above. Thus on February 13, 1936, a sworn statement from six medical attendants (including Abdel Mohsen El Wishy) pointed out that there "is no truth at all in the allegations . . . attributed to some of our former colleagues."

One ex-medical attendant swore, on April 14, 1936, that the "report [of Abdel Mohsen and his colleagues] is a mere lie and devoid of a single atom of truth." Several others declared that Abdel Mohsen "was a mere humbug" and that he "had intentionally fabricated this lie in order to exploit it together with his two colleagues . . . to their personal material benefit." Four medical attendants likewise swore that all the accusations were "mere fabrications and entirely devoid of truth." Still others declared that Abdel Mohsen and his friends were never, during their stay in Abyssinia, near the scene of the atrocities sworn to and could not possibly have witnessed any such events.

It is generally recognized that human testimony, even that of eye witnesses, is at best unreliable. And, as Ponsonby observes, "where bias, sentiment, passion, and so-called patriotism disturb the emotions, a personal affirmation becomes of no value whatsoever." As has been suggested, the Italian government logically attempted to avoid criticism on this score by securing its depositions from people of foreign extraction. According to evidence advanced by Abyssinia, however, there seem to be other forces, even more potent than patriotism, which lead to exaggeration or even complete fabrication. One Mahmoud Aly Ibrahim swore that he had been offered certain financial considerations and other "attractive promises" by an Italian agent to sign certain documents "embodying alleged barbarous actions on the part of the Abyssinians." Still another, Mohamed Riad, one of those to whom damaging statements against Abyssinia were attributed, declared that his signature had been secured under false pretenses.

Not only did Italian agents secure signatures by means of fraud, trickery, and financial remuneration, but force and compulsion were resorted to, if the Abyssinian charges are correct. One Dr. Belau, a Polish doctor, testified that he had been taken prisoner by the Italian forces in Abyssinia and, following considerable torture and rough treatment, had been forced to sign a false statement under threat of death. He signed, he said, "under constraint and in order to save his life." While Italy in this case denied the disavowal made by Dr. Belau, and even presented a counter-deposition, the more controversy rages about such points, the more one is inclined to doubt the authenticity and good faith of much of the evidence presented.

Finally, the Italian case does not seem too convincing when one considers the reputation that many of the men who made the depositions apparently had among their associates. Unreliable people can hardly be counted upon to give reliable testimony. Thus President Ismail Daoud, of the Egyptian Medical Mission, remarked on March 13, 1936, that "had Labib Hassan Ibrahim showed as much energy and enthusiasm in carrying out his duty as a cook as he showed in describing imaginary barbarous scenes, he would have still been working as a cook and receiving his monthly wages of £E6."

Effect of Italian Propaganda Efforts. With some minor exceptions, the Abyssinian government did not choose to counter Italy's charges with additional tales of individual atrocities. Rather, it adopted two other methods of approach. In the first place, as suggested above, it attempted to prove that many of the Italian accusations were either obviously untrue or completely misleading. In the second place, as the war progressed, it presented evidence to show that the Italian army was waging a war of extermination, and that Italy's policy of using poisonous gases and of bombarding unprotected towns was far more barbarous than any act of atrocity that individual Ethiopian soldiers might have committed.

In a telegram dated December 6, 1935, Emperor Haile Selassie complained that open towns (such as Dabat and Dessieh) were being bombarded by enemy planes. By March 29, 1936, some 54 cases had been reported. Italy was accused also of attacking towns with poisonous gases—chiefly mustard gas—of bombing Red Cross hospitals and ambulances, of bombing and burning a number of churches. On April 1, 1936, the Ethiopian government wrote the Secretary-General that Italian forces were "systematically killing women, old men, and children, destroying towns, villages, churches, and convents, and bombing hospitals and ambulances. The awful destruction of Harrar is but a single incident in this terrible war. These practices recall the carnage of ages which it was thought had gone never to return." Dozens of complaints were climaxed in June by the personal appearance of Haile Selassie in Geneva to denounce from the rostrum of the Assembly "the tortures inflicted upon Ethiopian people" by the invading hosts.

The reception accorded the Italian propaganda campaign in League circles is too well known to require elaboration at this point. While world statesmen accepted the atrocity stories and gruesome photographs as a further indication that the internal situation of Ethiopia called for extensive reforms, they seemed to agree that "a backward population can be assisted by other means than by guns and tanks." Atrocities in Abyssinia? To be sure. But any atrocities perpetrated by the Ethiopians were mild when compared with the use of poisonous gases and the bombing of open towns. As Mr. Bruce of Australia, president of the Council, pointed out on April 20, 1936, "all the charges that have been put forward . . . are hideous; but there is one thing . . . that stands out in its menace to humanity and civilization far above everything else, and that is the charge which has been made that poisonous and asphyxiating gases are being employed in this war."

Throughout the deliberations of the Council and Assembly concerning the Italo-Abyssinian dispute, the Italian delegation expressed no little bitterness that their memorandum of September 4, and subsequent atrocity data, had not been of greater weight in determining the League position. In the closing meetings of the Assembly, Baron Aloisi once more denounced the barbarous nature of the Ethiopian and complained that "neither the Council nor any of the committees appointed by it during the last month have taken the Italian memorandum into account. They have not even considered it."

Further bitterness was incurred by the Committee of Jurists appointed by the League to make a study of the alleged violations of "international law and morality" on the part of Abyssinia and Italy. Following the Committee's thorough comparison of the charges levied by both sides during the conflict, the Council, on April 20, 1936, prepared to adopt a resolution reminding the two parties that both were signatories of the Protocol of June 17, 1925, prohibiting the use of asphyxiating, poisonous, or other gases in war. The resolution made no reference to Abyssinian atrocities. This "oversight" again stirred Aloisi to action. Why "confine yourself to asphyxiating gases"?, he demanded.

"We have been protesting to the League of Nations for months against acts which are far more serious from the humanitarian point of view." As a result of his insistence, the resolution, as finally adopted, not only called attention to the Protocol of 1925, but also reminded Italy and Abyssinia that they were parties to other conventions "regarding the conduct of war." By adding this clause intended to cover the treatment of prisoners of war and of the dead on the battlefield, the Council officially took cognizance of the atrocities perpetrated against Italian soldiers by the Ethiopians. At any rate, the ruffled dignity of the Italian government had been smoothed somewhat.

As one might expect, Italy's propaganda technique met with even less success in the world press. A survey of some 35 leading periodicals in the United States discloses that the Abyssinian atrocities reported by Italy created not the slightest ripple in a country where German atrocities had been so gullibly devoured some two decades earlier. And while such journals as *Le Temps* and the *London Times* reported in an impartial manner what Rome referred to as the *"écrasante documentation italienne"* ["overwhelming Italian documentation"], the few minor atrocities designated from time to time (on both sides, incidentally) paled into insignificance when compared to the screaming headlines which called attention to Italy's methods of waging war.

The controlled German press likewise maintained an even keel. On several occasions, when the foreign press carried reports of atrocity stories perpetrated by one side or the other, German editors warned that such news could not be verified and should be read with great reservation. Somewhat typical is the attitude of *Der Angriff* in protesting against anti-fascist propaganda. Early in the war, *Der Angriff* called the attention of its readers to *Kriegsgreuelpropaganda* (war atrocity propaganda) and reminded the world of the *Greuellügen* (atrocity lies) so unfairly used against Germany during the World War. And, concluded *Der Angriff* in a leading editorial significantly entitled *Abgeschnittene Hände* [Cut-off Hands] since history had established the innocence of Germany in regard to World War atrocities, German papers should set themselves up as models of fairness in reporting the news.

Meanwhile in Italy Ethiopian atrocity stories played an important rôle in the propaganda campaign designed to (1) justify on legal and humanitarian grounds Italy's intervention in Ethiopia, (2) stimulate a more martial spirit among the Italian people, who had not entered the war with the desired amount of enthusiasm, and (3) afford an official and a legal justification (by invoking the doctrine of retaliation) for the bombing of open towns and the use of poisonous gases.

On September 5, 1935, Italian papers published long résumés of the memorandum submitted to the League of Nations, *Il Giornale d'Italia* devoting its first three pages to that topic. This was followed by a concentrated effort to emphasize the frightful living conditions in Ethiopia and the necessity for Italian intervention. The Italian government communication to the 16th Assembly proclaimed: "Italy views the work she has undertaken in Ethiopia as a sacred mission of civilization."

Apparently hopeful of achieving their goal in Abyssinia without conquering the entire country, the Italian armed forces did not resort to illegal methods of warfare on a wide scale before December and January. But when the Hoare-Laval plan fell to the ground, the die was cast. Throwing aside any semblance of restraint, *Il Duce's* war machine ruthlessly entered a new phase of the conflict designed to crush the opposition by fair means or foul.

Bombings and poisonous gases were readily justified. In the press of January 1, 1936, appeared the following statement of the Ministry of Propaganda in Rome: "The bombardment which has taken place on the Somali front is fully justified by the proved fact that two Italian aviators fallen at Dagabur have been killed, decapitated, and their heads carried in triumph to Harrar." The entire Italian press took up the cry. One editor called for a harder and more relentless type of war that would better respond to the inhumanity the warlike Abyssinians and their cruel chiefs had always shown. Another suggested that Italy had attempted to wage an honorable war based on the rules of international law. But "with these fearful atrocities," he said, "the enemy obliges us to make use of every possible method in order to combat them." Others, in calling attention to the Minniti case and other Abyssinian atrocities, insisted that the war be waged without mercy. For, as *Il Tevere* put it, a tent full of Swedes or British or League officials, or even all the criminal community of the fifty-odd sanctionist nations— "all that is not worth a single hair from the head of a decapitated Italian soldier."

The Ethiopian government apparently understood the tactics of its adversary. In a communication to the League of Nations dated January 3, 1936, it was charged that the Italian government, no longer able to deny certain crimes which had attracted world-wide attention, "is now attempting to justify them as reprisals against alleged acts of cruelty stated to have been committed by the Ethiopian authorities." Moreover, stated the communiqué, Italy was merely preparing world public opinion for the more intensive use it was about to make of illegal methods of warfare. Subsequent events seemed to substantiate Ethiopian assertions.

Italy based her case almost entirely on the necessity for reprisals. Her army, ran the Italian argument, had consistently obeyed the laws of war. The Ethiopian forces, with their "abominable atrocities"— decapitation, torture, emasculation, savagery, killing of non-combatants, etc.—had ignored the conventions concerning the conduct of warfare and were thus "in the legal position of being unable to appeal to them." The Italian authorities could not do otherwise than "punish every inhuman atrocity committed by its adversary in contempt of every principle of law and morality."

The Italo-Abyssinian affair dragged on to its unhappy end. Atrocity stories furnished good fuel for the controlled Italian press and provided within Italy both moral and legal grounds for the war of extermination against her "barbarous" adversaries. But in other countries new concepts of international law and morality, buttressed by important political factors, acted as adequate disinfectants against the Italian "germs of hate." Had not the members of the League of Nations guaranteed to protect the political independence and territorial integrity of all states within the League? Had not the signatories of the Kellogg Pact denounced war as an instrument of national policy? And by this same token, had not aggression been branded as a criminal act against international society—the crime above all other crimes?

Suppose, even, that some of the stories were true. Suppose that atrocities had been committed. Was not the initial act of aggression— launched without a sincere effort to settle the dispute in a peaceful manner, and carried on with an almost complete disregard for the law of war—far more illegal, far more inhuman, far more barbarous, than scattered acts of individual atrocity? The propaganda campaign of aggressor nations, frowned upon at the outset by world public opinion, must necessarily function within a narrowly limited framework. This case study of the use of Ethiopian atrocity stories by the Italian government is perhaps indicative of the limitations of that framework.

Some Economic Aspects of National Socialism in Germany

W. O. HENDERSON

⋙⋙⋙⋙⋙⋙⋙⋙⋙ *Published in 1939* ⋘⋘⋘⋘⋘⋘⋘⋘⋘

The coming to power of the Nazis has been explained in many ways. Some writers have stressed psychological factors, contending that as a result of the territorial losses suffered after World War I Germans developed a castration complex which the Nazis were able to exploit on a large scale. Some writers have emphasized economic considerations, claiming that Nazism was a plot by which German capitalists, fearful of communism, sought to preserve private property. Some writers have stressed religious influences, arguing that Lutheranism, with its encouragement of obedience to political authority, prepared the way for the Hitler regime. And other writers have argued in favor of other approaches and points of view. What matters, in any case, is that once the Nazis came to power they accented the nationalistic features of their program and toned down its socialistic features; they made clear their determination to reverse the verdict of Versailles. Proclaiming it their mission to make Germany strong once more, they quickly began to mobilize for total war. They undertook a rearmament program that was designed to end unemployment and at the same time to compel the rest of Europe to tremble and to yield each time the Nazis saw fit to demand concessions. In the article that follows, W. O. Henderson, the chief British expert in the field of modern German economic history, describes the repercussions of military preparedness on the conditions of German economic life in the early years of the Nazi regime.

Widely divergent views are held upon the economic results of the first five years of National Socialist rule in Germany. Some observers claim that strict control of the economic life of the nation and intelligent planning for the future have had admirable results. They

Reprinted by special permission from *German Life and Letters*, III (1939), 81-93. The footnotes which originally appeared with this essay have been omitted.

allege that there has been a striking reduction in unemployment and that workers now secure numerous benefits through the 'Strength through Joy' (*Kraft durch Freude*) movement. They point with pride to such spectacular public works as the new arterial motor roads (*Autobahnen*). They boast of the increase in national self-sufficiency of the new Germany and the growth of her economic power in Central and Eastern Europe. Others believe that the economic benefits supposed to have been gained by Germany are either exaggerated or illusory. They denounce Germany as a dishonest debtor. They claim that the revival of business has not been accompanied by the usual signs of prosperity such as rising wages and increased dividends. They consider that the German worker's standard of life has been seriously depressed and that his opportunities of resisting economic exploitation have been greatly reduced. They see German industry hindered by countless Government regulations and restrictions.

Among the reasons for these differences of opinion two deserve special mention since they are real obstacles to an understanding of the problem. First, it is difficult to secure precise statistical information concerning certain aspects of Germany's economic activities. Thus the annual budget statement is no longer published in the form that was customary before 1933. Secondly, the nature of the comments made by observers upon recent changes in Germany naturally depends upon their views regarding the objects of State economic policy. The fervent National Socialist regards self-sufficiency and preparedness for war as desirable in themselves. These objects should be ruthlessly pursued at all costs. Hostile critics tend to regard the extent of the material well-being of the mass of the people as the criterion by which to judge the success or failure of Germany's recent economic policy.

Although the policy of the National Socialist Government has been profoundly influenced both by the serious depression which crippled business when it assumed office and by its own philosophy

---

AUTARKIE: National self-sufficiency, a term much used in Nazi Germany. To achieve it was the main purpose of the Four Year Plan of 1936.

LABOR FRONT: Organization, headed by Robert Ley, which replaced the dissolved workers' parties and trade unions in Nazi Germany. It organized not only workers but also employers, and its function was to bring capital and labor together in order to achieve the objectives of Nazism.

concerning the objects of the economic activities of the State, it must be recognized that its work has also, in no small degree, been influenced by geographical and historical factors that deserve examination. Both German agriculture and industry have suffered from geographical difficulties. Much of the North German plain is not very fertile. The bogs (*Moore*) and heaths (*Geest*) west of the Elbe and the swampy valleys (*Urstromtäler*) east of that river present special difficulties to the farmer. Germany has important mineral resources, such as coal and iron, but many of them are near the frontiers of the Reich (e.g. the Silesian and Saar coalfields) and transport costs to the great centres of population are not inconsiderable.

An historical factor of some significance is that Germany's industrial revolution came considerably later than that of England or Belgium. The political disintegration of the country in the eighteenth and nineteenth centuries contributed to this. It was only in 1834 that the first serious step towards the economic unification of Germany was taken by the establishment of the Zollverein. Not until the 'eighties was that unification completed by the adhesion of Hamburg and Bremen to the German customs system. The building of German railways in the middle years of the last century greatly assisted economic progress. German manufacturers and merchants had the advantage of being able to learn from the experience of their English rivals who had already passed through an industrial revolution. But they were, for a time, hampered by lack of capital and perhaps also by the fact that foreign merchants (particularly English and Dutch) controlled much of Germany's trade with colonial regions.

It is partly owing to these geographical and historical factors and partly to the traditional military nature of the Prussian State that Germans have long been accustomed to a considerable measure of Government supervision and assistance in their economic activities. Dr. W. F. Bruck has recently observed that 'Mercantilism is the key-

---

WALTHER RATHENAU: German political leader who was in charge of raw-material supplies during World War I. Although opposed in 1918 to Germany's surrender, he became in the postwar years a major advocate of the policy of fulfillment, insisting that Germany should meet the reparations obligations imposed by the Versailles Treaty. Having antagonized nationalistic elements in Weimar Germany, he was assassinated in 1922.

note of Prussian Germany' and that 'expansionism, State protection in all great spheres of production and distribution, including State ownership of various undertakings, and general tutelage of the voluntarily obedient inhabitants, marked the development of Germany and especially Prussia from absolutism through constitutionalism up to totalitarianism.' Before the War the State played a not unimportant part in the economic development of the country. It pursued a fiscal policy of Protection. The shipping industry was encouraged by subsidies. The Prussian railways were nationalized. The State fostered technical education. Considerable sums were spent on recently acquired colonies which would, it was hoped, one day supply German manufacturers with many of their raw materials. The 'peaceful penetration' of the Balkans and Asia Minor had an economic as well as a political significance.

It is, however, not so much the economic policy of the State in the years before 1914 that has influenced the National Socialists in their attitude towards economic problems as the experience of the Great War and of the years that followed it. Probably no single factor contributed so much to Germany's defeat in the War as the Allied blockade. Starvation slowly sapped the morale of the people and lack of essential raw materials hampered military operations. The emergency forced the Government to adopt a policy of economic planning to make the country as self-supporting as possible. Walther Rathenau and Richard von Moellendorff carried out this early attempt to organize industry under State supervision. After the War the economic disabilities placed upon Germany by the peace settlement—losses of territory in Europe and overseas and the demand for Reparations—and the continued hostility of her former enemies encouraged the Weimar Republic to pursue a policy of national self-sufficiency and State planning. Under Hitler's régime this policy (*Autarkie*) has been greatly intensified for the National Socialists are determined that Germany shall never again be starved into submission by a war-time blockade.

Other economic and social developments during the Weimar period have influenced the National Socialists. First, the inflation which destroyed the savings of the middle classes and brought untold misery to them and to the workers has led to a determination to control the currency in such a way as to prevent a repetition of such a catastrophe. The National Socialists have in fact devalued the currency again but by severe exchange restrictions and price-fixing they have prevented any serious decline in the internal purchasing power of the Mark. Secondly, the economic and political strength of the workers in the Weimar period was a thorn in the flesh of the great capitalists. The National Socialists, by destroying the old trade unions and the former political parties of the Left, have driven "class-warfare" underground and have thus (in their own opinion) increased industrial efficiency. Thirdly, unemployment in Germany at the time of the world economic crisis became so serious as to threaten to bring about a condition of social anarchy. At the beginning of 1933 six million Germans were registered as unemployed and there may have been as many as a million more out of work who had in despair given up reporting at the Labour Offices. Here was an economic and social problem of the first magnitude and the National Socialists were determined to tackle it without delay.

The economic position of Germany when the National Socialists took office in 1933 may be summed up as follows. Germany had suffered very serious economic losses during the War and further severe burdens were placed upon her by the Peace. From being a creditor nation with a considerable income from foreign investments and shipping services she had become an impoverished debtor State. Subsequent recovery had been checked by the inflation, the French occupation of the Ruhr, the necessity of paying Reparations, and the difficulty of selling manufactured goods abroad owing to high tariffs. Foreign (particularly American) loans had staved off disaster for a time but the world economic crisis caused a great industrial depression in Germany and seriously increased unemployment. The difficulties of the War years and of the period that followed the conclusion of peace had led the Government to adopt measures of State economic planning, and both industries and agriculture received State encouragement at the expense of a considerable degree of State control. This was in the tradition of the old Mercantilist policy of the Prussian military State.

The National Socialists thus had two main objects in their economic policy. They desired, first, the abolition of unemployment. They were determined, secondly, to organize and supervise the economic life of the nation so that Germany should always be prepared for war. All other considerations had to give way before those two objects. The freedom of manufacturers and farmers to manage their own affairs as they pleased; the liberty of workers to organize themselves in independent trade unions and to strike for better conditions; the natural desire of men to improve their standard of living—these things were regarded as far less important than arming to the teeth and abolishing unemployment.

The unemployment problem was promptly tackled. Some of the youthful unemployed were absorbed in the Labour Service Corps and others had to work on the land (the "Land Help" and the "Land Year"). Only nominal wages were paid—a Labour Service Corps man received threepence a day pocket money—and it was argued that work of this kind was of great educational and social benefit to those undertaking it. Young persons in employment were also given this type of work so as to make room for older men in industry. The reintroduction of conscription removed a large number of young men from the labour market. By 1937 Germany probably had over three-quarters of a million men under arms. Measures were taken to spread available work over as many families as possible. Wives and daughters who could be supported by their husbands and fathers were discouraged from retaining paid employment. A check was placed upon extra leisure time earnings by those already fully employed. Efforts were made to create work by State guarantees and grants in aid to housing, road, canal, water-supply, water-power, railway, post-office and similar schemes. By the end of 1935 the rearmament programme had brought about an industrial boom and this rendered less necessary schemes to create work of the kind common in 1933-4. As a result of these measures unemployment declined from six millions in January 1933, to 1,877,000 in June 1935. It was estimated that one-third of these unemployed belonged to that "reserve of labour" from which industries recruit unskilled and casual workers as need arises. One-third were classed as "unemployable" for various reasons. One-third, though included in the unemployment statistics, actually had part-time employment or had independent means which covered at least part of their needs. In the circumstances a further reduction of unemployment appeared to present serious difficulties. But the continued increase in armaments and the further application of the other measures mentioned had, by March 1938, reduced the unemployed to only half a million. In September 1938—when the army was partially mobilized—unemployment in Germany (excluding Austria) fell to 156,000. The number of those out of work in Austria was less than 100,000. While every credit must go to the National Socialists for the vigour with which they dealt with a very serious problem it should be remembered that some of the plans adopted were worked out and even acted upon before they took office. Moreover some of those who were taken off the unemployment registers were not given work with wages in the ordinary sense. They were conscripted into the army, Labour Service Corps and other organizations and forced to work long hours for their keep and a little pocket money. In a free country where the workers are organized in trade unions some of these methods would not be possible.

While the unemployment problem has been solved to the satisfaction of the National Socialists only a certain measure of success has attended their efforts to achieve national self-sufficiency. It is by no means quite clear at exactly what degree of self-sufficiency National Socialists aim. Complete *Autarkie* would presumably mean that Germany had no foreign trade whatever and that the people would live in complete isolation from their neighbours. In fact Germany has a substantial foreign trade, and *in certain directions*, that commerce has been fostered by National Socialists by every means in their power. Perhaps the degree of *Autarkie* at which Germany aims may be defined as that measure of self-sufficiency which would enable the country to face a wartime blockade without suffering intolerable hardships.

Both agriculture and industry play their part in the National Socialist scheme for attaining self-sufficiency. National Socialists aim at a balanced national economy and have no wish to see in their own country that exceptional development of industry at the expense of agriculture that has taken place in England. They envisage German agriculture as producing enough food to make the country virtually independent of foreign foodstuffs and as maintaining a large healthy population on the land. Economic, social and military motives lie behind the National Socialist policy of fostering farming. German imports of foodstuffs and fodder have been drastically reduced. Efforts to cut down wheat and barley imports have been only partially successful. These imports had been virtually eliminated by 1936 but in the following year nearly 600,000 tons of wheat were imported. The imports of butter, eggs, lard and fodder have greatly declined. While the domestic production of wheat and barley has, on the whole, covered the decline in imports there have been periodic shortages of butter, eggs and lard. In April 1937 ration cards were introduced for bacon, lard and margarine. Moreover, the shortage of fodder has adversely affected the dairy industry and helps to explain the decline in the production of milk per cow between 1933 and 1935. The Government has made every effort to increase domestic agricultural production and it is estimated that five thousand million Marks was spent by the Reich between 1932 and 1937 to foster farming. It is doubtful to what extent the German drive for agricultural self-sufficiency has been successful and some controversy on the subject has arisen.

In the industrial field the drive towards national self-sufficiency has been characterized by a determination to exploit native natural resources to the utmost and to find substitutes for fuels and raw materials which cannot be produced in Germany. Lavish Government subsidies have been granted to increase the home production of such materials as lignite (brown coal), ores, wool and flax. Every effort has been made to increase the use of lignite for combustion under steam boilers—e.g. in power stations—and for the production of briquettes. Domestic products are being used instead of imported natural products. Thus rayon, flax and staple-fibre are taking the place of imported cotton, jute and sisal-hemp, while aluminium and bakelite are being used in place of copper and brass. In 1937 the textile industries secured a fifth of their materials at home compared with only six per cent. in 1932. The consumption of aluminium is about a hundred thousand tons a year compared with only 34,300 tons in 1933. The native production of bauxite (the main raw material for aluminium) has considerably increased. The use of imported goods is restricted. A typical regulation was one in 1937 which ordered breweries to use their horse waggons again so that pneumatic tyres might be saved. Various artificial products—such as artificial silk, synthetic rubber (*Buna*) and oil from coal—have been used. Some of these synthetic products are much more expensive and less durable than natural products. Regeneration processes have enabled shoddy (old wool), old tyres and scrap metal to be used again. Germany, however, still imports large quantities of raw materials. The "shortage" of raw materials, which it is attempted to remedy by the methods mentioned, is due partly to the heavy demands of the armaments industries and the consequent lack of important raw materials for ordinary civilian purposes. The cost of this aspect of the attempt to secure self-sufficiency has been very considerable not only to the Government but to manufacturers and consumers.

There are Germans who argue that economic planning to achieve national self-sufficiency would be more successful if the colonies they held before the War were returned to them. It is said that these overseas possessions would provide Germany with important raw materials and foodstuffs and would open up new markets for her manufactured articles. But the products of the former colonies are of no very great significance. Doubtless a German monopoly of the vanadium of South-West Africa, the sisal-hemp of Tanganyika (East Africa), the rubber and cocoa of the Cameroons, the phosphates of Nauru, and the copra of Samoa would be of some help in securing national self-sufficiency, but the economic benefits that Germany would gain by recovering her colonies should not be exaggerated. It may be observed that before the War Germany spent at least £100,000,000 in conquering and running her colonies; that none of the chief colonies were financially self-supporting; and that Germany's trade with her overseas possessions amounted to a mere half of one per cent. of her total commerce.

The National Socialist policy of subordinating everything to preparation for war—rearmament on a gigantic scale and efforts to secure self-sufficiency to withstand a blockade—has led to considerable changes in her foreign trade. Formerly Germany's foreign commerce was what one would normally expect in a highly industrialized country. Germany imported food, fodder, raw materials and half-finished goods and paid for them by the export of manufactured articles and of "invisible" exports (such as shipping services and the income derived from foreign tourists). Under Hitler's régime the imports of food and many raw materials have been cut down. Germany is now extremely anxious to obtain those materials which are essential to her armament industries. Other imports take a second place. The State controls foreign trade and foreign financial transactions. Foreign commerce is conducted almost entirely by bartering German goods for foreign goods under agreements made with nearly all the important countries of the world. Germany no longer buys in the cheapest market and sells in the dearest. She trades only with countries which are prepared to accept German goods in *direct* exchange for raw materials and foodstuffs. For certain transactions a vast amount of red tape is involved. It is said that on one occasion when German toys were bartered for ten thousand lbs of wool about 680 forms were filled up and eighteen months elapsed before the transaction was officially completed. Germany's foreign commerce declined somewhat in 1933 and 1934 but revived in the following year. Between January to September 1938, however, the value of Germany's imports was greater than that of her exports by RM164,100,000.

The problem of raising money to finance the National Socialist economic system was a serious one. When Hitler assumed power Germany was a debtor State with no accumulated reserves. To abolish unemployment, rearm on a vast scale, build great public works, construct factories to make unprofitable synthetic products, subsidize heavily both farming and certain export industries, and build up a vast administrative machine to make all this possible was an exceedingly costly enterprise. Some of the money was raised at the expense of Germany's foreign creditors. Not only did many foreign creditors lose some of their interest but both capital and interest were detained in Germany and might be spent only in Germany. Money due to foreign creditors was placed in various "blocked" accounts. Marks from these accounts were purchased at a heavy discount by the Government (through the Gold-Discount Bank) and the discount was used to subsidize exporters. One type of Mark derived from "blocked" accounts is familiar to foreign tourists. Visitors who enjoy a cheap holiday in Germany by purchasing Registered Marks benefit from the misfortunes of certain foreign creditors of Germany.

There are, however, limits to the amount of money that can be extracted from the pockets of foreigners and Germans themselves have had to pay heavily to finance their country's new economic policy. The Jews have been ruthlessly plundered. The Government's income from taxes and customs duties has been considerably augmented owing to the trade revival and to an increase in the burden of taxes of all kinds. It is estimated that the income from taxes levied by the central Government, federal State Government and municipalities was fifty per cent. higher in 1936-7 than in 1932-3. Further, Germans must invest their savings at home and not abroad. All savings are controlled by the Government either directly (e.g. if they are invested in State bonds) or indirectly (since all banks are controlled and business more or less supervised by the State). Business firms were forced to invest any surplus earnings above a six per cent. dividend in Government securities.

A huge administrative machine has been created to organize economic planning. Industry has been organized by "Estates"—for Industry and Trade, Handicrafts and Transport—by special Boards for certain manufactures which have to contend with a shortage of raw materials, and by Chambers of Commerce. Farming is controlled by the Agricultural (or Nutrition) "Estate." The activities of the workers are controlled by the Labour Front. Various organizations are concerned with the supply of foreign exchange. There is some overlapping in the functions of these, and other bodies, and their policies by no means always coincide. Thus the Agricultural Estate favours high prices for farmers' produce while the Labour Front desires low food prices. Chambers of Commerce try to obtain orders for local manufacturers while the special industrial Boards are interested in the export of certain types of goods rather than in the prosperity of any particular manufacturing region. Some of these bodies (such as the Labour Front) would more properly be described as organizations of the National Socialist Party. Indeed the existence of two great administrative machines—the Government civil service and the National Socialist Party organizations—is a peculiar feature of modern Germany and adds considerably to the national expenditure.

How have the workers fared under the new economic system? On the one hand unemployment has been greatly reduced and those out of work receive not only unemployment benefits but extra assistance through the "Winter Help" organization. The "Strength through Joy" movement provides the workers at low cost with various facilities —sport, entertainments, travel and so forth—for the enjoyment of their somewhat scanty leisure in a manner acceptable to the National Socialists. On the other hand the workers' standard of living has declined somewhat since wages have fallen, taxes and "voluntary" contributions to the Party have risen, and certain food prices have gone up. But the increase in the price of food has been mainly in eggs, butter and veal which hits the middle classes more than the workers. The prices of bread, sugar and potatoes have shown no marked increase. The reports of German Labour Inspectors for 1935 and 1936 show that working hours have been greatly extended. A forty-eight hour week is supposed to be the standard but exceptions are very numerous. In the metal, machinery and building trades a ten-hour day is usual. On public buildings skilled men have worked in twelve-hour relays. Even fifteen and sixteen-hour relays have been known. The old trade unions have been abolished and the opportunities of resisting exploitation by employers and by the all-powerful State are small.

Hitler's establishment of a Greater Germany by absorbing the Saar region (1935), Austria (1938) and the German-speaking parts of Czecho-Slovakia (1938) has increased the country's industrial and agricultural resources. The Saar region is 790 square miles in extent and has a population of over 800,000. It is a highly industrialized area which produced over a million and a half tons both of pig-iron and of steel in 1933. After being under international administration for fifteen years it was returned to Germany after a plebiscite. The German Government repurchased the French-owned mines. Austria has an area of 32,000 square miles and a population of six and a half million, of whom two millions live in Vienna. Her farming products are not likely to be of much help in making Germany agriculturally self-supporting but her resources of timber, hydro-electric power, coal and iron may assist Germany's armaments industries. Germany already draws a million tons of iron annually from Austria and the United Steelworks of Düsseldorf control Austria's chief mining company (the Alpine Montangesellschaft). Germany has also secured the gold and foreign currency (£19,000,000) accumulated by the former Austrian Government. By annexing the German-speaking parts of Czecho-Slovakia Germany has gained important coal and lignite deposits and some light industries such as textiles, glass, pottery and jewellery. These gains compensate Germany for some of her losses after the War—the iron of Lorraine, the textiles of Alsace, much of the coal of Upper Silesia, and the agricultural resources of Posen. The tourist trade of Austria and the Sudeten regions may provide some foreign exchange.

The economic achievements of the National Socialists in Germany may be summed up as follows. Unemployment has been virtually abolished in the sense that very few Germans are not working. But some of the work "found" for the unemployed is not work for normal wages but forced labour for food, shelter and a little pocket money. Imposing public works have been constructed. The mobilization of economic resources to bring about rearmament (*Wehrwirtschaft*) has led to the building up of a military machine so formidable that it has been possible to annex Austria and the German-speaking parts of Czecho-Slovakia by simply threatening war and without actually fighting. Hitler has boasted that Germany has already attained such a degree of self-sufficiency that she can face a wartime blockade. But Germany is short of fodder, certain foodstuffs and raw materials and a prolonged blockade would inflict great hardships upon her. These are substantial achievements. A price has had to be paid for them. German business men, bankers and farmers are controlled by the Government to a remarkable extent. The workers have to face low wages, a poor standard of living, long hours, and the complete loss of economic and political freedom. Huge Government and Party administrative machines impose a heavy burden upon the taxpayer. The energies of a whole people are ceaselessly devoted to preparations for war and Germany has become an armed camp.

History and Citizenship Training in National Socialist Germany

R. JOHN RATH

>>->>->>->>->>->>->>->>->>->>-> *Published in 1949* <<-<<<-<<<-<<<-<<<-<<<-<<<-<<<-<<<

The creators of the Third Reich were determined to direct not only its political and economic development but its cultural development as well. Like Stalin's Communists and Mussolini's Fascists, Hitler's Nazis feared dissent—a fear that was reflected in the conversion of the German educational system into one vast propaganda machine. Critical thinking—one of the principal objectives of education in a free society—was discouraged, and German youth was indoctrinated with hatred of freedom, democracy, humanitarianism, internationalism, and peace. The writings of many of the finest minds in the intellectual history of twentieth-century Europe were condemned; after all, according to Nazism, blood and race were the true sources of artistic inspiration. Germans could not read Albert Einstein, Henri Bergson, Benedetto Croce, Bertrand Russell, or Sigmund Freud, or the works of most of the truth-seeking historians of recent years. Instead, they were to read historical volumes that had been prepared in keeping with Nazi notions of "race science." In the essay that follows, R. John Rath, of the University of Colorado, describes the Nazi conception of ancient, medieval, and modern history and reveals the uses and abuses to which the past was subjected in the age of Hitler.

In expressing concern over the fact that some German teachers still have a pre-war attitude towards Hitler (International Conference on Comparative Education at Frankfurt, Germany, April 24, 1949), Dr. Alonzo Grace, who until September, 1949, was director of the United States Military Government education and cultural relations in Germany, was in reality recognizing the effectiveness of the National Socialist citizenship training program.

Reprinted by special permission from *Social Education*, XIII (1949), 309-314.

In accord with Nazi plans, between 1933 and 1945 all efforts in German schools were bent towards instilling in the youth a spirit of abject loyalty and obedience to the *Fuehrer* and the conviction that the German people were superior to all other nationalities. The youngsters were admonished always to follow the directions of their National Socialist leaders and were imbued with such so-called German values as self-reliance, loyalty, honor, self-sacrifice, and leadership and followership. They were told over and over again about the great historic accomplishments of the German people and were taught that all persons of German blood must be united together in a single political entity. The pupils were warned to be on guard against the machinations of the international- and political-minded Catholic Church to destroy the German soul, and were impregnated with an intense dislike for internationalism, pacifism, humanitarianism, democracy, capitalism, and Marxian Socialism. They were taught that morals are determined by race and not by religion and were trained always to be ready to serve the German nation and cheerfully to play their designated role in the German Folk-community. In countless ways it was pointed out to the German *Jungvolk* that the public interest always comes before private interests and that every single German is responsible for the welfare of the whole German race. Particularly was "a sense and feeling of race" burnt "into the hearts and minds" of the German school children. The young scholars were taught that each race has its own distinct soul and that history is nothing but a struggle between the different races of mankind for world hegemony. All efforts were directed towards convincing them of the omnipotence of the Nordic race and its most distinguished progeny, the Germans, and imbuing them with a keen desire to keep their race pure.

Although all subjects taught in the schools were used to instill into the younger generation the views and attitudes which the National Socialists thought they should have, the Nazis relied especially on the history courses taught in the German elementary and secondary schools[1] to implant their ideas in the future citizens of the Third Reich. In the opinion of Hitler and his minions, history exemplified

[1] History was taught for eight years in the German schools. The first course was given during the fifth year in the new eight-year continuation elementary schools and in the first grade in the principal (Hauptschulen) and secondary schools (Mittelschulen). The last course was taught during the last year in the secondary schools. The eight years during which history was taught were equivalent to the fifth to twelfth grades in American elementary and secondary schools.

the Nordic racial theory which was the foundation pillar of the National Socialist point of view.

Ancient History

In their courses in ancient history the school children were told of the physical prowess and inventive genius of their forebears which made them a mighty race of "peasants, seafarers, and warriors," who went far from home to conquer the lands of inferior races. Some went to Greece to build the brilliant culture which was eventually to flourish in the Greek peninsula. Others went to Italy, from where they subdued the whole Mediterranean basin. Some went east to make themselves masters of the Slav world; others, west, to become overlords of all Western Europe, England, and Ireland. Nordics even went to Asia Minor, where, under the name of Persians and Hittites, they built up vast world empires. Everywhere they went, the Nordic vanquishers at first took the greatest care to insure the genetic health, racial purity, and folk-community spirit of the ruling caste. Only members of the Nordic race were allowed to be farmers, land-owners, or citizens. All political leaders were Nordics, and the ruling group was strictly forbidden to intermarry with lesser breeds.

It was the Nordic element which raised Greek civilization to its pinnacle of greatness, the German youth were told. In Sparta the Nordic conquerors established a corporative social order in which the greatest care was taken to insure the racial purity and folk-community

---

The first history course taught in the German schools was an introductory course intended to give the young pupils simple pictures of the German people from ancient times to the present. The courses given on the level equivalent to the sixth, seventh, eighth, and ninth grades in American schools were devoted to the history of the German people from earliest times to the present. During the tenth, eleventh, and twelfth years the students were given a general overview of European and world history.

HOUSTON STEWART CHAMBERLAIN: Englishman who became a naturalized German citizen. Son-in-law of Richard Wagner, he upheld the composer's notions concerning the German mission. His racialism, antisemitism, and chauvinism were expressed in numerous volumes, most notably his *Foundations of the Nineteenth Century* (1899).

"FATHER" JAHN: German demagogue (d. 1852) who considered it his mis-

spirit of the Nordic ruling caste. Stringent laws protected the Spartan people against the miscreant Semitic capitalism prevailing in other parts of the Mediterranean world. In Athens, too, it was the Nordic element which controlled political, economic, intellectual, and social life. Only members of the Nordic race were allowed to be farmers, landowners, or citizens, and all political leaders were Nordics. The immortal attainments of the Greeks were wholly due to their sagacious exclusion of all non-Nordic elements from the political and cultural life of the country!

Unfortunately, the Nordic political and social order, so necessary for the fructification of civilization, did not long endure. Gradually a commercial spirit permeated the Greek world and destroyed the Nordic mode of living, based as it was on blood and soil. With the growth of trade, Oriental groups among the population began to play an important role in the economic and political life of the Greek peninsula. Races intermarried frequently, and racial differences disappeared. Men were no longer judged by blood and ancestry but by their intellectual training. An oligarchy of the racially elect was supplanted by a decadent democracy in which persons of non-Nordic stock were appointed to important state offices. The leaders of the Greek people were now corrupt and incompetent nonentities. Worse still, democracy and capitalism brought in their train a selfish and unpatriotic spirit of individualism, which rapidly permeated the whole population. People were no longer interested in serving their country. Enriching themselves and enjoying the blessings of an easy and peaceful life were their sole ambitions. Sacrificing themselves for their country no longer interested them, and mercenary armies took the place of the citizen militia. A rapid decline in the birth rate set in, and the Nordic blood in the Greek ruling classes soon became almost extinct.

The miscarriage of Alexander the Great's attempts to form a world empire turned out to be the final *coup de grâce*. A racially intermixed

---

sion to awaken in the German people consciousness of their nationality. His stress on the need for physical education and his attacks on foreigners and Jews endeared him to the Nazis.

ADOLF STÖCKER: German Lutheran minister, demagogue, and political leader (d. 1909). Founder of the Christian Socialist Workers' Party, he upheld a program of social reform, paternalism, and antisemitism.

Hellenistic culture took the place of the previous Nordic civilization in Greece. Hellenistic culture was nothing but intellectualism, "an uprooted mind, separated from blood and soil." Gone were all concepts of "Folk, home, customs, faith, state"—the ties which had previously held the people together. Greek society was rotten to the core. The way was wide open for a virile new power to conquer the Greek.

The people who became masters of the decadent Hellenistic world were the Romans, mighty Nordic conquerors who made the binding ties between blood and soil the basic unit of political life, who turned serving the Fatherland into the primary duty of every citizen, and who always married people with the purest Nordic blood in their veins. In the days of their pristine Nordic masculinity the Romans conquered the Italians and destroyed the degenerate, Semitic Carthaginians. But alas, as they spread their conquests into the East, the Romans fell under the influence of Hellenistic ideas. Semitic capitalism, with all its evils, now cast its malicious spell upon the Roman world. Wealthy financiers bought most of the land, and the sacred ties between blood and soil were broken. Politics became wholly dependent on high finance. More and more people remained single or childless, enabling foreign blood "to flow in in streams." Jewish prisoners were brought to Rome and freed. Their Semitic blood "further disintegrated the Roman nation." Once the racial basis of the Roman genius deteriorated and the vast majority of the population was nothing but the progeny of decrepit Orientals, Roman political life degenerated into base and destructive struggles for power between ambitious politicians supported by mercenary armies. Emperor Augustus tried desperately to revive the Nordic element in Roman life by striving to reawaken Roman patriotism, refusing to allow bachelors to become members of the Senate, conferring political honors only on persons having at least three children, and prohibiting Senators from marrying non-Nordics and emancipated slaves.

All his efforts were fruitless. The racial decomposition of the Roman stock had gone too far to be revived even by a leader like Augustus. Jews had already become the ruling group everywhere in the empire, while the Christian religion, with the emphasis on the differences between Christians and heathens, and not on the natural "racial-national or social differences" between people, was spreading Jewish religious and moral convictions throughout the Roman world. The

Nordic element in the empire was totally conquered by Orientals; hence there was only one possible future for the Roman empire: utter destruction!

Medieval and Early Modern History

In such a manner did the National Socialists pervert ancient history to convince future citizens of the Reich of the value of racial purity, physical prowess, and strong Nordic leadership, uncontaminated by lesser stocks. Medieval history was also changed at will to meet the citizenship-training purposes of Hitler's henchmen. The Medieval period of European history was represented to the school children as an era characterized by unending struggles to safeguard Germans against the attacks of Latin popes and to spread German blood and culture over all of Europe. The writers of the textbooks waxed eloquent over the Nazi-like virtues of the early German Folk—a new people formed through a merger of the Nordic and Phalic races of Central Europe during the time when the Mediterranean world was falling into decay. The early Germans were converted to Christianity, it is true, but they were won over to the Arian and not to the Roman Catholic form of Christianity. Their conversion to Arianism resulted in the establishment of a strong race barrier which preserved "German blood from being corrupted by the foreign races of the Mediterranean world." In quest of living space, the school children were told, racially pure and heroic German warriors overran the entire Roman Empire and brought German culture to the debilitated and vitiated Romans.

The Germanic invasions of the Roman Empire, however, did not bring in their train a permanent Germanization of the whole Latin world. In the Mediterranean region, "where the climate is not suited to the Nordic nature," the German invaders became soft. In Gaul, where the climate was more favorable, the leader of the Frankish invaders, Clovis, in a vainglorious ambition to create an absolutist Frankish dominion rather than a genuine German federal empire, did away with the existing barriers to intermarriage between Germans and Romans when he allowed his people to become converted to the Roman Catholic form of Christianity. The conversion of the Germans to Catholicism resulted in the disappearance of the old German heroic ethics, old German customs, and the sagacious old German laws which had prevented German freemen from marrying non-German slaves. Worse still, the introduction of monasticism into the German world by St.

Boniface, the pope's leading tool in his conspiracy to destroy the German people, undermined the German character by substituting Oriental notions of the eternal struggle between the spirit and the flesh for the old Germanic "ties of blood and soil," while Charlemagne's creation of the Holy Roman Empire and his conquest of the heathen Saxons, with all their uncorrupted Nordic virtues, dealt a death blow to the development of a German nation independent of the Roman Catholic Church.

For a time the counteroffensive of the Teutonic Vikings "against the Christian-Roman West" saved the Nordic world from utter annihilation, but the Vikings never succeeded in gaining permanent ascendancy in Europe because they had no great leaders, like Hitler, to direct their activities. The only tangible result of their invasion of Europe was that it enabled the German people to gain a new lease on life. Refreshed and revived by the addition of uncorrupted Viking-German blood to the German blood-stream, the reinvigorated Germans, under the leadership of the redoubtable Saxon kings Henry I and Otto I, created a genuine federal Nordic empire and struck out against and utterly defeated their Hungarian and Slav enemies, whose military genius had long been the terror of Europe, largely because German blood was dominant among their ruling families.

The rulers of the newly-created German empire also fought valorously to preserve the German world against the machinations of the pope to destroy it. For two centuries a titanic struggle for world supremacy was waged between the German emperors and the Roman popes. Alas for Germany, the Nazi children were informed, the pursuit of alien imperial interests by emperors like Otto III and Frederick II, who had non-German blood in their veins, weakened the Fatherland to such a lamentable extent that the struggles between the medieval emperors and popes resulted in the catastrophic destruction of the medieval German empire.

The theme of the Nazi version of medieval history was the never-ending strife between uncorrupted, dauntless Teutons and guileful, demoniacal Catholic prelates. The story of the growth of early modern capitalism was used to impress upon the minds of the young folk the fact that capitalism inevitably leads to ruthless greed, class hatred, and internationalism. The section devoted to the spread of Roman law to Central Europe contrasted the emphasis upon social responsibility in the age-old German national law with the irresponsible individualism in the Roman law code, while the account of the Renaissance extolled the writings and discoveries of various German intellectuals. The Protestant Reformation was portrayed as a fight "of the northern races against the Mediterranean world of ideas," during which Martin Luther freed "the Northern soul from the coercive religion of the South" and preserved the "purity of the German being." Luther's anti-Semitic voicings were eulogized. The knights' rebellion of Franz von Sickingen and Ulrich von Hutton was characterized as a glorious battle to win German racial independence by unifying the German people into a real empire. Tears were shed because the German princes refused to unite to prevent the pope and the Jesuits, the pope's chief props in his conspiracy to reestablish his world power, from winning back into the Catholic fold parts of Europe that had previously been converted to Protestantism. The main result of their deplorable lack of vision, it was emphasized to Hitler's *Jungvolk*, was the appreciable weakening of "the racial strength of the German people."

From the French Revolution to World War I

Similar Nazi distortions were presented to the youngsters about the French Revolution and the history of the nineteenth century. The French Revolution, with all its chaos and bloodshed and its nefarious ideas of the brotherhood of man, was, in the judgment of the textbook writers, nothing but the result of the fiendish plotting of Jewish Freemasons "to destroy the existing social and political order" as a preliminary to establishing "Jewish world control." With the Reign of Terror the Freemasons accomplished this aim in France. "The Nordic blood flowing in the veins of the free peasantry was to a great extent eradicated," and the Freemasons had already made great headway in propagandizing their villainous concepts in many parts of Europe when German patriots like Stein, Fichte, and Jahn succeeded in saving Europe from their intrigues by rekindling in the Germans a passionate love "for Fatherland, independence, and national honor" which stirred them into fighting a glorious war of liberation against the Jewish revolutionists.

Amor patriae saved the Germans from extinction, but it did not bring into being that German Fatherland which all Teutons so ardently desired. In spite of the efforts of German lovers of liberty, at the Congress of Vienna only a debile, meaningless Germanic Confederation was established. As a result, Prussia and Austria began a fraternal war against each other which was not ended until 1938, when Hitler "again led the old *Ostmark* [eastern frontier province; that is, Austria] home into the Reich."

The Nazi texts waxed enthusiastic over the early nineteenth century nationalist expressions of the *Burschenschaften* and smiled approvingly upon the racial ideas of some of the German Romantic writers. The German princes, however, were reprehended for repressing all manifestations of German nationalism and thereby pushing the German patriotic movement into the baneful paths of western liberalism. Prince Metternich was scolded for being a venal tool of the Jew Rothschild and an obsequious agent of the pope, and the 1848-49 revolutionists were denounced for falling victim to a radical Jewish liberalism which was never intended to be anything but a philosophy paving the way for Jewish world domination.

In the sections of the history texts dealing with the latter half of the nineteenth century, the Hapsburgs were castigated for combining with Hungarians and Slavs to undermine German interests in Central Europe. The success of the unification movement in Italy was attributed largely to the Nordic blood dominant in "the leaders and fighters for Italian unity." The German Empire, it was related to the students, was largely the creation of Bismarck, who courageously fought his Jewish and Freemason opponents in the Prussian legislature in "a spirit of genuine Nordic comitatus loyalty" to his emperor.

It was emphasized that the great accomplishments of Bismarck and other Nordics were undone by the Jews. The development of finance capitalism gave the Jews an opportunity to get control of most large German industrial concerns as well as much of the land which had been farmed before by German peasants. As a consequence, "German blood became detached from German soil" and the Germans lost all love for their homeland. The uprooted masses fell ready victims to the blandishments of radical Jewish Marxist leaders, who were working hard to create a condition of chaos in Germany that would enable the Jews easily to establish their miscreant rule over the German people. Few Germans saw through this diabolical Jewish complot against the German world. A handful of patriots like Wagner, Treitschke, Stöcker,

Schönerer, and Chamberlain cried out to their countrymen to wake up and face the perils confronting them, but their voices remained unheard.

Foreign politicians and their Jewish and Masonic allies helped the Jews in Germany to gain ascendancy over the German people. Fearing that the Germans in Southwest and East Africa would unite with the Boers to form a united Germanic kingdom in South Africa, the English began the Boer War to prevent the Germans from getting living space in Africa. Alarmed at Germany's growing commerce and her ever-increasing fleet, Edward VII, a member of the Masonic order, initiated a "network of agreements" against Germany "between leading Free-masons in England, France, and Russia" and saw to it that "most of the men of influence in these countries joined the lodges." After having accomplished this, the British sovereign went to Paris to make an understanding with his Masonic brother, Delcassé, to isolate Ger-many. Later he made a similar accord with Izvolsky, the Masonic minister of foreign affairs in Russia.

As soon as the triple entente against Germany was established, under the leadership of another Freemason, Lord Northcliffe, the Masonic press in the entente countries began a campaign of calumny against Germany, while the leaders of the international Masonic con-spiracy instructed their Jewish, Masonic, and Catholic cohorts in the German parliament to make use of every possible opportunity to sabotage the arming of Germany. At the same time, they induced a Serb plotter belonging to an organization similar to the Masonic order to create a cause for war by assassinating the Austrian Archduke, Franz Ferdinand. Once their Jewish and Masonic compatriots in Europe had forced Germany into war, "American Jewish high finance," fearing that a "German victory with the help of submarine warfare" would endanger their billions, forced the United States into the war.

History Since 1918

After the war was over, the German youth was informed, the Freemasons pronounced the death sentence upon Germany. Three of the "Big Four" who drafted the "Versailles dictate"—Wilson, Clemenceau, and Lloyd George—were high ranking Freemasons, and each of them had a Jewish adviser constantly at his side. They made a treaty which, in the words of Lloyd George, was calculated "to

squeeze out Germany shilling for shilling, ton for ton, like a lemon."
The Dawes and Young reparations plans, drawn up by agents of J. P.
Morgan, the king of Jewish international financiers, crowned the work
of the conspirators by making Germany nothing but "an exploitation
colony of international high finance."

In the meantime the Jews were at work in Germany itself. Long
before the end of the war the Jews concocted a plot to stab in the back
the courageous soldiers who fought in defense of their Fatherland.
As food became short in Germany, Jewish black marketeers sold it at
usurious prices. When the ministry of war threatened to send the black
marketeers to the front lines, "a leading German banker Jew (War-
burg)" warned "in a letter to the National Bank" that if this were done
the government would have to "assume that Jewish circles will have
less interest in the war loans than they had before." Meanwhile, the
Independent Socialists, "led by three Jews," began to agitate for peace
and for class warfare; Jews, Freemasons, Marxists, and Liberals circulated in Germany the poisonous Fourteen Points drafted by the
Freemason, Woodrow Wilson; and, finally, the enemies of the German
people plotted the November, 1918, revolution for the deliberate purpose of forcing the heroic German army to give up resistance.

After the war, the Jews, Marxists, and Freemasons completed their
work by shoving through the German national assembly a typically
Masonic constitution which had been drawn up by a Jewish political
scientist and which opened the road for the Jews to gain complete
control of German political, economic, and intellectual life. Thousands
of Eastern Jews streamed into the Fatherland, where they soon amassed
great fortunes. Before long eighty-five percent of all the leading political positions were in Jewish hands, and the Jews got complete control
of the press, the theater, the professions, and academic life.

It was the National Socialists who rescued Germany from the hands
of the Jews and their Masonic cohorts, the youngsters were told. All
Germans were overjoyed when Hitler came into power, abolished all
parties except the National Socialist, reestablished authoritarian leadership, created anew the sacred ties between German blood and German
soil, took measures to restore the genetic health of the German people,
and again restored as the guiding principle of German life the old
Teutonic maxim: "The public interest comes before private interests!"
It was Hitler alone who rescued the German people from the clutches
of misery and despair.

Hitler and his National Socialist followers wanted only peace, for they embodied the genuine desires of the German people, who, "by nature are not a warlike" but merely "a soldierly" people. It was otherwise with the leaders of the other European countries, who, instead of cooperating with Hitler in his efforts to bring peace and prosperity to the world, cruelly oppressed German racial brethren living outside the borders of the Third Reich. Under such circumstances there could be no peace and security. At the urgent requests of the German people in Austria and the Germans and Slovaks in Czechoslovakia, Hitler was constrained to send troops into those countries to rescue fellow Germans from their fiendish persecutors. The Poles, too, supported and egged on by the English and French, turned ever more savagely upon unfortunate German wretches, "made war preparations to conquer German lands, and finally attacked German territory." Upon this, the children were told, the only alternative for the Germans was to begin a counteroffensive against Poland. England and France declared war on Germany, and the German people were again plunged into a war for which they were not responsible.

Conclusions

Such was the historical nonsense crammed into the heads of the German youth in the National Socialist elementary and secondary schools! Hitler's *Jungvolk* was fed with little stories that made the tales of Jacob and Wilhelm Grimm sound amateurish by comparison. But no matter how nonsensical and stupid the historical propaganda injected into the younger generation in the Third Reich may seem to the American reader it would be foolish to dismiss it as the ravings of idiotic fanatics. Every little fiction inserted in the texts for the edification of the German youth was included for the deliberate purpose of inoculating the school children with reactions, prejudices, and a philosophy of life which the Nazis felt it necessary for them to have.

The characterizations of Christianity as a tool to spread Jewish moral convictions, the bewailing of the conversion of the heathen Germans to the Roman Catholic Church, and the fulminations against alleged papal conspiracies to destroy the German world were coolly calculated to imbue the German youth with a dislike for Christianity and a hatred for Catholicism. The loud harangues about the contributions of capitalism to the destruction of Greek and Roman civilizations were included to incite in the students a hatred for contemporary capitalistic societies. The epithets hurled against ancient and modern democracies were really thrown at Hitler's democratic enemies, while the castigations of Marxian Socialists were denunciations of Hitler's left-wing opponents.

Likewise, all the nostalgic panegyrics of primitive Nordic and German virtues and the illustrations of the need for good leadership and obedient followership were tools for fashioning fuglemen for the Nazi hierarchy and for convincing the German people of the need for totalitarian leaders like Hitler. The eulogies of the corporate social order and folk-community spirit in early Greece and Rome were to make the scholars ready to take their proper place in the Nazi corporate order, while the constant references to the desirability of a large peasant class rooted in the native earth were supposed to help win the students over to Darré's theories of blood and soil. The praise heaped upon the deeds of the Nordics and early Germans had one supreme purpose: to mold proud members of the German nation.

The allegations that Greek and Roman as well as other civilizations fell as a direct consequence of racial intermixture were included in the textbooks to convince Hitler's children of the need for the National Socialist racial legislation. The violent diatribes against Freemasons and Jews were intended to instill in the youth a violent hatred for Jews and to inspire in them a burning zeal to defend their Fatherland against its enemies, real or imagined. The depiction of history as a perpetual struggle of groups and races to destroy the German world was deliberately designed to make ardent militarists out of the younger generation.

For thirteen years the sole purpose of the history instruction in the German elementary and secondary schools was to mold the German youth into blind and obedient followers of Hitler and his minions. Is it any wonder that the United States Military Government officials in Germany are today deeply concerned over the anti-democratic prejudices and attitudes which are still lingering in the German people?

XXVI

World War II and Its Aftermath

֍֍֍֍֍֍֍֍֍֍֍֍֍֍֍֍֍֍֍֍֍֍֍

The Russo-German Treaty of 1939
L. B. NAMIER

Third Republic *versus* Third Reich
DAVID THOMSON

The Missing Pages of World War II
HANSON W. BALDWIN

Diagnosing the German Malady: The Events That Led Up to the Crime
SAMUEL J. HURWITZ

Soviet-American Relations Since the War
PHILIP E. MOSELY

֍֍֍֍֍֍֍֍֍֍֍֍֍֍֍֍֍֍֍֍֍֍֍

The Russo-German Treaty of 1939

L. B. NAMIER

⋙⋙⋙⋙⋙⋙⋙⋙⋙ *Published in 1949* ⋘⋘⋘⋘⋘⋘⋘⋘⋘

The Nazi transformation of the German economy into a war economy brought startlingly rapid results in the realm of international relations. Indeed, Hitler's diplomatic triumphs would have shocked even a Bismarck. As early as 1933 the Nazis withdrew from the Disarmament Conference and from the League of Nations. In 1935 they repudiated the disarmament clauses of the Treaty of Versailles and formally reintroduced conscription. One year later they reoccupied the Rhineland in violation of both the Treaty of Versailles and the Locarno Treaties. In March 1938 they annexed Austria, and in September they concluded the Munich Agreements. By March 1939 they took over Czechoslovakia and absorbed Memel. Poland was now obviously next in line. So it was that Britain and France finally took the Nazis seriously. They promised aid to the Poles, and it seemed that German aggression might at last be stopped. But then, in late August, came the announcement of the German-Russian Pact, and on September 1 the German attack on Poland began. It is no exaggeration to say that the Nazi-Soviet Pact stunned the world. After all the ravings and rantings of Hitler about Bolshevism and after all the Communist ravings and rantings about Nazism as the last gasp of German capitalism, it was hard for contemporaries to understand the Pact. Communists all over the world quickly worked up neat "explanations," but they convinced only those who wanted to believe them. Of course, the full story of the origins of the pact is still unknown, but the recent publication of many basic documents has made it possible to find out more about what really happened. In the present selection, L. B. Namier, the brilliant British historian, to whom reference has already been made (see page 868), tries to get behind the revolution in Nazi-Soviet diplomatic relations that ushered in World War II.

If there ever was a chance of avoiding a second world war, that chance lay in a defensive alliance between the Western Powers and Soviet Russia. If there was a way of making sure that there should be war, it was by concluding the agreement with the Germans precisely in the way knowingly chosen by the Soviet Government. The Ribbentrop-Molotov treaty negotiated and signed during the night of August 23 to 24, 1939, settled the issue. Looking back one wonders what it was that caused the Soviet Government to take that fateful decision which ultimately brought them to the brink of disaster, inflicted untold suffering on their own people, and devastated a large part of Russia.

This much must be said from the very outset in justice to all the three Governments concerned in the Anglo-French-Soviet negotiations of 1939, that circumstances were basically unfavourable to an agreement between them. At the end of the first world war, Soviet Russia had given up the alien fringe of the Tsarist Empire, and had moreover been forced to cede a wide stretch of White Russian and Ukrainian territory to Poland and Rumania. Even the voluntary renunciations were made with a hope that communist revolutions would re-integrate those countries in the Soviet system: but after twenty years the frontiers still remained as fixed in 1917-20. They had not been drawn by the Western Powers—in fact, Great Britain had opposed the expansion of Poland to the east beyond the so-called Curzon Line. None the less, if Russia meant to recapture certain territorities, or forcibly to Sovietise neighbouring countries, it was not for Powers which entertained friendly relations with them and professed League principles, to assist or abet Soviet action. The Germans, on the contrary, felt nowhere committed to the post-war settlement, and Hitler, devoid of moral scruples and unembarrassed even by his own passionate declarations of undying hatred of Bolshevism, was capable of any *volte-face*.

The immediate aim of the Western Powers in entering into negotiations with Russia in April 1939 was to secure a promise of aid should they become involved in war in discharge of the obligations they had assumed when guaranteeing Poland and Rumania against unprovoked German aggression. But there was latent hostility between these two countries and Russia, which found expression in the Polish-Rumanian

Reprinted by special permission from *The Listener*, September 1, 1949.

alliance directed solely against her. Neither desired the Russian help which the Western Powers were trying to secure for them: they feared that Russian troops, having entered their countries, would not leave again; and that Russia would try to recover certain territories and to Sovietise the rest. Those fears have been justified by subsequent events: yet they were as serious an obstacle to an Anglo-French-Soviet agreement as they would have been to action under it had it been concluded.

In the case of the Baltic states, it was a question of a neutrality which these tried scrupulously to preserve, but could not have defended. The Western Powers accepted the consequences of a similar awkward position in Belgium and Holland, which offered perfect cover to the Rhineland and Ruhr while Hitler was engaged elsewhere, but, without advance preparation, no effective obstacle to his offensive against France. The Soviet Government had no such delicacies. The guarantees which it tried to establish for the Baltic states, in spite of their protests, were to contain extensive safeguards even against German "indirect aggression", and to admit an occupation of military and naval bases in case of war. Britain was prepared to meet reasonable Russian demands by making "indirect aggression" cover "action accepted by the state in question under threat of force by another power and involving abandonment of its independence and neutrality". But the Soviet Government demanded that it should extend even to a *coup d'état* or to a political change favourable to the aggressor: which would have made Russia judge of the internal affairs of her small neighbours, and sanctioned her intervention. And this had a twist of its own as much as that of the Nazis. No complete agreement was ever reached about "indirect aggression"—a characteristic difficulty in the relations of the negotiating powers.

That difficulty sprang primarily from mutual lack of sympathy and from distrust. These were of course equally marked in Bolshevik-Nazi relations: yet in structure, spirit, and methods their two systems were

---

CURZON LINE: Eastern frontier laid down in 1919 between Russia and Poland. The Poles refused to accept it and demanded their old frontier of 1772. By the terms of the Peace of Riga of 1921 Poland secured an eastern boundary which approximated the boundary she had had on the eve of the partition of 1795. The German and Russian partition of Poland that followed the Battle of Poland in World War II roughly corresponded to the

nearer to each other than either was to Western democracy. Nazism was not incompatible with social revolution, nor Bolshevism with expansionist aggression; and one may well wonder what, except the special brand of nonsense which each had talked and fervently professed for years past, so deeply divided them. Perhaps without knowing it they continued, in fantastically irrelevant terms, the old contest of Slavs and Germans for the territories between the Baltic, the Adriatic, and the Black Sea. Still, agreements and conflicts between Nazis and Bolsheviks were possible in terms comprehensible and congenial to either; co-operation with the West would have put a serious strain on their temper and imagination.

The only inducement to the Soviet Government to close with the West would have been a feeling of certainty that such a diplomatic line-up would stop Hitler and save them from having to fight, for war—the favourite instrument of German policy—is not that of Bolshevism. But they had their usual doubts and suspicions. What if Hitler, encircled and curbed, attempted a coalition of "Imperialist capitalist Powers" against Soviet Russia? (That coalition is the perennial nightmare of the Bolsheviks.) Or alternatively, might he not, after all, risk an attack against the East, counting on the defensive military doctrine and mentality which the French had developed, and on the military unpreparedness of Britain? If the French sat tight in their Maginot Line, while Britain's main contribution was a naval blockade, Russia would have to bear the brunt of the fighting and of the defence of the Poles and Rumanians, who, to say the least, were no concern of hers. Further, extreme distrust undoubtedly suggested to the Russians the idea that the Western Powers, having got them into war with Germany, might leave them in the lurch, or finally make peace at their expense. A determined and sustained effort on the part of the Western Powers would have been required to dispel Russian doubts and suspicions, and even then it is by no means certain that it would

---

Curzon Line of 1919. By the provisions of the Yalta Agreement of 1945 the Line once more defined in general Poland's eastern frontier.

POLISH-RUMANIAN ALLIANCE: Treaty signed in 1921. Although expressed in general terms, it afforded protection specifically against Soviet Russia. The military convention which was annexed to it anticipated only the case of a Soviet attack.

have succeeded. But in fact the negotiations were conducted in a manner often inept and on the whole half-hearted (notwithstanding the many concessions ultimately made to the Russians): wherein a serious under-estimate of the Soviet military power, and over-estimate of that of Poland, played a part. And suspicions were a more formidable hindrance to an agreement between Russia and the West than between her and Germany: for the one might have meant to go tiger-shooting together, while the other did mean keeping away from the shooting and playing the jackal to the tiger.

"What could England offer Russia?" said a German diplomat to a Russian at the end of July, 1939, speaking from a brief. "At best, participation in a European war and the hostility of Germany, but not a single desirable end for Russia. What can we offer? Neutrality and staying out of a possible European conflict and, if Moscow wishes, a German-Russian understanding on common interests". . . . This pointed to territorial acquisitions in the Baltic area, in Poland, and in Rumania, such as it was morally impossible for the Western Powers to offer.

What, on the other hand, were the obstacles to a Nazi-Soviet agreement? Hitler victorious would clearly have been a deadly menace to Soviet Russia. And though the Russians probably, in common with everybody else including most German generals, overrated the defensive strength of France, and therefore the immunity or even advantages which they would be able to derive from a war between Germany and the West, the incalculable risks of a European war must have made them pause. Next there were the difficulties of approach between two parties long hostile and intensely suspicious of each other: each fearing that the other was not serious in any tentative advances which it made, but was merely fishing for material with which to blackmail the Western Powers into a more favourable agreement against the other side. Indeed, even after a Nazi-Soviet agreement had been concluded, Hitler, if given sufficient time, might have used it with a view to pulling off a super-Munich, ultimately, the Russians feared, directed against them. Supreme caution seemed therefore imperative.

It would in fact be difficult to imagine a more involved or a slyer game than that played by the Soviet Government between April and August, 1939. Whenever a step was taken toward the Western Powers or progress achieved in the negotiations with them, some counter-balancing approach was made to the Nazis, so that Hitler, in fear of effective encirclement, should not change front and attempt that coalition whose spectre obsessed the Bolshevik mind. As Western re-armament was proceeding apace, his best chance in a show-down with Poland was in 1939, and the season for it lay between the harvest and the autumn rains, that is, between the beginning of September and the middle of October. Therefore as the summer drew on, both the Western Powers and Hitler were becoming more intent on reaching an agreement with Russia. When at the end of July the announcement was made that the Allied Military Missions were proceeding to Moscow, the Germans redoubled their endeavours. And when on August 12, the day on which the military negotiations were opened, the Soviet Government informed the Germans that it was prepared to start political talks with them, the Germans threw all restraint to the winds: Ribbentrop, to clinch the matter, offered to come immediately to Moscow, and went on pressing, day by day, his offer on the Russians with ever growing insistence. The Russians now employed delaying tactics. It is by no means certain that they had meant to give their move of August 12 as far-reaching a significance as the Germans tried to put on it. At what exact juncture Stalin formed the decision to close with the Germans rather than with the West is not known even now, nor what it was that finally tipped the balance. But even if that decision had already been reached, the terrible weapon of an under-standing with Russia had to be withheld from Hitler till the advanced season would no longer allow time for blackmail but would force him to use it for one purpose only: an attack against Poland. As late as August 19, Molotov still refused to fix even an approximate date for Ribbentrop's journey, and only later in the day, apparently by order from Stalin, agreed to August 26 or 27. Finally, renewed German pressure, in the form of a personal telegram from Hitler to Stalin, made the Russians advance the date to August 23.

The rest presented hardly any difficulties. Hitler conceded whatever the Russians asked for; in fact, Ribbentrop was authorized to leave the Russians a free hand even with regard to Turkey and the Straits, but at this juncture the Russians did not raise the question. A secret protocol delimited spheres of interest: Finland, Estonia, and Latvia were to be in the Russian sphere, Lithuania in the German; a demarca-tion line across Poland assigned to Russia her White Russian and Ukrainian provinces, and also some ethnically Polish districts (which a month later Russia exchanged against Lithuania). Russia registered her interest in Bessarabia, and Germany her *désintéressement* in that area. The overt treaty took the innocent form of a non-aggression pact; yet its sense was patent to all and sundry. Hitler thought that his agreement with Russia would stop the Western Powers from giving the promised help to Poland. When he saw that it would not, he made a last confused bid for a second Munich. But time pressed: and eight days after the Nazi-Soviet agreement had been signed, Hitler opened his Polish campaign.

Third Republic *versus* Third Reich

DAVID THOMSON

⇝⇝⇝⇝⇝⇝⇝⇝⇝⇝ *Published in 1941* ⇜⇜⇜⇜⇜⇜⇜⇜⇜⇜

Like World War I, World War II brought many surprises. And one of the greatest of these was the speedy military defeat of France. Within less than a year of the outbreak of hostilities, the Third French Republic capitulated to the Third Reich. Despite one of Churchill's most stirring appeals, despite General de Gaulle's plea that the struggle continue, defeatism triumphed, the Pétain regime came to power, and the Third French Republic, which had been born in defeat, died in defeat. Hardly had the collapse taken place than a heated debate got under way. Why had the Third Republic fallen? Who had been its gravediggers? Writers pointed to the success of German propaganda efforts; to inadequate military leadership, to the fantastic faith in the invulnerability of the Maginot Line, to the antiquated character of French military preparations; to the divisions in the French nation, to the fear of Communism, and to the fear of socialism of the Léon Blum variety. In the present selection David Thomson, one of the ablest of contemporary British students of the history of the Third Republic, discusses the fall of France and analyzes the facts and forces that lay behind the disasters of May and June 1940.

I t is nearly a year since the collapse of France. Yet how many people in Britain could give an accurately brief explanation of why France fell? Many excellent books have already appeared, purporting to explain it. Certain general truths emerge very clearly from these books. But these truths have not yet "got across" to the general public. This is partly because subsequent events have absorbed popular attention; but partly, too, because enemy and partisan propaganda have succeeded remarkably well in confusing the issue.

Reprinted by special permission from *The Contemporary Review*, CLIX (1941), 668-675.

It was natural and inevitable that, in the first moments of chagrin and stupefaction after the sudden collapse of France, everyone both here and in France should ask himself the question, "Who is to blame for this disaster?" As soon as the question was asked, back came a babble of conflicting replies. "The incompetent and treacherous brass-hats," said the French Radical. "The Communists and pacifists and Jews," cried the French Right-wing sympathisers. "Perfidious Albion," retorted many of the French military and naval leaders, and—of course —"King Leopold." "It's the corruption and rottenness of the Third Republic," explained many Englishmen; "the blindness of French leaders and the incompetence of their administration is notorious. Why on earth didn't they extend the Maginot Line?" All these explanations were, of course, judiciously encouraged in the appropriate quarters by Nazi propagandists, who in this respect at least showed great impartiality. They were content that anybody should be blamed for the Fall of France except the Nazis themselves. In this way the one really important fact was overlooked: that the fall of France was due above all to plain military defeat, in the production of which various other factors played an important but subsidiary part. The right question to ask ourselves is not, "Who was to blame?" but rather "How did the German military machine achieve this surprising and complete disintegration of France?" It is idle to indulge in recriminations and to try to affix blame for the disaster on anything except its most obvious cause—the ruthless brutality and overwhelming efficiency of the German war machine.

Most of those who have studied the collapse at close range emphasise this fact. "The part played by personalities," writes M. André Maurois in *Why France Fell,* "was not the essential cause of the defeat. That cause . . . was lack of preparation, military, diplomatic and industrial, on the part of the Allies." "It was the inevitable result," declared General de Gaulle, "of the shock of an encounter between an

---

CAGOULARDS: Hooded ones. Members of an armed secret society who, with Nazi support, conspired to overthrow the Third French Republic. Though their plot was exposed in 1937, their prosecution was halted, for men close to Marshal Pétain were involved, and Pétain was still highly admired as the hero of Verdun.

STAVISKY CASE: A political scandal of 1934 that grew out of the involvement

army organised on outworn principles and an army organised for modern mechanical warfare." "The French," writes Reuter's war correspondent, Mr. Gordon Waterfield, "went down with their hands tied behind their backs. They were all mobilised and had to obey the orders of an incompetent general staff and of a government which became a 'peace at any price' government." The blunders and miscalculations of the French General Staff: their obsession with defence rather than offence, their gross neglect of the great new factors of the tank and the aeroplane, their pathetic belief that "time is on our side" —all these are too well known already to need further emphasis here. But less clearly realised is the *political* inappropriateness of this "Maginot mentality"; and it is this fact which proved so fatal to France. We must distinguish between the military defeat of May and the capitulation of June 1940. To explain why the one led so decisively to the other, we must take into account one consideration which the General Staff had forgotten, and which alone makes both events comprehensible.

It is that France, without knowing it, was fighting a war on two fronts. Of these her Eastern Front, with its great fortifications, was the less important. The other was the home front. Hitler had from the first concentrated on this front, for he had said, "I shall disintegrate their war." His attacks on the Maginot Line were, in this larger strategy, more in the nature of a feint, to make France concentrate on the defensive. The one strategy which France could not afford to adopt, in the circumstances of 1939, was a defensive strategy. Hitler was able to knock out the French armies in six weeks on the "Western Front" because he had already spent six years disintegrating her morale and destroying her soul, on the home front. And if we want to examine how and why he was able to do this we must look beyond the events of the last six years. We must remember that the present is always the

---

of a number of politicians in the questionable deals carried on by Stavisky, a clever financial manipulator. As a result of the scandal, France was faced for a time with serious civil disorders. Although a center coalition cabinet soon took charge, it was ominous that in a democracy there should be so little faith in political parties and politicians, and that it should be popular to wear lapel buttons with the words "I am not a Deputy."

result of the whole of the past, and not merely of the immediate past. And any foreshortened view is bound to distort the picture.

There is a rounded completeness about the history of the Third Republic which does not need to be added to by such carefully staged performances as Hitler's dictation of the armistice terms of 1940 in Foch's railway-carriage at Compiègne. On September 1st, 1870, the gunfire died away round Sedan, and the Emperor Napoleon III surrendered his armies to Bismarck. This event began a train of events which led to the completion of the German Empire and, eventually, to the setting-up of the Third Republic. The German Reich and the Third Republic of France, born in the same storm of events, were henceforth destined to have the most intimate influence on one another. On May 15th, 1940, the German armies again broke through into France on the Meuse, enveloping Sedan, and again starting a train of events which led to the fall of the Third Republic. The story of the Republic in the intervening seventy years is dominated by certain constant forces which, in their logical persistence and fatality, give the story an atmosphere of doom reminiscent of the highest tragedy. It is not enough, therefore, merely to trace the working of these forces back to 1933, or even to 1914. Only by viewing the story in all its dramatic completeness can we understand the situation in France to-day.

The two great themes of the drama, reduced to their simplest terms, are the external menace to French nationalism, which came from Germany, and the internal menace to French democracy, which came from social tensions between social classes, economic groups and political parties. The Republic lived only by incessant manoeuvring, aimed at striking some balance between these two interacting forces. The countless political parties and the recurrent cabinet shuffles, which gave French politics their peculiar "musical-chairs" atmosphere, were simply the expression of this uneasy shifting, this inherent urge to find a new centre of gravity, a new harmony between these forces. Indeed, the Republic suited France because it was the only political system which could allow for this constant readjustment of forces. France of the 1870's, after the collapse of the Second Empire and the experience of the Paris Commune, was splintered into various groups and ideologies reluctant to co-operate with one another. The Republican régime was accepted, as Thiers put it, "because it divides us least." In this sense the recurrent Cabinet crises which so worried English observers (chiefly because so many of them failed to realise that a French Cabinet crisis was something far less serious than the collapse of a British Cabinet) were in fact an expression of the resilience and stability of the Republic, rather than of its instability: just as the wobblings of a tight-rope walker are a sign of his skill in keeping his equilibrium.

Precisely because she was on a tight-rope, France always felt vulnerable. Because of the joint operation of these two forces, pulling her now one way, now the other, France was ever thrown into a posture of defence. Her foreign policy, for example, always revealed a nervous anxiety, a sort of feminine fickleness, which often proved irritating to her Allies. The "Maginot mentality" did not begin with the Maginot line: it was there from the first, inherent in the whole character of the Third Republic. Marianne lacked the self-assurance of that more stolid lady, Britannia. And so at a time (in the 1920's and 1930's) when Britannia, like a famous film-star, was proclaiming that she wanted to be alone, Marianne was trotting around Europe, making friends with all sorts of other people—with the Little Entente of Roumania, Czechoslovakia and Yugoslavia, with Italy, and even with the U.S.S.R. She became entangled in various engagements, in the hope of having as many friends as possible in time of need. Britannia refused to take the German menace seriously, and never fully understood the inner conflicts of Marianne. She only became irritated by these fretful demands for guarantees of "security," which lay behind all French diplomacy.

The interaction of these two forces, the external menace to national independence and the internal menace to democratic government, is very clearly illustrated by the political history of the Third Republic in the forty years between 1875 and 1914. Two general lessons should have been learnt from the events of these years. First, the twofold menace could be met so long as most Frenchmen were even more devoted to the democratic ideal than they were to nationalism. It was this popular support for democratic methods and institutions which enabled the Republican governments to overcome so successfully the succession of crises which they had to meet from the militarist, clerical and reactionary forces of the Right. The attempts of Marshal Mac-Mahon in 1877 to prolong his period of power as President; the more picturesque menace of the Minister of War, General Boulanger, who formed his "League of Patriots" and tried in 1887 to mobilise the old sentiments of Bonapartism and, by combining them with nationalist hatred of Germany, to turn them against the Republic; and, finally, the supreme test-case of Alfred Dreyfus, which brought to a climax the internal tensions between democrats and nationalists: all these crises were in turn overcome. In each instance it was the democratic faith and vision of men like Jules Grévy, Jules Ferry, Clemenceau and Zola, which saved the Republic and, with it, the integrity and independence of the French nation. The memories of the disastrous dictatorship of Napoleon III combined with popular desire for revenge against Germany to keep France loyal to the existing régime.

The second lesson to be learnt from these years was that the price of democracy is constant watchfulness. In France there was an inner discord between democracy and nationalism of a kind that England has scarcely known since the eighteenth-century fears of the "redcoats." By the very circumstances of its birth the Third Republic was committed to the economic burdens and social tensions involved in rapid rearmament and strenuous measures of national defence. Liquidation of the indemnity to Germany; frontier fortification: a large standing army and navy; peacetime conscription; popular lust for revenge: these were the legacies of the Franco-Prussian War to the Republic. They were legacies which could in no way be avoided. But they meant granting more and more power to the militarist groups and leaders, who were the sworn enemies of democracy. It was a cruel dilemma. Conscription, for example, which by a Law of 1872 was made compulsory between the ages of twenty and forty, and was for a period of five years, had the result of placing the effective civilian population at the command of the military authorities. Even as eventually reorganised by the Law of 1912, universal conscription in France meant that the army leaders were able to dispose of all Frenchmen for twenty-five years of their lives, and had complete control of them for two years. So long as the military power was closely associated with the anti-republican clerical forces, either by birth or by education, this involved great internal tension and constant watchfulness on the part of the civil power and the politicians. But the parliamentarians upheld their cause, preserved the Republic, and won the approval of democrats everywhere by asserting clearly the superiority of civil and political justice to all claims of "national prestige" and "military honour." Zola blew sky-high the pretensions of Machiavellian *étatisme* [state power] and military totalitarianism in France. But then came the Great War.

For the previous forty years French foreign policy had been dominated by a great desire—revenge on Germany for Sedan, for the loss of Alsace and Lorraine, for the humiliation of German soldiers tramping down the Champs-Élysées. It had also been dominated by a great fear—the fear of isolation and encirclement, which it had been the persistent aim of Germany to achieve. It was this fear of encirclement which made the two forces distracting France so difficult to reconcile. Could France make herself strong enough to preserve her independence only by sacrificing her democratic spirit and institutions? That was the question which haunted French politics. Again France was thrown on to the defensive—at home to defend the Republic, abroad to defend France. She sought alliances; for Germany, in her anxiety to isolate and encircle France, was also seeking allies. Thus arose that complex system of great European alliances which did so much to bring about the Great War, and, once it had begun, to make it a world war.

At the cost of great devastation of territory and the loss of one and a half million men, France won this war. But her defensive attitude, and the old interaction of external fear and internal tension, remained. It was nothing new. It was a continuation of the same process, and there is a consistency in the whole history of the Third Republic. France was awarded immense reparations in 1919; but a large part of them was never paid. She was left with a falling population, the irreparable loss of a million and a half men, a legacy of economic problems which aggravated internal tensions, and the clear knowledge that Germany would now plan revenge on her. She was able to understand the certainty of this revenge better than any other people, because she knew how revenge had filled her own thoughts after 1870. She was doomed to remain as anxious, apprehensive and defensive as before. She constantly sought "security" in the ways already described. By demanding security even before disarmament she fell foul of British opinion, which imagined that disarmament should precede security. As soon as French and British policy fell out of step, the whole success of the League of Nations was brought into jeopardy, for the League could only work successfully if based on Anglo-French collaboration.

In January 1933 began the real battle between Third Republic and Third Reich. There came into power in Germany a leader pledged to revenge, who had written, "France is and will remain the implacable enemy of Germany." *Mein Kampf* had ended with an exhortation to all Germans to "rally together for a last decisive contest with France," and its author had added, in words ominous for the future of Europe, "Of course it is here presumed that Germany sees in the suppression of France nothing more than a means which will make it possible for our people to expand in another quarter." From this time the last great challenge to the Third Republic was inevitable. For the external menace and the internal tensions became more and more closely linked together. And they now worked in the same direction. Now every political or financial crisis in France played into the hands of Hitler, and was ruthlessly exploited by Nazi propaganda. It mattered little whether the crisis was deliberately provoked by Fascist and semi-Fascist parties under encouragement from Hitler, such as the Stavisky riots of February 1934 and the Cagoulard plots of 1936, or whether they arose spontaneously from internal difficulties, such as the stay-in strikes, promoted by Communist and other agitators in 1936. Everything which helped to disrupt France, to perplex public opinion, discredit parliamentarians and dislocate French production was grist to the mill of Nazi strategy and propaganda. France was in a cleft stick, and whatever she did could be turned to her discredit. Above all it was fatal for her to order wholesale mobilisation and then to adopt a strategy of waiting and boredom.

The external menace was now, at last, identical as a political force with the internal threat to the Republic. One by one the guarantees of security were torn from her. Hitler had rearmed Germany and reintroduced conscription; he had remilitarised the Rhine; he had, in 1935, made a naval treaty with Britain behind France's back; first Austria and then Czechoslovakia, France's best ally in Eastern Europe, had been absorbed; the League as an agency of "collective security" had completely broken down. And whilst the traditional double menace to French security was thus moving in one direction, and her bulwarks of security were torn away, the one element which had saved France in the early days of the Republic was now lacking. With a few very notable exceptions, the leaders of French democracy were lacking in that democratic vision and faith which had saved her before. There were even some who said, "Better Hitler than Blum." There were others, like Paul Baudouin, who spoke of "the Christian regeneration of an impious France—through military defeat." The old clerical menace reared its head. One power fused all these elements into one great overwhelming force, "to disintegrate their war"—and to disintegrate with it both the French nation and the Third Republic. It was Nazi propaganda, operating in the favourable conditions of a "war of rot" and the vacuum created by an over-zealous censorship. It only needed the military break-through on the Meuse to precipitate the whole process of disintegration. France fell apart. The tight-rope walker was pushed; but she had first lost all her sense of balance.

France fell, it must be repeated, in the face of overwhelming weight of men and machines and military equipment. But the speed of that fall and the extent of that collapse can be explained only by this conjunction of historical tendencies and political forces which I have tried to analyse. France fell when her leaders and large sections of her people ceased to place democratic values first and nationalist considerations second. . . .

The Missing Pages of World War II

HANSON W. BALDWIN

Published in 1949

Before the twentieth century, documents dealing with the outbreak and course of a war were usually kept secret for many decades after the event. On the eve of World War I, for example, remarkably few documents concerning the Franco-German War of 1870-1871 were available. During World War I and in the years that followed, however, this practice of keeping diplomatic and military documents secret was in large part abandoned. The reason was, of course, that revolutions had taken place in Russia, Austria-Hungary, and Germany; and with the overthrow of the Romanovs, Habsburgs, and Hohenzollerns, the new governments proceeded to publish large numbers of documents dealing with the origins and conduct of the war in the hope of discrediting the old regimes and improving the position of the new revolutionary regimes. The example of Russia, Austria, and Germany was followed by the other participants, and the result was that the people who fought World War I soon had access to accurate information concerning the struggle that had done so much to shape their lives. What happened to the generation of World War I has also happened to the generation of World War II. Once more the early publication of documents has proceeded on a large scale; and so there is available a good deal of accurate information relating to the origins and conduct of the war. Nevertheless, there are still many fundamental questions that cannot be answered. In the bibliographical essay that follows, Hanson W. Baldwin, the learned and provocative military analyst of the New York *Times*, reviews the more important literature of World War II, emphasizing not only what is known about the struggle but also what is yet to be known. It should be noted that Baldwin's article appeared in September, 1949.

Ten years ago Thursday the Nazi legions marched, their tank tracks clanged and Polish horsemen died in brave and futile defiance. Ten years ago yesterday New York's summer heat was slowly fading and the airborne voice of England's King was heard solemnly rallying his people for the dark days ahead, for a war no longer confined to the battlefield. Ten years ago began the widest ranging war in history: Hundreds of campaigns; 10,000 battles; 20,000,000 dead; kings and nations hurled to destruction; winged fleets shattering the ancient monuments of civilization; navies far-flung across the seven seas.

From this most gigantic of man's struggles against man have burgeoned vast libraries of books to which we are adding daily. It is already clear that World War II has been correctly described as the best documented war in history. Nearly every facet of the war has received factual treatment. Only four years after the end of the war we have a pretty comprehensive knowledge of what it was all about, how it was fought and the scars it left upon the people who fought it. This is, indeed, an achievement; never before have a war's participants been quite so frank so soon after the event.

But, the ringing cadences of Winston Churchill excepted, there is, as yet, no modern Homer, no Macaulay, no Gibbon to chronicle World War II. Much of the vast panorama of conflict has been laid before us, brushed on in sweeping strokes from an inexhaustible palette. The ministers and marshals have spoken. The powers behind the scenes have pulled aside some of the ironic curtains. There have been revelations ranging from the acerb comments of Vinegar Joe Stilwell to the military monody of a bishop's dour son who rose to be a Field Marshal and Viscount of Alamein.

In no one volume or series of volumes, however, have all the threads been pulled together. The history of this war is still a vast, sprawling and disparate thing. Many important kernels of fact can be gleaned only by carefully winnowing through dozens of sources. There are still tremendous gaps in our knowledge. The shadows of secrecy obscure battles, policies and leaders. The outstanding gaps are in the politico-military realm. The records of JCS and CCS—the American Joint Chiefs of Staff and the Anglo-American Combined Chiefs of Staff—

Reprinted by special permission from the New York *Times Book Review*, September 4, 1949.

have never been published. Their most important papers will probably be kept secret during our lifetime. Not all the Roosevelt papers are yet available. Neither are the full records of any of the famous wartime conferences: Quebec, Yalta, Teheran and the rest.

When Prof. William L. Langer's exhaustive political history of the war appears, many lacunae will be filled. Mr. Langer, who is Coolidge Professor of History at Harvard, has already, apart from his main work, given us in "Our Vichy Gamble" a book that illuminates one salient aspect of American wartime policy better than any other work. His forthcoming volumes, which are being prepared under the sponsorship of the Council on Foreign Relations, are likely to take a long time to prepare, but his first volume is virtually completed.

Other gaps are being filled all the time. Winston Churchill's rather personal panorama of the war years stands, of course, at the top of any list. Long after more pedantic works have been published and forgotten Mr. Churchill's volumes will hold their place. They are not precise history; the author sometimes indulges the great man's penchant for ratiocination and justification. There are definite and sometimes major errors of omission and commission. But these books are sentient things. Here is subjective history at its best, written by a man unashamed of sweeping, impressionistic brush strokes and Victorian grandeur of phrase.

Robert Sherwood's "Roosevelt and Hopkins" and ex-Secretary Henry L. Stimson's "On Active Service," written with McGeorge Bundy, are the best of the American crop of high-level books about the war. But they must be supplemented—if one is to get the broad picture—by such books as the tedious Cordell Hull memoirs, James M. Byrnes' pedestrian but important "Speaking Frankly" and "The Strange Alliance," by Maj. Gen. John R. Deane, head of our military mission to Moscow at the climax of the war.

Even so, no single book this reviewer knows of satisfactorily explains two of the main military reasons behind the concessions made to Russia at Yalta—to exemplify the gaps still existing in the war's history. These were: An erroneous intelligence estimate of the Japanese strength in Manchuria, and failure of our experts to calculate and assess the logistic problems of American bomber bases in Siberia.

Various important books reveal the war as seen by our enemies. Most of these are derived from studies of enemy documents or interviews with German and Japanese leaders. Such books as "The Goebbels

Diaries," Milton Shulman's "Defeat in the West," Liddell Hart's "The German Generals Talk," Anthony Martienssen's "Hitler and His Admirals" and Asher Lee's "The German Air Force" should be read in conjunction with "The Ciano Diaries" and Allen W. Dulles' "Germany's Underground."

No books of quite comparable character, giving the Japanese side of the picture, are yet available—although, for the patient student, the two-volume "Interrogations of Japanese Officials," compiled by the Naval Analysis Division of the United States Strategic Bombing Survey and published by the Government Printing Office, provide valuable source material.

Most of the now-it-can-be-told personal memoirs by the medaled commanders have been disappointing. Field Marshal Montgomery's two volumes are, like their author, dry and repressed. They contribute virtually nothing that is new to the informed student of war; little of interest to the general reader. One cannot escape the feeling that General Eisenhower's plan to be objective and fair in "Crusade in Europe" has led him to pull his punches. His aide, Captain Harry Butcher, in that strangely mixed book of chitchat and high-level strategy, "My Three Years With Eisenhower," is somewhat more frank.

"The Stilwell Papers"—because they are the well-edited diaries and letters of a distinct personality, and because their author was a two-fisted fighting man—are among the more valuable recollections of the top commanders. "The Brereton Diaries," by that bantam cock-of-the-walk Air Force general who saw a great slice of the war, also make a contribution. And Maj. Gen. Sir Francis de Guingand, who was Monty's Chief of Staff, has given us, in "Operation Victory," a careful, readable and outspoken work. This is history as de Guingand saw it—one of the best of the British war books.

Yet there are glaring gaps in this field, too. No work has yet come from that master of sonorous communiqués, the great American proconsul in Japan. But these are preparing books of reminiscences: Admiral William D. Leahy, President Roosevelt's Chief of Staff; Admiral Ernest J. King, wartime Commander in Chief of the Fleet; Gen. H. H. Arnold, the Air Force leader, and Gen. Omar N. Bradley. Of these, General Bradley's book, which will probably not be published until his retirement from active duty, gives great promise of decided literary merit.

The monumental volumes of the Army's official history—three out of a projected ninety-nine volumes have so far appeared—stand in sharp contrast to the plethora of personal histories. The Government Printing Office publishes these volumes under the general title, "The U. S. Army in World War II," and they are examples of military objectivity. But they have the faults, as well as the virtues, of official history. "Okinawa, the Last Battle"—the only volume dealing with combat yet issued—is a scholarly, painstaking job that lays most of the cards on the table. Earlier volumes, dealing with organization and training, have seemed to slough over or omit some important details.

All stagger under prodigious and pedantic minutiae. They are not for the general reader. Their purpose, which they admirably fulfil, is to serve as the basic source material for military historians. But the ideal historian must go outside their pages if he is to present history whole; these books provide only the bones of facts. They deal adequately with the tangibles of war; scarcely at all with the intangibles. And who is to say which is the more important?

The Army's full-length studies are supplemented by smaller monographs dealing with selected battles, issued in the "American Forces in Action Series." These are models of their kind. The Marine Corps has issued booklets on "The Defense of Wake" and "Marines at Midway," two of a series of operational monographs which will eventually form an official history of the Marines in the war. An unofficial history written with access to the Corps' files has been published by Fletcher Pratt as "The Marines' War." It is vivaciously readable, and it recaptures the battlefield drama.

The Navy has followed its own course. Samuel Eliot Morison's "History of United States Naval Operations in World War II" (three volumes published; ten to go) is "unofficial"—with full official help. Morison does not hesitate to analyze and criticize. He writes with verve of the sea he loves. His books are easier than the Army's to read. But there are faults in the Morison history. The latest volume, "The Rising Sun in the Pacific," suffers from too great a compression of naval operations. A disproportionate amount of space is given to political sequences. Some of the puzzling earlier events of the war are unmentioned or unexplained.

Professor Morison's works are admirably supplemented by the "Battle Report" series of Captain Walter Karig. There is duplication, but, in general, Karig and his co-authors have tried to concentrate on the human interest side of the war. Dr. Robert G. Albion, who is now Professor of History of Harvard, is at work on an administrative history of the Navy. He has taken the word "administrative" broadly. The inner wartime workings of the Navy Department—and perhaps some of the factors that motivated the Joint Chiefs of Staff—will be discussed.

"The United States at War," issued by the Government Printing Office for the Bureau of the Budget, deserves study as a source document. It traces in broad outline our war program in Washington.

The numerous reports of the United States Strategic Bombing Survey and the official history of the Air Force may never be widely read. But they are important. The Strategic Bombing Survey—it was official, too—studied the war in Europe and in the Pacific. Its title is something of a misnomer, since its reports also cover Pacific naval campaigns and other subjects. Service rivalry and personal politics mar some of the reports. Not all conclusions are supported by facts. They give, however, one of the best records of the meaning of total war.

Two out of seven thick volumes on "The Army Air Forces in World War II" have been published by the Chicago University Press. They are edited by professional historians, formerly Air Force historical officers. They are careful, complete and straight-forward. The first volumes speak frankly. Volume II, for example, points out that "Eighth Air Force claims [of German fighters shot down] were far more exaggerated than even their severest critics had assumed."

Many unit and divisional histories have appeared. They are mainly interesting only to participants and military historians. A few stand out, such as "The Eighty-fourth Infantry Division in the Battle of Germany," by Theodore Draper, who also wrote a good book on the fall of France, "The Six Weeks' War." Another superior job is "Danger Forward," the wartime history of the First Division. It contains material of interest to all readers, since each battle is first described by a war correspondent and then by an officer of the division.

Individual battles and episodes of war have received the attention of authors innumerable. Outstanding in literary craftsmanship or historical excellence are: John Hersey's "Hiroshima"; Robert Edward Merriam's "Dark December," the story of the Battle of the Bulge;

James A. Field's "The Japanese at Leyte Gulf" and Comer Vann Woodward's "The Battle for Leyte Gulf."

This review is not concerned with fiction or foreign books dealing solely with the operations and politics of other nations. But—to make just two exceptions—"Stalingrad" and "Day Without End" may be mentioned as mirrors of wartime life that are probably as factual as any history. "Stalingrad," by Theodor Plievier, deals with the disintegration of the German Sixth Army and should be read as a companion piece to Alexander Werth's "The Year of Stalingrad." "Day Without End," by Van Van Praag, deals with the disintegration of an American platoon commander in the hedgerow fighting in Normandy.

The scope of "Stalingrad" is tremendous, but the frame is factually accurate; the scope of "Day Without End" is small in the vast inferno of a world war, but its theme—war as seen by man and the effects of war on man—is universal.

A survey of the books about this most terrible of wars reveals, then, four major areas of obscurity:

1. The first—and greatest—is the Russian front. Despite the availability of mounds of German documents dealing with the Russian campaign, very little about it that is comprehensive, objective and readable has been published.

2. The second area of ignorance covers the high-level discussions, deliberations and decisions that guided the course of the war: Casablanca, Quebec, Yalta, Teheran and so on; the proceedings of JCS and CCS; the Moscow meetings; the work of the European Advisory Commission, or (with the exceptions of Joseph Clark Grew's "Report from Tokyo" and "Ten Years in Japan," and one volume of John Gilbert Winant's "Letter from Grosvenor Square,") the work of our embassies. This whole area may be filled by Professor Langer, but we have no comprehensive picture yet.

3. The third area of ignorance concerns our defeats. In Mr. Merriam's "Dark December" some of the mystery surrounding the Battle of the Bulge is dispelled. But there has been no comparably frank treatment of the first Battle of Savo Island; of Bataan; of the Philippines; of the Netherlands East Indies (where American forces also fought), of the Kasserine Pass, or Kiska.

4. The fourth great blank is the role that Gen. Douglas MacArthur

played in the war; here is a famous and controversial figure, variously described in terms that range all the way from adulation to scorn, who has had no adequate, thorough, revealing and yet fair appraisal.

Above all, this tenth anniversary reveals the need for balanced history, for history that pulls all the threads together. There has been plenty of subjective, personal history, either of the war correspondent's "I-was-there" variety or the "Everybody-was-wrong-but-me" school (like General Chennault's book, "Way of a Fighter"). There has been plenty of the objective, dry-as-dust, statistical treatment. What is lacking is balanced history—subjective enough to comprehend the important intangibles, objective enough to weigh and assess the fundamental tangibles of man's greatest inhumanity to man.

Diagnosing the German Malady

The Events That Led Up to the Crime

SAMUEL J. HURWITZ

→»-→»-→»-→»-→»-→»-→»-→» *Published in 1947* «-«-«-«-«-«-«-«-«-«

It is no surprise that there is a mountain of books, pamphlets, and magazine articles dealing with "the German problem." After all, it was the famous blank check that Germany gave to Austria-Hungary in the period of the Sarajevo crisis that played a decisive part in precipitating World War I. And it was the numerous acts of aggression committed by Nazi Germany that brought on World War II. In short, German policies in the twentieth century have caused untold grief for millions of people. Small wonder, therefore, that in the period of both World Wars I and II hundreds of books and articles centering on "the German question" were published in allied countries. Many of these, to be sure, were products of a sort that their authors would not have been proud to acknowledge in later years. So emotional and even hysterical was their tone and so absurd were many of the contentions they set forth that they are valuable mainly for the evidence they provide of the bitterness, resentment, and hatred which German policies were capable of arousing. On the other hand, some of the wartime books and articles dealing with Germany were models of thoughtful analysis. In the present bibliographical essay, Samuel J. Hurwitz, of Brooklyn College, one of the most promising young scholars in the field of twentieth-century European history, surveys and evaluates some of the more important works that sought to clarify the German problem in the period of World War II.

I t is understandable that we should have a flood of books on German history, all bearing the imprint of a kind of compulsive urgency. By common consent the core of the ills that beset our time is Germany. Since Germany has been guilty of every crime but suicide, and balks

Reprinted by special permission from *Commentary*, IV (1947), 178-186. The author has made a few minor changes in the present version of his essay.

at that, we demand from history some simple rational explanation to afford us consoling deliverance from the sense of past catastrophe and an ominous future.

But even more practical considerations motivate our interest. If we are to cure Germany, the plague-spot of Europe, we must know the cause of her malady. The key to the answer of "what to do about Germany" depends on our diagnosis of the nature of the German problem, characterized more than eighty years ago by Constantin Frantz, a German publicist, as "the most somber, the most complicated, the most comprehensive problem of all recent history."

Unfortunately, some historians are physicians who announce the prognosis first, and then construct the diagnosis to fit, with little respect for the facts of the case record. Lord Vansittart is of the school that seems satisfied to offer reiterated allegations as a substitute for historic truth. But, lacking the brazenness of Hitler and Goebbels, he tries to reinforce his repetitive assertions with "historic evidence," and fails where they succeeded. Writing the foreword to a history of Germany by a Pole writing under the very English pen name of W. M. Knight-Patterson (*Germany from Defeat to Conquest*, New York, Macmillan, 1946), Vansittart holds that "everyone who thinks that the Germans are as other people, only misled, is an enemy of other people. . . . Here is the proof and the story." (Whatever the demerits of the book—and it has many—it is better than the thesis of Lord Vansittart's foreword.)

A well-known British historian, F. J. C. Hearnshaw, entitles his story *Germany the Aggressor Throughout the Ages* (New York, Dutton, 1942). To him, Germany is "chronically dangerous" and "easily misguided." Though definitely writing a "war book," Hearnshaw cannot entirely cast off his cloak of learning and understanding, and the result is a medley of fact, fiction, and imprecation. Somewhat similar in tone, if more academic and more substantial, is the work of an American university professor who offers us *The German Record— A Political Portrait* (William Ebenstein, New York, Rinehart, 1945). Professor Ebenstein, who is not without hope that Germany "can change"—if but slowly—rejects, by writing his book, his own counsel on the German problem, namely, "to declare a moratorium of, say, two years, on books, articles, and lectures on the Germans and the problems they present to the world." Disappointing, too, is S. H. Steinberg's

A Short History of Germany (New York, Macmillan, 1945), a political narrative that sometimes substitutes exhortation for explanation.

The president of Hunter College, George N. Shuster, has for many years been concerned with the future of Germany and the world. His *The Germans: An Inquiry and An Estimate* (New York, L. Mac-Veagh-Dial) was published in 1932; and in 1944, in collaboration with Arnold Bergstraesser, he wrote *Germany: A Short History* (New York, W. W. Norton, 1944). Both works are characterized by a breadth of understanding and humaneness too often lacking in works dealing with Germany. The sickness of which Hitlerism is such a horrible example is seen as not restricted to that country. Yet one may question a diagnosis which assumes (in 1932) that "Dr. Bruening has been nothing short of a godsend to his countrymen and even to us," even though his government "probably ruled against the wishes of the majority of Germans . . . by reason of the police power it was able to marshal." Even in 1944, Bruening is still staunchly defended, and the "basic explanation for the triumph of Hitlerism" is "found not in the realm of rational calculation, economics, for example, but in that of ethical absolutes," although "the conflict between social ideals and economic realities" is admitted.

An undercurrent of economic ideas, if not realities, influences Wilhelm Ropke's *Die Deutsche Frage* (Ehlenbach—Zürich, Switzerland, 1945). It is in many respects a superior work; much of what Ropke says is valid and relevant: he recognizes the importance of Germany to Europe and the wider significance of National Socialism, as well as the connection between regimentation and proletarization on the one hand and nationalism and totalitarianism on the other. Ropke is opposed to large-scale industry and monopoly, but his solution appears as impossible as it is archaic: to do away with "regimentation and proletarization." He wants a confederation of autonomous states with

---

FRIEDRICH EBERT: Leader of the Social Democratic Party and first president of the Weimar Republic (d. 1925). He took the stand that in the postwar atmosphere socialist objectives must be subordinated to two other goals: the strengthening of the position of the Republic and the hastening of the reconstruction of Germany.

SPARTACISTS: German communists, led by Karl Liebknecht and Rosa Luxem-

an economic structure that is "pronouncedly anti-collectivist." How to reverse the growth and tendencies of two hundred years of industrialization is not explained. Ropke does face up to the problem of modern production and totalitarianism, of the incidence of an economy which operates mechanically if not automatically; but his attempt to deal with the problem has about it the earmarks of the incantations of a witch doctor called upon to purge a patient of "evil spirits."

Veit Valentin's *The German People* (New York, Knopf, 1946) is a book as pretentious as it is shallow, full of errors and downright inanities, made all the more glaring by a very awkward translation. More of a chronicle than a history, it is a mere catalogue of names, events, and dates. Valentin's account reminds one of Ambrose Bierce's definition of history as "an account mostly false, of events mostly unimportant, which are brought about by rulers mostly knaves, and soldiers mostly fools."

Historians, no angels, have not feared to tread, but psychiatrists have rushed in with heavy step.

A practicing psychiatrist, Richard L. Brickner (*Is Germany Incurable?* Philadelphia, Lippincott, 1943), explains the German problem as one of group paranoia. He solemnly tells us that the "deliberate massacre of all Germans is of course intolerable," but offers no other specific remedies. A member of the Department of Psychiatry at Columbia University, David Abrahamsen (*Men, Mind, and Power*, New York, Columbia, 1945), offers us such helpful explanations as the following: "Life in the dark forests affected the thinking of the German tribes; they felt that the woods were full of secret beings who induced fear in the people living there. . . ." The German language is so full of harsh sounds because of "the belief that it was unmanly to talk nicely and smoothly. . . ." "It apparently did not occur to [Hitler] that he was conquering an entire country [Austria] in order to revenge himself on his father. . . ." "If [the Germans] could develop a taste

---

burg, who attempted to overthrow the German Republic in 1919. Their Berlin rebellion was quickly crushed.

LORD VANSITTART: British Foreign Office official who believed that a hard peace settlement should be imposed on Germany after World War II. Among other things, he favored the de-industrialization of Germany and its transformation into a country of farmers.

for democracy, then they would be able to want a democracy." The Germans are "materialistic, aggressive, and submissive" and also "romantic, seclusive, and idealistic."

Gerhart Eisler and two collaborators have written *The Lesson of Germany* (New York, International, 1945), "a guide, a modest attempt to interpret the past history of Germany which will enable the reader better to study and understand the future course of the German people in the light of their past." Unfortunately, after the reader has gone more than 200 pages, the authors deny the significance of Germany's past altogether. However, one can hardly quarrel with such a conclusion when it is based on such an account of Germany's past as these authors give.

We do not quite turn to the sublime with two other books, but one has real promise; the other represents substantial achievement. The first is *Germany: A Self Portrait* (New York, Oxford, 1944) which Harlen R. Crippen has edited with frequent editorial remarks. His comments alone are worth the price of the book. Though one may quarrel with his selections, my major criticism is not concerned with these, but rather with the fact that the hard-headed Mr. Crippen has been much too close-fisted with his own introductions and editorial remarks. Attacking "bargain-counter racism," he sees the "obscene and criminal Third Reich" as "the manifestation of the profound maladjustments in German society." While his approach is analytical, his mood and style are impressionistic; but some real insights result. His summary of the period before 1914 and his review of conditions between the wars express in a very few pages a terrible indictment of German—and world—society. It is to be hoped that *Germany: A Self Portrait* will be followed by *Germany: A Portrait*.

A distinguished example of historical writing is A. J. P. Taylor's *The Course of German History* (New York, Coward McCann, 1946). Though it is dogmatic and arrogant, and Taylor's wartime passions and resentments often get the better of his temper and tongue, *The Course of German History* demonstrates that the nature of the German problem rests in the history of the German people, who, like other peoples, have been shaped and influenced by social, economic, and political forces rather than by innate characteristics—racial or otherwise. Nurture, not nature, is the basis of the evil, and Taylor attempts to portray the influences that have shaped Germany and the

Germans. He is not always successful, he is often exasperating, and he is sometimes illogical, yet there does emerge from his frequently brilliant pages, as from no other book, the *history* of Germany, the story of its development.

Significant is the geographical setting. In the center of Europe, Germany lacks geography: without natural frontiers, the German plain is intersected by great rivers that serve to divide, but neither to confine nor protect. Germany is in the center ethnographically as well. The artificiality and impermanence of its frontiers have made it the stamping ground of the peoples of Europe. No study of the "national character" of the Germans can ignore these influences; yet no serious study can see them as the all-controlling factors.

More important were the great geographical discoveries of the 16th century. In most of Western Europe this was a time of commercial prosperity, of national consolidation, the period of the rise of the modern state. The central location of Germany had made it for a time the highway and the *entrepôt* of world trade. But this very central position was to prove her undoing. The discoveries of the explorers of the 16th century shifted world commerce from land to sea, and thus spelled the decline of Central Europe. The collapse of Germany was inherent in the opening of the Cape route to India. The effects of the Lutheran Reformation only compounded the disastrous consequences.

As was to be true later in 1848, the masses took too literally the words of reform and revolution. Luther, shocked by the Peasants' Revolt of 1525, turned to the princes and bolstered their fading power. The revival of feudal authority was a concomitant of the decline in trade, of the reversion to a more self-contained and stagnant economy; the Lutheran Reformation by strengthening that tendency helped to sunder Germany. Elsewhere in Western Europe, religious changes reinforced national power, but Lutheranism failed to establish itself as the religion of all Germans and thus accentuated disunity.

Sorely burdened, Germany left alone might yet have attained that nationhood achieved by her contemporaries, but the latter, fearing their own weakness as their neighbor became stronger, intervened. The Thirty Years' War (1618-48) wasted Germany. The remarkably stable Peace of Westphalia (whose provisions remained generally operative for 150 years) made vested the interest of those who profited by a divided Germany. The result was that the multitudinous German states prospered—in the persons of their princes—while the people languished.

It is not strange that France, Germany's strongest neighbor, always had a profound influence on the course of German history. France prevented German unity in the 17th century; in the 19th she acted as a spur to German unification. In one respect the French Revolution realized the aims of Richelieu—the destruction of the feudal lords and the centralization of power in the national state. But while Richelieu had sought to keep Germany divided, the French Revolution tended to unite her, even if only against the French. This unity was impossible on any firmer basis because of the lag in commercial and industrial development, and the economic backwardness of the bourgeoisie. There is reality behind the epigram: "The French rule the land, the English the sea, and the Germans the clouds." Napoleon soon defeated the German coalition, but permitted the survival of Prussia.

Bolstered by the final defeat of France, and jealously guarding their prerogatives, the Prussian and Austrian ruling classes engaged in a campaign against nationalism and liberalism. As Taylor puts it, "the classes that ruled Prussia would dig their own graves provided that they retained a monopoly of wielding the spade." Yet economic necessities could not be ignored. With political unification thwarted, economic cooperation was established by the *Zollverein*. An economic ersatz for political unification, it was not a durable substitute. The revolutionary events of 1848 constituted an attempt to incorporate in political reality the economic facts of German life. The revolutions of 1848, inside and outside of Germany, were essentially middle class. Everywhere industrialism had bred a rising bourgeoisie, discontented and frustrated by the old forms of society, eager for a new world in its own image.

Not wholly successful anywhere, the revolutions of 1848 nevertheless set the stage for further advances everywhere except in Germany. There the fiasco led to disastrous consequences. The lack of success in Austria was just as complete, yet it was not fatal; it was but symptomatic of the industrial backwardness of the huge, sprawling, and incoherent Austrian Empire. Doomed to relative impotence, Austria did not develop the contradictions inherent in the functioning of a modern industrial economy within a feudal state. But for Germany, the failure of the middle class to realize its "rendezvous with destiny" —or at least with history—was to have tragic results.

The revolution was doomed to failure by circumstances beyond the control of any of its participants. The Germans sought to become, and were becoming, like everyone else, but much too late and hence too much. German industrialism was a late growth, vaulting where others grew slowly and integratedly. This belated but sudden growth of industry in Germany had created a working class that was less *bourgeois* in its outlook than the working class of other countries. Late industrialization had created large units. The small-scale enterprises so characteristic of Great Britain and France, which were the result of a relatively slow process of industrialization, were absent in Germany. Hence the German workers, employed in relatively large-scale establishments, with little hope of ever becoming capitalists themselves, were much more class-conscious than their counterparts in other countries. That more than anything else perhaps explains the appearance of a Marx in Germany.

Taylor ignores the reasons, but he is aware of the significance: ". . . the cause of national union must be adorned with the attractions of socialism. This was the program of Marx and Engels, to which they devoted the rest of their lives, until their national starting-point was almost forgotten. They advocated socialism so as to cause a revolution; only much later did their followers suppose that they had advocated revolution in order to accomplish socialism." On the other hand, it was their fear of socialism that haunted the German middle classes for the next century. And it was the failure of 1848 that robbed them of faith in their own political capacities. The fiasco of '48 and its "proof" of the inherent dangers of political action made the German middle classes not merely tired, but afraid.

While the events of 1848 set the pattern, the crisis of the 1860's in Prussia saw it finally completed. The 1860's were the period of liberalism's great—and, in the light of subsequent events, final—opportunity to seize control of events in Germany. But the Prussian liberals, obsessed by the incubus of 1848, dared not press their advantage. This difficulty of the German bourgeoisie was Bismarck's opportunity, and he exploited it to the full.

Although Mr. Taylor brings forth little that is new to the well informed, his portrayal of Bismarck's motives and actions must be much in the nature of a revelation to generations of American college students: Bismarck, his fanciful *Memoirs* notwithstanding, had not the slightest intention of unifying Germany when he assumed office as Prussian Chancellor. Nor did he, at the outset, favor war with Austria. His only program was the preservation of the Junker social order; what he would have most preferred was a return to the age of Metternich. A unified, single German national state was nowhere in his picture. Events forced his hand. Strength was needed against an Austria that had not given up its own "German policy." With strife inevitable, Bismarck took the initiative. The Seven Weeks' War of 1866 eliminated the Austrian bugbear, and the gratitude of the Prussian liberals was unbounded. By a vote of more than three to one, the Prussian parliament forgave Bismarck for his sins against the constitution. Liberalism had not disappeared; it simply disqualified itself as a force in German history. As nothing succeeds like success, the course of German history was now clear. Liberalism had sold its birthright, but for fifty years it had rich porridge.

The Franco-Prussian War of 1870-1 was "inevitable": Bismarck had to consolidate his gains; France needed to expiate her inept policies and "solve" her internal problems. The crushing defeat administered to France resolved any doubts about the future of German policy. The constitution of the German Reich, proclaimed not in Germany but in France's Hall of Mirrors in Versailles, reflected the almost fictional character of German unification. A product essentially of the aristocracy, it was a loose confederation rather than a modern constitution based upon centralization of power. It was not a "dictatorship of Prussia" as Taylor dogmatically asserts. Nor is Taylor fully emancipated from the stock version, often repeated by the Germans themselves in a breast-beating mood, of the absolute impotence of the Reichstag (elected, incidentally, by universal manhood suffrage and by secret ballot, whereas in Great Britain, for example, the secret ballot was not attained until 1872 and universal manhood suffrage not until 1918). The Chancellor and the Bundesrat might fume and rant, but the only menace that the Reichstag faced was dissolution, with later re-election if the Reichstag members truly represented the wishes of their constituents. That is not to say that the Reichstag's powers were comparable to those of the British House of Commons or the French Chamber of Deputies: unlike those bodies, the Reichstag had no direct control over the Chancellor and the ministers of state. The distinction is significant, but it should not blur the fact that the Reichstag possessed real power. (Nor should it be overlooked that the growth of cabinet government in Great Britain has tended to curtail the actual powers of the House of Commons.) It is preposterous to hold that "the government of Germany was as autocratic as the government of Tsarist Russia."

But such extravagant statements do not seriously detract from Taylor's keen analysis of the reasons for the introduction in Germany of direct universal manhood suffrage—opposed by the liberals of the 19th century. Both the liberals and Bismarck anticipated that universal suffrage would swamp the liberals, and their fear was Bismarck's hope. It was precisely because German unification was achieved, at best, with the passive resistance of the liberals, that the fruits of unification were not liberal. The liberals accepted the constitution because it gave them unification—and prosperity. The workers gained the vote—and social legislation.

The retarded unification of Germany was responsible for the failure of liberalism to take hold. Liberalism was on the wane in Western Europe after 1870, its best assets shrinking, its liabilities ever more apparent. Freedom of the individual, the dignity of man, could not be attained in a social order that thrived on inequality and exploitation. "Liberal" capitalism proved a contradiction in terms, and the faith that gave such spirit and buoyancy to most of the first hundred years after the French Revolution was ebbing. If one date and one event must be taken as the pivotal point, it was the crash of 1873, from which free capitalism never fully recovered. The lag characteristic of social institutions embalmed liberalism in Britain and France. Not perfectly, and even less in France than in Britain, but sufficient unto the day. (To be sure, even Britain showed evidences of strain on the eve of 1914, and the masses, as well as recalcitrant aristocrats who sought in a last desperate gamble to hold on to a show of power, chafed, while the middle class itself was progressively losing its confidence. But the resources of capitalism in Britain were not yet exhausted, and the sense of continuity, the pride of history, helped keep British society relatively well balanced.)

In Germany, the middle classes had in 1848 rejected a unification that carried in it the seeds of democracy and revolution. In the 1860's they were confronted not merely with the possibility but with the fact of a unification that carried with it aristocratic rule. They acquiesced, to their economic glory but to their everlasting social and political humiliation. The formal proclamation of a unified German state in 1871 left the German middle classes with a sense of inferiority, shame, and guilt—a state of mind from which they never recovered and which their economic success all the more emphasized. Hence their grumbling, but also their restraint in never actually challenging Bismarck's power. They achieved all their demands—except political and social power. To make things easier for them and to insure his own retention of power, Bismarck conjured up specters: France, the Catholics, the Social Democrats—all served, each in its time, to the point of exhaustion. By 1890 dictatorship seemed the only alternative, but the young and ambitious William II dismissed the "Iron Chancellor" and sought to resolve internal difficulties by winning over the masses to the cause of German glory.

Everywhere in Europe—and in the United States, too—this was the period of imperialism and demagogic chauvinism. The resemblance between Theodore Roosevelt and William II is striking. By 1890 pose had replaced pomp. Bismarck had not lacked either, but William II was even more of a poseur. His policy was the logical continuation of 1871, just as Hitler's policy was the logical continuation of 1890. The dismissal of Bismarck was approved by the Chief of the German General Staff, "who believed that a more demagogic policy would strengthen the army and so enable Germany to take a more forceful line in foreign affairs."

For four years Chancellor Caprivi carried out a policy which, though it was more demagogic than real, proved too strong for the Junkers and National Liberals. Provoking extreme resistance, Caprivi could only remain in power by overthrowing the existing order. For this almost no one was prepared, and Germany returned to a more conservative policy under Hohenlohe and his successors. But it was already too late for that and that alone. A whipping boy had to be found; internal tensions and discontents had to be sublimated if the social order was to remain unchanged. "World Policy"—bluster and alarms—served as the great outlet and distraction. Bismarck's policy, much exaggerated, became the touchstone of success. The French and the British did not neglect to act likewise—but Germany, with internal strife more pronounced, was forced into a position much more exaggerated.

This policy lasted a dozen years and broke down in 1906. The failure of the Algeciras Conference marked the end of successes won by mere threat of force. Ultimately, the decision rested with strength itself, not merely the show of strength. The slogan "the Fatherland is in danger" continued to rally the country, but was becoming ineffectual in foreign affairs. Worse, it helped to make war unavoidable. Crippen best catches the mood: "The crazy zig-zags by which war was several times averted only served to strengthen the popular illusion that war was an illusion. Hairbreadth escapes encouraged the German rulers to engage in further rash enterprises—for bellicose acts and warlike words were usually followed by substantial concessions from other powers. And when thirteen years of the century had passed, the proudest boast of the Hohenzollerns was that there had been no war, and it was implied, there would be none. It was a thin story, but the Germans along with other nations wanted to believe."

As with the liberals, the ubiquitous policy of the "lesser evil" had infected the German Social Democrats, despite their socialist catechisms. The unanimous Reichstag vote for war credits (after 96 out of the 110 Social Democratic deputies had previously, in a secret caucus, decided to support the government) came as a shock to Lenin, but merely proved that Bernstein's plea for a revision of Marxism was a more realistic appraisal of the Social Democratic position in Germany. Mass education, popular suffrage, social insurance, and a standard of living higher than that in any other of the Continental countries had undermined revolutionary ideology. The German worker was a German first and foremost, and the laggards were rallied by the cry that the "Cossacks" would sweep down into Germany. And certainly the German working class did not wish to exchange the Kaiser for the knout.

Though they might differ as to aims, all Germans entered into the war of 1914 with high hopes. But as the war dragged on, unanimity was shattered; as hardships increased, so did discontent. As the home front grew more querulous under the strain of war, and the civilian government more inept, the army was forced to take over real control.

The failure of the German war effort meant the end of army rule. The military leaders were no "die-hards"; they were ready, willing, and anxious to relinquish the reins when they themselves failed. The dispatch with which the government of Germany was transformed into a democratic republic is more attributable to the consent of the army than the ardent desire of the Social Democrats to assume power.

Shuster and Bergstraesser are at their best in describing the events of 1918 and 1919. Few really wanted the revolution but "one must not assume that the army command used revolution as a strategic device to transfer blame for the debacle on other shoulders. . . . It had simply lost its nerve." Here, clearly, was a revolutionary situation, the opportunity for revolution so often looked forward to by the Social Democrats. But the Social Democrats and their millions of followers who had laboriously acquired a stake in German society saw in this situation only a threat to their own stability, and proceeded, not to revolution, but to save a society of which they felt themselves to be an integral part. No less than Ebert, who, as he himself said, "hated revolution like sin," the German working class viewed with horror the possibility of revolution—with its expected uprooting and chaos; their abhorrence was made all the greater by the events in Russia. So long as the former ruling class did not press its demands, so long as the German working class achieved its major aims of peace and a democratic political organization, so long was the "revolution" successful and so long was it unnecessary to destroy the former ruling class physically.

As a matter of fact, the Social Democrats could not eliminate the Junkers and their adherents without destroying themselves. For close on the heels of the Social Democratic revolution was the terror of an uprising on the Russian model. And it seemed plain to socialists and democrats, even as early as the end of 1918, that the Russian Revolution was a perversion of socialism. Having no other resources with which to resist the extreme Left, the government established an alliance with the High Command in order to preserve order. The Spartacists, unable to attain their ends by democratic means, preached—and practiced—violence almost as an end in itself. Against their own better judgment their leaders followed the irresponsible crowds—to death and destruction.

The Social Democrats were trade-union leaders, not revolutionaries; they endeavored to preserve the German state and most of its institutions. They sought a democratic regime, the ideal of 1848. And, indeed, the Weimar Constitution of 1919 was the most democratic constitution ever adopted by any state. All power resided in the people, and there were no "due process of law" clauses to prevent socialization. But neither did it provide for socialism automatically. The German people could have it, but first they must want it, and whether they did or not could be ascertained through the democratic process. Whatever the reason, this they never did. Even in the first post-revolution election, in January, 1919, the Social Democrats did not have a majority, nor would fusion with the more radical socialist groups have given them a majority. And the socialist vote, of every persuasion (the Spartacists, numerically insignificant, "boycotted" the election), reached its high-water mark in the election of January 1919. Never was it possible to achieve socialism in Germany *by parliamentary means*—a fact that has generally been ignored.

If democratic socialism was unachievable, so was reaction impossible without the destruction of the values of those groups in Germany which favored a middle-class republic along much the same lines as did analogous groups in the United States, France, and Great Britain. But the failure of democratic capitalism and the seeming impossibility of democratic socialism catapulted more and more German citizens into the ranks of a party which was bound to no past, and which, rootless and unfettered by coherent principles, could chameleon-like assume the colors of the moment. As rationality and responsibility failed in meeting the problems thrown up by the Great Depression, the party of irrationality and irresponsibility reaped the harvest. For between them, the inflation and the depression destroyed—figuratively if not literally—that class in Germany which has everywhere been the champion of democracy and liberalism.

There was an integral and causal connection in the 19th century between the middle class, democracy, and liberalism. The great question of our time is whether this trinity still holds. Karl Marx, who had emphasized the original historical connection between capitalism and liberalism, held not merely that socialism, democracy, and liberalism were compatible, but that their synthesis was inherent and necessary if liberalism was to survive. He became a socialist for the very reason that, as he held, capitalism stifled liberalism. To him socialism was true liberalism, that liberalism which proclaimed the dignity of the individual as the *sine qua non*.

The failure of the Russian Revolution was chiefly responsible for the German "disenchantment" with socialism; the failure of democratic capitalism created the void in accepted values. National Socialism sought to occupy this vacuum.

The economic crisis that began in 1929 was worldwide, but its effects in Germany were greater than anywhere else. With fewer re-sources—material and spiritual—to meet the collapse, it is natural that the consequences were more catastrophic. It is true, as Taylor says, "there was no reason at all why [the crisis] should justify a nationalistic policy and rearmament . . ." but it did result in just that, and not only in Germany. The question of "justification" is somewhat irrelevant. Wherein Germany differed was not in the policy, but in the degree of its application. Fully and even extravagantly applied, it was the policy of fascism or National Socialism—or totalitarianism.

Because of its previous history and the greater impact of the depression, the road to dictatorship was easier to mark out in Germany than in other countries. But one individual who must bear great responsibility for bringing Germany to the precipice from which there was no return is Chancellor Bruening. Beginning in 1930, Bruening followed a method of ruling by emergency decrees—not over the protest of the Reichstag, it is true, but without its consent. This method paralyzed the republic; the policies were fatal. Retrenchment which involved the slashing of wages and social services completed the demoralization of those groups that had still remained loyal to the Republic and that now found it more and more impossible to countenance a state ruled by decrees—decrees, moreover, which served but to complete their economic ruin. Disheartened by the turn of events and having no faith in Communism, the democratic working class had the alternative of acquiescence and apathy, or National Socialism. Whichever they chose, Hitler found the going easy.

The British workers, too, had felt themselves betrayed by Mac-Donald in 1931, but MacDonald ruled through Parliament, and parliamentary majorities could be changed. Bruening ruled over Parliament and there was nothing to change, short of revolution. In Britain the middle class still had faith in Parliament and "democracy"; both could be turned to their own cause. Not so in Germany. Only dictatorship could be trusted in time of crisis. Fascism was not unique to Germany but its success was. And it succeeded in Germany because the pre-conditions were there: the breakdown of traditional values, the unwillingness—and perhaps inability—to embrace social revolution, and a literate and desperate population that could accept Caesarism.

For fascism—the negation of individual personality—requires active participation by the many. That is why Italian fascism was such a sham: Mussolini's histrionics may have amused but they never seriously moved the great masses, who could no more "appreciate" and share in fascism than they could in democracy. The aspirations of Italian fascism were beyond Italy's possibilities. A long-suffering, less literate population could not accept—nor could Mussolini successfully fashion, in an economically backward country—that synthesis summed up in the words "National Socialism." In Germany, however, men grasped desperately for meaning, for a philosophy of living that was more consonant with their actual mode of behavior than the democratic liberalism of the 19th century which had failed them in the crucial test. Consequences notwithstanding, men sought a mythology, in the best sense of the word, to synthesize their experience, to organize their values, to make the events of their time intelligible.

The events in Germany provide the lessons of our time. Do they but adumbrate the future? Whether or not we are our brother's keeper, is his illness our illness? I think it was Dorothy Thompson who remarked some years back that the Jews were like everyone else, only more so. A haunting fear that this may be even more true of the Germans—and an effort to avoid the basic issues thus posed—may explain much in our current thinking about the nature of Germany's past. The malady of our age can be glossed over and even denied if it can be made apparent that the Germans are like no one else and even more so.

If one may paraphrase Mussolini, it is Germany that is now the stinking corpse. Unable to be buried, unable to be ignored, with the smell of its death pervasive, Germany dead seems still to pollute the world as much as Germany living and aggressive. A horrible, if unvoiced, suspicion that her death rattle may have marked the final agony of Western civilization has focused attention on her as a case history. To prove the uniqueness of Germany, to divorce her from the stream of world history—that, apparently, has become the task. Eagerly and desperately, we have reached out for a formula that would provide a solution for our difficulties without requiring us to recast our lives or our society. The "devil theory" is probably as old as man, and age has not attenuated its appeal.

The significant problem in the study of Germany's past (and present and future) is to recognize that Germany belongs, in its development, to the community of nations. Simply to outlaw Germany by fiat, as so many historians have done, is not only intellectually shallow and invalid; what is worse, it tends to lull us into a false sense of security and prevent even an attempt at a proper remedy.

Any study that is to explain Germany's history as well as our own cannot *a priori* rule out those features which are common to our civilization. That is not to say that Germany's past is exactly like our own, or that of Great Britain, or France—or Russia. The commercial decline of the German states in the 16th century, the Lutheran Reformation, the failure of the revolution of 1848, Bismarck, Versailles, postwar inflation and depression, all played their part in a culmination that was peculiar to Germany. But each of these factors is itself the product of forces that acted on all the Western European countries, influencing them at different times and with different strength. The process of industrialization, for example, operated in all countries, creating, weakening, or strengthening groups with special interests and special political drives, and leading to common political configurations.

Germany, if we look at history with the eyes of historic objectivity, is neither "different" nor "the same." Each country unquestionably has institutions peculiar to itself, products of its special historical development and growth. But the underlying and fundamental unity of the forces which make up our modern civilization forces itself into any analysis which is intended to make more clear the true conditions of our era. The task of the historian—or of anyone else who is concerned with our world—is to present a frame of reference by which we can evaluate similarities and differences. Only then can we judge, for example, whether fascism is generic in modern industrial society, and what institutions (political, social, economic, and cultural—if these can be separated) make society more readily susceptible to the blandishments of those who pretend to ride "the wave of the future." What must we do to avoid having the bell toll for us?

"A fable agreed upon," was Napoleon's characterization of history. If the history of Germany cannot quite support the sins of the world, its historiography—history as written—too often now seeks to achieve this purpose. Germany, an outcast in the world, finds its counterpart in Germany an outcast in history. But this is the easy, dangerous way. More objective history will lead to a better understanding of the German case; and that in turn may help us to a deeper, truer understanding of the unsolved problems of the world we live in, and to an avoidance of perils that may lie latent in our own American industrial society.

Soviet-American Relations Since the War

PHILIP E. MOSELY

➤➤➤➤➤➤➤➤➤ *Published in 1949* ⬅⬅⬅⬅⬅⬅⬅⬅⬅

In Tsarist times the United States and Russia got along remarkably well. Since the two countries had, as a rule, little to do with each other, the opportunities for friction were few. Even in the years after the Bolshevik Revolution, relations between Russia and the United States caused little concern to the rest of the world. As in the past, the two powers had relatively little to do with each other; the United States did not even recognize the Soviet government until 1933. It was only in the period of World War II that Russo-American relations ceased to be sporadic and became continuous. For with the falling out between the Communists and the Nazis and with the American entry into the war, the United States and Russia found themselves allies; and it was in their years as allies that suspicions and tensions increased. Russian attacks on the United States and Britain for their slowness in launching a second front, and absurd Russian claims that they alone were fighting the good fight against the Nazi enemy, augured ill for the future. And when Germany and Japan were finally defeated the world found itself faced with one problem that loomed larger than any other: Russo-American relations. Americans were convinced that Russia was aiming at world revolution. And Russians, fed on the time-worn myth of the U.S.S.R. as a beleaguered fortress of socialism in a hostile capitalist world, were convinced that Wall Street was out to destroy them. It is this deterioration of Russo-American relations that Philip E. Mosely considers in the present essay. Professor of international relations at Columbia University's Russian Institute, Mosely is one of the most thoughtful of present-day writers on Russian diplomatic history.

The problem which now dominates all aspects of postwar politics is that of the antagonism between American and Soviet politics. If there is a ballot on admitting new members to the United Nations, or a decision to be taken on reconstruction in Germany, it cannot be discussed on the merits of the case. Each position is taken with an eye to its effect upon the two contending greatest powers.

The extreme polarization of power is reflected along sensitive frontiers, as in Norway and Iran. It cuts across critical areas of homogeneous nationalities, as in the cases of Germany, Austria, and Korea. It is paralleled in dangerous fissures within many national communities and is reflected in the continuing unrest within Soviet satellites and in the struggles of the Communist parties in France and Italy, in Greece and China. The factors of conflict, which have been traced in several articles in this volume, have been tumultuous and remain dangerous.

The dangers are increased by the fact that both Soviet and American centers of power are largely self-contained; the outlook and purposes of each of these powers are generated internally, are secreted from its own way of life. The intentional or unforeseen repercussions of their acts affect many other peoples in their most sensitive interests and aspirations. In addition, each of these two great powers finds it difficult to arrive at a coherent judgment of the power and intentions of the other.

Soviet Ideas of the United States

When the Soviet leaders look at America, they think primarily of its great economic power. No doubt, they are rather well informed

Reprinted by special permission from *The Annals of the American Academy of Political and Social Science*, CCLXIII (1949), 202-211.

COMINFORM: Communist Information Bureau. Its establishment in 1947 was a major reflection of the deterioration of relations between Russia and the Western powers. It consists of representatives from each affiliated national Communist Party; and its official function is to "organize and exchange experience and, in case of necessity, coordinate the activity of communist parties on foundations of mutual agreement."

MORGENTHAU PLAN: Scheme developed toward the end of World War II by the American Secretary of the Treasury. Germany was to cease to be a

of its strength in specific skills and of its inventiveness. Their insistence upon the validity of a single philosophy prevents them from understanding the political and social experience and outlook which form the underpinning of American society. In applying with extreme rigor the system of piece-rate rewards and penalties to their own workers, they overlook the fact that in America differential incentives to workers rest on a high minimum standard of living. Admitting the technical superiority of American industry, always measuring their own achievements against American statistics, the Soviet leaders also believe unshakably that the American economy is certain to be pounded to pieces from within. And since the United States is now the only other great power, they wait impatiently for the time when that power will disintegrate and American policy will be paralyzed by internal stresses.

The duality in the Soviet evaluation of American strength was clearly shown in the question of a postwar loan. The Soviet representatives were eager to secure a very large loan—figures of six to ten billion dollars were bandied about—and admitted freely that Soviet reconstruction would be immensely facilitated by the inflow of American equipment. On the other hand, they were absolutely convinced that this loan was not something for which they would have to make an effort, even an effort to maintain some degree of diplomatic decorum. They were certain that America would come hat in hand, begging them to accept a large loan, solely for the purpose of staving off a catastrophic depression at home. They felt they would be doing a favor to American manufacturers by giving their rickety economic system a few years of grace. Holding these views, the Soviet leaders assumed that their own offensive against American interests and sentiments was in no way incompatible with the obtaining of a loan.

A similar opaqueness has shaped the Soviet leaders' understanding

land of heavy industry and was to become an agricultural country. Her domestic economy and foreign trade were to be subjected to long-term controls. She was to cede several provinces to neighboring countries, and her remaining territory was to be partitioned into three states. Although the plan did much for a time to shape official American thinking concerning the German problem, its harsh proposals become increasingly embarrassing from the American point of view—especially when Soviet-American relations proceeded to deteriorate.

of American policies in the postwar world. They can recognize that Americans are basically oriented inwards and find it hard to be concerned steadily with world affairs. They know that the United States did not take the initiative in starting either of the world wars in this century. From the full and open discussion of policy which goes on in this country, they can see that most disputes revolve around the question of finding the best way to prevent a new war. Yet the Soviet leaders insist that America is the center of a new and active conspiracy to unleash a new world war.

Believing that the Soviet system alone has solved the inner contradictions of industrial society and that it is bound to expand into ever wider areas and some day to encompass the world, the Soviet leaders conclude that any forces which are outside Soviet control are, potentially or in reality, a menace to their ambition and to their regime. Professing to believe that the non-Soviet world envies the achievements of the Soviet Union and desires to destroy their system, they assume that the forces of the non-Soviet world are bound, sooner or later, to coalesce around the strongest non-Soviet power. Power beyond Soviet control and "anti-Soviet" power tend to become identified in their way of thinking.

In 1941 the Soviet leaders fully expected Britain and the United States to sit idly by while Hitler attempted to destroy the Soviet regime, or even to join with him. The prompt support which the Soviets received in a time of greatest danger, the great contributions of supplies, and the constant efforts to promote closer co-operation did not shake their faith in the dogma of "capitalist encirclement." In February 1946 this basic tenet was reaffirmed by Marshal Stalin as the central point in the postwar Soviet program.

Reasoning From Unsound Premises

The trouble about Soviet reasoning is not that it is illogical—it is usually too strictly logical—but that its premises ignore or distort simple facts which are readily discernible to minds which have not been subjected to the process of "Bolshevist hardening." If "lasting peace" is declared to be possible only under the Soviet system, then, logically, only the Soviet Union and its obedient satellites can be considered truly "peace-loving" countries. Whatever "subjective" horror of war may be expressed by "capitalist" leaders, their governments, "objectively" analyzed, are engaged in "warmongering." Anyone who criticizes or opposes Soviet claims and actions is, of course, "spreading anti-Soviet slander," "undermining peace," "promoting fascism," or "destroying Allied unity." This syllogism rests in turn on an assumption, which cannot be questioned or criticized in areas under Soviet control, that a small group of leaders in command of the regime has, through self-appointed apostolic succession to Lenin, a monopoly of wisdom and virtue.

Of course, the faculty of reasoning logically from unprovable hypotheses to untenable conclusions is not confined to any one group of men, although it seems to appear most often under conditions of absolute power. Such a faculty is dangerous when its pronouncements monopolize access to men's minds, including the minds of those who direct or serve the dictatorship.

There is a continual danger in the Soviet leaders' habit of taking action upon a set of facts which appear as facts to them alone. An even more serious danger lies in the marshaling and interpreting of a commonly perceived body of facts in accordance with a rigidly enforced philosophy, adherence to which is the password to authority and responsibility within the Soviet system.

Some American Misconceptions About the Soviet Union

Most Americans cannot make up their minds as to whether the Soviet Union is strong or weak. Because the Soviet war effort was greatly assisted through lend-lease, many Americans suppose that the Soviet Union cannot wage a major war on the basis of its own production. This assumption overlooks the fact that up to the turning of the tide at Stalingrad, the Soviet armies had received relatively small quantities of supplies from abroad. Throughout the war, the basic tools of war—artillery, tanks, planes—were almost entirely of Soviet manufacture. It would be short-sighted to suppose that Soviet capacity to wage war is far smaller, or is not actually substantially greater, than it was when the Soviet forces broke the German onslaught.

It is sometimes assumed that a denial of technical equipment and knowledge derived from the West will slow down or even disrupt the development of Soviet industry. It must, however, be assumed that in the production of machine tools the Soviet Union is "over the hump" in the process of industrialization. Failure to obtain abroad certain specialized or more modern types of equipment may delay or hamper but cannot prevent the broad development of Soviet industry on the basis of skills already acquired. Finally, the ratio of total industrial power to war potential varies considerably under diverse systems. The Soviet system gives its leaders great leeway in deciding what proportion of industrial power shall be directed towards military needs.

A contrary assumption is also advanced that the Soviet leaders may lightheartedly engage in a new trial of strength by war, as soon as they feel confident of thereby gaining some immediate and decisive advantage. Their real range of choice seems to lie somewhere between two extremes. It is unrealistic to suppose that they would make concessions from their basic program, either to secure economic aid or to win favor in the eyes of the non-Soviet world. It is also unreasonable to assume that the urge to extend their system to new areas will lead them into war without considering the effect of war upon the low Soviet standard of living or without reflecting on the possibly unpredictable outcome of a war against a powerful, highly ingenious, and relatively impregnable enemy.

If the Soviet leaders have, since 1945, steadily weighted their choice in favor of a relentless political offensive against the non-Soviet world, this may be due in large part to their habit of subordinating economic considerations to factors of power. It may be due to a short-run assumption that the economic advantages which might be gained immediately through a more conciliatory policy are of minor importance to them when compared with the great extension of political power on which they are gambling. It may also be assumed that they have felt sure that a policy of strong pressure offered no risk to their basic security, since the American military machine was being dismantled with great haste and there was no other power to challenge their ambitions.

Because the Soviet Government rules through a centralized dictatorship and severely limits the range of suggestion or criticism allowed to its citizens and to supporters abroad, an American readily assumes that the system is inherently weak, maintained only through the constant stimulation of fear. This impression of political instability has been enhanced by the sensational abandonment of Soviet allegiance by individual citizens and by the much less publicized refusal of several hundreds of thousands of its citizens to return to the Soviet

Union. To people accustomed to a regime which periodically submits to the judgment of the voters, these facts suggest weakness, hence, a necessity for such a regime to avoid war at all cost.

This interpretation, natural in American eyes, overlooks many unfamiliar factors: a long tradition of rule by a strong and irresponsible power, the tradition of combining incessant persuasion with coercion, and absence of conscious formulation of alternative programs despite widespread discontent with privations and injustices. It would be short-sighted to disparage the substantial level of disciplined action achieved under the Soviet regime or to assume that internal discontent would be an important factor, especially in a short test of strength. In any major war, of course, a defeated and occupied country may undergo a change of regime, and new currents may come to the surface. In Russia today, or anywhere in Europe, few of these currents would be tender of individual rights.

Popular Appeal of Communism

It is hard for Americans to realize that Communism meets with acceptance and even fanatical support in many segments of the population. Communism remains a powerful force in France and Italy, for American gifts and economic recovery do not reach far into the basic factors making for discontent. Backward countries may be attracted to the Soviet recipe of quick action through dictatorship, rather than to the American method of piecemeal improvement and changes brought about through consent. Where problems of overpopulation, absence of technical skills and capital, and age-old accumulations of social and national resentments set discouragingly high barriers to modernization, the appeal of Communism is bound to remain strong. There it is judged by its promises of "progress"—not by the as yet unknown effects which may follow from the quality and direction of the "progress" it offers. The Soviet leaders choose to regard American democracy as a "conspiracy." It would be equally dangerous for Americans to assume that their own type of democracy is universally admired and desired, and that the strength of Communism resides only in a centralized conspiracy of force.

Since the Soviet leaders accept the duty of spreading their system and rejoice at the appearance of each new "people's democracy," it is easily and widely assumed that this political ambition motivates its leaders at all times with an unvarying emotional intensity. It is difficult to judge the emotional intensities within the Politburo, but it is clear from the record that the outward pressure of Soviet expansionism has fluctuated rather widely over the past thirty-one years. This intensity may vary in the future.

A relative relaxation of the outward thrust may come about in one of several ways. It may arise from a discouraged recognition of solid and impassable barriers erected in its path; or it may develop from the operation of internal factors. In the case of an ideology which offers the only "scientific" basis for prediction, repeated failures to predict accurately may result in the growth of skepticism towards the doctrine of infallibility itself. Or, when a militant ideology has outlived the generation which formulated it in the heat of revolutionary struggle, and becomes the property of a generation which docilely received the tradition ready-made, the fervor of the revolutionary "fathers" may not pass integrally into the postrevolutionary "sons."

The written word of revelation may remain sacrosanct, but if it is believed with, say, 10 per cent less fervor by a new generation, the compulsion to act hazardously on behalf of the doctrine may slacken. As a dogma becomes more rigid, it may not evoke the same desire to act. Since about 1937, Soviet dogma has achieved a remarkable posture of rigidity, unnatural in a people of quick mind and ranging curiosity. Meanwhile, since no confident prediction of a slackening of the Soviet urge to messianic expansion can be made, it has become necessary to act on the assumption that this urge can be restrained only by constructing external barriers and setting clear warning signals.

Soviet-American Relations During the War

During the stress of common danger a limited degree of co-operation was established between the Soviet Union and the United States, and a modest amount of combined planning for the postwar period was accomplished. During the war the American Government made many efforts, not always well directed, to win the confidence of a very distrustful group of leaders and to lay the groundwork of a postwar community of interest. It was agreed to establish a new security organization, dominated by the great powers, and specific agreements were reached concerning the postwar occupation and control of Germany and Austria. Some limited successes were achieved, and it could not be said with finality that the Soviet leaders were determined to go their own way in the postwar world and to ignore completely their allies' constant invitations to co-operative action. It can be said that in this phase the Soviet Government insisted on safeguarding its own strength, security, secrecy, and independence of decision, yet was willing, when none of these factors was directly involved, to make limited commitments to joint action. This phase lasted through the Yalta Conference, which marked the high point in the prospects for closer understanding and co-operation.

A fortnight after Yalta there occurred a significant shift in the emphasis of Soviet policy. While the slogan of "Allied unity" continued to be chanted in every key by Soviet propagandists, there took place a rapid ebbing in any signs of Soviet consideration for the interests or hopes of the western Allies. In direct violation of the recently signed Yalta agreements, the Soviet Government proceeded to impose governments of its own choosing upon the smaller countries of eastern Europe. In violation of another part of the Yalta agreement it gave its full support to the minority Lublin regime in Poland, and signed with it a close alliance and a unilateral agreement defining Poland's western boundary, again in disregard of a specific agreement with its allies. At this very time it also backed away, in a significant respect, from implementing the agreement to co-operate with its allies in the postwar control of Germany.

After the signing, in November 1944, of the Allied agreement for establishing joint control over postwar Germany, the three governments of Great Britain, the Soviet Union, and the United States had agreed orally to set up immediately a nucleus of the future control machinery. The three, later four, nucleus control groups could thus, in advance, become accustomed to working together, could adjust their diverse administrative conceptions and establish their twelve working divisions, and would be ready to begin operations within a few days after the German surrender. The Soviet representative on the European Advisory Commission, in London, informed his colleagues that the Soviet nucleus group was being selected, that it was nearly complete, that it was almost ready to join the American and British groups. At Yalta Marshal Stalin agreed to expedite the arrival of the nucleus group, and about ten days later his representative in London informed his American colleague, with obvious satisfaction, that the Soviet group would arrive on a fixed day. Shortly after, the Soviet delegate sent a subordinate to inform the American delegation that the Soviet group was not coming at all. Viewed in retrospect, this reversal was merely one additional sign pointing to a strong trend towards unilateral Soviet policy everywhere in Europe.

FACTORS IN POST-YALTA SHIFT

There may be several partial explanations of this post-Yalta shift from limited co-operation to an attitude of sharp rivalry. As Soviet troops entered German territory, the dominant voice in Soviet policy may well have passed from the Foreign Ministry, which had until then been responsible for planning the occupation on the agreed basis of joint Allied action, into the hands of the powerful economic ministries, bent on squeezing every bit of economic relief out of Germany, and of the secret police, responsible directly to the Politburo for enforcing Soviet control in occupied areas. Another factor may have been the strong Soviet expectation of a rapid withdrawal of American forces from Europe.

At Yalta, American officials had insisted that the United States Government could not commit its people to any specific and continuing responsibilities in Europe, and that American forces would be withdrawn across the ocean just as rapidly as the availability of shipping would permit. At that stage the Morgenthau "Plan," which dominated official thinking about the German problem, showed no trace of any concern for Germany's longer-range future. Turning Germany into a "pastoral" country would, of course, have left Communism as the sole hope for German survival. Knowing after Yalta that American power would be withdrawn with utmost speed from Europe, the Soviet leaders could also, and did, treat with contempt American protests, even President Roosevelt's personal appeals to Stalin, concerning the open and frequent violations of the Yalta agreements on eastern Europe.

The same factors must have encouraged the Soviet leaders, after digesting the experience of Yalta, to hope that France and Italy, where the native Communist parties were far stronger and better organized than in Poland, Hungary, or Rumania, would also come under Russian Communist domination. In addition, throughout 1944-46 one of the strongest arguments of Communist supporters in western Europe was that America, though it appeared strong and friendly, was an unreliable friend, that its armies were nonexistent in time of peace and its economic assistance would melt away in a postwar economic crisis of its own, while the Soviet Union would remain close at hand and would know how to reward its adherents and punish its opponents.

As the Moscow Politburo wrote to the obstreperous Belgrade Politburo in 1948, the way in which the war ended had, "unfortunately," made it impossible for the Soviet Union to establish "people's democracies" in Italy and France. But if they could not be established in western Germany, France, and Italy by the expeditious means of Soviet military assistance, the same goal might still be achieved through combined pressure from within and without, provided American support were withdrawn and American policy reverted to transoceanic isolationism.

Soviet-American Relations, 1945-47

The new phase, of Soviet initiatives and intensive Soviet pressure, which began shortly after Yalta, continued into the spring of 1947. During this period Soviet policy was based on the assumption that France was beyond recovery, that Britain was done as a great power, and that the United States was about to isolate itself from European affairs or fall into economic impotence. At Potsdam there were still some slight traces of willingness on the part of Soviet leaders to give a hearing to the views of their allies and to compromise in minor details. But it was at Potsdam that the Soviet leaders gave frank expression to a program of expansion which, if achieved, would have made their power supreme in Europe and in the eastern Mediterranean.

To list the Soviet demands, flatly presented or delicately adumbrated at Potsdam, is to outline the policy which the Soviet leaders have pursued since 1945 with remarkable persistence. In Germany they wanted to rewrite the Allied agreement on zones of occupation by setting up a separate Ruhr region under three-power control, with a veto assuring them of a high degree of bargaining power. They wanted to slap a ten-billion-dollar reparations mortgage on Germany, regardless of its effects on the survival of the German people or on the American taxpayer. A completely unmanageable mortgage of this kind would have given them unlimited opportunities to promote the Sovietization of all Germany through hunger blackmail. Marshal Stalin tried hard to secure a release from the

Yalta agreements concerning eastern Europe and to secure a carte blanche for whatever he might do there. The Soviet delegation pressed for an immediate confirmation of the Polish-German boundary which the Soviet Government had laid down; it reluctantly agreed to consider the boundary as provisional in return for Allied support of Soviet annexation of part of East Prussia.

The Soviet leaders also made it clear that they wanted control of the Turkish Straits, and expressed their "interest" in the Dodecanese Islands. They pressed for the immediate removal of British troops from Greece, and at the same time asked to be relieved of the obligation, signed in 1942, to remove their troops from northern Iran after the end of the war. Stalin did gain a definite advantage in this respect, for he now secured consent to keep his forces in Iran until six months after the end of the war against Japan—not against Germany as had been assumed until then. Stalin's main argument was that "it [Iran] is too near Baku." Marshal Stalin also said he was "definitely interested" in the Italian colonies, but postponed asking for a trusteeship over Tripolitania until six weeks later, at the London Conference of Foreign Ministers. Shortly after Potsdam the Soviet Government also demanded, without success, an equal share in the occupation of Japan.

The Potsdam demands were set forth in a matter-of-fact manner, without the propaganda orchestration which was applied after the going became rough. Nevertheless, they added up to a very substantial program: a stranglehold on the Ruhr and on the entire German economy; an uncontested domination of the one hundred million people of eastern Europe; domination of the eastern Mediterranean through control of Greece, Turkey, and Tripolitania; and domination of Iran.

To the great perplexity and anger of the Soviet leaders, this second phase, outlined at Potsdam, was successful only in those areas where Soviet forces were on the ground at the close of the war. Elsewhere the execution of the program was averted through delaying actions, improvisations, evasion, and by the growth of an awareness in western Europe and America that Soviet ambitions had grown far beyond the "natural" sphere of a concern for security.

In the beginning of the second phase, American opinion was extremely sensitive to any disparagement of Soviet actions or intentions. In the wave of sympathy for Soviet sacrifices in the war, of enthusiasm for Soviet courage, and in the passionate hope that a solid basis of Allied understanding had been found, American sentiment discredited or ignored many facts which, added together, suggested that the Soviet leaders saw no obstacles in the path of their ambition to extend and entrench their power in a world which had been devastated and hollowed out by Nazi brutality and by war. By the end of this phase, which was marked by the Truman Doctrine and the Marshall plan, the pendulum had swung so far, under the hard impact of evidence of the Soviet challenge for power, that anyone who admitted the possibility of ever settling any dispute with the Soviet Government was likely to fall under suspicion of favoring "appeasement."

The Third Phase

In the third phase, the United States broke with ancient tradition to offer specific assistance and to furnish specific guarantees to countries which lay in the path of Soviet expansionism. Overcoming its scruples concerning the governments in Greece and Turkey, it came to their assistance. The alternative would have been acquiescence in the establishment of a Communist-dominated regime in Greece and the submission of Turkey to Soviet overlordship, either through Soviet control of the Turkish Straits and of the highlands of eastern Anatolia, or through the installing of a "friendly" regime, according to the Soviet definition. By this decision the United States undertook to deter the Soviet Government from any sudden move to control the eastern Mediterranean.

The United States embarked on a far broader program of strengthening the economic and social structure of western Europe, although the program, announced tentatively in June 1947, went into effect only in 1948. Instead of joining the Committee of European Economic Co-operation and demanding a large share of American aid for itself and its satellites, the Soviet Government mobilized its supporters in opposition. Its attacks were not fully consistent. It asserted, on one hand, that the program was only a bluff and was bound to fail, and in the same breath denounced it as the spearhead of military aggression directed against the Soviet Union. To offset the attractions of the Marshall plan among its satellites, it established the Cominform in September 1947 and rounded out its control of the Soviet bloc by the Communist seizure of power in Czechoslovakia in February 1948, and by a pact of mutual assistance with Finland in April. The nervous insistence of the Soviet leaders on complete subservience of subsidiary Communist regimes, and their difficulties in securing a reliable picture of the true situation through their over-indoctrinated agents, were high-lighted in the falling away, or rather the kicking away, of the Yugoslav member of the Soviet bloc in June. The Soviet correspondence with the Yugoslav Politburo has shown clearly that the only "nationalism" that can be tolerated within the Soviet orbit is Soviet nationalism.

The movement in western Europe for self-protection against Soviet pressure moved steadily forward in 1948 and 1949, from Bevin's speech in January 1948 to the Franco-British agreement for mutual assistance, to the five-power Brussels Pact, and to the signing of the twelve-power North Atlantic Treaty on April 4, 1949. In bolstering western Europe against the massive land power of the Soviet Union, the United States had to choose between two approaches. It could have encouraged the formation of a Western European Union, in the hope that over a period of years this advanced and populous region would become strong enough to be, in itself, a deterrent to a possible Soviet attack or threat of attack, without becoming too closely bound to American policy. Western Europe might, it was hoped, emerge as a "third force," standing between the Soviet and American centers of power and able to deal effectively with both.

In the short run, however, western Europe has proved too weak to make adequate provision for its own security. It requires American support if it is to constitute even a moderately powerful deterrent. In addition, western Europe is unable to cope with the economic and political rehabilitation of western Germany except with American co-operation. In American policy the consolidation of western Europe and the recovery of Germany have become increasingly closely associated. In order to provide a firm barrier against Soviet domination of western Europe it has become necessary to avert a Soviet domination of all Germany. In order to attract western Germany to the side of the Atlantic powers it is necessary to promote the emergence of an effective economic and political regime in western Germany.

Since 1947 the Soviet Union has lost the momentum of military and ideological expansion in Europe, and political initiative has passed to western Europe and the United States. In China, on the other hand, the American effort to bring together Nationalist and Communist forces, to help in the strengthening of an effective central government, capable of active efforts at reform and of protecting China's national independence, was a failure. Parallel to the effort in Germany, there has been a shift in the occupation of Japan towards more strenuous promotion of economic recovery. The Soviet Government has constantly denounced American policy in Germany and Japan as a plot to acquire additional allies for an attack on the Soviet Union. Since both occupied countries are completely disarmed, these accusations are somewhat wide of the mark. However, the question of how the security of these two countries may be assured poses a serious dilemma. Certainly, there are strong misgivings about permitting any form of rearmament, but it is doubtful if the United Nations, which they can enter only with Soviet approval, can offer sufficient assurance of their continued independence.

Retrospect and Prospect

Looking back to Yalta and Potsdam, the Soviet leaders must realize that the successes which they anticipated have, in many instances, eluded their grasp. The hardening of American policy has been due to successive shocks administered by the Politburo. Their relative lack of success they owe, in large part, to their failure to understand the nature of the American polity and the underlying motives of American action abroad. They have underestimated the repugnance with which Americans view the destruction of the national independence of small but proud peoples. They have overestimated the elements of instability operating within the American economy. The mysterious workings of a democratic public opinion which first praises them to the skies and then turns on them, while they feel they have remained themselves throughout, they explain away by reference to a malevolent "conspiracy." Attributing to others their own habits of thought, they are certain that there is an American "Politburo" which secretly manipulates the press, the economy, and the Government. The fact that the location, the membership, and the operations of this Politburo remain undiscoverable, they attribute to that well-known tradition of American ingenuity.

Beyond the building of adequate deterrents to Soviet expansion, American policy has another duty. It has a difficult path to walk in these next years, strengthening the supports of a tolerable democratic peace and at the same time avoiding provocative actions and gestures. There is no better gift to the Soviet propagandists than speculation in the press by an American officer on how many atomic bombs it would require to "eliminate" the Soviet capacity to make war. American policy makers must likewise be prepared to state the terms on which they would be willing to settle specific problems through negotiation. Such terms have been stated repeatedly with respect to Austria and Korea. When the western German state is a going concern, the United States and its allies must be prepared eventually to negotiate for a reunification of Germany on terms guaranteeing its independence, or else allow the eastern and western German states to work out terms for their own unification.

Even after the American people were pitchforked by Japanese and German aggression into a war for national survival, it was far from clear that they would accept, after the war, any continuing responsibilities beyond their ocean borders. In 1945 they assumed that the United Nations, if firmly supported, would suffice to keep the peace and that they, as a nation, need have no concern for developments abroad beyond some temporary assistance in economic recovery. If the Soviet leaders had curbed their own postwar ambitions, they would have profited by a great fund of good will in America. If, in 1945 and 1946, the Soviet leaders had been less cocksure of the validity of their "scientific" prognosis and had met American interests and sentiments a part of the way, a continuing basis for correct and fairly co-operative relations might have been laid. This did not occur. The philosophy of world-wide expansion, which the Soviet leaders had muted down during the co-operation with Hitler, was turned on full-blast against their recent allies. In their gamble, the Soviet leaders threw into the discard those human *imponderabilia* which even Bismarck considered as important in the conduct of successful policy as the possession of great power.

XXVII

Science and Religion in the Twentieth Century

Freud and Psychology
EDNA HEIDBREDER

Fifty Years of Atomic Physics
HENRY D. SMYTH

A Historian Looks Ahead; The Future of Christianity in the Light of Its Past
KENNETH SCOTT LATOURETTE

Freud and Psychology

EDNA HEIDBREDER

⇒⇒⇒⇒⇒⇒⇒⇒⇒ *Published in 1940* ⇐⇐⇐⇐⇐⇐⇐⇐⇐⇐

Probably the study of human behavior is almost as old as human behavior, and the written discussion of human behavior is doubtless as old as literature. Indeed, the man who would deny that Homer, Euripides, and Shakespeare were subtle psychologists would be foolhardy. Nevertheless, it is probably safe to say that psychology, as a subject for systematic study, as an organized body of knowledge, dates mainly from the labors of Wilhelm Wundt, whose *Principles of Physiological Psychology* (1874) gave a great impetus to the development of experimental psychology. It is ironic, however, that widespread popular interest in the new study was connected mainly with the writings of a man who had no interest in the psychology of his time: the Viennese doctor Sigmund Freud (1856-1939). One of the seminal minds in the intellectual history of modern Europe, Freud has been the subject of innumerable controversies. And whether the controversialists support Freud or denounce him, his powerful influence has continued to make itself felt—and not only in the fields of psychology and psychiatry. Twentieth-century art, literature, biographical writing, and religious thought—all have shown the impact of his ideas. In the present essay, Edna Heidbreder, of Wellesley College, discusses Freud's contribution to psychology. Author of a valuable history of modern psychological thought, she writes with a sense of moderation that is rare in evaluations of Freud's achievements.

The death of Sigmund Freud has reminded the world anew of his extraordinary role in the broadening and deepening of psychological inquiry. Yet his influence on psychology was a very small part of the total effect he produced on the intellectual life of

Reprinted by special permission from *The Psychological Review*, XLVII (1940), 185-195. The footnotes which originally appeared with this essay have been omitted.

his age. In some of the arts, in literature especially, the impress of his teachings is one of the distinctive marks of the day. In the social sciences, too, notably in anthropology and sociology, the signs of his influence are unmistakable and familiar. In psychiatry, as everyone knows, he effected a revolution. Problems of ethics and aesthetics have been reviewed in the light of his theories, and the implications of his doctrines have by no means escaped the attention of students of philosophy and religion. Even such impersonal disciplines as logic, mathematics, and the physical sciences take on, as human enterprises, a special significance when seen from his point of view. But most remarkable of all is his effect on the thought of everyday life. Much of the Freudian terminology has found its way into common speech; and a general, though vague, notion of his interpretation of human nature is part and parcel of the common thought of the age.

It would be a mistake to regard Freud's influence on psychology as constituting a problem essentially different from that of his influence on any other field. For it was not as a psychologist that Freud influenced psychology. Neither was it as a man of letters that he influenced literature, nor as an anthropologist that he influenced anthropology. In every case his action was that of a force from without. Even psychiatry is no exception to the rule, for it was not by working in the professional tradition that he exerted his influence on his own profession. His development in psychiatry was always outside the regular line of professional advancement, and when eventually he was recognized by fellow psychiatrists in Zurich, the main direction of his thought had been definitely and firmly set. He had even acquired a group of disciples in Vienna and elsewhere, and the time had passed, if indeed it had ever existed, when Freud could be absorbed by a professional group as a member on an equal footing with other members.

His capacity for maintaining a course of action without the support and encouragement of his profession was an essential factor in his achievement. Whatever else his teachings may be, they are those of a man working at his own task in his own way. Nothing in his career is more remarkable than the complete trust he placed in his own perceptions. As one reads his comments on those who did not wholly agree with him, one is struck by the fact that it apparently did not occur to him that divergences from his own opinion might be anything but errors—errors due to an inability, temperamental or otherwise, to understand and accept what he so plainly saw to be true. In marked contrast to his repeatedly demonstrated readiness to change his theories when his own observations and reflections required it, was his resentment of changes suggested by others, especially those who had once been his followers. Apparently he could accept the contributions of disciples while they remained disciples; but the give and take between colleagues on terms of equality seems to have been foreign to his nature.

Without his independence of professional support and professional conventions, Freud could not have accomplished his task. Without it, he could never have maintained the novel and difficult direction of attention which gave his contributions their distinctive character. For the uniqueness of his achievement was determined by the fact that he saw human beings neither as common sense saw them nor as they appeared to the eyes of any existing profession. He addressed himself to problems of human nature which were not quite the problems anyone else had seen; his interest was attracted by a field of observation not exactly that which anyone else had explored or even clearly noted; and he gradually evolved a conceptual system which, derived from his personal observation in his special field, came nowhere near engaging smoothly with the accepted conceptions of any professional group. In a sense, of course, Freud was working on an age-old problem, that of inner conflict. In a narrower and more professional sense he was observing the material every psychiatrist must perforce observe. But his attention was caught by occurrences and connections no one else had made focal and steadily regarded, and in reflecting on them he made explicit and welded into a connected (though not closely articulated) system, facts and relationships which others had overlooked or had only dimly sensed or had noted and reported as fragmentary observations.

Perhaps Freud's most striking intellectual characteristic is his utter absorption in the class of facts he had set himself to understand. At any rate it was this absorption, unhampered as well as unsupported by professional tradition, that gave his theory both its strangeness and

HERMANN EBBINGHAUS: German experimental psychologist (d. 1909) who used nonsense syllables. His memory experiments, published in 1885, were the first significant attempt to apply scientific methods to the study of the factors that govern learning and forgetting. His researches inspired many later investigations.

pretations. It is this obscure relevance to common knowledge that made Freud's teachings credible, though not always acceptable, to the man in the street; and it is in his role as man in the street, not on the basis of his special knowledge, that a psychologist pays attention to Freud.

But more than vague relevance to common knowledge was needed to give Freud's theories the importance they attained. An essential part of Freud's contribution is the form in which he presented his teachings, a form which made statable for open and public discussion events which occurred in hidden private worlds. In brief he invented a mythology and a terminology. By the liberal use of analogy and metaphor he constructed a world of symbols well adapted to the human propensity for thinking in terms of concrete situations: a world not of abstractions, difficult to conceive and attend to, but of picturable persons and objects and places, as easy to think and talk about as the world of a novel or drama, and somewhat similar in its appeal to human interest. By reference to this world layman and scientist alike found it possible to formulate the problems of depth psychology. It is profoundly significant that the Freudian terminology has been widely adopted, and that even among psychologists who find Freud's explanations worthless, there are many who find his terminology indispensable. Whether the terminology would have become current without the mythology is a question. The mingling of the two is now a *fait accompli*, and a source both of strength and of confusion in the Freudian system.

It is a source of strength because, as has just been suggested, it takes advantage of the mode of thought which human beings find easiest and most effective. By using a terminology which externalizes inner conflicts, by presenting them imaginatively as if they were situations like those encountered in the external world, Freud did much toward placing the emotional entanglements of human beings in a context in which they could be looked at objectively and recognized as problems for scientific investigation. The confusion arises from the fact that the device is not only helpful but dangerous, offering as it does an ever present temptation to reification. Imagined objects and situations may all too readily be thought of as actually existing. Furthermore, when used as symbols, they involve the risk of surrounding the concept with irrelevant implications. They place before the reader more than is there in order to make him see that something is there. The question then rises, Can the excess, which is merely arbitrary and may therefore be misleading, be effectually cleared away or at least rendered harmless? Can products of the imagination be transformed into scientific concepts?

Murray's *Explorations in Personality* is an attempt to come to terms with this problem by one whose main interests are in clinical rather than in academic psychology. But academic psychologists are concerned with a problem similar in general outline. Among these are men of such different interests and academic backgrounds as Tolman, Lewin, and G. W. Allport—all far more impressed than Freud by the requirements of science, but all finding the conventional systems of psychology inadequate to the problems with which they deal. Thus from within academic psychology itself there has come a demand for concepts suitable to dynamic problems. Perhaps not the least of Freud's achievements is the impetus he has given to a movement in which he seems to have had no interest whatsoever, a movement toward a revision of the theoretical framework of academic psychology for the accommodation of problems in dynamics.

But while gaining attention for some aspects of human nature, Freud needlessly thrust others into the background. Absorbed in the psychology of the primal urges, he paid little attention to the implications of the fact that the human animal is capable of intelligent action. Yet one of the conspicuous differences between human beings and other animals is the greater extent to which the human species employs the mode of adaptation called intelligence. No other species develops arts, sciences, and philosophies; no other species produces and destroys civilizations. To ignore such conspicuous differentiae of a species is as one sided and unrealistic as to ignore those characteristics which place it in the same class with other animals.

Of course Freud did not ignore the intellectual processes completely, but in comparison with the non-rational urges they seemed to him unimportant. It is significant that he never worked out a very clear position with respect to the intellectual processes. At first he rather vaguely regarded them as associated with the ego, admitting that there was much in the ego that he did not understand. Thus he conceived of the ego as more or less effectively opposing the libido, and at the same time he thought of the intellectual processes as subservient to the libido. Rationalization and autistic thinking he regarded as typical intellectual activities. It is unfortunate and somewhat strange that the intellectual operations as such did not arouse his curiosity, for the very occurrence of such practices as rationalization and day dreaming suggests that intellectual activities are not incapable of imposing their own conditions. Does not rationalization suggest that there are intellectual demands which must be satisfied, even when the main object of the intellectual activity is to serve the non-rational impulses? And is not some explanation required for the fact that imperious primal urges can be satisfied, even temporarily and partially, by such flimsy stuff as day dreams? At any rate a field of inquiry is indicated concerning lines of relationship between cognitive activities and the primal urges.

As a matter of fact, a recognition of something of the sort is implied in the direction Freud's own thought has taken. In his later theories he posited, largely as a result of a study of the ego trends, a far greater complexity of organization, a far more intricate system of interrelationships among the parts of the personality, than that pictured in the simple opposition of ego and libido. The old theory seemed inadequate to the complexities of a creature capable of going beyond the pleasure principle. In consequence Freud developed the concept of an elaborate organization consisting of the ego, super ego, and id. The new theory, while keeping the emphasis unmistakably on non-rational urges, nevertheless definitely recognized in the cognitive and intellectual processes distinctive and essential and complicating factors involved in the production of conflicts and in the formation of the personality. It also recognized strong alliances as well as bitter conflicts between the rational and non-rational components of human nature.

It is impossible, of course, to foresee the lasting outcome of Freud's system, but the general character of his contribution is easily discernible. Like Copernicus and Darwin—the comparison has become inevitable—he put the facts of common observation in a setting which profoundly altered their meaning, and which introduced into both science and common knowledge radically new perspectives. But unlike Copernicus and Darwin, Freud presented his theories in a form unsuitable to scientific verification and use. The situation abounds in difficulties and recalls the half despairing advice given by Willian James in another connection: "The only thing then is to use as much sagacity as you possess and to be as candid as you can."

Fifty Years of Atomic Physics

HENRY D. SMYTH

➤➤➤➤➤➤➤➤➤➤➤ *Published in 1946* ᐸᐸᐸᐸᐸᐸᐸᐸᐸᐸ

The achievements of science in the first half of the twentieth century were unbelievably great—so great that even the most extravagant worshipers of science in the age of Darwin would have found it hard to believe the scientific wonders that were yet to be. No triumph of twentieth-century science, however, was in a class with the release of atomic energy; so eminent a scientist as Arthur Compton has described it as probably "the supreme gift of physical science to the modern age." The first important use of atomic energy came, of course, in the form of the bomb the explosion of which, in August 1945, in the city of Hiroshima brought a rapid end to World War II and thus doubtless saved innumerable lives. Yet however much the wartime uses of atomic energy impressed contemporaries, there was no question that in the long run its peacetime implications would be far more meaningful; it bade fair to transform many features of twentieth-century man's way of life. Yet what had made the release of atomic energy possible? Mainly it was the cooperation of thousands of scientists all over the world. Indeed, if anyone ever needed to be convinced of the internationalism of science, the release of nuclear energy offered the best possible illustration. For any survey of the main developments in the history of atomic physics drives home emphatically the extent to which scientific knowledge has refused to recognize the existence of national boundaries. It is this point, among others, that Princeton's distinguished physicist Henry D. Smyth makes in his sketch of the growth of atomic physics.

Introduction

Since this is the first paper of a two-day session devoted to the atomic bomb, it seems appropriate to me to devote my talk to the development of atomic physics in the past fifty years in an attempt to

Reprinted by special permission from *Proceedings of the American Philosophical Society*, XC (1946), No. 1, 1-6.

its scope—on the one hand, putting it out of line with the intellectual mores of the day, and on the other, by keeping it close to the concrete and the actual, making it relevant to a wide range of human interests. Freud's disregard of the accepted rules of science and scholarship is notorious. Using the special tools of no profession or craft, he had recourse to a method more akin to common observation and common sense than to the specialized techniques of any of the established intellectual disciplines. Fundamentally his observations were like those involved in the social perceptions and judgments of everyday life—more sensitive and more shrewd, of course, and inevitably marked by his personal preoccupations—but dependent nevertheless on the ordinary operations of social intelligence. It is interesting that his special method uses the commonest mode of social communication. Psychoanalysis is carried on by means of talk, conversation. Indeed, much of the strength of Freud's theories and practices lies in the fact that his methods were *un*technical and *un*specialized, and therefore kept him close to the familiar actualities of common life and common sense.

Yet it would be manifestly absurd to identify Freud's theories with the insights of common sense. Rather they were the outcome of explorations into the subsoil of common sense; and if for this reason they are relevant to the whole range of human endeavor, they are for the same reason difficult to place with reference to existing bodies of knowledge and modes of procedure, not excluding those of common sense. It is extraordinarily difficult to describe Freud's method in any but negative terms. Perhaps the nearest approach to a positive description may be found in Emerson's phrase 'man thinking.' 'Thinking in unhabitual ways' is another phrase that suggests itself as appropriate, especially when it is recalled that Freud's inquiries have been directed toward the very facts concerning which conventional modes of thought have been most subject to the pressure of habit and custom. Freud's task required the difficult and delicate adjustment of focusing just off the usual fixation point; of maintaining a line of regard almost co-

---

SIR FRANCIS GALTON: English scientist (1822-1911) who stands as a pioneer in the history of the investigation of heredity, mental imagery, and individual differences. His main contribution to psychology was his use of statistical methods in the measurement of individual differences.

inciding with, yet always distinct from, the one favored by habit and common practice. Furthermore his observations were a personal enterprise, one in which he neither utilized, nor indeed felt the need for, the safeguards which the sciences find indispensable.

No psychologist need be told that this mode of observation was not one approved by the psychology of Freud's day. It is a commonplace that when psychology emerged as a science, its goal and direction, along with its method and assumptions, were determined by the physical sciences of the nineteenth century. No more impersonal psychology has ever existed than that which developed in the first psychological laboratories. There is a sense in which its special method, introspection, represents the height of objectivity and detachment, requiring as it does the observation of events defined as available only in immediate experience, with the same disregard for personal values and implications demanded of an experimenter observing any event, say a falling body, in the external world. The introspection of the early laboratories was not self-exploration and insofar as psychoanalysis was precisely self-exploration for the person analyzed, it ran directly counter to the approved methods of the psychology of the time. It would be difficult to find a task in sharper contrast with that of the 'observer' in a psychological laboratory than that required of a patient undergoing psychoanalysis.

This difference in method and outlook becomes especially significant when one considers how closely Freud's career coincides in time with the rise and development of psychology as an experimental science. Freud was born in 1856, four years before the publication of Fechner's *Elements of Psychophysics*, the book commonly regarded as the first achievement of a definitely experimental psychology. By the time he had reached university age, the early classics in psychology had been written. During his own student days at Vienna, Wundt's famous laboratory was opened at Leipzig, and in the decade of the eighties—the formative period of his professional life—such notable pioneer studies in psychology were appearing as Galton's researches on imagery and association, Ebbinghaus' monograph on memory, and the contributions of James and Lange to the theory of the emotions now known by their names. The list might be extended but it has gone far enough to exhibit in an account of Freud's work the character of 'not belonging.' Yet imagery and association, memory and emotion, are processes of vital importance to the Freudian theories and to the success of psychoanalysis as therapy.

The fact is that Freud's interests were so completely outside the psychology pursued by professional psychologists that he was altogether unaffected by their activities. To be sure, there was a time when he acknowledged the usefulness of the free association experiment which Jung introduced from the psychological laboratory. But in his *History of the Psychoanalytic Movement*, written after the break with Jung, his comment on this importation is entirely unenthusiastic and constitutes the only reference to experimental psychology in the entire account. It is interesting too that the five lectures entitled *The Origin and Development of Psychoanalysis*, given at Clark University at the invitation of G. Stanley Hall, likewise contain only one reference to a psychological study; a reference, moreover, which seems an expression of courtesy rather than of an interest in the findings of psychologists. Freud's indifference, furthermore, persisted throughout his career. It remained completely unaltered when psychology itself changed, partly by enlarging its field and including problems similar to his own. The mere suggestion that his attitude might have been otherwise is slightly absurd. It is interesting, nevertheless, as additional evidence of his extraordinary absorption, that a whole new intellectual movement arose and developed in a field presumably related to his own, without arousing his curiosity or even attracting his serious attention.

It is interesting, too, that psychology did not meet indifference with indifference, but paid far more heed to Freud than to most of its own workers. Why then did Freud, who had no interest in psychology, become one of the most potent influences in the psychology of his day?

An obvious answer, and one that is less trivial than it seems, is that psychologists would have been blind and deaf to what was going on in the world about them if they had not noticed the tremendous stir Freud was creating concerning topics presumably within their own field.

Many psychologists, of course, are almost that. In other words, many of them are almost as absorbed in their special problems as Freud was in his, and some of the problems are such that they can be profitably investigated without reference to the teachings of Freud. It is well to recognize that this is the case. If psychology is defined as the work psychologists are doing, it becomes a mere matter of empirical fact that there are portions of psychology which have been as unaffected by Freud, as Freud's teachings have been unaffected by psychology. This means, among other things, that the subject matter of psychology is not limited to problems of personal adjustment. It is well that this point be explicitly stated since it is one that most psychoanalysts and some psychologists seem to find either inconceivable or incredible. Yet in the *difference* between the tasks of psychologists and psychoanalysts lies the reason for their different attitudes toward each other. Psychoanalysts, whose activities and thoughts are centered about a special problem which is both practical and pressing, can afford to work at this problem with little concern for what most psychologists are doing. Psychologists, however, undertaking a more detached but more comprehensive survey of human nature, find it impossible not to listen to Freud. Even the most specialized workers find it hard to be unaware of the total field of which their problems are a part. They can therefore be only 'almost' as absorbed in a special problem as Freud. Psychologists know too that the field Freud explored is one in which their own efforts have been most fruitless. It is interesting to find a symposium on Freud's concepts which includes among its participants a number of psychologists whose chief contributions and characteristic interests are elsewhere. Psychologists do not find it possible to ignore Freud and his theories, as Freud and his followers have found it possible to ignore psychology. Psychology, aiming at comprehensiveness, is aware of incompleteness.

A sense of the incompleteness of psychology, however, does not explain the positive appeal of Freud's teachings. Not everything that promises to deepen and vitalize psychological knowledge gains from psychologists the respectful hearing they have given this theory based on methods and conceptions so different from their own.

There is no escaping the fact that the Freudian theories found their way into psychology without the backing of accepted, or acceptable, scientific evidence. They entered with no support but that of common knowledge about human nature, knowledge neither more nor less accessible to psychologists than to anyone else. There is a sense in which Freud's teachings were unfamiliar to few, in which despite their boldness and originality, they were often heard even at first with something like recognition. To be sure, Freud's theories were considered bizarre. No one had seen exactly what Freud had seen and no one had seen all that Freud had seen; yet many had noticed something sufficiently similar to arouse their willingness and eagerness to listen to his interpretations. It is this obscure relevance to common knowledge that made Freud's teachings credible, though not always acceptable, to the man in the street; and it is in his role as man in the street, not on the basis of his special knowledge, that a psychologist pays attention to Freud.

But more than vague relevance to common knowledge was needed to give Freud's theories the importance they attained. An essential part of Freud's contribution is the form in which he presented his teachings, a form which made statable for open and public discussion events which occurred in hidden private worlds. In brief he invented a mythology and a terminology. By the liberal use of analogy and metaphor he constructed a world of symbols well adapted to the human propensity for thinking in terms of concrete situations: a world not of abstractions, difficult to conceive and attend to, but of picturable persons and objects and places, as easy to think and talk about as the world of a novel or drama, and somewhat similar in its appeal to human interest. By reference to this world layman and scientist alike found it possible to formulate the problems of depth psychology. It is profoundly significant that the Freudian terminology has been widely adopted, and that even among psychologists who find Freud's explanations worthless, there are many who find his terminology indispensable. Whether the terminology would have become current without the mythology is a question. The mingling of the two is now a *fait accompli*, and a source both of strength and of confusion in the Freudian system.

It is a source of strength because, as has just been suggested, it takes advantage of the mode of thought which human beings find easiest and most effective. By using a terminology which externalizes inner conflicts, by presenting them imaginatively as if they were situations like those encountered in the external world, Freud did much toward placing the emotional entanglements of human beings in a context in which they could be looked at objectively and recognized as problems for scientific investigation. The confusion arises from the fact that the device is not only helpful but dangerous, offering as it does an ever present temptation to reification. Imagined objects and situations may all too readily be thought of as actually existing. Furthermore, when used as symbols, they involve the risk of surrounding the concept with irrelevant implications. They place before the reader more than is there in order to make him see that something is there. The question then rises, Can the excess, which is merely arbitrary and may therefore be misleading, be effectually cleared away or at least rendered harmless? Can products of the imagination be transformed into scientific concepts?

Murray's *Explorations in Personality* is an attempt to come to terms with this problem by one whose main interests are in clinical rather than in academic psychology. But academic psychologists are concerned with a problem similar in general outline. Among these are men of such different interests and academic backgrounds as Tolman, Lewin, and G. W. Allport—all far more impressed than Freud by the requirements of science, but all finding the conventional systems of psychology inadequate to the problems with which they deal. Thus from within academic psychology itself there has come a demand for concepts suitable to dynamic problems. Perhaps not the least of Freud's achievements is the impetus he has given to a movement in which he seems to have had no interest whatsoever, a movement toward a revision of the theoretical framework of academic psychology for the accommodation of problems in dynamics.

But while gaining attention for some aspects of human nature, Freud needlessly thrust others into the background. Absorbed in the psychology of the primal urges, he paid little attention to the implications of the fact that the human animal is capable of intelligent action. Yet one of the conspicuous differences between human beings and other animals is the greater extent to which the human species employs the mode of adaptation called intelligence. No other species develops arts, sciences, and philosophies; no other species produces and destroys civilizations. To ignore such conspicuous differentiae of a species is as one sided and unrealistic as to ignore those characteristics which place it in the same class with other animals.

Of course Freud did not ignore the intellectual processes completely, but in comparison with the non-rational urges they seemed to him unimportant. It is significant that he never worked out a very clear position with respect to the intellectual processes. At first he rather vaguely regarded them as associated with the ego, admitting that there was much in the ego that he did not understand. Thus he conceived of the ego as more or less effectively opposing the libido, and at the same time he thought of the intellectual processes as subservient to the libido. Rationalization and autistic thinking he regarded as typical intellectual activities. It is unfortunate and somewhat strange that the intellectual operations as such did not arouse his curiosity, for the very occurrence of such practices as rationalization and day dreaming suggests that intellectual activities are not incapable of imposing their own conditions. Does not rationalization suggest that there are intellectual demands which must be satisfied, even when the main object of the intellectual activity is to serve the non-rational impulses? And is not some explanation required for the fact that imperious primal urges can be satisfied, even temporarily and partially, by such flimsy stuff as day dreams? At any rate a field of inquiry is indicated concerning lines of relationship between cognitive activities and the primal urges.

As a matter of fact, a recognition of something of the sort is implied in the direction Freud's own thought has taken. In his later theories he posited, largely as a result of a study of the ego trends, a far greater complexity of organization, a far more intricate system of interrelationships among the parts of the personality, than that pictured in the simple opposition of ego and libido. The old theory seemed inadequate to the complexities of a creature capable of going beyond the pleasure principle. In consequence Freud developed the concept of an elaborate organization consisting of the ego, super ego, and id. The new theory, while keeping the emphasis unmistakably on non-rational urges, nevertheless definitely recognized in the cognitive and intellectual processes distinctive and essential and complicating factors involved in the production of conflicts and in the formation of the personality. It also recognized strong alliances as well as bitter conflicts between the rational and non-rational components of human nature.

It is impossible, of course, to foresee the lasting outcome of Freud's system, but the general character of his contribution is easily discernible. Like Copernicus and Darwin—the comparison has become inevitable—he put the facts of common observation in a setting which profoundly altered their meaning, and which introduced into both science and common knowledge radically new perspectives. But unlike Copernicus and Darwin, Freud presented his theories in a form unsuitable to scientific verification and use. The situation abounds in difficulties and recalls the half despairing advice given by Willian James in another connection: "The only thing then is to use as much sagacity as you possess and to be as candid as you can."

Fifty Years of Atomic Physics

HENRY D. SMYTH

⋙⋙⋙⋙⋙⋙⋙⋙⋙⋙ *Published in 1946* ⋘⋘⋘⋘⋘⋘⋘⋘⋘⋘

The achievements of science in the first half of the twentieth century were unbelievably great—so great that even the most extravagant worshipers of science in the age of Darwin would have found it hard to believe the scientific wonders that were yet to be. No triumph of twentieth-century science, however, was in a class with the release of atomic energy; so eminent a scientist as Arthur Compton has described it as probably "the supreme gift of physical science to the modern age." The first important use of atomic energy came, of course, in the form of the bomb the explosion of which, in August 1945, in the city of Hiroshima brought a rapid end to World War II and thus doubtless saved innumerable lives. Yet however much the wartime uses of atomic energy impressed contemporaries, there was no question that in the long run its peacetime implications would be far more meaningful; it bade fair to transform many features of twentieth-century man's way of life. Yet what had made the release of atomic energy possible? Mainly it was the cooperation of thousands of scientists all over the world. Indeed, if anyone ever needed to be convinced of the internationalism of science, the release of nuclear energy offered the best possible illustration. For any survey of the main developments in the history of atomic physics drives home emphatically the extent to which scientific knowledge has refused to recognize the existence of national boundaries. It is this point, among others, that Princeton's distinguished physicist Henry D. Smyth makes in his sketch of the growth of atomic physics.

Introduction

Since this is the first paper of a two-day session devoted to the atomic bomb, it seems appropriate to me to devote my talk to the development of atomic physics in the past fifty years in an attempt to

Reprinted by special permission from *Proceedings of the American Philosophical Society*, XC (1946), No. 1, 1-6.

recall to your minds the background in which the atomic bomb development rests. It is, in fact, just fifty years since the discovery of x-rays, a discovery which marked the beginning of the era of atomic physics. That period of fifty years is split in two by the First World War and terminates with the second. Let us begin by going back to the state of atomic theory in 1895.

ATOMIC THEORY IN 1895

The idea that all matter was made up of indivisible particles goes back to the time of the Greek philosophers. After many fluctuations of philosophical popularity it finally was put on a solid foundation of experimental chemistry in the nineteenth century. By 1895 the idea that matter consisted of atoms of some ninety different elements was reasonably well established. It had also been suggested that electrical charge was atomic. Attempts had been made from the kinetic theory of gases to estimate the number of molecules in a given quantity of gas and thereby the size of molecules. In fact, the first estimate was made by an Austrian, Loschmidt, in 1865. Using later determinations of this number and the experimental results on electrolysis, an estimate had been made of the electrical charge carried by a single ion in solution. But all these quantitative data were uncertain and there were still many who did not accept the atomic hypothesis with enthusiasm.

THE STATE OF PHYSICS IN 1895

Furthermore, the question of whether or not atoms existed and the question of their structure, if anyone was so bold as to raise it, were considered the province of chemistry. The future of physics was estimated as follows:

> While it is never safe to affirm that the future of physical science has no marvels in store, even more astonishing than those of the past, it seems probable that most of the grand underlying principles have been firmly established and that further advances are to be sought chiefly in the rigorous application of these principles to all the phenomena which come under our notice.

This statement has been attributed to Professor Michelson; at least it appeared annually in the catalogue of the University of Chicago from about 1893 to 1906. Assuming what I might call a normal lag between a university catalogue and the views of a university faculty, this probably represents Michelson's views from say 1890 to 1900.

Discoveries Between 1895 and 1900

I have already mentioned the discovery of x-rays. It was made by Roentgen in Germany in 1895. His work was published and the news spread through the scientific world. As a consequence of this news, Becquerel in France discovered that uranium was radioactive. As is well known, work on radioactivity was carried on by the Curies and later by many others in many countries.

The third great discovery of this period was not so clear-cut. It was the discovery of the electron. The phenomena of cathode rays had been known for some thirty or forty years. In fact, there was a controversy between two schools of thought: the particle school and the wave school. Stoney had suggested the atomism of electrical charge as had Maxwell before him and suggested the name electron for the atom of charge. Assuming that cathode rays were charged particles, Schuster had measured the ratio of charge to mass of these particles by their magnetic deflection. (I might here mention that the principle involved in Schuster's experiment is the same as used in mass spectrographs, in cyclotrons, and in the mighty electro-magnetic mass separators at Oak Ridge.) By 1899 J. J. Thomson had measured more accurately both the ratio of charge to mass and the velocity of cathode rays. The velocity had also been measured in Germany by Wiechert using a high-frequency method. The velocities proved to be very great—of the order of one-tenth of the velocity of light. In other experiments the electrical charge carried by each particle had been determined and found to be approximately the same as that carried by a single ion in electrolysis. Perhaps most important of all, it had been shown that electrons could be obtained from all kinds of materials and that, whatever their source, they were always identical in charge and mass. Thus, electrons appeared as the first universal constituent of matter.

Developments Between 1900 and the First World War

ATOMIC STRUCTURE

The idea that all matter was made of a few fundamental constituents was an old one. In particular, Prout in 1815 had suggested that the atoms of all elements were built up in some way from the lightest one, hydrogen. Prout's hypothesis was based on the belief that all chemical atomic weights were integral multiples of that of hydrogen, and it was given up when more exact atomic weight determinations gave values that were clearly not integral. The discovery that electrons were constituents of all elements gave renewed impetus to the study of atomic structure.

Evidently x-rays, cathode rays, and radioactivity all originated in some sort of atomic disruption. Yet their first contribution to the knowledge of atomic structure came from their use as probes to feel out the structure of other atoms rather than from a study of their own origin. Thus the study of the scattering of x-rays by different substances enabled Thomson to estimate how many electrons were in the atoms of different elements, while Rutherford's study of the scattering of the high-speed alpha particles revealed the distribution of mass and charge within the atoms.

Further evidence that all atoms might be made of the same particles in different arrangements came from the detailed study of the radioactive transformations. Such study showed that one radioactive element changes spontaneously into a different chemical element either by giving off an alpha particle or a beta particle and that all the radioactive elements go through series of successive transformations, eventually forming lead. Furthermore, it was proved that alpha particles are helium atoms that have lost two electrons.

As a result of many researches along these lines in Germany, France, Holland, England and a few in this country, the general picture of atomic structure which we now have was proposed by Rutherford in 1911. It is interesting to note that a similar idea had been suggested by Nagaoka of Japan in 1904. Rutherford's idea was that most of the mass of the atom was concentrated in a small nucleus which was positively charged and around which was a system of negatively charged electrons. By the time of the First World War, this picture had been confirmed and amplified by Mosley's discovery of x-ray spectra and by Bohr's theory of the arrangement of the electrons. The idea of isotopes, first introduced by Soddy in the radioactive field, had begun to be applied to nonradioactive elements, but its importance really belongs to the postwar epoch. Summarized briefly, the first twenty years of the atomic era established the existence of atoms, the existence of electrons, the general structure of atoms and its variation from element to element, but did not say much about the structure of the nuclei of atoms or about the possibilities of transmuting one kind of atom into another.

QUANTUM THEORY AND THEORY OF RELATIVITY

It was not only the experimental physicists who were busy between 1895 and 1915. In 1901 Planck in Germany proposed the quantum theory in its first form. Essentially this theory suggests that radiant energy is atomistic in character, or at least that the processes of absorption and emission of radiation occur in discontinuous steps or quanta. This theory was later developed by Einstein and others, and in particular was the keystone of Bohr's theory of atomic structure which I have already mentioned; for atomic bomb purposes, an even more significant theoretical development was the suggestion by Einstein in 1905 that matter and energy were related by the equation, $E = mc^2$. This equivalence of matter and energy arose from the theory of relativity as developed by Einstein at that time. It is interesting to note that in his paper Einstein suggests that experimental proof of his equation might be found in the phenomena of radioactivity. The direct experimental proof, however, was not forthcoming for twenty-five years.

THERMIONICS

Although the work on the emission of electrons by hot bodies that was done in this period is not very directly involved in atomic bomb development, I mention it because it is fundamental to the whole electronics industry which has been of great importance indirectly to the atomic bomb project.

PRINCIPAL CENTERS OF ACTIVITY IN THIS ERA

The first scientific journal in this country devoted exclusively to physics was founded in 1893. The American Physical Society was not founded until 1899. I am afraid this corresponds to the relatively small proportion of the work I have been reviewing which was done in this country. The great centers of research in physics were Cambridge and Manchester in England, Leyden in Holland, and various German universities. With a few notable exceptions such as Millikan and Michelson, the great names are European names: Rutherford, Bohr, Geiger, Richardson (an Englishman who worked in this country), Wien, Zeeman, Lorentz, Planck, Einstein, the Curies, etc.

The Period Following World War I

In the years immediately following the First World War the greatest activity in physics had to do with spectroscopy; that is to say, with the wave length of light emitted by various atoms under various circumstances. Such studies, coupled with simultaneous theoretical calculations, clarified our knowledge of the outer electronic structure of the various kinds of atom. It was possible to correlate these results with chemical information and to interpret chemical behavior in terms of electronic arrangement. These researches have little bearing on the atomic bomb project except through their influence on the development of the laws of quantum mechanics which govern not only the outer structure of an atom but the nucleus as well.

THE STUDY OF ISOTOPES

In the early 1920's Aston measured the exact masses of the atoms of many of the elements in the periodic table. As a result of these studies it was established that a given chemical element might have several isotopes; that is, atoms of different masses but the same chemical properties. Furthermore, it was observed that the masses of these isotopes were very nearly integral multiples of the mass of the hydrogen atom, the nucleus of which is called a proton. This suggested that all atoms were made up of two kinds of particles: electrons and protons; that the nuclei of atoms contained an integral number of protons which determined their mass and a smaller number of electrons of negligible mass but which neutralized the charges of some of the protons. The remaining positive charge on the nucleus determined the number of electrons in the outer system of the atom and therefore its chemical properties. We shall see presently that this picture is now modified.

BINDING ENERGIES

Aston did observe that the masses of the atoms were not quite exactly integral multiples of the mass of the proton. To explain this, Einstein's principle of the equivalence of mass and energy was invoked. According to this view, when particles are bound together in a nucleus their total mass is less than when they are free. This change in mass represents the energy released when the nucleus is synthesized, and, vice versa, represents the amount of energy that has to be used to break a nucleus into its component parts. Moreover, Aston found that there was a considerable variation in the binding energy per particle in different nuclei and that, in general, the nuclei of atoms in the middle part of the periodic table were more tightly bound than either the very light or very heavy nuclei. This led to the conclusion that, if a way could be found to break up heavy nuclei into medium-weight ones or to synthesize very light nuclei into medium-weight ones, energy would be released. Calculations showed that the amount of energy involved was very much larger than the amount involved in chemical reactions which depend only on rearrangement of the outer structure of the atoms. This was the first suggestion that there might be vast sources of untapped energy in atomic nuclei.

THE FIRST ARTIFICIAL TRANSMUTATION OF ELEMENTS

In 1919 Rutherford announced that he had succeeded in changing a few atoms of nitrogen into atoms of oxygen by bombarding them with alpha particles, and that in the course of this change a hydrogen nucleus or proton was ejected. Before Rutherford's experiments no attempt to produce nuclear changes artificially or to alter the rate of the natural nuclear changes in radioactive materials had succeeded.

Rutherford's experiments were on a minute scale and depended on alpha particles from rare radioactive substances. Consequently, progress was slow in this field. A good many similar experiments were performed, but there was no indication that nuclear energy could be released on a practical scale. However, between 1920 and 1932 technical developments in high-voltage equipment such as the development of the Van de Graaff generator and the cyclotron made it possible to produce artificial particles of almost as great energy as the alpha particles from radioactive substances.

SUMMARY OF THE STATE OF PHYSICS IN 1931

By the end of the first ten or twelve years after World War I the field of spectroscopy was beginning to be clearly understood. Quantum mechanics had been developed to such a point that progress was relatively slow and the field of nuclear physics was still limited by dependence on natural radioactive materials. No one would have made such a statement as that quoted at the beginning of this paper, for techniques were improving and it seemed likely that new discoveries would be made; but certainly new discoveries in theoretical and experimental physics were needed to revitalize research. Such discoveries came in a rush in 1932.

THE YEAR 1932

In 1932 Chadwick of England discovered the neutron. Like most scientific discoveries, this was in the nature of an extension, explanation, and clarification of previous experiments made earlier the same year by Irene Curie and F. Joliot in Paris and in 1930 by Bothe and Becker in Germany. The neutron is a particle of approximately the same mass as a proton but carrying no charge. As in the case of electrons, alpha particles, and x-rays, the discovery of the neutron promoted our knowledge of atomic structure in two ways. It could be used as a projectile to explore the structure of atoms, even to enter the atomic nuclei and disrupt them; also its existence could be used to simplify the picture we had of atomic structure—more specifically of nuclear structure. We now believe that all atomic nuclei are made of protons and neutrons, that the number of protons determines the atomic number and therefore the chemical nature of the atom, and that the nature of the nucleus depends on both the number of protons and the number of neutrons; and, in fact, in some cases the same numbers of protons and neutrons may be differently arranged so that nuclei having the same atomic number and the same mass number may have different nuclear properties. Up to the time of the discovery of neutrons the only heavy (as compared to electrons) projectiles which could be fired at atomic nuclei were the proton and the alpha particle. Both of these are positively charged and are therefore strongly repelled by the nuclei of the elements of high atomic number. The great advantage of the neutron as a projectile is its lack of charge.

Other major events in physics in 1932 were the discovery of the positron by Anderson and the discovery of heavy hydrogen by Urey, Brickwedde, and Murphy. Both these discoveries were made in this country. Finally, it was in the year 1932 that Cockcroft and Walton, in Rutherford's laboratory in England, first succeeded in producing nuclear changes by artificially-produced high-speed particles, and in proving by direct experiment that Einstein's equation, $E = mc^2$, was valid in nuclear changes.

The discovery of artificial radioactivity by Curie and Joliot in France was not made until 1934, but it really belongs in this general group of developments.

THE RISE OF PHYSICS IN THE UNITED STATES

It may be well at this point to digress from the main story in order to examine the change in the conditions of physics in this country. It was by no means an accident that heavy hydrogen and the positron were discovered by Americans. After the First World War interest in both theoretical and experimental research in physics increased greatly in this country. In particular, the establishment of national research fellowships by the Rockefeller Foundation, working through the National Research Council, gave an opportunity for many of the better young men to spend one to three years after receiving their Ph.D. in research at the leading universities in this country or abroad. The habit of research so developed persisted, and the influence of these men, both directly and indirectly, has been very great. Experimental physics, which had always been relatively strong, flourished particularly, with the resulting development of the Van de Graaff generator, the cyclotron, the mass spectrograph, and other devices. Theoretical physics, which had been almost nonexistent in this country before the war, also began to develop healthily. Yet it must be reported that most of the great discoveries in fundamental physics in the period between the two wars were made in Europe.

PRACTICABILITY OF ATOMIC POWER IN 1939

The discovery of the neutron and the multiplication of cyclotrons and the high-voltage devices rapidly led to many experiments on nuclear disintegration. Einstein's notion of the equivalence of matter and energy was repeatedly verified in this country and abroad. Yet in all these experiments the amounts of material involved were minute and the amounts of nuclear energy released were small compared to the energy expended in the experiment as a whole. It was evident that some sort of chain reaction among nuclei was needed to release appreciable quantities of energy. Such a chain reaction was indeed postulated by Bethe as the probable source of energy in the sun. His hypothesis suggested a series of six successive nuclear reactions, the net effect of which was the transformation of hydrogen into helium and the release of vast amounts of energy. Speculation was rife as to the possibilities of achieving a similar series of reactions in the laboratory, but no progress was made until the discovery of uranium fission.

The Discovery of Uranium Fission

Beginning in 1934 Fermi in Rome studied the effect of neutron bombardment on the heaviest elements, in particular, uranium. The results were puzzling and were not properly interpreted until 1939 when Hahn and Strassmann in Germany proved that an isotope of barium was produced by neutron bombardment of uranium. This discovery was soon interpreted by Frisch and Meitner in Copenhagen, and their interpretation was verified there and in this country. It was shown that the absorption of neutrons by uranium resulted in the splitting or fission of the uranium nucleus into two approximately equal parts and that this act of fission released from one to three neutrons. Since the fission was itself caused by neutrons, the possibility of a chain reaction was at once apparent. Also, since the fission released enormous amounts of energy, millions of times greater than the energy released by the most violent explosives, the possibility of useful production of energy from nuclei became a probability. Interest in this discovery was of course world-wide, and its investigation was pursued by scientists in all countries with the result that a considerable body of information had already been published in the literature by the middle of 1940. Since that time most of the work has been done in secret, but it may be of interest to quote from my report[1] the summary of what was generally known about fission in 1940.

Definite and Generally-Known Information on Fission

All the following information was generally known in June 1940, both here and abroad:

(1) That three elements—uranium, thorium, and protoactinium—when bombarded by neutrons sometimes split into approximately equal fragments, and that these fragments were isotopes of elements in the middle of the periodic table, ranging from selenium $(Z=34)$ to lanthanum $(Z=57)$.

(2) That most of these fission fragments were unstable, decaying radioactively by successive emission of beta particles through a series of elements to various stable forms.

(3) That these fission fragments had very great kinetic energy.

(4) That fission of thorium and protoactinium was caused only by fast neutrons (velocities of the order of thousands of miles per second).

[1] *Atomic Energy for Military Purposes*, Princeton Univ. Press, 1945.

(5) That fission in uranium could be produced by fast or slow (so-called thermal velocity) neutrons; specifically, that thermal neutrons caused fission in one isotope, U-235, but not in the other U-238, and that fast neutrons had a lower probability of causing fission in U-235 than thermal neutrons.

(6) That at certain neutron speeds there was a large capture cross section in U-238 producing U-239 but not fission.

(7) That the energy released per fission of a uranium nucleus was approximately 200 million electron volts.

(8) That high-speed neutrons were emitted in the process of fission.

(9) That the average number of neutrons released per fission was somewhere between one and three.

(10) That high-speed neutrons could lose energy by inelastic collision with uranium nuclei without any nuclear reaction taking place.

(11) That most of this information was consistent with the semiempirical theory of nuclear structure worked out by Bohr and Wheeler and others; this suggested that predictions based on this theory had a fair chance of success.

Summary

1940 marked the end of forty-five years' work on atomic physics. Starting from a general notion that atoms probably existed, chemists and physicists had proved their existence and shown that they were built of protons, neutrons, and electrons, had developed the laws which govern the arrangement of the electrons, in the outer structure, had developed the general picture of the nuclear atom, had learned something of nuclear structure, and finally had learned how to change one kind of nucleus into another—in other words, to transmute one element into another. They had released nuclear energy in the laboratory and had made the discoveries which would probably lead to the release of nuclear energy on a large scale, thus tapping a source of energy unknown on the earth except in the rare radioactive elements. In the last twenty years of this period of advance science in this country had begun to reach maturity, and a large number of chemists and physicists competent in the field of atomic structure had been trained. But these men were still largely dependent on Europe for fundamental advances and, in many cases, for training.

Conclusion

In this paper I have not tried to review the actual development of the atomic bomb itself. This has been covered in many discussions of both a technical and popular nature in the past few months. Nor shall I try to look into the future, either scientifically or politically. I hope that the later papers on this program will consider the great questions which have been raised by the development of the atomic bomb; I do believe that the enormous strides made by the international cooperation of scientists up to 1940 and by the national cooperation of scientists, engineers, industrialists, and military men in the past five years may teach us something. I believe they show what men can do to solve very difficult problems by working together and they give us hope that men working together may solve the even more difficult political problems that face us.

A Historian Looks Ahead; The Future of Christianity in the Light of Its Past

KENNETH SCOTT LATOURETTE

➤➤➤-➤➤➤-➤➤➤-➤➤➤-➤➤➤-➤➤➤-➤➤➤-➤➤➤ *Published in 1946* ᚹᚹᚹ-ᚹᚹᚹ-ᚹᚹᚹ-ᚹᚹᚹ-ᚹᚹᚹ-ᚹᚹᚹ-ᚹᚹᚹ

The first half of the twentieth century was a time of troubles for the Christian churches of Europe. First, the growth of science was accompanied by a growth of both agnosticism and atheism. For, although scientific discoveries confirmed some people in their belief in God, those discoveries encouraged in other people doubt or disbelief. Secondly, the growth of Marxism served to undermine the Christian churches of Europe. For hand in hand with Marxism went the belief that orthodox religion was a form of spiritual oppression—a weapon devised by the exploiting classes in order to keep the exploited classes in their place. In the years after the Bolshevik Revolution Russia became the scene of a more or less constant campaign designed to uproot traditional religion; and the notorious Society of the Godless was vigorous in carrying out its program of antireligious propaganda. Christianity suffered no less serious reverses in Nazi Germany. True, Hitler frequently made appeals for divine inspiration and guidance. But Nazism did not accept Christianity with its stress on humility and humanitarianism and with its concept of a just and loving God. And although Nazism sought to use the churches as a political instrument, it sought, too, to replace Christianity by the Hitler brand of paganism. Yet in spite of the reverses that the Christian churches suffered in many parts of Europe in the first half of the twentieth century, Christianity continued to make up for its European losses in other parts of the world. The fact, however, that western Europe was on the decline and that the United States and Russia were assuming increasing importance had serious implications for the future. In the present article, Kenneth Scott Latourette, of whose contributions to church history mention has already been made (see page 933), discusses some of the major developments in the recent history of Christianity and on the basis of these developments ventures a number of predictions concerning the future of Christianity.

What can the past tell us of the future of Christianity? Prophecy is notoriously fallible, especially for far distant years. Historians have seen so many predictions disproved by the event that they are wary of venturing upon the dangerous role of forecasters. Yet trends have a way of continuing. We may not be able to depict with accuracy the details of things to come. We may, however, by observing the directions which movements have been taking in the recent past and by noting the forces which are operating to modify them, be able to foretell the main courses which they are to follow for the decades immediately before us. Certainly those who essay to shape policies must attempt such analyses. By their knowledge of the past historians should be of assistance in providing both facts about what has transpired and conjectures to aid in plotting the paths to be pursued.

As the record of the last century and a half, and especially of the last thirty years, is surveyed a number of trends are to be seen. Some of these have persisted and have been strengthened across the passing decades. They have continued through the comparatively peaceful nineteenth century and the stormy decades since 1914. Having known both fair and foul weather and having increased rather than diminished during the latter, presumably they are to be with us for an indefinitely long period. Others might have been forecast during the nineteenth century, but have first become apparent in more recent years. Because of their nature and the circumstances in connection with which they have arisen they seem to be only at their beginning and are probably to be more prominent as the years pass. These trends are not necessarily in any logical order. They are proceeding concurrently. Some seem to be reciprocally contradictory. Any order in which they are arranged is, therefore, more for the convenience of the observer than because it is inherent in the structure of the world.

One continuing trend is the increasing influence which Christianity exerts in the life of mankind. If we are to make an appraisal of the effect of any religion or, indeed, of any set of ideas in the total stream of human history which will be worthy of respect, we must endeavor to achieve it against a global background. Striking gains or losses in a particular area may have great significance, but they may be more than offset by developments in other regions. This is notably true of Christianity. Its announced scope is the human race. To an amazing

Reprinted by special permission from *Church History*, XV (1946), 3-16.

degree it has attained world-wide extension. In this it has been more successful than has any other religious faith or, indeed, than has any other idealistic movement. If we are correctly to measure its advance or recession, we must not center our attention upon any one nation or continent or even upon any one major segment of mankind, such as the Occident or the Orient. We must, rather, traverse the entire earth and seek to arrive at our judgment with a comprehensive perspective. Could we penetrate the veil of death, we would have to do more. We would be constrained to take into account what the fruits of the Christian faith have been in lives beyond the short span of our present stage of existence. This, however, is quite beyond the facts with which the historian deals.

As one attempts to make an appraisal of the place of Christianity in the stream of history, one becomes aware that the faith has grown in its effect upon the human race and that that advance has been especially marked in the nineteenth and twentieth centuries.

In the first five centuries, Christianity was confined mainly to the Roman Empire. Winning the nominal allegiance of that realm was a major achievement, but in the other great civilized areas of the globe, such as India and China, the faith was either unknown or was represented only by very small minorities. Nearly all of primitive mankind, which then covered most of the land surface of the globe, was completely untouched. Even in the Roman Empire many phases of life were affected very little, if at all.

The severe blows dealt Christianity by the collapse of the Roman Empire and the invasions were relatively more costly in territory than any losses which the faith has since suffered. Especially were the Islam-bearing Arab conquests disastrous. Yet even in these dark centuries Christianity was being carried across Asia to China, was regaining lost ground in Britain, and was making fresh advances in several parts of Western and Central Europe and in the upper reaches of the valley of the Nile.

In the eleventh, twelfth, thirteenth, and fourteenth centuries Chris-

---

KARL BARTH: Contemporary Swiss Protestant theologian. He has criticized attempts to hasten the establishment of God's Kingdom on earth, and he has insisted that the course of history would be changed only by the sudden eruption of supernatural forces. Not surprisingly, his "theology of crisis" has often served as a conservative political force.

tians were to be found from China in the East to Greenland and possibly, through the Northmen, to North America on the West. To be sure, over most of this vast territory Christians were scattered minorities. Only in a few sections of Western Asia and in parts of Europe did they constitute a majority of the population. Yet in Europe, and particularly in Western Europe, Christianity was having a more profound effect upon more aspects of culture than it had had in the Roman Empire.

In the fourteenth and fifteenth centuries sharp losses were experienced. Christian communities died out in Greenland, and, if they had ever existed there, in North America. They disappeared from China and Central Asia. Carried by the Ottoman Turks, the Crescent advanced against the Cross in Asia Minor and the Balkans. In Western Christendom the morale of the Church declined. The great papal schism rent the church into factions and the worldly Renaissance popes seemed to deny its true mission.

In the sixteenth, seventeenth, and eighteenth centuries, in contrast, Christianity had a phenomenal spread. Through the expansion of European peoples and active missions it was firmly planted in the Americas, won footholds, albeit slight ones, along the shores of Africa, south of the Equator, added to its minority constituencies in India, became potent in Ceylon, was introduced to Japan, won the majority of the Filipinos, gained footholds in the East Indies, was carried across Siberia, and was reintroduced to China in such fashion that it has never since disappeared from that Empire. Christianity continued to be influential in Europe and made itself strikingly felt in the Americas, partly in the colonies of Europeans and partly in ameliorating the impact of the white man upon the Indians.

In the nineteenth century, Christianity continued its astonishing advance. In the Western hemisphere it became much more prominent, especially by accompanying the westward march of the frontier in the United States. Here it helped shape the life of the new nation and was especially important in education, morals, and social reform, including

---

ECUMENICAL MOVEMENT: The movement in the direction of a world-wide and united Christendom. Its chief outward and visible sign is the World Council of Churches. Backed by all of Christendom, with the exception of the Roman Catholic communion, it is probably the most significant development in recent church history.

the emancipation of the Negro. Christianity penetrated most of Africa and was the major factor in the termination of the slave trade. It gained headway among the highly civilized peoples of Southern and Eastern Asia.

In the twentieth century, in spite of two world wars and sweeping revolutions, Christianity has registered additional advances. The majority of Christians are still among Occidental peoples in Europe, the Americas and Australasia, but the percentage of Christians among non-European peoples has more than doubled. The increase has been notable in Negro Africa, but it has also been striking in India, China, several lesser lands in Asia, and the East Indies. Christianity is better rooted among more non-European peoples than it has ever been. Its effects upon non-Occidental cultures have increased. This has been seen in China, but it is also marked in India, Africa, and the islands of the sea.

The advance across the centuries has not been steady. It has, rather, been by great pulsations. Yet it has been advance. Presumably, even though it may be interrupted by occasional recessions, advance will continue. This seems especially probable in view of its accelerated pace in the past century and a half. The Christian tide gains momentum as it moves forward.

By a contradiction and paradox, the advance of Christianity faces growing opposition. Never has the faith found the world friendly. Always its gains have been made against active hostility. In the twentieth century that hostility has mounted. This has been peculiarly true in much of what we had learned to call Christendom. The closing decades of the eighteenth century and the nineteenth and twentieth centuries saw the most extensive geographic spread which Christianity had yet displayed. They also witnessed a more open repudiation of the faith in communities traditionally committed to it than had been known at any time since the great Moslem advances. This was partly through the religious scepticism engendered by the prevalence of the scientific method. It was also in large degree because the Church was deemed to be opposed to movements represented by political liberalism, as in France, and to the totalitarian control of society by a Nazi or a Communist party.

Other threats to Christianity in its hereditary strongholds have come not so much through open hostility as through indifference, absorption in activities which crowd out religion, vast shifts of population which take millions away from their accustomed church connections, and war.

To many, religion, including Christianity, has seemed to be irrelevant to their main interests. The millions who have moved into the new industrial and commercial cities have, by their migration, been separated from the church life in which they were reared. A large proportion of them have not formed new church affiliations and their children have come to maturity without religious instruction. The wars of the twentieth century have militated against Christianity. This is partly because of the fashion in which war absorbs those engaged in it to the neglect of religious instruction and worship. Then, too, war has uprooted millions from their familiar associations. Many of those in the armed services, in spite of chaplains, loosed from accustomed restraints and taught to kill, depart from Christian ideals of property, sex, and the sanctity of life.

Because of this opposition and defection, Christians are more a self-conscious minority set in an indifferent or hostile world than at any time since the first three centuries. That minority is much more widespread than ever before. It is active. In non-Occidental lands and in some Occidental lands it is growing. But it is a minority.

Yet that minority has not given over the vision of witnessing to the Gospel throughout the world. Large elements in it seek to bring the entire race into discipleship and to permeate all mankind with Christian ideals. Probably a larger proportion of Christians than at any previous age of the Church are committed to fulfilling the Great Commission in all the sweeping and breath-taking program recorded in the closing verses of Matthew's Gospel. By no means all Christians are so committed. Indeed, only a minority of the Christian minority thus envision the scope and command of their faith. Yet that minority appears to be growing.

This effort to win and transform the entire world, indifferent or hostile though that world is, has in it promise for the continued growth of the Christian community. Were Christians ever to become content with remaining a minority, they would become encysted, in-growing communities. The faith would be carried on from generation to generation by heredity and in time would become sterile. One only needs to look at the old churches in the Moslem world or some of the smaller groups, such as the Mennonites in Europe, to foresee what the fate of Christianity would be. That Christians are not so content, but insistent upon striving to win all men to their faith and teaching them all that Christ commanded, augurs well for the future extension of the influence of Christianity in the life of mankind.

A series of trends arises from the decline of Western Europe and the passing of power from Western Europe to what has been the periphery of that region, the United States and Russia. Beginning with the closing decade of the fifteenth century, European and especially Western European peoples progressively became dominant throughout the globe. In the fore part of the present century that hegemony reached its peak. European peoples had flooded into the Americas and Australasia and had given rise to new nations. They controlled almost all of Africa, the islands of the four seas, and much of Asia. Western Europe was the chief center of wealth and culture. Presumably that position of leadership would have been lost, although slowly, even without the disasters brought by war. The Americas were gaining in population. The natural monopoly of the mechanical appliances which were prominent in enabling Europe to achieve its dominance was being lost through the acquisition of machines by other peoples. The two world wars of the present century have borne particularly heavily on Western Europe and by their destruction have hastened the relative decline of that area. The strongest nations are no longer there. Even Great Britain has receded from the place which she held in the pre-1914 and pre-1939 world. Russia, profiting by much of what came to her from Western Europe in ideology and technical skill, and the United States, predominantly of peoples of Western European descent, are the great powers of the generation immediately ahead. We have only begun to see what this shift in wealth, culture, and control is to mean. Most of us are as yet only dimly aware of the implications for the Christian Church.

One of the most startling consequences for Christianity is probably to be the relative decline of the Roman Catholic Church and the continued passing to Protestantism of leadership in the Christian forces. The older Eastern churches, with the exception of the Russian Orthodox Church, have been waning for about eight centuries. The Revolution of 1917 dealt the Russian Orthodox Church body blows from which it is probably not soon, if ever, to make more than a partial recovery. Between the eleventh and the nineteenth century, the leadership of the Christian world was mainly in Roman Catholic hands. Especially was the geographic extension of the Christian faith primarily through the Roman Catholic wing of the Christian movement. In the nineteenth century Christianity spread relatively more rapidly through Protestants than through Roman Catholics. This was true whether the expansion was by migration of European, traditionally Christian peoples, or by the conversion of non-Christian, non-Occidental folk. Yet Roman Catholic Christianity was still spreading rapidly. The bulk of the funds and personnel for Roman Catholic missions have been derived from Western Europe. There, too, is the administrative center and there have been most of the creative thought and the origin of the large majority of the new orders, congregations, and societies of the Roman Catholic Church. The sharp decline of Western Europe, particularly that wrought by the recent war, cannot fail to bring a diminution in funds and numbers of missionaries from that region. In the decline in morals and education, and in the disturbed political and economic conditions which characterize Western Europe, the Roman Catholic Church will be among the sufferers. Western Europe is probably not fully to recover the position which it has lost. The Roman Catholic Church will, therefore, be permanently weakened in its traditional main stronghold.

That loss is probably not fully to be made good from the Americas or from other areas. The largest body of professing Roman Catholics outside of Europe is in Latin America. In that region the Roman Catholic Church is notoriously passive and lacking in vitality. It provides very few missionaries, even for the non-Christian Indians at its own door. Most of the missionaries on its frontiers are from Europe. It is of very slight assistance in the world-wide extension of the Christian faith. Roman Catholics in the United States will in part make good the loss, for here is a vigorous section of the Church which is growing in wealth. Yet in the United States Roman Catholics are a minority and probably have about reached the height of their percentage of the population. Accessions from Europe, the chief source of their strength, have been reduced to a trickle by the immigration laws of the United States. The Church is chiefly urban and is suffering from the declining birth rate which is a feature of modern city life. Some converts are won from Protestantism, but their numbers are probably more than balanced by leakages either to Protestantism or to irreligious secularism. Canadian Roman Catholics, although aggressive and of increasing prominence in that Dominion, are too few to effect much change in the world scene. The younger branches in Asia and Africa, while mounting in numbers and in indigenous leadership, are too weak to redress the losses in Europe.

The Roman Catholic Church, it need hardly be said, is not to die out. It still shows great vigor in its inner life of the spirit and its organizations. It will continue to grow. Presumably, however, that growth is to slow down and to be only on its periphery. The Roman Catholic Church has been wounded severely at its very heart.

In contrast, Protestant Christianity is probably to continue to increase. It had a phenomenal expansion in the nineteenth century. That growth was closely associated with the prominence of the British Isles and the might and extent of the British Empire. Great Britain was, and is, predominantly Protestant. Its increase in wealth and power in the nineteenth century was paralleled by religious awakenings within British Protestantism. The British Empire is not as outstanding as it was at the beginning of the twentieth century. However, it is still scattered over much of the globe. The numerical strength of Protestantism in the British Isles seems to have declined. Yet Great Britain continues to be among the chief powers and its churches display vigor and initiative. Protestant Britain has not suffered as severely from the wars of the present century as has Roman Catholic Western Europe.

In the decades immediately ahead, Protestant Christianity is almost certainly to have its chief center in the United States. During the latter part of the nineteenth and thus far in the twentieth century, its numerical and financial strength in that country has been mounting. It is the dominant faith of that land. If it can match its opportunity with a vital inner life, it will share in the growing prominence of the United States in the world. "The American century" is probably journalistic exuberance. Yet it has back of it so much of supporting fact that it cannot be lightly dismissed. In industrial, financial, air, and naval might the United States leads the world. In this she parallels the position of Great Britain in the nineteenth century. Should that leadership be accompanied by revivals within the Protestantism of the land as was the nineteenth century industrial, commercial and financial hegemony of Great Britain, the place of Protestantism in the world scene will be largely augmented. This will be especially the case since Protestantism continues vigorous in the British Isles and the Dominions, is still strong in Northwestern Europe, and has been growing rapidly in the non-Occidental portions of the globe.

Whether such an awakening will occur in the Protestantism of the United States we cannot yet know. The increase of the percentage of Protestant church membership in the country seems to have been accompanied by a watering down of the quality of Christian living and a decline in religious literacy. Perhaps that is to be expected of mass conversions such as the one which in the last century and a half has been in progress in the United States. It certainly was seen in the corresponding mass conversion of the Roman Empire in the first five centuries of Christian history. The moral and spiritual sag which is the aftermath of war will make itself felt, as it did after World War I. Yet signs of life are present. These are seen in student circles, still numerically small, in the growth of support for the Ecumenical Movement, in the efforts at relief for Europe and Asia, and in the recouping of the depleted staffs of the foreign missionary societies.

Out of the sufferings of European Protestants, moreover, may come a new life which will make itself felt in the Protestantism of the United States. After the blows dealt by the Thirty Years War, and in part because of them, came the Pietist revival in Germany and the Moravians of Herrnhut. Through them the Evangelical Revival in Great Britain was given additional impetus. So the faith and the heroism of European Protestants under the Nazi yoke are already heartening many American and British Protestants.

Protestantism displays several features which seem to suggest that in the next few generations it will become increasingly the main stream of Christianity. It is more flexible than is either the Roman Catholic or Eastern Christianity. Hence it can better adapt itself to the changing conditions of the new age and especially to the non-Occidental cultures in which its "younger churches" are found. It also appears to be sufficiently tied to historic Christianity not to become denatured. Through the Anglican communion and much of the Lutheran and Reformed tradition it seems too firmly grounded in the long development of the past to succumb to the temptation fully to conform itself to new and possibly transient environments. The growing Ecumenical Movement is binding Protestant Christianity together and preventing it from being fragmented into national churches which sacrifice their soul to the state. Through some phases of its activities Protestantism is reaching out in unprecedented fashion to draw Christians of non-Protestant communions into a world-fellowship, and yet without the sacrifice of their confessional loyalties. This is seen here and there in the Young Men's Christian Associations, the World's Student Christian Federation, the National Conference of Christians and Jews, one or more of the missionary conferences (as in the Rhodesias, where Protestants and Roman Catholics cooperate), the Fellowship of St. Sergius and St. Albans, and in the membership of the Federal Council of the Churches of Christ in America and the World Council of Churches.

Moreover, the rapid spread of Protestantism by its missions seems to presage an enlarging future. In Latin America and the Philippines Protestantism is growing more rapidly at the expense of a nominal Roman Catholicism than has the Roman Catholic Church or any Eastern church at the expense of Protestantism since the seventeenth century. For the past century and a half it has been expanding on all the continents among non-Christian non-Occidental peoples. At its outset Protestant Christianity was confined almost entirely to the people of Northwestern Europe and the British Isles. Until the nineteenth century, it was still all but identified with the peoples of these areas and their overseas colonies, then small in population. It has become world-wide.

Whether Protestant Christianity will rise to the opportunity presented by the advantages offered it by the present position of the United States and by its nineteenth and twentieth century achievements, the historian ought not confidently to predict. He can, however, point out the possibility and suggest that the trend has been in that direction.

Another trend is the changing character of Protestant Christianity. This in part issues from the world-wide extension of Protestantism and from the rise to prominence of Anglo-Saxon Protestantism and especially of the Protestantism of the United States. Protestantism is becoming more weighted on the left wing, radical phases of the movement, more ecumenical and less regional, more inclusive and less a sectarian division, and more varied and yet finding a comprehensive unity which permits and even encourages diversity.

Protestantism is more world-wide and less a sect than it has ever been. It never fully deserved its traditional name. From almost the very first the term Protestant was a misnomer. Protestantism was not primarily a protest against the Roman Catholic Church. It was a congeries of revivals which were too potent to be held within the old wine skins of that Church. In some of its phases, as in Lutheranism and Anglicanism, it held to much which had come down to it through the old Church. Indeed, as we all know, to many Anglicans the term Protestant is abhorrent and emphasis is placed on the Catholic tradition. The Reformed departed further from the Roman heritage, but still held to much which was associated with the historic development of the Church. The radicals endeavored to disregard all that intervened between the first century and their day and to return to what they believed they found in the New Testament and only to that. Yet no form of Protestantism was precisely like anything which had gone before. Here was a new, creative movement issuing from the Christian stream. However, at the beginning Protestantism, as we have suggested, was the religion of only a small segment of the globe. It has now become extended over the globe. There are few non-Occidental lands where it is not represented, not by churches made up of European, British, or American residents, although such churches are to be found, but from the native-born population.

In seeming contrast with this world-wide character, Protestantism is becoming more Anglo-Saxon and American. The decline of Western Europe, the continued prominence of Great Britain and the British Dominions, and the growing strength of the United States have reduced the proportionate place which the churches of Continental Europe hold in Protestantism. To be sure, some of the ablest leadership still is from the Continent and the influence of the theology associated with the name of Barth is evidence of the importance of Western Europe in Protestant thought. However, these had emerged before the recent world war. That cataclysm cannot fail to have serious repercussions on the leadership, both in thought and in action, of the on-coming generation of European Protestants. More and more, too, the financial undergirding of the world-wide work of the Protestant churches will come from the United States. Probably an increasing proportion of the chief centers of theological training and thought are to be in the United States.

The enlarging prominence of American Christianity means the growing strength of the radical wing of Protestantism. In Western Europe, Protestantism has been chiefly represented by Lutheran and Reformed churches. In the British Isles, in spite of the prominence of Non-conformity in England, it has been predominantly Anglican and Reformed. European and even British Protestantism, then, has been mainly that which had departed the least widely from the Catholic tradition. In contrast, in the United States more than half of the Protestant church membership is from those bodies, such as the Baptists, Methodists, Disciples of Christ, and Congregationalists, which are near the extreme left of the movement. Lutherans and Anglicans are in the small minority. Even with the addition of Presbyterians and Reformed the conservative wing of American Protestantism is in the minority. From the radical wing come a majority of the missionaries who are propagating Protestant Christianity in other lands. This means that the world-wide Protestantism of the decades ahead is probably to depart further from the Christianity of pre-Reformation days than has that of Western Europe and the British Isles. Presumably, the trend will be augmented as the "younger churches" in non-Occidental countries mount in strength.

As we suggested a few paragraphs above, Protestantism is becoming more varied and more inclusive. It is also finding a growing unity. It already displays more diversity than Christianity has ever before done. Yet it is rapidly moving toward a unity which both permits and transcends variety. The combination is something quite new in Christian history. If "catholic" is employed in the sense of universality and ecumenicity, Protestantism is more catholic than it or any other form of Christianity has ever been.

Is Christianity ever to bring all of mankind to its allegiance and into conformity with its ideals? Are all men everywhere sometime to be obedient? Are the disciples to succeed in their commission of teaching all nations to observe all that their Lord commanded them? Are all things to be brought into subjection to Christ? Is Christ to triumph in all aspects of life?

Some features of the record of Christianity appear to give the lie to such hopes. Several of the colossal ills of mankind have attained their largest dimensions in regions and among peoples where Christianity has had the longest approach to free course. We recall at once Negro slavery and war. Moreover, the sobering reflection is borne in upon us that it may be partly because of Christianity that these evils attained such appalling magnitude. Negro slaves were especially numerous in the New World. The sources of the slaves were discovered by the Portuguese voyages initiated by Henry the Navigator, who was in part impelled by a Christian purpose. The discoverer of the New World saw in his name, Christopher, a divine commission. It is quite possible that the additional courage required for persistence in his westward voyage was derived from the sense of mission and the confidence that God's power could be depended upon for the fulfilment of the task. Modern wars are so extensive and destructive because of the mechanical appliances made possible by science. From Christianity have come in part, particularly through the forming of the western European mind since the conversion of Europe, the discipline of thought and the confidence in the dependability and orderliness of the universe and in man's ability increasingly to understand and use that universe, which have brought science into being. The forces released by Christianity, misapplied through man's sin, have on occasion been used for man's hurt. The longer Christianity operates the more destructive do the perversions become.

On the other hand, the record has in it much to confirm faith and hope. Christianity seems only barely to have begun its course. It is gaining in momentum and has seen its widest extension in the past century and a half. Only recently has it become world-wide and even now in non-Occidental lands it is represented by small although growing minorities. In spite of palpable weaknesses it is displaying great vigor. During the present century its influence upon mankind as a whole has been mounting. If the analysis is correct which declares that it has contributed to movements which, twisted by man's greed and fear, have wrought damage before which the imagination stands benumbed, it is clear that these same achievements, such as geographic and scientific discoveries, can be and have been employed to further man's welfare. We must also recall that if some of man's continuing ills have had unprecedented extent in what we formerly denominated Christendom, the Christian faith has nerved men to the most hopeful efforts in history to combat these ills. Thus the campaigns which brought to an end Negro slavery and the slave trade came out of Christian revivals, notably the Evangelical Awakening in Great Britain and the Great Awakening and the Finney revival in the United States. The pioneers in the development of international law and in the nineteenth and twentieth century peace movements were moved and sustained by a profound Christian faith. The modern world-wide nursing profession and the new medical profession of China had their birth in the Christian faith.

The historian ought not to attempt to predict the final outcome. However, he can reasonably venture some generalizations. He knows that the nature of the ideals of Christianity are such that neither as individuals nor as societies can men fully attain them within this life. The Gospel holds forth the promise of eternal life which has only its beginning this side of the grave. The historian has shown that Christianity is a mounting force in the life of mankind. Here, "within history," it is making itself felt over a wider and wider area. Unless a long time trend is checked that growth will continue. This the historian can confidently expect. The details he may not know. New periods of reverse may come. Severe losses may be suffered in some lands and in some aspects of life. Yet, viewed against the background of nineteen centuries, the outlook is for an ever increasing prominence of Christianity in the affairs of men.